Microsoft Security Copilot

Master strategies for AI-driven cyber defense

Bi Yue Xu
Rod Trent

<packt>

Microsoft Security Copilot

Portfolio Director: Vijin Boricha

Relationship Lead: Anindya Sil

Program Manager and Growth Lead: Ankita Thakur

Project Manager: Gandhali Raut

Content Engineer: Tazeen Shaikh

Technical Editor: Nithik Cheruvakodan

Copy Editor: Safis Editing

Indexer: Tejal Soni

Proofreader: Tazeen Shaikh

Production Designer: Pranit Padwal

First published: July 2025

Production reference: 2190825

Published by Packt Publishing Ltd.
Grosvenor House
11 St Paul's Square
Birmingham
B3 1RB, UK.

ISBN 978-1-83588-452-2

www.packtpub.com

I dedicate this book to my extraordinary mother, Xu Yun. Like a phoenix soaring from the ashes, she transformed the obstacles and hardships of her youth in China into a life defined by determination, courage, and inspiring achievement.

Equally, I dedicate this book to my fearless leader and mentor, Pavan Ethhiraj. Thank you for always seeing my potential, even when I couldn't.

– Bi Yue Xu

This book is dedicated to Megan—my guiding algorithm, whose steady logic helps me navigate life's complexities. To Alex, Rachel, Eric, and Elly—your insights and curiosity continually refine my thinking. To Reid and Meredith—may your data be rich, your minds curious, and your hearts empathetic. And to my entire family—you are my Copilot, co-authoring a life of meaning with me.

– Rod Trent

Contributors

About the authors

Bi Yue Xu is a seasoned Principal Security Cloud Solution Architect at Microsoft, with over 15 years of experience in cybersecurity. Specializing in Digital Forensics and Incident Response, she was a Certified Windows Forensics Examiner (EnCE) and held multiple security certifications, including GREM, GCFA, GCIA, GWAPT, GCWN, SC100, SC200, SC900, and others. Bi Yue's expertise is showcased in her work, from designing and developing a comprehensive four-day Defender for Endpoint training course, which has been delivered to over 300 organizations across 44 countries since its inception two years ago, to creating custom KQL detection and hunting queries, and even uncovering attacks related to zero-day.

I would like to extend my heartfelt thanks to my family for their patience, understanding, and unwavering support as I poured long hours into writing this book, often at the expense of missing family events. I am also grateful to Daniel P. Huynh and Aastha Sahni for their insightful feedback and the time they devoted to reviewing this book. Lastly, I would like to thank the entire Packt team for their support during the course of writing this book.

Rod Trent is a Senior Product Manager for Microsoft, where he focuses on the intersection between Security and AI. In his spare time, Rod writes KQL queries, authors fiction and nonfiction books, shares proud stories about his grandkids, boasts about his Six Million Dollar Man addiction, and teaches AI to behave.

About the reviewers

Daniel P. Huynh is a cybersecurity expert and army veteran, currently serving as a Principal Product Manager at Microsoft. With a distinguished career in incident response and security operations, he has made significant contributions to both the private sector and the U.S. Army. Daniel holds Computer Science degrees from the United States Military Academy at West Point and the Naval Postgraduate School, along with numerous industry certifications. Renowned for his leadership and dedication, Daniel is committed to mentoring the next generation of cybersecurity professionals while driving innovation and excellence in the field.

Aastha Sahni is a seasoned cybersecurity professional with over seven years of experience, specializing in identity and access management, application security, SIEM, threat hunting, Azure cloud, and vulnerability management. She began her career as an engineer, transitioned to a technical trainer role, and is now a tenured security analyst at Microsoft.

In addition to her technical expertise, Aastha is a passionate advocate for diversity and inclusion, empowering women in cybersecurity through initiatives such as the BBWIC Foundation, which she founded. She also extends her impact as a mentor at WiCyS, TopMate, and WomenTechNetwork. Aastha has been an ambassador for Snyk, actively contributing to the cybersecurity community, and has served on the board of the Diana Initiative.

Table of Contents

Chapter 2: Unveiling Security Copilot through Its Embedded Experience 23

Chapter 3: Navigating the Security Copilot Platform 73

Chapter 5: The Art of Prompt Engineering 177

Chapter 6: The Power of Promptbooks in Security Copilot 223

Chapter 9: Harnessing Security Copilot within the Microsoft Ecosystem 367

Chapter 10: Frontline Tales with Security Copilot 421

Chapter 11: The Pricing Model in Security Copilot 479

Chapter 12: Unlock Your Book's Exclusive Benefits 523

Appendix A – Security Copilot Agents 527

Preface

Be at the forefront of cybersecurity innovation with Microsoft Security Copilot, where advanced **artificial intelligence** (**AI**) tackles the intricate challenges of digital defense. This book unveils Security Copilot's powerful features, from AI-powered analytics revolutionizing security operations to intelligent orchestration that streamlines incident response and threat management. Through real-world case studies and frontline stories, you'll learn how to truly harness AI advancements and unlock the full potential of Security Copilot within the expansive Microsoft ecosystem.

Designed for security professionals navigating increasingly sophisticated cyber threats, this book equips you with the skills to accelerate threat detection and investigation, refine your security processes, and optimize cyber defense strategies. You will discover that Security Copilot is more than just a tool; it is your trusted partner in the fight against cyber threats, empowering you to work smarter, respond faster, and stay ahead of ever-evolving threats.

By the end of this book, you'll have become a Security Copilot ninja, confidently crafting effective prompts, designing promptbooks, creating custom plugins, and integrating logic apps for enhanced automation.

Who this book is for

This book is for cybersecurity professionals at all experience levels, from beginners seeking foundational knowledge to seasoned experts looking to stay ahead of the curve. While readers with basic cybersecurity knowledge will find the content approachable, experienced practitioners will gain deep insights into advanced features and real-world applications.

What this book covers

Chapter 1, Elevating Cyber Defense with Security Copilot, introduces you to the world of AI, outlining its evolution from foundational principles to cutting-edge technologies. The chapter details how AI is fueling innovative advancements with a specific focus on Microsoft Copilot.

Chapter 2, Unveiling Security Copilot through Its Embedded Experience, formally introduces Security Copilot to you by showcasing it in action. It highlights Security Copilot's core features across various embedded experiences and provides an introduction to the standalone experience.

Chapter 3, Navigating the Security Copilot Platform, walks through Security Copilot's onboarding process and reviews its user interfaces after you have become acquainted with the platform. Following that, it presents a case study to demonstrate how Security Copilot can be applied in a real-world security incident investigation, offering a hands-on view of its practical use.

Chapter 4, Extending Security Copilot's Capabilities with Plugins, highlights how plugins enable Security Copilot to expand and adapt to diverse needs. The chapter covers the preinstalled plugins as well as third-party offerings. It also provides insights into the development and use of custom plugins designed to address specific security requirements.

Chapter 5, The Art of Prompt Engineering, takes a closer look at the techniques behind crafting clear, well-structured prompts. It introduces practical strategies for building effective prompts and shares best practices to support successful prompt engineering.

Chapter 6, The Power of Promptbooks in Security Copilot, introduces promptbooks by exploring their role within the platform. This chapter highlights a range of prebuilt promptbooks, then offers guidance on creating custom ones tailored to specific security scenarios. It concludes with sample promptbooks and practical tips to support effective implementation.

Chapter 7, Automation and Integration – The Next Frontier, introduces the **Security Copilot Logic Apps connector** and demonstrates its integration with **Azure Logic Apps workflows** that enable more customizable automation. This chapter also covers how Security Copilot can harness organization-specific insights through its file upload feature and the **Azure AI Search** plugin.

Chapter 8, Cyber Sleuthing with Security Copilot, brings together the key concepts covered in earlier chapters by walking through a real-world **Microsoft Defender XDR** incident investigation. It also offers practical insights and strategies, including the use of custom plugins and the chaining of promptbooks, to enhance investigation workflows.

Chapter 9, Harnessing Security Copilot within the Microsoft Ecosystem, presents additional case studies that demonstrate the practical application of Security Copilot. It illustrates how the platform supports analysts in examining user behavior, tracking suspicious activity, and detecting signs of account compromise. It also highlights how Security Copilot can streamline device comparisons and identify policy conflicts through its Intune plugin.

Chapter 10, Frontline Tales with Security Copilot, continues with additional case studies that highlight Security Copilot's real-world impact. It demonstrates how the platform can track attacker infrastructure and transform threat intelligence into actionable insights. It also illustrates how Security Copilot delivers strategic guidance to help chief information security officers to stay ahead of emerging threats.

Chapter 11, The Pricing Model in Security Copilot, walks through the role of **Security Compute Unit** (**SCUs**) in the Security Copilot ecosystem. It details Security Copilot's pricing structure and cost calculation. It also offers practical guidance on cost optimization and highlights strategies to improve efficiency.

To get the most out of this book

- It's ideal to have some familiarity with the following foundational technologies and concepts. If you're new to these topics, don't worry; key ideas are introduced and explained throughout the book. That said, a basic understanding will make it easier to contextualize the material and follow along more effectively:
- A general understanding of cybersecurity operations and concepts, such as incident response, threat detection, and the attack life cycle
- A working knowledge of Microsoft Defender security solutions
- Some familiarity with scripting or automation workflows, such as **Kusto Query Language** (**KQL**) or Azure Logic Apps
- A basic awareness of AI concepts, including **large language models** (**LLMs**), prompt engineering, and generative AI, though *Chapter 1* will give you an introductory refresher

Download the example code files

The code bundle for the book is hosted on GitHub at `https://github.com/PacktPublishing/Microsoft-Copilot-for-Security`. We also have other code bundles from our rich catalog of books and videos available at `https://github.com/PacktPublishing`. Check them out!

Download the color images

We also provide a PDF file that has color images of the screenshots/diagrams used in this book. You can download it here: `https://packt.link/gbp/9781835884522`.

Conventions used

There are a number of text conventions used throughout this book.

`CodeInText`: Indicates code words in text, database table names, folder names, filenames, file extensions, pathnames, dummy URLs, user input, and Twitter/X handles. For example: "For instance, when inquiring about error code `0xC7D14FBA`, Security Copilot explains that this error occurs because the app installation failed due to the necessary file being deleted before the process finished."

User prompts are written as follows:

```
Can you explain in more detail about the following event:
services.exe modified service image file from to %COMSPEC% /C
"powershell.exe -EncodedCommand QwA6AFwAUwBjAHIAaQBwAHQAcwBcAFIAZ
QBuAGEAbQBlAFAAbwB3AGUAcgBzAGgAZQBsAGwALgBwAHMAMQA=" for service
WDUAPJKVADPWOQLFGQSH
```

Copilot outputs are displayed as:

> The provided command line script executes a file named "jyglecpm.1v0.exe" in a hidden window. It then uses the '-encodedCommand' parameter to run a base64-encoded command. The base64 string decodes to a PowerShell script located at 'C:\Scripts\ExportADFSTokenSigningCert.ps1'. This suggests that the script is likely used to execute a hidden process and then run a PowerShell script, possibly for malicious purposes.

A block of code is set as follows:

```
Table = <tablename>
Time/Date range = <time range>
Query = <query processing example: the top medium severity alert and the
number of times is shows up in the data>
Display = <how the results are displayed example: just the alert name and
the times it shows up>
```

Bold: Indicates a new term, an important word, or words that you see on the screen. For instance, words in menus or dialog boxes appear in the text like this. For example: "Scroll to the bottom of the **Manage Sources** page, and within the **Custom** section, you'll find an **Add plugin** option."

Warnings or important notes appear like this.

Tips and tricks appear like this.

Get in touch

Feedback from our readers is always welcome.

General feedback: If you have questions about any aspect of this book or have any general feedback, please email us at `customercare@packt.com` and mention the book's title in the subject of your message.

Errata: Although we have taken every care to ensure the accuracy of our content, mistakes do happen. If you have found a mistake in this book, we would be grateful if you reported this to us. Please visit `http://www.packt.com/submit-errata`, click **Submit Errata**, and fill in the form. We ensure that all valid errata are promptly updated in the GitHub repository at `https://github.com/PacktPublishing/Microsoft-Copilot-for-Security`.

Piracy: If you come across any illegal copies of our works in any form on the internet, we would be grateful if you would provide us with the location address or website name. Please contact us at `copyright@packt.com` with a link to the material.

If you are interested in becoming an author: If there is a topic that you have expertise in and you are interested in either writing or contributing to a book, please visit `http://authors.packt.com/`.

Share your thoughts

Once you've read *Microsoft Security Copilot*, we'd love to hear your thoughts! Scan the QR code below to go straight to the Amazon review page for this book and share your feedback.

`https://packt.link/r/1835884539`

Your review is important to us and the tech community and will help us make sure we're delivering excellent quality content.

1

Elevating Cyber Defense with Security Copilot

Welcome to Microsoft Security Copilot! In this book, you'll embark on an exciting journey into the world of next-generation cyber defense powered by AI. This opening chapter takes you to the fascinating world of **Artificial Intelligence** (**AI**) and illustrates how it has evolved over time. You'll gain insights into the technological advancements that have shaped AI, starting with the foundational principles of **machine learning** and progressing to more sophisticated technologies, including **deep learning**, **generative AI**, and **large language models** (**LLMs**). These technological breakthroughs have contributed to the powerful AI capabilities we use today.

By exploring the core concepts behind AI, you'll gain a clearer understanding of how it operates behind the scenes. This deeper insight will enhance your knowledge and confidence in using AI tools such as **Microsoft Security Copilot**, allowing you to apply your understanding of AI principles to effectively utilize these tools.

You'll also gain a comprehensive view of how Microsoft is harnessing AI through its suite of Copilot solutions to drive the development of innovation and practical applications, as well as its significant role in enhancing cybersecurity to protect your digital assets and infrastructure.

We will cover these topics through the following sections in this chapter:

- AI evolution – core principles and generative advances
- Introducing Microsoft Security Copilot
- Discovering Microsoft Security Copilot

Getting the most out of this book – get to know your free benefits

Unlock exclusive **free** benefits that come with your purchase, thoughtfully crafted to supercharge your learning journey and help you learn without limits.

Here's a quick overview of what you get with this book:

Next-gen reader

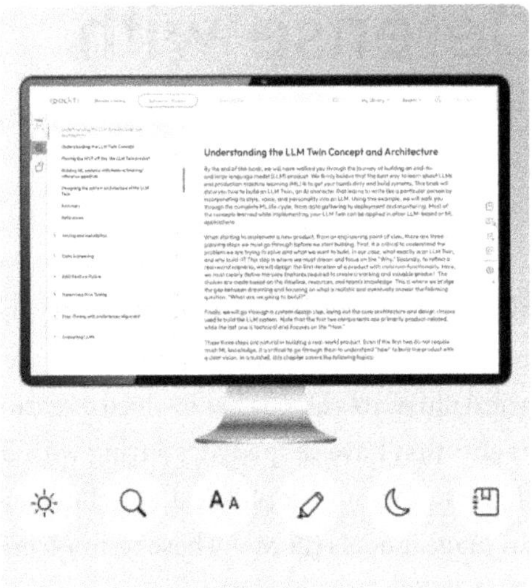

Figure 1.1: Illustration of the next-gen Packt Reader's features

Our web-based reader, designed to help you learn effectively, comes with the following features:

Multi-device progress sync: Learn from any device with seamless progress sync.

Highlighting and notetaking: Turn your reading into lasting knowledge.

Bookmarking: Revisit your most important learnings anytime.

Dark mode: Focus with minimal eye strain by switching to dark or sepia mode.

Interactive AI assistant (beta)

Figure 1.2: Illustration of Packt's AI assistant

Our interactive AI assistant has been trained on the content of this book, to maximize your learning experience. It comes with the following features:

✦ Summarize it: Summarize key sections or an entire chapter.

✦ AI code explainers: In the next-gen Packt Reader, click the Explain button above each code block for AI-powered code explanations.

Note: The AI assistant is part of next-gen Packt Reader and is still in beta.

DRM-free PDF or ePub version

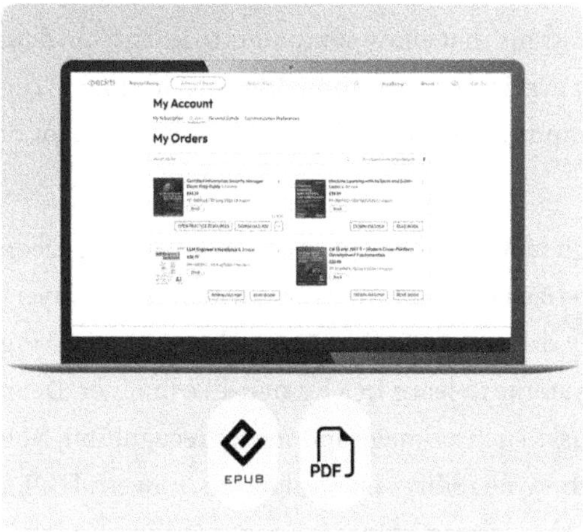

Figure 1.3: Free PDF and ePub

Learn without limits with the following perks included with your purchase:

Learn from anywhere with a DRM-free PDF copy of this book.

Use your favorite e-reader to learn using a DRM-free ePub version of this book.

AI evolution – core principles and generative advances

AI is the grand umbrella term that encompasses all forms of computational systems that can perform tasks that normally require human intelligence. AI encompasses a wide range of subfields, including **machine learning**, **deep learning**, **neural networks**, **Natural Language Processing (NLP)**, and **robotics**. Its applications are diverse, ranging from medical diagnosis and financial analysis to self-driving cars and virtual personal assistants.

The term *artificial intelligence* was first introduced by John McCarthy in 1956 during the *Dartmouth Conference*, marking the birth of AI as a field of study. AI gained momentum with the rise of machine learning, which focused on developing algorithms that allow computers to learn from data and make predictions or decisions without being explicitly programmed for specific tasks. The availability of large datasets and advances in computing power facilitated the development of more complex machine learning models.

The mid-2000s marked a significant breakthrough in AI with the advent of deep learning. Deep learning, a branch of machine learning, is characterized by neural networks with multiple layers. It began to gain prominence around 2006, largely driven by Geoffrey Hinton's groundbreaking work in developing techniques that enabled AI systems to learn in a human-like manner. Deep learning models achieved remarkable success in tasks such as image and speech recognition, NLP, and gaming. This era's progress was propelled by the availability of large datasets, powerful GPUs, and improved algorithms, all of which facilitated the training of increasingly complex models.

Generative AI, which can generate content that closely resembles human creation, saw significant advancements in 2014. It began with the capability to create realistic images from noise maps. Over time, it has evolved to craft an extensive variety of content, spanning from textual compositions and imagery to video clips, musical pieces, and synthesized speech.

The early 2020s were marked by an AI boom, particularly with the advancements in deep learning and the development of LLMs. These models are capable of summarizing, reading, or generating text in a manner similar to human communication, which has led to a substantial expansion of generative AI systems. Advanced chatbots such as ChatGPT, Copilot, and LLaMA have contributed greatly to the AI landscape, transforming our interaction with technology and unlocking unprecedented levels of efficiency and creative potential.

AI continues to advance at an unprecedented pace. However, its core components are deeply interconnected, starting with the broad foundation of AI and progressing to more specialized areas such as machine learning, deep learning, and, ultimately, specialized models such as generative AI and LLMs. The core components of AI and their relationships are outlined next, illustrating how each one is interconnected within the broader AI ecosystem:

- AI is the broad field – the "umbrella"
- Machine learning is a core component of AI – it's a method within AI
- Deep learning is a specialized subcomponent of machine learning
- Generative AI is an application area (or functional branch) of deep learning
- LLMs are a specific type of generative AI – very specialized components built on top of deep learning architectures

The following diagram offers a visual guide to these core AI components:

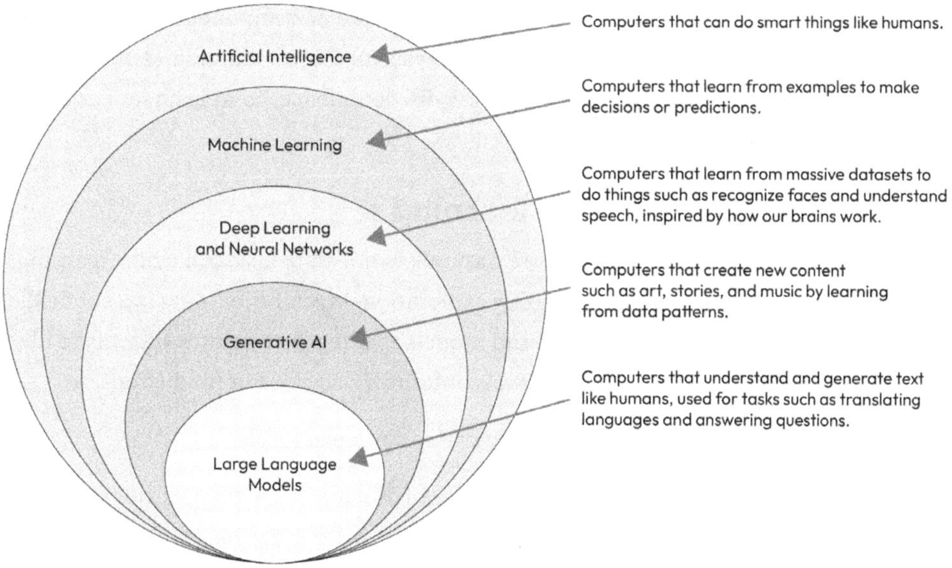

Figure 1.4 – Visual guide illustrating the layers within AI systems

Note that this visual guide depicts the core components of AI in layers, with each component in an inner layer being a subset of the component in the outer layer. Each layer also builds upon the capabilities of the outer layer, illustrating how each foundational technology, such as machine learning, paved the way for more advanced developments, such as deep learning.

As AI continues to advance, its transformative impact is being felt across a wide range of industries. In healthcare, AI is revolutionizing the sector by helping doctors with diagnoses, creating personalized treatment plans, and accelerating the pace of drug discovery. Banks and financial institutions are leveraging AI's power to detect fraudulent activities, execute algorithmic trades, and manage risks. In the automotive industry, AI is behind the wheel of self-driving cars and boosting safety with advanced driver-assistance systems. Retailers are tapping into AI to tailor customer recommendations, streamline inventory management, and automate client services. In the manufacturing sphere, AI is used to optimize supply chain logistics, enable predictive maintenance, and ensure quality control through cutting-edge analytics and robotic automation.

The applications of AI across industries highlight its transformative potential and the ongoing technological evolution. While AI-powered tools and systems have already made a significant impact, the ongoing research and development continue to overcome present limitations and unlock new possibilities, paving the way for innovations that could revolutionize industries and everyday life.

With AI continuing to evolve, understanding the technologies driving this transformation becomes crucial. In the next few sections, we will delve into the core AI components that have shaped modern AI. By gaining a clear understanding of how each of these technologies works, you'll be better prepared to use them more effectively and with confidence, as AI is no longer a magical black box that just works.

The emergence of machine learning

As we explore the fascinating world of AI, we naturally come to focus on machine learning, the foremost fundamental concept in our ongoing exploration. Machine learning is a subfield of AI. It involves the development of algorithms and models that teach computer systems to identify patterns in data and use this knowledge to make informed decisions or predictions.

Let's illustrate the concept of machine learning with a simple example.

Imagine you give your friend Alex a bunch of pictures of different animals, cats, dogs, and rabbits, and you tell him which animal is which for each picture. As Alex examines the images, he begins to recognize patterns: cats have pointy ears and whiskers, dogs have floppy ears and snouts, and rabbits have long ears and fluffy tails.

Through repeated observation, Alex becomes pretty good at guessing which animal is which just by looking at their features. Now, if you show Alex a new picture of an animal he hasn't seen before, he can apply what he's learned about these patterns to make an educated guess—it might be a cat because of the pointy ears and whiskers, for example.

This process mirrors machine learning, where algorithms are trained on data to recognize patterns, such as features in animal pictures, and use these patterns to make predictions or decisions about new data that they haven't seen before. This ability to learn from data and predict outcomes is what makes machine learning such a powerful tool across various fields.

Let's look at a more technical example that illustrates machine learning, focusing on the relationship between input data and outcomes. Imagine we have a dataset containing information about houses: their sizes in square feet and their corresponding prices. The goal is to build a machine learning model that can predict the price of a house based on its size.

We start by collecting the dataset, such as house sizes and their prices. We prepare this data, ensuring it's suitable for a machine learning model. We then select an algorithm that can predict continuous values, such as house prices based on size. By feeding the algorithm with the dataset, it learns the relationship between house size, the input, and house price, the output. During training, the model fine-tunes its parameters to reduce the prediction error. Once trained, the model can estimate the price of a new house by applying the patterns it has learned.

For instance, if the model has learned that a house's price increases by $10,000 for every additional 100 square feet, it can predict that a 1,500-square-foot house might be priced at $150,000 more than a house with 1,400 square feet. This demonstrates how machine learning algorithms can learn from data and make predictions on new, unseen data.

To summarize, in machine learning, the goal is to use an algorithm that can predict outputs from inputs. This algorithm is learned from examples of past input-output pairs. Once learned, this algorithm can then be used to predict what the output would be for new input data that the model hasn't seen before.

The rise of machine learning has been a driving force in the acceleration of AI. The momentum gained by AI with the advent of machine learning is profound, as it shifted the focus from rule-based programming to data-driven learning. This transition allowed computers to evolve from performing predefined tasks to making predictions and decisions based on data analysis. The importance of machine learning in this context is its role in enabling AI systems to uncover insights and patterns within vast datasets that were previously unattainable with traditional computing methods. This capability has not only propelled AI forward but also opened new possibilities and applications, making AI more versatile and effective across various domains.

The rise of deep learning and neural networks

Now that we have seen how machine learning works in general, you may wonder about real-world scenarios where we encounter all sorts of data, such as images, text, and audio, and other forms of unstructured information. The traditional machine learning models often find these unstructured datasets challenging, as they typically require significant manual effort to process.

This is where deep learning comes in. Deep learning is a subset of machine learning that excels in interpreting and learning from unstructured data. You can think of deep learning as the whiz kid of machine learning that is good at making sense of messy data. It uses layers upon layers of artificial neural networks, like a deep stack of filters. Each layer learns different aspects of the data, allowing the system to process and understand all of that unstructured information. These layers help deep learning models to identify complex patterns and make smart predictions or decisions. *"For example, deep learning is what driverless cars use to process images and distinguish pedestrians from other objects on the road or what your smart home devices use to understand your voice commands."* (Microsoft, *What Is Deep Learning?*, `https://azure.microsoft.com/en-us/resources/cloud-computing-dictionary/what-is-deep-learning`).

Artificial neural networks are composed of layers of interconnected *neurons* that the input signal goes through one after another to predict the outcome. For example, in the following diagram, to identify whether it's a flower in the picture, the image passes through multiple layers of neurons (depicted as circles) to generate a prediction:

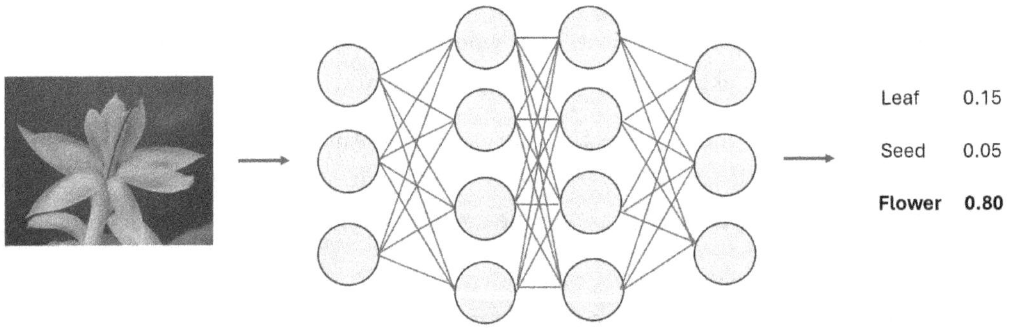

Figure 1.5 – Visualizing artificial neural networks

Deep learning algorithms are inspired by the structure and function of the human brain, and they are capable of automatically learning patterns and representations from data. These deep neural networks learn from vast amounts of diverse data, enabling them to automatically extract increasingly abstract features from raw data, making them highly effective for tasks such as image and speech recognition and NLP.

Deep learning enables machines to process and recognize patterns in data in ways that are inspired by human cognition, but at a much larger scale and scope. The advent of artificial neural networks has enhanced AI technology considerably, allowing machines to tackle previously insurmountable tasks, thus revolutionizing our use of technology in processing and engaging with intricate data.

Introducing generative AI

Generative AI is a fascinating branch of AI that specializes in creating new content. Leveraging deep learning techniques, it extracts patterns from training data to create new instances that mimic the original dataset. This innovative technology excels at producing diverse outputs that can be text, images, music, and so on, based on the patterns it has learned from the training data. Generative AI has attracted significant attention for its potential to produce realistic and creative outputs, revolutionizing industries such as art, entertainment, design, and scientific research.

At the core of generative AI are several key technologies and methodologies. Neural networks serve as the backbone of generative AI. These computational models are inspired by the complex network of neurons in the human brain. In the context of generative AI, these networks use their learned knowledge to create new content. Imagine them as skilled apprentices who, after analyzing countless paintings, can create entirely new artworks that blend elements from various styles they've observed.

The **Transformer models**, including OpenAI's **Generative Pre-trained Transformer** (**GPT**) series, have become a cornerstone of modern generative AI. The Transformer model is like a super-smart assistant that excels at understanding and generating content. Imagine you're asking this assistant a question. It carefully analyzes each word and its context in your question to figure out what you're asking for, then provides an answer.

For instance, if you ask, "Which state is Seattle in?" the Transformer model analyzes the question by focusing on important words such as *state* and *Seattle*. It understands that you're asking about Seattle's location. Using its extensive knowledge of language and information from vast amounts of text, it finds the most likely answer. In this case, based on its training, it knows Seattle is in the state of Washington and generates an answer, "Seattle is in Washington state."

The Transformer model, as its name implies, takes input data and generates contextually relevant responses. It is skilled at processing language by understanding the relationships between words and generating responses that are contextually relevant and informative. It can generate clear and relevant text, such as writing articles, answering questions, or composing poetry. The model can condense long pieces of articles into concise summaries while retaining the essential information.

It can understand questions posed in natural language and provide accurate answers based on the context provided. Beyond translation, the Transformer model can comprehend and interpret the nuances of language, aiding in tasks such as sentiment analysis and classification.

Besides Transformer models, there are other popular techniques for implementing generative AI, enabling its wide-ranging applications in fields such as NLP, image and video generation, music composition, and beyond.

In image and video generation, generative AI creates art, realistic images, and videos for advertising and media production. In music and audio generation, it composes music across genres, synthesizes sound effects, and generates natural-sounding voices for virtual assistants and audiobooks. In text generation, generative AI aids in creative writing by producing poems, stories, and articles, while enhancing chatbots and virtual assistants for more natural interactions. In scientific research, generative AI accelerates drug discovery by predicting molecular structures and designing new materials with specific properties. *"The use of artificial intelligence (AI) is proving to be a game-changer when it comes to medicine with the technology now helping scientists to unlock the first new antibiotics in 60 years"* (Oceane Duboust (2023) Euronews, *Scientists discover the first new antibiotics in over 60 years using AI* `https://www.euronews.com/health/2023/12/31/scientists-discover-the-first-new-antibiotics-in-over-60-years-using-ai`).

LLMs

In earlier sections of this chapter, we covered machine learning, a branch of AI. Machine learning enables machines to make predictions or decisions without being explicitly programmed for each specific task. Then, we explored deep learning, a subset of machine learning, that utilizes multi-layered or "deep" neural networks to analyze complex patterns in data. Deep learning is particularly good at recognizing patterns in unstructured data such as images, sound, and text. We then discussed generative AI, which leverages deep learning techniques to produce original and creative content. It generates outputs that can be text, images, music, and so on, based on the patterns it has learned from the training data.

You may now be curious about the roles of ChatGPT and Microsoft Copilot within the extensive AI ecosystem. To understand this further, it's important to discuss another key element known as LLMs.

LLMs are a specialized form of generative AI, and they excel in generating text that closely resembles human writing. These models, such as GPT, represent an advanced application of the Transformer model architecture, but scaled up significantly in terms of model size and training data.

These models are trained on extensive datasets drawn from a variety of sources, with each model's capabilities shaped by the data it has been exposed to, including its training cutoff date. By predicting the next token (which can be a word or part of a word) in a sequence, these models become powerful tools for understanding and generating human language. They can be used for a variety of tasks, such as text completion, translation, summarization, question-answering, and code generation.

LLMs predict the next word in a sentence by considering the words that come before it. This is done by calculating the probability of each possible next word based on the patterns it has learned during training. The model uses these probabilities to generate the most likely next word, which leads to the creation of coherent and contextually appropriate sentences.

In the grand scheme of AI, LLMs represent the cutting-edge of what's possible with generative AI and deep learning, pushing the boundaries of how machines understand and create human-like text. They are a powerful tool in the AI toolkit, enabling a wide range of applications from automated content creation to sophisticated conversational agents.

ChatGPT and Microsoft Copilot are both technologies that leverage LLMs to assist users in accomplishing tasks more efficiently. While both technologies understand and generate human language, they serve different purposes and operate within different scopes. ChatGPT, part of the OpenAI family, is designed to engage in conversational dialogue and perform a range of language-related tasks, including creative writing, problem-solving, and coding assistance. Microsoft Copilot, on the other hand, is specifically integrated into the Microsoft ecosystem. It aims to streamline workflows and enhance productivity by assisting with tasks across the suite of Microsoft applications, such as summarizing emails, drafting documents, and managing meetings.

At their core, ChatGPT and Microsoft Copilot employ sophisticated AI through LLMs for natural language tasks. These models leverage deep learning and generative AI methods to handle linguistic data in ways that mirror human-like comprehension and innovation.

Understanding natural language processing

You may have noticed that we mentioned NLP a few times in the previous sections. NLP is a core field within AI that focuses on empowering computers to understand, interpret, and generate human language effectively. By ensuring interactions are both meaningful and contextually aware, NLP enhances the way machines engage with and respond to human communication. It is like giving computers the superpower to understand, interpret, and talk to us in our own language. NLP is a key component behind how your phone understands your voice commands, how spam filters keep your inbox clean, and even how virtual assistants such as Siri or Alexa chat with you like a friend.

At its heart, NLP uses clever tricks from machine learning to teach computers how to handle the complexities of human language. Imagine algorithms that can read through mountains of text to figure out whether an email is important or junk, or sift through customer reviews to tell you how people feel about a product. These tools use patterns from tons of examples to make smart decisions about language.

But it doesn't stop there. Deep learning turbocharges NLP by letting computers learn intricate linguistic features directly from raw text data, diving deep into how language works. Think of it like teaching a computer to spot sarcasm or understand the subtleties in a poem. Neural networks, the brains behind deep learning, learn these things by crunching through tons of sentences, spotting patterns, and building their own understanding of language rules.

Then there's generative AI, which not only understands what we say but can also create new text that is coherent, contextually appropriate, and often indistinguishable from human writing, with LLMs leading the way. These techniques advance NLP by improving both language generation and understanding.

NLP integrates various methodologies from machine learning, benefits from advancements in deep learning for understanding complex language patterns, utilizes techniques from generative AI for text generation, and pushes the boundaries with state-of-the-art LLMs for advanced natural language understanding and generation tasks.

Putting it all together

With a foundation laid across the core components of AI, spanning machine learning, deep learning, generative AI, LLMs, and NLP, it's clear we are witnessing a profound transformation. AI has evolved from basic data processing to machines capable of producing original, human-like creativity. Machine learning provides the basic tools for pattern recognition and prediction, which are enhanced by deep learning's ability to learn from unstructured data. Generative AI then elevates these capabilities, producing original content that mirrors human ingenuity, while LLMs channel this creative force into sophisticated, human-like language applications.

Now that we've explored each of these core AI components, let's take a step back to see the bigger picture, examining how these components interconnect and observing the synergy they share:

- AI is the grand umbrella term that encompasses all forms of computational systems that can perform tasks normally requiring human intelligence. This includes reasoning, learning, perception, problem-solving, and language understanding.

- Machine learning is a subset of AI. It involves the development of algorithms and models that enable computer systems to recognize patterns in data and use them to make informed decisions or predictions.
- Deep learning, a subset of machine learning, advances these principles. It uses neural networks with multiple layers (hence *deep*) to learn from vast amounts of diverse data, especially unstructured data. These neural networks are structured in a way that mimics the human brain's neural networks, hence the term *neural*. Deep learning allows the machine to learn from complex patterns and perform tasks such as image and speech recognition.
- Generative AI leverages deep learning techniques to focus on creating new content. Based on the patterns it has learned from the training data, it generates outputs that can be text, images, music, and so on. Generative AI models can produce original and creative content, and they are particularly useful in fields such as design, art, and content creation.
- LLMs are a specialized type of generative AI that processes and generates human-like text, at a level of sophistication that approaches human understanding and inventiveness. LLMs are built using deep learning techniques, particularly neural networks known as Transformers, which are adept at handling sequential data such as text. LLMs can perform a wide variety of NLP tasks, such as translation, summarization, question-answering, and conversation.

> Important note
>
> This perspective offers a simplified understanding of AI components. The field of AI is complex, encompassing other definitions that we have not discussed.

Having introduced AI and some of its core components, let's dig deeper into the practical applications of AI in the real world. In the next section, we will take a closer look at how Microsoft is leveraging AI to develop innovative solutions, particularly within the Microsoft Copilot family.

Introducing Microsoft Security Copilot

The Microsoft Copilot family consists of a variety of solutions that enhance productivity across different services. These include Microsoft 365 Copilot, Dynamics 365 Copilot, Copilot in Power Platform, Security Copilot, and GitHub Copilot. Each member of the Copilot family brings its own unique capabilities to the table.

Microsoft Copilot employs an LLM based on OpenAI's GPT framework to generate and interpret human-like text. This advanced model allows Copilot to understand and respond to user inputs with precision. Its conversational interface is crafted to be user-friendly and mirrors the interaction style of ChatGPT, ensuring an accessible chat experience for users.

In the next few sections, we'll dive into a selection of solutions from the Microsoft Copilot family. Keep in mind, though, that this is just a glimpse of Microsoft's rapidly growing Copilot ecosystem. The goal is to highlight a few flagship products that showcase the diverse applications of AI. It is important to be aware that Microsoft continues to introduce new enterprise Copilot offerings across a variety of platforms and services, while existing solutions are constantly evolving with new features and enhanced capabilities. By the time you're reading this, the Copilot lineup has likely expanded even further with additional updates. Furthermore, be aware that product names and branding may change over time, as is often the case with Microsoft's ever-evolving technology landscape.

Microsoft 365 Copilot

Microsoft 365 Copilot acts as a powerful personal assistant right within your Microsoft 365 apps – be it Word, Excel, PowerPoint, Outlook, Teams, and more. This personal assistant is seamlessly integrated into your daily work tools. It can help you to draft documents, summarize emails, create presentations, manage meetings, keep track of tasks, review content, analyze data, and conduct web research to name a few.

Let's say your inbox is overflowing with emails. You need to get to the gist of them, but reading through each one is time-consuming. Microsoft 365 Copilot can summarize your emails, giving you the key points in a concise format. It's like having a personal assistant who sifts through your emails and gives you a brief on the important stuff.

Imagine you're in a Teams meeting with several colleagues discussing a new project. As the discussion unfolds, Microsoft 365 Copilot is there in real time, summarizing key points and suggesting action items. Suppose you attend the meeting late due to a prior engagement. Microsoft 365 Copilot can provide a summary of what you've missed, allowing you to catch up quickly and participate effectively. As the meeting draws to a close, Microsoft 365 Copilot helps wrap up by providing a summary of the key points discussed and identifying the next steps, including tasks assigned to specific people.

Microsoft 365 Copilot is also a powerful tool for task and project management. It assists you in managing your tasks by setting reminders for important deadlines, keeping track of your to-do list, and suggesting the most efficient order to complete your tasks.

Additionally, it aids in project management by providing realistic, AI-generated task plan recommendations, which can expedite the project creation process and ensure the timely completion of tasks.

There are some amazing examples and innovative ways to utilize Microsoft 365 Copilot out there. Whether you're drafting a report, crunching numbers, or brainstorming for your next big project, think of Microsoft 365 Copilot as your work assistant, always prepared to help, inspire, and simplify your workday.

Dynamics 365 Copilot

Dynamics 365 Copilot provides interactive, AI-powered assistance across business functions. It acts as a powerful personal assistant right within your Dynamics 365 apps, much like Microsoft 365 Copilot does within the Microsoft 365 apps. It is designed for professionals in sales, service, marketing, operations, and supply chain management, empowering individuals to focus more on the most rewarding aspects of their work and less time on mundane tasks.

Imagine you're a sales representative and you've just finished a productive meeting with a potential client. You have a lot of follow-up tasks to do, such as sending a personalized thank you email, updating the opportunity record with the latest discussion points, and scheduling a follow-up meeting. Normally, this would take a considerable amount of time, but with Dynamics 365 Copilot, you can handle all these tasks effortlessly. *"AI helps write email responses to customers and can even create an email summary of a Teams meeting in Outlook. The meeting summary pulls in details from the seller's CRM such as product and pricing information, as well as insights from the recorded Teams call"* (Charles Lamanna (2023), Microsoft, *Introducing Microsoft Dynamics 365 Copilot, the world's first copilot in both CRM and ERP, that brings next-generation AI to every line of business*, `https://blogs.microsoft.com/blog/2023/03/06/introducing-microsoft-dynamics-365-copilot/`). Lastly, you can instruct Copilot to find a suitable time for the next meeting based on your calendar availability and send a meeting request to the client, all done through natural language commands.

It's not just about sales. Dynamics 365 Copilot extends its capabilities across a variety of business functions. In customer service, it drafts contextual answers to queries, providing agents with AI-powered expertise. For finance teams, it streamlines tedious accounting tasks. And in marketing, it helps create compelling content that resonates with the audience. Dynamics 365 Copilot, when integrated within Microsoft Supply Chain Center, can proactively monitor external factors such as weather and financial trends that could disrupt supply chains. It uses predictive insights to identify and alert on affected orders, and can draft emails to notify partners, enabling swift action to mitigate potential issues before they arise.

Copilot in Power Platform

Copilot in Power Platform is a suite of AI-powered tools that help you create apps, automate workflows, and analyze data, all with the ease of conversational language. It's like having a tech-savvy friend who can translate your ideas into reality, without you needing to know the nitty-gritty of coding. *"Now, if you can imagine your solution, you can simply describe it in everyday language, and copilot can create it for you via an intuitive and intelligent low code experience"* (Charles Lamanna (2023), Microsoft, *Power Platform is leading a new era of AI-generated low-code app development*, `https://www.microsoft.com/en-us/power-platform/blog/2023/03/16/power-platform-is-leading-a-new-era-of-ai-generated-low-code-app-development/`).

Let's say you run a small bakery, and you want to keep track of your daily sales, inventory, and customer feedback. You describe your needs to Copilot, and just like that, it whips up an app tailored for your bakery. This app not only logs sales and tracks inventory but also gathers customer sentiments through a friendly chatbot.

So, whether you're a seasoned developer or a business owner with no coding experience, Copilot in Power Platform is your ally, turning your ideas into digital solutions. It's not just about building apps; it's about empowering you to create, innovate, and solve problems in a way that liberates you from technical constraints such as coding.

GitHub Copilot

GitHub Copilot can be perceived as an AI-based coding assistant, a companion that helps you write better code by suggesting entire lines or blocks of code as you type, guiding you through the syntax and semantics, much like a seasoned navigator guiding a ship through uncharted waters.

Imagine you're working on a project, and you need to write a function to calculate the Fibonacci sequence, a series of numbers where each number is the sum of the two preceding ones. Instead of spending time trying to remember how to write this function from scratch, you turn to GitHub Copilot. GitHub Copilot, understanding your intent, suggests a complete function that does exactly that. It's like having a knowledgeable coding partner who not only understands what you want to do but also helps you do it faster.

Now, you might be wondering how GitHub Copilot compares to Copilot in Power Platform, as they both offer AI-based coding assistance. GitHub Copilot and Copilot in Power Platform serve different purposes and operate within distinct environments, catering to different user needs.

GitHub Copilot is an AI pair programmer that helps you write code faster, drawing context from comments and code to suggest individual lines or whole functions instantly. While GitHub Copilot is focused on assisting with coding tasks, Copilot in Power Platform is about enabling users to build apps and workflows without requiring coding skills, or with minimal coding involved. Both tools leverage AI to simplify and expedite their respective tasks, but they cater to different aspects of the software development and app creation processes. GitHub Copilot is for writing code, and Copilot in Power Platform is for building no-code/low-code solutions.

In conclusion, the Microsoft Copilot family demonstrates how AI-driven solutions can enhance productivity across various platforms and services. From Microsoft 365 Copilot and Dynamics 365 Copilot to Copilot in Power Platform and GitHub Copilot, each member brings distinct capabilities to streamline workflows and improve efficiency. In the next section, let's turn our attention to Security Copilot, the digital security assistant leveraging AI to defend against cyber threats and enabling a rapid response.

Discovering Microsoft Security Copilot

In today's dynamic cybersecurity landscape, a security specialist needs to be highly skilled and knowledgeable across a wide range of areas. For instance, in incident response, the responder must be well versed in various attack techniques to effectively analyze vast amounts of data and logs to uncover subtle indicators of attack. The responder needs to be skilled in scripting languages, including PowerShell, Visual Basic Script, and JavaScript, and even embedded macros, as these tools are frequently leveraged by cyber adversaries. A good understanding of operating systems is crucial too, as the responder must be able to quickly recognize anomalies. For instance, while `lsass.exe` is a normal Windows system process for managing and verifying user logins and security credentials, having multiple instances running could signal a potential threat. The responder must also be skilled at identifying malicious exploitation of Windows net commands, along with commonly abused tools such as scheduled tasks, PowerShell, or **PsExec** (`https://learn.microsoft.com/en-us/sysinternals/downloads/psexec`). Proficiency in **registry keys** is vital for detecting malicious code hiding in a registry key. This is merely the tip of the iceberg. From phishing scams to network breaches, and fileless attacks to driverless attacks, the breadth of knowledge required is staggering. No single person can master it all.

This is where Security Copilot steps in, to empower and assist security professionals. As an example, Security Copilot can analyze complex commands and scripts, summarize their actions, and provide clear explanations. This capability enables security teams to understand the script functionality without the need for manual reverse engineering. This ability to quickly grasp malicious scripts or commands allows the security teams to react promptly, make informed decisions, and minimize the damage. This capability is particularly beneficial since there are often very few people in the security teams who can quickly reverse engineer complex scripts, especially scripts that are obfuscated or encoded.

In addition to analyzing scripts, Security Copilot can also examine files. During an investigation, security analysts must sift through numerous files, particularly executable and less common ones, to pinpoint any malicious files. Leveraging Security Copilot significantly reduces investigation time and the risk of overlooking malicious files.

On top of this, Security Copilot has extensive knowledge about a wide array of attacks. This includes information about established and emerging attack methods, tactics, techniques, and procedures used by **threat actors**, **Indicators of Compromise** (**IOCs**), **exploited vulnerabilities**, and contextual threat intelligence data from **Microsoft Defender Threat Intelligence**. Given the complexity and diversity of attack techniques, responders often face challenges in acquiring the depth of knowledge necessary to effectively identify all indicators of attack. Security Copilot can help support security professionals by providing extensive attack expertise.

As illustrated in the following screenshot, security analysts can turn to Security Copilot to uncover ways attackers might move laterally across an organization. The question posed to Security Copilot and its response are highlighted in the screenshot:

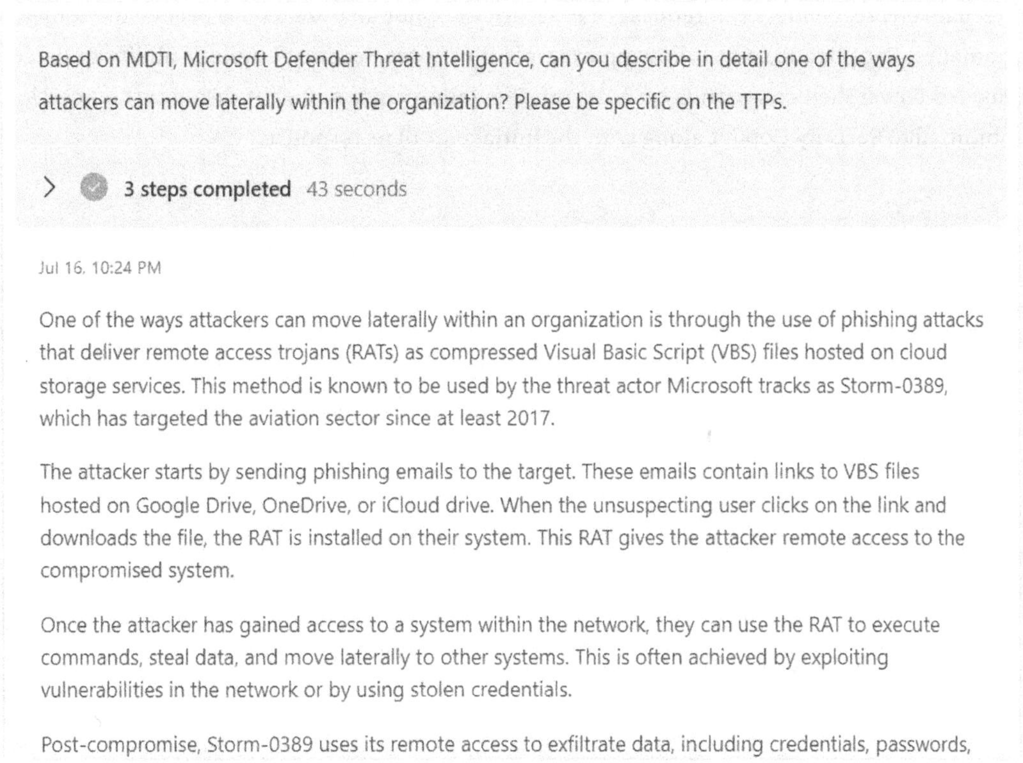

Figure 1.6 – Interacting with Security Copilot

Note

Keep in mind, Security Copilot is an AI solution that is always learning and improving. The responses you receive for the same prompt may differ from those shown here.

Alternatively, responders can request that Security Copilot analyze device events and look for anomalies. For instance, the following example illustrates Security Copilot's ability to detect encoded PowerShell commands on a device. The following screenshot displays the question submitted to Security Copilot along with the initial part of its response:

Figure 1.7 – Security Copilot examines device events

The following screenshot presents the remainder of Security Copilot's response, including its findings and additional comments. Security Copilot notes: **The command lines are Base64 encoded and are part of a PowerShell command. This is a common technique used by attackers to obfuscate their actions and evade detection. It's recommended to further investigate these events for potential security threats.**

Figure 1.8 – Security Copilot detects an encoded command line

As an AI assistant, Security Copilot excels across many different areas. Its abilities in security incident investigation are only a small part of what it can do. This book provides an in-depth tour of its comprehensive features, enabling you to fully utilize Microsoft Security Copilot and enhance your cybersecurity measures with sophisticated AI tools. Through practical case studies, you'll learn how to deploy advanced AI solutions for tackling security challenges and elevating your cyber defense tactics.

Summary

This chapter explored the evolution of AI, tracing its development from early machine learning techniques to the advanced field of generative AI. Key concepts such as deep learning, neural networks, and LLMs were introduced, highlighting how these advancements have transformed AI capabilities. It also showcased the integration of AI into various Microsoft solutions to drive the development of innovation and practical applications. Additionally, this chapter introduced Security Copilot, setting the stage for a more detailed exploration of its role and features in the following chapters.

Additionally, this chapter aimed to demystify AI by revealing the core concepts and underlying mechanisms that make it work. By gaining a clearer understanding of how AI operates behind the scenes, you recognize that AI is not a magical black box, but technologies grounded in clear, logical processes. This insight will enhance your confidence in using tools such as Microsoft Security Copilot, enabling you to apply your AI knowledge to use these tools more effectively.

In the next chapter, we will dive into the specifics of Security Copilot, demonstrating how it enhances security across various Microsoft platforms. Building on the foundational AI principles covered in this chapter, you'll gain a deeper understanding of AI's role in cybersecurity.

Further reading

- Microsoft, *What is deep learning?* – `https://azure.microsoft.com/en-us/resources/cloud-computing-dictionary/what-is-deep-learning`.
- Oceane Duboust (2023) Euronews, *Scientists discover the first new antibiotics in over 60 years using AI* – `https://www.euronews.com/health/2023/12/31/scientists-discover-the-first-new-antibiotics-in-over-60-years-using-ai`.
- Charles Lamanna (2023), Microsoft, *Introducing Microsoft Dynamics 365 Copilot, the world's first copilot in both CRM and ERP, that brings next-generation AI to every line of business* – `https://blogs.microsoft.com/blog/2023/03/06/introducing-microsoft-dynamics-365-copilot/`.
- Charles Lamanna (2023), Microsoft, *Power Platform is leading a new era of AI-generated low-code app development* – `https://www.microsoft.com/en-us/power-platform/blog/2023/03/16/power-platform-is-leading-a-new-era-of-ai-generated-low-code-app-development/`.
- PsExec – `https://learn.microsoft.com/en-us/sysinternals/downloads/psexec`.

2

Unveiling Security Copilot through Its Embedded Experience

This chapter formally introduces you to **Security Copilot**. You will witness it in action, uncover its powerful capabilities, and learn how it enhances your security operations. Throughout this chapter, you'll gain a solid understanding of Security Copilot's core features within its embedded experience, along with an introduction to its standalone experience. This will set the stage for a more in-depth exploration of its advanced functionalities in the upcoming chapters. Get ready to see how this smart assistant can transform your security operations and support your team's success.

In this chapter, as we delve into Security Copilot, we will cover the following key topics:

- Security Copilot – your ultimate security assistant
- Leveraging Security Copilot in Microsoft Defender
- Integrating Security Copilot with Microsoft Entra
- Exploring Security Copilot within Microsoft Purview
- Enhancing security with Microsoft Defender for Cloud
- Utilizing Security Copilot in Microsoft Intune
- From the embedded experience to the standalone experience

Want to try out the prompts, custom plugins, and promptbooks featured in this book? Take a look at the book's GitHub repository at `https://github.com/PacktPublishing/Microsoft-Copilot-for-Security`.

Security Copilot – your ultimate security assistant

Security Copilot serves as a remarkably handy, resourceful, and intelligent assistant for security professionals. Whether you're seeking insights into the tactics and tools used by threat actors, trying to identify attacks, investigating incidents, or looking for actionable recommendations, Security Copilot can provide guidance and information that are insightful, clear, and easy to understand.

Security Copilot plays a key role in investigating security incidents, analyzing suspicious files or scripts, assessing risky users, and proactively hunting for threats. Once the investigation is complete, it generates detailed reports to document the findings!

Security Copilot is also highly effective at gathering threat intelligence, identifying anomalies, and pinpointing attack surfaces. Additionally, it supports insider risk management, aids in eDiscovery, provides device details, assists device troubleshooting, helps with managing device policies and settings, and so much more.

Some of Security Copilot's capabilities are built right into Microsoft security solutions. This is known as the **embedded experience**. It acts like a smart assistant within the Microsoft solutions, providing real-time and context-specific insights, supporting security teams along the way without disrupting the workflow.

You can pivot from Security Copilot's embedded experience to the dedicated portal of Security Copilot, which offers a robust and comprehensive set of resources for in-depth analysis and security management. This is referred to as the **standalone experience**. It acts as a single pane of glass where you can access capabilities and features from all available solutions, including threat intelligence feeds, Microsoft security solutions, and third-party tools. It offers extensive data and insights for thorough analysis across a broad spectrum of information, with all features from the embedded experience also accessible within the standalone portal.

Whether it's the embedded or the standalone experience, Security Copilot acts as your royal assistant, guiding and supporting you at every step. To better understand what Security Copilot is and what it offers, let's start by exploring its core capabilities in the embedded experience. This will provide a solid overview of Security Copilot before we dive into its more advanced aspects.

Leveraging Security Copilot in Microsoft Defender XDR

Microsoft Defender XDR is an enterprise defense suite designed to offer integrated protection against advanced threats. It unifies detection, prevention, investigation, and response across endpoints, identities, emails, and applications to effectively safeguard against complex attacks. Think of it as a highly advanced, digital security guard that not only looks for potential threats but also takes action to stop them and helps recover any affected areas.

Security Copilot is seamlessly integrated into Microsoft Defender XDR to enhance security operations and incident response. Embedded directly in the Microsoft Defender XDR portal, Security Copilot leverages the power of AI to assist security teams to do the following:

- **Summarize incidents**: Compile details from all related alerts and analyst notes into a clear and concise incident summary. This allows a quick understanding of the scope and impact of security incidents, bringing the analyst up to speed with all pertinent information.
- **Use guided responses**: Guide the analyst through the recommended investigation and remediation actions based on the incident details.
- **Analyze scripts, codes, and registry keys**: Break down complex scripts, command lines, and registry keys, offering a clear and straightforward explanation that is easy to understand.
- **Analyze files**: Examine files for malicious content or suspicious behavior.
- **Generate KQL queries**: Create advanced queries to hunt for threats across the network.
- **Summarize device information**: Get an overview of a device's security posture and any unusual activities.
- **Summarize identities**: Get contextual insights into a user in the organization, including security concerns and potential anomalies.
- **Create incident reports**: Document findings and actions taken during an investigation.

Let's explore the features that Security Copilot adds to Microsoft Defender XDR. The following sections are designed to offer an understanding of how these functions enhance security operations and improve incident management efficiency.

Incident summary

As soon as you start examining a security incident in the Microsoft Defender XDR portal, Security Copilot is already present, seamlessly integrated, and ready to assist. It automatically generates a summary of the incident, providing a clear overview of the attack. The incident summary lays out the attack timeline, illustrates the stages of the attack, and highlights key details, all of which help you to quickly grasp the extent and progression of the attack that unfolded.

In the case of a particularly serious incident with many alerts involved, the incident summary generated by Security Copilot helps you understand the entire extent and nature of the attack, despite the complexity and volume of the alerts. For instance, as shown in the next screen capture, the incident involves 34 correlated alerts, affects 8 different assets, and includes over 50 suspicious entities. Security Copilot appears alongside the main incident page. It offers a concise summary that helps the security analyst quickly understand the full impact of the attack. Key events are clearly highlighted, helping to bring analysts up to speed with all relevant details:

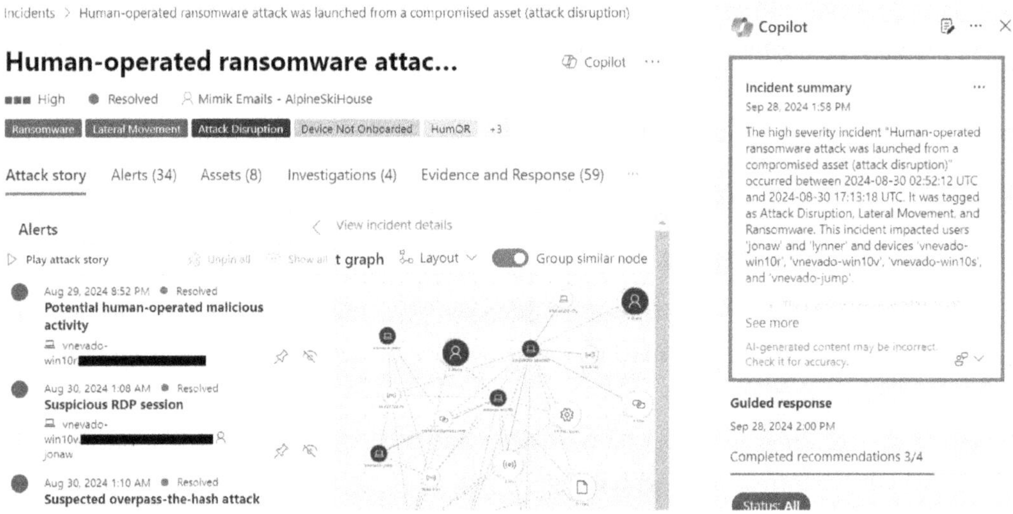

Figure 2.1 – Incident summary

Quick tip: Need to see a high-resolution version of this image? Open this book in the next-gen Packt Reader or view it in the PDF/ePub copy.

The next-gen Packt Reader and a **free PDF/ePub copy** of this book are included with your purchase. Scan the QR code OR visit `packtpub.com/unlock`, then use the search bar to find this book by name. Double-check the edition shown to make sure you get the right one.

In the full incident summary report shown next, you can see that the Security Copilot incident summary includes a high-level view of the attack, outlining its nature as a human-operated ransomware attack, and its severity. It details the start and end times of the attack and the sequence of significant activities, broken down by the stages of the attack. Each stage is associated with specific timestamps and affected assets, showing how the attack progressed over time.

Incident summary

The high severity incident "Human-operated ransomware attack was launched from a compromised asset (attack disruption)" occurred between 2024-08-30 02:52:12 UTC and 2024-08-30 17:13:18 UTC. It was tagged as Attack Disruption, Lateral Movement, and Ransomware. This incident impacted users 'jonaw' and 'lynner' and devices 'vnevado-win10r', 'vnevado-win10v', 'vnevado-win10s', and 'vnevado-jump'.

The incident began at 2024-08-30 02:52:12 UTC with potential human-operated malicious activity on 'vnevado-win10r' (Windows 10). At 2024-08-30 07:03:47 UTC, 'Orchestrator.ps1' was created on 'vnevado-win10v' (Windows 10) by 'SYSTEM'. Shortly after, at 2024-08-30 07:08:46 UTC, a suspicious RDP session was detected on 'vnevado-win10v', involving 'mimikatz.exe', 'powershell.exe', and IP 10.0.0.132.

- **DefenseEvasion:** At 2024-08-30 07:10:19 UTC, 'lynner' attempted to authenticate against 'VNEVADO-DC' from 'vnevado-win10v', indicating a suspected overpass-the-hash attack.
- **Execution:** At 2024-08-30 07:10:34 UTC, a suspicious PowerShell command line was executed on 'vnevado-win10v', followed by the creation of 'mimidrv.sys', 'mimikatz.exe', 'mimilib.dll', 'mimilove.exe', and 'mimispool.dll' by 'powershell.exe'.

- **CredentialAccess:** At 2024-08-30 07:10:39 UTC, 'mimikatz.exe' accessed 'lsass.exe' on 'vnevado-win10v', and Defender detected 'HackTool:Win32/Mimikatz!pz'. At 2024-08-30 07:11:42 UTC, 'mimikatz.exe' modified the LSASS process memory. At 2024-08-30 07:14:46 UTC, Defender terminated and quarantined 'mimikatz.exe'.
- **LateralMovement:** At 2024-08-30 07:24:37 UTC, possible lateral movement was detected involving IP 10.60.0.63 on 'vnevado-jump' (Windows Server 2016). At 2024-08-30 07:48:23 UTC, suspicious remote activity was detected on 'vnevado-win10s' (Windows 10) involving 'vssadmin.exe' and 'net.exe'. At 2024-08-30 07:49:07 UTC, possible ransomware activity was detected on 'vnevado-win10r', involving 'unsmoking.txt.lockbit' and IP 10.60.0.63.
- **CredentialAccess:** At 2024-08-30 07:49:20 UTC, there was a possible attempt to access the Primary Refresh Token (PRT) on 'vnevado-win10s' and 'vnevado-win10r' using 'BrowserCore.exe' and 'powershell.exe'.
- **LateralMovement:** At 2024-08-30 07:51:07 UTC, a hands-on-keyboard attack involving multiple devices was detected, impacting 'vnevado-win10r'. At 2024-08-30 07:56:11 UTC, lateral movement using SMB remote file access was blocked on 'vnevado-win10s'.

Guided responses

After the incident summary, Security Copilot offers tailored guidance for responding to the incident through its guided responses feature: "*Copilot in Defender uses AI and machine learning capabilities to contextualize an incident and learn from previous investigations to generate appropriate response actions*" (Microsoft, *Triage and investigate incidents with guided responses from Microsoft Copilot in Microsoft Defender*, `https://learn.microsoft.com/en-us/defender-xdr/security-copilot-m365d-guided-response`). The guided responses capability empowers security teams to apply response actions with confidence and speed, reducing the time and effort needed to resolve incidents.

Guided responses offer recommendations across four response categories: **Triage**, **Containment**, **Investigation**, and **Remediation**.

The **Triage** category within the guided responses feature offers recommendations on the appropriate incident classification. As illustrated in the next screenshot, Security Copilot suggests classifying an incident as a **true positive** because it recognizes that the organization has previously categorized similar incidents in this manner. To provide further clarity on this recommendation, Security Copilot also lets you view similar incidents:

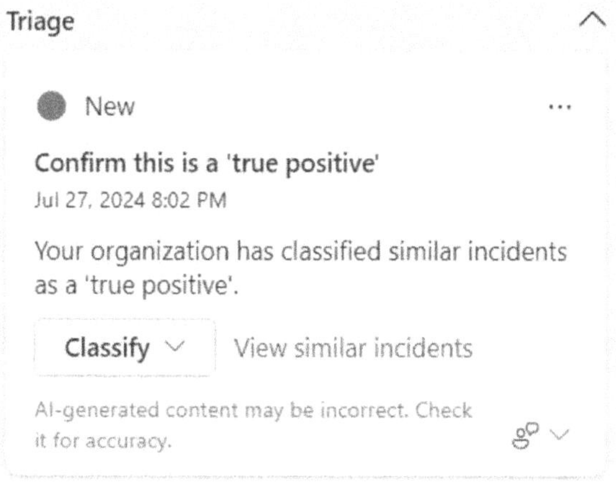

Figure 2.2 – Triage within the guided responses

The **Containment** category within guided responses provides recommended actions to limit the damage caused by the compromise, preventing the attack from affecting other systems, networks, or data within the organization. For example, as shown in the following screenshot, Security Copilot suggests isolating devices from the network as part of the containment strategy. Again, it provides a rationale and explanation for this recommendation:

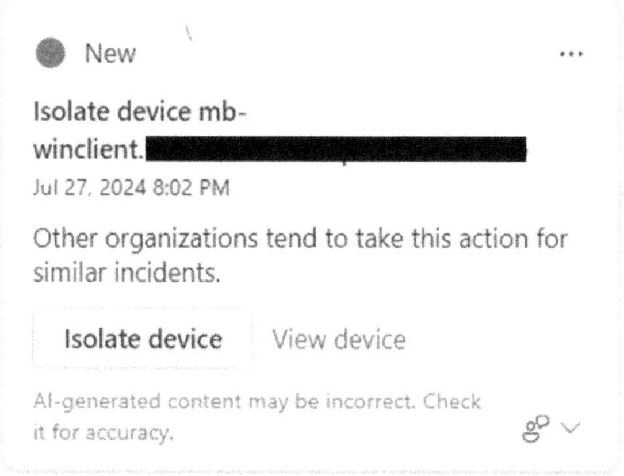

Figure 2.3 – Containment within the guided responses

The **Investigation** category within guided responses provides suggested actions for gathering more insights and conducting further investigations. As shown next, Security Copilot advises reaching out to the user to confirm their activity as the next step in the incident investigation.

It also prepares a message to send to the user that includes detailed information from the incident to provide additional context:

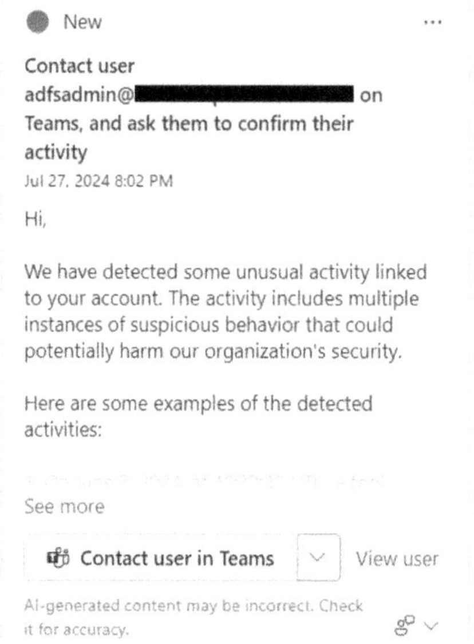

Figure 2.4 – Containment within the guided responses

The **Remediation** category in the guided responses feature suggests response actions to address or resolve threats identified during the incident. Security Copilot can recommend resetting the user password to prevent the attacker from accessing the compromised account. This step is crucial in halting further damage or data exfiltration. Security Copilot can also advise disabling the user account, as seen in the next screenshot. Disabling a compromised account prevents both the user and any attacker using that account from accessing systems and data. This immediate action is vital for containing the incident and stopping any ongoing malicious activities:

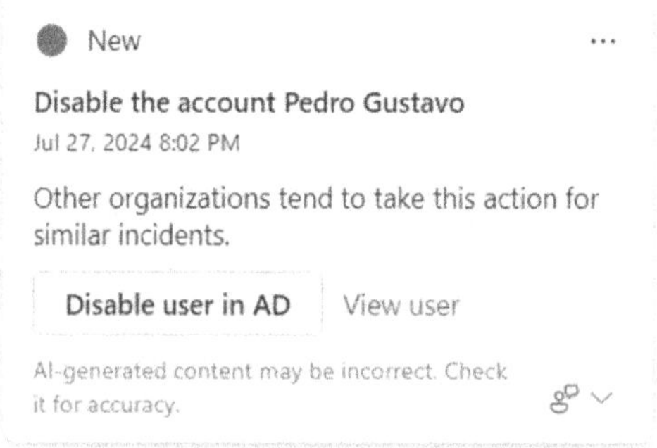

Figure 2.5 – Remediation within the guided responses

The guided responses feature of Security Copilot assists the security team throughout the incident investigation cycle, enhancing their efficiency and effectiveness. However, it's important to note that recommendations provided as a part of guided responses are not meant to be inclusive of all the possible steps an analyst should take. They're meant to serve as a starting point. Besides, guided responses, Security Copilot offers more advanced capabilities to support investigative efforts. Let's continue exploring in the next few sections.

Scripts, command lines, and registry keys analysis

The script analysis feature in Security Copilot allows for the examination of scripts, command lines, and registry keys. This capability enables security teams to thoroughly examine and comprehend complex scripts, malicious command lines, and more, that are frequently employed in sophisticated cyber-attacks.

During an investigation, an incident responder often relies on Defender for Endpoint's **Timeline** feature to review events that occurred on a device. *Defender for Endpoint is one of the security solutions within Microsoft Defender XDR.* It enables the responder to examine process activities to identify the malicious execution of files. Along with process events, Defender for Endpoint also records the associated process command-line information. This often provides crucial context for determining whether the process is being used for malicious purposes. For instance, while PowerShell is utilized by IT teams, security professionals, and attackers alike, simply discovering its execution is not sufficient to determine whether it is used for malicious purposes. Instead, an examination of the PowerShell command line helps to recognize its intent and identify potentially harmful actions.

Understanding PowerShell commands requires a solid grasp of PowerShell and considerable experience. In this context, Security Copilot becomes an invaluable tool. It examines the PowerShell command line, providing a simple and direct explanation of the PowerShell commands in question. This feature aids security analysts in promptly determining whether the PowerShell execution is being employed for malicious activities.

What's even more impressive is that Security Copilot can analyze obfuscated or encoded scripts and command lines. This capability greatly helps security analysts by saving them the time and effort needed to decode such complex commands. De-obfuscation and decoding demand specialized skills that are often scarce within security teams.

As shown in the next screenshot, the PowerShell command line is lengthy and appears to be encoded. Security Copilot translates and summarizes this complex command line into a clear, easily understandable description:

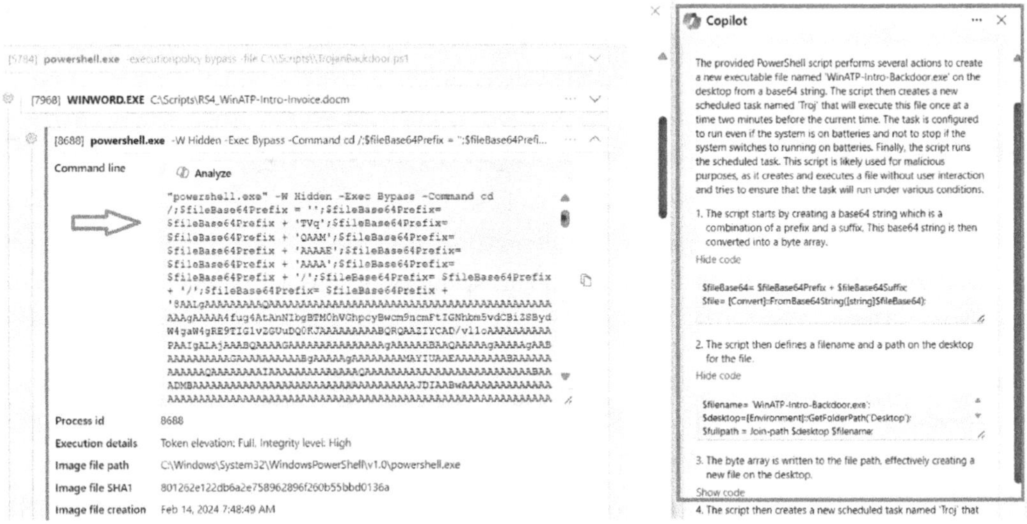

Figure 2.6 – Encoded command-line analysis

Here is a complete copy of the analysis from Security Copilot. You can see that it breaks down the encoded PowerShell commands and makes them easier to understand. This detailed explanation uncovers the intent behind the script, which helps security analysts quickly grasp its purpose:

> The provided PowerShell script performs several actions to create a new executable file named '`WinATP-Intro-Backdoor.exe`' on the desktop from a base64 string. The script then creates a new scheduled task named 'Troj' that will execute this file once at a time two minutes before the current time. The task is configured to run even if the system is on batteries and not to stop if the system switches to running on batteries. Finally, the script runs the scheduled task. This script is likely used for malicious purposes, as it creates and executes a file without user interaction and tries to ensure that the task will run under various conditions.
>
> The script starts by creating a base64 string which is a combination of a prefix and a suffix. This base64 string is then converted into a byte array.
>
> 1. The script then defines a filename and a path on the desktop for the file.
> 2. The byte array is written to the file path, effectively creating a new file on the desktop.
> 3. The script then creates a new scheduled task named 'Troj' that will execute the newly created file. The task is set to run once at a time two minutes before the current time.

4. The script modifies the settings of the scheduled task to allow it to start even if the system is running on batteries and not to stop if the system switches to running on batteries.
5. Finally, the script runs the scheduled task.

The **Script analysis** feature in Security Copilot is available for any process with a command line in Defender for Endpoint. This feature greatly assists security analysts while they review process execution events during an investigation. As analysts are sifting through a large number of device events, they can ask Security Copilot to quickly analyze the command line of a process, review the analysis summary, understand its purpose, and then decide whether the process appears suspicious or not.

As another example, in the next screenshot, there is a device event where `svchost.exe` created the process `gpupdate.exe`. The command line for `svchost.exe` reads: `svchost.exe -k netsvcs -p -s Schedule`. To quickly understand the function of this command, the responder can click the **Analyze** button in the **Command line** section of the process, allowing Security Copilot to generate a summary of the command:

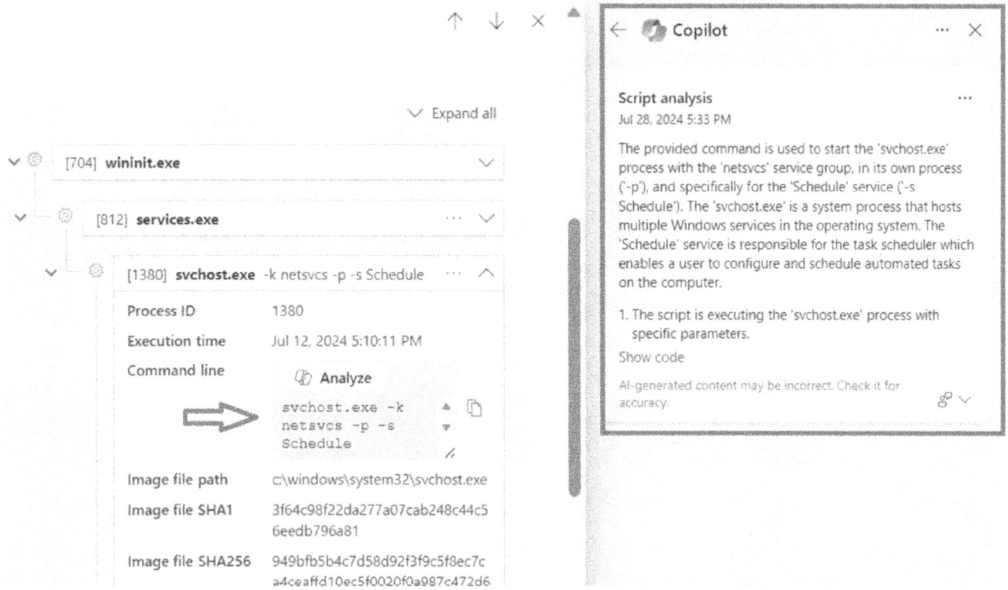

Figure 2.7 – Command line analysis with Security Copilot

For your reference, here is the Security Copilot analysis copied from the previous screenshot:

> The provided command is used to start the 'svchost.exe' process with the 'netsvcs' service group, in its own process ('-p'), and specifically for the 'Schedule' service ('-s Schedule'). The 'svchost.exe' is a system process that hosts multiple Windows services in the operating system. The 'Schedule' service is responsible for the task scheduler which enables a user to configure and schedule automated tasks on the computer.
>
> 1. The script is executing the 'svchost.exe' process with specific parameters.

`svchost.exe` is a Windows system process that manages multiple Windows services. Since it handles many crucial background tasks, it's often targeted by malware. Attackers might exploit or disguise their malicious software within this process to avoid detection. In these situations, having Security Copilot quickly analyze its behavior can be very helpful for security analysts.

Optionally, the Script analysis feature also highlights the MITRE ATT&CK techniques identified within the script, helping analysts to quickly understand the adversarial tactics being used and assess the potential impact of malicious activities.

In addition to analyzing scripts and command lines, Security Copilot can also examine registry keys and their values, as seen in the next screenshot:

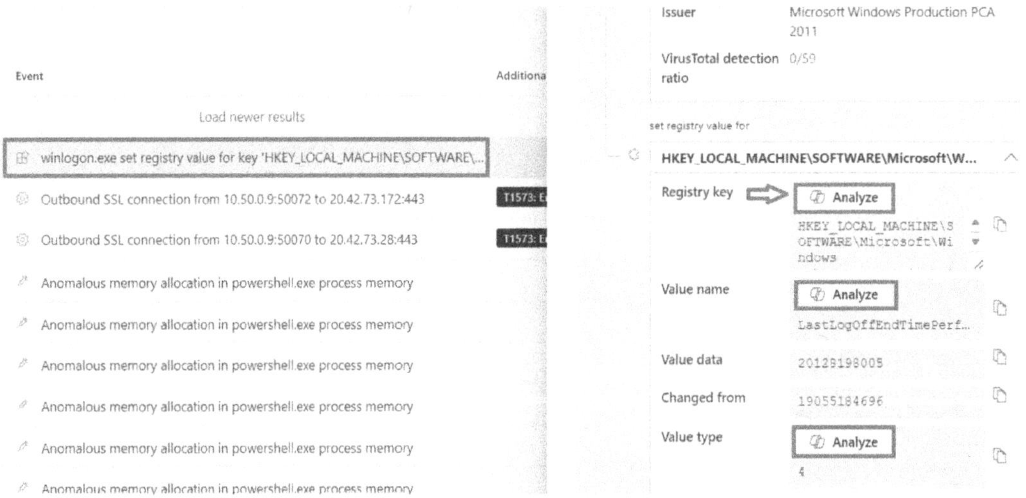

Figure 2.8 – Registry key analysis

Registry keys are another area commonly exploited by attackers. Threat actors may create or modify registry keys to ensure their malware survives reboots. For example, they might add entries to the `Run` or `RunOnce` registry keys to launch malicious programs automatically when the device starts.

By altering registry keys, attackers can change system settings or permissions to gain higher privileges. For example, they might modify registry values related to user permissions to escalate their access level. Malicious actors can hide their activities by altering registry keys that control system visibility and notifications. For instance, they might disable security alerts or hide the presence of malicious files and processes from the user.

It's challenging to be familiar with every registry key to quickly and accurately detect malicious usage. Security Copilot, as your assistant, provides analysis on registry keys that allows for a more thorough and rapid inspection of the behaviors and configurations that could be indicative of security threats or breaches.

In the case when the registry key is used for malicious purposes, Security Copilot not only explains its function and behavior but also warns that this registry location is a common location used by malware for persistence. The next screen capture depicts the analysis of a suspicious registry key event:

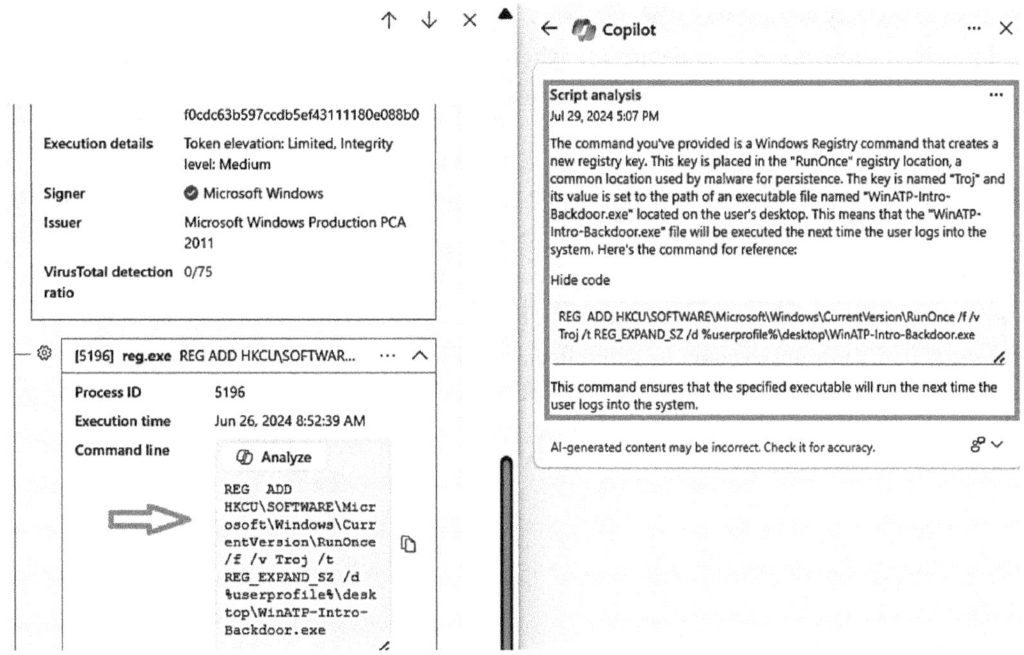

Figure 2.9 – Registry key analysis

File analysis

The incident summary generated by Security Copilot provides a foundation for understanding the scope of an incident. The guided responses feature within Security Copilot then offers actionable steps to triage, contain, investigate, and remediate incidents. On top of this, Security Copilot presents script analysis options to support further in-depth investigative efforts. Furthermore, once suspicious files are identified, Security Copilot helps security teams quickly evaluate and analyze them with its file analysis feature.

The file analysis feature lets the security analyst pick a file in Microsoft Defender and have Security Copilot examine and analyze it. A detailed report is then generated. This analysis report provides an overview of the file, including any detection names if it is flagged as malicious. The report typically includes essential details such as certificates and signers, as well as a summary of the file's contents that contributed to its evaluation. It often highlights strings within the file, lists the API calls it makes, and provides information on relevant certificates. This thorough analysis equips the security analyst with the necessary insights to effectively evaluate the file's impact and intent, making it easier to determine whether the file poses a threat. This is particularly useful for tracking and resolving attacks that use malicious files to mimic legitimate or system files to evade detection.

For example, Microsoft Defender reports a file named `mimikatz.exe` as malware. The security analyst needs to validate Microsoft Defender's verdict and ensure that the file is indeed malicious. Rather than spending excessive time manually analyzing the file, the analyst can turn to Security Copilot to quickly and thoroughly evaluate the file. As shown in the next screen capture, you can request Security Copilot to generate a detailed analysis report for the `mimikatz.exe` file:

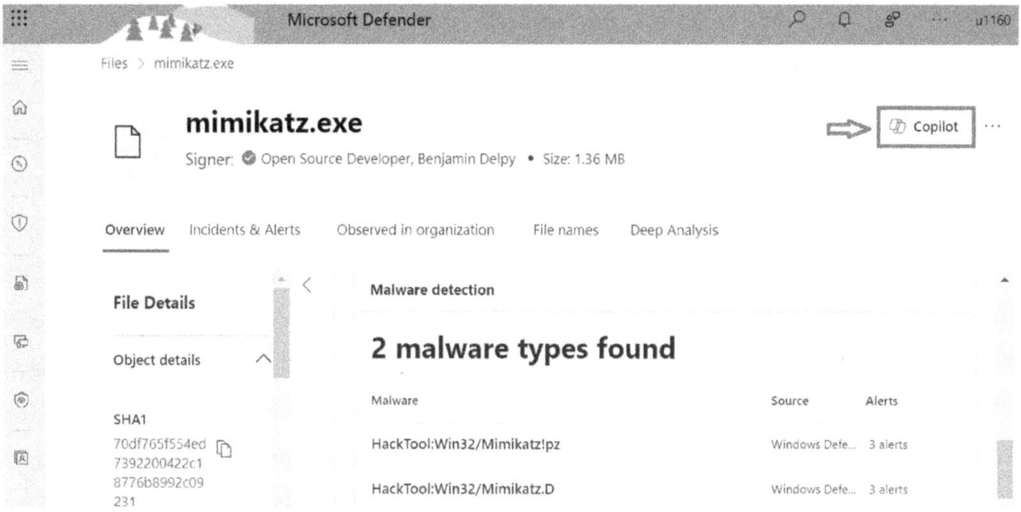

Figure 2.10 – File analysis

The report from Security Copilot indicates that the file is detected as malicious by 63 out of 74 engines in VirusTotal, including Microsoft's, and is flagged as `HackTool:Win32/Mimikatz!pz`. The file has a valid certificate from Open Source Developer but importing functions with potential security risks, such as unauthorized data access and privilege escalation. You can view part of the analysis report here as a reference:

Overview

The file has been detected as malicious by 63 out of 74 engines in the VirusTotal static scan, including by the Microsoft engine as HackTool:Win32/Mimikatz!pz. The digital certificate is valid and signed by Open Source Developer, Benjamin Delpy, with a thumbprint of 30258528ee8476dc9b68486668959cff820e8e3b. The malware determination confirms the file as malware. The PE metadata reveals an image size of 1351680 and the company name as gentilkiwi (Benjamin DELPY).

API calls

The file under scrutiny imports several functions from DLLs, some of which have potential security implications.

The file imports 'CDLocateCSystem' from 'cryptdll.dll', typically used to locate cryptographic systems. Misuse could lead to unauthorized data access or cryptographic system manipulation.

'BuildSecurityDescriptorW' from 'advapi32.dll' is also imported. This function builds a security descriptor, a data structure with security information for a securable object. Misuse could lead to privilege escalation or unauthorized access.

The file imports 'SCardGetAttrib' from 'winscard.dll', used to retrieve current reader attributes. Misuse could lead to unauthorized smart card data access.

'I_NetServerTrustPasswordsGet' from 'netapi32.dll' is also imported. This function retrieves server trust passwords, which could be exploited for unauthorized network resource access.

Lastly, the file imports 'CryptImportKey' from 'advapi32.dll', used to import cryptographic keys. Misuse could lead to unauthorized encrypted data access.

These functions could lead to security risks such as unauthorized data access, privilege escalation, or security mechanism bypassing. Further investigation is recommended to assess potential security implications.

Based on this report, the security analyst can likely determine that the file is indeed malicious.

From this demonstrated example, you can see that the file analysis feature in Security Copilot enables security teams to quickly conduct in-depth examinations of potentially malicious files. This capability empowers analysts from all levels to complete their investigation with a shorter turnaround time, significantly boosting efficiency, particularly when time is critical in addressing security incidents.

Whether the file is seen in the Defender for Endpoint timeline, accessed through its file page, or flagged as suspicious in an incident, the security analyst can request Security Copilot to analyze the file and generate a detailed report.

Device summary

Once a security analyst identifies something suspicious about a device, they can request Security Copilot to generate a device summary. This summary provides details on the device's security posture, vulnerable software, and any unusual behaviors. With this information, the analyst can quickly evaluate the device's risk level and understand potential threats from vulnerabilities, misconfigurations, or other anomalies.

Additionally, the device summary may offer extra context that supports incident investigation, enabling security teams to act promptly to address potential threats and decide on appropriate response actions.

When you navigate to the device page in Microsoft Defender, Security Copilot automatically generates the **Device summary** information and displays it in the **Copilot** side pane on the right:

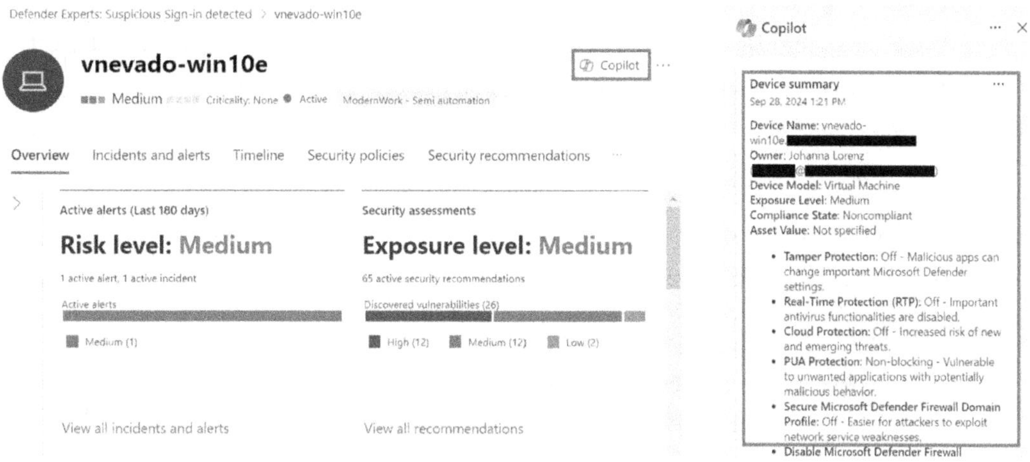

Figure 2.11 – Device summary

For instance, from the detailed device summary shown next, Security Copilot points out a couple of concerns: key settings, such as **Tamper Protection**, **Real-Time Protection**, **Cloud Protection**, and **Microsoft Defender Firewall**, are all disabled, leaving the system vulnerable to malware and network attacks. Additionally, the device has high-severity vulnerabilities in Firefox and OpenSSL, increasing the risk of exploitation:

Device Name: vnevado-win10e.[redacted]

Owner: Johanna Lorenz ([redacted]@[redacted])

Device Model: Virtual Machine

Exposure Level: Medium

Compliance State: Noncomplian

Asset Value: Not specified

- **Tamper Protection:** Off - Malicious apps can change important Microsoft Defender settings.
- **Real-Time Protection (RTP):** Off - Important antivirus functionalities are disabled.
- **Cloud Protection:** Off - Increased risk of new and emerging threats.

- **PUA Protection:** Non-blocking - Vulnerable to unwanted applications with potentially malicious behavior.
- **Secure Microsoft Defender Firewall Domain Profile**: Off - Easier for attackers to exploit network service weaknesses.
- **Disable Microsoft Defender Firewall notifications (Domain profile)**: Off
- **Disable Microsoft Defender Firewall notifications (Private profile)**: Off
- **Disable merging of local Microsoft Defender Firewall connection rules (Public profile)**: Off
- **Attack Surface Reduction (ASR)**: Off - Increased risk from common attack techniques and malicious software.

Vulnerable software

- **Firefox 128.0.0.0**: High severity
- **OpenSSL 3.3.0.0**: High severity

Intune policies

The device is noncompliant due to the Device Risk policy. Specifically, the setting Windows10CompliancePolicy.DeviceThreatProtectionRequiredSecurityLevel is noncompliant.

In conclusion, the device summary from Security Copilot gives analysts a quick overview of a device's security posture when suspicious activity is detected. It highlights vulnerable software and unusual behaviors, enabling rapid risk assessment and identification of potential threats.

Advanced hunting using KQL

Kusto Query Language (**KQL**) is a query language used to retrieve and analyze data in various Microsoft solutions such as Microsoft Defender and Microsoft Sentinel. It is designed to handle large volumes of data efficiently and allows users to perform complex queries and analytics on log and telemetry data. KQL is known for its powerful querying capabilities, including filtering, sorting, aggregating, and joining data.

Advanced hunting is a feature in Microsoft Defender XDR designed to identify and investigate threats throughout an organization's environment. It utilizes KQL to search through large datasets for signs of suspicious or malicious activities. It enables security analysts to create custom queries to detect and investigate potential threats, trends, and anomalies that might not be captured by standard security alerts or automated processes.

Advanced hunting is very powerful, but to fully leverage its capabilities, a good understanding of KQL is necessary. Threat hunters or security analysts who are not yet proficient in KQL can turn to Security Copilot to draft KQL queries for them. Additionally, Security Copilot offers detailed explanations of the query to show the underlying logic. This cuts down the time needed to create a hunting query from scratch, allowing security teams to concentrate more on identifying and investigating threats.

When you open the **Advanced hunting** page in Microsoft Defender, Security Copilot appears on the right-hand side, offering several sample Copilot instructions called **prompts** to assist you in crafting and refining your queries.

If you choose a sample prompt such as **Show the top 5 devices with the most network connection failures,** Security Copilot then generates a KQL query as shown in the next screenshot:

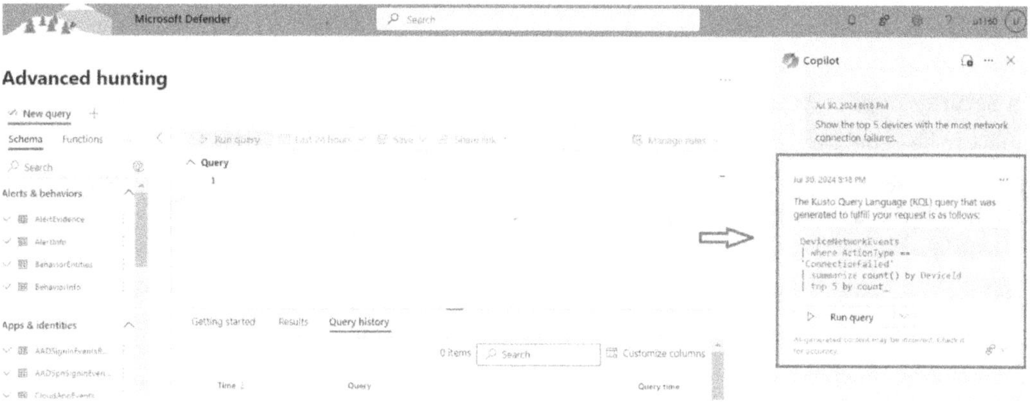

Figure 2.12 – Security Copilot generates a KQL query

Once you click the **Run query** option, Security Copilot transfers this KQL query into the **Advanced hunting** pane and executes it:

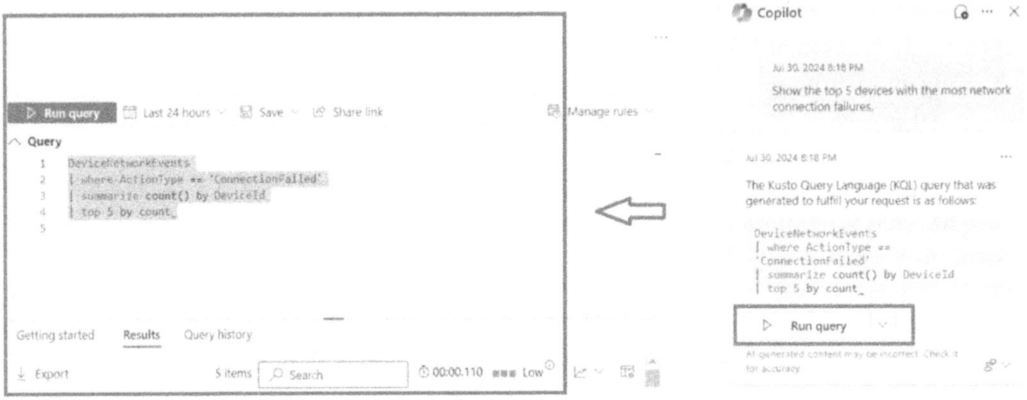

Figure 2.13 – Security Copilot executes a KQL query

In Security Copilot, you can input your own **natural language prompt** to request a new KQL query to be generated. For example, you can ask:

```
From the DeviceEvents, can you summarize all the action types and sort
them in ascending order?
```

As shown next, Security Copilot generates a KQL query for you, which is then executed in **Advanced hunting**. The result output displays a list of action types from the `DeviceEvents` data table, sorted in ascending order, which matches the request specified in your prompt:

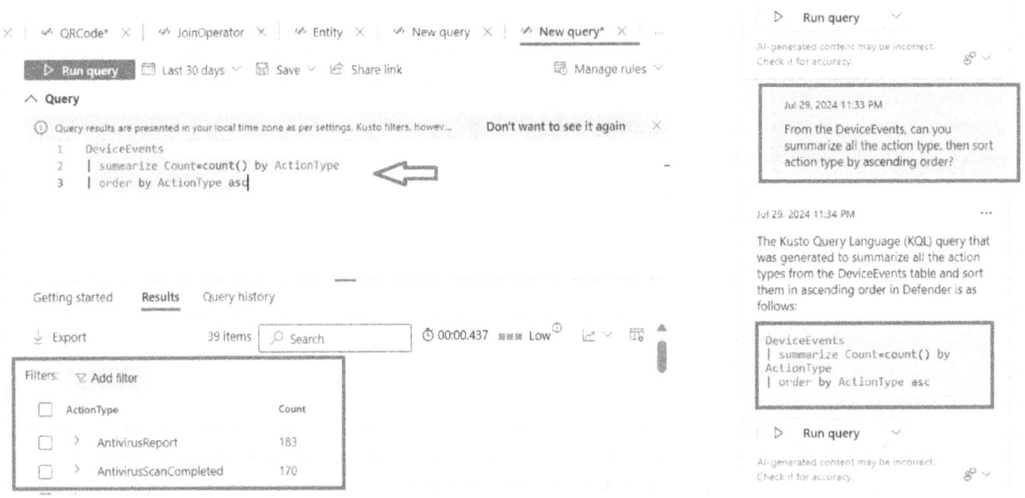

Figure 2.14 – Security Copilot generates and then executes the KQL query

It's important to note that Security Copilot does not always produce the correct KQL query. You can use the query generated by Copilot as a starting point or reference, but you need to verify its accuracy. For more information about KQL or to master it, you can refer to its documentation repository at `https://learn.microsoft.com/en-us/kusto/?view=microsoft-fabric`.

Incident reports

Writing incident reports can be a dreaded task for many security professionals. It's often time-consuming and tedious, requiring a thorough review and the compilation of all relevant logs. In some cases, preparing the incident report can take longer than the actual investigation. This is why many security analysts are thrilled that Security Copilot now generates detailed incident reports for them!

Using Security Copilot, security teams can generate an incident report with a single click by selecting the report icon in the **Copilot** side panel. Security Copilot creates a detailed report that includes key timestamps such as incident creation and closure, as well as the timing of the first and last events. The report outlines the investigation and remediation actions taken, including specific actions such as device isolation, disabling a user, and soft deletion of emails. It also details the analysts involved in the response, the classification of the incident, and the reasons for this classification. Follow-up steps such as recommendations, open issues, or next actions noted by the analysts are also included in the report.

The incident report can be copied to the clipboard, posted to the activity log, or exported as a PDF. When exporting the incident report as a PDF, you have the option to customize the report by including or excluding information such as the overview, attack story, scope, evidence and response, and supporting data.

The following screenshots of the incident report are provided as a reference to highlight some of its details. The complete incident report is available in the GitHub repository for this book and can be accessed at `https://github.com/PacktPublishing/Microsoft-Copilot-for-Security/blob/main/Other/Incident%20Report%20-%20Chapter%202.pdf`.

The first screen capture displays the detailed incident summary in the incident report:

Incident summary

The high severity incident titled 'Multi-stage incident involving Execution & Lateral movement on multiple endpoints reported by multiple sources' occurred between 2024-06-07 09:16:21 UTC and 2024-06-07 10:39:50 UTC.

- At 2024-06-07 09:00:19 UTC, on the device 'mb-adfs' (WindowsServer2022), the 'SenseCM.exe' process (running as SYSTEM) created multiple files including 'PolicyEnforcer.ps1', 'AntiVirus.psm1', and 'EDR.psm1'.
- At 2024-06-07 09:16:18 UTC, on the device 'mb-winclient' (Windows10), the 'powershell.exe' process created the file 'Midnight182.ps1' under the user 'kdickens'.
- **Discovery**: At 2024-06-07 09:16:21 UTC, a suspicious sequence of exploration activities was detected on 'mb-winclient' involving the IP 10.2.0.4 and processes including 'powershell.exe' and 'whoami.exe', impacting users 'pgustavo' and 'kdickens'.
- **DefenseEvasion**: At 2024-06-07 09:16:21 UTC, a process was injected with potentially malicious code on 'mb-winclient', involving the file 'Midnight182.ps1' and the IP 10.2.0.4, impacting users 'pgustavo' and 'kdickens'.
- **Execution**: At 2024-06-07 09:16:22 UTC, a malicious PowerShell Cmdlet was invoked on 'mb-winclient' involving the file 'Midnight182.ps1' and impacting user 'kdickens'.
- **LateralMovement**: At 2024-06-07 09:16:22 UTC, suspicious hands-on keyboard user behavior was detected on 'mb-winclient' involving the process 'powershell.exe' and impacting user 'kdickens'.

Figure 2.15 – Incident summary in the incident report

The incident report also includes a graph that illustrates the attack story, as demonstrated in the next screenshot:

Attack story graph

MITRE categories	Number of alerts	Impacted assets	Evidence
6	30	8	6

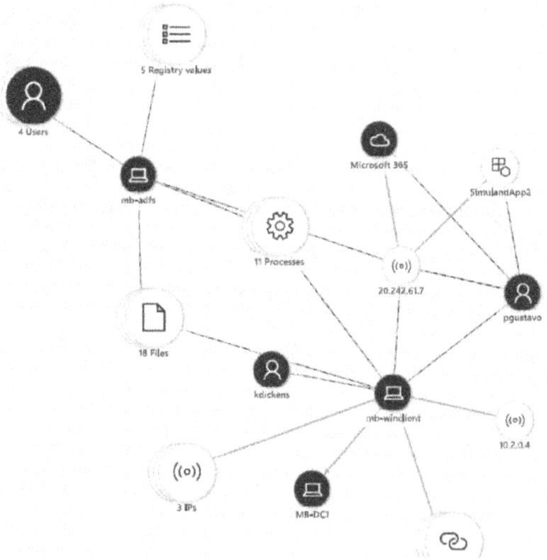

Figure 2.16 – Attack story graph in the incident report

The incident report displays alerts and their threat categories, organized according to **MITRE ATT&CK** tactics:

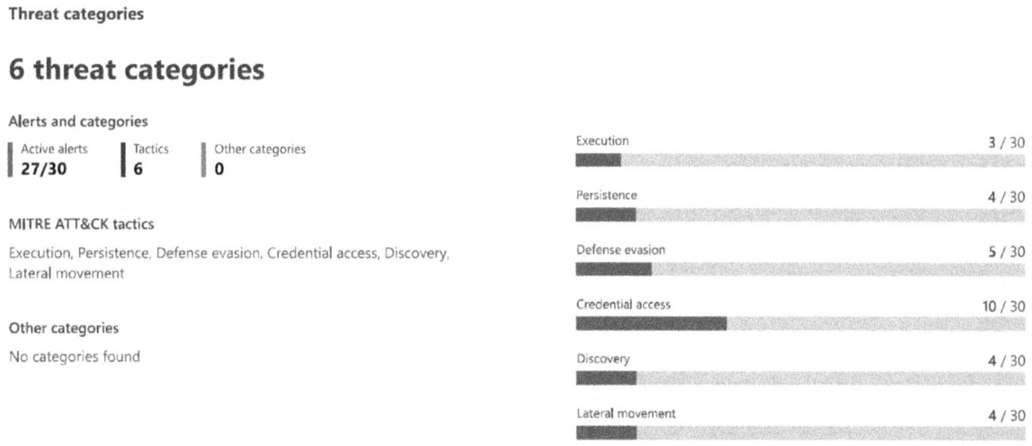

Figure 2.17 – Threat categories in the incident report

After observing how Security Copilot integrates with Microsoft Defender XDR to enhance security operations and incident response, you likely appreciate the power of AI in increasing the effectiveness and efficiency of security teams. Next, let's explore how Security Copilot integrates with **Microsoft Entra** to further support and strengthen security measures.

Integrating Security Copilot with Microsoft Entra

Microsoft Entra is designed to help organizations manage and secure who has access to their digital resources. It simplifies the process of verifying user identities and controlling their access to various systems and information. Think of it as a digital gatekeeper that ensures only authorized individuals can get into the right places, helping to protect sensitive data and support secure operations. Microsoft Entra includes a range of products designed to secure access for a variety of identities, including employees, external partners, and customers, from anywhere, to any resource across clouds and on-premises.

Microsoft Entra ID Protection is a part of the broader Microsoft Entra suite. Microsoft Entra ID Protection identifies when a user's behavior or login attempts seem suspicious or unusual, which could signal a possible threat. For instance, if a user suddenly tries to access sensitive information from an unexpected location, Entra ID Protection can flag this as *risky* and help the organization take steps to prevent any potential security breaches.

If a user account is compromised and appears on the internet, such as on the dark web, Microsoft Entra ID Protection triggers a *leaked credentials* alert. This alert indicates that the user's account and credentials may no longer be trusted, as they could be used by attackers to gain access. Consequently, Entra ID Protection flags this user as risky: "*This risk detection indicates that the account's valid credentials leaked. The leak can occur when someone uploads the credentials in public code artifact on GitHub, or when the credentials are leaked through a data breach. When the Microsoft leaked credentials service acquires credentials from GitHub, the dark web, paste sites, or other sources, they're checked against current valid credentials in Microsoft Entra ID to find valid matches*" (Microsoft, *Securing workload identities*, `https://learn.microsoft.com/en-us/entra/id-protection/concept-workload-identity-risk`).

In addition to these two scenarios just described, Microsoft Entra ID Protection can identify a user as risky in various other situations. To assist security analysts in managing and understanding these diverse scenarios, Security Copilot, embedded in Entra, provides a summary for each risky user. This summary includes an explanation of why the user is deemed risky and a list of recommended next steps for investigation and preventing future incidents. Access to additional help and documentation is also provided by Security Copilot.

As an example, the *Risky user* report in Entra ID Protection provides a list of users who have been flagged as risky due to suspicious or potentially harmful activities. By selecting a user from the *Risky user* report, you can then navigate to that user's **Risky User Details** page. Security Copilot is already present there, providing the user summary for you.

In this example, the summary by Security Copilot highlights that user Cameron has been flagged for three recent high-risk activities, detected through Microsoft Entra threat intelligence, and signs of suspicious behavior such as anonymous IP addresses and password spray attacks. Each risky sign-in lacked multi-factor authentication and involved unfamiliar IP addresses and locations:

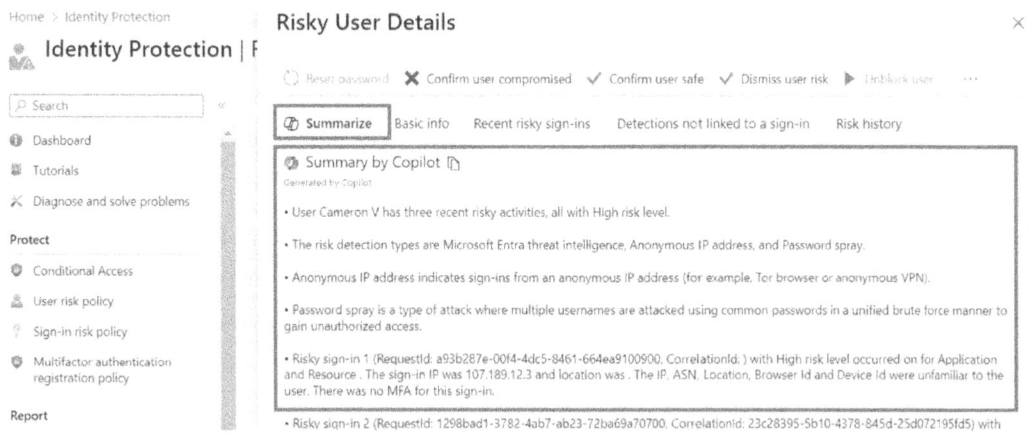

Figure 2.18 – Ricky user summary

In the Microsoft Entra admin center, clicking the **Copilot** button by the navigation bar opens up the Security Copilot side panel. As shown in the next screenshot, Security Copilot offers suggested questions to ask such as **List user sign-ins that failed in the last 24 hours** or **How does Microsoft determine Risky Users?**. There is also an option to provide your own questions to get tailored insights:

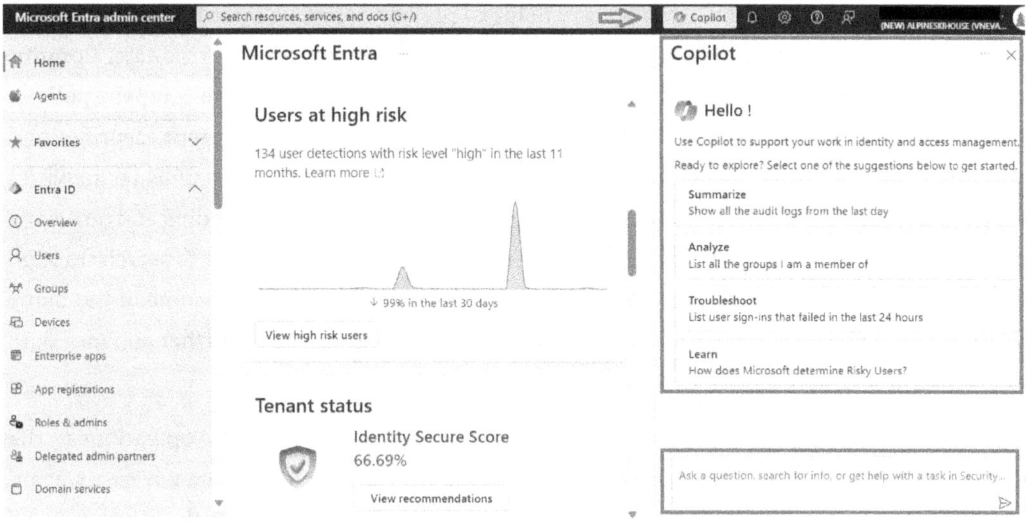

Figure 2.19 – Security Copilot embedded in Entra admin center

Additionally, with the Security Copilot Entra **plugin**, analysts can also access user details, sign-in logs, audit logs, group information, and more to support their investigations and identify other suspicious activities. Further details on Security Copilot plugins (including the Entra one) will be covered in *Chapter 4*. A detailed case study highlighting additional capabilities and features of the Security Copilot Entra plugin will be presented in *Chapter 9*.

Now that you've observed how Security Copilot integrates with Microsoft Defender to improve security operations and incident response, and how it helps security analysts manage and understand risky users in Microsoft Entra, let's explore how Security Copilot applies the same capabilities to data and compliance within **Microsoft Purview**.

Exploring Security Copilot within Microsoft Purview

Microsoft Purview is a tool designed to help organizations in managing and protecting their data. It tracks where data is stored, and ensures it is organized, secure, and meets regulatory requirements. It acts as a smart assistant by keeping data organized and secure, while also simplifying the management and protection of important information. It is a comprehensive solution for data governance, security, and compliance.

Purview provides a range of essential features to assist organizations in managing their data efficiently. Its **Data loss prevention** feature helps to prevent sensitive information from being accidentally shared or leaked by automatically detecting and protecting at-risk data. **Communication compliance** ensures that users' messages and interactions adhere to company policies and regulations, helping maintain proper standards. **Insider risk management** identifies and addresses potential threats from within the organization by monitoring for unusual activities that might indicate internal risks. And **eDiscovery** simplifies the process of finding and retrieving important information during legal investigations or audits, making it easier to search through large volumes of data for relevant documents and evidence. These are just some of the many features offered by Purview; there are additional capabilities designed to further enhance data management and security.

Security Copilot brings the same set of capabilities we have seen for security operations to the world of data and compliance. Integrated directly into Purview, it equips data governance and compliance experts with generative AI capabilities, significantly enhancing the efficiency and speed of their investigations. Now, let's take a closer look at these features and how they can be utilized.

Data loss prevention alert investigation

The **data loss prevention** (**DLP**) feature in Microsoft Purview helps protect sensitive information from being accidentally shared or leaked. It works by monitoring and controlling how data is used and shared across the organization. If it detects that sensitive information, such as personal details or financial data, might be at risk, it can block or alert the security teams to prevent potential leaks. Essentially, DLP ensures that important information stays secure and only reaches the people who should have access to it.

Investigating DLP alerts can feel like solving a jigsaw puzzle, with pieces scattered across various data sources including applications, cloud services, emails, endpoints, and chat. The process is further complicated by the various rules and conditions of each policy that must be analyzed and understood. This can be challenging for data security analysts.

One way Security Copilot can assist is by offering a comprehensive summary of the DLP alert. It provides key details, including policy rules, sources, files involved, and more. Additionally, the summary pulls the user risk levels from **Insider risk management**, providing integrated insights across data security solutions. These summaries provide the analysts with a good starting point for further investigation.

On the **Alerts** page of the **Data loss prevention** solution in Purview, you can select the **Get a summary from Security Copilot** option to generate a summary of the alert, as seen in the next screen capture:

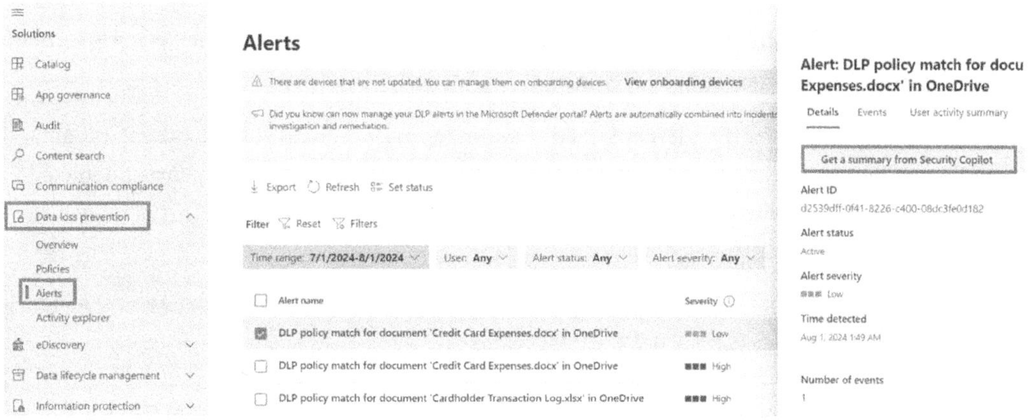

Figure 2.20 – Getting a summary of a DLP alert

For instance, with the **DLP policy match for document 'Credit Card Expenses.docx' in OneDrive** alert, the summary shown in the next screen capture provides key information that helps the analyst to quickly understand the impact and specifics of the issue. It identifies the alert as low severity for a document in OneDrive that is linked to the user Natasha. The summary includes details about the specific policy and rule that triggered the alert. It also notes that the file contains content that is blocked from sharing under this policy. This concise overview helps the analysts understand the context and scope of the alert, enabling them to assess and address the issue effectively:

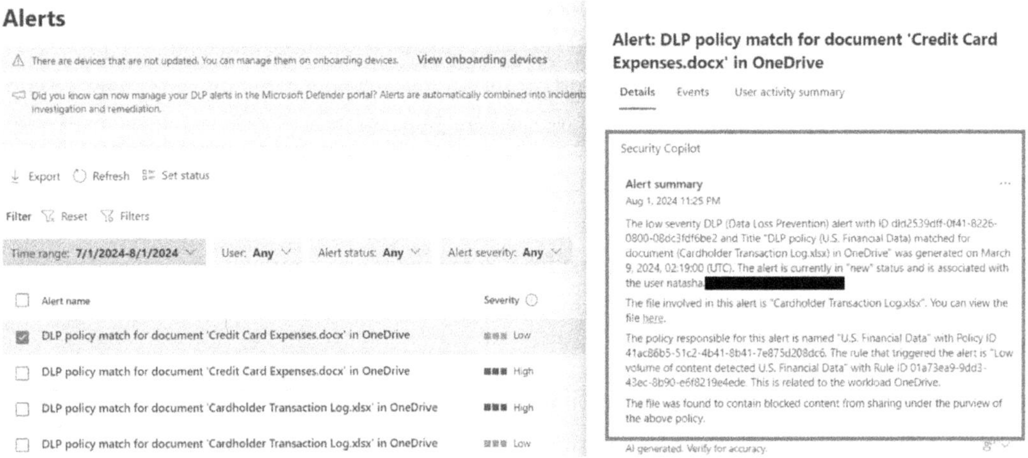

Figure 2.21 – The summary of a DLP alert

The specific policy and the rule that triggered the alert, as documented in the Security Copilot summary, are provided next for your reference:

> The policy responsible for this alert is named "U.S. Financial Data" with Policy ID 41ac86b5-51c2-4b41-8b41-7e875d208dc6. The rule that triggered the alert is "Low volume of content detected U.S. Financial Data" with Rule ID 01a73ea9-9dd3-43ec-8b90-e6f8219e4ede. This is related to the workload OneDrive.
>
> The file was found to contain blocked content from sharing under the purview of the above policy.

eDiscovery

The **eDiscovery** feature in Purview helps organizations locate and manage critical information for legal or compliance purposes. For instance, if a company is involved in a legal dispute and needs to find all emails and documents related to the specific project, eDiscovery in Purview can quickly search through all its digital content to identify and gather the relevant files.

This ensures that important information is not overlooked. Essentially, eDiscovery streamlines the process of tracking down and organizing data needed for legal cases or compliance audits.

Legal investigations can take hours, days, or even weeks to sift through the list of evidence collected in review sets. This process often requires expensive resources, such as outside counsel, to manually review each document and assess its relevance to the case.

With Security Copilot, analysts can quickly obtain a comprehensive summary of the conversations in the review set with just a single click. Review sets typically range from a few dozen to several thousand files, especially in large-scale investigations. By providing a contextual summary of items in a review set, Security Copilot greatly helps the analyst to quickly identify relevant information, saving valuable time and making the investigation process more efficient.

For example, the snippet in the next screenshot shows a portion of a review set in eDiscovery:

Figure 2.22 – A portion of a review set in eDiscovery

Imagine the time needed to read through the emails in this review set to piece together and understand what happened. In contrast, Security Copilot provides a contextual overview of the items in the review set. This summary, as illustrated next, saves analysts significant time by quickly highlighting useful information and capturing the key details from the review set:

> The conversation you provided involves two individuals, Seungin and Nina. They discuss a confidential acquisition of two companies, BitDefender and Frostvision, by another company named Contoso. Seungin shares this insider information with Nina, predicting that this acquisition will cause a surge in Contoso's stocks. They plan to capitalize on this information by purchasing stocks in BitDefender and Frostvision. Seungin advises Nina to keep this information confidential and not to act too hastily. Nina agrees to this plan and offers to split the profits with Seungin, intending to move the funds to offshore accounts. They both agree to keep their agreement a secret.

Additionally, Security Copilot offers prompts to assist in identifying relevant details, key participants, or important topics for further investigation. Here are a few examples of the prompts you may encounter:

- **Please identify key participants**
- **Please identify key topics**
- **Please identify action items**

Insider risk management

Insider risk management (IRM) in Microsoft Purview helps organizations to identify and address potential risks that come from within the company. It monitors activities and behavior to spot any unusual or suspicious actions that might indicate internal threats, such as data theft or policy violations. For example, if an employee is accessing a large volume of sensitive information they don't normally work with or is trying to share confidential data outside the company, IRM can flag these activities for further review. By analyzing patterns and behaviors, it helps organizations detect and manage these risks before they become serious problems, ensuring a safer and more secure work environment.

Investigating an insider risk alert involves a significant amount of effort due to the extensive details that must be reviewed. Analysts need to sift through a variety of logs, including the activities that triggered the alert, user information, and historical data. To fully understand why a user was flagged as high risk, they must examine detailed records and risk factors, often navigating through a large amount of information. Additionally, it can be difficult to know where to begin the investigation, especially when risky activities span over a long period.

Again, the comprehensive summary provided by Security Copilot offers key details, including alert severity, user details, and much more! These summaries help accelerate investigations by helping the analysts quickly gain context into user intent and timing of risky activities, enabling the analysts to tailor the investigation with specific dates in mind and quickly pinpoint sensitive files at risk.

For example, from the alert summary shown next, Security Copilot indicates that this high-severity alert involves a user flagged as high risk due to substantial activities related to potential data theft. Key information includes the specific policy triggered by an HR offboarding event and the nature of the user's activities, such as cumulative exfiltration of sensitive data. The summary details the specific risk factors, such as sending 30 emails with attachments and accessing 14 sensitive SharePoint files, along with an HR event marking the user's resignation date. This organized presentation of relevant data allows analysts to quickly assess the situation, understand the severity, and focus their investigations on the most pertinent issues.

For your reference, here's the Security Copilot summary for the Purview IRM alert:

> The alert with Id: 86e52569-5953-4272-82b4-c8dae7e8cc0d is a High severity Insider Risk Management alert involving isaiah detected on April 21, 2023 21:39:29 (UTC). The policy "Potential data theft – Employee Departure" was triggered when an HR Offboarding event was detected. The user's activity that led to this alert getting generated was identified as Cumulative Exfiltration. The alert is in Confirmed state and is being investigated. The alert also has a case "Case 034: Potential data leak" associated with it.
>
> The user is considered High risk based on the following risk factors:
>
> - **Emails with attachments sent outside the organization (March 6, 2024 23:59:59 UTC)** - User is found to be sending 30 emails with attachments outside the organization. The emails contained priority content and were sent to 1 recipient. A total of 30 emails were sent and 1 of them contained sensitivity info.
> - **Sensitive SharePoint files accessed (March 6, 2024 23:59:59 UTC)** - User is found to be accessing 14 sensitive SharePoint files. The files contained priority content and were accessed from 1 SharePoint site with sensitivity label applied. A total of 5 instances of sensitivity info were found in the files.
>
> Additionally, an HR event was detected on March 8, 2024 (UTC) indicating that the user's resignation date has been set.

Communication compliance

Microsoft Purview's **Communication compliance** feature helps organizations ensure that their employees' communications meet company policies and legal regulations. It monitors emails, chats, and other messages to make sure they follow the rules and standards set by the organization. For instance, if an employee uses inappropriate language or makes discriminatory remarks in a company chat, the system will flag this as a potential violation. Compliance teams are then alerted to review and address the issue. This feature helps maintain professional communication practices and prevents issues by ensuring all interactions comply with organizational guidelines.

Reviewing communication violations can be time-consuming, particularly with lengthy content such as meeting transcripts, email attachments, Teams files, or extensive text. Although **Communication compliance** helps by identifying timestamps and highlighting matched conditions, there's still a significant amount of text for the analyst to sift through. However, with Security Copilot, the analyst can get a comprehensive summary of an alert with just a single click!

The summary generated by Security Copilot helps to speed up the investigation by highlighting high-risk communications. The next screen capture demonstrates using the prompt:

```
Summarize this message and supported attachments in the context of Stock
manipulation category detected
```

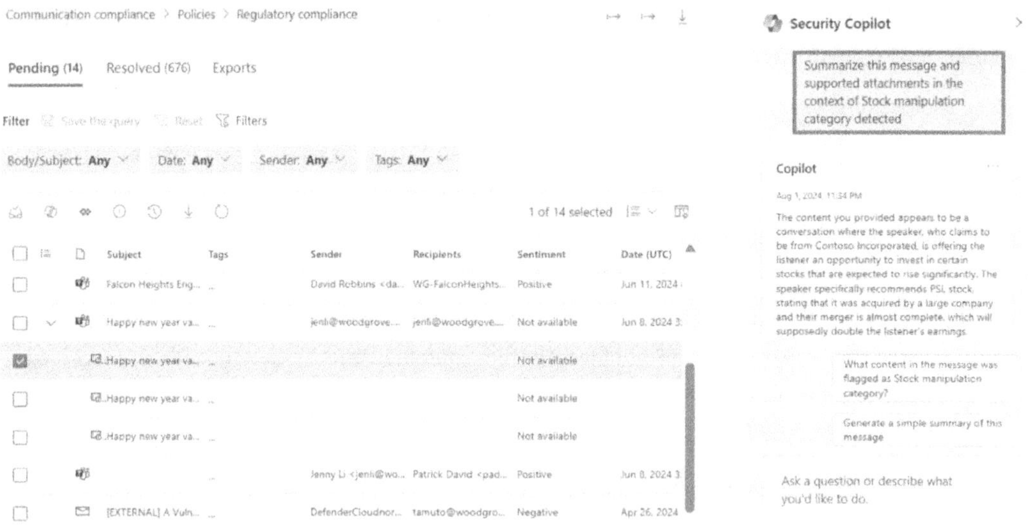

Figure 2.23 – Summarize the message and supported attachments

For example, the alert summary, as illustrated next, helps the analyst by providing key details about the conversation. It highlights that the speaker is recommending specific stocks with promises of significant returns. The statements flagged in the example suggest potential stock manipulation, as they guarantee substantial gains and hint at insider information about a merger. By outlining these crucial points, the Security Copilot summary allows the analyst to quickly assess the nature of the communication and determine whether it violates compliance policies or regulations, streamlining the review process:

> The content you provided appears to be a conversation where the speaker, who claims to be from Contoso Incorporated, is offering the listener an opportunity to invest in certain stocks that are expected to rise significantly. The speaker specifically recommends PSL stock, stating that it was acquired by a large company and their merger is almost complete, which will supposedly double the listener's earnings.
>
> This conversation could potentially be seen as an attempt at stock manipulation, as the speaker is making recommendations to buy certain stocks with the promise of significant returns. The lines, 'I am offering you this deal ahead of time. So you can get that latest and greatest even among our valued customers. The stocks I recommend are guaranteed to rise to the moon soon.' and 'Here's the first recommendation. I'll give you PSL stock. PSL was acquired by large company and between you and me, their merger is almost complete. If you add it in your investment portfolio, you will double the earnings that you are currently seeing.' support this rationale.

You can also ask Security Copilot follow-up questions – for example, `Does this violation indicate unauthorized disclosure?` As shown next, Copilot confirms that it does appear to disclose confidential information that is not yet public knowledge. Yet again, this helps accelerate the investigation time!

> The content you provided does seem to indicate a potential violation of the 'Unauthorized disclosure' category. The speaker mentions, "PSL was acquired by large company and between you and me, their merger is almost complete. If you add it in your investment portfolio, you will double the earnings that you are currently seeing." This statement appears to disclose confidential or internal information about a merger that is not yet public knowledge, which could be considered unauthorized disclosure.

Additionally, Security Copilot provides prompts or suggested questions that you can ask for further clarification – for instance, `What content in the message was flagged as Stock manipulation category?`

At this point, we have demonstrated that Security Copilot, when integrated with Microsoft Purview, enhances security analysts' ability to analyze large volumes of security data with greater efficiency and speed. This refined analysis greatly assists in identifying potential threats and unusual activities. Now, let's explore how Security Copilot can further support you within **Microsoft Defender for Cloud**.

Enhancing security with Microsoft Defender for Cloud

Microsoft Defender for Cloud is a comprehensive security solution designed to protect cloud environments. It acts as a guardian for businesses, continuously monitoring and evaluating the security of their cloud-based systems and data. It helps identify potential threats and vulnerabilities, offering insights and recommendations to strengthen security posture and resilience.

Microsoft Defender for Cloud significantly enhances security and compliance by continuously assessing cloud resources against best practices and regulatory standards. It provides actionable recommendations to address vulnerabilities and compliance gaps, such as enabling encryption or adjusting network settings.

Embedded in Defender for Cloud, Security Copilot offers powerful ways to manage and address security recommendations displayed on Defender for Cloud's recommendations page, assisting security teams in analyzing them. You can ask Security Copilot to do things such as `Display risks for publicly exposed resources`, `reveal risks for critical resources`, or perform other specific tasks. The results help us to narrow down the recommendations and to focus on the most relevant ones. The following screen capture shows a selection of suggested prompts you can request Copilot to execute:

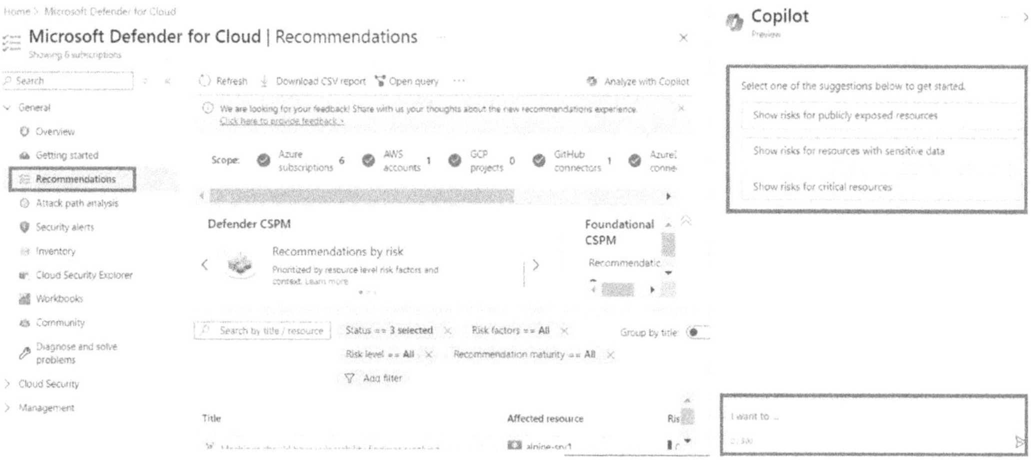

Figure 2.24 – Security Copilot prompt suggestion in Defender for Cloud

For any specific recommendation, Security Copilot can summarize it to offer a clear overview of the associated risks and vulnerabilities. The next screenshot demonstrates how to request a summary from Security Copilot with a single click:

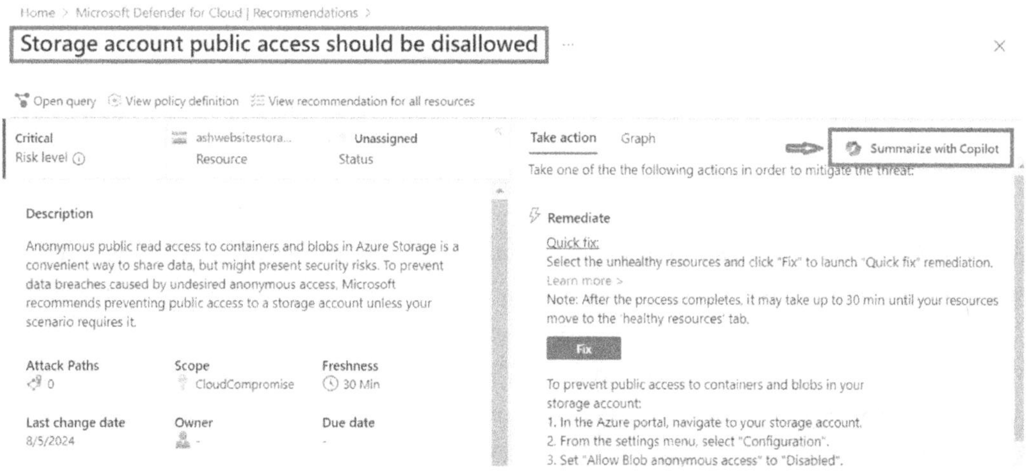

Figure 2.25 – Summarize recommendation with Copilot

The summary generated by Security Copilot presents the recommendation information in an easy-to-understand manner, allowing security teams to quickly grasp the key details and prioritize remediation efforts effectively. For your reference, the next screenshot captures the recommendation summary generated by Security Copilot:

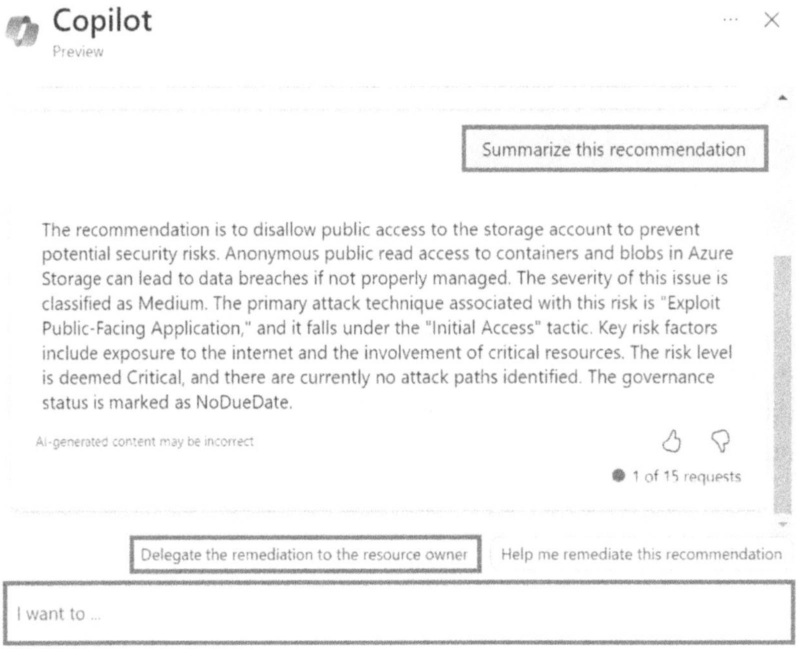

Figure 2.26 – Recommendation summary generated by Security Copilot

As shown in the previous screenshot, if needed, you can always supplement the Copilot summary with additional prompts or questions for Security Copilot. Furthermore, after Security Copilot summarizes a recommendation, it then assists the security teams with the remediation process. Security Copilot provides suggested prompts, such as **Help me remediate this recommendation**, allowing the analysts to request further action from Copilot. The security teams can then review the suggested remediation details and follow the provided instructions to address the recommendation. If there are uncertainties or additional guidance is needed, Security Copilot can be queried for further information using additional prompts.

If a script is included in the remediation step, the security analyst can choose the **Run** option inside the Security Copilot panel to apply the remediation, as illustrated in the next screen capture:

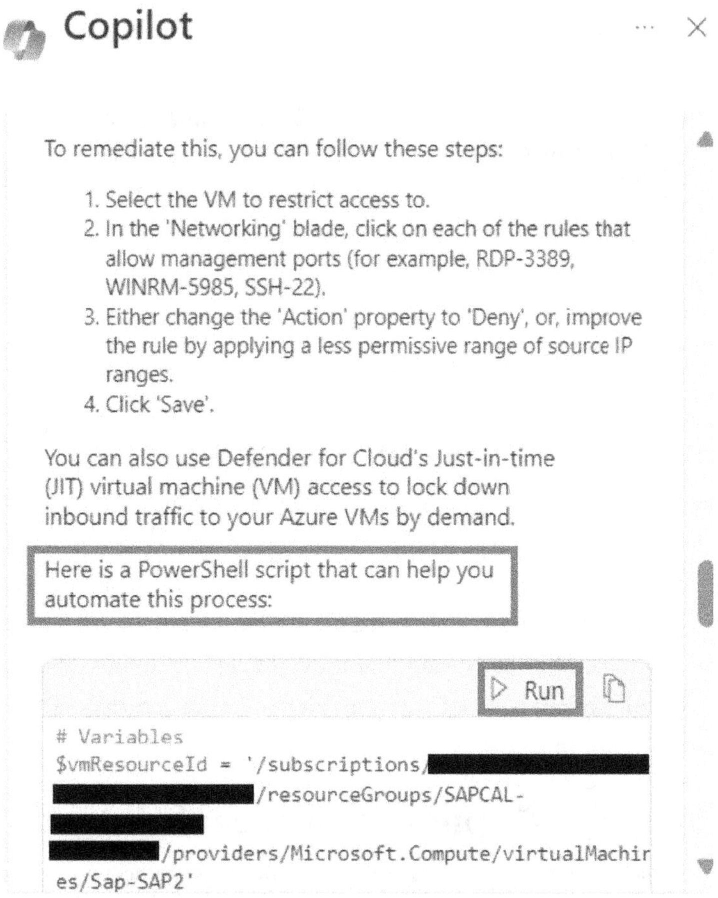

Figure 2.27 – Running the script to apply the remediation

Additionally, within Security Copilot, recommendations can be assigned to other team members, ensuring that specific issues are handled by the appropriate experts:

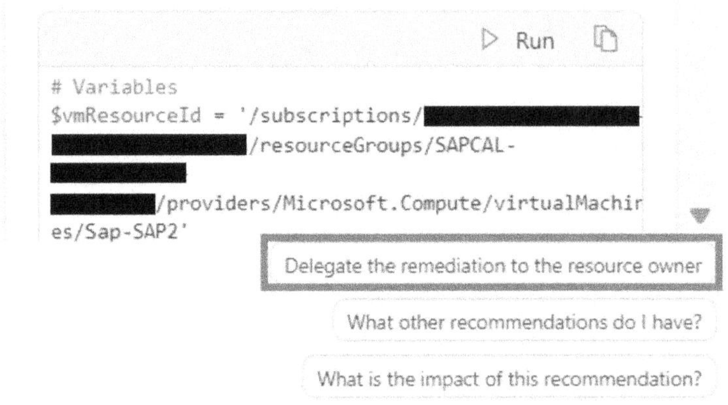

Figure 2.28 – Delegating the remediation

In summary, Security Copilot can analyze all the recommendations, enabling you to leverage these analytical insights to focus on specific recommendations in Defender for Cloud. Security Copilot also provides concise summaries of these recommendations, making it easier to understand and prioritize them. It supports the remediation process and allows for delegating tasks to the appropriate team members, ensuring that the right experts address the identified issues effectively. Next, we will explore how Security Copilot assists the security and IT teams when it is integrated into **Microsoft Intune**.

Utilizing Security Copilot in Microsoft Intune

Microsoft Intune is a solution that helps organizations manage and secure their employees' devices and applications. Think of it as a central control panel that allows a company to ensure that smartphones, tablets, and computers are used safely and effectively. It helps administrators set up policies to protect sensitive information, manage which applications can be used, and ensure that all devices comply with security standards. By using Intune, companies can maintain control over their technology while making sure that employees have the tools they need to do their jobs securely and efficiently.

Endpoint security policies, such as those for Defender Antivirus, Attack Surface Reduction, App Control for Business, disk encryption, Windows firewall, and others, can be defined and configured within Intune. These policies are designed to enhance device security and reduce risk.

Embedded within Intune, Security Copilot supports security teams in managing policies and settings. It provides summaries of policies, evaluates their impact on users, devices, and overall security, and explains specific configuration settings within Intune. Additionally, it excels at identifying potential policy conflicts. Security Copilot also helps IT admins manage and troubleshoot devices efficiently.

Policy and settings management

For any existing Intune policies, Security Copilot provides a summary that offers an overview of the policy details. This summary covers the policy's configurations, the users and groups it applies to, and its specific settings. This information provides insights into what the policy entails and how its configurations impact users and devices. The next screenshot displays the summary generated by Security Copilot:

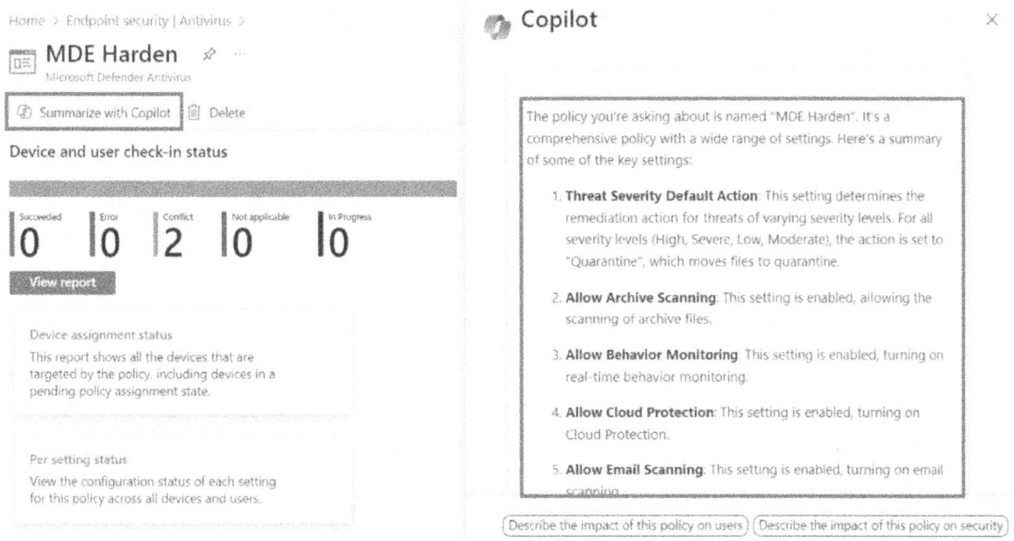

Figure 2.29 – Summary of an Intune policy

For the same Defender policy, Security Copilot offers additional commands, known as prompts, that can be used to request further actions or information. For instance, you can ask Security Copilot to describe the impact of this policy on users. As illustrated in the following snippet, Security Copilot dutifully provides a detailed assessment of how this policy affects user experience:

The policy "MDE Harden" has a wide range of settings that could impact users in various ways. Here's a detailed analysis:

1. **Threat Severity Default Action:** All threats, regardless of their severity level, are set to be quarantined. This means that any detected threats will be moved to a secure location, preventing them from causing harm. However, this could potentially lead to false positives being quarantined, which might disrupt user activities if legitimate files are incorrectly flagged.
2. **Allow Archive Scanning:** This setting is enabled, allowing the scanning of archive files. This enhances security by detecting threats within compressed files, but it might slightly increase the time required for scans.
3. **Allow Behavior Monitoring:** This setting is enabled, providing real-time behavior monitoring. This can detect and stop malicious activities based on their behavior, but it might cause performance impacts if many activities need to be monitored.

You can then request Security Copilot to explain the impact of this policy on security. A sample of Copilot's response is provided next:

The policy "MDE Harden" has a wide range of settings that could significantly impact the security of your system. Here's a detailed analysis:

1. **Threat Severity Default Action:** This setting quarantines threats of all severity levels. This can improve security by promptly dealing with threats, but it could potentially disrupt user activities if legitimate files are incorrectly flagged.
2. **Allow Archive Scanning:** This setting scans archive files, enhancing security by detecting threats within compressed files. However, it might slightly increase the time required for scans.
3. **Allow Behavior Monitoring:** This setting turns on real-time behavior monitoring, which can detect and stop malicious activities based on their behavior. However, it might cause performance impacts if many activities need to be monitored.

You can also ask Security Copilot to explain a specific configuration setting in an Intune policy, as illustrated in the next screenshot:

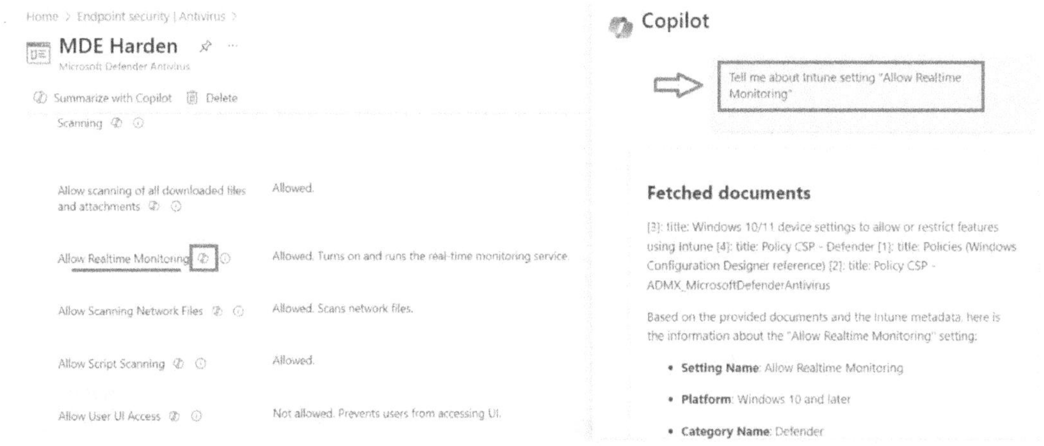

Figure 2.30 – Asking Security Copilot about a specific configuration setting

Again, Security Copilot provides detailed information about the configuration setting along with reference links. This reduces the time and effort required to search through a large number of online documents for similar information, which is often less comprehensive than the insights provided by Security Copilot.

In the Security Copilot window, there are many more pre-drafted commands or questions, known as prompts, available for use. Users can access these prompts by selecting the prompt guide and choosing from the existing list of options. For instance, you can pick **Has this setting been configured in any other policies?** from the prompt guide to look for potential policy conflicts within Intune. This makes it even easier to navigate and manage settings. More Security Copilot features for Intune will be covered in *Chapter 9* through a detailed case study.

Device details and troubleshooting

With Security Copilot integrated into Microsoft Intune, IT administrators can effectively manage and troubleshoot devices. When accessing a specific device in Intune's device blade, Security Copilot appears on the device's **Overview** page, ready to assist. It provides three main features: **Explore device**, **Compare to another device**, and **Analyze error code**, as seen in the next screenshot:

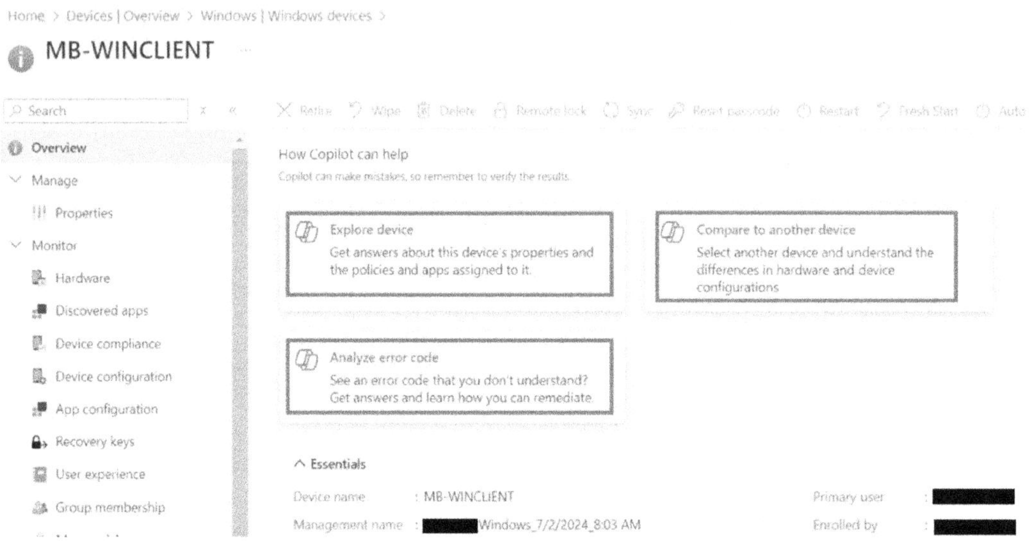

Figure 2.31 – Security Copilot embedded in the device page

You can leverage Security Copilot to explore a device, gather detailed information such as installed apps and group membership, and more. Additionally, you can request Security Copilot to compare this device with another sometimes similar or identical device, to identify differences and guide your investigation. Security Copilot can also be used to analyze error codes.

Through the **Explore device** option, you can ask Security Copilot to provide a device summary, policies assigned to this device, apps on this device, primary user, group membership, and more, as shown next:

Figure 2.32 – Security Copilot provides device insights

The device summary provides detailed information about the device, including its OS, model, type, user, compliance status, and reasons for non-compliance. Security Copilot can also display either managed apps or discovered apps for this device. It also lists configuration profiles, compliance policies, or app configuration policies on this device.

Security Copilot helps to resolve issues with specific devices by comparing working and non-working devices. By comparing a functioning device with a malfunctioning one, you can pinpoint differences and troubleshoot the problematic device. Alternatively, when examining a suspicious device, you can compare it with a similar or identical device to understand discrepancies and to guide your investigation. There are a few comparison types, as illustrated in the next screenshot:

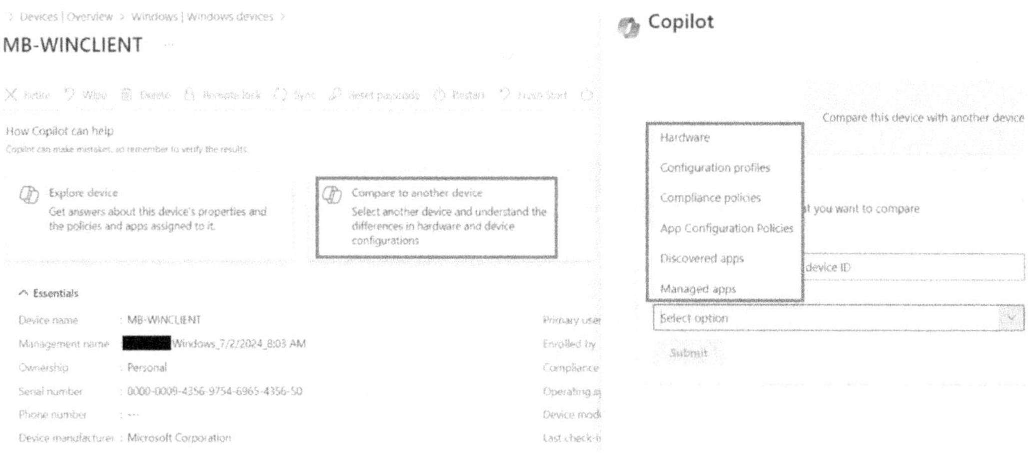

Figure 2.33 – Options to compare to another device in Security Copilot

Security Copilot interprets error codes and offers detailed explanations and troubleshooting steps to assist IT professionals in resolving issues related to device configuration profiles, compliance policies, app installations, and more. For instance, when inquiring about error code `0xC7D14FBA`, Security Copilot explains that this error occurs because the app installation failed due to the necessary file being deleted before the process finished. This typically happens if there is a significant delay between downloading the app and attempting to install it. Security Copilot additionally provides troubleshooting steps.

In summary, we've looked into how Security Copilot, embedded within Intune, empowers security and IT teams by simplifying policy and setting management, summarizing their impact on users and devices, and identifying potential conflicts. It also enables IT admins to manage and troubleshoot devices more efficiently.

The Security Copilot features you have reviewed so far are built right into the Microsoft security solutions. This is referred to as the embedded experience. As you've seen, these Copilot capabilities enhance the functionality of the Microsoft products they are integrated with and act as an assistant to security teams, offering support and guidance to analysts while they're using the solution.

> **Note**
>
> Due to fast-paced Security Copilot development, these features are representative of some of the capabilities within the embedded experiences and new features are continuously being added to improve functionality and usability.

In addition to the embedded experience, you can pivot to the dedicated Security Copilot portal, known as the standalone experience. This standalone environment offers even more advanced features and capabilities. In the next section, let's take a quick look at it and get acquainted with its features.

From the embedded experience to the standalone experience

The Security Copilot capabilities embedded within a specific Microsoft product are designed to work exclusively with that solution. Consequently, with the embedded experience, you can only access the Security Copilot knowledge and capabilities that are directly relevant to the product you're working with. For example, if you're using Security Copilot within the Microsoft Defender XDR solution, the Copilot features available are specific to Defender's capabilities.

While the embedded experience is product-specific, you can switch to Security Copilot's standalone experience, which allows you to access and make use of different security solutions simultaneously through a unified interface. This consolidated platform provides an integrated and streamlined experience for you. It enables you to leverage the full range of Security Copilot capabilities from Microsoft and non-Microsoft solutions, eliminating the need to switch between different technologies or interfaces. Additionally, the standalone experience not only offers all the capabilities found in the embedded mode but also provides many additional advanced and powerful features not present in the embedded experience.

As we explore the standalone experience available at `https://securitycopilot.microsoft.com/`, it's essential to get familiar with the key concepts and terminologies that are commonly encountered there. For the next few sections, let's review these terms to get a better understanding of the standalone experience.

Plugin

In Security Copilot, a **plugin** provides a set of specialized AI functionalities that extend the core capabilities of Security Copilot. These plugins enable Security Copilot to access and utilize features and data from integrated security solutions, offering more comprehensive and tailored security insights and support. For example, there is the Microsoft Defender XDR plugin in Security Copilot, as well as plugins for Intune, Microsoft Entra, and third-party solutions such as ServiceNow or AbuseIPDB.

Plugins transform Security Copilot from a static product into a dynamic, customizable platform. First, plugins allow Security Copilot to connect with a wide range of security solutions, from both Microsoft and third-party providers. You can easily enable or disable plugins within Security Copilot. When a plugin is turned off, Security Copilot will no longer use that solution. This modular approach allows you to tailor the platform to your needs. Furthermore, it offers greater flexibility and adaptability over time as new plugins, including your own custom ones, are introduced.

The screenshot shown next showcases various Microsoft plugins:

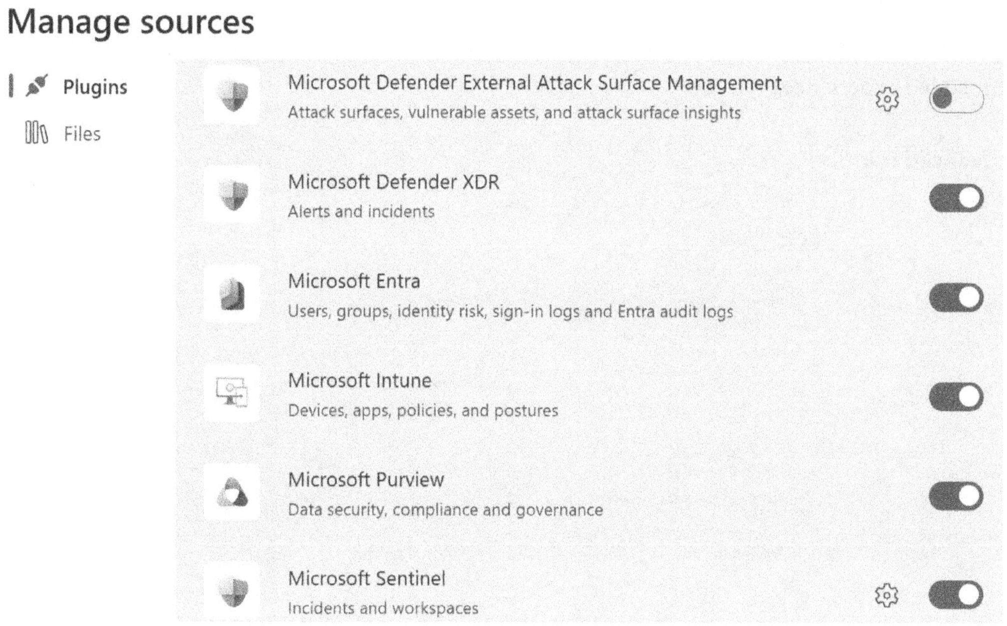

Figure 2.34 – Microsoft plugins

Capability/skill

A **capability**, also referred to as a **skill**, is a specific feature or function that a plugin provides. It highlights what the plugin can do. For instance, the Microsoft Defender XDR plugin includes capabilities such as incident summarization, guided response, scripts and code analysis, KQL query generation, incident report creation, and more.

Each plugin allows Security Copilot to access capabilities or skills tied to the particular data source to which the plugin is connected. These unique capabilities or skills enhance Security Copilot's overall functionality, making it more flexible and adaptable to different needs.

Prompt

A **prompt** is a specific instruction given to Security Copilot to generate a response, perform a task, or take action based on the input provided. For instance, a prompt could request Security Copilot to summarize a policy, create a hunting query in KQL, or address a recommendation. Essentially, the prompt directs Security Copilot's capabilities to address specific needs, allowing you to get targeted insights and relevant support.

The following screenshot shows several of the prompts suggested by Security Copilot in the embedded experience:

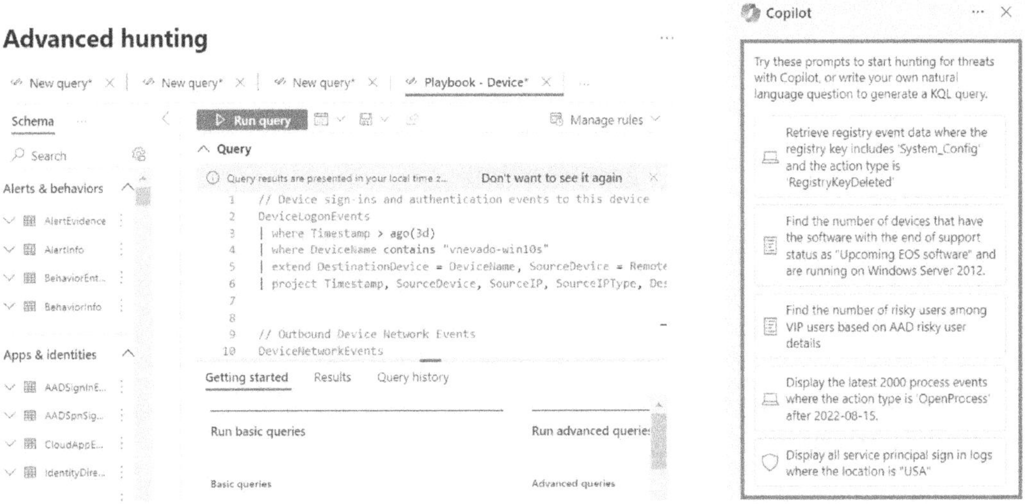

Figure 2.35 – Security Copilot prompts

Prompts are used in both the embedded and the standalone experiences. In the embedded experience, prompts can be automatically generated by Security Copilot or entered by users. In the standalone environment, user-entered prompts are the primary method for interacting with Security Copilot, although suggested prompts are also available on the main landing page and throughout your working sessions in Copilot.

There are various collections of sample prompts you can reference online. One is the main Microsoft Security Copilot **prompt library** at `https://github.com/Azure/Security-Copilot/tree/main/Sample%20Prompts`. Another good online resource is `https://aka.ms/CfSPromptLibrary`. All the prompts featured in this book can be found at `https://github.com/PacktPublishing/Microsoft-Copilot-for-Security/tree/main/Prompts`.

Promptbook

A **promptbook** is a collection of prompts that have been put together to accomplish a set of specific tasks. Think of it as a playbook with a ready-to-use template that runs a series of prompts in sequence to complete various tasks for analysts.

Here is an example of a promptbook that analyzes an IP address using different threat intelligence sources such as **Microsoft Defender Threat Intelligence** (**MDTI**), VirusTotal, CrowdSec, and Shodan. Notice this promptbook requires the user to provide input:

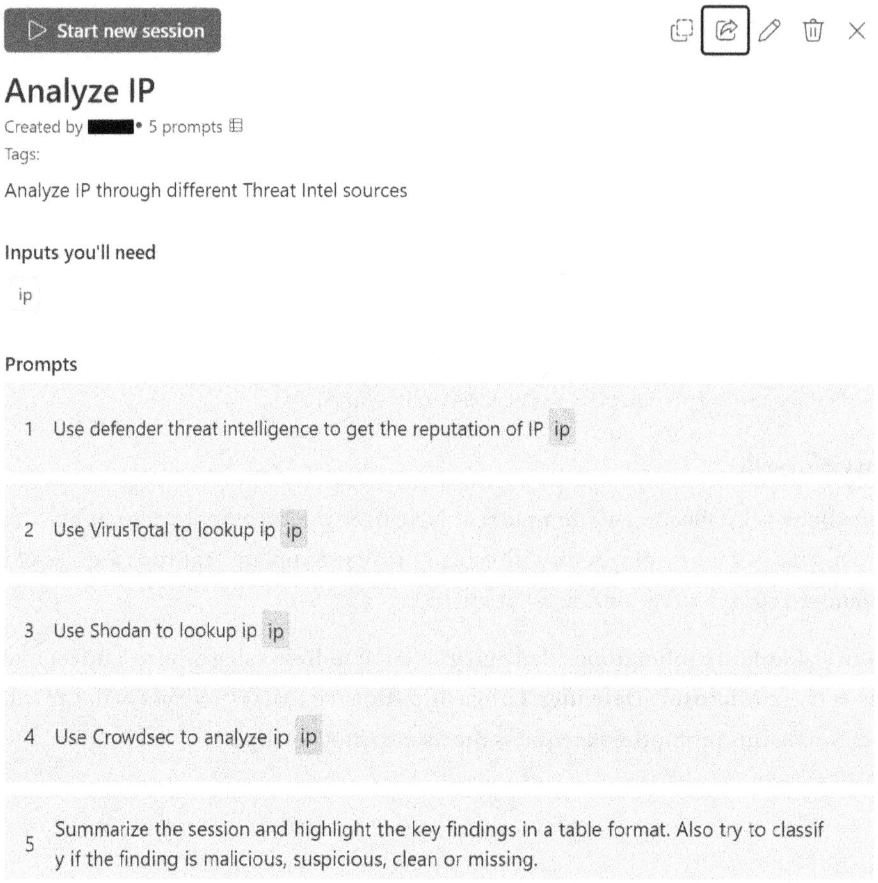

Figure 2.36 – Security Copilot promptbook

The promptbook first asks the user to enter the IP address to be analyzed. Then, the first prompt in the promptbook queries MDTI to obtain the IP's reputation. Additional prompts then use other security tools, such as VirusTotal and Shodan, to further investigate the IP. The last prompt asks Security Copilot to generate a report and highlight key findings.

Session

A **session** is a distinct interaction period with Security Copilot, where an analyst's engagement is tracked and managed. It captures the sequence of the analyst's prompts and responses. Sessions are designed to provide continuity, allowing analysts to pick up where they left off, review previous interactions, and maintain context throughout their work.

As analysts enter prompts and receive responses from Security Copilot, they may have follow-up requests based on the information provided. Copilot maintains the context within the session, allowing it to provide relevant answers to these subsequent requests. *This context-aware interaction ensures that the conversation flows logically and that each response builds upon the previous ones, creating a cohesive and efficient experience for the user.*

In the standalone experience of Security Copilot, you can manage your sessions with search and filter options, and rename or delete sessions. You can also view sessions created by embedded experiences. This ensures a consistent and integrated experience across both the embedded and standalone platforms.

The next screenshot displays a list of various sessions, including those that have been renamed:

Figure 2.37 – Security Copilot sessions

The Security Copilot session can be shared with others. Sharing a session enhances collaboration within security teams. It enables multiple users to work together, review information, and make decisions. Session sharing is particularly useful for security reviews and incident investigations, as it allows for input from various team members. Additionally, session sharing serves as an effective training tool to show new team members how to manage different security scenarios.

Furthermore, sessions are retained indefinitely. As the list grows, you may want to consider deleting obsolete sessions or renaming older ones to make it easier to find the specific session later on. Alternatively, you have the option to convert commonly used sessions into promptbooks. Details on how to do this will be covered in *Chapter 6*.

At this point, we have covered the key concepts and terminologies of the standalone environment. To fully showcase its advanced features, a more in-depth approach is needed. Therefore, throughout this book, we will gradually dive into these features, providing detailed explanations and practical illustrations along the way.

Summary

This chapter has provided an introduction to the capabilities and features of Security Copilot, giving you a better understanding of what it is and how it operates, especially when it is embedded in Microsoft security solutions. The thorough introduction allows you to see how Security Copilot can serve as a smart assistant, transforming security operations and empowering your team's success. This foundational knowledge of Security Copilot's core features and benefits will prepare you for a more in-depth exploration of its advanced functionalities in the upcoming chapters.

With a solid understanding of Security Copilot in place, in the next chapter, we will focus on its onboarding and setup. You'll be guided through the onboarding process and be introduced to Security Copilot's user interfaces, assisting you to navigate the tool effectively. Lastly, to help you become more familiar with how Security Copilot works in practice, you will go through a case study and experience firsthand how Security Copilot can be applied in a real-life security incident investigation.

3

Navigating the Security Copilot Platform

The previous chapter highlighted some of the key capabilities and features of **Security Copilot**, formally introducing the tool to you. It provided a detailed explanation of what the tool is and how it functions. You were able to see Security Copilot in action when it is embedded within various Microsoft security solutions. You also became familiar with essential concepts and terminologies relevant to Security Copilot's standalone experience. This introduction showcased how Security Copilot can serve as a handy, resourceful, and smart assistant, transforming security operations and empowering security professionals.

After becoming acquainted with Security Copilot and exploring its functionalities, you may be eager to set it up and start enjoying its benefits. To get started, in this chapter, we will go through Security Copilot's onboarding process and review its user interfaces, enabling you to navigate the tool more efficiently and effectively. By understanding the setup and customization of the tool, you will be better equipped to meet your specific security needs and ensure that you can maximize its AI capabilities.

In the final section of the chapter, we will present a case study to showcase how Security Copilot can be used in an actual security incident investigation. This will give you a more interactive demonstration of how the tool functions in real-world scenarios, helping you gain a better understanding of its application and how it supports security operations in practice.

With this in mind, the upcoming sections of this chapter will navigate you through the journey:

- Setting the stage – technical requirements and onboarding
- Navigating the user interfaces
- Case study – harnessing Security Copilot in defending against cyber threats

> Want to try out the prompts, custom plugins, and promptbooks featured in this book? Take a look at the book's GitHub repository at `https://github.com/PacktPublishing/Microsoft-Copilot-for-Security`.

Setting the stage – technical requirements and onboarding

Before setting up Security Copilot, there are a few prerequisites to keep in mind. First, you will need an active Azure subscription, as Security Copilot is hosted in Azure. Additionally, you must ensure that you have the necessary permissions and access rights within your Azure environment to configure and manage the service. It's also important to estimate the expected usage of Security Copilot.

If any of this seems overwhelming or confusing, don't worry; we'll explore them in more detail next to help you get started and guide you through the setup process.

Getting ready for onboarding

To start the onboarding process, you'll need an Azure subscription, which operates much like a utility account but for Microsoft's Azure cloud services. Just as a utility account handles billing and management for electricity or water, an Azure subscription manages and pays for the Azure services used. With Security Copilot hosted on Azure, the subscription is essential for accessing and setting up the service.

Security Copilot operates on a provisioned capacity model. Its costs are incurred based on the number of **Security Compute Units** (**SCUs**) allocated and any additional overage usage. Each task performed by Security Copilot consumes a specific amount of SCUs. The more complex or numerous the tasks, the more SCUs are consumed. To help with managing the cost, you can estimate the expected SCU usage by monitoring the overall usage dashboard available in the Security Copilot portal.

SCUs can be purchased either through the Security Copilot portal or via Azure, during the initial setup or at a later time. "*Microsoft recommends provisioning 3 SCUs per hour to start your Security Copilot exploration*" (Microsoft, *Microsoft Security Copilot pricing*: `https://azure.microsoft.com/en-us/pricing/details/microsoft-copilot-for-security/`). Your actual SCU needs vary depending on the Security Copilot features you use and the number of users. Typically, each embedded experience requires one SCU, while running prompts in the standalone experience requires at least three additional SCUs. If you're using promptbooks and logic apps, you should plan for three to five more SCUs.

During the initial phase, as you use Security Copilot and begin integrating it into your daily processes, you'll gain a better understanding of your actual SCU requirements. SCUs can be easily scaled up or down to adjust to your processing needs.

Besides SCUs, you might frequently encounter the term **capacity**. In the context of Security Copilot, capacity refers to an Azure resource that contains SCUs. It denotes the amount of computing power allocated for managing and analyzing security tasks, encompassing the SCUs required to perform these operations effectively.

A more in-depth discussion of the Security Copilot pricing structure, the role of SCUs in cost management, and the usage dashboard can be found in *Chapter 11*. For now, let's move on to the onboarding process for Security Copilot.

Onboarding Security Copilot

Onboarding to Security Copilot involves a two-step process: first, provisioning the capacity, and second, setting up the default environment.

Step 1 – provision capacity

There are two options for provisioning capacity: either directly within Security Copilot or through Azure. Regardless of the option you choose, you'll need to enter the same information and fill out the same fields with each method. Although the user interfaces differ, the details you provide, such as Azure subscription name, capacity name, and other relevant information, are consistent across both methods.

You can follow the steps outlined next to reach the capacity provisioning page in Azure:

1. Go to Azure at `https://portal.azure.com/`.
2. In the Azure search bar, type `security copilot` and then select the Azure service, **Microsoft Security compute capacities**, as illustrated here:

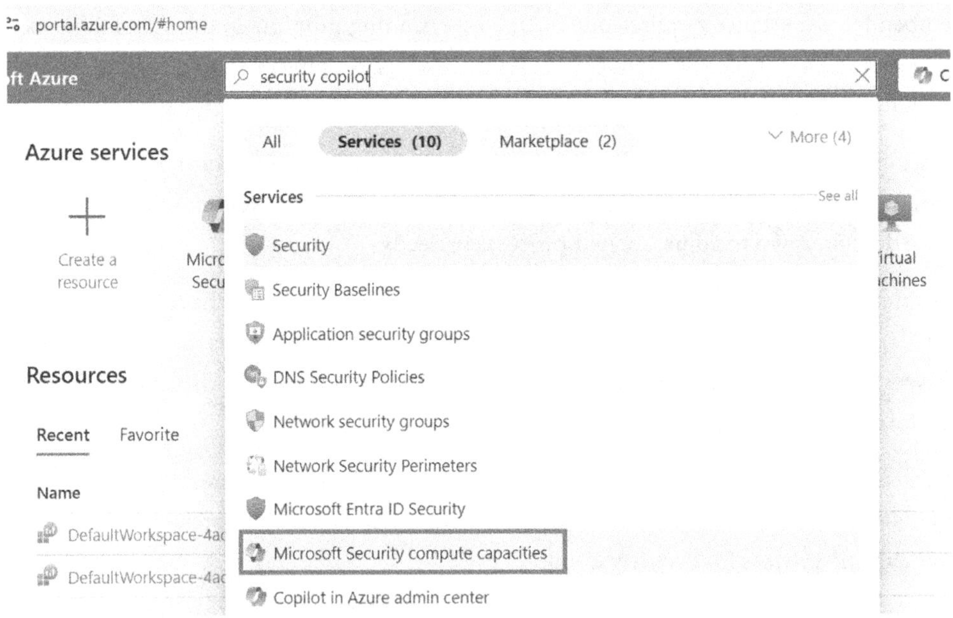

Figure 3.1 – Microsoft Security Copilot compute capacities

3. The Security Copilot capacity provisioning page, as shown next, then appears:

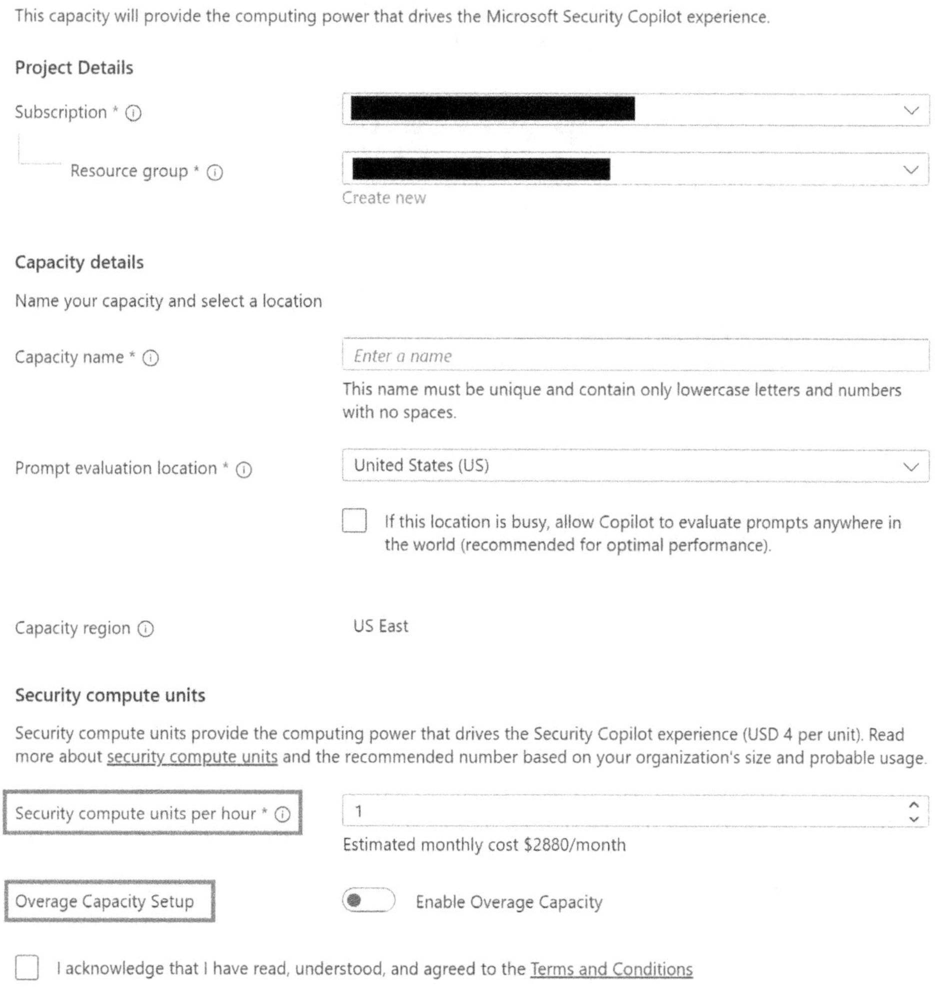

Figure 3.2 – Security Copilot capacity provisioning in Azure

To get to the capacity provisioning page directly within Security Copilot, simply visit the Security Copilot portal at `https://securitycopilot.microsoft.com`.

4. The capacity provisioning wizard then appears to guide you through the process. The main sections of the wizard page are displayed in the next screenshot:

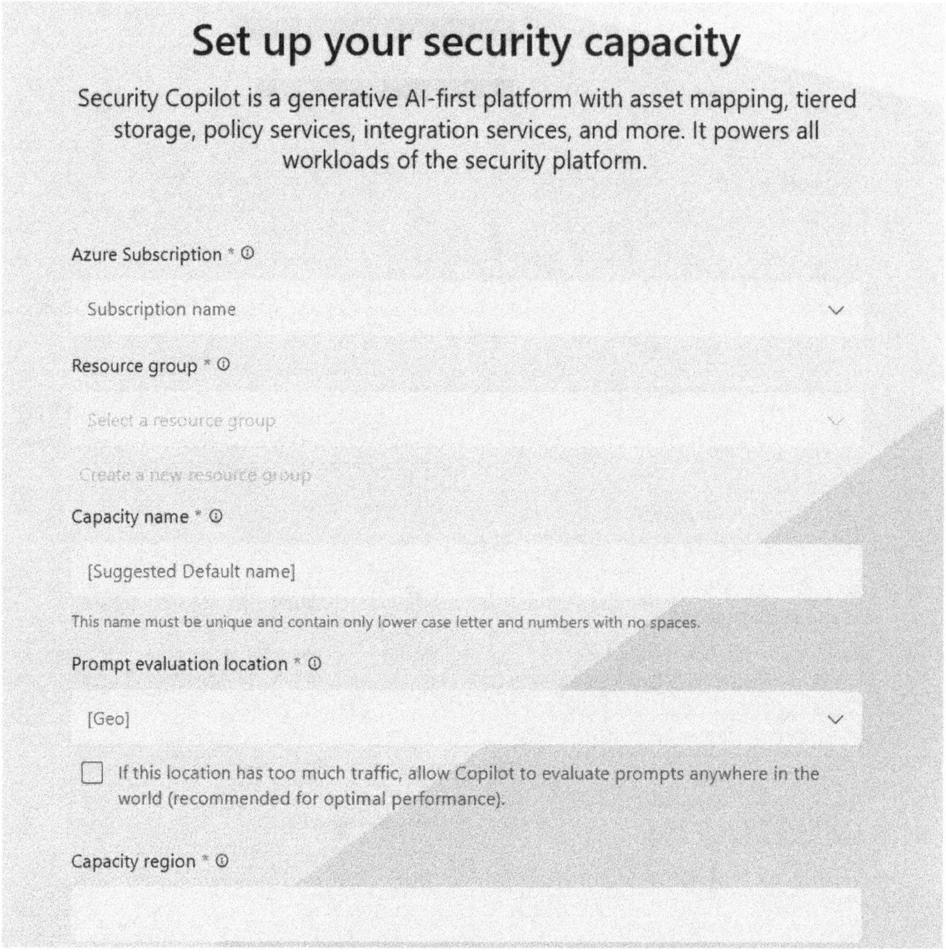

Figure 3.3 – Capacity provisioning in Security Copilot

5. The last section of the wizard page is displayed next. It lets you select the number of SCUs:

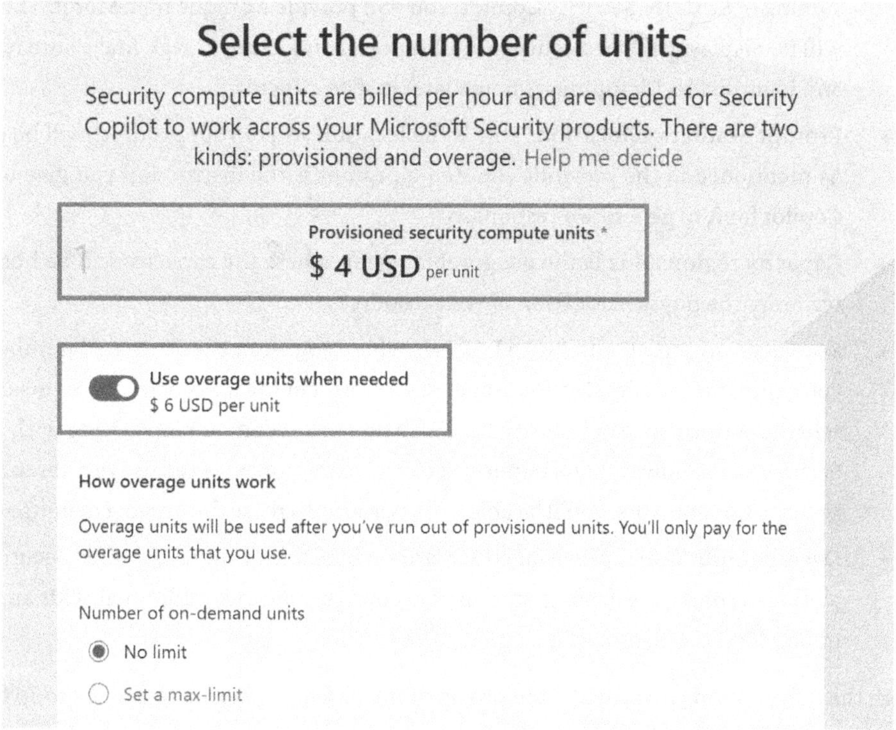

Figure 3.4 – The last section of the wizard page

As you navigate through the capacity provisioning wizard, there are specific details you need to provide to complete the process:

- **Azure Subscription**: The name of the Azure subscription where you host and manage your Security Copilot resources and associated costs.
- **Resource group**: The name of the Azure resource group where the Security Copilot resources will be deployed. A resource group is a container that holds related resources for an Azure solution and allows you to manage them collectively, including their lifecycle, permissions, and policies.

- **Capacity name**: Capacity is a specific resource within Azure that deals with the provisioning of SCUs for Security Copilot. You will provide a unique name for it. This capacity will be displayed in the Security Copilot portal and Azure portal. Make sure it is unique and identifiable. Changing its name later can be difficult.
- **Prompt evaluation location**: This is the location where your prompts will be evaluated. As mentioned in the previous chapter, a prompt is the instruction you give to Security Copilot for it to generate a response.
- **Capacity region**: This is the geographic region where the capacity will be hosted. It determines the physical location of your resources.
- **Security Compute Units (SCUs)**: This is where you enter the estimated number of SCUs you expect for Security Copilot usage. SCUs represent the units of resources needed for the reliable performance of Security Copilot. Microsoft recommends starting with a baseline of three SCUs. However, it's important to estimate your expected usage prior to setting up Security Copilot. Note, you'll be able to increase or decrease the number of units at any time.
- **Overage units**: If your provisioned SCUs are exhausted during unexpected Security Copilot workload spikes, the overage amount you configure ensures additional SCUs are available to handle the demand.

With the information you provide, the provisioning process creates a resource group for the Microsoft Security Copilot service within your Azure subscription. The SCUs are then allocated as an Azure resource within that resource group.

As you can see from the previous three screenshots, the provisioning process is simple and straightforward. Microsoft recommends provisioning the capacity within the Security Copilot portal.

Important note

Since capacity provisioning is handled through Azure, you need to be an Azure subscription owner or contributor to provision capacity, regardless of whether you are using Security Copilot or Azure to do so.

Note that having a *Global Administrator* role in Microsoft Entra does not automatically grant access to Azure subscriptions or resources. Entra roles (such as *Global Administrator*) and Azure RBAC roles (such as *Owner* or *Contributor*) are separate and managed independently. If you're provisioning with a *Global Administrator* account and encounter errors, be sure to verify that your account has the necessary Azure subscription permissions.

After you've completed the capacity provisioning process, the next step is to configure the default environment for Security Copilot.

Step 2 – setting up the default environment for Security Copilot

To set up the default environment, you need to be at least a *Security Administrator* or a *Global Administrator*, and you need to provide the following key information:

- **SCU capacity**: Select the capacity of SCUs previously provisioned
- **Data storage**: Confirm the geographic location where your collected data will be stored
- **Data sharing options**: You can opt in or opt out of data sharing options, as shown in the following screenshot:

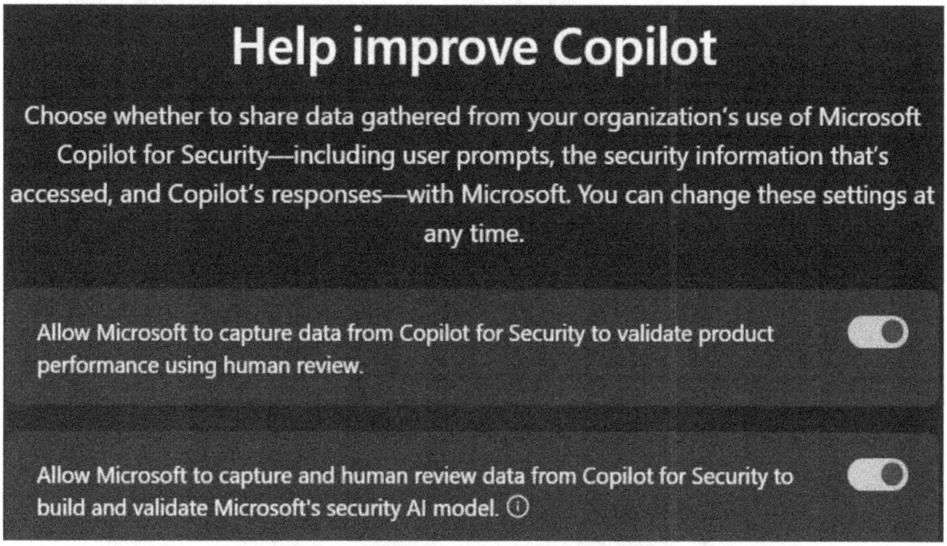

Figure 3.5 – Security Copilot data sharing options

- **Roles**: Select the roles that are authorized to access Security Copilot, as shown in the next screenshot:

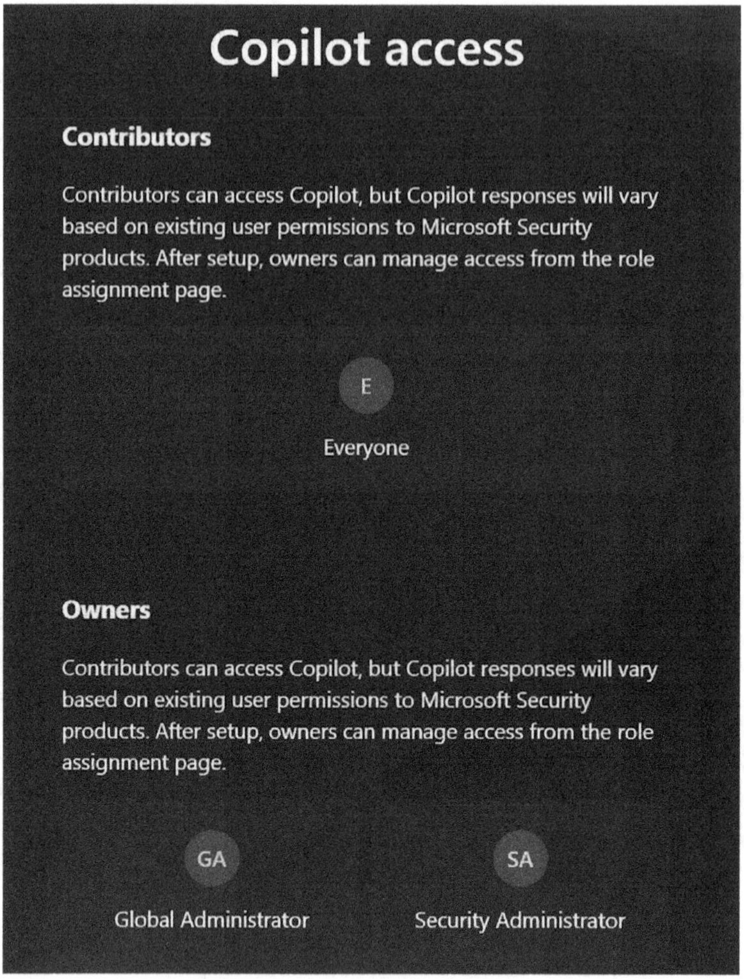

Figure 3.6 – Security Copilot default roles

> Note
>
> Role assignments in Security Copilot are not permanent and can be updated to reflect changes in responsibilities or organizational needs.

Once all the required information has been provided, the setup process is then complete. You can begin using Security Copilot immediately.

With Copilot ready for you to explore, the next section will provide you with a detailed look at its user interfaces to help you navigate them more effectively.

Navigating the user interfaces

The user interfaces in Security Copilot's embedded experience and standalone environment differ significantly in their design and functionality. In the embedded experience, Copilot's user interface is integrated within the specific security solution, providing a streamlined and compact view that aligns with the host environment's layout. This integration often limits customization options and restricts access to only the Security Copilot's core functionalities necessary for the embedded context.

In contrast, the standalone experience of Security Copilot provides a dedicated environment that operates independently. It is not influenced or limited by the design or functionality of an external application. This independent interface allows for greater customization options. It lets you access a broader range of advanced features and functionalities that go beyond those available in the embedded experience. This flexibility enables a more tailored user experience, with a layout that supports a comprehensive view of features and facilitates more adaptable workflows.

The embedded experience – key aspects explained

The previous chapter focused on Security Copilot's embedded experience, providing a detailed walkthrough of its features and capabilities within various Microsoft security solutions. In the process, you have likely become familiar with many of the user interfaces of the embedded experience. Rather than revisiting them in detail, this section will focus on their key aspects to help you retain and review the important points. This will help you navigate and utilize these user interfaces more effectively for optimal performance.

For instance, within the embedded experience, you will often notice the Copilot icon appearing within certain features of that solution. This icon signifies that Security Copilot is ready to offer assistance and insights.

As illustrated in the next screenshot, the Copilot icon indicates that Security Copilot is embedded in the **Microsoft Entra ID Protection** solution. It provides the **Summarize** option, which offers a summary of the risky user details for a potentially compromised user account:

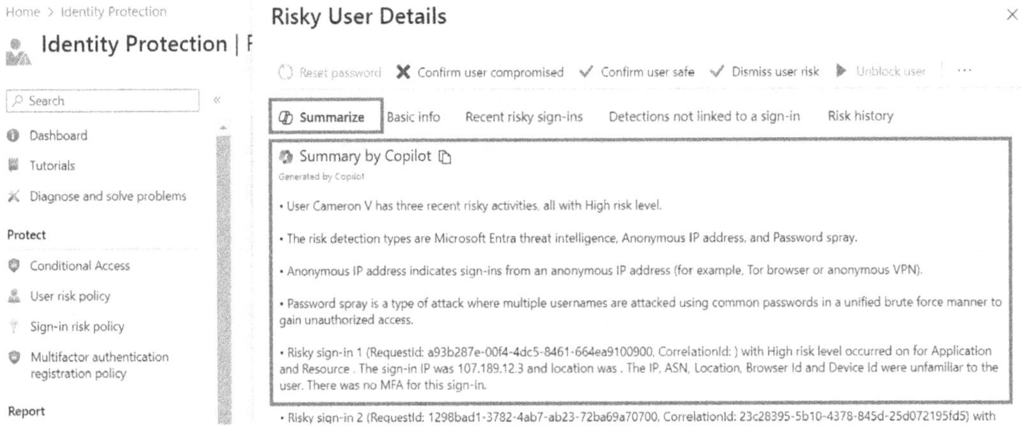

Figure 3.7 – Security Copilot embedded experience

Quick tip: Need to see a high-resolution version of this image? Open this book in the next-gen Packt Reader or view it in the PDF/ePub copy.

The next-gen Packt Reader and a **free PDF/ePub copy** of this book are included with your purchase. Scan the QR code OR visit `packtpub.com/unlock`, then use the search bar to find this book by name. Double-check the edition shown to make sure you get the right one.

In some instances, such as with the Security Copilot's incident summary feature in **Microsoft Defender XDR**, Security Copilot can be automatically activated. More often, however, you'll need to manually click the Copilot icon to initiate its function. The next screenshot demonstrates this manual process: when you click the Copilot icon next to a security setting, the **Copilot** pane on the right side will display a prompt such as, **Tell me about Intune setting 'Allow Realtime Monitoring'**. Security Copilot then retrieves the relevant documents for that specific setting:

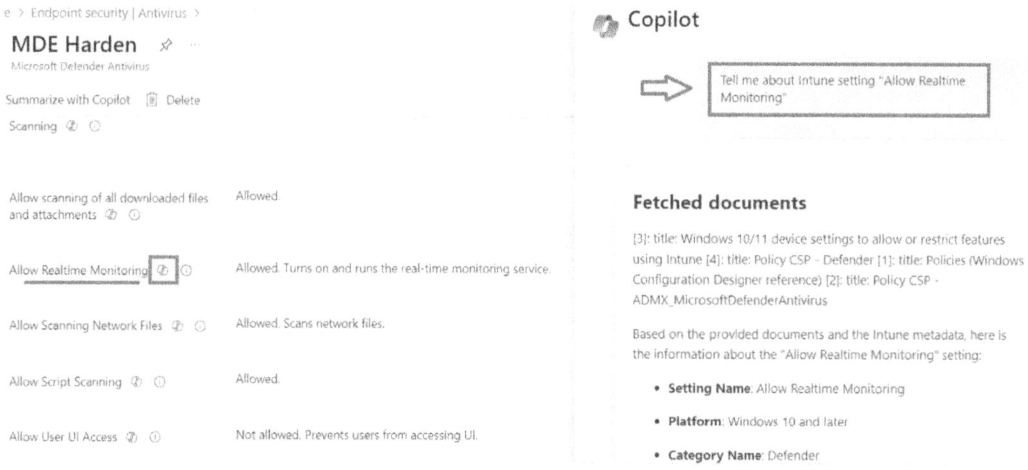

Figure 3.8 – Manually starting Security Copilot by clicking its icon next to a security setting

Sometimes, Security Copilot not only delivers the requested information but also follows up with additional recommended prompts that you can use to interact further with Copilot, such as the annotated prompts shown in the next screenshot:

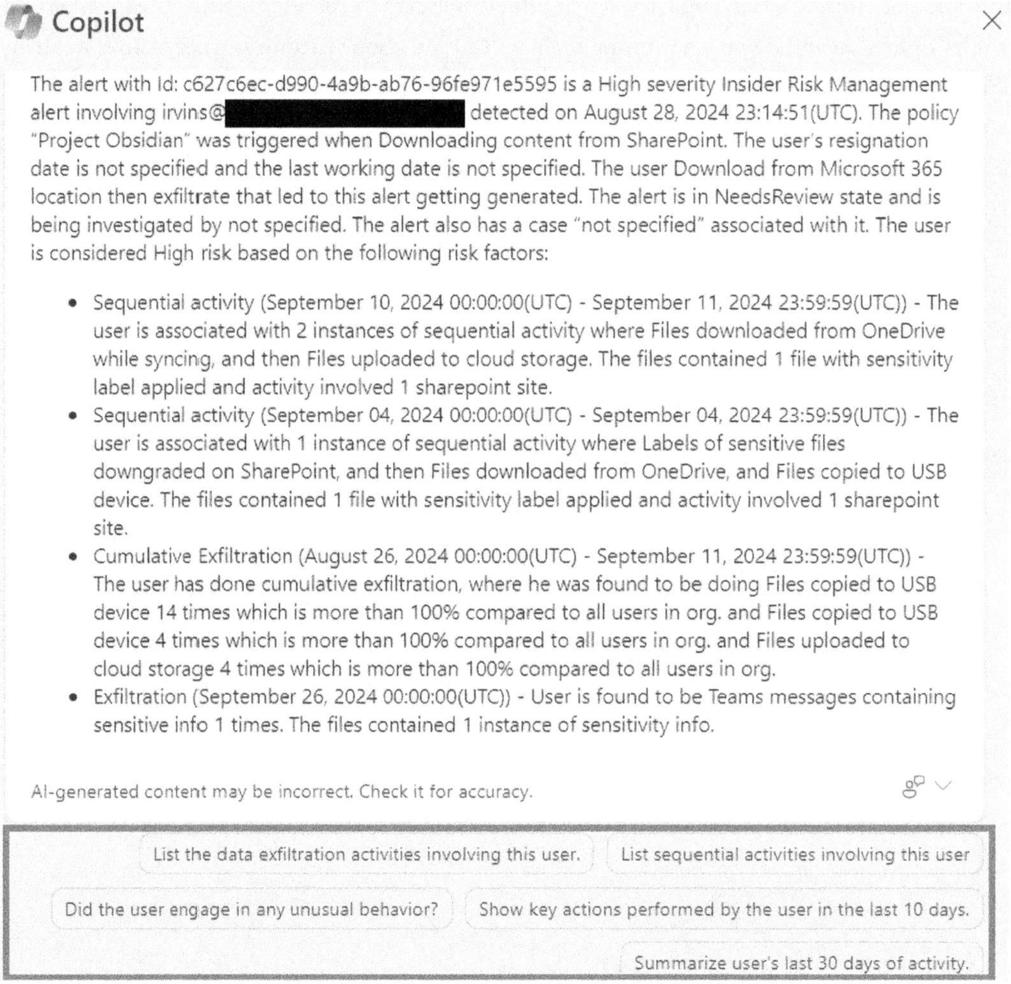

Figure 3.9 – Additional recommended prompts from Security Copilot

In certain cases, you are also able to interact directly within the **Copilot** pane, as seen in the next screenshot:

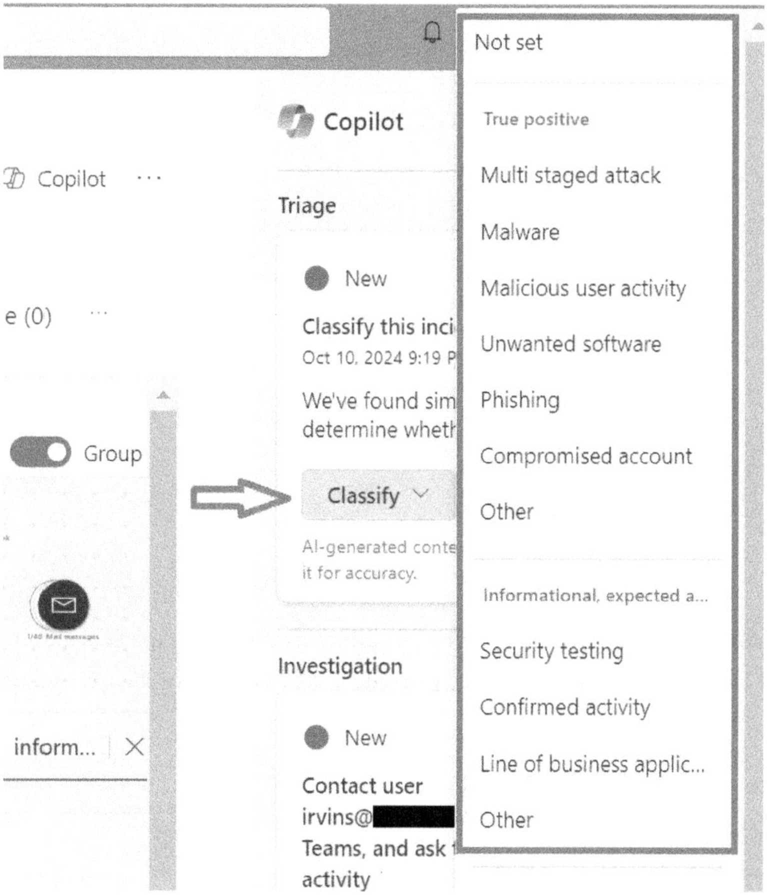

Figure 3.10 – Interacting with Security Copilot

You might have noticed that there is usually an ellipsis right inside the **Copilot** pane. As illustrated in the next screenshot, clicking on the ellipsis reveals additional options, such as the ability to copy Copilot's response for further review. You can also request Copilot to regenerate its response if needed:

Figure 3.11 – Security Copilot ellipsis

You can effortlessly transition from Security Copilot's embedded experience to its standalone environment by choosing **Open in Security Copilot**, as illustrated in the next screenshot:

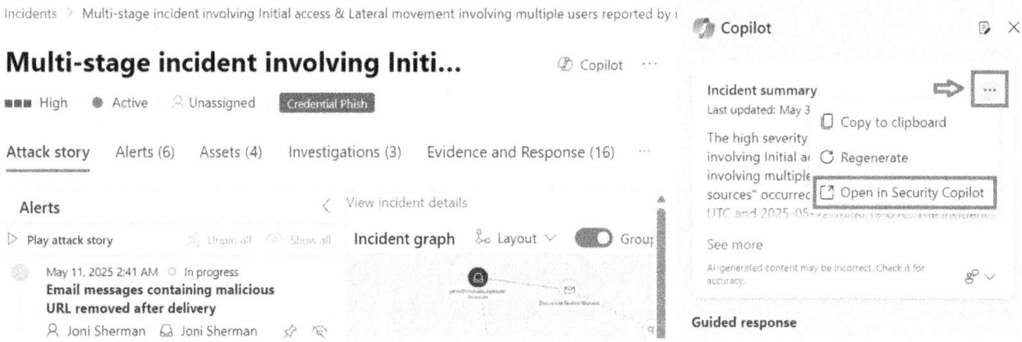

Figure 3.12 – Pivoting from Copilot's embedded experience to its standalone mode

Note

In the embedded experience for Security Copilot, its user interfaces are designed to be simple and straightforward. Customization options are typically limited, as the interface is intended to integrate seamlessly with the host application. This design ensures that the **Copilot** interface is consistent with the host environment, making key Security Copilot functionalities easily accessible without extensive personalization. While this approach prioritizes a seamless user experience and focuses on essential features, it offers fewer opportunities for modification compared to the standalone experience.

The standalone experience

The design and layout in Security Copilot's standalone environment are quite different from the embedded experience. In the standalone mode, its interface is more customizable, allowing for a tailored and flexible experience, with options to adjust the layout to better meet individual needs. This setup allows a dedicated space for the user to fully explore and leverage Copilot's advanced features.

When you sign in to the standalone environment of Security Copilot at `https://securitycopilot.microsoft.com/`, the home screen, shown in the next screenshot, presents a list of prompts or promptbooks for you to explore:

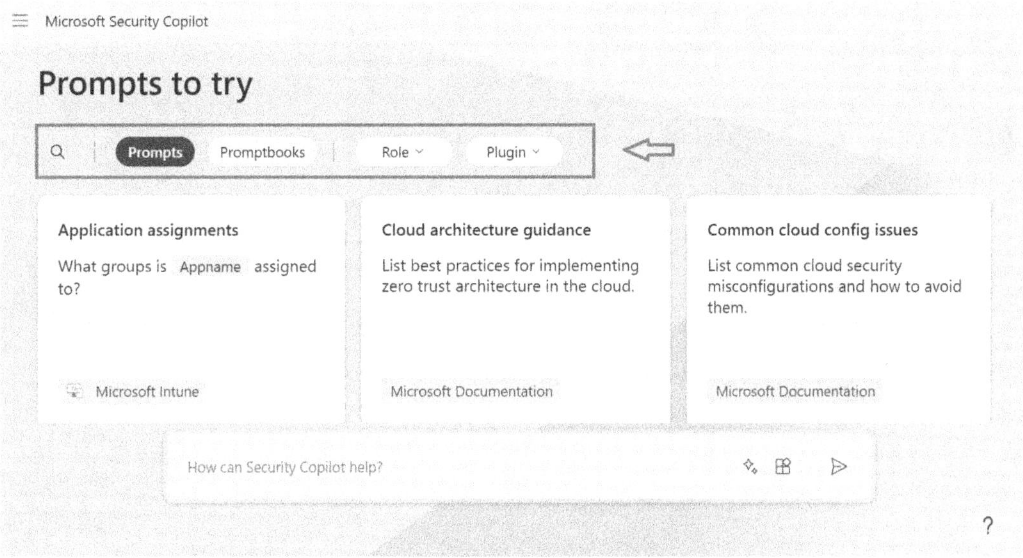

Figure 3.13 – Security Copilot standalone experience home screen

You can further narrow down the prompts or promptbooks by filtering them according to the plugin involved and/or the analyst's role. The next screenshot illustrates how the recommended prompts are filtered using two selected plugins, **Incident Analysis** and **Microsoft Defender XDR**:

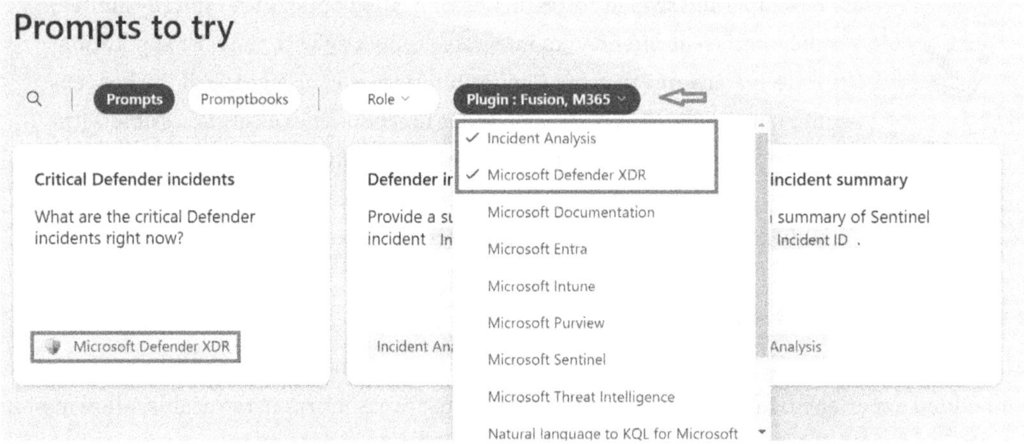

Figure 3.14 – Prompts filtered by selected plugins

In addition, the following screenshot shows that a specific promptbook named **Microsoft User Analysis** appears on the home screen when the **Identity Administrator** role is selected:

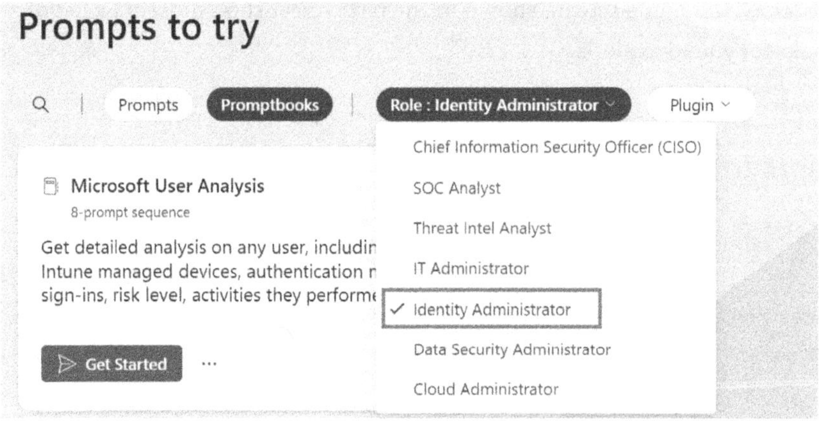

Figure 3.15 – Narrowing down promptbooks by the analyst's role

On the home screen, let's explore three main menu options:

1. Home menu
2. Prompt bar
3. Additional resources (represented by a question mark icon)

They are outlined and can be seen in the next screenshot:

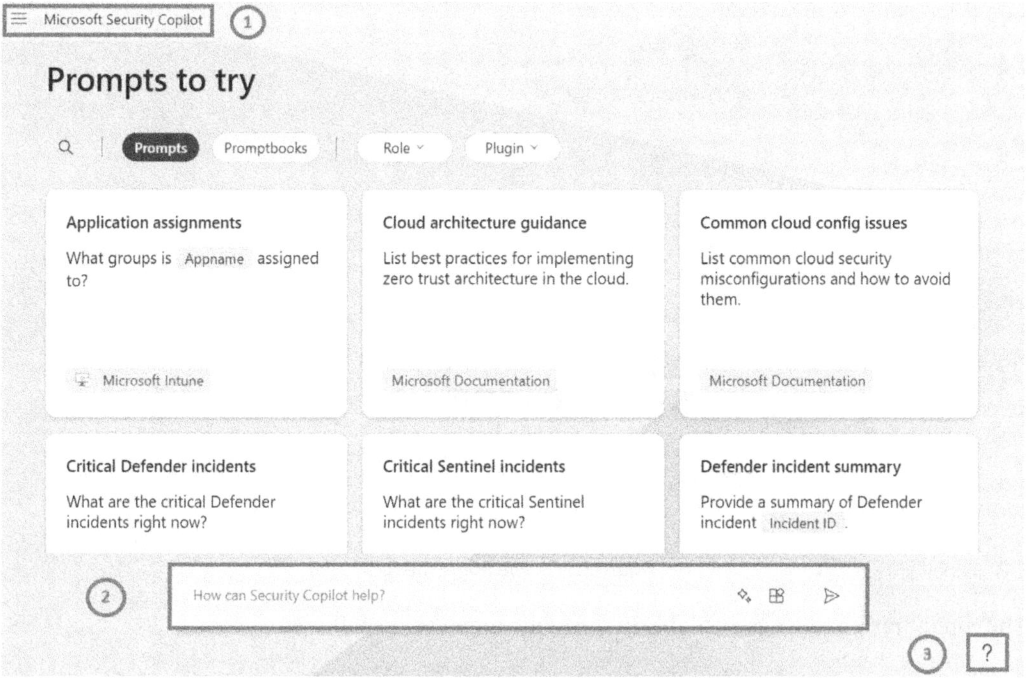

Figure 3.16 – Main menu options on the home screen

The home menu is located in the upper-left corner of the home screen. It provides access to the main features and settings of Security Copilot. This is illustrated in the next screen capture:

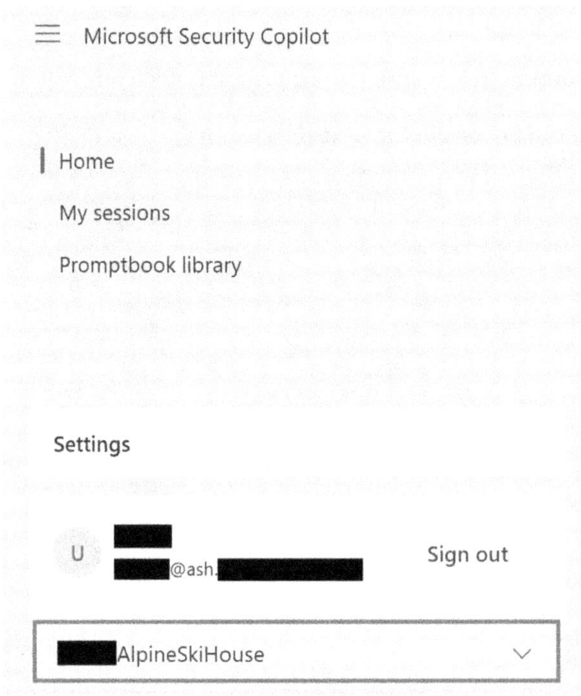

Figure 3.17 – The home menu

The configuration settings available in the home menu are as follows:

- **Home** takes you back to the main home screen page, where you can start drafting a new prompt.
- **My sessions** displays a list of your past Security Copilot sessions, including those from embedded experiences. In there, you can manage your sessions using search and filter options, as well as rename or delete sessions as needed.

- **Promptbook library** lists your own promptbooks, those shared within your organization, and Microsoft promptbooks. Within this section, you can search for specific promptbooks, duplicate existing ones, and share promptbooks as needed. We will explore promptbooks and the promptbook library in greater detail in *Chapter 6*.
- **Settings** include three categories: **Preferences**, **Data and Privacy**, and **About**. The **Preferences** section allows you to configure configurations such as choosing a theme (light, dark, or high contrast) for your Copilot user interface and setting your time zone and language preferences.
- At the bottom of the home menu is the current tenant (outlined in the previous screenshot). You can switch the tenant to access security data in a different tenant. This feature allows authorized external or guest accounts to conduct sessions using your tenant data.

The prompt bar is located at the bottom of the home screen. You can use it to enter prompts to direct Copilot to perform tasks. The prompt bar also features two additional menu icons: **Prompts** and **Sources**. The next screenshot shows the **Prompts** icon:

Figure 3.18 – The Prompts icon

The **Sources** icon is shown in the following screenshot:

Figure 3.19 – The Sources icon

The **Prompts** option helps you to get started by offering a selection of promptbooks. These promptbooks provide structured guidance and examples to assist you in creating and using prompts effectively within Security Copilot. Additionally, clicking on the **Prompts** option leads to the **SYSTEM CAPABILITIES** function. This is illustrated next:

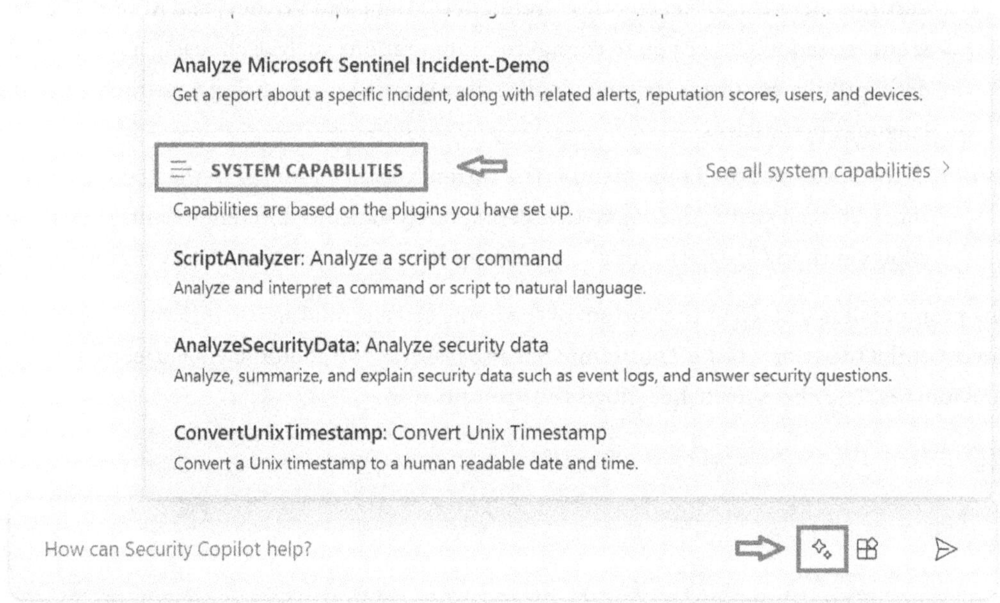

Figure 3.20 – The SYSTEM CAPABILITIES function in the standalone experience

Whenever a new tool is introduced, there's often curiosity about its capabilities and the value it can provide. With the embedded experience of Security Copilot, its functions are clearly displayed and presented to you through the user interfaces. In the standalone experience, you're tapping into its vast amount of knowledge and information to gain insights and support. But exactly what does Security Copilot know? What questions can you ask Copilot through its standalone experience?

This is where the **SYSTEM CAPABILITIES** function becomes your guide for getting acquainted with Security Copilot. It showcases the knowledge and information Copilot possesses, highlights the features Copilot offers, and provides a detailed overview of what Copilot can accomplish with each plugin. It can serve as your starter guide to understanding the full extent of Security Copilot's capabilities, particularly those not covered in the embedded experiences.

The screenshot of the **SYSTEM CAPABILITIES** function, as shown next, highlights some of Copilot's capabilities, especially those not featured in the embedded experience:

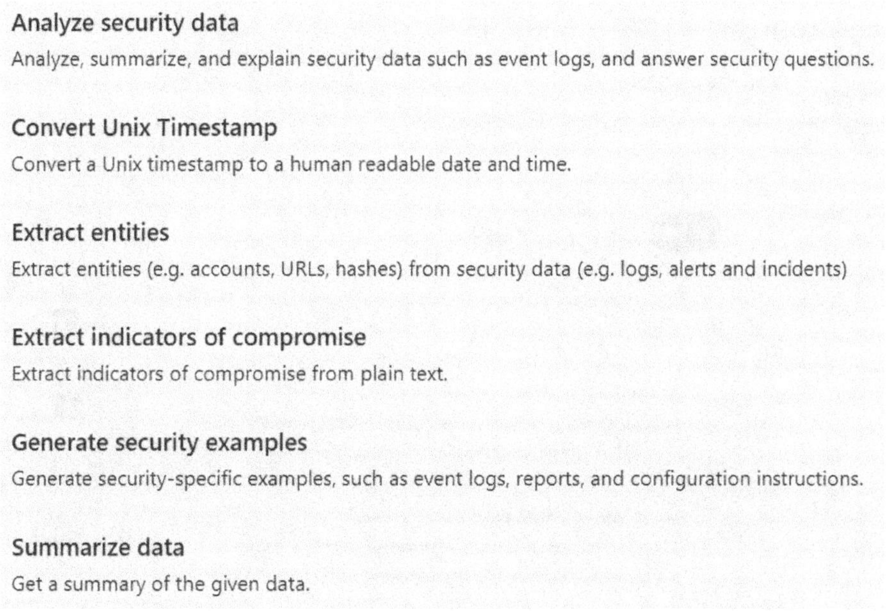

Figure 3.21 – Some system capability examples

The next screen capture displays some additional functions mentioned in **SYSTEM CAPABILITIES**:

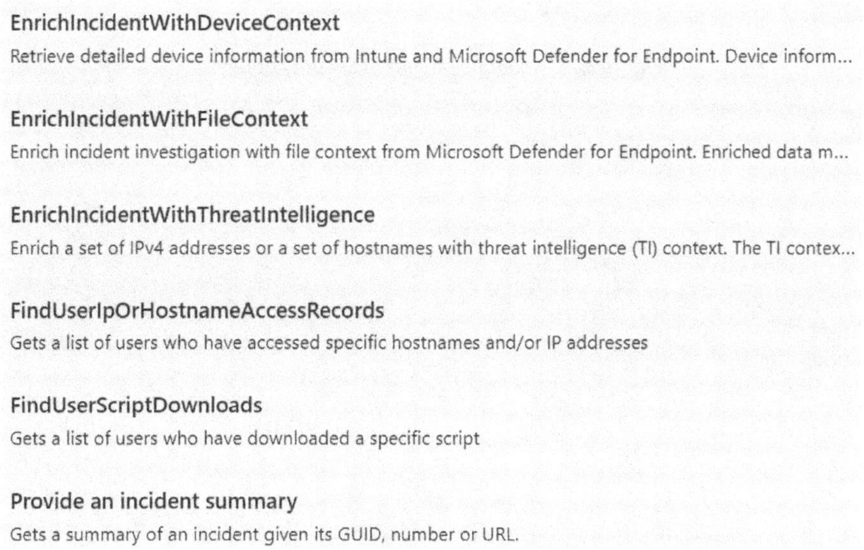

Figure 3.22 – Additional system capability examples

As mentioned earlier, the prompt bar also includes a menu option called **Sources.** As illustrated in the next screenshot, this menu option lets you manage different plugins:

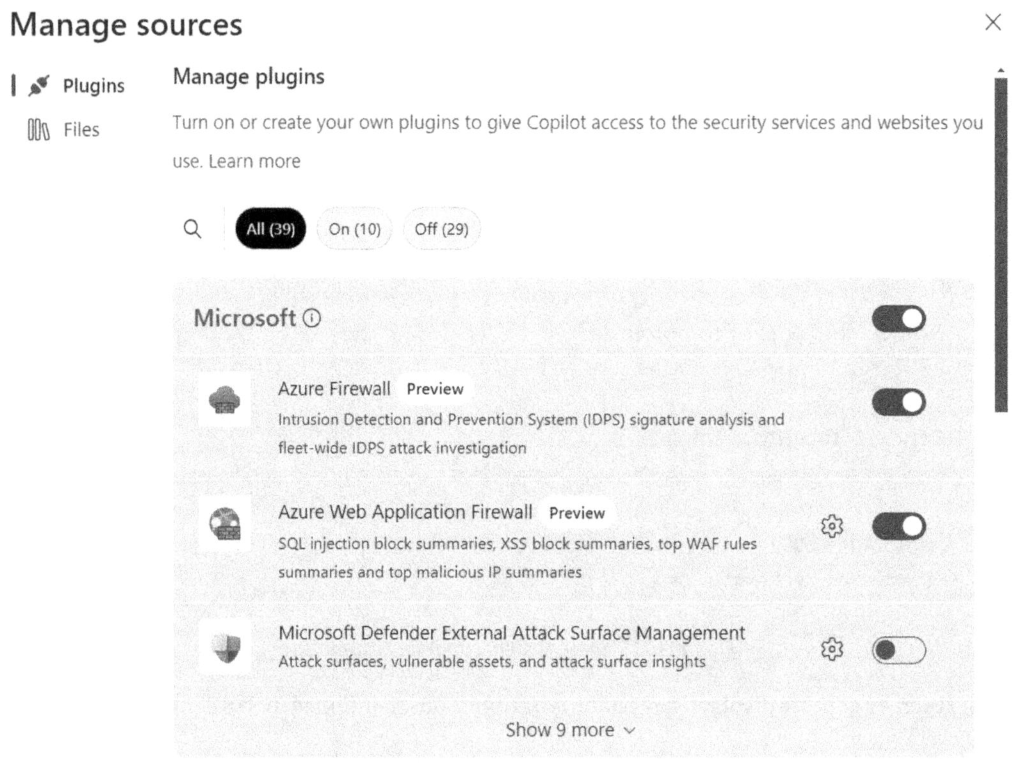

Figure 3.23 – Manage plugins in Security Copilot

Here, you can activate your own plugins as well. This is illustrated next:

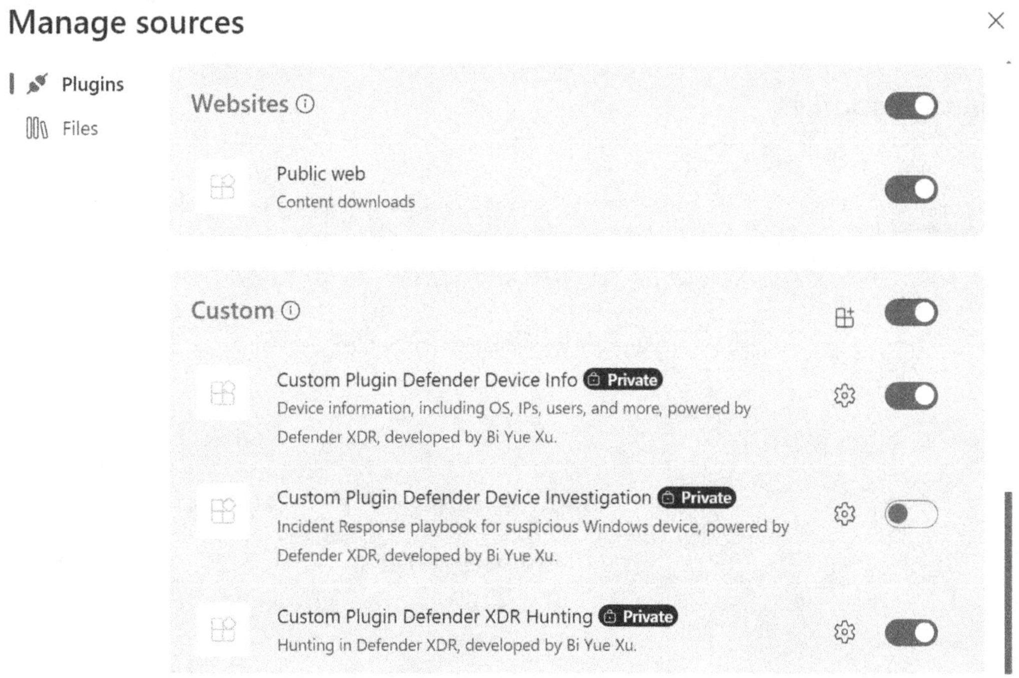

Figure 3.24 – Public web and custom plugin

From the previous screenshot, you may have seen a **Public web** plugin, located just above the **Custom** plugin section. It is a special plugin designed to integrate information from the public web. Security Copilot can be configured to access and retrieve information from publicly available sources on the internet. This capability enables Copilot to access up-to-date information and deliver insights and recommendations based on the latest emerging threats or vulnerabilities. This results in more informed advice and support for your security strategies and decisions.

In addition to managing plugins, the **Manage sources** menu provides the **Files** option to let you upload your own internal files to add organizational knowledge for Security Copilot, as shown in the next screenshot:

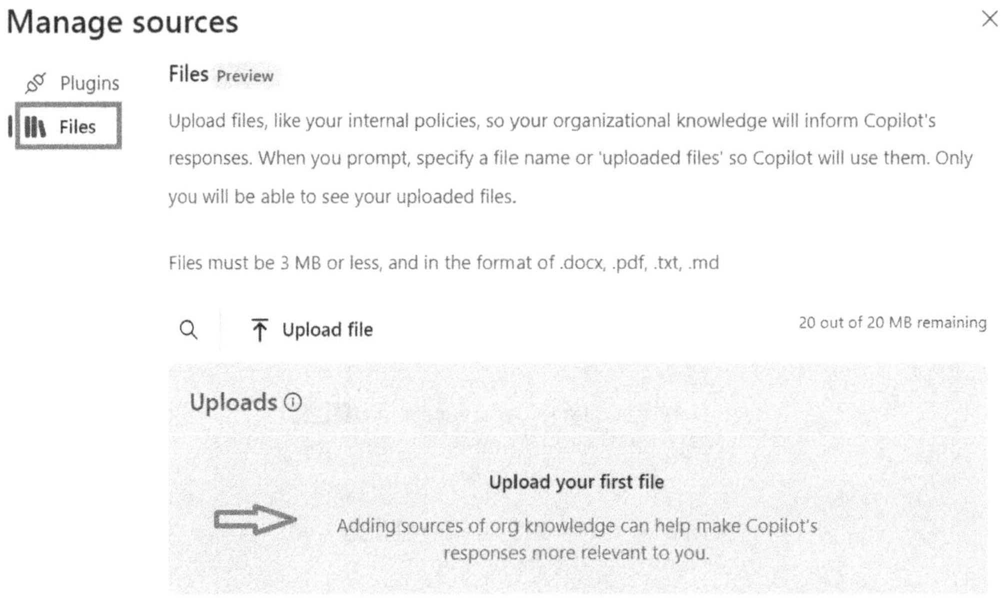

Figure 3.25 – The Files option in the Sources menu option

By uploading and incorporating these files into Security Copilot, you enable it to use your proprietary information to enhance Copilot's response and support. This integration allows Security Copilot to deliver advice and actions that are more relevant and contextually informed based on the specific content of your organization. For instance, if Copilot has access to your internal guidelines or recent vulnerability reports, it can use this information to offer more accurate and tailored recommendations, enhancing its ability to address your organization's unique needs and challenges.

Lastly, we have the *additional resources* menu option in the lower-right corner of the home screen, indicated by a question mark icon. This menu offers access to a range of supporting materials for Security Copilot, including documentation, training videos, and additional support resources. This is shown in the next screenshot:

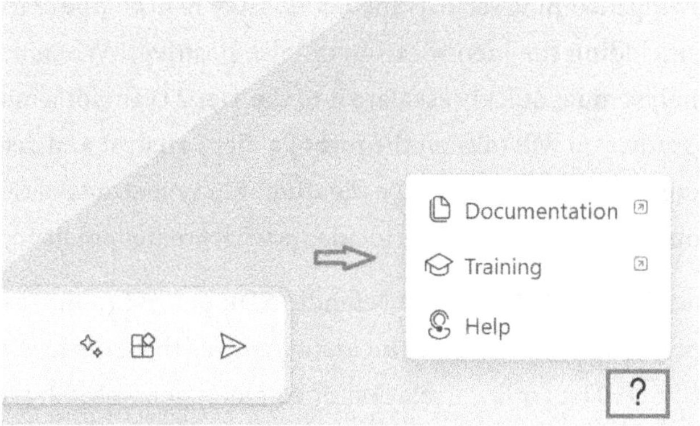

Figure 3.26 – The additional resources menu option

The **Documentation** function leads you to the official Microsoft resources for Security Copilot. The **Training** function leverages videos and visual tutorials to guide you in learning about and using Security Copilot effectively. The **Help** function offers the self-help widget to provide articles related to your query and allows you to submit a support case. The *additional resources* menu option, outlined in red and shown as a question mark icon in the previous screenshot, is designed to help you maximize your use of Security Copilot by providing essential resources and support.

Now that you're getting familiar with both the embedded experience and the standalone mode and have reviewed their user interfaces for more efficient navigation, in the next section, let's use a case study to illustrate how Security Copilot can support you throughout the security incident investigation.

Case study – harnessing Security Copilot in defending against cyber threats

In a typical **Security Operations Center (SOC)** environment, Tier 1 analysts are responsible for monitoring and reviewing incoming security incidents. They're in charge of the initial triage and basic investigations, including the identification of false positives. When a critical incident is detected, the Tier 1 analyst must quickly escalate it to the Tier 2 team for a more thorough investigation. In this case study, you will take on the role of a Tier 1 analyst and discover how Copilot can support you throughout the incident investigation. Many features of Security Copilot are designed to enable you to assess and manage incidents with greater efficiency and effectiveness.

Let's use a security incident in the Microsoft Defender XDR portal for our case study. As shown in the next screen capture, this high-severity incident involves three devices, four user accounts, and one email inbox. It consists of a correlation of 25 alerts generated by different Microsoft security solutions. This incident, titled **Multi-stage incident involving Initial access & Lateral movement on multiple endpoints reported by multiple sources**, appears complex, extensive, and intimidating:

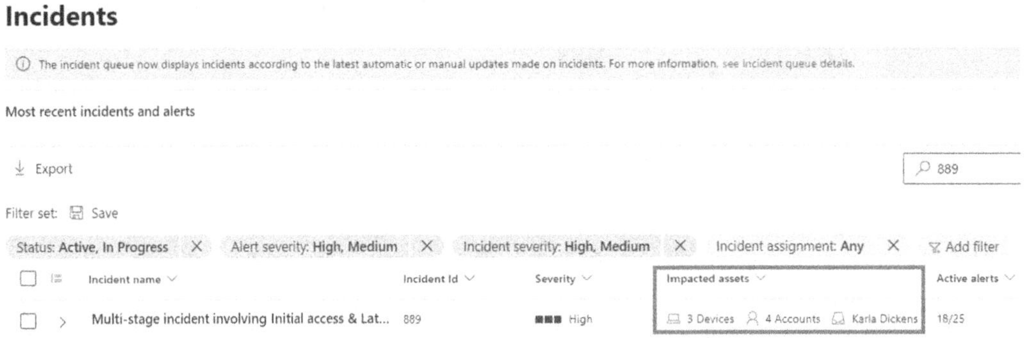

Figure 3.27 – The security incident in the case study

As soon as you start examining this incident in the Microsoft Defender XDR portal, Security Copilot is already present on the incident page, as shown in the next diagram. It automatically generates a summary of the incident, providing a clear overview of the attack.

Additionally, it offers tailored guidance for responding to the incident through its **Guided response** feature, which is also accessible on the incident page:

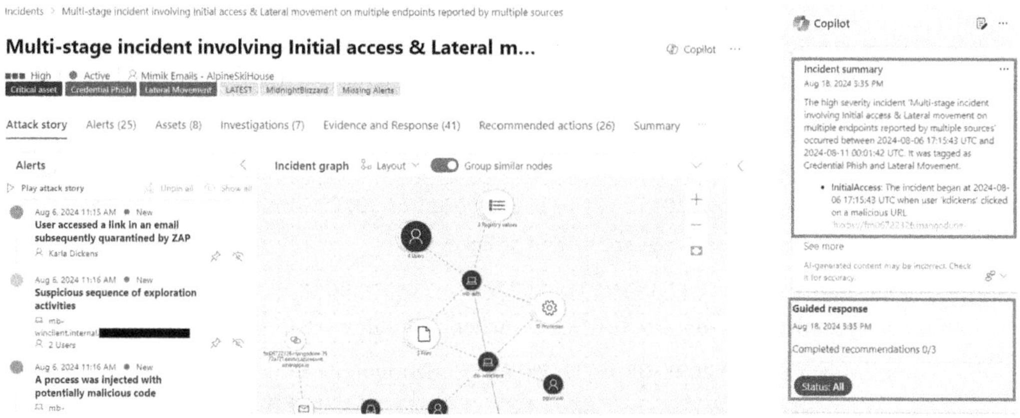

Figure 3.28 – Incident summary and guided response provided by Copilot

Rather than sifting through all 25 alerts in the incident to understand the attack, let's review the summary provided by Security Copilot first. You can copy the **Incident summary** information for further review using Copilot's **Copy to clipboard** option. This feature is illustrated in the next screenshot:

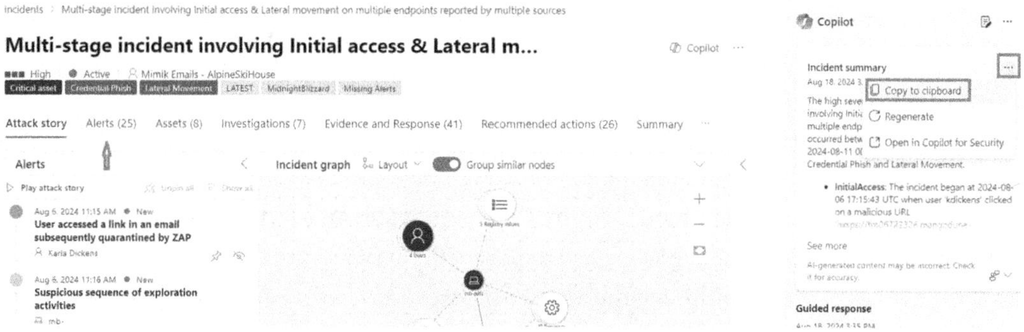

Figure 3.29 – The Copy to clipboard option

For your reference, here is the full **Incident summary** information copied from Security Copilot:

> The high severity incident 'Multi-stage incident involving Initial access & Lateral movement on multiple endpoints reported by multiple sources' occurred between 2024-08-06 17:15:43 UTC and 2024-08-11 00:01:42 UTC. It was tagged as Credential Phish and Lateral Movement.
>
> - **InitialAccess:** The incident began at 2024-08-06 17:15:43 UTC when user 'kdickens' clicked on a malicious URL 'hxxps://fm06722326.mangodune-7572a721.eastus.azurecontainerapps.io/'.

- **Discovery:** At 2024-08-06 17:16:17 UTC, a suspicious sequence of exploration activities was detected on 'mb-winclient' (Windows 10), involving the processes 'whoami.exe', 'powershell.exe' (running as SYSTEM), and impacting users 'pgustavo' and 'kdickens'.
- **DefenseEvasion:** At 2024-08-06 17:16:20 UTC, a process was injected with potentially malicious code on 'mb-winclient' (Windows 10), involving the files 'ContosoADFSadmincreds.ps1', 'Midnight161.ps1', and impacting users 'pgustavo' and 'kdickens'.
- **Execution:** At 2024-08-06 17:16:20 UTC, a malicious PowerShell Cmdlet was invoked on 'mb-winclient' (Windows 10), involving the files 'ContosoADFSadmincreds.ps1', 'Midnight161.ps1', and impacting users 'pgustavo' and 'kdickens'.
- **CredentialAccess:** At 2024-08-06 17:17:07 UTC, a suspected DCSync attack (replication of directory services) was detected on 'mb-winclient' (Windows 10), impacting user 'pgustavo'.
- **LateralMovement:** At 2024-08-06 17:17:09 UTC, an ongoing hands-on-keyboard attack via Impacket toolkit was detected on 'mb-adfs' (Windows Server 2022), involving the processes 'lsass.exe' (running as SYSTEM), 'powershell.exe' (running as SYSTEM), and impacting users 'LocalSystem' and 'adfsadmin'.
- **Persistence:** At 2024-08-06 17:17:10 UTC, suspicious service creation was detected on 'mb-adfs' (Windows Server 2022), involving the process 'services.exe' (running as SYSTEM), and impacting user 'adfsadmin'.
- **CredentialAccess:** At 2024-08-06 17:18:20 UTC, an ADFS private key extraction attempt was detected on 'mb-adfs' (Windows Server 2022), impacting user 'adfsadmin'.
- **DefenseEvasion:** At 2024-08-11 00:01:42 UTC, an attempt to hide the use of a dual-purpose tool was detected on 'mb-adfs' (Windows Server 2022), involving the file 'jyglecpm.1v0.exe', and impacting user 'adfsadmin'.

As seen from the incident summary, Security Copilot provides an overview of the incident that helps you quickly understand the scope and impact of the attack. It groups the suspicious events into distinct attack stages, outlining the attack's progression from initial access to lateral movement and persistent access. Each stage is detailed with specific timestamps and a concise summary of the events. In a typical investigation, the Tier 1 analyst would need to create a similar incident outline manually. With Copilot, this process is now automated and much faster.

After reviewing the incident summary, it's clear that this is a highly involved incident with multiple sophisticated attacks. As a Tier 1 analyst, your goal is to quickly assess the attacks, rule out the false positives, determine the incident impact, and decide whether it needs to be escalated to the Tier 2 team. Let's dive into some of the incident investigation and see how Security Copilot can assist throughout the process.

Initial access, discovery, and defense evasion

The *initial access* occurs when the attacker gains entry into the target system or network. In this case, the attacker employs a common attack tactic by tricking the user to click on a malicious link, to establish the initial foothold within the user's corporate network. For your reference, the initial access point, as outlined in the Security Copilot incident summary, is provided next:

> **InitialAccess:** The incident began at 2024-08-06 17:15:43 UTC when user 'kdickens' clicked on a malicious URL 'hxxps://fm06722326.mangodune-7572a721.eastus.azurecontainerapps.io/'.

Once the attackers gain access to the corporate network, they need to gather information about the environment – for instance, running the `whoami.exe` Windows process to gather details about the current user's identity and environment. Executing `whoami/groups` shows the groups to which the current user belongs, revealing the user's access level and permissions within the system. This process is documented during the **Discovery** phase in the Security Copilot incident summary, as shown next:

> **Discovery:** At 2024-08-06 17:16:17 UTC, a suspicious sequence of exploration activities was detected on 'mb-winclient' (Windows 10), involving the processes 'whoami.exe', 'powershell.exe' (running as SYSTEM), and impacting users 'pgustavo' and 'kdickens'.

So far, the attack techniques encountered are standard and frequently observed. For a Tier 1 analyst, these techniques are familiar and well-known, making the investigation relatively simple.

However, starting from the *defense evasion* phase, as documented in the Security Copilot incident summary, things may get a bit tricky. You see a process injection event in the alert:

> **DefenseEvasion:** At 2024-08-06 17:16:20 UTC, a process was injected with potentially malicious code on 'mb-winclient' (Windows 10), involving the files 'ContosoADFSadmincreds.ps1', 'Midnight161.ps1', and impacting users 'pgustavo' and 'kdickens'.

What might **a process was injected with potentially malicious code** indicate? What's a process injection? Let's consult with Security Copilot. You can switch from its embedded experience to Copilot's standalone mode. This allows you to ask Security Copilot various questions using its prompt feature.

Upon switching to Security Copilot's standalone environment, you are directed to the Copilot session where the incident summary is already present. In this session, you can generate additional follow-up prompts.

This is illustrated in the next screenshot, with the prompt outlined:

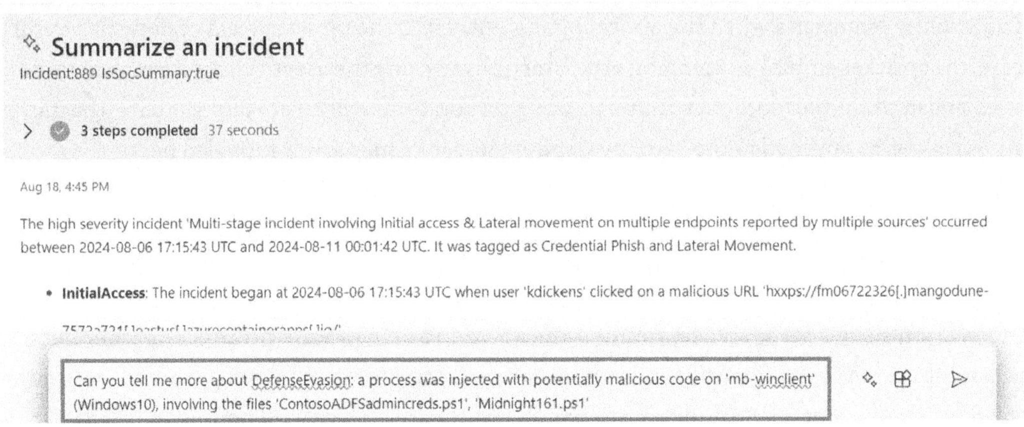

Figure 3.30 – Consulting with Copilot via its prompt feature

The response from Copilot provides an overview of process injection and its characteristics, as displayed in the next screen capture:

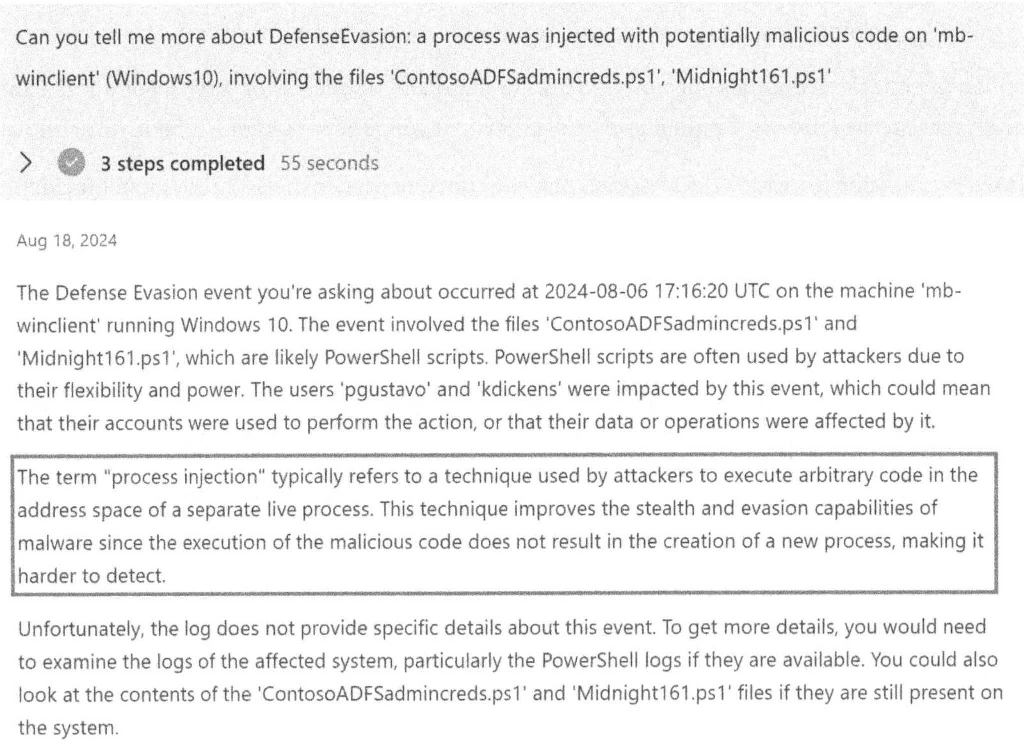

Figure 3.31 – Response from Security Copilot

The process injection overview may still be somewhat abstract. You can follow up with Copilot for a more detailed description using the prompt seen in the next screen capture:

Can you describe in detail about the technique used by attackers to execute arbitrary code in the address space of a separate live process.

Figure 3.32 – Asking Copilot with a follow-up prompt

With the response from Copilot, you have a better understanding of process injection. The next screenshot presents a portion of the response from Security Copilot:

2. **Crafting the Payload**: The attacker then crafts a payload, which is the piece of code they want the system to execute. This could be anything from code that creates a backdoor in the system, to code that simply crashes the system.

3. **Injection**: The attacker then injects this payload into the system or application. This is often done by inputting the code into an insecure form or data entry point in the application, or by tricking the system into loading a file containing the malicious code.

4. **Execution**: If the attack is successful, the system will then execute the injected code, thinking it is part of the normal program. This allows the attacker to carry out their intended action (e.g., gaining unauthorized access, extracting sensitive data).

Figure 3.33 – More detailed response from Security Copilot

The information from Security Copilot adds more context and insights for this alert, enabling you, the Tier 1 analyst, to start a more thorough investigation immediately.

Back to the Microsoft Defender XDR portal, analysts typically leverage the Defender for Endpoint **Timeline** feature to investigate the event that might have triggered the **a process was injected with potentially malicious code** alert. The next screenshot shows that in the **Timeline** section, Defender recorded a device event, **powershell.exe executed a script**. This event led Defender for Endpoint to immediately detect and report **powershell.exe process contains suspicious patterns in AMSI content related to 'Process Injection' and other techniques.**

This then led to the triggering of the process injection alert:

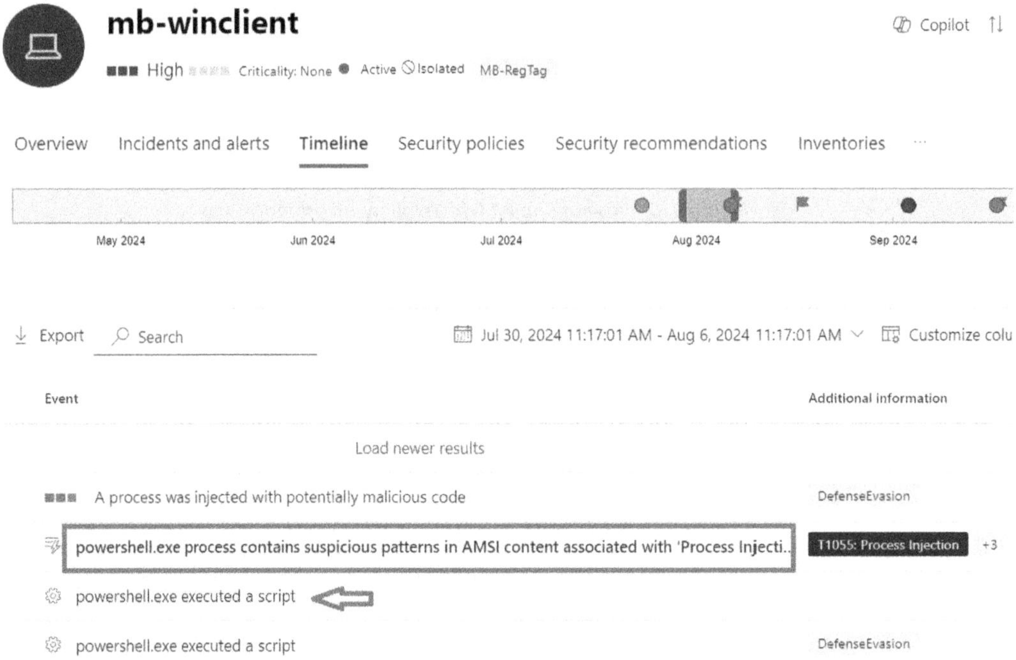

Figure 3.34 – Defender for Endpoint Timeline

Defender also provides the detailed PowerShell process commands that you can ask Security Copilot to analyze, as shown in the next screen capture:

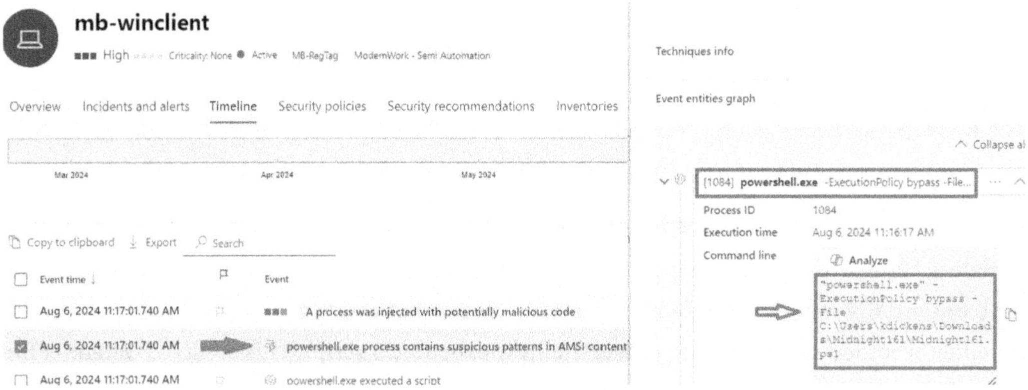

Figure 3.35 – Asking Security Copilot to analyze the PowerShell command line

With Security Copilot's information on process injection, combining the details from the device events, especially that the PowerShell script was executed from the user's downloads directory, it's clear that this is likely a malicious attack rather than a false positive. The use of a more advanced technique of process injection suggests that this case should be escalated to the Tier 2 team for further investigation.

In Defender's **Timeline** feature, security analysts typically review device events that occurred around the time the security alert was triggered to identify any additional malicious activity. This process is both time-consuming and labor-intensive. Security Copilot can handle the heavy lifting for you. Let's return to Security Copilot's standalone environment and use its prompt feature to accomplish this.

The prompt seen in the next screenshot instructs Security Copilot to use a Defender KQL query to retrieve all device process events from around the time of the process injection activity. It then asks Copilot to analyze these events for any signs of suspicious activity:

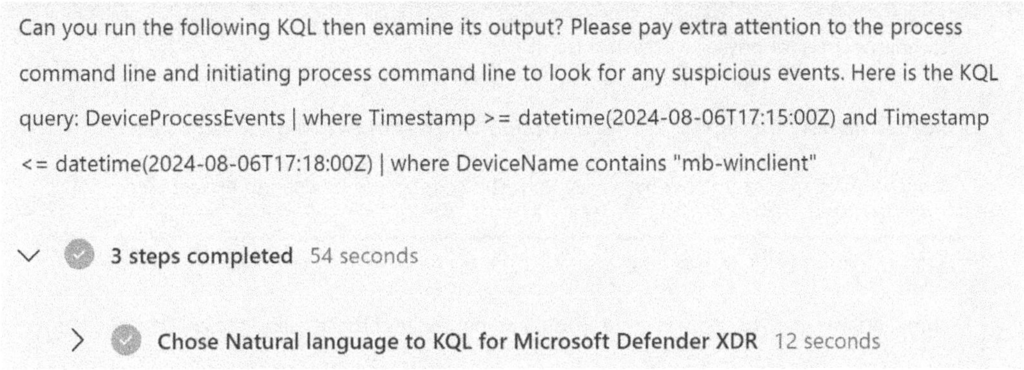

Figure 3.36 – Security Copilot prompt

As shown in the next screen capture, Security Copilot has flagged a few events that are worth investigating further, with one in particular that stands out:

Upon examining the process command line and initiating process command line, several events stand out:

1. At 2024-08-06T17:15:43.2841119Z, Microsoft Edge was launched with a URL that was accessed via a safe link. This could be the initial access point for the attacker.
2. At 2024-08-06T17:16:17.2236813Z, a PowerShell script named 'Midnight161.ps1' was executed. This script could be part of the attacker's toolkit.
3. At 2024-08-06T17:16:29.4285926Z and 2024-08-06T17:16:56.6809837Z, PowerShell was used to start another PowerShell process with elevated privileges (runas verb). This is a common technique used for privilege escalation.
4. At 2024-08-06T17:16:58.7137936Z and 2024-08-06T17:17:01.9498066Z, a script named 'ContosoADFSadmincreds.ps1' was executed. This script could be used to extract credentials.
5. At 2024-08-06T17:17:33.3585749Z and 2024-08-06T17:17:33.2111318Z, the 'csc.exe' (C# compiler) was used to compile code. This could be a sign of the attacker compiling malicious code on the fly.

These events suggest that the attacker used PowerShell scripts and privilege escalation to perform malicious activities on the 'mb-winclient' device.

Figure 3.37 – Response from Security Copilot

The suspicious event highlighted in the previous screenshot may warrant further investigation. You can ask Security Copilot to further investigate it by using the following prompt in Copilot's standalone experience:

Can you run the following KQL then examine its output? Please pay extra attention to the process command line and initiating process command line to look for 'csc.exe' (C# compiler) was used to compile code. Then display the relevant event here. Here is the KQL query: DeviceProcessEvents | where Timestamp >= datetime(2024-08-06T17:15:00Z) and Timestamp <= datetime(2024-08-06T17:18:00Z) | where DeviceName contains "mb-winclient"

Figure 3.38 – Security Copilot prompt

Security Copilot then provides more details on the events related to `csc.exe`, as shown in the next screenshot:

Upon examining the process command line and initiating process command line, several events stand out:

1. At 2024-08-06T17:17:33.3582409Z, 'csc.exe' (C# compiler) was used to compile code. The command line used was "csc.exe" /noconfig /fullpaths @"C:\WINDOWS\TEMP\3j555zka\3j555zka.cmdline". This could be a sign of the attacker compiling malicious code on the fly.

2. At 2024-08-06T17:17:33.2107333Z, 'csc.exe' (C# compiler) was used to compile code. The command line used was "csc.exe" /noconfig /fullpaths @"C:\WINDOWS\TEMP\anulltrs\anulltrs.cmdline". This could be a sign of the attacker compiling malicious code on the fly.

These events suggest that the attacker used 'csc.exe' (C# compiler) to compile code on the 'mb-winclient' device.

References

Figure 3.39 – Response from Security Copilot

This investigation may take some time to finish. However, as a Tier 1 analyst, you can conclude that this is likely a malicious event involving a sophisticated attack technique. The Tier 2 team will need to carry out a more in-depth investigation. In the meantime, you can move on to the next security alert.

Credential access

The Security Copilot incident summary also identifies a suspected `DCSync` attack as part of `CredentialAccess` activity. The snippet from the incident summary is shown next:

> **CredentialAccess:** At 2024-08-06 17:17:07 UTC, a suspected DCSync attack (replication of directory services) was detected on 'mb-winclient' (Windows 10), impacting user 'pgustavo'.

What is a `DCSync` attack? Rather than spending a lot of time researching it online, you can leverage Security Copilot's standalone experience to quickly get an idea of what it is and how it works. The next screenshot displays the question you can ask Copilot, along with some of its responses:

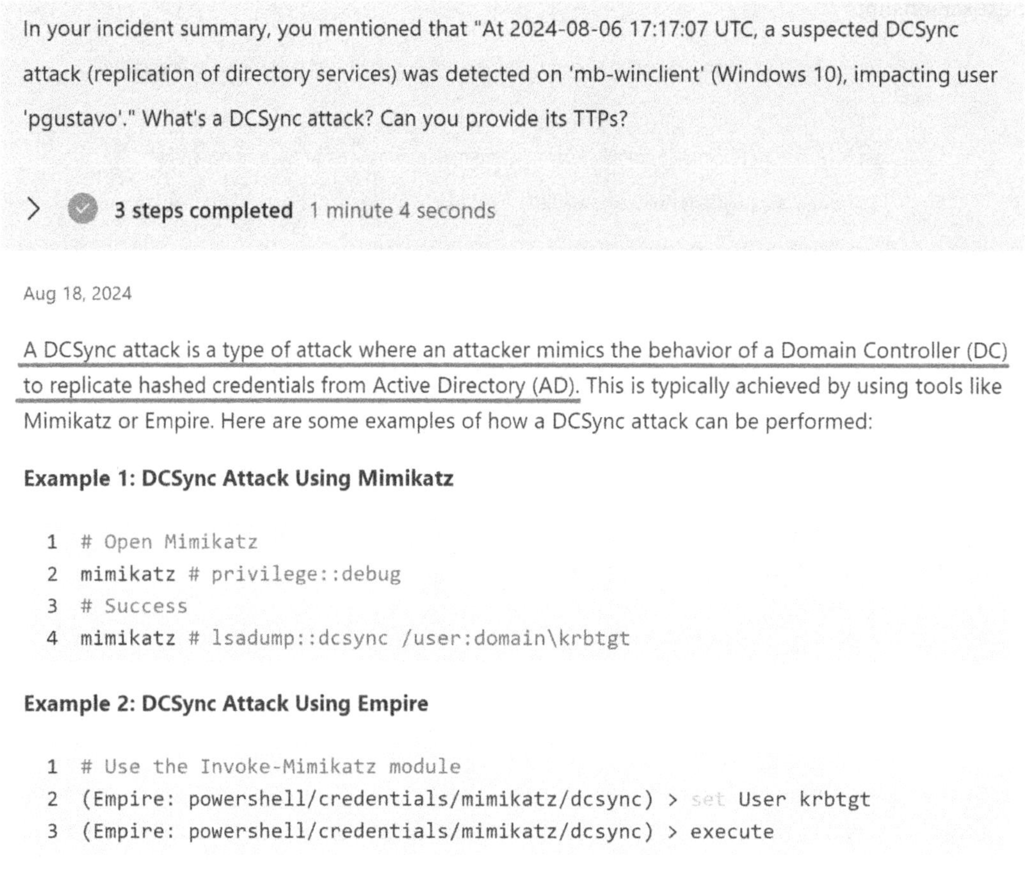

Figure 3.40 – Security Copilot prompt and responses

Security Copilot first provides an overview of the `DCSync` attack with some specific examples. It then walks you through the steps involved in a typical `DCSync` attack, as seen in the next snapshot:

The Tactics, Techniques, and Procedures (TTPs) of a DCSync attack typically involve the following steps:

1. **Initial Access**: The attacker gains access to a system within the network. This could be through spear-phishing, exploiting a vulnerability, or using stolen credentials.
2. **Privilege Escalation**: The attacker escalates their privileges to that of a domain administrator or an account with similar permissions.
3. **Credential Dumping**: The attacker uses tools like Mimikatz or Empire to perform the DCSync attack, which tricks the domain controller into syncing the hashed credentials of the target account.
4. **Lateral Movement**: With the stolen credentials, the attacker can move laterally across the network, accessing other systems and furthering their reach within the network.
5. **Persistence**: The attacker establishes a method of maintaining their access to the network, such as creating a backdoor or scheduling tasks that will re-establish their connection if it is lost.
6. **Exfiltration**: The attacker may exfiltrate data from the network, either for their own use or to sell on the dark web.
7. **Command and Control (C2)**: The attacker maintains communication with the compromised systems, often using a C2 server to remotely control the systems and execute commands.
8. **Defense Evasion**: The attacker takes steps to avoid detection, such as disabling security software, clearing logs, or using stealthy malware that can evade traditional antivirus solutions.

These steps provide a general overview of the TTPs associated with a DCSync attack. However, the specific actions and tools used can vary depending on the attacker and the specifics of the network environment.

Figure 3.41 – Steps involved in a typical DCSync attack

After reviewing the information provided by Security Copilot, you should have a better understanding of the key aspects of a `DCSync` attack and how it operates. If there are more questions or if further clarification is needed, you can always use Copilot's prompt feature in its standalone mode to gain additional support.

Once you have a solid understanding of the `DCSync` attack, you can apply this insight to assist the security incident investigation. Back in the Microsoft Defender XDR portal, when you examine the alert story for the **Suspected DCSync attack** alert, you'll likely notice something is off when the end user sends a replication request to a domain controller, as seen in the screen capture:

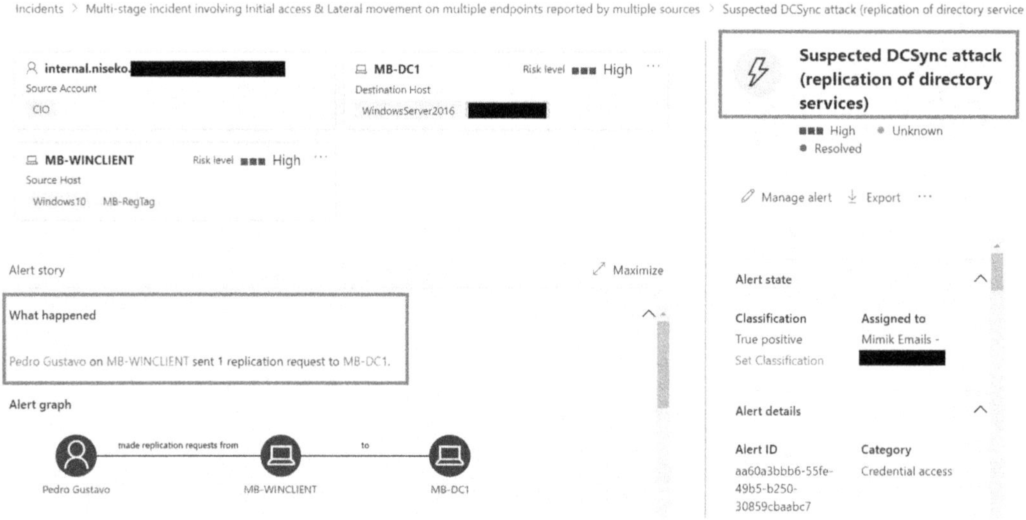

Figure 3.42 – Suspected DCSync attack alert

You can confirm your suspicion with Copilot by entering the following prompt in Copilot's standalone mode:

```
Is it common for a regular user on a Windows 10 device to sent a
replication request to a DC?
```

Note

As seen in the next screen capture, Security Copilot confirms that "**it is not common for a regular user on a Windows 10 device to send a replication request to a Domain Controller (DC). In a typical Active Directory environment, only Domain Controllers replicate data amongst themselves.**"

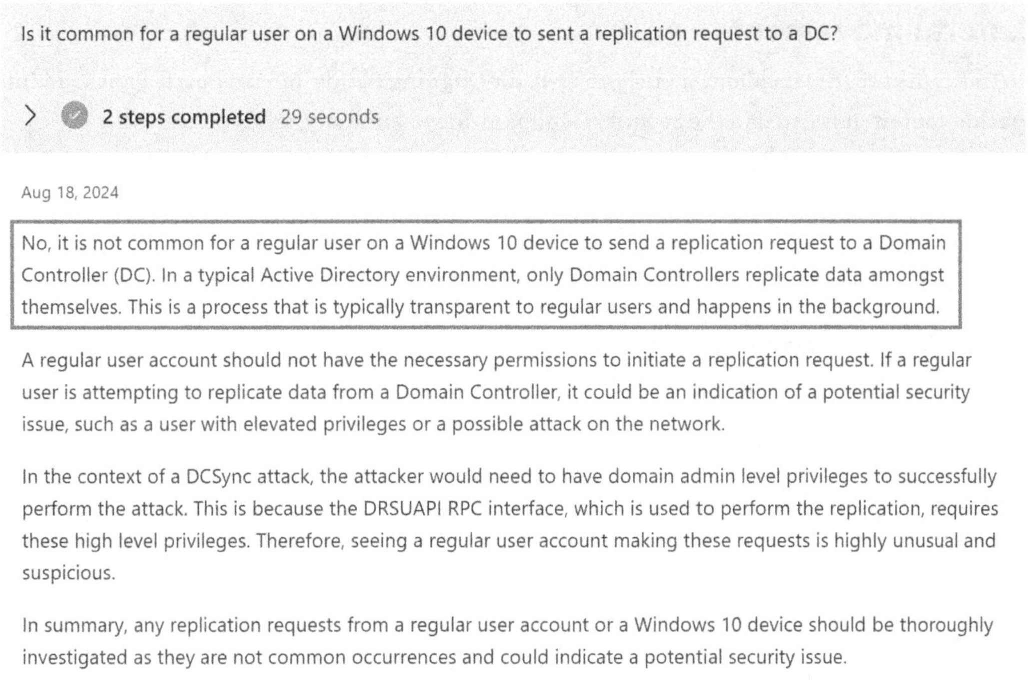

Figure 3.43 – Response from Security Copilot

At this point, you likely can confirm this is a true security incident, not a false positive. Given the nature of the attack, it will require further investigation by the Tier 2 team.

Without help from Security Copilot, researching and confirming whether suspicious behavior is truly malicious can be time-consuming and labor-intensive. However, with Copilot, it is faster and more straightforward to confirm malicious activities.

Additionally, its explanations offer more context, helping the Tier 1 analyst assess the impact and severity of the incident. This enables the analyst to quickly decide whether the incident needs to be escalated to the Tier 2 team or not.

Now, let's move on to the lateral movement stage of the attack.

Lateral movement

In this same security incident, there is an alert for **Ongoing hands-on-keyboard attack via Impacket toolkit**. It is listed in the Security Copilot incident summary, as seen next:

> **LateralMovement:** At 2024-08-06 17:17:09 UTC, an ongoing hands-on-keyboard attack via Impacket toolkit was detected on 'mb-adfs' (Windows Server 2022), involving the processes '`lsass.exe`' (running as SYSTEM), '`powershell.exe`' (running as SYSTEM), and impacting users 'LocalSystem' and 'adfsadmin'.

In the Microsoft Defender XDR portal, the alert description provides a brief description of the Impacket toolkit, as shown next:

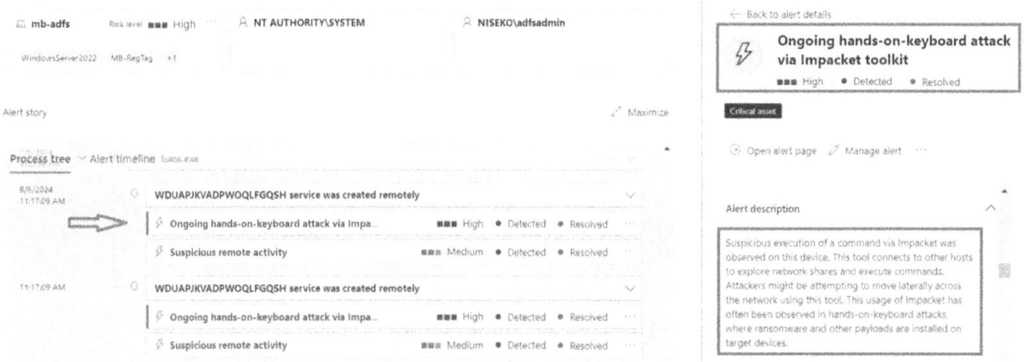

Figure 3.44 – Alert description in Microsoft Defender portal

The description of the Impacket toolkit in the Microsoft Defender portal is helpful. However, for more detailed information, you can turn to Security Copilot's standalone experience and ask the following:

```
Can you tell me more about the Impacket tool? Where is it used most often?
How is it exploited by attackers?
```

Copilot provides a more thorough description of this toolkit. While Impacket is a legitimate tool, Security Copilot emphasizes that it can also be exploited by attackers. As shown in the next screen capture, Security Copilot includes several examples to illustrate this point:

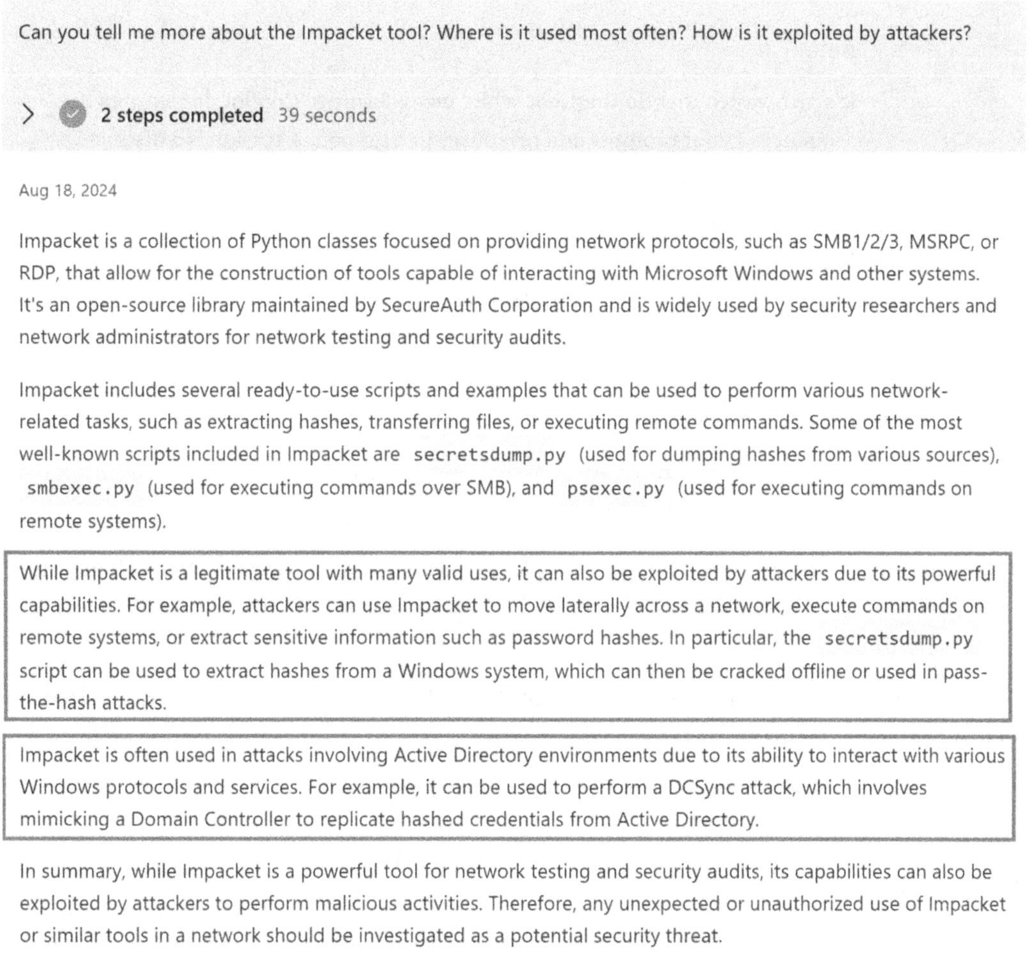
Can you tell me more about the Impacket tool? Where is it used most often? How is it exploited by attackers?

> 2 steps completed 39 seconds

Aug 18, 2024

Impacket is a collection of Python classes focused on providing network protocols, such as SMB1/2/3, MSRPC, or RDP, that allow for the construction of tools capable of interacting with Microsoft Windows and other systems. It's an open-source library maintained by SecureAuth Corporation and is widely used by security researchers and network administrators for network testing and security audits.

Impacket includes several ready-to-use scripts and examples that can be used to perform various network-related tasks, such as extracting hashes, transferring files, or executing remote commands. Some of the most well-known scripts included in Impacket are `secretsdump.py` (used for dumping hashes from various sources), `smbexec.py` (used for executing commands over SMB), and `psexec.py` (used for executing commands on remote systems).

While Impacket is a legitimate tool with many valid uses, it can also be exploited by attackers due to its powerful capabilities. For example, attackers can use Impacket to move laterally across a network, execute commands on remote systems, or extract sensitive information such as password hashes. In particular, the `secretsdump.py` script can be used to extract hashes from a Windows system, which can then be cracked offline or used in pass-the-hash attacks.

Impacket is often used in attacks involving Active Directory environments due to its ability to interact with various Windows protocols and services. For example, it can be used to perform a DCSync attack, which involves mimicking a Domain Controller to replicate hashed credentials from Active Directory.

In summary, while Impacket is a powerful tool for network testing and security audits, its capabilities can also be exploited by attackers to perform malicious activities. Therefore, any unexpected or unauthorized use of Impacket or similar tools in a network should be investigated as a potential security threat.

Figure 3.45 – Response from Security Copilot

As seen in the previous screenshot, Security Copilot also highlights a specific attack scenario, pointing out that **Impacket can be used to carry out a DCSync attack**. And, as the Tier 1 analyst, you have just confirmed that a `DCSync` attack is involved in the same security incident.

Note

It's also worth mentioning that while using Security Copilot, it captures the sequence of your prompts and responses in a session. A session is a distinct interaction period with Security Copilot, during which Copilot retains the context of the conversation. This allows it to provide relevant answers to subsequent requests, ensuring that the conversation flows logically and that each response builds upon the previous ones. This could be the reason why Security Copilot specifically points out that Impacket can be used to perform a `DCSync` attack.

Persistence

As we proceed with the incident summary generated by Security Copilot, the next security alert there is a suspicious service creation event that occurred during the attack's *persistence* stage:

> **Persistence:** At 2024-08-06 17:17:10 UTC, suspicious service creation was detected on 'mb-adfs' (Windows Server 2022), involving the process 'services.exe' (running as SYSTEM), and impacting user 'adfsadmin'.

If you start examining this alert in the Microsoft Defender portal, you will notice that Defender for Identity, Defender for Endpoint EDR, and Defender XDR all generated similar alerts, likely for the same suspicious event, as seen in the next screen capture:

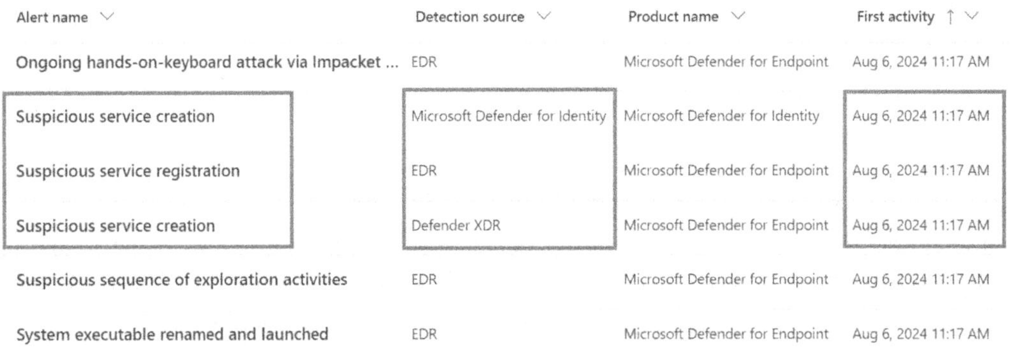

Figure 3.46 – The alerts in the Defender incident

Let's first take a look at the **Suspicious service creation** alert triggered in **Microsoft Defender for Identity** (**MDI**), as shown next:

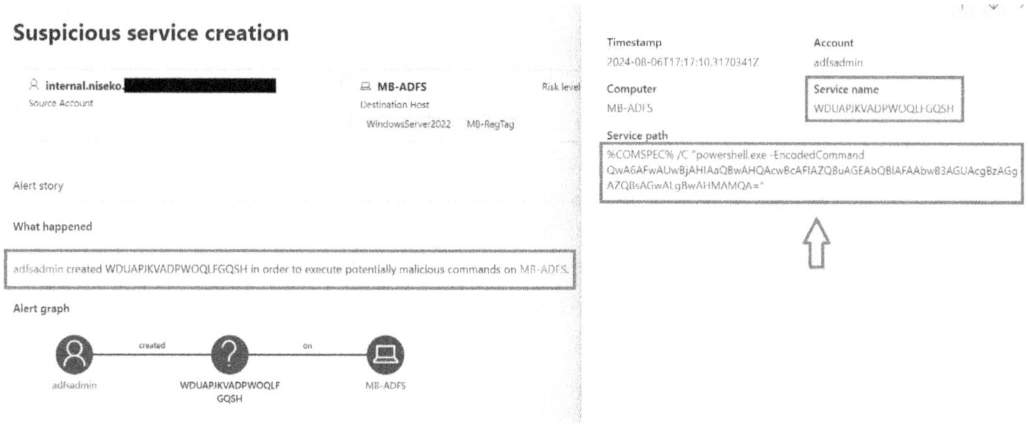

Figure 3.47 – The MDI Suspicious service creation alert

The service path listed in the alert looks suspicious and it is encoded. Let's use the following prompt to consult with Security Copilot and understand its purpose:

```
Can you decode then tell me more about this service path: %COMSPEC% /C
"powershell.exe -EncodedCommand QwA6AFwAUwBjAHIAaQBwAHQAcwBcAFIAZQBuAGEAb
QBlAFAAbwB3AGUAcgBzAGgAZQBsAGwALgBwAHMAMQA="
```

The next screen capture displays the response from Security Copilot:

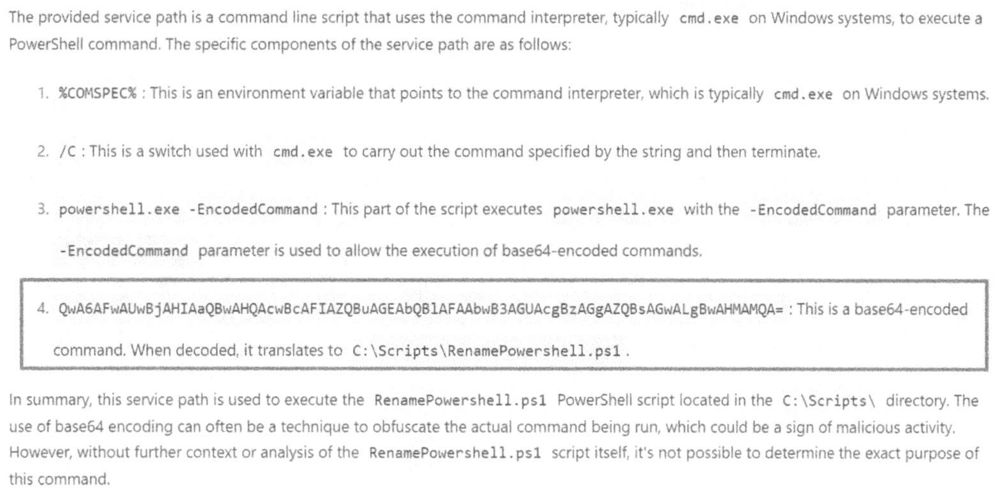
The provided service path is a command line script that uses the command interpreter, typically `cmd.exe` on Windows systems, to execute a PowerShell command. The specific components of the service path are as follows:

1. `%COMSPEC%` : This is an environment variable that points to the command interpreter, which is typically `cmd.exe` on Windows systems.
2. `/C` : This is a switch used with `cmd.exe` to carry out the command specified by the string and then terminate.
3. `powershell.exe -EncodedCommand` : This part of the script executes `powershell.exe` with the `-EncodedCommand` parameter. The `-EncodedCommand` parameter is used to allow the execution of base64-encoded commands.
4. `QwA6AFwAUwBjAHIAaQBwAHQAcwBcAFIAZQBuAGEAbQBlAFAAbwB3AGUAcgBzAGgAZQBsAGwALgBwAHMAMQA=` : This is a base64-encoded command. When decoded, it translates to `C:\Scripts\RenamePowershell.ps1` .

In summary, this service path is used to execute the `RenamePowershell.ps1` PowerShell script located in the `C:\Scripts\` directory. The use of base64 encoding can often be a technique to obfuscate the actual command being run, which could be a sign of malicious activity. However, without further context or analysis of the `RenamePowershell.ps1` script itself, it's not possible to determine the exact purpose of this command.

Figure 3.48 – Response from Security Copilot

> Note
>
> Security Copilot provides a detailed breakdown of the service path. It identifies the encoded command as `base64` encoding and decodes it for you. It then concludes with a summary: **this service path is used to execute the Rename-Powershell.ps1 PowerShell script located in the C:\Scripts\ directory.** The use of `base64` encoding can often be a technique to obfuscate the actual command being run, which could be a sign of malicious activity.

This information is helpful. Let's continue examining the other related security alerts. The **Suspicious service registration** alert triggered in **Microsoft Defender for Endpoint (MDE)** likely pertains to the same suspicious activity that is just looked at. This alert provides a little bit more information and mentions **services.exe modified service image file**, as shown next:

Figure 3.49 – The MDE Suspicious service registration alert

Using the following prompt, let's see what Security Copilot can find out:

```
Can you explain in more detail about the following event: services.
exe modified service image file from to %COMSPEC% /C "powershell.exe
-EncodedCommand QwA6AFwAUwBjAHIAaQBwAHQAcwBcAFIAZQBuAGEAbQBlAFAAbw
B3AGUAcgBzAGgAZQBsAGwALgBwAHMAMQA=" for service WDUAPJKVADPWOQLFGQSH
```

The screenshot shown next displays Copilot's response:

The event you're referring to indicates that the `services.exe` process, which is a critical system process responsible for starting, stopping, and interacting with system services, has modified the image file path of a service named `WDUAPJKVADPWOQLFGQSH`.

The new image file path is `%COMSPEC% /C "powershell.exe -EncodedCommand QwA6AFwAUwBjAHIAaQBwAHQAcwBcAFIAZQBuAGEAbQBlAFAAbwB3AGUAcgBzAGgAZQBsAGwALgBwAHMAMQA="`. This is a command line script that uses the command interpreter, typically `cmd.exe` on Windows systems, to execute a PowerShell command.

The specific components of the service path are as follows:

1. `%COMSPEC%` : This is an environment variable that points to the command interpreter, which is typically `cmd.exe` on Windows systems.
2. `/C` : This is a switch used with `cmd.exe` to carry out the command specified by the string and then terminate.
3. `powershell.exe -EncodedCommand` : This part of the script executes `powershell.exe` with the `-EncodedCommand` parameter. The `-EncodedCommand` parameter is used to allow the execution of base64-encoded commands.
4. `QwA6AFwAUwBjAHIAaQBwAHQAcwBcAFIAZQBuAGEAbQBlAFAAbwB3AGUAcgBzAGgAZQBsAGwALgBwAHMAMQA=` : This is a base64-encoded command. When decoded, it translates to `C:\Scripts\RenamePowershell.ps1`.

In summary, this service path is used to execute the `RenamePowershell.ps1` PowerShell script located in the `C:\Scripts\` directory. The use of base64 encoding can often be a technique to obfuscate the actual command being run, which could be a sign of malicious activity. However, without further context or analysis of the `RenamePowershell.ps1` script itself, it's not possible to determine the exact purpose of this command.

It's worth noting that changes to service image file paths, especially those involving scripts or unusual locations, can be a sign of malicious activity. In this case, the `services.exe` process has been instructed to launch a PowerShell script whenever the `WDUAPJKVADPWOQLFGQSH` service is started, which is unusual behavior and could potentially be malicious. Further investigation would be required to determine the nature of this activity.

Figure 3.50 – Response from Security Copilot

Copilot's findings for this **Suspicious service registration** alert closely align with its analysis of the **Suspicious service creation** alert triggered in MDI. This confirms the suspicion that the two alerts from different security solutions are both reporting the same malicious activity. However, because the MDE alert points out a `services.exe` modified service image file and this detail is included in the prompt to Copilot, Security Copilot can now provide additional insights in its analysis that weren't present in the previous report.

Note

With the help of Security Copilot, you now have a clear picture of this malicious activity: the `services.exe` process has been set to run `RenamePowershell.ps1` whenever the `WDUAPJKVADPWOQLFGQSH` service is started. For your reference, the following snippet is taken from Copilot's last response:

It's worth noting that changes to service image file paths, especially those involving scripts or unusual locations, can be a sign of malicious activity. In this case, the services.exe process has been instructed to launch a PowerShell script whenever the WDUAPJKVADPWOQLFGQSH service is started, which is unusual behavior and could potentially be malicious.

This example also highlights the importance of effective prompting. The more specific the information you provide to Copilot, the more relevant and precise the response you're likely to receive.

Additionally, this example further emphasizes Microsoft Defender XDR's capability in integrating and correlating data across various Defender solutions. When different Defender tools detect the same malicious activity, they generate individual alerts. Microsoft Defender XDR then aggregates these alerts into a unified incident. This correlation helps to provide a comprehensive view of the threat.

Credential access

Let's review one more alert from the incident summary provided by Security Copilot: a suspicious credential access event involving an ADFS private key extraction. Its incident summary snippet is shown next:

CredentialAccess: At 2024-08-06 17:18:20 UTC, an ADFS private key extraction attempt was detected on 'mb-adfs' (Windows Server 2022), impacting user 'adfsadmin'.

In the Microsoft Defender XDR portal, in addition to the alert story, the device timeline also shows the events that led to the alert being triggered. For this one, the device event, **jyglecpm.1v0.exe ran an LDAP query**, triggered the **ADFS private key extraction attempt** alert.

A section of the device timeline is displayed in the next screenshot:

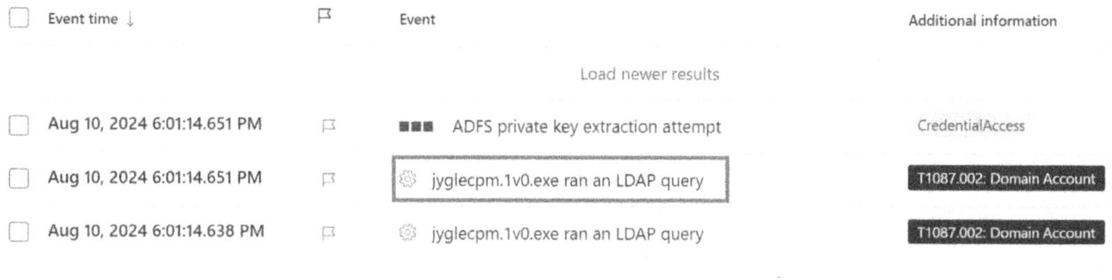

Figure 3.51 – The device timeline

To further investigate this device event, one option is to utilize Security Copilot to analyze the command line for the `jyglecpm.1v0.exe` process that ran the LDAP query. You can perform this directly within the Microsoft Defender portal, leveraging the embedded experience of Security Copilot. Alternatively, in standalone mode, you can paste the command line into the Copilot prompt and request analysis.

The next screenshot illustrates the progression from the event shown in the device timeline to the display of its suspicious command line, then to its analysis within Security Copilot's embedded experience:

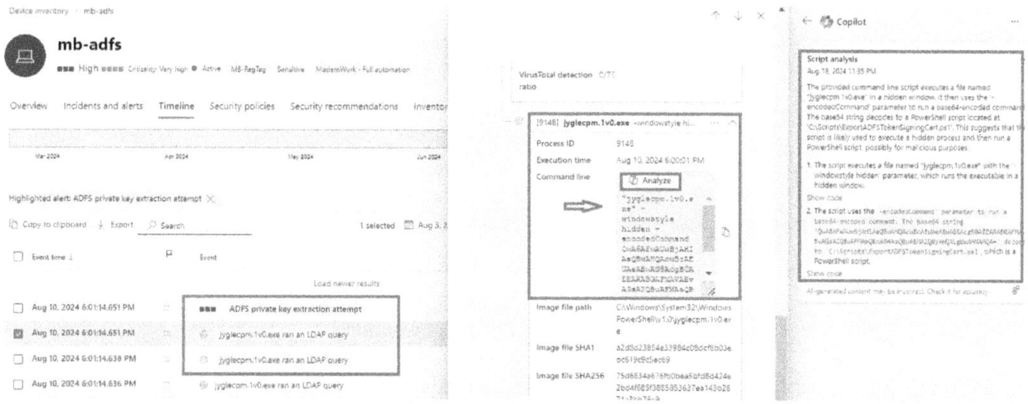

Figure 3.52 – Copilot command-line analysis

Security Copilot offers a detailed analysis of this process command line. An excerpt of the analysis is provided next for your reference since it's difficult to read in the screenshot:

The provided command line script executes a file named "jyglecpm.1vO.exe" in a hidden window. It then uses the '-encodedCommand' parameter to run a base64-encoded command. The base64 string decodes to a PowerShell script located at 'C:\Scripts\ExportADFSTokenSigningCert.ps1'. This suggests that the script is likely used to execute a hidden process and then run a PowerShell script, possibly for malicious purposes.

From the Copilot analysis, you can sense something wasn't right when `jyglecpm.1v0.exe` performed the LDAP query. To further investigate, you can first get a sense of what the normal LDAP operations are by prompting Copilot with the following questions in its standalone experience:

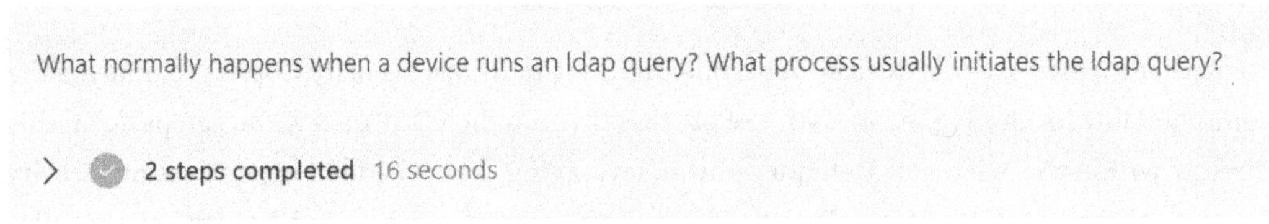

Figure 3.53 – Security Copilot prompt

The next screenshot displays the information returned by Copilot:

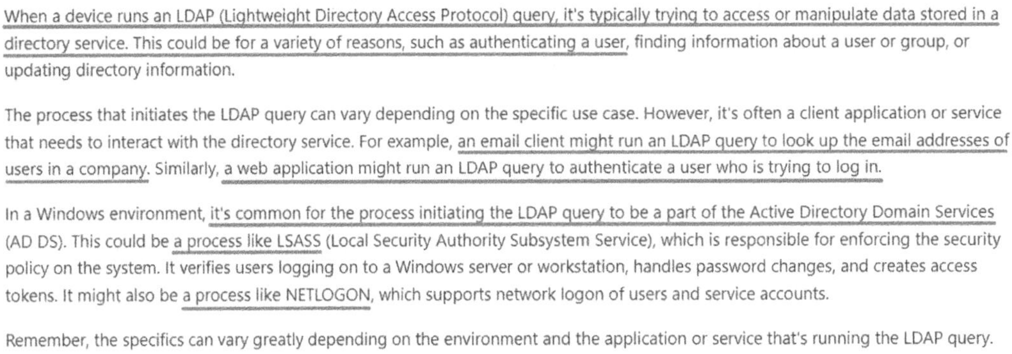

Figure 3.54 – Security Copilot response

Based on Copilot's explanation, you quickly gain an understanding of LDAP and how it operates. LDAP queries are typically initiated by client applications or services that need to access data stored in a directory service. For instance, an email client might perform an LDAP query to retrieve the email addresses of users within an organization.

Now you may be wondering why an unfamiliar and rarely seen process such as `jyglecpm.1v0.exe` needs to run an LDAP query to access data in a directory service. It is especially suspicious with its encoded command line. Let's continue to consult with Security Copilot.

The prompt is shown in the next screen capture:

Can you tell me if this is normal LDAP operation based on the following command line in the LDAP query:

"jyglecpm.1v0.exe" -windowstyle hidden -encodedCommand

QwA6AFwAUwBjAHIAaQBwAHQAcwBcAEUAeABwAG8AcgB0AEEARABGAFMAVABvAGsAZQBuAFMAaQBnAG4AaQBuAE
MAZQByAHQALgBwAHMAMQA=

Figure 3.55 – Security Copilot prompt

Security Copilot, leveraging its vast amount of knowledge, reports that the command-line script does not resemble a typical LDAP operation. Its full response is displayed in the next screen capture:

The command line script you provided does not appear to be a normal LDAP operation. It executes a file named "jyglecpm.1v0.exe" in a hidden window, which means the process will run in the background without displaying a window to the user. This is not typical behavior for LDAP operations, which usually involve network communication to access and manage directory information.

Moreover, the script uses the `-encodedCommand` parameter to run a base64-encoded command. The base64 string decodes to `C:\Scripts\ExportADFSTokenSigningCert.ps1`, indicating that a PowerShell script named "ExportADFSTokenSigningCert.ps1" located in the "C:\Scripts" directory is being executed. This script might be used to export the ADFS (Active Directory Federation Services) token signing certificate.

While ADFS is a part of Microsoft's Active Directory suite and is used in some LDAP environments, the exporting of a token signing certificate is not a standard LDAP operation. This could potentially be used for malicious purposes such as token forging. Therefore, this command line script does not appear to be a normal LDAP operation and may warrant further investigation.

Figure 3.56 – Security Copilot response

> **Important note**
>
> Without the assistance of Security Copilot, the process of determining whether the behavior is truly malicious can be time-consuming and labor-intensive. Traditional methods often involve extensive manual research, analysis, and investigation, which can delay the identification of true threats. However, with Copilot, this process becomes significantly more efficient and straightforward.

The additional context and explanations offered by Security Copilot can assist Tier 1 analysts in quickly understanding the nature and severity of the incident. As a result, they can make informed decisions on whether the incident requires escalation to the Tier 2 team. By leveraging Security Copilot, Tier 1 analysts not only can expedite the identification of true security threats but also ensure that appropriate actions are taken promptly, thus optimizing the overall incident response process.

Summary

In this chapter, you were introduced to the processes for setting up and customizing Security Copilot, as well as navigating its user interfaces. The chapter concluded with a real-life case study of a security incident investigation, allowing you to observe Security Copilot's application in real-world security scenarios and understand the synergy between its various components. By gaining a clear understanding of both the embedded and standalone experiences, you can better leverage the platform's AI capabilities to address your specific security needs.

In the next chapter, you will explore how various plugins extend Security Copilot's functionalities. It will cover both pre-installed Microsoft plugins and third-party options, as well as the development of custom plugins tailored to unique security requirements. This will build on the foundation you've established, enhancing your ability to adapt the tool to your specific needs.

4

Extending Security Copilot's Capabilities with Plugins

Security Copilot was developed as a comprehensive framework designed to enhance an organization's security posture by seamlessly connecting to its systems. This framework leverages advanced AI capabilities to provide tailored insights and proactive security measures.

In this chapter, we will explore the world of **plugins** that extend the capabilities of Security Copilot, showcasing how they enhance Copilot's functionality and adaptability to meet diverse security needs.

Plugins are a key differentiator for Security Copilot. Unlike other solutions that focus solely on developing standalone products, Security Copilot is strategically designed as both a platform and a product. Rather than being confined to a fixed set of features, it can be expanded and tailored to diverse needs through its wide range of plugins. This modular approach enables Security Copilot to provide a more versatile and integrated experience. As we explore the plugins for Security Copilot, we'll start by examining the **preinstalled Microsoft plugins**, providing a thorough understanding of their features and applications. Next, we'll look into **non-Microsoft plugins**. Moreover, this chapter will provide insights into the development and utilization of **custom plugins** tailored to specific security needs. Through this exploration, you will develop the skills to effectively use plugins and even create your own, empowering you to further enhance and refine your security strategies with the support of Security Copilot.

The following key areas outlined in this chapter will guide you through the discovery and exploration:

- Exploring Security Copilot plugins
- Unleashing the power of preinstalled Microsoft plugins

- OpenAI and beyond – Delving into non-Microsoft plugins
- Crafting your own – The world of custom plugins

Want to try out the prompts, custom plugins, and promptbooks featured in this book? Take a look at the book's GitHub repository at https://github.com/PacktPublishing/Microsoft-Copilot-for-Security.

Exploring Security Copilot plugins

A plugin is a set of specialized capabilities designed to enhance and extend Security Copilot's functionality. Essentially, it provides new security features to expand the core capabilities of Security Copilot, allowing Copilot to address a wider range of security challenges. For instance, some of Microsoft Defender XDR's features can serve as a plugin for Security Copilot. Capabilities in Intune and Microsoft Entra, as well as third-party solutions such as ServiceNow, Jamf, Darktrace, and AbuseIPDB, can also be used as plugins for Security Copilot.

Imagine your Security Copilot solution as a high-tech car. The plugins are like a set of premium accessories that you can add to customize and boost your car's performance. These accessories – whether they're preinstalled or available from other providers – allow you to tailor the system to better meet your needs.

To give you a better idea about the plugins, here's a short sample list of Microsoft and non-Microsoft plugins available for Security Copilot:

- Microsoft Defender XDR
- Microsoft Defender Threat Intelligence (MDTI)
- Microsoft Defender External Attack Surface Management (EASM)
- Microsoft Entra
- Microsoft Purview
- AbuseIPDB
- CyberArk Privilege Cloud
- Darktrace
- Intel 471 Threat Intelligence
- Jamf
- Red Canary
- Tanium
- UrlScan

In addition, you can further enhance Security Copilot's features by creating your own plugins.

The plugins allow Security Copilot to evolve from a fixed set of features into a more dynamic ecosystem. You can pick and choose from a range of available plugins. This flexibility allows you to tailor your setup by including only the plugins that meet your needs and disabling those that are unnecessary. This modular approach transforms Security Copilot from a static product into a versatile platform with a broad range of options. As the Security Copilot marketing team puts it, *"we are building a platform and a product."* This strategy ensures that as Security Copilot evolves, its functionality will continue to grow with new plugins, offering greater adaptability and customization.

Capabilities (or skills) of each plugin

Each plugin offers a set of capabilities, often called **skills**, that Security Copilot can utilize. For instance, the Microsoft Defender XDR plugin includes capabilities such as incident summarization, guided response, scripts analysis, and incident report creation.

Whenever you ask Security Copilot a question through its prompt feature, it will choose the most suitable plugin based on its capabilities/skills to provide an answer to your question. As an example, if you ask Copilot to summarize a Microsoft Defender incident, it selects the Microsoft Defender XDR plugin, as illustrated in the next screenshot:

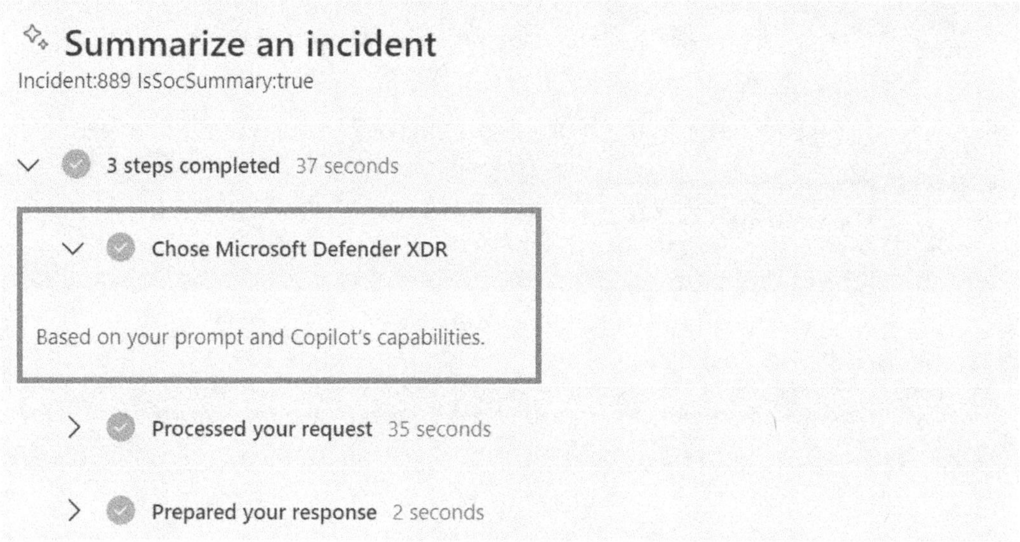

Figure 4.1 – Selecting the plugin that best fits your prompt

In some instances, if there is no suitable plugin, not even the Generic one, Security Copilot defaults to using the standard GPT model in Azure OpenAI Service, as shown in the following screenshot:

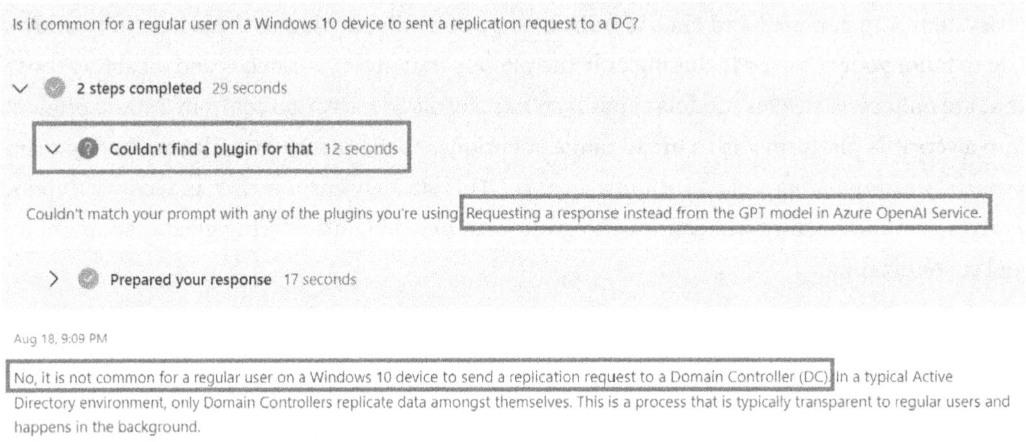

Figure 4.2 – Security Copilot defaults to using the standard GPT model in Azure OpenAI Service

To get an overview of the capabilities or skills offered by a plugin, you can use the **SYSTEM CAPABILITIES** option from the **Prompts** menu to view a list of plugins and their associated skills, as shown in the following screenshot:

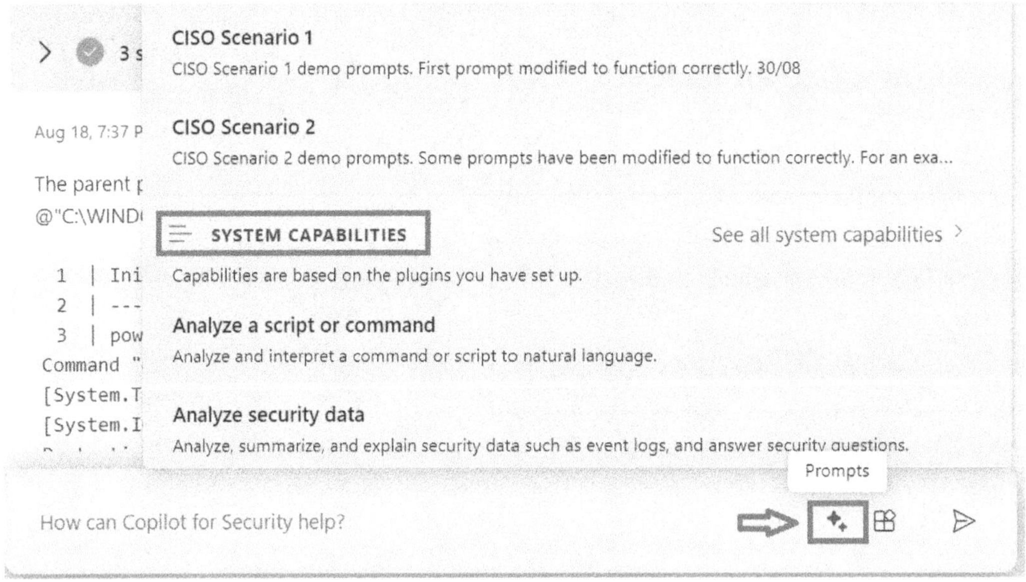

Figure 4.3 – SYSTEM CAPABILITIES

Important note

Microsoft is continually enhancing and updating Security Copilot's capabilities. As a result, the plugins and their associated skills listed under **SYSTEM CAPABILITIES** are subject to change over time. Consequently, the information presented in this book, such as the plugin name or a specific skill, may not always reflect what appears in the most current version of Security Copilot.

Up to this point, you have been briefly introduced to plugins in Security Copilot. To further showcase how these plugins enhance Copilot's functionality and adaptability to various security needs, we'll examine them in more detail next. We'll start by looking into the specific features and advantages of some of the Microsoft plugins in the next section.

Unleashing the power of preinstalled Microsoft plugins

Security Copilot supports a wide array of **Microsoft plugins**. The specific plugins and features available to you are determined by the Microsoft services and configurations your organization has in place. Depending on the Microsoft solutions assigned to your role or organization, you may have access to any of the plugins listed here:

- Azure AI Search (Preview)
- Azure Firewall
- Azure Web Application Firewall (Preview)
- Microsoft Defender External Attack Surface Management
- Microsoft Defender Threat Intelligence
- Microsoft Defender XDR
- Microsoft Entra
- Microsoft Intune
- Microsoft Purview
- Microsoft Sentinel
- Natural Language to KQL for Microsoft Defender XDR

Note

The preceding list includes plugins that are in preview as of March 2025. These plugins have not yet reached **General Availability (GA)**.

Security Copilot uses a special method called **on-behalf-of authentication** to interact with other Microsoft services that your organization already uses. Think of it like this: when you use Security Copilot, this method lets Copilot access other Microsoft tools or services on your behalf, using the permissions you already have. Essentially, it's like giving Security Copilot the ability to use your access rights to seamlessly integrate and work with those other services, without you needing to log in separately to each one. This means Security Copilot can automatically utilize the available plugins without requiring any additional setup from you.

This also means that Security Copilot relies on your access permissions to use the plugins. Even if a plugin is enabled in your Security Copilot settings, if you do not have the appropriate permissions, the plugin will not function as intended. Alternatively, the plugin will have all the permissions you maintain, which should highlight the importance of applying the principle of least privilege and securing your credentials.

By default, users have access to preinstalled Microsoft and non-Microsoft plugins. They can manage their own plugin settings, such as turning plugins on or off and setting up required authentication methods. Additionally, administrators with the owner role can enforce organization-wide plugin restrictions. This includes controlling which existing and new plugins are available to users, as well as determining who can add and manage custom plugins.

Assuming you have activated all the Microsoft plugins and have the appropriate access, let's examine some of the plugins, particularly those not in preview, in the next few sections.

Security Copilot Defender XDR plugins

Microsoft Defender XDR, also known as Microsoft Defender, is an advanced security solution that protects organizations from a wide array of cyber threats. It provides comprehensive monitoring and safeguards the entire IT environment. This includes endpoint security through Microsoft Defender for Endpoint, email protection against phishing and malicious messages via Microsoft Defender for Office, and user account security with Microsoft Defender for Identity. Additionally, it extends protection to cloud applications with Microsoft Defender for Cloud Apps. By integrating with these security tools and services, Defender XDR provides a unified approach to threat detection and response, combining insights from multiple sources to effectively address and mitigate potential risks across the organization's digital assets.

Microsoft Defender XDR also includes a powerful feature known as **advanced hunting**. Utilizing **Kusto Query Language (KQL)**, this tool serves as an advanced analytics engine for the organization's cyber telemetry data.

It enables security teams to quickly and thoroughly analyze data from various sources, including activities from emails, devices, users, and network traffic. As a result, it significantly accelerates the investigation process, detection, and threat hunting.

The Microsoft **Defender XDR plugin** in Security Copilot, leveraging the advanced capabilities of AI and the extensive features within Microsoft Defender XDR, offers many additional enhanced security functionalities to support security teams.

In *Chapter 2*, we demonstrated how the Microsoft Defender XDR plugin enables seamless integration of Security Copilot into the Microsoft Defender portal, assisting security teams with the following enhanced capabilities:

- **Summarize incidents**: Security Copilot compiles details from all related alerts into a clear and concise incident summary
- **Use guided responses**: Security Copilot guides the analyst through the recommended investigation and remediation actions based on the incident details
- **Analyze scripts, codes, and registry keys**: Security Copilot breaks down complex scripts, command lines, and registry keys, offering a clear and straightforward explanation that is easy to understand
- **Analyze files**: Security Copilot examines files for malicious content or suspicious behavior
- **Generate KQL queries**: Security Copilot creates advanced queries to hunt for threats across the network
- **Summarize device information**: Security Copilot provides an overview of a device's security posture and any unusual activities
- **Create incident reports**: Security Copilot documents findings and actions taken during an investigation to generate an incident report

> Note
>
> The standalone experience of Security Copilot includes all the plugin capabilities/skills of Defender XDR available in the embedded mode, along with many additional capabilities not offered in the embedded experience.

In addition, the capabilities/skills of Defender XDR are divided into two separate plugins: the **Microsoft Defender XDR plugin** and the **Natural Language to KQL for Microsoft Defender XDR plugin**.

The Microsoft Defender XDR plugin is designed for incident analysis and investigation, while the Natural Language to KQL for Microsoft Defender XDR plugin focuses on generating KQL queries for analyzing data from Microsoft Defender XDR.

The **SYSTEM CAPABILITIES** menu option in Security Copilot outlines the core capabilities or skills offered by the two Microsoft Defender XDR plugins, as shown here:

Microsoft Defender XDR:

- **Analyze a file:** Inspect a file using available information, including API calls, certificates, and strings
- **Generate an incident report:** Get a report about an attack and your response, including who took action and when
- **Generate guided response:** Get step-by-step response recommendations for an incident
- **List incidents and related alerts:** Get the list of incidents or find specific incidents
- **Summarize the security state of the device:** Get device insights, security issues, and other important information

Natural Language to KQL for Microsoft Defender XDR:

- **Generate Microsoft Defender XDR KQL Queries:** Generates and runs KQL hunting queries using Microsoft Defender XDR data

In *Chapter 3*, you assumed the role of a tier 1 analyst in a case study to see how Security Copilot can assist in incident investigations. This time, we will revisit the same incident from that case study. However, you will now take on the role of a tier 2 analyst to explore how Microsoft Defender XDR plugins can support you throughout the investigation.

Note

The walk-through provided in this section is intended to demonstrate some of the possible steps a tier 2 analyst might take during an investigation, but it is not all-inclusive. Individual tier 2 analysts may follow different workflows, use alternative prompts, or craft different KQL queries based on their investigative approach and the specifics of the incident.

The incident summary provided by Security Copilot reveals that the incident started when the user clicked on a URL in an email, as illustrated here:

- **InitialAccess**: The incident began at 2024-08-06 17:15:43 UTC when user 'kdickens' clicked on a malicious URL 'hxxps://fm06722326[.]mangodune-7572a721[.]eastus[.]azurecontainerapps[.]io/' in an email that was later quarantined by ZAP.

Figure 4.4 – The initial access description in Copilot's incident summary

The next alert then reports a suspicious sequence of exploration activities involving the `'whoami.exe'` and `powershell.exe` processes.

- **Discovery**: At 2024-08-06 17:16:17 UTC, a suspicious sequence of exploration activities was detected on the device 'mb-winclient' (Windows10), involving the processes 'whoami.exe', 'powershell.exe' (running as SYSTEM), and impacting users 'pgustavo' and 'kdickens'.

Figure 4.5 – The description of the discovery stage in Security Copilot's incident summary

> As a tier 2 analyst, you need to investigate what occurred after the user clicked on the malicious link in the email, leading to a sequence of exploratory activities on the same device.

In Microsoft Defender, each email is assigned a unique identifier called the **network message ID**. Referencing this ID, you can request Security Copilot to retrieve basic information about this email for a quick review.

The following screenshot shows the Security Copilot prompt fetching email entities. Notice that in this instance, Copilot selects the Natural Language to KQL for Microsoft Defender XDR plugin to pull the email entity information:

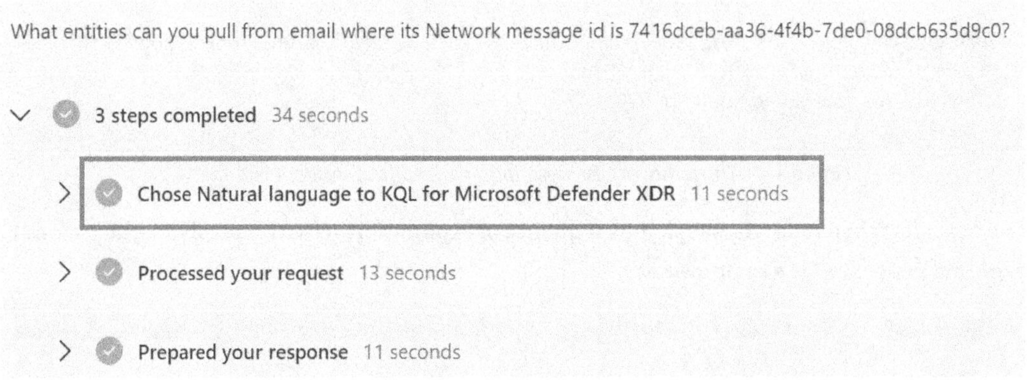

Figure 4.6 – Request Security Copilot to fetch email data

Security Copilot then provides details about this email, including the subject, the sender's email address, the domain, and the IP, as illustrated in the following screenshot:

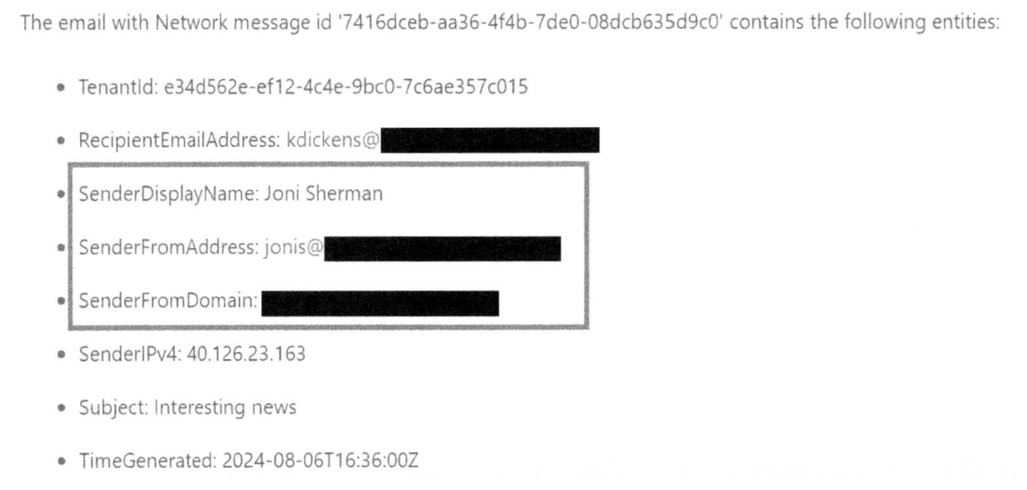

Figure 4.7 – Security Copilot provides details about this email

Security Copilot's response doesn't include details about URLs or file attachments in the email. You can follow up to request this information. The specific Copilot prompt is displayed in the following screenshot:

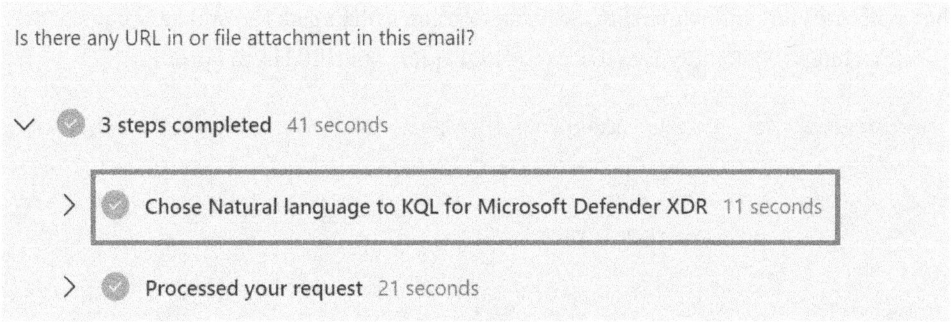

Figure 4.8 – Follow-up request for Security Copilot

This time, Security Copilot extracts the URL from the email, as shown next. This demonstration also illustrates that when a prompt isn't clear or detailed enough, Copilot may not give the relevant answers. However, you can always use a follow-up prompt to get the information you need:

Figure 4.9 – Security Copilot extracts and displays the URL included in the email

Using the Natural Language to KQL for Microsoft Defender XDR plugin, Security Copilot is able to pull the suspicious email and its associated entities for you to review quickly. You now know that the email was sent by an internal user, has the subject line of **Interesting news**, and contains a suspicious link that the user clicked on.

As a tier 2 analyst, your next step is likely to determine whether any files were downloaded or executed as a result of the user clicking on the link. There is a KQL query that security teams can use to identify file download activities following such link clicks. You can now request Security Copilot to run this KQL query and report on its findings.

As shown in the following screenshot, Security Copilot, utilizing its Natural Language to KQL for Microsoft Defender XDR plugin, executes the KQL query specified in the prompt:

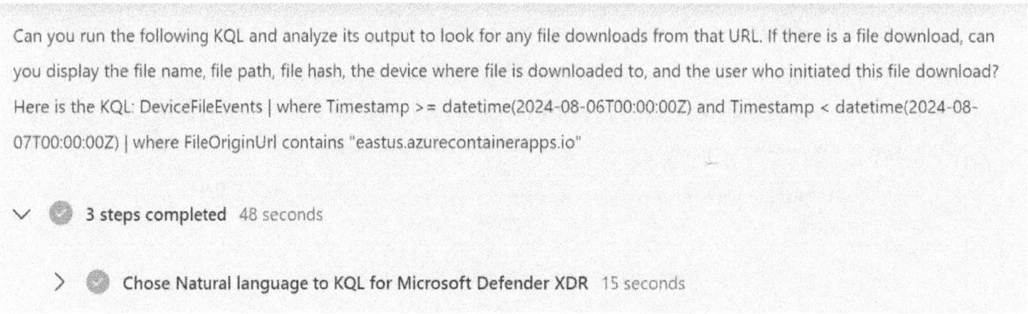

Figure 4.10 – Security Copilot to execute the KQL query and then analyze the resulting data

The response provided by Security Copilot indicates that the file, `Midnight161.zip`, was downloaded to the `C:\Users\kdickens\Downloads\` directory on that user's device. This is illustrated in the following screenshot. Verifying the timestamp of the URL click confirms that it matches the time of the file download. *You now have a suspicious file to investigate*:

Figure 4.11 – Security Copilot reports that the file, Midnight161.zip, was downloaded

You can request Security Copilot to assess this downloaded file's reputation, prevalence, and other relevant details. The prompt shown next asks Security Copilot to evaluate the downloaded file:

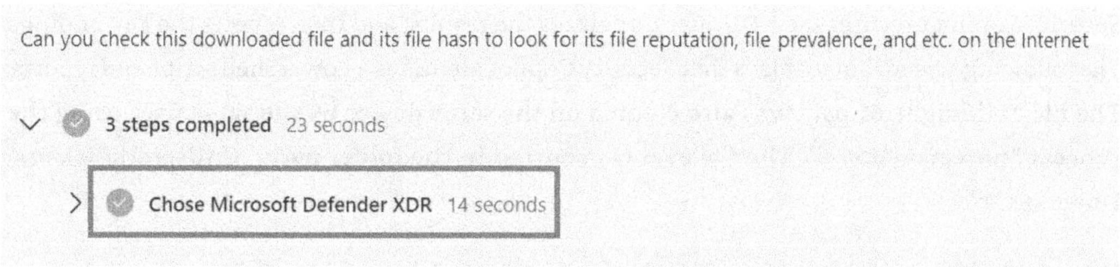

Figure 4.12 – Ask Security Copilot to evaluate the downloaded file

The response generated by Security Copilot is shown in the following screenshot:

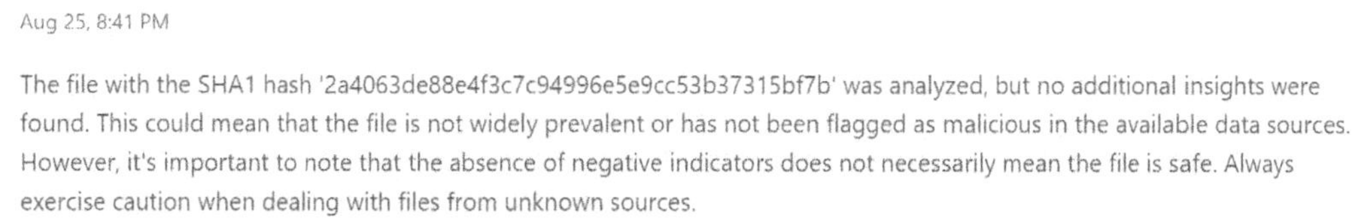

Figure 4.13 – Responses from Security Copilot

> **Important note**
>
> Often, if a file is downloaded from a website but is relatively unknown with very low prevalence, it may indicate that the file is suspicious.

Let's ask Security Copilot to execute another KQL query to review any file creation, modification, or deletion events that occurred during the day of the incident, specifically those involving files with the `Midnight161` keyword in their names. The Security Copilot prompt and the plugin used are shown in the following screenshot:

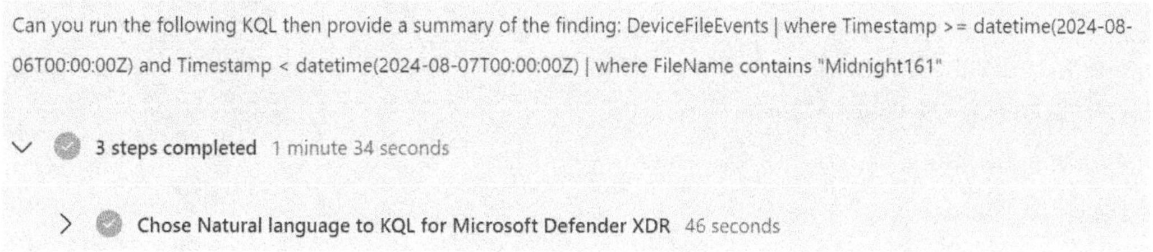

Figure 4.14 – The Security Copilot prompt and the plugin used

Security Copilot executes the KQL query, analyzes the results, and then reports the key findings. The following screenshot displays that Security Copilot identifies a PowerShell script and reports: **The file "Midnight161.ps1" was also created on the same device by the same user using the process "powershell.exe". The file events occurred in the folder path "C:\Users\kdickens\Downloads"**:

The query was specifically looking for file events related to "Midnight161" within the specified time frame. Here are the detailed records:

Export to Excel

TenantId	ActionType	AppGuardContainerId
e34d562e-ef12-4c4e-9bc0-7c6ae357c015	FileRenamed	
e34d562e-ef12-4c4e-9bc0-7c6ae357c015	FileCreated	
e34d562e-ef12-4c4e-9bc0-7c6ae357c015	FileRenamed	
e34d562e-ef12-4c4e-9bc0-7c6ae357c015	FileCreated	

From the output, we can see that the file "Midnight161.zip" was renamed, created, and modified multiple times on the device "mb-winclient.internal.[redacted]". The actions were initiated by the user "kdickens" from the domain "niseko" using the process "msedge.exe". The file "Midnight161.ps1" was also created on the same device by the same user using the process "powershell.exe". The file events occurred in the folder path "C:\Users\kdickens\Downloads".

Figure 4.15 – Security Copilot's response and the identification of a new PowerShell script, Midnight161.ps1

By examining the KQL results through the **Export to Excel** option or by expanding the results listed in Security Copilot, as shown in the following screenshot, you are able to review the time-stamps of the two files, `Midnight161.zip` and `Midnight161.ps1`, to confirm that they were created around the same time:

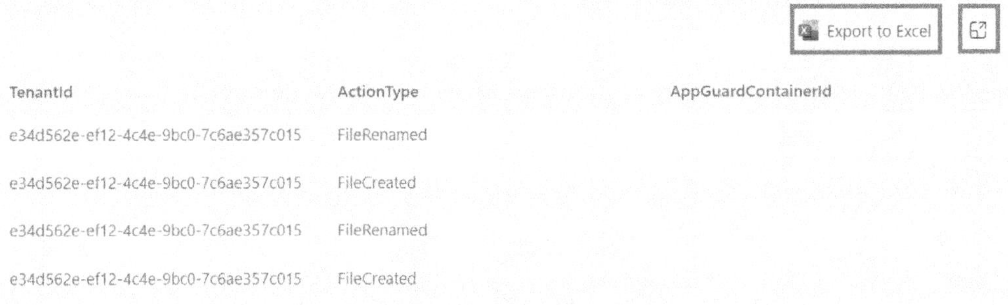

Export to Excel

TenantId	ActionType	AppGuardContainerId
e34d562e-ef12-4c4e-9bc0-7c6ae357c015	FileRenamed	
e34d562e-ef12-4c4e-9bc0-7c6ae357c015	FileCreated	
e34d562e-ef12-4c4e-9bc0-7c6ae357c015	FileRenamed	
e34d562e-ef12-4c4e-9bc0-7c6ae357c015	FileCreated	

Figure 4.16 – Security Copilot allows you to fully analyze its KQL output

You now have one additional file to investigate, `Midnight161.ps1`.

Leveraging the Natural Language to KQL for Microsoft Defender XDR plugin, Security Copilot can extract process, file, registry, network, and other device events containing the `Midnight161` keyword. It then analyzes these events and displays the ones that are related to PowerShell execution. The KQL query along with the Security Copilot prompt is shown in the following screenshot:

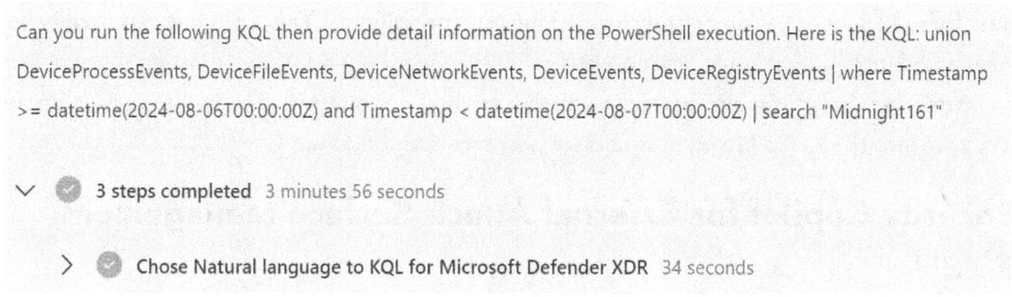

Figure 4.17 – The Security Copilot prompt and the plugin used

As illustrated in the following screenshot, Security Copilot identified that the `Midnight161.ps1` PowerShell script was run by the user `kdickens`. This script established network connections to two external sites and it also executed `whoami.exe`. Note that the execution of `whoami` is highlighted in the second alert within the incident summary provided by Security Copilot, which reports the suspicious sequence of exploration activities:

Figure 4.18 – Security Copilot's findings related to PowerShell execution

With this additional context from Security Copilot, you now have a clearer understanding of the events that unfolded after the user clicked on the link. You can determine that after the click of the email link, a file named `Midnight161.zip` was downloaded to the device.

Then, a file named `Midnight161.ps1` was created around the same time, which ran `whoami.exe` to collect information about the user environment.

It's quite impressive how Security Copilot can enhance incident investigations with its Microsoft Defender XDR plugins. Later in this chapter, as well as in other chapters, we will demonstrate how these KQL queries can be transformed into custom plugins. These plugins can then be incorporated into promptbooks for more efficient investigation workflows. Additionally, you can chain different promptbooks together to further streamline your investigation process. For now, let's dive into the EASM plugin next and see how it can support you.

Security Copilot for External Attack Surface Management plugin

An organization's external and public-facing assets, such as its website and online applications, are vulnerable targets for attackers. Since these elements are publicly accessible on the internet, it is easier for attackers to spot potential vulnerabilities, such as outdated software, unprotected services, or misconfigured settings. This visibility allows attackers to focus on these weaknesses to gain unauthorized access or to exploit the organization's systems.

Microsoft Defender EASM is designed to provide a view of the attack surface of your organization's external-facing digital assets, much like how attackers would see from the outside in. Imagine your company as a large and well-guarded building. The goal is to make sure that no one can sneak in through the unlocked door or open window. Microsoft Defender EASM acts like a team of security experts who walk around the building, examining every possible entry point to identify any weaknesses.

Defender EASM works by scanning and analyzing the organization's digital presence seen on the internet, everything from websites and applications to cloud services and network configurations. It then provides detailed insights about potential risks and vulnerabilities, helping businesses to address these issues before they can be exploited by malicious actors. By identifying and assessing these vulnerabilities, Microsoft Defender EASM enables organizations to be more proactive in protecting and securing their external digital assets, addressing weaknesses before they can be exploited.

Security Copilot can further enhance Defender EASM functionalities by offering detailed insights into vulnerabilities and asset statuses. It helps to identify external-facing assets affected by specific **Common Vulnerabilities and Exposures (CVEs)**, or with high **Common Vulnerability Scoring System (CVSS)** scores, prioritizes risks based on their severity, and offers a comprehensive view of the attack surface.

Security Copilot also simplifies asset management with natural language queries and highlights expired domains and SSL certificates. By integrating these capabilities, Security Copilot allows for more effective risk prioritization and proactive security measures, ultimately improving the management and protection of your external digital assets.

Please note that Security Copilot is not embedded in the Microsoft Defender EASM console. However, you can still access and use its plugin through Security Copilot's standalone experience.

The **SYSTEM CAPABILITIES** menu option in Security Copilot outlines some of the Defender EASM core capabilities available within the standalone portal:

- **Get assets impacted by CVE:** Identify the assets that a CVE impacts, their details, and when they were observed.
- **Get assets impacted by CVSS:** Identify the assets that a CVSS score impacts, their details, and when they were observed.
- **Get attack surface insights:** Learn about high-, medium-, or low-priority insights impacting attack surfaces.
- **Get attack surface summary:** Discover what assets are in an attack surface.
- **Get EASM assets:** Get assets based on a natural language query.
- **Get expired domains:** Learn about expired domains, their details, and assets for attack surfaces.
- **Get expired SSL certificates:** Learn about expired SSL certificates, their details, and associated assets for attack surfaces.
- **Get Microsoft Defender EASM general information:** Learn about Microsoft Defender EASM's features, data, and other details.
- **Get SSL certificates using SHA-1:** Learn about SSL certificates using SHA-1, their details, and associated assets.

Note

The features available in EASM differ based on whether you have a free or paid license. This also affects the EASM plugin functionality within Security Copilot. As an example, the free license provides access to pre-built attack surface insights, but it may not allow you to search for your organization's specific attack surface if it's not part of the predefined data. The next few examples will showcase EASM capabilities within Security Copilot when using a paid license.

For example, by using the Defender EASM plugin in Security Copilot's standalone mode, you can request a summary of the attack surface for your organization's external-facing digital assets. The Security Copilot prompt utilizing this plugin is illustrated in the following screenshot:

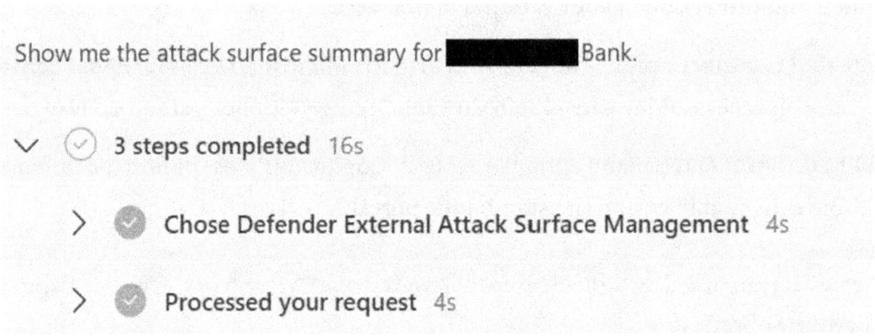

Figure 4.19 – The Security Copilot prompt

The response generated by Security Copilot, shown next, reveals a complex online environment with 268 confirmed domains and 7,374 hosts, indicating a substantial infrastructure:

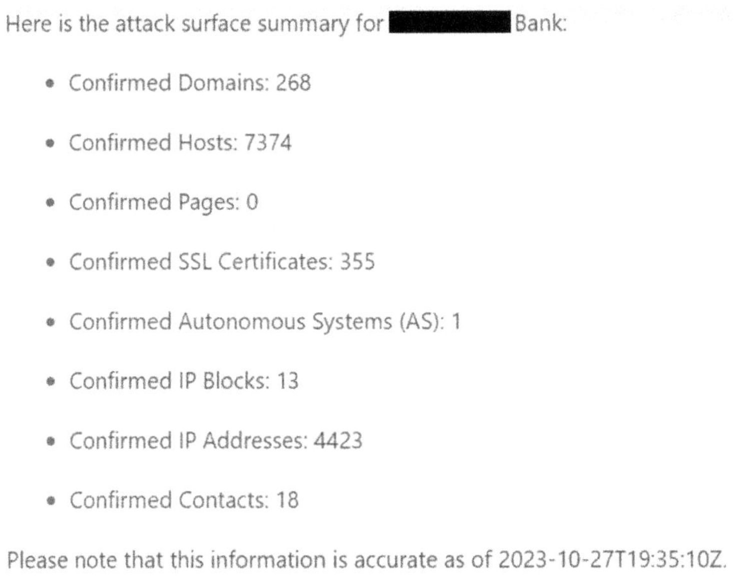

Figure 4.20 – Response from Security Copilot

Despite this extensive network, from Security Copilot's response, it's noteworthy that there are no confirmed web pages associated with these hosts, which could suggest a focus on backend operations or security considerations. The organization holds 355 confirmed SSL certificates, highlighting a commitment to secure communications and data protection.

You can then ask Security Copilot to list expired SSL certificates for your externally facing resources. These certificates may signal **shadow IT** or abandoned assets that are not known by security teams. Shadow IT refers to the use of technology, applications, or services within an organization without the approval or knowledge of the IT department. While employees may adopt these tools to enhance productivity, it can lead to security risks and compliance issues since they may not meet the organization's security standards. As shown in the following screenshot, Security Copilot identifies the expired SSL certificates for you:

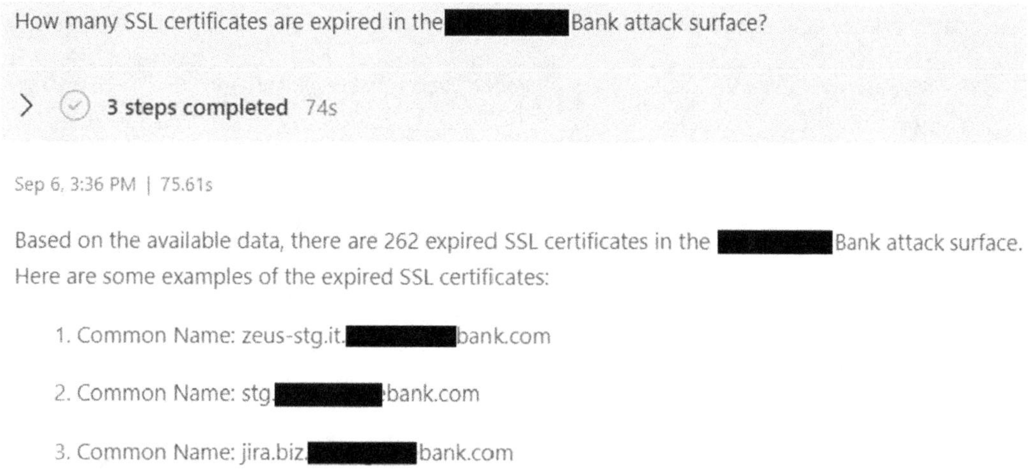

Figure 4.21 – Security Copilot lists expired SSL certificates

Once you have identified the expired SSL certificates, you can then ask Security Copilot to list which related assets might have high-severity vulnerabilities. For instance, you can prompt Security Copilot for a list of vulnerabilities associated with a host tied to the expired SSL certificate, as shown next:

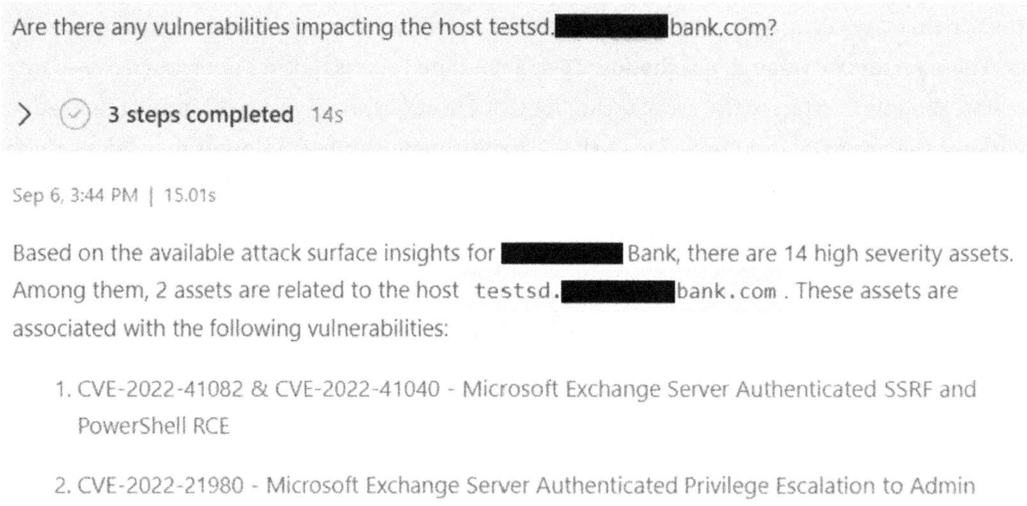

Figure 4.22 – Security Copilot lists vulnerabilities associated with a host

Next, you can prompt Security Copilot to get a list of recommended mitigation steps for the CVEs:

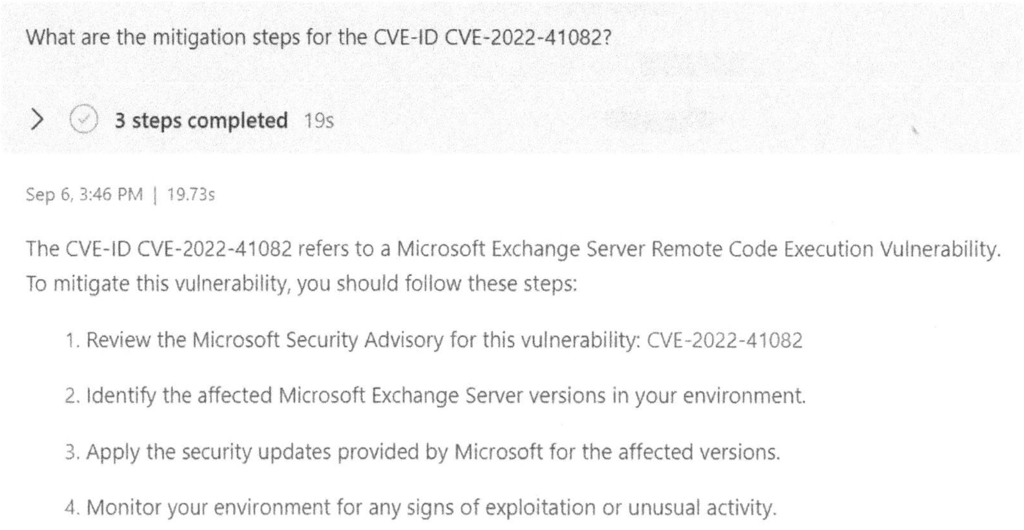

Figure 4.23 – Security Copilot to provide mitigation steps for a CVE

Finally, after gathering sufficient information from Security Copilot, you can request it to generate a report, covering the specific topics discussed. A sample prompt is shown next:

```
Create a report for this Security copilot session and include sections
for: an overview of MDEASM, the summary of the attack surface for the
organization, list of expired Domains and whois info, the list of common
names from expired SSL certificates, describe the vulnerabilities on the
host testsd.wbank.com with CVSS scores, detailed steps for mitigating
vulnerabilities on testsd.wbank.com
```

While Defender XDR offers a comprehensive and unified approach to detecting and responding to threats within an organization's infrastructure, EASM is dedicated to identifying and managing vulnerabilities and risks that are exposed from outside the organization. Next, we will explore how the Microsoft Threat Intelligence plugin in Security Copilot can further assist you in identifying and addressing threats.

Security Copilot Threat Intelligence plugin

Picture your house in a neighborhood. Traditionally, a basic alarm system might alert you if someone breaks a window or opens a door. MDTI is like a comprehensive upgrade of your system to include not only alarms but also advanced surveillance that watches for suspicious behavior in and around your neighborhood. This upgraded system, as an illustrative example of MDTI, gathers data on past criminal activities and the specific traits of repeat offenders. For example, if offenders are known to drive a black sports car with a distinctive decal, this system will alert you if a black sports car with that same decal shows up in your neighborhood. In the realm of cybersecurity, the black sports car represents an **Indicator of Compromise (IOC)**, which is any signal used to identify attackers or the malware they employ. This allows you to take action before a potential threat fully materializes.

MDTI gathers intelligence data from various sources, including internal research, external threat feeds, and industry partnerships, to provide insights into emerging threats and tactics. An equivalent analogy would be for this upgraded system from the previous example to incorporate information from local law enforcement and neighborhood watch groups.

MDTI not only offers comprehensive protection through threat analysis and identification but also extends its capabilities to monitoring and evaluating the infrastructure used by attackers. It tracks the tools, networks, and tactics employed by cybercriminals. If attackers shift to new infrastructure, such as different IP addresses or new domains, or begin using upgraded malware, the system provides updated threat intelligence on the attacker's new infrastructure, enabling the monitoring and detection of these specific threats and cybercriminals for your organization.

In essence, MDTI is a vast and dynamic repository that is continuously updated with threat data. *"Defender Threat Intelligence enables security professionals to directly access, ingest, and act upon our powerful repository of threat intelligence built from 78 trillion signals and more than 10,000 multidisciplinary experts worldwide."* (Microsoft Defender Threat Intelligence, `https://www.microsoft.com/en-us/security/business/siem-and-xdr/microsoft-defender-threat-intelligence`). This extensive collection of data is used to assist security teams in detection, analytics, and incident response, helping to uncover and neutralize modern adversaries and cyber threats, including ransomware.

With the MDTI plugin integrated into Security Copilot, you can now tap into its vast amount of knowledge on threats, attack techniques, adversary profiles, and more to assist you during incident investigation, threat detection, and hunting.

As an example, you may request Security Copilot to provide an overview of the latest threats to your organization, as shown in the following screenshot:

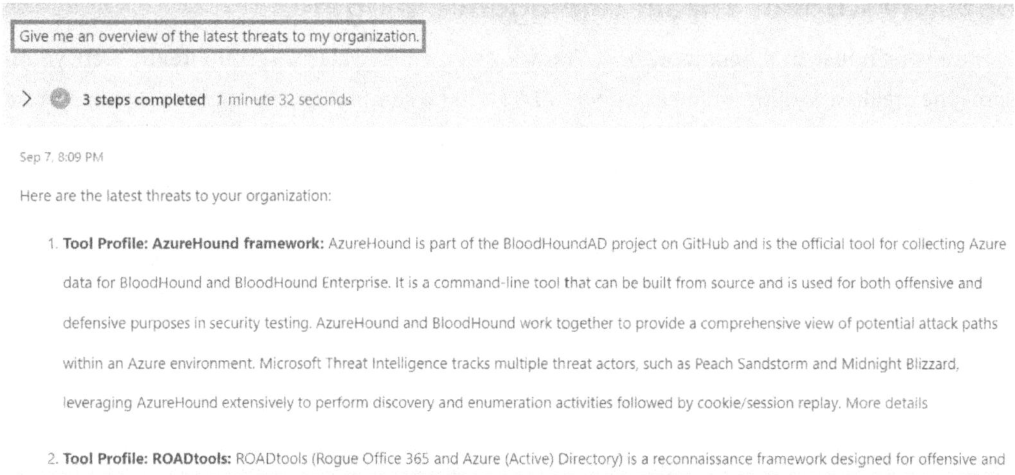

Figure 4.24 – The Copilot prompt utilizing the MDTI plugin

You may then consult Security Copilot for more detailed information on why this poses a threat to your organization, as illustrated next:

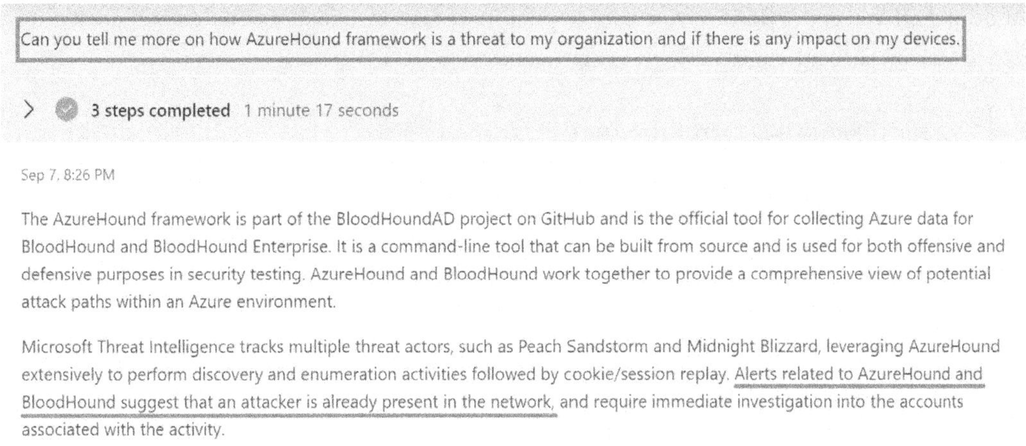

Figure 4.25 – Another Security Copilot prompt example utilizing the MDTI plugin

To get more specific information on this threat, you can request Security Copilot to provide the **Tactics, Techniques, and Procedures (TTPs)** associated with this threat, as well as the IOCs. Following that, you can ask Security Copilot to generate the detection rules for you. An example Copilot prompt is shown in the following screenshot:

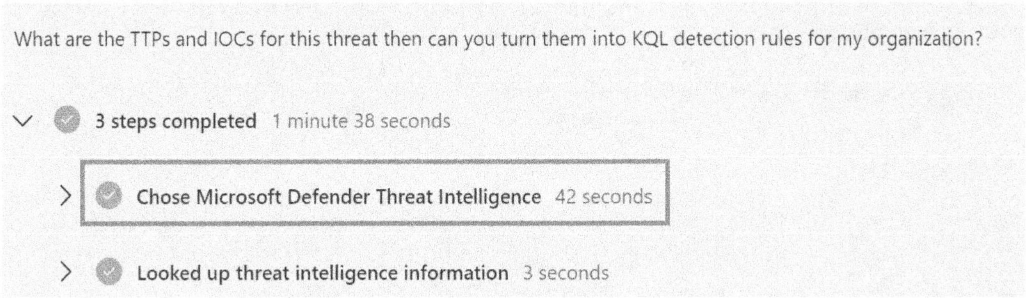

Figure 4.26 – The Copilot prompt utilizing the MDTI plugin

The following screenshot displays a KQL query suggested by Security Copilot:

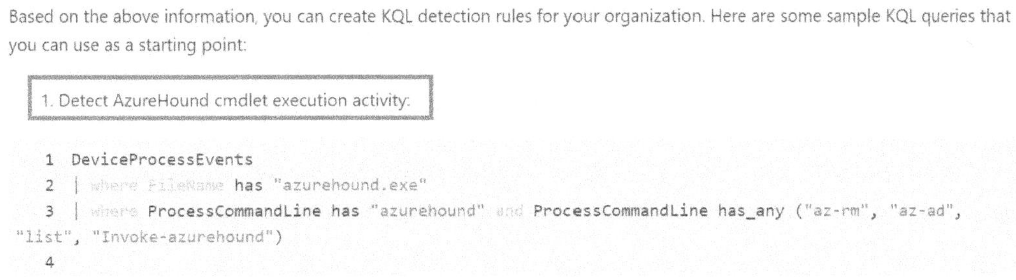

Figure 4.27 – A detection rule provided by Security Copilot

Another KQL query provided by Security Copilot in its response focuses on detecting reconnaissance activity through network logs, as shown next:

2. Detect reconnaissance activity using network logs:

```
DeviceNetworkEvents
| where RemoteUrl in ("login.microsoftonline.com", "graph.microsoft.com")
| where InitiatingProcessCommandLine has_all ("list", "-u" , "-p") or InitiatingProcessCommandLine has_all ("list", "--u" , "--p")
or InitiatingProcessCommandLine has_all ("list", "--app" , "--secret") or InitiatingProcessCommandLine has_all ("list", "-app" , "-secret")
or InitiatingProcessCommandLine has_all ("list", "-app" , "--cert") or InitiatingProcessCommandLine has_all ("list", "-app" , "-cert")
or InitiatingProcessCommandLine has_all ("list", "-j") or InitiatingProcessCommandLine has_all ("list", "--j")
| where InitiatingProcessFolderPath !contains "Microsoft"
| summarize dcount(RemoteUrl) by bin(Timestamp, 1m), InitiatingProcessFileName, DeviceId
| where dcount_RemoteUrl == 2
```

Figure 4.28 – Another detection rule provided by Security Copilot

During an investigation, if you encounter a suspicious domain or IP, you can leverage Security Copilot's MDTI plugin to quickly gather relevant information for you. First, you can prompt Security Copilot to check the reputation of the suspicious domain, for instance, **weinsteinfrog[.]com**, as seen next:

What is the reputation for domain weinsteinfrog.com?

> 3 steps completed 18 seconds

Sep 7, 10:28 PM

The domain `weinsteinfrog[.]com` has a reputation score of 100, which classifies it as malicious. This domain has been associated with two rules:

1. MDTI Intel Article: Citrine Sleet exploiting Chromium zero-day with a severity of 5.
2. Cyber Threat Intelligence: Citrine Sleet with a severity of 5.

Please note that the domain name has been defanged for security reasons, replacing "." with "[.]".

Figure 4.29 – Check the reputation of a suspicious domain

From Security Copilot's response, you learn that this domain, **weinsteinfrog[.]com**, is considered malicious and has been linked to **Citrine Sleet exploiting Chromium zero-day**.

For further analysis, you can request Security Copilot to list the web components for this domain. The Security Copilot prompt and some of its responses are displayed in the following screenshot:

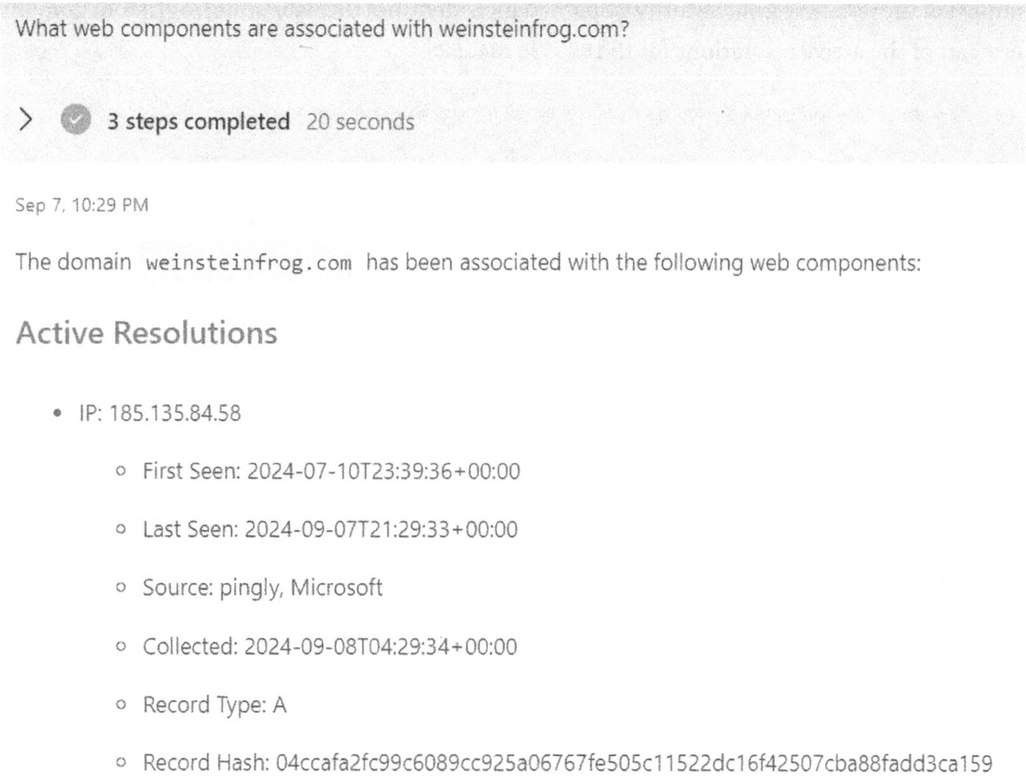

Figure 4.30 – Grab web components for the suspicious domain

From Security Copilot's results, you obtain an IP address, `185.135.84.58`, associated with the suspicious domain, **weinsteinfrog[.]com**. Now, you can request Security Copilot to pull passive DNS data for this IP address.

> Note
>
> Passive DNS records historical data on domain-to-IP mappings, enabling security analysts to observe how an IP address has resolved to various domains over time. This can help to identify additional malicious domains that can be used as IOCs.

To start, you can ask Security Copilot for passive DNS data related to the IP address `185.135.84.58`, including the relevant dates. The following screenshot displays the prompt along with the first snippet of the response from Security Copilot, which identifies the **weinsteinfrog[.]com** domain as a part of the active resolutions for IP `185.135.84.58`:

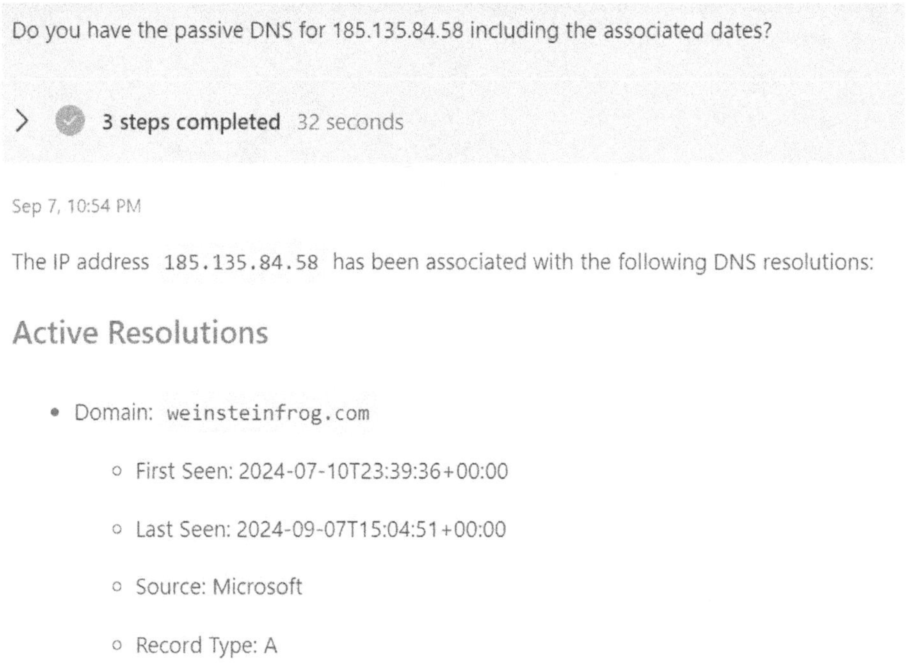

Figure 4.31 – Security Copilot prompt to pull passive DNS data along with its response

The following screenshot displays additional responses generated by Security Copilot, specifically the inactive resolutions. From there, it is quite easy and fast to identify another domain, **www.voyagorclub[.]space**, that has recently been linked to the IP address `185.135.84.58`:

Inactive Resolutions

- Domain: `www.voyagorclub.space`
    - First Seen: 2024-07-10T20:40:56+00:00
    - Last Seen: 2024-09-04T05:52:17+00:00
    - Source: Microsoft
    - Record Type: A
    - Record Hash: e6434c3dbd3922faa8391df5ab73f5b5923d5fb5a20086bb17e2a6d8bc9b5c3d
- Domain: `www.weinsteinfrog.com`
    - First Seen: 2024-07-15T09:20:49+00:00
    - Last Seen: 2024-09-04T05:52:17+00:00
    - Source: Microsoft
    - Record Type: A
    - Record Hash: 9818a81444b4c63b714460b41f9504990f16d596efb208bdbf044cdd9091a0ce

Figure 4.32 – Another domain discovered via passive DNS data

Next, you can consult with Security Copilot to check on the reputation of this newly discovered domain, **www.voyagorclub[.]space**. As seen in the following screenshot, Security Copilot reports that this domain is also highly suspicious:

What is the reputation for domain www.voyagorclub.space?

> **3 steps completed** 20 seconds

Sep 8, 10:14 AM

The domain `www.voyagorclub[.]space` has a reputation score of 69, which classifies it as suspicious. This domain has been associated with one rule:

1. TLD: Infrastructure hosted by this TLD is frequently associated with suspicious behavior with a severity of 3.

Please note that the domain name has been defanged for security reasons, replacing "." with "[.]".

Figure 4.33 – Security Copilot prompt to check domain reputation and its response

Given Security Copilot's assessment of this domain and the fact that the infrastructure hosted by this top-level domain is often linked to suspicious behavior, you may consider adding this domain to your investigation or detection rule as well.

Up to this point, you've observed how Security Copilot can deliver threat intelligence tailored to your organization and provide responses that are updated with the latest threat information. Additionally, Security Copilot allows you to quickly pivot and identify further IOCs.

What you've seen so far represents a subset of the capabilities offered by the MDTI plugin within Security Copilot. This plugin provides many more features beyond what's been mentioned. In a later chapter, we will use a real-life case study to further highlight its additional functions. Meanwhile, the **SYSTEM CAPABILITIES** menu option for this plugin serves as a reference for some of its capabilities or skills you can leverage:

- **Get CVE details by IDs:** Get the details and remediation for a list of CVE IDs
- **Get CVE details by keywords:** Get a list of terse info for CVEs related to a keyword, or if no keyword is provided, a list of recent CVEs
- **Get CVE mitigation:** Get the mitigation or remediation steps of a given CVE
- **Get DNS resolutions by hostname:** Get the DNS resolutions of a given hostname
- **Get DNS resolutions by IP address:** Get the DNS resolutions of a given IP address
- **Get intelligence profile indicators of compromise:** Get the IOCs related to a given intelligence profile
- **Get reputation for indicators of compromise:** Get the reputation details for a list of indicators of compromise.
- **GetRelatedIncidentsByQuery:** Returns the related incidents/alerts in a given time period for matching Threat Analytics reports.
- **Look up threat intelligence:** Look up threat intelligence information like intelligence profiles, articles, and threat analytics.

Before we wrap up our discussion on the MDTI plugin, please note that this feature is also accessible within the embedded experience of Security Copilot as shown in the following screenshot:

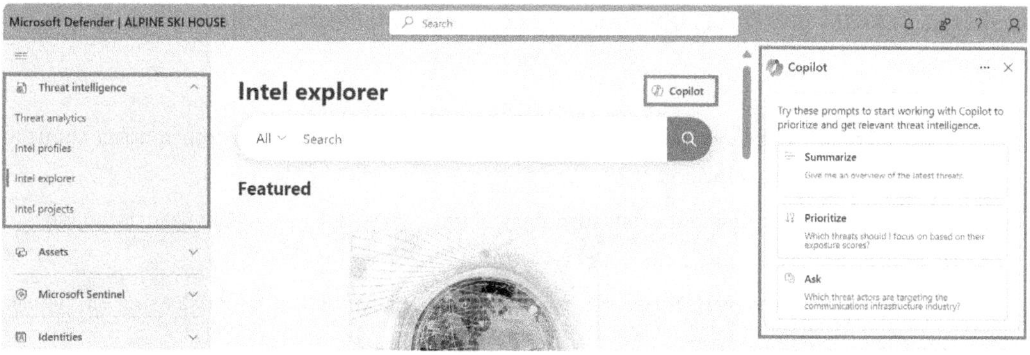

Figure 4.34 – Security Copilot embedded in the Microsoft Defender Threat Intelligence console

Having seen the Microsoft Threat Intelligence plugin in action, next, we will explore how the Microsoft Purview plugin can assist in safeguarding data within the organization.

Security Copilot Purview plugin

Microsoft Purview is a comprehensive solution designed to help organizations to manage and understand their data. It provides tools to classify and organize information, making it easier to see where sensitive data is located and how it is being used. This is particularly useful for ensuring that data is properly protected and compliant with regulations. Microsoft Purview helps businesses gain insights into their data landscape, making it simpler to manage and safeguard their information.

Microsoft Purview **Data Loss Prevention** (**DLP**) is a set of strategies and tools aimed at preventing sensitive information from being accidentally or intentionally shared or lost. DLP policies are used to monitor and control how data is handled and shared. By setting up rules and alerts, DLP helps to ensure that confidential information remains secure and is not exposed to unauthorized individuals. This protects against data breaches and helps maintain compliance with privacy laws and regulations.

In *Chapter 2*, we looked into the Security Copilot features provided by the Purview plugin that are embedded directly within the Purview console. The standalone experience of Security Copilot includes all the embedded capabilities, as well as additional ones not offered in the embedded experience.

Again, the **SYSTEM CAPABILITIES** option lists the core capabilities of the Purview plugin, as shown here:

- **Ask Microsoft Purview documentation:** Ask questions or search for information about Microsoft Purview solutions.
- **Get Microsoft Purview data risk summary:** Summarizes risk of the data associated with the security incident or a Data Loss Prevention alert.
- **Get Microsoft Purview user risk summary:** Provides an overview of user risk using Purview Insider Risk Management.
- **Summarize Microsoft Purview alerts:** Summarizes Microsoft Purview alerts from Purview Data Loss Prevention and Insider Risk Management.
- **Triage Microsoft Purview alerts:** Retrieves recent Purview Data Loss Prevention alerts based on severity and status.
- **Zoom into Microsoft Purview data risk:** Identifies attributes like labels or activities for the data in the context of Microsoft Purview.
- **Zoom into Microsoft Purview user risk:** Provides information about the user's activities from Purview Insider Risk Management.

These core skills offer a solid foundation for understanding the types of questions you can pose to Security Copilot. However, the scope of your interactions with Copilot is not limited to these initial queries. You can explore and test a broader range of prompts. For instance, instead of using the **Triage Microsoft Purview alerts** prompt listed in the **SYSTEM CAPABILITIES** menu option, you can ask Security Copilot with this prompt:

```
What are the critical Purview Data Loss Prevention alerts for my
organization that I need to be aware of?
```

The response from Security Copilot is displayed in the following screenshot:

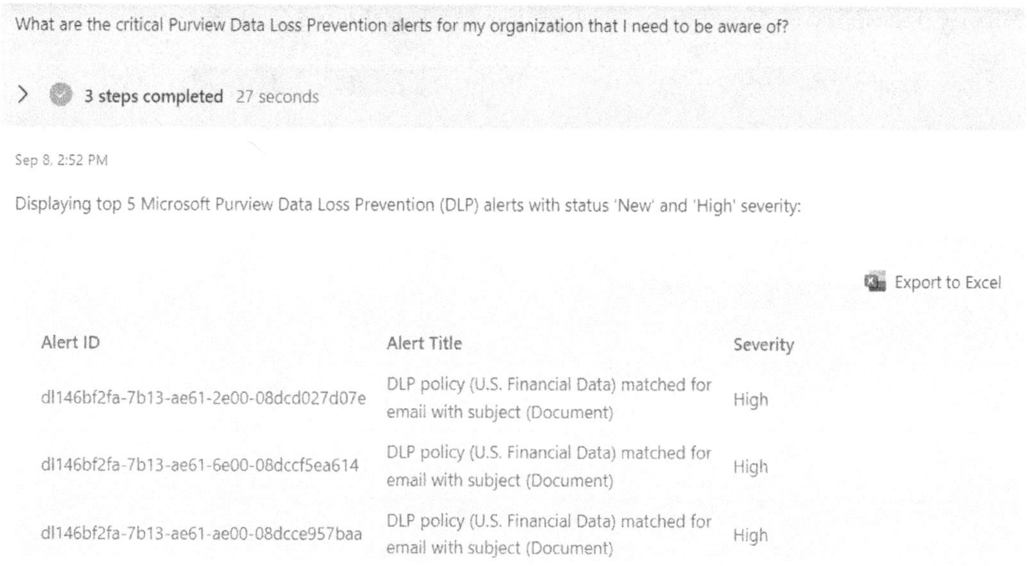

Figure 4.35 – The Security Copilot prompt and its responses

To gain more insights into a specific alert, you can then request Security Copilot to provide more detailed information. The following screenshot displays an example Security Copilot prompt and its reply:

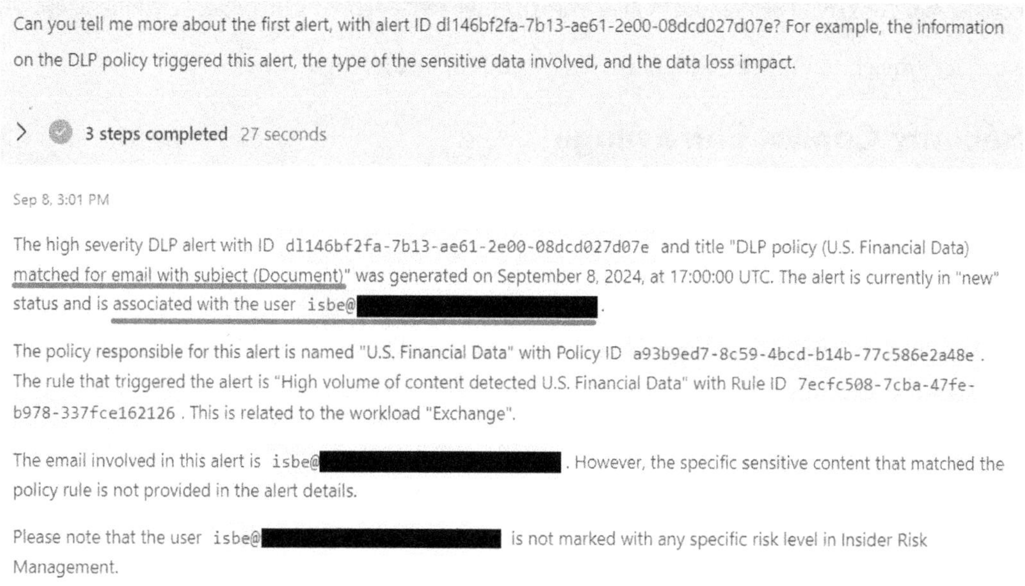

Figure 4.36 – The Security Copilot prompt and its responses

You may then start your investigation with prompts such as the one displayed next:

Figure 4.37 – The Security Copilot prompt and its responses

There are many prompt examples and resources you can reference when developing your own prompts. A good starting point would be the Security Copilot GitHub resource at `https://github.com/Azure/Copilot-For-Security/tree/main/Sample%20Prompts/Microsoft%20Purview`.

Next, let's dive into the Microsoft Entra plugin and explore its capabilities.

Security Copilot Entra plugin

Microsoft Entra is a comprehensive identity and access management solution that secures digital identities and facilitates the management of access to systems and data. Think of it as a central hub where businesses can effectively manage user accounts, ensure secure sign-ins, and control access to sensitive information and resources. Entra also provides log data that is crucial for tracking and investigating security incidents. These logs offer detailed records of user activities and sign-ins, allowing administrators to quickly identify and address potential security threats.

Whether you're monitoring user activities, managing access, addressing identity risks, or investigating compromised accounts, Security Copilot provides you with the insights and tools to stay ahead. Utilizing data from Entra users, groups, sign-in logs, audit logs, diagnostic logs, and more, Security Copilot makes it simple to detect and analyze any unusual activities that could indicate a security issue.

It enhances your ability to assess and manage risks, respond to security incidents with greater efficiency, and maintain a clearer view of access controls and user activities.

Security Copilot offers insight into user profiles, including contact details and authentication methods. This helps you to manage user accounts more effectively and respond quickly to any authentication issues. As an example, the following screenshot illustrates the Security Copilot prompt requesting user data:

Using the Microsoft Entra plugin, can you generate a summary about user, [redacted].co?

Figure 4.38 – The Security Copilot prompt

Security Copilot responds with detailed user information, including the user's name, email address, ID, job title, department, company name, and account status. This is shown next:

The user with the display name "Karla Dickens" has the following details:

- Given Name: Karla
- Surname: Dickens
- Email: [redacted].co
- User Principal Name: [redacted].co
- ID: [redacted]
- Job Title: Account Manager
- Account Status: Enabled
- Created Date and Time: 2024-06-19T14:46:09Z
- Company Name: Niseko
- Department: Sales

Figure 4.39 – The Security Copilot responses

Additionally, Security Copilot gives you a clear picture of any risks associated with individual users. You can access detailed summaries of user accounts and risks, understand the reasons behind flagged accounts, and dive into the factors driving these assessments.

If you need to review sign-in logs, through Security Copilot, you can easily find information on user login attempts, including detailed data from specific dates or recent periods. This feature is valuable for detecting suspicious sign-ins or understanding login patterns.

In addition to monitoring sign-ins, Security Copilot enables you to investigate failed login attempts and the reasons behind them, track authentication methods, and check terms of use agreements. This thoroughness ensures that any security gaps are identified and addressed promptly.

When it comes to oversight and auditing, Security Copilot simplifies the process of examining changes within your system. Whether it's modifications to applications, user groups, or security policies, you can view comprehensive audit logs detailing who made changes and when. This transparency is crucial for maintaining security and compliance, as it allows for accurate tracking of alterations and helps pinpoint any irregularities.

Once again, the **SYSTEM CAPABILITIES** option in Security Copilot highlights the key features offered by the Microsoft Entra plugin that you can reference:

- **Explore a summary of a user's active risk with Entra ID Protection:** View a detailed summary of a Microsoft Entra ID user's risk
- **Explore diagnostic log collection in Microsoft Entra:** View settings for diagnostic log collection and streaming of activity logs in Microsoft Entra ID
- **Explore Microsoft Entra audit log details:** View changes to applications, groups, users, and licenses in Microsoft Entra ID
- **Find group details in Microsoft Entra:** View Microsoft Entra ID group ownership and membership details
- **Find sign-in logs in Microsoft Entra:** View Microsoft Entra ID sign-in log details, including policy evaluation results
- **Find user details in Microsoft Entra:** View contact information, authentication method registration, and account details for users
- **Investigate identity risks with Entra ID Protection:** View details of Microsoft Entra ID users with high, medium, or low risk of compromise

Other plugins

Security Copilot comes with additional Microsoft plugins preinstalled. As of March 2025, these plugins are as follows:

- **Microsoft Intune**: Devices, apps, policies, and postures
- **Azure Firewall: Intrusion Detection and Prevention System (IDPS)** signature analysis and fleet-wide IDPS attack investigation
- **Azure Web Application Firewall** (Preview): SQL injection block summaries, XSS block summaries, top WAF rules summaries, and top malicious IP summaries
- **Microsoft Sentinel**: Incidents and workspaces
- **Azure AI Search** (Preview): Indexed data

For your information, the following are some of the core capabilities that the Microsoft Intune plugin brings to Security Copilot:

- **Analyze device configuration error code**: Get detailed information about a device configuration error code
- **Describe device configuration policy**: Summarize and assess the impact of a Microsoft Intune policy
- **Get assignment scope for app or policy**: Get a summary of the number of users and devices that an app or policy is assigned to
- **Get device configuration differences between two devices**: Get a summary of similarities and differences in the configuration of two managed devices
- **Get device group memberships**: Summarize the group memberships of a managed device
- **Get discovered or managed apps for device**: Get a list of Intune managed apps, or software applications, installed on a managed device
- **Get Microsoft Intune Devices**: Get a summary of managed devices with key information for a user
- **Get policies assigned to a device**: Get info on policies assigned to a managed device, including device config and app config
- **Learn about policy setting**: Get detailed info about a device configuration policy setting, including best practices
- **Learn where my policies use a specified setting**: Get info about whether any existing device configuration policies contain a specified setting
- **Understand why a device has app or policy**: Get info about why a managed device has a policy or app by checking its group memberships

Alongside the Microsoft plugins, Security Copilot also includes other built-in plugins. Additionally, there is an extensive array of non-Microsoft plugins available in Security Copilot. Furthermore, you can create your own custom plugins. We will explore these options in more detail in the next few sections.

OpenAI and beyond – Delving into non-Microsoft plugins

The plugin mechanism allows Security Copilot to interact with various external systems and databases, extending Copilot's functionality beyond its core capabilities. This feature sets it apart from competitors as Security Copilot functions both as a product and a platform. Rather than being restricted to a fixed set of functions, Security Copilot can be expanded and tailored through a wide range of plugins. This modular approach provides flexibility and adaptability to address diverse needs.

The **SYSTEM CAPABILITIES** option in the prompt menu lets you view the list of plugins and their features. In addition to Microsoft plugins, there are also built-in plugins such as the **Generic plugin** and the **Public Web plugin**. Next, let's dive into these two additional plugins.

Built-in plugins in Security Copilot

The Generic plugin is a **GPT-style** plugin that takes input in the prompt and drops it on the AI model. As a built-in plugin, neither the Generic plugin itself nor its skills can be turned off in Security Copilot. Additionally, it acts as a catch-all plugin – when Security Copilot can't find a specific plugin to handle a prompt, Copilot automatically defaults to the Generic plugin.

The Generic plugin is often used in Security Copilot. For instance, in the case study from *Chapter 3*, this plugin was frequently called to handle prompts, as illustrated in the next three screenshots.

The following first screenshot illustrates that Security Copilot picks the Generic plugin when offering a response regarding the defense evasion technique related to process injection:

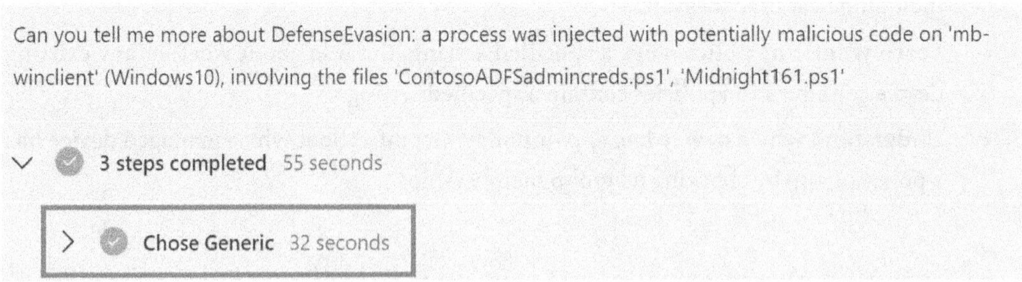

Figure 4.40 – The Generic plugin utilized to provide information on process injection

The following second screenshot shows that Security Copilot employs the Generic plugin when asked about the DCSync attack and its TTPs:

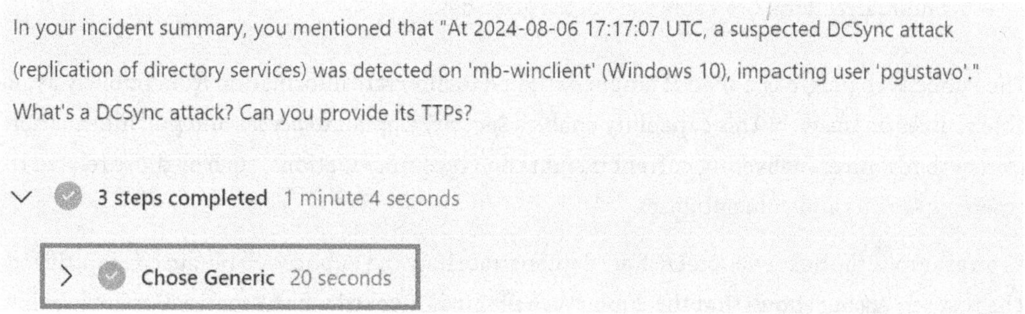

Figure 4.41 – The Generic plugin utilized to provide information on a DCSync attack

The third screenshot demonstrates Security Copilot's ability to recognize encoded commands and even decode them through the Generic plugin:

Figure 4.42 – The Generic plugin utilized to decode and analyze service path

The Generic plugin provides a range of capabilities. In addition to those highlighted in the case study, you can learn more about this plugin by referencing its features, shown here, listed in the **SYSTEM CAPABILITIES** menu option and experimenting with different prompts:

- **Analyze a script or command:** Analyze and interpret a command or script to natural language.
- **Analyze security data:** Analyze, summarize, and explain security data such as event logs, and answer security questions.
- **Convert Unix Timestamp:** Convert a Unix timestamp to a human readable date and time.
- **Extract entities:** Extract entities (e.g. accounts, URLs, hashes) from security data (e.g. logs, alerts and incidents).
- **Extract indicators of compromise:** Extract indicators of compromise from plain text.

- **Generate security examples:** Generate security-specific examples, such as event logs, reports, and configuration instructions.
- **Summarize data:** Get a summary of the given data.

The Public Web plugin is a special plugin designed to integrate information from publicly available sources on the web. This capability enables Security Copilot to access and pull information from web resources, delivering current insights and recommendations, such as those related to emerging threats and vulnerabilities.

As an example, the next two screenshots demonstrate how the Public Web plugin can be utilized. The first screenshot shows that the Public Web plugin is invoked when Security Copilot is being asked to reference an external web page that talks about vulnerabilities from the Microsoft September 2024 Patch Tuesday and to provide insights:

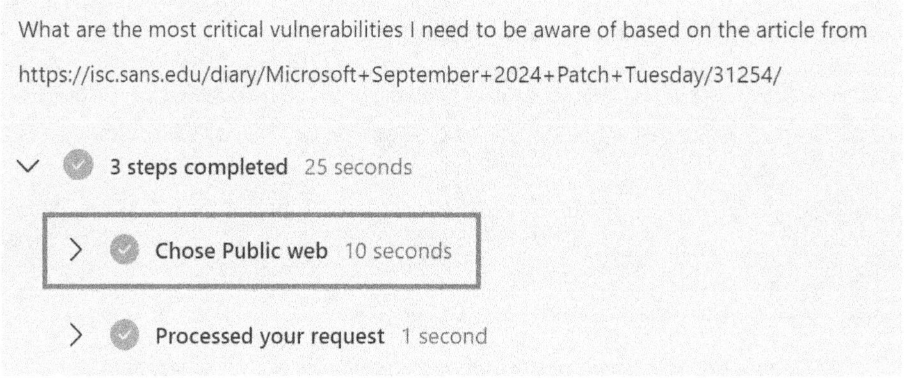

Figure 4.43 – The Security Copilot prompt utilizing the Public Web plugin

The next screenshot illustrates that Security Copilot reviews the external web page and then delivers the requested insights based on the user prompt:

Based on the article from the SANS Internet Storm Center, the most critical vulnerabilities from the Microsoft September 2024 Patch Tuesday are:

1. **CVE-2024-43491**: This is a "downgrade" vulnerability. An attacker can remove previously applied patches and exploit older vulnerabilities. This issue only affects Windows 10 Version 1507, which is EOL. It appears to differ from the similar vulnerabilities (CVE-2024-38202 and CVE-2024-21302) made public by Alon Leviev during Blackhat this year. These two vulnerabilities appear to remain unpatched.
2. **CVE-2024-38014**: A Windows Installer issue could lead to attackers gaining System access.
3. **CVE-2024-38217**: Yet another "Mark of the Web" bypass that is already exploited and could be used to trick a victim into installing malware.

Figure 4.44 – Security Copilot summarizes critical vulnerabilities based on a public resource

Alongside the Microsoft and other built-in plugins, Security Copilot also has an extensive array of non-Microsoft plugins, developed by different organizations. Let's take a look at them next.

Non-Microsoft plugins

Non-Microsoft plugins in Security Copilot are developed by Microsoft's partners and other supported external providers. These plugins provide valuable extensions to Security Copilot, helping you to enhance your security measures with tools and information from trusted external sources.

Non-Microsoft plugins extend Security Copilot's capabilities by offering specialized capabilities and integration with external sources. For instance, these plugins can bring in advanced analytics and specialized threat detection, or connect with other security systems. By incorporating the plugins, Security Copilot can tap into a wide variety of external sources, including additional threat intelligence feeds or vulnerability databases. As a result, Security Copilot can deliver a broader range of insights and recommendations.

As of March 2025, the official Microsoft documentation lists the following non-Microsoft plugins for Security Copilot:

CIRCL Hash Lookup	AbuseIPDB	Cybersixgill	Netskope	SGNL
CyberArk Privilege Cloud	CrowdSec CTI	Red Canary	Forescout	Jamf
Pure Signal Scout	TufinMate	Darktrace	Saviynt	Aviatrix
Intel 471 Threat Intel	ReversingLabs	Silverfort	Tanium	Shodan
Valence Security	GreyNoise	Whoisfreaks	UrlScan	IPinfo
Quest Security Guardian	IP Geolocation	CheckPhish	Cyware	Splunk

Table 4.1 – A list of non-Microsoft plugins for Security Copilot

You can set up, enable, or disable these non-Microsoft plugins through the **Plugins** option located within the **Manage sources** section, as shown in the following screenshot. This is also where you manage your Microsoft plugins:

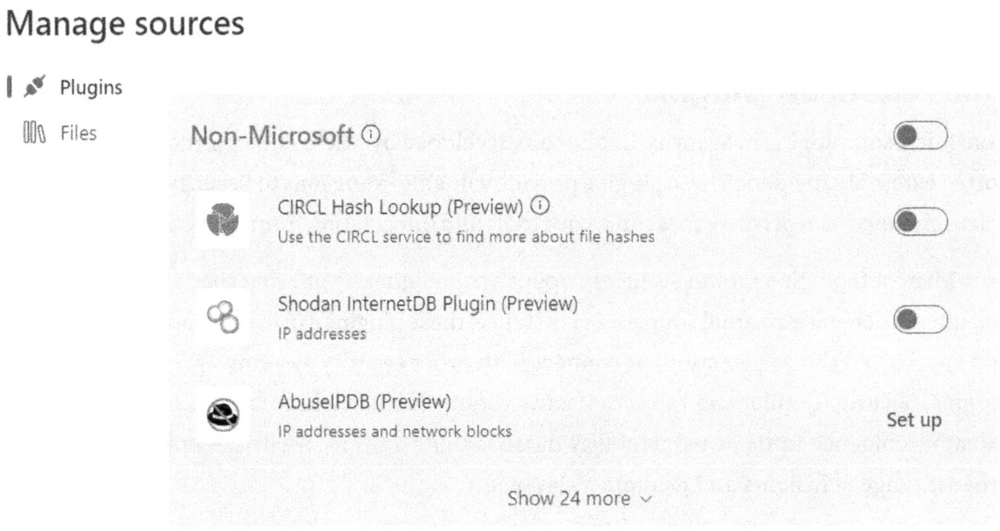

Figure 4.45 – Manage non-Microsoft plugins in Security Copilot

Note

As previously mentioned, administrators with the Owner role also have the authority to manage and enforce plugin restrictions across the organization. Using the **plugin** settings blade in the Security Copilot standalone portal, they can control which Microsoft and non-Microsoft plugins are made available to users.

The features of each third-party plugin are well documented and can be accessed through the *Non-Microsoft plugins for Microsoft Security Pilot* page at `https://learn.microsoft.com/en-us/copilot/security/plugin-other`.

Additionally, the Microsoft Security Copilot GitHub repository includes a **Community Based Plugins** section, where additional non-Microsoft plugins are shared. The following screenshot displays some of the plugins available there:

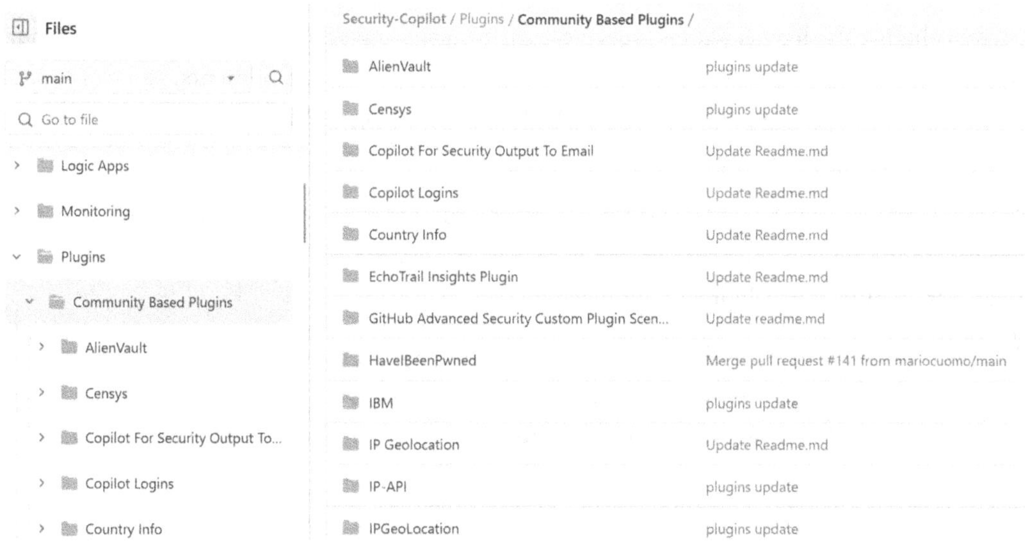

Figure 4.46 – Community Based Plugins

You can access this repository at `https://github.com/Azure/Security-Copilot/tree/main/Plugins/Community%20Based%20Plugins`. The non-Microsoft plugins there include those developed by IBM, AlienVault, SentinelOne, and more, with the collection continuously growing. These plugins are well documented. For example, the IBM plugin page offers an overview of IBM X-Force Threat Intelligence. It explains how to invoke this custom Security Copilot plugin and details the various skills available within it. You'll also find sample prompts for retrieving threat reports, threat group profiles, DNS records, WHOIS information, and more.

Having explored the various plugins available, including those from Microsoft and third parties, it's now time to consider the option of creating your own custom plugins. Let's take a look at this process next.

Crafting your own – The world of custom plugins

Security Copilot lets you create your own custom plugins. Custom plugins empower you to extend Copilot's functionalities beyond the preinstalled and non-Microsoft plugins. By utilizing the custom plugin framework, security teams can create new features and capabilities, as well as share and reuse others' custom plugins. This approach significantly enhances Security Copilot's overall adaptability, unlocking new possibilities along the way.

Custom plugins also let you address specific security needs or workflows that are unique to your organization. By adding functionalities tailored to your specific requirements, you can create solutions that meet unique organizational challenges, resulting in more efficient workflows and innovative strategies that tackle security concerns.

There are different options available for developing custom plugins. Let's take a look at one of these methods here. In the next two chapters, we will dive into custom plugins in more detail and cover additional development approaches.

Earlier in this chapter, we looked into how to use Security Copilot to execute KQL queries and analyze the resulting data as part of the analyst's investigation workflow. One of the KQL queries is to search for file downloads that occur after a user clicks on a suspicious email link, as illustrated in the following screenshot:

Figure 4.47 – Security Copilot prompt that uses KQL query to track file downloads

Rather than copying and pasting the KQL query each time you run this workflow in Security Copilot, you can convert it into a custom plugin. Automating the process with a custom plugin not only saves time and effort but also more conveniently highlights a feature in Security Copilot that may not be known by others. Additionally, this modular approach simplifies the sharing of new features, greatly enhancing Security Copilot's capabilities for everyone.

Now, let's walk through the steps in creating the new plugin. We will be adding a new KQL skill or capability to this custom plugin that can be triggered from the Security Copilot console and using it in combination with other prompts.

Creating this plugin is straightforward. First, you need to create a **YAML** file to define the KQL query. YAML is a human-readable language that is often used for writing configuration files. For your reference, the YAML file for this plugin is available for download through this book's GitHub repository at `https://github.com/PacktPublishing/Microsoft-Copilot-for-Security/blob/main/Plugins/MyYMLTest.yml`. The following screenshot also displays the YAML file for this plugin:

```yaml
Descriptor:
  Name: MyTestPlugin
  DisplayName: Test Plugin for Copilot Book
  Description:  This is a test for our Copilot for Security book developed by Bi Yue Xu

SkillGroups:
  - Format: KQL
    Skills:
      - Name: ListDownloadedFiles
        DisplayName: List files downloaded
        Description: List files downloaded to this device in the last 3 days with the device name as the input
        Inputs:
          - Name: devicename
            Description: Provide the name of the device you want to look for file download activities
            Required: true
        Settings:
          Target: Defender
          Template: |-
           DeviceFileEvents
           | where DeviceName contains '{{devicename}}'
           | where Timestamp > ago(3d)
           | where isnotempty(FileOriginUrl) and ActionType == "FileCreated"
           | project Timestamp, DeviceName, ActionType, FileName, FolderPath, FileOriginUrl, InitiatingProcessFileName
           | sort by Timestamp desc
```

Figure 4.48 – The YAML file for the custom plugin

The first section of the YAML file, as shown next, specifies the name and description of the custom plugin. The name you provide in the `DisplayName` field will be displayed as the custom plugin's name in the Security Copilot console:

```yaml
Descriptor:
  Name: MyTestPlugin
  DisplayName: Test Plugin for Copilot Book
  Description:  This is a test for our Copilot for Security book developed by Bi Yue Xu
```

Figure 4.49 – The first section of the YAML file

The next section of the YAML file defines the skills or capabilities of the custom plugin. In this case, only one skill is specified and the skill name is `List files downloaded`, as illustrated in the following screenshot.

Notice that as this is a KQL-based custom plugin, the skill group format is set to `KQL`:

```
Descriptor:
  Name: MyTestPlugin
  DisplayName: Test Plugin for Copilot Book
  Description:  This is a test for our Copilot for Security book developed by Bi Yue Xu

SkillGroups:
  - Format: KQL
    Skills:
      - Name: ListDownloadedFiles
        DisplayName: List files downloaded
        Description: List files downloaded to this device in the last 3 days with the device name as the input
        Inputs:
          - Name: devicename
            Description: Provide the name of the device you want to look for file download activities
            Required: true
        Settings:
          Target: Defender
          Template: |-
           DeviceFileEvents
           | where DeviceName contains '{{devicename}}'
           | where Timestamp > ago(3d)
           | where isnotempty(FileOriginUrl) and ActionType == "FileCreated"
           | project Timestamp, DeviceName, ActionType, FileName, FolderPath, FileOriginUrl, InitiatingProcess
           | sort by Timestamp desc
```

Figure 4.50 – The next section of the YAML file

To configure the specific skill, you have the option to specify its input. In this case, a single input parameter, `devicename`, is defined. Next, you need to include the KQL query in the `Template` section, where the query will use `devicename` as its input. This is illustrated in the following screenshot:

```
Descriptor:
  Name: MyTestPlugin
  DisplayName: Test Plugin for Copilot Book
  Description:  This is a test for our Copilot for Security book developed by Bi Yue Xu

SkillGroups:
  - Format: KQL
    Skills:
      - Name: ListDownloadedFiles
        DisplayName: List files downloaded
        Description: List files downloaded to this device in the last 3 days with the device name as the input
        Inputs:
          - Name: devicename
            Description: Provide the name of the device you want to look for file download activities
            Required: true
        Settings:
          Target: Defender
          Template: |-
           DeviceFileEvents
           | where DeviceName contains '{{devicename}}'
           | where Timestamp > ago(3d)
           | where isnotempty(FileOriginUrl) and ActionType == "FileCreated"
           | project Timestamp, DeviceName, ActionType, FileName, FolderPath, FileOriginUrl, InitiatingProcess
           | sort by Timestamp desc
```

Figure 4.51 – Define the skill in the YAML file

After creating the YAML file, you can upload it to Security Copilot. With just a few clicks, the custom plugin should be added. You should be able to follow the steps outlined next to upload the YAML file to your Copilot instance and add in your first custom plugin:

1. Select the **Sources** icon in the prompt bar, as shown in the following screenshot:

Figure 4.52 – Select the Sources icon in the prompt bar

2. Scroll to the bottom of the **Manage Sources** page, and within the **Custom** section, you'll find an **Add plugin** option. This is illustrated in the following screenshot:

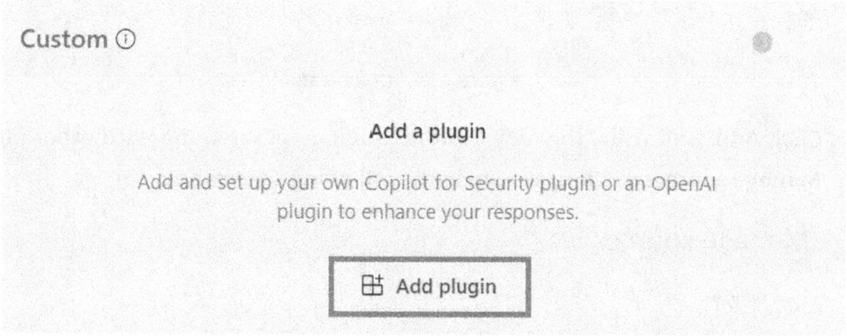

Figure 4.53 – The Add a plugin option within the Custom plugin section

3. Click on **Add plugin** and then choose **Copilot for Security plugin**, as illustrated in the following screenshot:

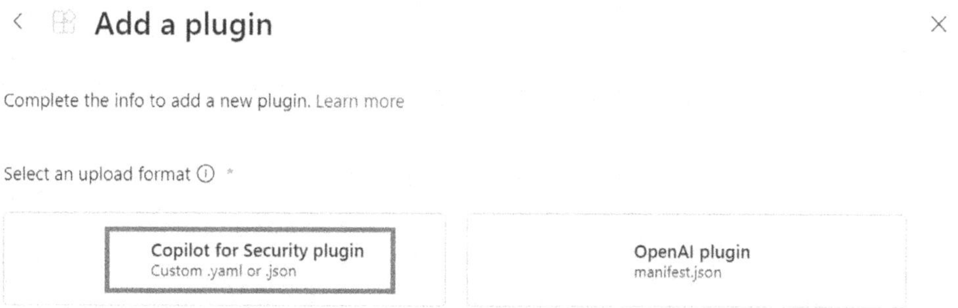

Figure 4.54 – Choose Copilot for Security plugin

4. Upload the YAML file. For this example, we will use `MyYMLTest.yml`, which is available for download in this book's GitHub repository:

Figure 4.55 – Upload MyYMLTest.yml

5. Click **Add**. And voilà, the new custom plugin appears along with other plugins in the **Manage sources** section, as seen in the following screenshot:

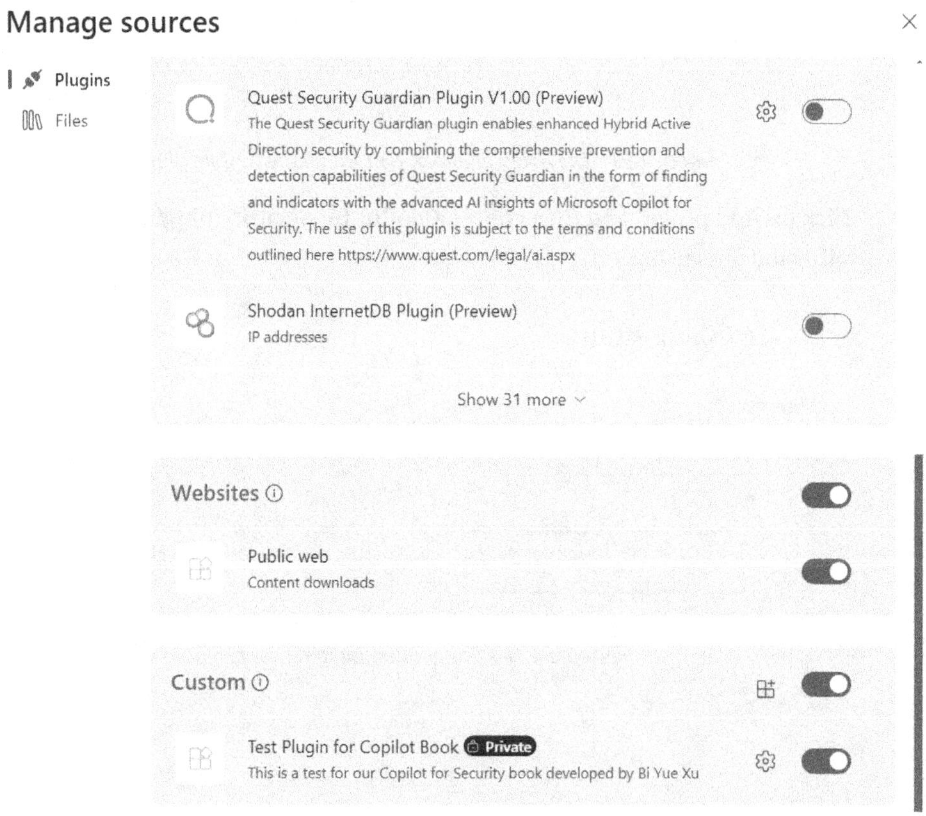

Figure 4.56 – The new custom plugin has been added

If you navigate to the **SYSTEM CAPABILITIES** menu option within Security Copilot, you will also find this new plugin listed there, as demonstrated in the following screenshot:

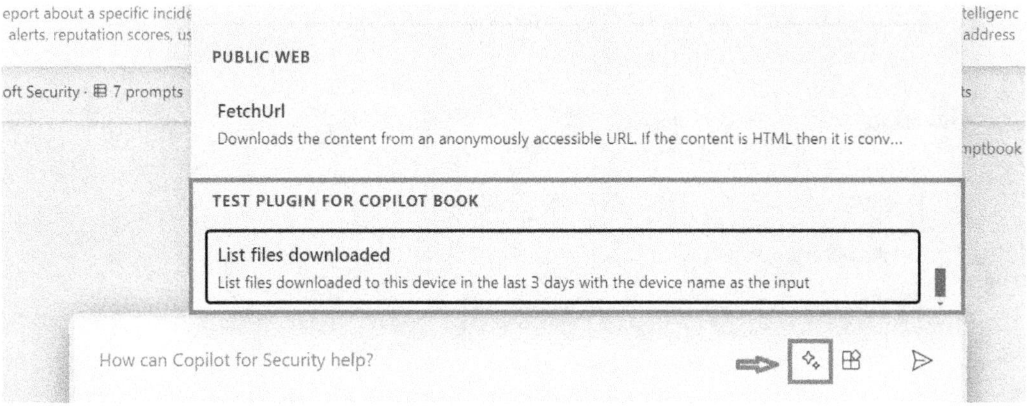

Figure 4.57 – New custom plugin seen in SYSTEM CAPABILITIES

Simply click on the capability or skill for this plugin, and **List files downloaded** will let you run it from the prompt bar, as seen in the following screenshot:

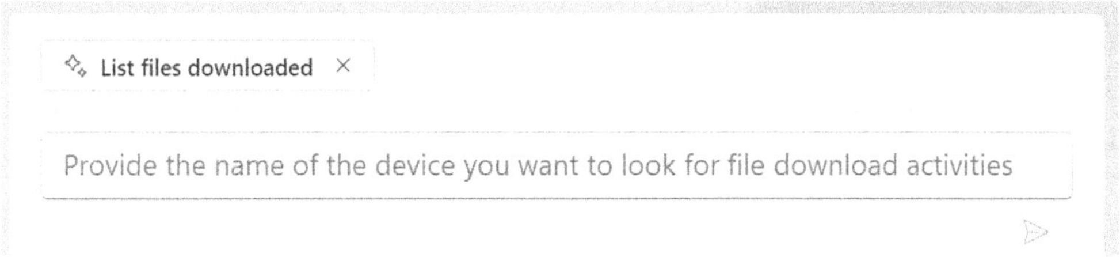

Figure 4.58 – Clicking List files downloaded lets you run it from the prompt bar

Security Copilot's output displays files downloaded to that specific device, as shown in the following screenshot:

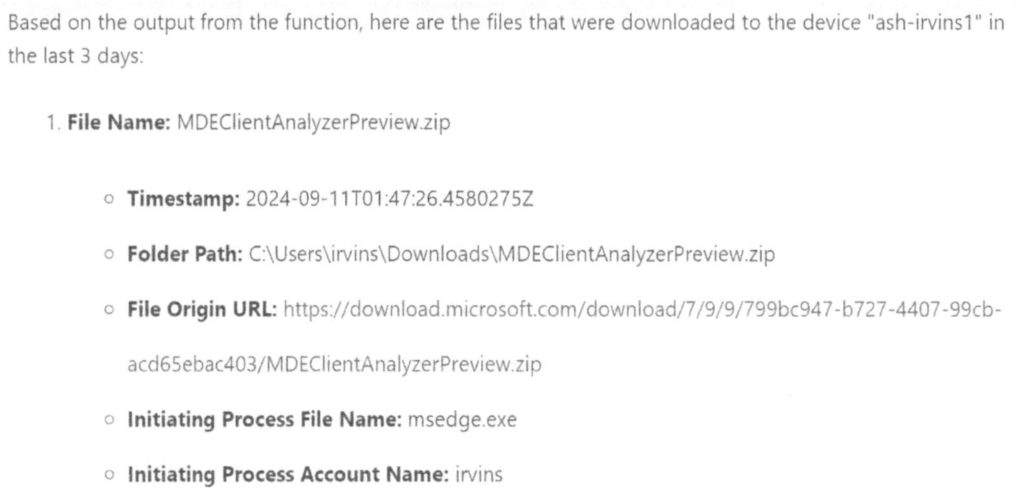

Figure 4.59 – Security Copilot shows the file downloaded to that specific device

Alternatively, you can use natural language to instruct Security Copilot to execute this plugin, as seen in the following screenshot:

Figure 4.60 – Instruct Security Copilot to run this plugin using natural language

There are different ways of creating custom plugins; what we've explored is just one approach. In the next two chapters, we'll revisit custom plugins while we dive into Security Copilot prompts and promptbooks.

The following are a few examples of custom plugins:

- **CfSAllinOne**: This plugin combines different plugins into a single, all-in-one effort to capture and respond with Security Copilot activity. This plugin will be updated as additional monitoring activity is made available and identified.

- **Use IP-API with Copilot for Security**: The API is simple and free and can be configured to return all of the following for an IP address: `status`, `message`, `continent`, `continentCode`, `country`, `countryCode`, `region`, `regionName`, `city`, `district`, `zip`, `lat`, `lon`, `timezone`, `offset`, `currency`, `isp`, `org`, `as`, `asname`, `reverse`, `mobile`, `proxy`, `hosting`, and `query`.
- **WHOIS Services for Copilot for Security**: Since WHOIS data is a powerful tool for cybersecurity professionals, it is very helpful that we can use this information with Security Copilot.

You can find these custom plugin examples in the Microsoft Security Copilot GitHub repository at `https://github.com/Azure/Security-Copilot/tree/main/Plugins`. Additionally, there are custom plugins created specifically for this book. They are available in this book's GitHub repository at `https://github.com/PacktPublishing/Microsoft-Copilot-for-Security/tree/main/Plugins`.

Summary

In this chapter, you were introduced to the different plugins available in Security Copilot. You have explored the preinstalled plugins from Microsoft, helping you to gain a deeper understanding of their features and capabilities. You also become familiar with non-Microsoft plugins. Additionally, you gained insights into the development and utilization of custom plugins. Throughout the chapter, you've learned about the functionalities of these plugins, experiencing firsthand how they can enhance and extend the capabilities of Security Copilot.

In the next chapter, we will illustrate how prompts play a crucial role in shaping the interaction between users and Security Copilot. You'll learn how to develop the skills needed to create effective prompts. This will equip you with the knowledge and abilities to design well-structured prompts that effectively guide Security Copilot in assisting with security-related tasks.

5

The Art of Prompt Engineering

Up to this point, you've explored many features of Security Copilot. You've seen how Security Copilot functions in both its embedded experience and the standalone mode. Through case studies and examples, you've gained practical insights into the workings of Security Copilot and understand the synergy between its various components. You have also been introduced to various plugins that extend the capabilities of Security Copilot.

Throughout this learning journey, Security Copilot prompts have been consistently mentioned and utilized, highlighting their critical role in the Copilot experience. In this chapter, we will take a closer look at **prompts**. You'll develop the skills to craft effective prompts and adopt best practices in prompt engineering.

As we proceed through this chapter, the following key topics related to prompts will be discussed:

- The science of prompt creation
- Crafting effective security prompts
- Prompt engineering best practices and error handling

By the end of this chapter, you'll be equipped to create well-structured prompts that effectively guide Security Copilot in providing assistance with security-related tasks.

> Want to try out the prompts, custom plugins, and promptbooks featured in this book? Take a look at the book's GitHub repository at `https://github.com/PacktPublishing/Microsoft-Copilot-for-Security`.

The science of prompt creation

Through the examples and case studies in previous chapters, you've seen Security Copilot in action. In these scenarios, prompts are used extensively. To explore the significance of prompts and their impact, let's start by defining what a Security Copilot prompt is.

You can think of a prompt as the instruction or request you give to Security Copilot, indicating the specific information or action you need. Essentially, a prompt is how you communicate your requirements to the AI, directing Security Copilot to generate a relevant response.

There are different aspects to consider regarding prompts; let's discuss them in more detail in the next few sections.

Unlocking Security Copilot for smart prompting

To write effective prompts in Security Copilot, you should understand the information and knowledge Security Copilot has, as well as its capabilities.

Just like with any other security solution, having a solid grasp of the tool's capabilities enables you to use it more effectively. For analysts, a good understanding of security copilot's knowledge base and capabilities serves as a foundation for effective interaction with copilot. This knowledge can directly influence how you tailor your prompts to elicit the most relevant and accurate responses.

Suppose security analysts are tasked with reviewing emerging security threats and identifying those affecting the organization. They can use the **Microsoft Threat Intelligence plugin** in security copilot to gather information about each new threat, analyze the data, and then manually determine its impact on the organization. However, a more effective prompt would be to directly ask security copilot to provide an overview of the latest threats to their organization, as shown in the next screen capture. This would save analysts from the lengthy process of sifting through threat data and drawing conclusions manually. With a well-crafted prompt, copilot can handle the work for them instead:

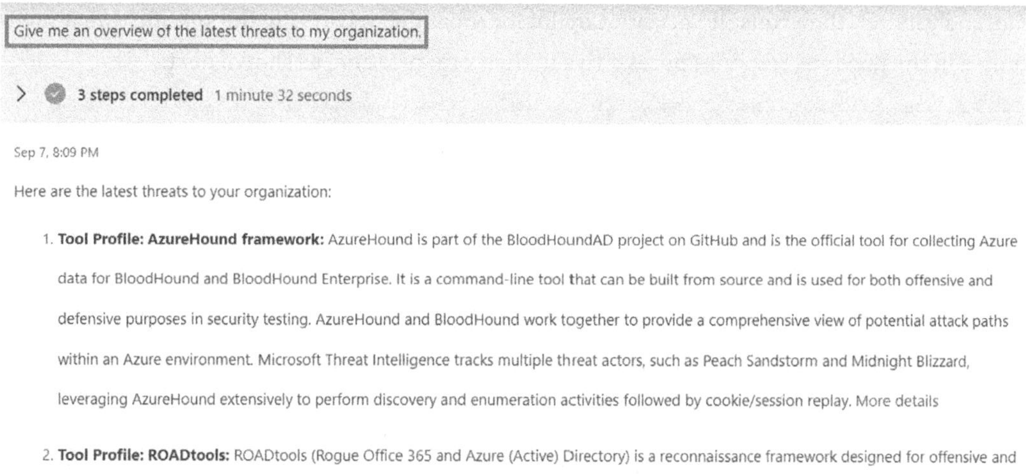

Figure 5.1 – A more efficient prompt

Quick tip: Need to see a high-resolution version of this image? Open this book in the next-gen Packt Reader or view it in the PDF/ePub copy.

The next-gen Packt Reader and a **free PDF/ePub copy** of this book are included with your purchase. Scan the QR code OR visit `packtpub.com/unlock`, then use the search bar to find this book by name. Double-check the edition shown to make sure you get the right one.

The analysts can then consult Security Copilot for more details on why the specific threat mentioned in the previous response poses a risk to their organization, as shown next:

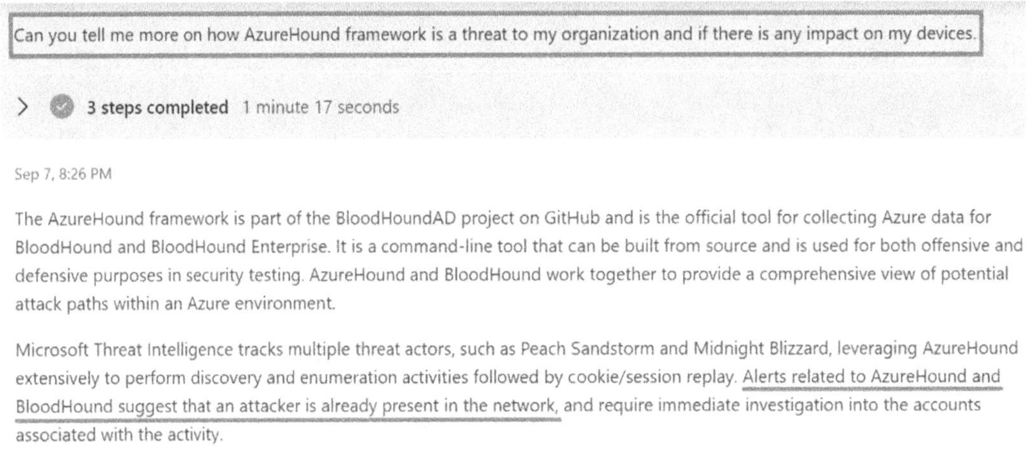

Figure 5.2 – Another Copilot prompt example

Now, you might be wondering, *How can I gain a better understanding of Copilot's knowledge base and capabilities to create more efficient prompts?* The features and capabilities of Security Copilot that you explored in previous chapters provide a good foundation. The examples and case studies presented in those chapters, as well as in future ones, should help you get a better idea of what Security Copilot can do and how it can support you.

In addition to the content in this book, there are plenty of online resources available to help you learn and understand the capabilities of Security Copilot. These resources include tutorials, blog posts, GitHub repositories, and more. You'll also find a wealth of prompt samples for reference. A detailed list of these resources is provided in *Chapter 11* and *Appendix B*. This will give you the information you need to further your learning and make the most of Security Copilot in your work.

Furthermore, as highlighted in *Chapter 4*, the **System Capabilities** menu option in the standalone experience of Security Copilot is another excellent resource to help you explore Copilot's capabilities. It outlines the knowledge that Security Copilot possesses and provides sample prompts to guide you. By exploring this menu option, you can tailor your prompts to elicit the most relevant and accurate responses, ultimately enhancing your experience with the tool.

In conclusion, a solid understanding of the knowledge and capabilities of Security Copilot helps you know what prompts to write. Next, we will uncover how the use of natural language in prompts sets Security Copilot apart from traditional tools.

The power of natural language in prompts

Security Copilot prompts are written in natural language, meaning they resemble human communication. This lets you frame your questions and requests in a conversational style. Unlike programming languages that follow strict rules and structures, natural language is flexible and context-dependent.

Using natural language in prompts reduces the need for technical jargon or strict syntax. Many traditional tools require users to follow rigid command structures or specific syntax, which can be frustrating. If you type a command incorrectly or omit a necessary parameter, the tool may return an error or fail to execute. *Natural language eliminates the need to remember the exact syntax. It lets you focus on your intent instead of specific keywords or formats.* This shift reduces stress and fosters a more positive user experience.

With natural language, you can also phrase your prompts in various ways while still achieving the same or a similar outcome. This flexibility makes it easier to express your needs. Different users may have different ways of articulating the same question or request, and natural language accommodates these variations, ensuring that communication remains effective.

For instance, in Copilot, you can invoke the **Device Current and Past IPs** skill or capability listed in the **System Capabilities** menu option, as illustrated next:

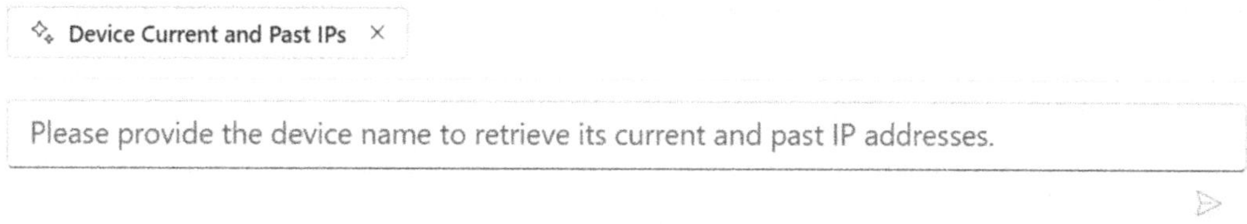

Figure 5.3 – Invoking the Device Current and Past IPs skill

Let's use the **sp4-irvins** device for our example, seen next:

Figure 5.4 – Entering the parameter required for the skill

Security Copilot executes this skill or capability, then provides a list of IPs for the **sp4-irvins** device. However, rather than navigating to the **System Capabilities** menu to invoke this skill, you can also use natural language in the prompt bar to ask Copilot to launch this specific skill and retrieve IPs for the **sp4-irvins** device, as displayed next:

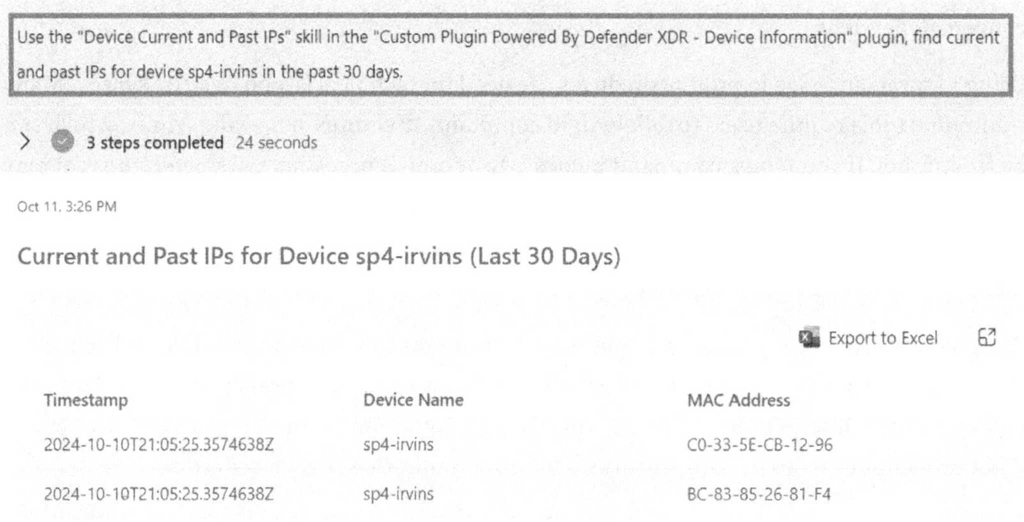

Figure 5.5 – Using natural language to invoke a skill

You can rephrase your prompt and still get Security Copilot to invoke the same skill and deliver the same result. The updated prompt is displayed next:

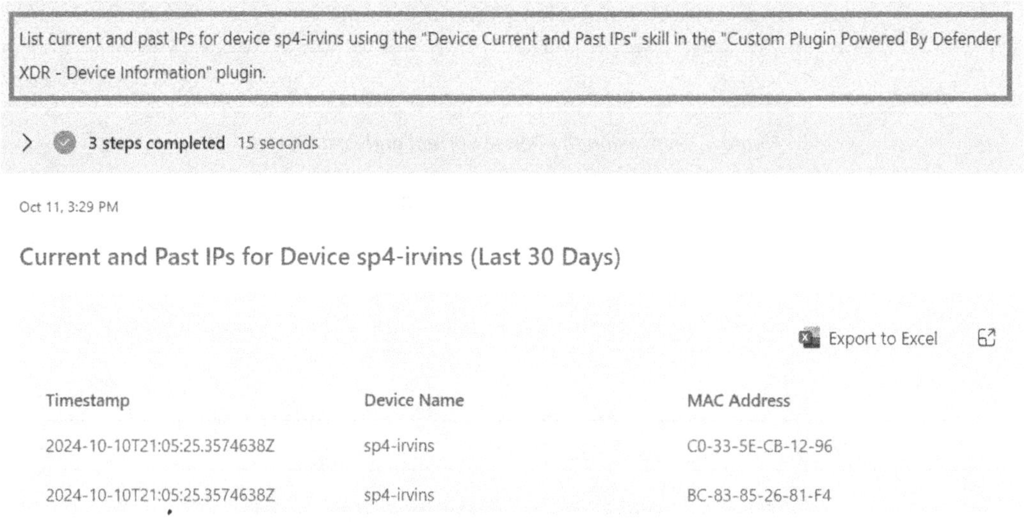

Figure 5.6 – A slightly different prompt but with the same result

The screenshot shown next displays yet another different prompt that still invokes the same capability and produces the same output:

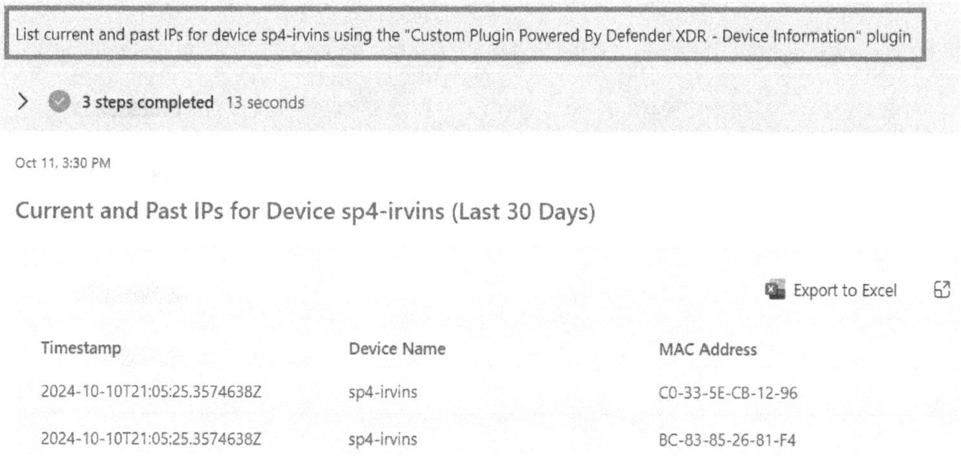

Figure 5.7 – Yet one more different prompt, but still the same result

> A quick note
>
> For those wondering why the IP column isn't visible in the three previous results, Security Copilot often does not show all columns in its displayed output. To view the complete results, you'll need to click the *enlarge* icon, as seen in the next screenshot.

Figure 5.8 – Using the enlarge icon to view the full results

For your reference, the full output, including the IPs, is shown next:

Export to Excel

Timestamp	Device Name	MAC Address	IP Address
2024-10-10T21:05:25.3574638Z	sp4-irvins	C0-33-5E-CB-12-96	169.[redacted]
2024-10-10T21:05:25.3574638Z	sp4-irvins	BC-83-85-26-81-F4	192.[redacted]
2024-10-10T21:05:25.3574638Z	sp4-irvins	BC-83-85-26-81-F5	169[redacted]
2024-10-10T21:05:25.3574638Z	sp4-irvins	BE-83-85-26-80-F5	169[redacted]
2024-10-09T11:05:15.4148509Z	sp4-irvins	BE-83-85-26-85-F5	169[redacted]

Figure 5.9 – The complete output data

Since Security Copilot is powered by advanced AI to generate responses, it's also important to know that running the same prompt often produces slightly different results. You may notice variations in wording, formatting, or specific details, even when the prompt remains unchanged. While the core information typically stays consistent, these small variations are a normal part of how generative AI works.

Now that you've seen how natural language works within Security Copilot, let's shift our focus to how context and session awareness can further enhance Security Copilot's capabilities.

Context awareness and session awareness

Security Copilot is designed to understand what users are asking through the context of their prompts. When you interact with Security Copilot, its contextual awareness feature enables it to interpret your intent based on the information you provide. For example, if you request `logs from yesterday`, Security Copilot recognizes that you're looking for recent log data.

Beyond being context-aware, Security Copilot also maintains awareness within each user session. As described in *Chapter 3*, a session represents a single continuous interaction between the user and Security Copilot. Throughout the same session, Security Copilot keeps track of the user's inputs, queries, and the overall context of the conversation, allowing it to retain and reference information from earlier prompts.

For instance, if you've previously inquired about a list of vulnerable devices and then ask to check the status of the third device later on, Security Copilot can leverage that earlier context of the device list and understand exactly which device you're referring to. If you change topics or refer back to something you mentioned earlier, Security Copilot can adjust its responses to stay aligned with the ongoing conversation.

By retaining context from previous interactions in the same session, Security Copilot can follow the dialogue's thread and conversation flow, allowing users to build on earlier interactions without repeating background details. The conversation in the Copilot session, therefore, feels more natural and connected, like an ongoing dialogue rather than a series of disconnected questions. Additionally, understanding the context allows Security Copilot to tailor its answers to specific circumstances, providing insights that align with the user's current needs.

For example, the prompt shown in the next screenshot asks Security Copilot to use a skill in a custom plugin to report the sensitive files detected on a device. In response, Security Copilot provides a list of sensitive file events for that device over the last 30 days:

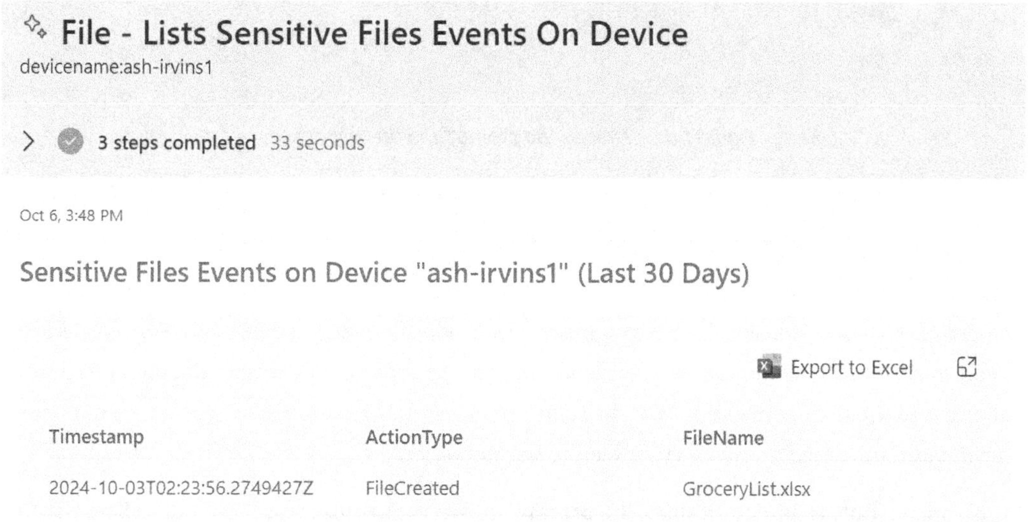

Figure 5.10 – Sensitive file events on a device

The next screenshot displays a follow-up prompt requesting Security Copilot to analyze the sensitive file events from the earlier prompt, focusing on the file hashes to identify any files that share the same hash but have different filenames:

> Using the Copilot for Security Generic plugin, can you evaluate the sensitive files events you just provided? Look through the file hash for ALL the files and identify the file with same file hash but different file name.
>
> > 3 steps completed 1 minute 5 seconds

Oct 6, 3:49 PM

Files with Identical Hashes but Different Names

The following files have the same SHA256 hash but different file names:

Export to Excel

File Name	SHA256
GroceryList.xlsx	6893a10ce49f66871a9dc1de57b323f1346511862204479c92fa61dcfab46be0
EmployeeInfo_EDM.xlsx	6893a10ce49f66871a9dc1de57b323f1346511862204479c92fa61dcfab46be0

Figure 5.11 – A follow-up prompt and the response

As shown in the previous screenshot, Security Copilot reviews the results from the earlier prompt and identifies two sensitive files with matching file hashes but different names: `GroceryList.xlsx` and `Employeelnfo_EDM.xlsx`.

Context and session awareness also encourage users to ask more nuanced questions, knowing that Security Copilot understands the prior context. This leads analysts to explore topics more deeply, confidently delving into areas they may not have initially considered. It also enables analysts to ask more relevant and informed questions that lead to better responses.

Here's an example to illustrate this. The prompt shown in the next screenshot asks Security Copilot to retrieve events related to device tampering attempts, then analyze them, and provide a summary highlighting any suspicious activity:

> Can you pull device tampering attempt events using the Device Tampering Attempt skill in the Device IR Playbook plugin, with device name as cpc-u126-wajb21? Then analyze these events, provide a summary with anything that seem suspicious?

Figure 5.12 – The prompt in this example

The first half of Security Copilot's response includes a list of detailed tampering attempt events, as shown next:

Tampering Attempts on Device: cpc-u126-wajb21

Summary of Tampering Attempts (Last 30 Days)

Export to Excel

Timestamp	ActionType	RegistryKey
2024-09-15T21:05:05.569678Z	TamperingAttempt	HKEY_LOCAL_MACHINE\SOFTWARE \POLICIES\MICROSOFT\WINDOWS DEFENDER\POLICY MANAGER
2024-09-15T21:05:05.5723768Z	TamperingAttempt	HKEY_LOCAL_MACHINE\SOFTWARE \POLICIES\MICROSOFT\WINDOWS DEFENDER\POLICY MANAGER
2024-09-15T21:05:05.573254Z	TamperingAttempt	HKEY_LOCAL_MACHINE\SOFTWARE \POLICIES\MICROSOFT\WINDOWS DEFENDER\POLICY MANAGER

Figure 5.13 – The first half of Security Copilot's response

The second half of the response is Security Copilot's analysis, displayed in the next screenshot. Security Copilot notes that the consistent pattern of registry modifications suggests a potential automated script rather than a direct attack. It also highlights that, although `svchost.exe` is a legitimate process, its involvement in registry modifications should be monitored carefully:

A total of 6 tampering attempts were detected on the device "cpc-u126-wajb21" in the last 30 days.

Analysis

All tampering attempts involved modifications to the Windows Defender Policy Manager registry keys. The initiating process for all attempts was `svchost.exe` , a legitimate Windows process, running under the `SYSTEM` account. The status of all attempts was marked as "Ignored," indicating that these changes were not blocked or flagged as critical by the system.

While `svchost.exe` is a legitimate process, its use in registry modifications should be monitored closely, especially if these changes are unexpected or unauthorized. The consistent pattern of registry modifications suggests a potential automated script or policy change rather than a direct attack.

No immediate suspicious activity was detected beyond the registry modifications by `svchost.exe` .

Figure 5.14 – The second half of Security Copilot's response

You can then follow up by asking Security Copilot to provide examples of when the `svchost.exe` process has been involved in tampering attempts. The next screenshot shows the prompt, along with the first example provided by Security Copilot:

Can you give some examples of suspicious tampering attempts using svchost.exe in the wild?

> **3 steps completed** 25 seconds

Oct 12, 2:17 PM

Examples of Suspicious Tampering Attempts Using svchost.exe

Example 1: Unusual Network Activity

Log Entry:

```
Timestamp: 2023-10-01 14:23:45
Process: svchost.exe
Source IP: 192.168.1.100
Destination IP: 203.0.113.45
Destination Port: 8080
Protocol: TCP
```

Figure 5.15 – Example of suspicious tampering attempts

There are more examples provided by Security Copilot, as seen next:

Example 2: Unauthorized File Modification

Log Entry:

```
Timestamp: 2023-10-02 09:15:30
Process: svchost.exe
File Path: C:\Windows\System32\drivers\etc\hosts
Action: File modification
Details: Added multiple entries redirecting legitimate domains to malicious IP addresses
```

Example 3: Abnormal Process Creation

Log Entry:

```
Timestamp: 2023-10-03 11:45:12
Parent Process: svchost.exe
Child Process: cmd.exe
Command Line: cmd.exe /c powershell -ExecutionPolicy Bypass -File C:\malicious_script.ps1
Activity: Execution of a PowerShell script
```

Figure 5.16 – Additional examples of suspicious tampering attempts

Assume you're surprised by the second example, which links the modification of the `hosts` file in the `etc` directory to a tampering attempt; you can then provide Copilot with a more targeted prompt related to **Example 2**. The next screenshot shows the prompt you can use to ask Security Copilot about it:

Can you dive into Example 2: Unauthorized File Modification more? How can modifying file C:\Windows\System32\drivers\etc\hosts being considered suspicious tampering attempt?

Figure 5.17 – The targeted Copilot prompt

Security Copilot then provides a more detailed explanation of **Example 2**, as illustrated next:

Example 2: Unauthorized File Modification

Why Modifying the File **`C:\Windows\System32\drivers\etc\hosts`** is Suspicious

Modifying the `hosts` file can be considered a suspicious tampering attempt because this file is used to map hostnames to IP addresses. Unauthorized changes to this file can redirect legitimate domain requests to malicious IP addresses, potentially leading to:

- **Phishing Attacks**: Redirecting users to fake websites that look like legitimate ones to steal credentials or personal information.
- **Malware Distribution**: Redirecting users to malicious sites that host malware, leading to infections.
- **Data Interception**: Redirecting traffic to malicious servers to intercept and manipulate data.

In the given example, `svchost.exe` was used to add multiple entries in the `hosts` file, redirecting legitimate domains to malicious IP addresses. This kind of activity is often indicative of an attempt to compromise the system or deceive users.

Figure 5.18 – Security Copilot provides a more detailed explanation

This example shows how context and session awareness lead users to ask more follow-up questions. As a result, analysts often dive deeper into specific topics and explore areas they may not have considered at first.

Moreover, by understanding the context of prompts and tracking the conversation flow during a session, Security Copilot reduces confusion. If you use a word that could mean different things, the system can pick the most likely meaning based on what you've discussed so far. This leads to clearer communication and fewer misunderstandings, making it easier for you to get the information you need.

That said, it's important to note that Security Copilot sessions are isolated. For example, while in the second session, Security Copilot cannot reference the information from the first session. Essentially, every new session begins with a clean slate. Therefore, it's best to approach each new session as if you are starting a conversation with a stranger. This is the current product design as of May 2025, though future developments may lead to changes in how session continuity is handled.

Lastly, here's a fun fact about prompts in Security Copilot. You may have spotted some typos and grammatical errors in the prompts we've reviewed. Nonetheless, Security Copilot is still able to accurately interpret these prompts and provide accurate responses.

Now that we have covered the core concepts of prompting in Security Copilot, let's explore how to create effective prompts next.

Crafting effective security prompts

Just as crafting an effective question requires careful thought and clarity, creating a well-designed prompt follows the same principles. The quality of your input directly influences the quality of the output you receive; in other words, good input leads to good output. To ensure you get the most relevant and insightful responses, it's important to keep a few key criteria in mind when crafting your prompts.

Microsoft recommends considering the following elements when writing a prompt:

- **Goal**: An effective prompt should have a clear goal that conveys your desired outcome. Here's an example: `I need to know how do I start my investigation for this incident, what should I start looking into?`
- **Context**: Providing context, such as background information or setting the scene, can enhance the quality of the response. As an example, consider the following prompt: `You mentioned: "Review the initial compromise on 'vnevado-win10r' at 2024-08-30 02:52:12 UTC." Can you provide more detailed guidance on how to perform this review?`
- **Expectations**: Expectations can be the desired response, whether it's a list of action steps, a summary, or an analysis. Here is an example: `Can you provide a list of action steps to identify signs of how the attacker gained access to this device?`
- **Source**: This indicates which data source or plugin Security Copilot can utilize. Here is an example: `Using the MDTI plugin, can you tell me more about domain vectorsandarrows[.]com?`

Building on the prompt recommendation just discussed, let's review a few prompts and Copilot's responses to help you understand how prompts can assist during an investigation.

First, after Security Copilot summarizes an incident, you can follow up with a prompt that conveys your desired *goal*, for example, asking how to start the incident investigation. The prompt shown next illustrates this approach:

> I need to know how do I start my investigation for this incident, what should I start look into?

Figure 5.19 – The prompt with a clear goal

Copilot then presents a list of steps and important areas to focus on, as displayed next:

> To start your investigation for Incident 1661, focus on the following key areas:
>
> 1. **Initial Compromise and Lateral Movement**:
>   - Review the initial compromise on 'vnevado-win10r' at 2024-08-30 02:52:12 UTC.
>   - Investigate the suspicious RDP session on 'vnevado-win10v' at 2024-08-30 07:08:46 UTC, involving 'mimikatz.exe' and 'powershell.exe'.
> 2. **Credential Theft**:
>   - Examine the execution of 'mimikatz.exe' and the access to the LSASS service on 'vnevado-win10v' at 2024-08-30 07:10:39 UTC.
>   - Look into the multiple attempts to access the Primary Refresh Token (PRT) on 'vnevado-win10s' and

Figure 5.20 – Security Copilot provides recommendations

As seen in Security Copilot's response, the first recommendation is **Review the initial compromise on 'vnevado-win10r' at 2024-08-30 02:52:12 UTC**. However, Security Copilot does not offer details on how to accomplish this. You can write a follow-up prompt by first providing some *context*, such as the Copilot recommendation, then specifying your *expectations*, such as needing a playbook. The prompt is displayed in the next screenshot:

> You mentioned: "Review the initial compromise on 'vnevado-win10r' at 2024-08-30 02:52:12 UTC." Can you provide a playbook for looking for signs of how the attacker gained access to this device?

Figure 5.21 – The prompt that provides context and sets expectations

This time, Security Copilot provides a detailed playbook for investigating the initial compromise on the **vnevado-win10r** device, as requested in your prompt. This is illustrated next:

Playbook for Investigating Initial Compromise on 'vnevado-win10r'

1. Preparation

- Ensure you have the necessary permissions to access logs and systems.
- Gather tools: SIEM, EDR, antivirus software, and forensic tools.

2. Identification

- **Timestamp:** 2024-08-30 02:52:12 UTC
- **Device:** vnevado-win10r

3. Data Collection

- **System Logs:**
    - Collect Windows Event Logs (Security, Application, System).

Figure 5.22 – Security Copilot provides a detailed playbook in its response

As you investigate this incident, you can request Security Copilot to extract **indicators of compromise (IoCs)** related to it, as shown next:

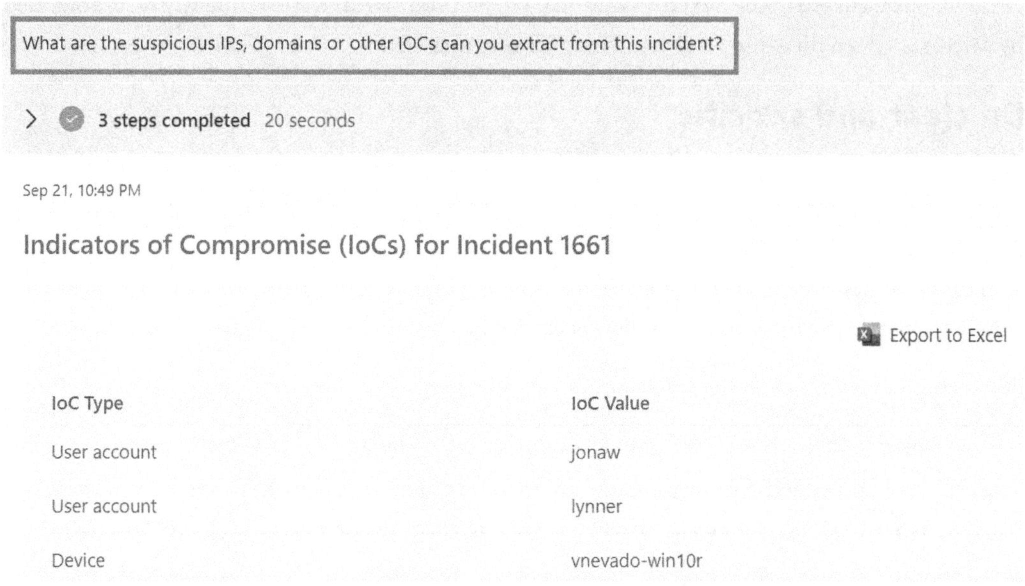

Figure 5.23 – Prompt that requests Copilot to extract IoCs

For any notable IoCs, such as an external domain, you can specifically request the MDTI plugin in Security Copilot as the *source* to provide further threat intelligence information. This is illustrated in the next screenshot:

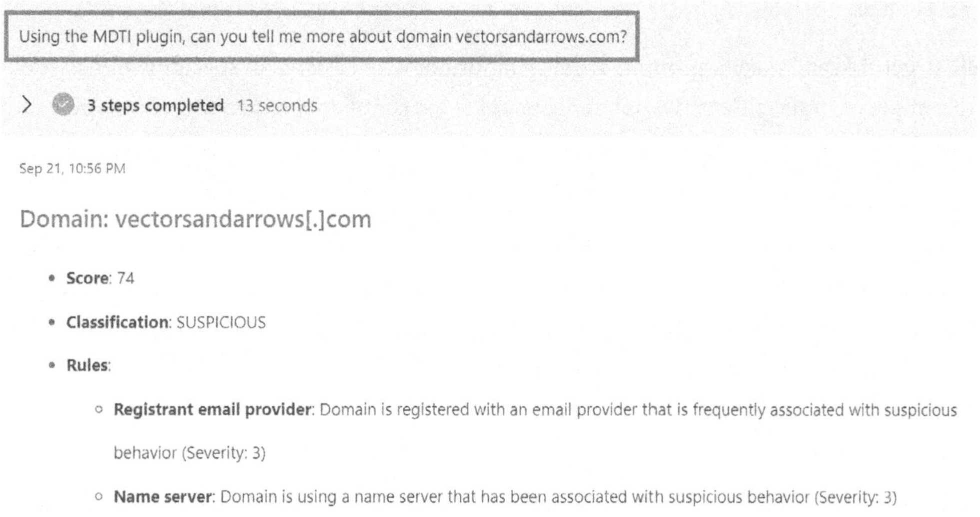

Figure 5.24 – A prompt that indicates which plugin to use

This investigation example highlights the four key elements of crafting an effective prompt: goal, context, expectations, and source. There are also additional tips for writing your own prompts. This will be discussed in the next few sections. We will start with those frequently recommended by Microsoft, then dive into additional helpful suggestions.

Be clear and specific

In Security Copilot, it's essential to start with clear and specific prompts. This is particularly important at the beginning of a session, since each session starts fresh with no prior context. The more precise and specific your information, the more targeted the response. Vague prompts lead to vague answers, while detailed requests often yield richer, more nuanced insights. Always consider the specific information or perspective you want and state it clearly in your prompt.

For example, take a look at the two prompts shown next:

- **Vague prompt:** `What can you tell me about a security incident?`
- **Clear and specific prompt:** `Can you provide details on the security incident involving the 'vnevado-win10r' device that occurred on August 30, 2024?`

The first prompt is vague and open-ended, which may lead to a broad and unhelpful response. The second prompt is clear and specific, asking for particular information about a certain incident, which helps Security Copilot deliver a more targeted and useful answer.

The need for clear and specific prompts also applies when shifting to a new topic in the middle of a session. Unless you indicate a change in focus, Copilot assumes you're continuing the same topic. For instance, you might say `Now switch to incident 1983`... to signal the change.

Well-structured and specific prompts are also important when asking for specific actions, working with complex or multiple entities, referencing uploaded content, or requesting correlation and investigation support. In these cases, vague prompts may lead to incomplete or off-target responses.

For example, when requesting specific outputs, a prompt such as `List last 3 days alerts by severity in a table` provides clearer direction. When dealing with complex entities, you should specify which systems, users, or timeframes you mean, such as `How are managed apps on this device, workstation1, different from device workstation3?` If using uploaded or external data, providing context about the source and your goal is key, for instance, `In the uploaded files, referencing 'Cobalt Strike.docx', can you list`.... Finally, when asking for correlation or investigation guidance, clearly define what you want to uncover, such as `Correlate risky user activity with sign-in anomalies.`

Please note, once context has been established within a session, you can take a more conversational approach. Security Copilot maintains awareness of the ongoing discussion in a session, so brief follow-ups such as `Any IoCs related to that incident` or `Any related alerts?` are typically understood without repeating previous details.

Next, let's discuss another tip: the benefits of using iteration in prompts.

Use iteration to refine prompts

Iterate on your prompts to achieve better results. Initial prompts may yield general or broad responses, but refining your later prompts allows you to hone in on the specific information you need. By continuously adjusting and clarifying your prompts, you can guide the conversation toward more detailed insights and actionable intelligence.

Here's an example that demonstrates the effectiveness of iteration. The initial prompt and the Security Copilot response are seen in the following screenshot:

Figure 5.25 – The initial prompt and the Security Copilot response

Next, we have a follow-up prompt and its corresponding response:

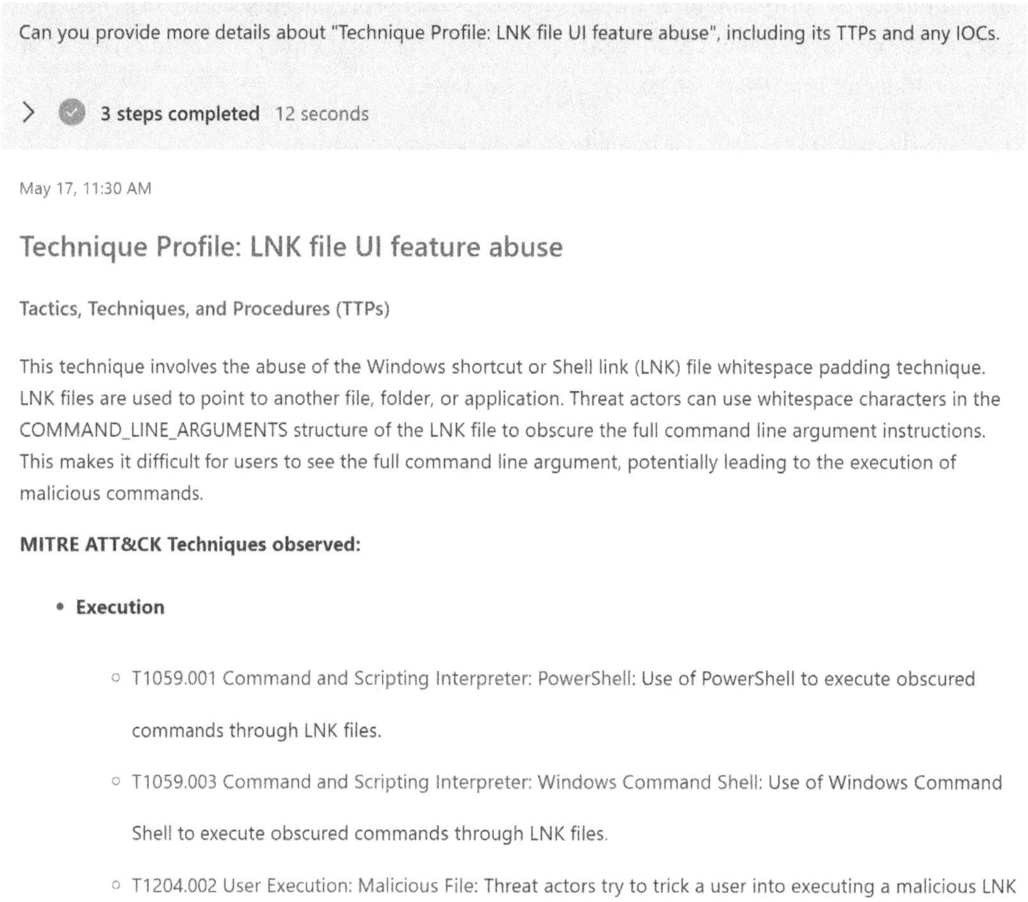

Can you provide more details about "Technique Profile: LNK file UI feature abuse", including its TTPs and any IOCs.

> 3 steps completed 12 seconds

May 17, 11:30 AM

Technique Profile: LNK file UI feature abuse

Tactics, Techniques, and Procedures (TTPs)

This technique involves the abuse of the Windows shortcut or Shell link (LNK) file whitespace padding technique. LNK files are used to point to another file, folder, or application. Threat actors can use whitespace characters in the COMMAND_LINE_ARGUMENTS structure of the LNK file to obscure the full command line argument instructions. This makes it difficult for users to see the full command line argument, potentially leading to the execution of malicious commands.

MITRE ATT&CK Techniques observed:

- **Execution**
  - T1059.001 Command and Scripting Interpreter: PowerShell: Use of PowerShell to execute obscured commands through LNK files.
  - T1059.003 Command and Scripting Interpreter: Windows Command Shell: Use of Windows Command Shell to execute obscured commands through LNK files.
  - T1204.002 User Execution: Malicious File: Threat actors try to trick a user into executing a malicious LNK

Figure 5.26 – The follow-up prompt and its corresponding response

In this example, the initial prompt generates a general overview, but the analyst then realizes more specific information is needed. The follow-up prompt iterates on the first by clarifying the request, leading to a more targeted and informative response. This process allows the user to continuously test prompts and refine them based on the responses received. This iterative approach enhances the effectiveness of prompts, helping to achieve the desired outcome.

Now, let's move on to the next tip on utilizing context.

Leverage context to narrow down focus

The way you frame your prompts can influence Security Copilot's data search process. Adding context to your requests, such as background details, scope, or specific parameters, helps Copilot narrow down where it looks for data. This ensures the information retrieved is relevant and actionable.

For instance, consider the two prompts displayed next:

- **Basic prompt**: `Analyze user behavior in the past week.`
- **More effective prompt**: `Analyze user behavior for the past week in Microsoft Sentinel, and focus on unusual login patterns.`

The basic prompt is quite broad and could yield generic insights. The improved prompt narrows the search to a specific platform and highlights the particular aspects you want to investigate. By giving Security Copilot clear parameters, you ensure that the analysis is both relevant and actionable, enabling you to address specific concerns more effectively.

Let's move on to the next tip, often mentioned by Microsoft.

Use positive instructions to boost efficiency

When working with Security Copilot, focusing on positive instructions can improve the effectiveness of your prompts. Positive instruction refers to providing clear, actionable guidance about what you want Security Copilot to accomplish, rather than focusing on what not to do. Since Security Copilot is designed for action, articulating your desired outcomes leads to more productive results.

For instance, consider the following two prompts:

- **Restrictive prompt**: `Don't show me any inactive accounts.`
- **Positive instruction prompt**: `Please provide a list of active user accounts along with their last login dates.`

The positive instruction clearly outlines what you want Security Copilot to accomplish. Since Copilot is designed for action, specifying your desired outcomes in this way leads to more productive results, helping you gather the information you need efficiently.

Having covered the importance of positive instructions, we have now summarized the key recommendations commonly highlighted by Microsoft. Next, let's explore some additional tips.

More tips for crafting effective prompts

Here are some additional recommendations to make your prompts more effective. As you gain experience with Security Copilot, you'll develop your own strategies to share with others:

- **Prioritize key information**: Identify the most critical elements of your inquiry and prioritize them in your prompt. Highlighting essential information helps guide Security Copilot to focus on what truly matters.
- **Use action-oriented language**: Frame your prompts with action verbs to clearly indicate the tasks you want Security Copilot to perform. This approach encourages a more direct response and clarifies your expectations. For instance, consider this prompt: `Identify the top three vulnerabilities in the wild and recommend mitigation strategies.`
- **Specify the desired format**: If you have a particular format in mind for the response (such as a list, a summary, or a detailed report), make that clear in your prompt. This helps set expectations for the output. For example, try this prompt: `Please summarize the incident report in bullet points, highlighting key findings and recommendations.`
- **Specify stakeholders**: Mention any specific stakeholders or departments relevant to your request. This can help tailor the response to your organizational context. For example, consider this prompt: `What security measures should the IT department implement to safeguard sensitive data?`
- **Include timeframes**: Adding a timeframe can help narrow the focus of the information you're requesting. This is particularly useful for tasks that require recent data or trends. For instance, here's a prompt you might use: `What were the most significant security breaches reported in the last quarter?`
- **Ask for comparisons**: Encouraging Security Copilot to compare different datasets or incidents can provide deeper insights. Framing your prompt this way can lead to more informative responses. Consider this prompt as an example: `Compare the recent malware attacks on healthcare vs. financial sectors, focusing on methods used and impacts.`
- **Encourage exploration**: Invite Security Copilot to explore broader implications or related topics. This can yield insights that may not be immediately obvious and can enrich your understanding. For instance, you might try a prompt such as the following: `What are the emerging trends in cybersecurity threats, and how might they impact my organization in the next year?`

- **Test different angles**: If the initial response isn't satisfactory, rephrase your question from a different perspective. This can sometimes lead to more insightful answers. For example, instead of asking `What are the risks of my current system?`, try asking `What potential vulnerabilities exist in my current system architecture?`
- **Combine multiple requests**: If relevant, combine multiple related inquiries into a single prompt. This can help Security Copilot provide a more comprehensive answer without needing to follow up. For instance, here is a prompt you might use: `List the recent phishing campaigns targeting our organization and outline the measures taken to counter them.`

> Note
>
> Security Copilot can handle multiple requests or instructions within a single prompt, as long as the required data comes from a single plugin. However, when a prompt relies on information from multiple plugins, Security Copilot does not do well. For instance, asking for incidents from Microsoft Defender and device data from Intune in the same prompt may not produce accurate results, as the current design supports only one plugin per prompt. In cases where such combined queries do succeed, it typically relies on one plugin and the generic GPT capabilities to, for example, outline the measures taken to counter them.

In conclusion, incorporating strategies to craft effective prompts can enhance your experience with Security Copilot. The tips shared empower you to guide the conversation more effectively, leading to better responses and deeper insights. Building on this foundation, embracing openness can further encourage creativity, allowing for even more innovative and dynamic exchanges with Security Copilot. Last but not least, let's explore this idea next.

Openness encourages creativity

Adopting an open mindset while interacting with Security Copilot can lead to surprising insights and new discoveries. Security Copilot is an AI with a vast amount of knowledge and is designed specifically to enhance cybersecurity efforts. It is also continually improving and becoming more capable. Don't hesitate to ask Security Copilot new questions or request different tasks; you may be pleasantly surprised by what it knows and can do for you. Consider it as your intelligent assistant in the security realm, always ready to help. When you find yourself stuck or in need of assistance during an investigation or analysis, give Security Copilot a try.

For instance, while investigating an incident, you may encounter unfamiliar events or cryptic log data. Rather than conducting time-consuming and stressful research on your own, consider reaching out to Security Copilot. The author did just that and was pleasantly surprised by how effective Security Copilot was. Many of the new prompts used to explore what Security Copilot can do are featured in a case study presented in *Chapter 3*.

One example mentioned in that case study is when the analyst observes a user on a Windows device sending a replication request to the domain controller, as shown in the next screenshot:

Figure 5.27 – Device sending a replication request to the domain controller

Rather than learning and researching about **domain controllers** and the **domain replication process**, the analyst can turn to Security Copilot and directly ask whether this behavior is normal.

Security Copilot not only gives a clear answer but also provides a detailed explanation, as shown next:

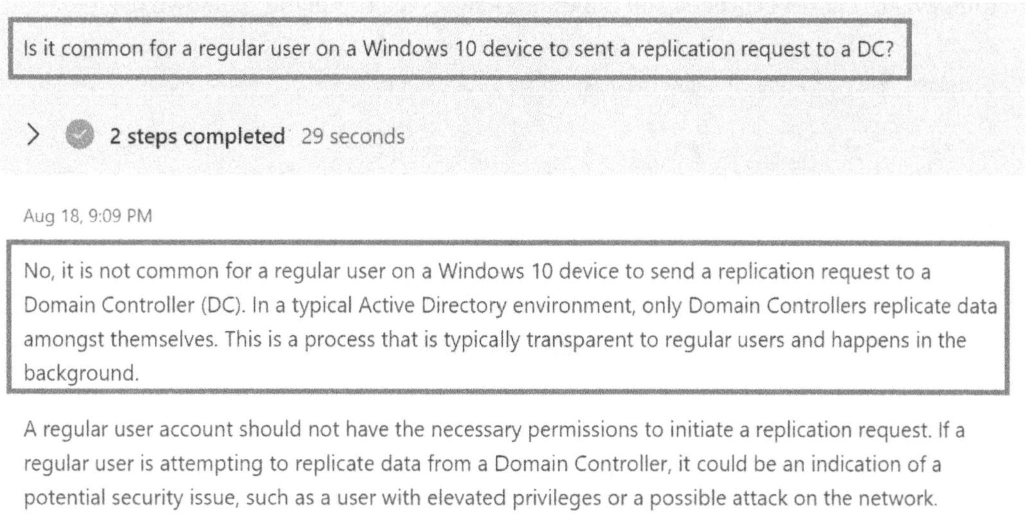

Figure 5.28 – A new prompt used in Security Copilot

Another example involves requesting Security Copilot to run a KQL query to retrieve detailed process events from a device, followed by a request for Security Copilot to analyze the process data for any encoded command lines. The prompt is displayed in the next screenshot:

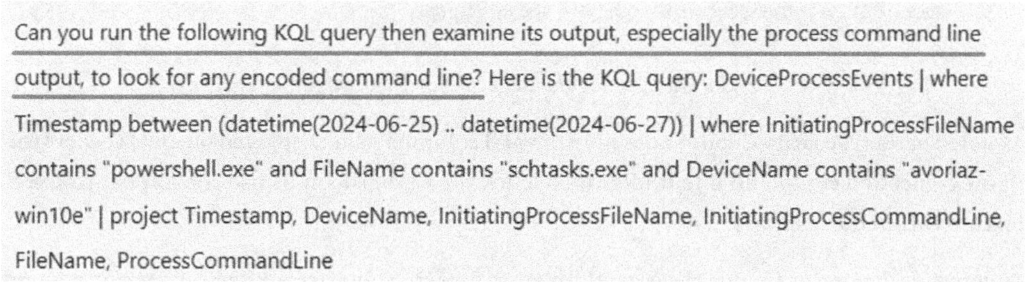

Figure 5.29 – A Security Copilot prompt containing a KQL query

Security Copilot then reviews all the process events and points out the encoded command-line output, which is Base64 encoded and is part of a PowerShell command, as shown next:

The query returned a total of 2 rows, all of which are displayed below:

Export to Excel

Timestamp	DeviceName	InitiatingProcessFileName
2024-06-26T14:48:36.9677982Z	avoriaz-win10e.[redacted]	powershell.exe
osemary\Desktop\WinATP-Intro-Backdoor.exe /ST 14:46 /F		
2024-06-26T14:52:32.417074Z	avoriaz-win10e.[redacted]	powershell.exe

Upon examining the `InitiatingProcessCommandLine` column, it is evident that there are encoded command lines. The command lines are Base64 encoded and are part of a PowerShell command. This is a common technique used by attackers to obfuscate their actions and evade detection. It's recommended to further investigate these events for potential security threats.

Figure 5.30 – Security Copilot identifies Base64-encoded command lines

As noted earlier, Security Copilot does not show all columns in its displayed output. To view the Base64-encoded command line it identified, click the *enlarge* icon or use the **Export to Excel** feature within the response.

To conclude, having examined the essential elements of crafting effective security prompts along with various helpful tips, we will now shift our focus to best practices in prompt engineering in the next section.

Prompt engineering best practices and error handling

While knowing how to formulate effective prompts is helpful, following best practices can further improve your results. Effective prompt engineering can enhance your interactions with Security Copilot.

By implementing best practices and mastering error handling, you can navigate potential challenges more effectively. In the following sections, we will dive into some of the best practices and provide examples to illustrate how to refine your approach for maximum effectiveness.

Harnessing Security Copilot's knowledge and capabilities

Security Copilot excels in many areas that may sometimes go unnoticed. To get the most value out of Security Copilot, you are encouraged to explore and make the most of its capabilities. For your reference, here's a rundown of some areas where Security Copilot excels. You can craft specific prompts to leverage these capabilities:

- **Information at your fingertips:** Security Copilot provides you with a wealth of cybersecurity insights, including attack techniques, vulnerabilities, threat intelligence, trends, recommendations, playbooks, and much more. Think of Security Copilot as your trusted and reliable assistant in cybersecurity, equipped with encyclopedic knowledge and ready to support you with any questions you may have. This empowers you to quickly grasp important information and stay informed.
- **Support for incident response:** When a security incident occurs, Security Copilot can assist you with incident response. It can help you assess the situation, prioritize tasks, provide a playbook for responding to incidents, outline the actions you can take, protocols for internal and external communication, and more. If you find yourself stuck or needing guidance during your analysis or investigation, give Security Copilot a try.
- **Dissecting attack techniques:** Security Copilot excels at breaking down and explaining various attack methods, techniques, typical attacker behaviors, and associated IoCs, enabling faster investigation and more informed response decisions.
- **Spotting suspicious behavior:** Security Copilot is great at sifting through log data to identify suspicious activities, including unusual processes and events, while also extracting key IoCs and entities such as IPs, URLs, file hashes, domains, and so on.
- **Script analysis:** Security Copilot excels at analyzing complex scripts, command lines, registry keys, and much more. It can break down the logic and flow of scripts, identifying key functions, suspicious behaviors, and hidden operations. This helps you quickly understand the script's intent without manual review. As it analyzes scripts, Security Copilot also extracts relevant IoCs and presents them in a clear, actionable format for further investigation.

- **Decoding obfuscated content and reverse engineering**: Malicious scripts often use obfuscation techniques, such as Base64 encoding, string manipulation, or dynamic execution, to evade detection. Security Copilot can automatically decode and de-obfuscate them, revealing the real code and intent beneath the layers.
- **General data analysis**: Security Copilot can help you analyze compromised user account events, evaluate device policies, configuration, and status, distinguish between normal activity and potential threats for suspicious behavior detected, and more.
- **Creating and analyzing KQL queries**: Security Copilot can help you create KQL queries. It can also analyze queries, breaking down their functionality to help you understand how they work and what results they produce.
- **Helpful recommendations**: Security Copilot can offer you practical advice, including the following:
    - Suggested actions
    - Steps for remediation
    - Preventative measures

  Please note that, depending on the prompt and context provided, the recommendations can be specifically tailored or broader to reflect general best practices. They may not cover every specific action required for remediation or preventative measures.
- **Reporting and summarization**: Security Copilot can generate clear reports and summaries for you. This includes summaries for public documents or an incident report at the end of your Copilot session. It can also tailor its content to suit the intended audience.
- **Strengthening security posture**: Security Copilot helps you figure out whether your organization is vulnerable to known threats, prioritizes risks, and offers clear steps to address them.
- **Data correlation**: Security Copilot is able to correlate different sets of data, enhancing your understanding of security incidents.
- **Ensuring compliance**: You can use Security Copilot to verify compliance with security policies and regulations, ensuring that all aspects are being monitored effectively.
- **Deep, product-specific insights into Microsoft solutions**: Because Security Copilot is tightly integrated with Microsoft products, it can surface detailed insights into product configuration settings that are not commonly found in public documentation.

Security Copilot, as an AI solution, can significantly enhance your cybersecurity efforts. By focusing on its features, particularly the lesser-known ones, you can maximize its effectiveness. You'll notice different prompts leveraging these capabilities and features as we explore additional case studies in *Chapters 8*, *9*, and *10*.

Now, let's shift our focus to the next best practice recommendation, pertaining to plugins.

Choose your preferred plugin

When working with Security Copilot, utilizing specific plugins can enhance your experience by tailoring the tool to meet your unique needs. Each plugin is designed to address particular tasks or provide specialized functionalities.

In the standalone experience of Security Copilot, you can select a specific skill or capability within a plugin to complete a specific task. This is achieved through the **System Capabilities** menu, which you can access from the prompt bar.

However, rather than navigating to the **System Capabilities** menu every time to select the right plugin and its specific skill, you can also specify what you would like to use by directly mentioning it in your prompt. This not only saves you a few clicks each time but also enables automation.

For instance, you can structure your prompt by stating the specific plugin you would like Security Copilot to use: `Using the Copilot for Security Generic plugin, can you…`. The next screenshot illustrates this:

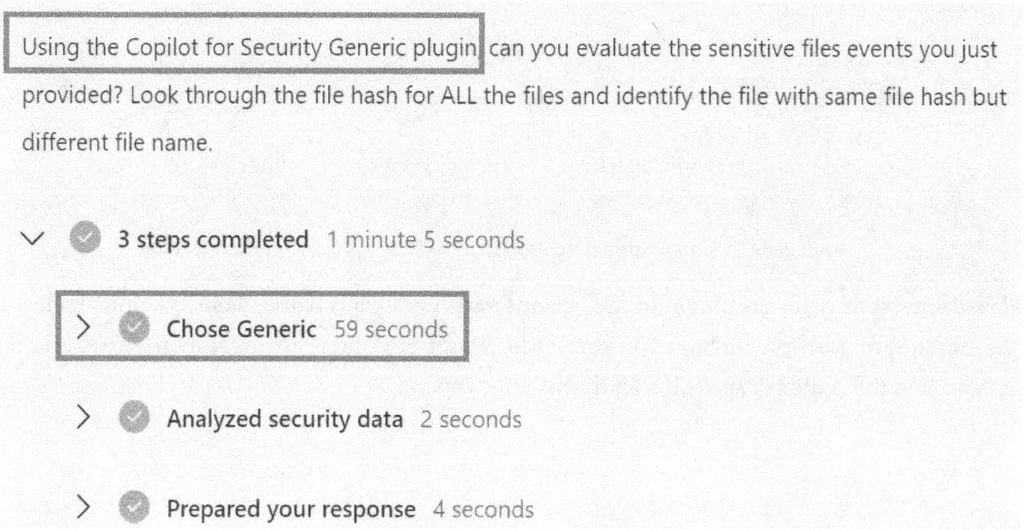

Figure 5.31 – Instruct which plugin you would like to use in a prompt

This approach is particularly useful when you have to provide multiple parameters for the skill in a plugin. As an example, the following screenshot illustrates how a plugin skill requires the analyst to manually fill in three parameters:

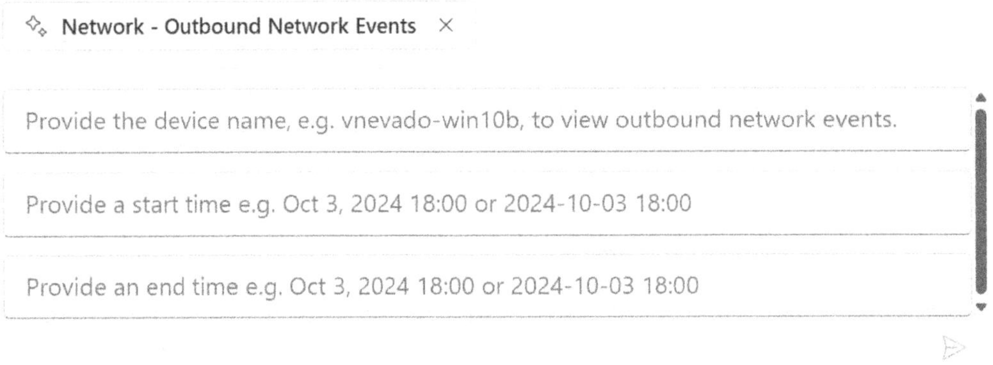

Figure 5.32 – Parameters needed for a plugin skill

Instead, it's much faster and more efficient to use natural language to specify the skill, the plugin, and all the parameters directly within the prompt, as shown next:

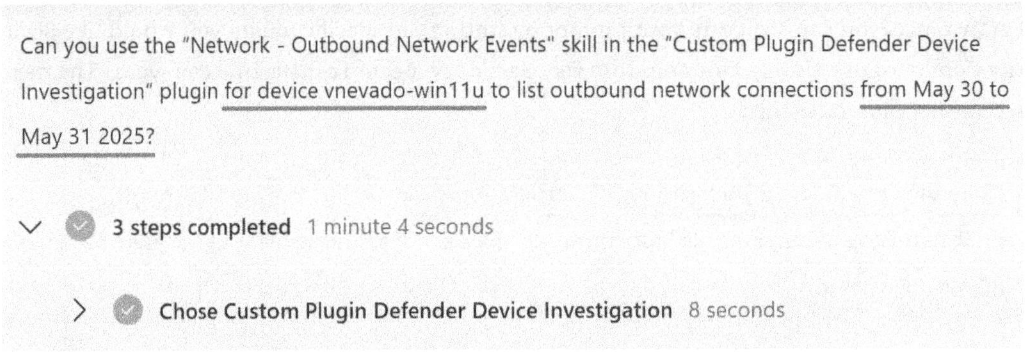

Figure 5.33 – Using natural language to set skill, plugin, and parameters

Please note, specifying the plugin in the prompt may not always work. Security Copilot selects the most appropriate plugin based on keywords in your prompt, previous responses within the session, and the skills or capabilities it deems relevant.

This limitation is illustrated in the next screenshot:

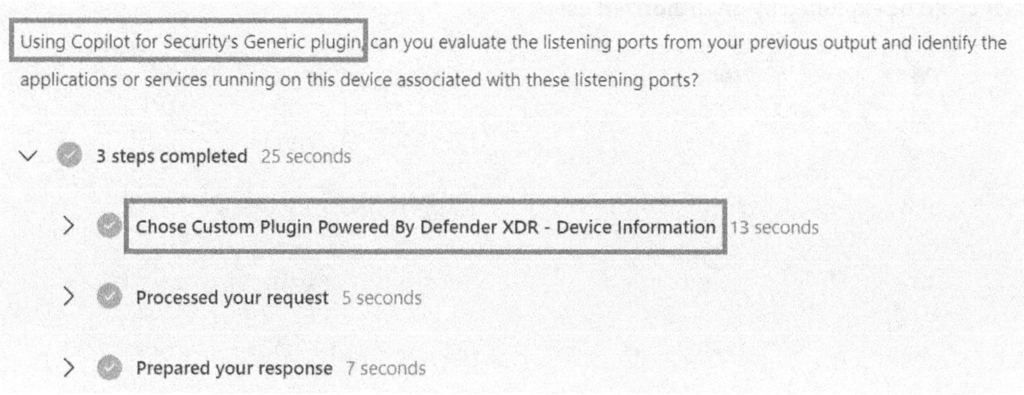

Figure 5.34 – Security Copilot picks a different plugin than the one specified in the prompt

One helpful tip to solve this problem is to be more specific in your prompt and avoid using keywords that might trigger a different plugin. The new prompt, displayed next, adds additional context about what needs to be accomplished, which helps Security Copilot select the desired plugin:

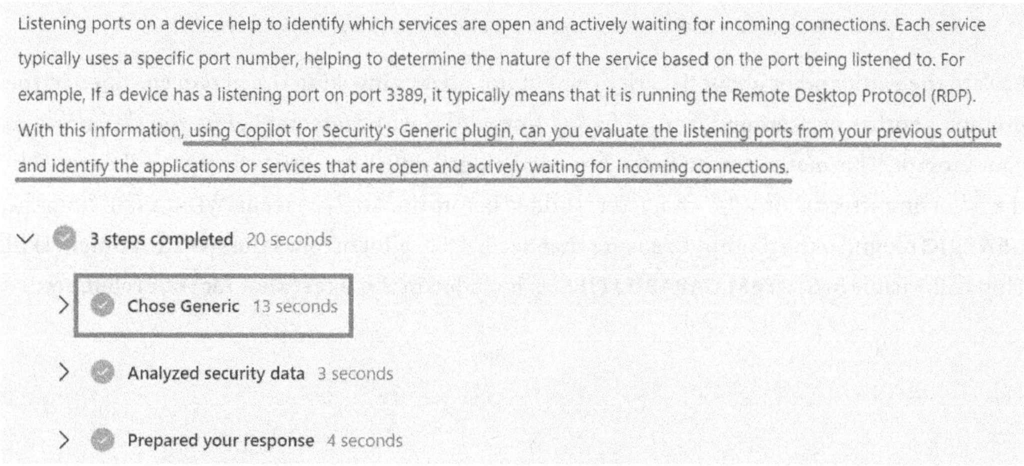

Figure 5.35 – Being more specific and avoiding using keywords may help

Here's an interesting observation for your awareness: the response from Security Copilot outlines the applications and services currently waiting for incoming connections. You can see that **Remote Desktop Protocol** (**RDP**) is active and accepting connections on this device.

This information can be crucial for security monitoring, as it highlights potential entry points that could be exploited by unauthorized users:

Port	Process	Application/Service
135	svchost.exe	RPC Endpoint Mapper
139	ntoskrnl.exe	NetBIOS Session Service
445	ntoskrnl.exe	Microsoft-DS (Active Directory, SMB)
3389	svchost.exe	Remote Desktop Protocol (RDP)
5040	svchost.exe	Windows Event Collector
7680	svchost.exe	Unknown Service
42050	microsoft.sharepoint.exe	Microsoft SharePoint

Figure 5.36 – RDP is active and accepting connections on this device

Back to the earlier point about Security Copilot not always invoking the plugin specified in the prompt, another workaround is to add a "/" (forward slash) character before the skill name in your prompt. This method ensures the intended plugin skill is invoked reliably. As illustrated in the following screenshot, a "/" character is added before the **AnalyzeSecurityData** skill from the **GENERIC** plugin in the prompt to ensure that Security Copilot invokes the specified plugin skill. This skill, visible in **SYSTEM CAPABILITIES**, is included in the screenshot for your reference:

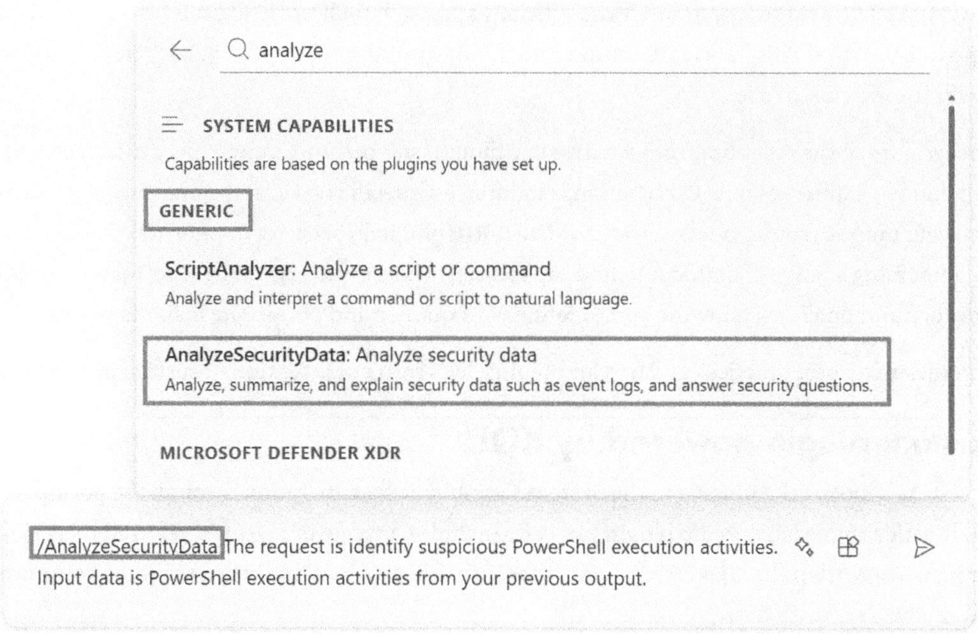

Figure 5.37 – A "/" character is added before the AnalyzeSecurityData skill in the prompt

When this prompt is executed, Security Copilot invokes the **AnalyzeSecurityData** skill within the **GENERIC** plugin, as illustrated in the next screenshot:

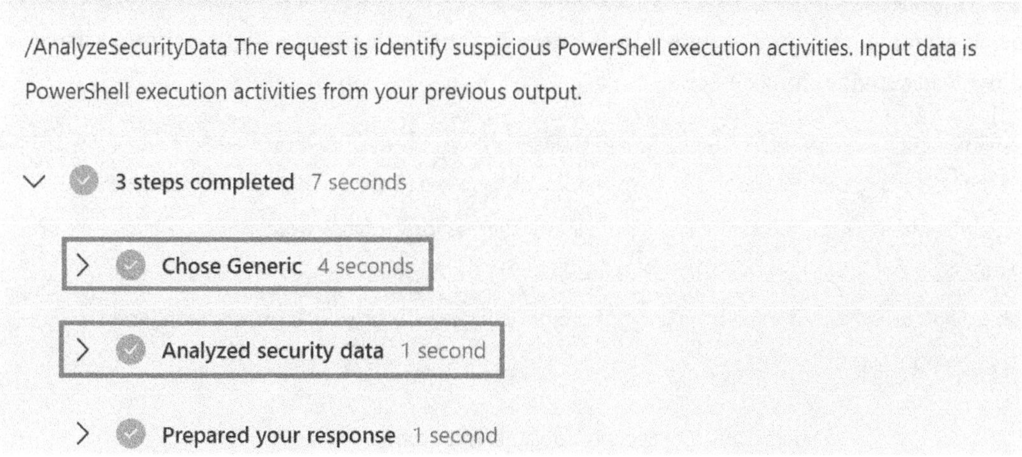

Figure 5.38 – Security Copilot invokes the AnalyzeSecurityData skill within the GENERIC plugin

As of May 2025, a more streamlined and efficient approach to direct skill invocation is available in private preview. This new feature functions similarly to the "/" approach but offers improved reliability and ease of use.

Furthermore, if the response from a particular plugin isn't meeting your expectations, consider switching to a different one. Each plugin is tailored for specific tasks, and some may align better with your unique requirements. Often, the **GENERIC** plugin in Security Copilot acts as a catch-all, encompassing a range of undocumented capabilities. This versatility can help you access a wider array of functionalities, allowing you to refine your queries and obtain the insights you need.

After reviewing best practices and tips for plugins, let's turn our attention to custom plugins next.

Custom plugin powered by KQL

If you take a look at the plugins in the **System Capabilities** menu option through the prompt bar, you'll notice that each specific plugin typically includes a range of features, referred to as skills. For instance, within the **GENERIC** plugin, there are skills such as **Analyze a script or command** and **Analyze security data**.

Additionally, you've seen how a KQL query can be incorporated in a prompt to retrieve specific events and data for Security Copilot to analyze. While this method is effective, a more efficient approach is to convert the KQL query into a skill in a custom plugin. This way, rather than executing the KQL query directly in the prompt, you can simply call the skill in the custom plugin to run it.

As an example, the prompt shown in the next screenshot features a KQL query that lists file download activities for a device.

Can you run the following KQL query to report on file download activities? Then examine its output. Here is the KQL query: DeviceFileEvents | where Timestamp between (datetime(2024-10-03) .. datetime(2024-10-04)) | where DeviceName contains "ash-irvins1"| where isnotempty(FileOriginUrl) and ActionType == "FileCreated"| project Timestamp, DeviceName, ActionType, FileName, FolderPath, FileOriginUrl, InitiatingProcessFileName, InitiatingProcessAccountName, InitiatingProcessCommandLine | sort by Timestamp desc

Figure 5.39 – The Security Copilot prompt containing a KQL query

It's cumbersome to copy and paste the KQL query into a prompt every time. By converting this KQL query into a custom plugin, you can directly call it through a skill in a custom plugin.

The next screenshot illustrates that a skill called **ListFilesDownloaded** is available in a plugin named **CUSTOM PLUGIN DEFENDER DEVICE INVESTIGATION**. The plugin can be accessed through the **System Capabilities** menu option via the prompt bar:

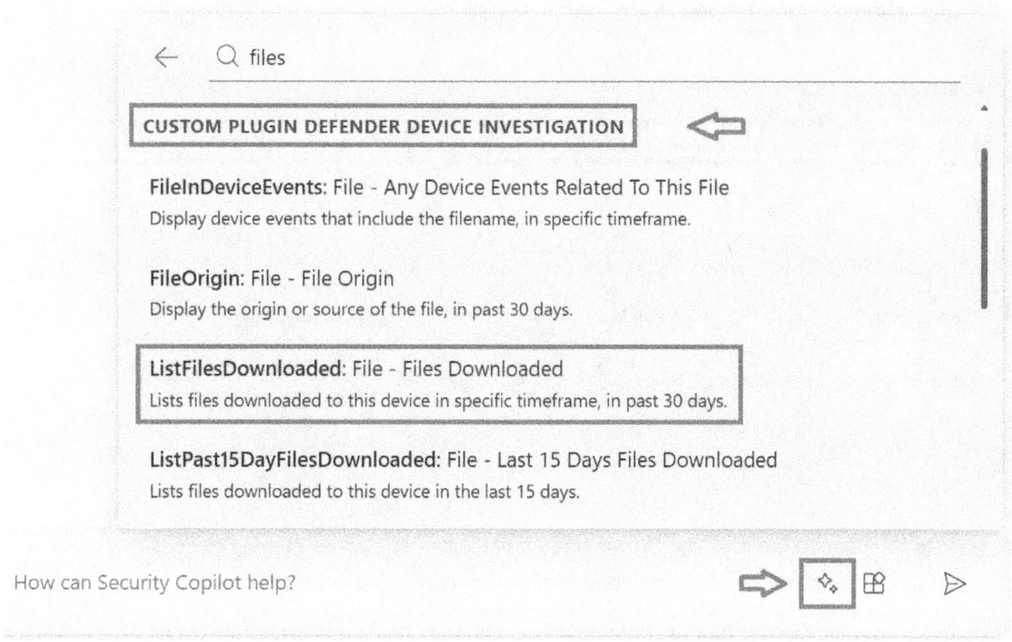

Figure 5.40 – The KQL query is converted into a skill

Once you select and run this skill, Security Copilot provides the same file download activities as the previous prompt containing the KQL query, as shown next:

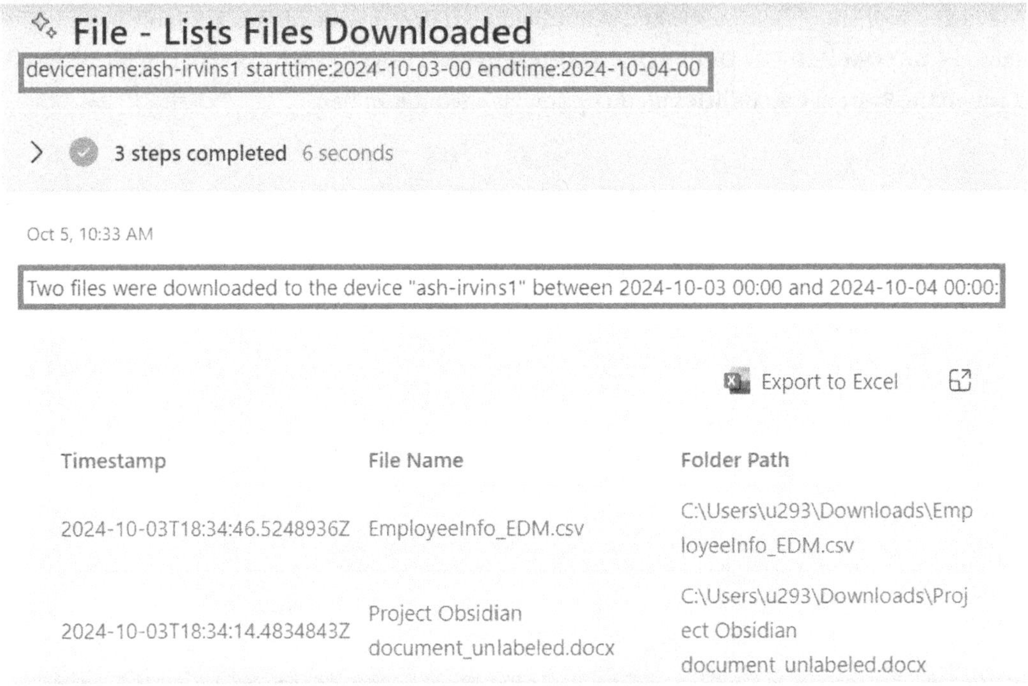

Figure 5.41 – File downloaded activities reported by Security Copilot

A skill in the custom plugin also offers additional advantages. For starters, it can be reused often across various projects or teams. Additionally, it can be easily shared with anyone who needs it. Plus, Security Copilot can call the custom plugin at any time, ensuring smooth integration into existing workflows.

There are several types of custom plugins: API based plugins, GPT-based plugins, and KQL-based plugins. Our focus here is the KQL-based plugin, which, as you've seen, enables you to define the KQL query as a skill in a custom plugin.

Creating a KQL-based plugin is simple and straightforward. The overall process can be summarized in three steps:

1. Identify the KQL query you want to include in the custom plugin.
2. Add the KQL query into a YAML template file.
3. Upload the YAML file to Security Copilot.

There are many resources available to help you find or develop KQL queries during *step 1*. For *step 2*, adding the KQL query to a YAML file is also straightforward.

A YAML file uses plain text and a straightforward structure to describe data. It offers a simple way to organize and store information in a format that is easy to read and understand. Think of it like a neatly arranged list or a recipe. The next screenshot shows a snippet of a YAML file defining a custom plugin titled **Custom Plugin Defender Device Investigation**. One of the skills outlined in the YAML file is also visible in the screenshot: **ListFilesDownloaded**.

Figure 5.42 – A snippet of a YAML file

You can include many KQL queries in a YAML file, with each query serving as a separate skill for the custom plugin. For your reference, here is a list of skills for this particular custom plugin named **Custom Plugin Defender Device Investigation**:

- **File - Last 15 Days Files Downloaded**
- **File - Lists Files Downloaded**
- **File - Lists Sensitive Files Events**
- **Process - Process Executions Summary**
- **Process - Detailed Process Executions**

- **Lateral Movement - RDP To Device**
- **Lateral Movement - Last 10 Days RDP To Device**
- **Lateral Movement - Logon To Device**
- **Lateral Movement - Logons To Device In Last 10 Days**
- **Network - Outbound Network Events**
- **Network - Inbound Network Events**
- **Network - Device Listening Ports**
- **Device Events - Scheduled Task Events**
- **Device Events - User Account Events**
- **Device Events - User Account Added Or Removed From Local Group**
- **Suspicious Activities - ASR Rules Triggered**
- **Suspicious Activities - Device ASMSI Script Detection**
- **Suspicious Activities - Exploit Guard Events**
- **Suspicious Activities - Network Protection Events**
- **Suspicious Activities - Device Tampering Attempts**

This custom plugin's YAML file, along with several others, is available for you to download from this book's GitHub repository at `https://github.com/PacktPublishing/Microsoft-Copilot-for-Security/tree/main/Plugins`. Please note, these YAML files contain KQL queries designed to run in the Microsoft Defender XDR's Advanced Hunting environment.

You then upload YAML files to your Security Copilot environment in order to use these custom plugins. The procedure for uploading a YAML file to Security Copilot is outlined in *Chapter 4*, and it only takes a few clicks to complete.

The KQL-based plugin lets you extract specific cyber telemetry data from various sources using KQL queries. You can then use other Security Copilot plugins to analyze this data. Additionally, these prompts can be automated through promptbooks, which we will discuss in *Chapter 6*.

Now that you've explored custom plugins with KQL, let's dive into how using a KQL template in your prompts can help Security Copilot generate more accurate KQL queries.

Using a KQL template for Security Copilot

KQL is a robust and versatile query language built to enable efficient analysis of large datasets. Its ability to quickly process and extract insights from a vast amount of data in real time makes it an invaluable asset for organizations.

You've discovered that a KQL query can be integrated into a prompt to retrieve specific data for Security Copilot to analyze. Even more powerful, you've seen firsthand how a KQL query can be transformed into a custom plugin, unlocking additional functionality.

In addition to these capabilities, Security Copilot can also generate KQL queries for you. However, there may be instances where it doesn't produce the desired query. This can happen because the KQL syntax and available data can vary depending on the environment in which it's used. For example, the schema tables and fields in KQL queries for **Microsoft Defender XDR** can differ from those in **Microsoft Sentinel**.

As a best practice, using a template in your prompts can help provide Security Copilot with the necessary information, thereby reducing confusion and enabling it to generate more accurate KQL queries.

For example, as mentioned in the blog post *Tip: Using KQL Request Templates for Copilot for Security* (`https://rodtrent.substack.com/p/tip-using-kql-request-templates-for`), you can use the following template to generate a proper KQL query for Microsoft Sentinel:

```
Table = <tablename>
Time/Date range = <time range>
Query = <query processing example: the top medium severity alert and the
number of times is shows up in the data>
Display = <how the results are displayed example: just the alert name and
the times it shows up>
```

Quick tip: Enhance your coding experience with the **AI Code Explainer** and **Quick Copy** features. Open this book in the next-gen Packt Reader. Click the **Copy** button **(1)** to quickly copy code into your coding environment, or click the **Explain** button **(2)** to get the AI assistant to explain a block of code to you.

The next-gen Packt Reader is included for free with the purchase of this book. Scan the QR code OR go to `packtpub.com/unlock`, then use the search bar to find this book by name. Double-check the edition shown to make sure you get the right one.

The template lets you provide the necessary information for Security Copilot to generate more accurate KQL queries based on your requirements, such as the specific schema table to use or the intended outcome.

While using a template can help Security Copilot generate more reliable KQL queries, it's also important to consider how AI behavior in Security Copilot can influence its results. Let's take a closer look at that next.

AI in action – expect variability in your results

Since Security Copilot is AI-powered, running the same prompt just minutes apart can produce slightly different results, often in the wording or formatting of the output.

In some cases, there may be more differences. For example, the KQL query specified in the prompt may not be identical to the KQL query executed by Security Copilot. This is because Security Copilot interprets the input from the prompt to generate a tailored query, which often differs in syntax from the original query. Therefore, the output may not always align precisely with your expectations.

The following screenshot demonstrates that Security Copilot executed a modified version of the KQL query specified in the prompt:

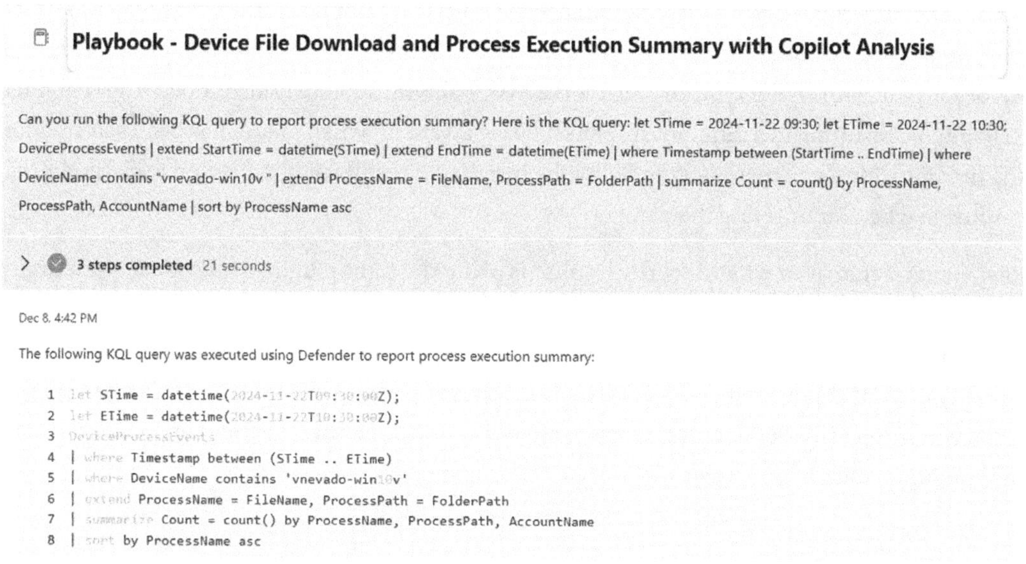

Figure 5.43 – The KQL query in the prompt differs from the one executed by Security Copilot

Furthermore, running the same prompt days or months apart may lead to even more noticeable differences, especially if the underlying data has changed or the AI model has been updated. This variability is a natural outcome of AI systems that adapt to new information and data inputs.

For this reason, it's a good idea to keep your old Security Copilot sessions, as they may contain historical responses that can't be recreated later. These past sessions can be useful for reviewing previous results, preserving investigation evidence, spotting trends over time, or referencing specific details that may no longer be accessible due to data changes or model updates.

With this in mind, let's shift focus to the next section, which covers common errors you may encounter in Security Copilot and tips on how to address them.

Common error handling

If the response from Security Copilot isn't what you expected, check which plugin was invoked. Choosing the right plugin is important, as the Copilot response can vary depending on the plugin used. If Security Copilot selects an unintended plugin, or it fails to choose one and times out, you can guide Security Copilot by explicitly specifying the desired plugin and its skill in the prompt, as covered earlier in this chapter.

Different security solutions can offer similar insights. For instance, both Microsoft Defender XDR and **Microsoft Defender Threat Intelligence** (**MDTI**) provide vulnerability data, though their approaches and focus areas differ. As noted earlier, Security Copilot results may vary based on the plugin selected. For a prompt such as `Give me an overview of the latest threats to my organization`, Copilot typically selects the MDTI plugin, but it may also choose the Defender XDR plugin, resulting in a different response. Being aware of which plugin has been selected for the prompt allows you to understand why the insights or results may differ and avoid potential confusion when interpreting the data.

Keep in mind that even when Security Copilot is using the right plugin, its response sometimes can still be less than ideal; perhaps the wording or formatting is not what you prefer. In such cases, try to run the prompt again, as you may receive a different but more useful result. Since Security Copilot is powered by AI, its responses can vary even when you use the same prompt. Skills within Security Copilot plugins try to answer questions as best as they can, but variations in formatting, details, and items may vary.

> Note
>
> Currently, Security Copilot can only access data from one plugin at a time. For example, when you request the latest threats in the prompt, Security Copilot can gather this data either from the MDTI plugin or the Defender XDR plugin, but not both. Security Copilot does not have visibility across all data sources when responding to a prompt. Work is underway for future capability to allow Security Copilot to retrieve data from multiple plugins at the same time. This will enable Security Copilot to pull and correlate insights across more than one source, leading to more comprehensive results.

Security Copilot sometimes may not respond as effectively when the prompt is written in a language other than English. In such cases, try replacing key terms with their English equivalents or consider rewriting the prompt entirely in English for better results.

At times, Security Copilot can be sensitive to the exact wording used in a prompt. For instance, asking it to list the total number of incidents *closed* in the last 7 days may not yield a response. However, replacing the word *closed* with *resolved* allows Security Copilot to respond as expected. This is because, in Microsoft Defender XDR, incidents can be *resolved*, but there is no option to *close* them.

The following screenshot displays the Security Copilot prompt using the keyword *closed*, which results in an error:

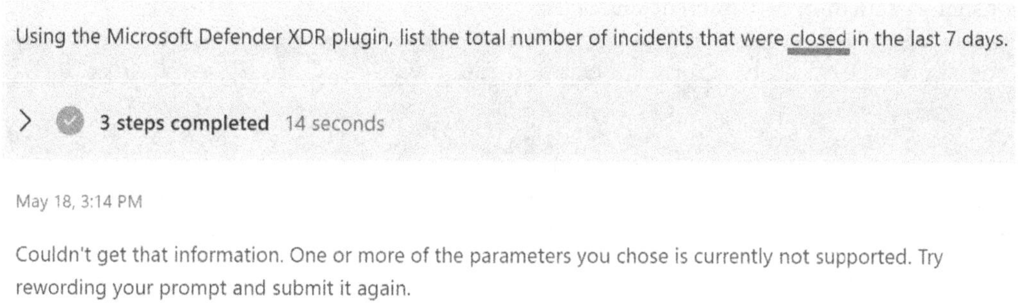

Figure 5.44 – Security Copilot prompt containing the keyword "closed"

As shown next, the same prompt, with the keyword *closed* replaced by *resolved*, runs successfully and returns results:

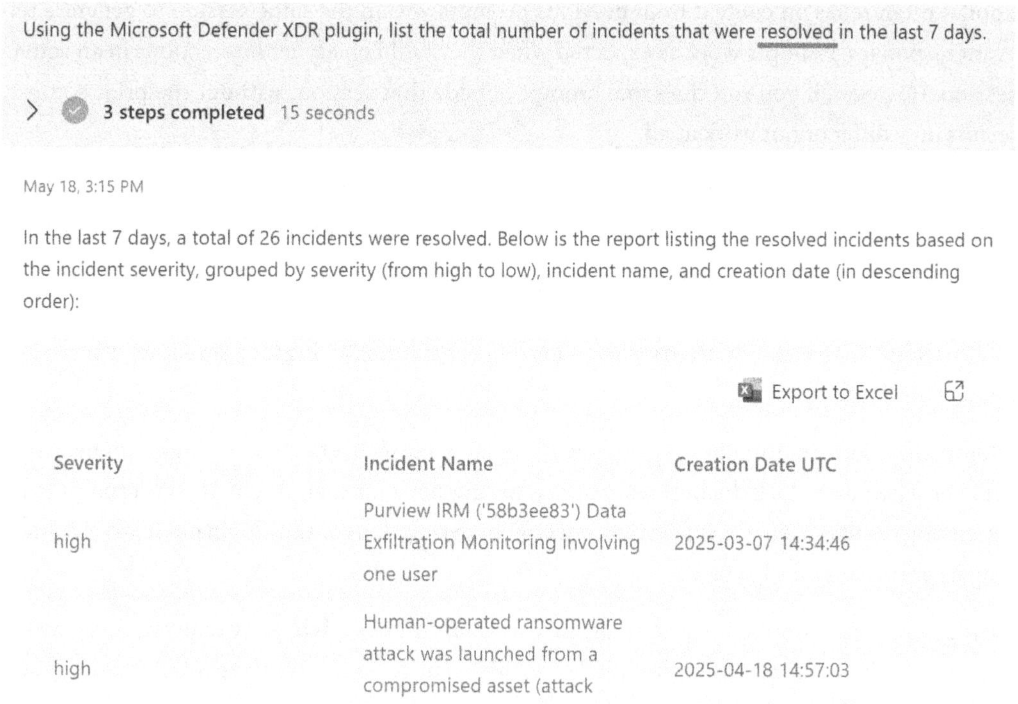

Figure 5.45 – Security Copilot prompt containing the keyword "resolved"

Sometimes, Security Copilot struggles with processing multiple requests in a prompt, even when only one plugin is invoked. For example, the following prompt results in an error because it asks for sign-in data from two different source IPs:

```
For the past 25 days, based on the sign-in activity for user Lee Gu,
can you provide the date and time when user Lee Gu signed in from IP
137.117.84.85 and 20.185.147.193?
```

In such cases, having Security Copilot perform only one task may fix the issue. In this example, once the prompt is revised to request sign-in data from just one source IP, Security Copilot executes successfully:

```
For the past 25 days, based on the sign-in activity for user Lee Gu,
can you provide the date and time when user Lee Gu signed in from IP
137.117.84.85?
```

Another consideration to keep in mind is Security Copilot's session awareness capability. Security Copilot often relies on context from previous prompts within the same session to generate relevant responses. Prompts work as expected when they build on earlier interactions in an active session. However, if you run the same prompt outside that session, without the prior context, results may differ or not work at all.

Security Copilot is great at tracking and retaining information discussed during a session. However, it can occasionally become fixated on previously provided information, which may hinder its responsiveness to new requests within the same session. If you notice that Copilot isn't behaving as expected, starting a new session can often help reset its context and clear any lingering information. This fresh start often resolves any odd behavior, allowing for a smoother interaction moving forward.

Additionally, Security Copilot may not always reliably notify users when a plugin has been disabled or when users lack the necessary access permissions for that plugin. If your prompt isn't generating results when you expect it to, check your permissions or the plugin menu to see which plugins are enabled or disabled.

If the prompt execution returns an error, such as **Couldn't complete your request**, this may be because the allowed limit has been exceeded. While Security Copilot may suggest rewording your prompt, it actually implies that you should narrow down the scope of your prompt, for instance, try adjusting the search timeframe to a shorter duration.

The screenshot shown next displays the error message. Notice that the timeframe set for this prompt is from September 10th to October 5th:

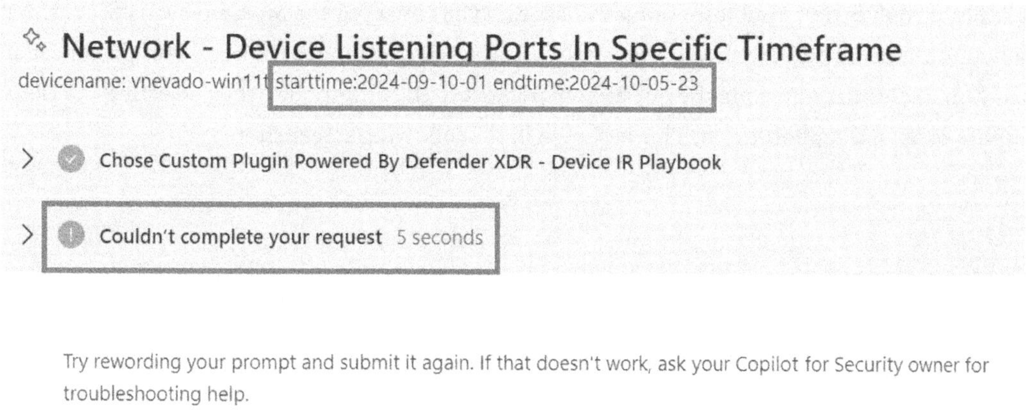

Figure 5.46 – Error message seen in Security Copilot

If you run the exact same prompt but with a shorter timeframe, such as from October 3rd to October 5th, it executes successfully. This is illustrated in the next screenshot:

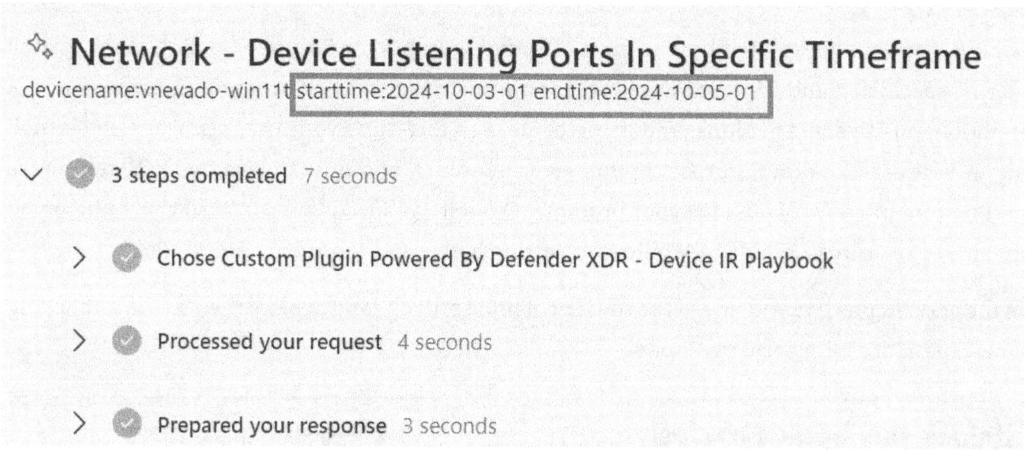

Figure 5.47 – Prompt successfully runs when the timeframe is shorter

Broad prompts that attempt to ask for too much information or retrieve a large volume of data can be difficult for the system to handle. Keeping your request more targeted not only helps to avoid errors but also improves response time and makes the results easier to work with.

The error-handling tips we've covered so far aren't limited to just Security Copilot's standalone experience. They can also apply in the embedded experiences where prompting is supported, such as in MDTI, Advanced Hunting in Microsoft Defender XDR, and others.

Finally, if you've tried troubleshooting the issue on your own but the problem persists, consider opening a support ticket with Microsoft. You can do this by heading to the bottom-right corner of the home screen and clicking the question mark next to the prompt bar, then selecting the **Help** option to open a support ticket. This is shown in the following screenshot:

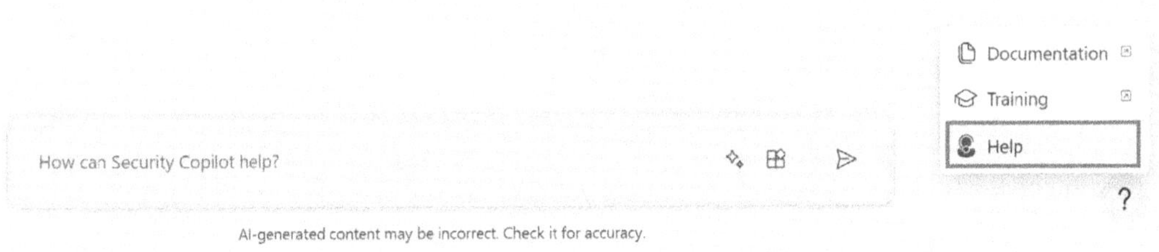

Figure 5.48 – Using the Help option to open a support ticket

Having covered common error handling techniques, let's now summarize the key takeaways from this chapter.

Summary

In this chapter, we explored how to craft effective prompts for Security Copilot, emphasizing clarity, specificity, and context awareness for optimal results. We discussed the importance of iteration, positive instructions, and using context to fine-tune your queries. You also learned about best practices for Security Copilot, error handling, and how to leverage KQL templates and custom plugins to enhance your prompts. Overall, we discussed practical tips to help you maximize Security Copilot's capabilities, ensuring better and more accurate results.

In the next chapter, we will unveil the concept of promptbooks and explore their role in enhancing your experience with Security Copilot.

6

The Power of Promptbooks in Security Copilot

In the previous chapter, we discussed how prompts play a critical role in Security Copilot, acting as a bridge to communicate your requirements and directing the AI to generate relevant and effective responses.

By grouping various prompts together, we can further streamline and enhance the Security Copilot experience. This is accomplished through the idea of a **promptbook**. In this chapter, we will examine the role of promptbooks in Security Copilot, showcasing the range of prebuilt options available and offering guidance on how to create custom promptbooks designed for specific security scenarios.

To guide you through promptbooks and explore their applications, we'll break this chapter into four key sections:

- Demystifying promptbooks – an introduction
- The prebuilt promptbook arsenal
- Tailoring custom promptbooks for security needs
- Promptbooks in action – sample promptbooks and tips

> Want to try out the prompts, custom plugins, and promptbooks featured in this book? Take a look at the book's GitHub repository at `https://github.com/PacktPublishing/Microsoft-Copilot-for-Security`.

Demystifying promptbooks – an introduction

In Security Copilot, a promptbook is essentially a collection of predefined prompts that execute automatically in a designated order to accomplish a specific set of tasks.

Imagine you're planning a party and have a list of tasks to complete. You create a checklist that includes steps such as sending invitations, arranging catering, and setting up decorations, all in the proper order. Similarly, a promptbook functions in a comparable way as the checklist, but with more automation. As an example, the screen capture shown next illustrates a promptbook designed for vulnerability impact assessment:

Prompts (4)

1. Summarize <CVEID> in a short narrative. Indicate if this vulnerability if a remote code execution and if it impacts devices on the Internet. Finally, include a bullet point list of impacted technology for easy reference.
2. Identify any threat intelligence articles or threat actors associated with <CVEID>. Summarize the content and include links to the source content.
3. What mitigations can I put in place to defend against <CVEID>? Lead with specific mitigations and end with generic ones.
4. Write me an executive summary report for the vulnerability, threat actor insights, and recommendations for someone who is less technical.

Figure 6.1 – A promptbook for vulnerability impact assessment

This promptbook consists of four predefined prompts. When it is executed with a given vulnerability, the first prompt summarizes the vulnerability. The next prompt then identifies any relevant threat intelligence data associated with it. The third prompt provides mitigation strategies to defend against this vulnerability. The final prompt delivers an executive summary report of the findings.

Each prompt within the promptbook is configured to execute sequentially, with the current prompt building upon the responses generated by the previous ones. The promptbook functions like a workflow engine that organizes and automates task sequences. This allows analysts to effectively manage and execute a series of interconnected tasks, reducing manual effort and ensuring streamlined processes.

A promptbook can serve multiple functions. It can automate repetitive tasks or act as a structured guide to ensure all necessary actions are completed. Mainly, a promptbook can function as a ready-to-use security playbook that streamlines various aspects of an investigation.

For instance, when responding to a security incident, one or more promptbooks can guide you through the investigation process: from initial incident response and data collection to escalation protocols and post-incident reporting. Each prompt is interconnected, ensuring that the necessary context and information flow seamlessly from one action to the next.

By utilizing promptbooks to automate the sequences of actions typically outlined in security playbooks, routine tasks are transformed into streamlined processes. This approach guides analysts through predefined investigation steps, ensuring that important actions are not overlooked while enhancing efficiency for security teams.

Additionally, promptbooks can be customized to align with your organization's specific workflows, allowing teams to create tailored sequences that reflect their unique processes and compliance requirements. This customization ensures that your security operations are not only efficient but also aligned with your organizational goals.

As we delve deeper into promptbooks and their applications, it will be helpful to start with specific promptbook examples. In the next section, let's examine promptbooks created by others, including those developed by Microsoft, to see their application in different security scenarios.

The prebuilt promptbook arsenal

Upon signing in to your Security Copilot standalone console, you will find a list of promptbooks available for you to use. These include promptbooks that your organization has specifically shared with you, tailored to meet your team's unique needs and workflows. Additionally, you will find global promptbooks that Microsoft has made available to everyone using Security Copilot.

There are multiple ways to access these promptbooks. On the Security Copilot home page in the standalone experience, selecting **View promptbook library** will take you to the list of promptbooks, as illustrated in the next screenshot:

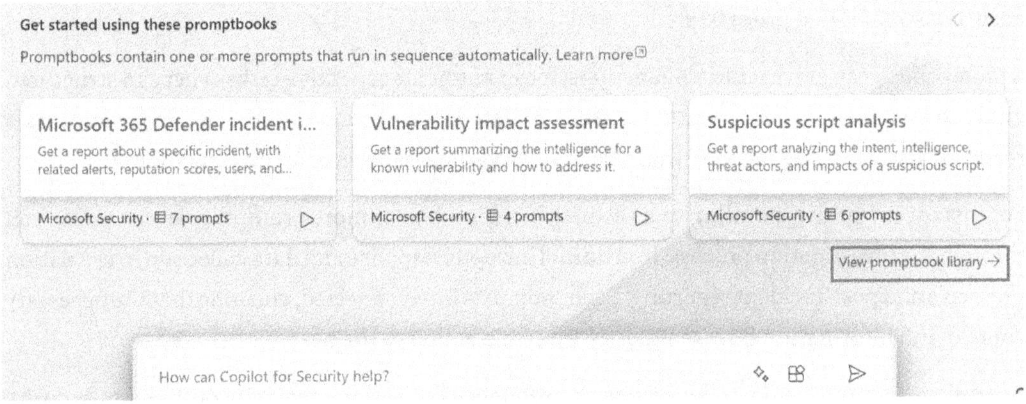

Figure 6.2 – View promptbook library on the Security Copilot home page

Another option is to click the **Prompts** icon in the prompt bar, which then displays a list of promptbooks along with the **See all promptbooks** option. This is illustrated in the next screen capture:

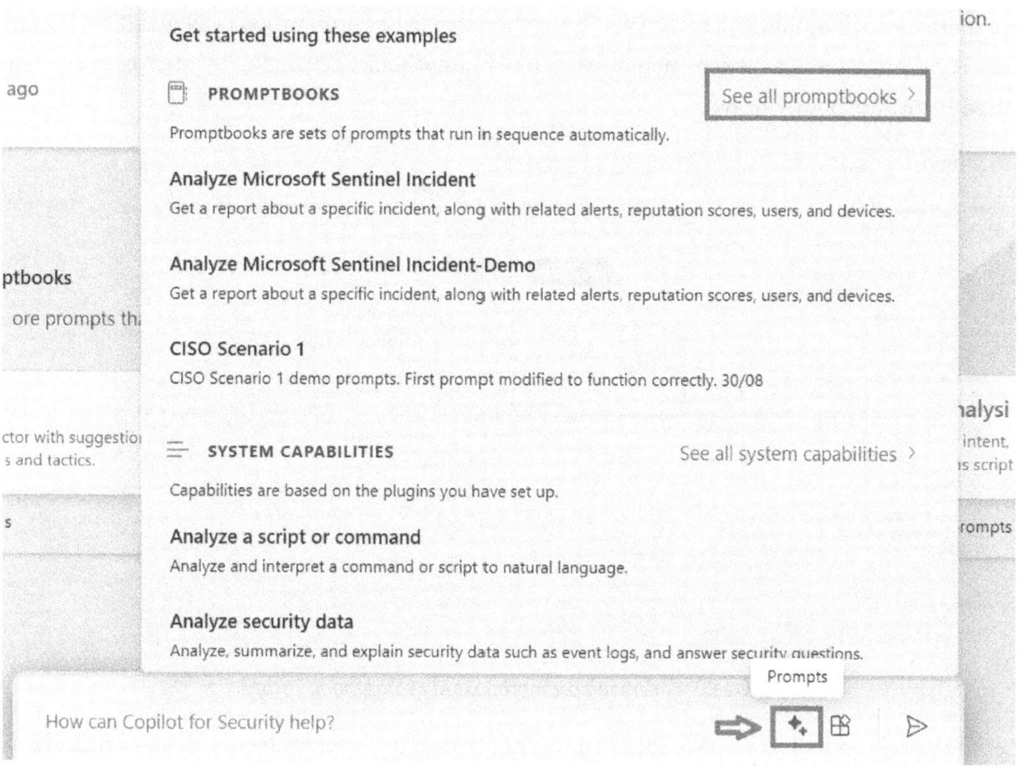

Figure 6.3 – The See all promptbooks option

Lastly, on the Security Copilot home page, the hamburger menu in the upper-left corner takes you to the **Promptbook library** option to access the promptbooks. This is shown in the next screenshot:

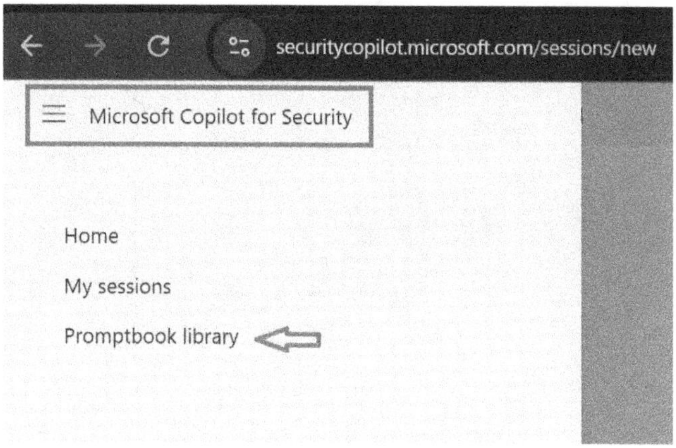

Figure 6.4 – The Promptbook library option from the main menu

No matter which option you select, you'll see the same list of promptbooks available for you to use. For example, the next screenshot lists a few promptbooks developed by Microsoft and featured in **Promptbook library**:

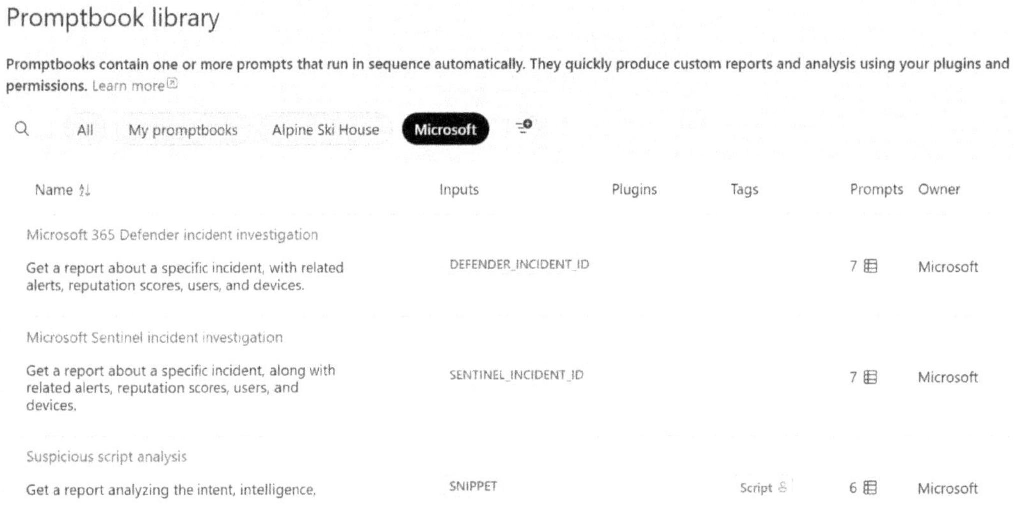

Figure 6.5 – Microsoft promptbooks in Promptbook library

Let's take a closer look at some of these promptbooks next to better understand their capabilities and applications.

Microsoft promptbook – Microsoft 365 Defender incident investigation

The **Microsoft 365 Defender incident investigation** promptbook, provided by Microsoft, is designed to assist analysts in conducting incident investigations within the Microsoft 365 Defender platform.

There are seven predefined prompts in this promptbook, as shown next:

1	Summarize Defender incident <DEFENDER_INCIDENT_ID>.
2	Tell me about the entities associated with that incident.
3	What are the reputation scores for the IPv4 addresses on that incident?
4	Show the authentication methods setup for each user involved in that incident. Especially indicate whether they have MFA enabled.
5	If a user is listed in the incident details, show which devices they have used recently and indicate whether they are compliant with policies.
6	If any devices are listed in the previous output, show details from Intune on the one that checked in most recently. Especially indicate if it is current on all operating system updates.
7	Write an executive report summarizing this investigation. It should be suited for a non-technical audience.

Figure 6.6 – The seven predefined prompts in this promptbook

In a typical investigation, analysts usually start by reviewing the incident alerts and relevant data to get a good overview of the attack. To complement this investigation approach and support the analysts, the first prompt in this promptbook (for all prompts in the following paragraphs, refer to *Figure 6.6*) provides a detailed incident summary.

After a quick review of the incident, analysts then start their investigation into the attack. At some point during the investigation, they proceed to analyze the suspicious entities to gain more context, leverage identified malicious entities to connect the dots, and discover additional suspicious entities or behaviors. To further streamline this process, the second prompt in this promptbook (*Figure 6.6*) automatically retrieves the impacted entities in the incident. In this scenario, Security Copilot typically provides detailed reports on the affected devices, user accounts, IP addresses, files, or URLs associated with the incident.

The promptbook then proceeds to conduct basic investigations on key entities for analysts. The third predefined prompt assesses the reputation of the IP addresses identified in the earlier prompts. The fourth prompt evaluates the authentication methods for potentially compromised user accounts. The fifth prompt reviews the recent devices used by the impacted users, while the sixth prompt gathers details from Intune about these devices.

Finally, the promptbook wraps up with an executive report that highlights the findings derived from the prompts' responses.

This promptbook serves as a good example showcasing how Security Copilot can streamline incident investigation. By offering structured prompts, it supports and guides analysts throughout the investigation process.

To run this promptbook, one of the options is to click **Start new session**. This will launch the promptbook in a new Security Copilot session. Alternatively, a promptbook can also be invoked in an existing session. Most promptbooks require some form of input. For this specific promptbook, you will need to enter the incident ID to fill the **DEFENDER_INCIDENT_ID** field. This process is illustrated in the next screen capture:

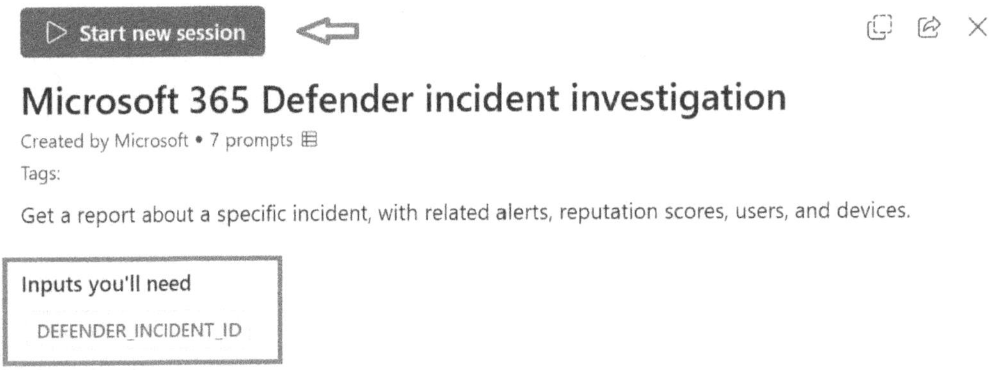

Figure 6.7 – Leveraging Start new session to run the promptbook

Now that you've taken a good and close look at this promptbook, let's quickly review a couple of other promptbooks developed by Microsoft in the next few sections. By illustrating these additional promptbook examples, you should be able to gain a clearer understanding of what promptbooks are, along with their features and benefits.

Microsoft promptbook – Suspicious script analysis

The **Suspicious script analysis** promptbook is also developed by Microsoft for anyone to use. It details what the script does, infers the intent, extracts threat intelligence data and indicators from the script, and offers response actions along with a summary of the findings.

This promptbook includes six predefined prompts, displayed in the next screenshot:

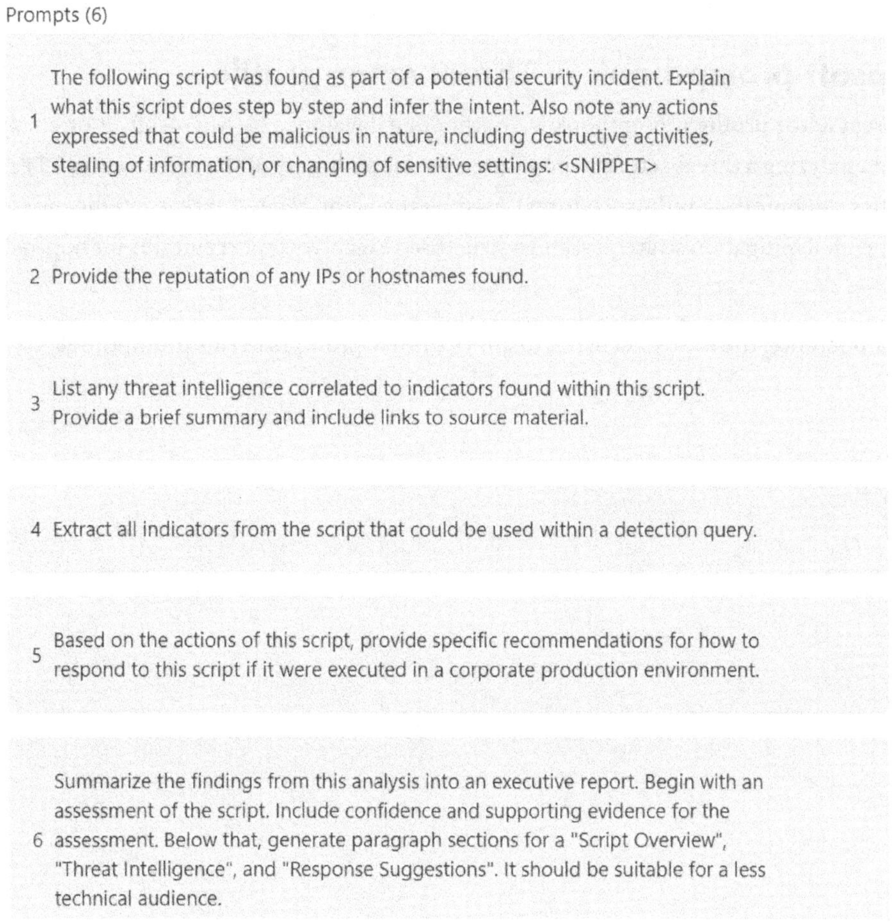

Figure 6.8 – The six predefined prompts in this promptbook

During incident investigation, this promptbook comes in handy for malicious script analysis. Script analysis is one of the powerful features offered by Security Copilot. By offering detailed insights into a script's functionality and intent, it enables security teams to quickly assess the nature of the script and its potential impact. Typically, only a handful of analysts on a security team have the expertise to understand and interpret various scripts, such as PowerShell, JavaScript, VBScript, batch scripts, Python, and others. But now, Security Copilot can quickly decipher and interpret different scripts. The promptbook further enhances this ability by also extracting threat intelligence information and indicators from the scripts, along with the recommendations that equip analysts with actionable steps to mitigate risks.

While this promptbook can be helpful, Microsoft offers additional promptbooks that support security teams. Next, let's take a look at another one for a different security scenario.

Microsoft promptbook – Threat actor profile

The **Threat actor profile** promptbook is another one developed by Microsoft. It offers a framework for analyzing a threat actor by providing a profile summary of the threat actor, **TTPs** (short for **tactics, techniques, and procedures**) used by the actor, related threat intelligence articles, recommended mitigation strategies, and a structured executive report suitable for non-technical audiences.

For your reference, the next screenshot displays the five prompts in this promptbook:

1	Give me a profile summary of <THREATACTORNAME>. Include an executive summary at the start.
2	Summarize the TTPs of this actor using MITRE ATT&CK techniques. Format the output as a bullet point list starting with the technique name and number and include a brief summary. Each technique should be linked directly to the MITRE ATT&CK website.
3	If there are TI articles related to this threat actor, provide a list and summary of them and include links to source material.
4	Based on the actor TTPs, what would be good mitigation or defense methods to protect against this threat actor? Begin with more specific examples and end with generic ones. Format as a table with sections for "category", "description", which includes the work to be done, and "reason" with an example why this related to the threat actor.
5	Summarize the threat actor insights into an executive report. Begin with metadata points for the threat actor including aliases, suspected origin country, industries targeted, vulnerabilities exploited, and tools leveraged. Each of these should be CSV and brief. Below that, include a bullet list of key points about the threat actor as an executive summary. Below that, create paragraph sections for an overview, TTPs, and mitigation strategies. It should be suitable for a less technical audience.

Figure 6.9 – The five predefined prompts in this promptbook

Similar to the other promptbooks we've discussed, this one is also located in the Security Copilot's promptbook library and available for your use. In addition, there are other Microsoft promptbook resources you can utilize. Let's take a look at some of them next.

Microsoft GitHub promptbooks

There are additional Microsoft promptbooks available for you to use. However, most of them are not included in the Security Copilot promptbook library. Instead, you can access and copy these promptbooks from the Microsoft Security Copilot GitHub repository at `https://github.com/Azure/Copilot-For-Security/tree/main/Promptbook%20samples`.

One of the promptbooks available on Microsoft GitHub is **Entra Risky User investigation** (`https://github.com/Azure/Copilot-For-Security/blob/main/Promptbook%20samples/Entra%20Risky%20User%20investigation.md#entra-risky-user-investigation`). This promptbook evaluates whether the identified user is deemed risky. It details the user's authentication methods, recent login attempts with IP addresses, IP reputation assessments, associations with known threat actors, and group memberships. Finally, it offers remediation recommendations and an executive summary of the findings.

This promptbook requires two inputs: the user UPN and the username. Its eight prompts are listed in the next screenshot:

1 Generate a report based on Entra plugin, Is the user <userupn> considered risky? If yes, list the reasons.

2 What authentication methods are enabled for the user <userupn>?

3 Retrieve and list all login attempts made by the user within the past 30 days, along with the corresponding IP addresses used for each login attempt.

4 Provide the reputation of any IPs or hostnames found.

5 If any IP address is found, validate its association with any known Threat actor?

6 List the groups user <username> is part of.

7 Recommend remediation steps to mitigate the user risk.

8 Generate an executive report summarizing insights on a potentially risky user. Commence with metadata details for the user, encompassing their User Principal Name (UPN), suspected country of origin, configured authentication method, and any recorded failed login attempts. Follow this with a bullet-point list outlining key areas requiring remediation to address the identified risks. Subsequently, craft a coherent paragraph elucidating mitigation strategies aimed at ameliorating the highlighted concerns.

Figure 6.10 – The Entra Risky User investigation promptbook

Another promptbook available in the Microsoft GitHub repository is titled **High Risk Assets from the External Attack Surface** (`https://github.com/Azure/Copilot-For-Security/blob/main/Promptbook%20samples/High%20Risk%20Assets%20from%20the%20External%20Attack%20Surface%20Promptbook.md#high-risk-assets-from-the-external-attack-surface`). This promptbook leverages the **Microsoft Defender External Attack Surface Management** and **Microsoft Defender Threat Intelligence** plugins to identify high-risk assets that have been recently targeted. The prompts in this promptbook are shown next:

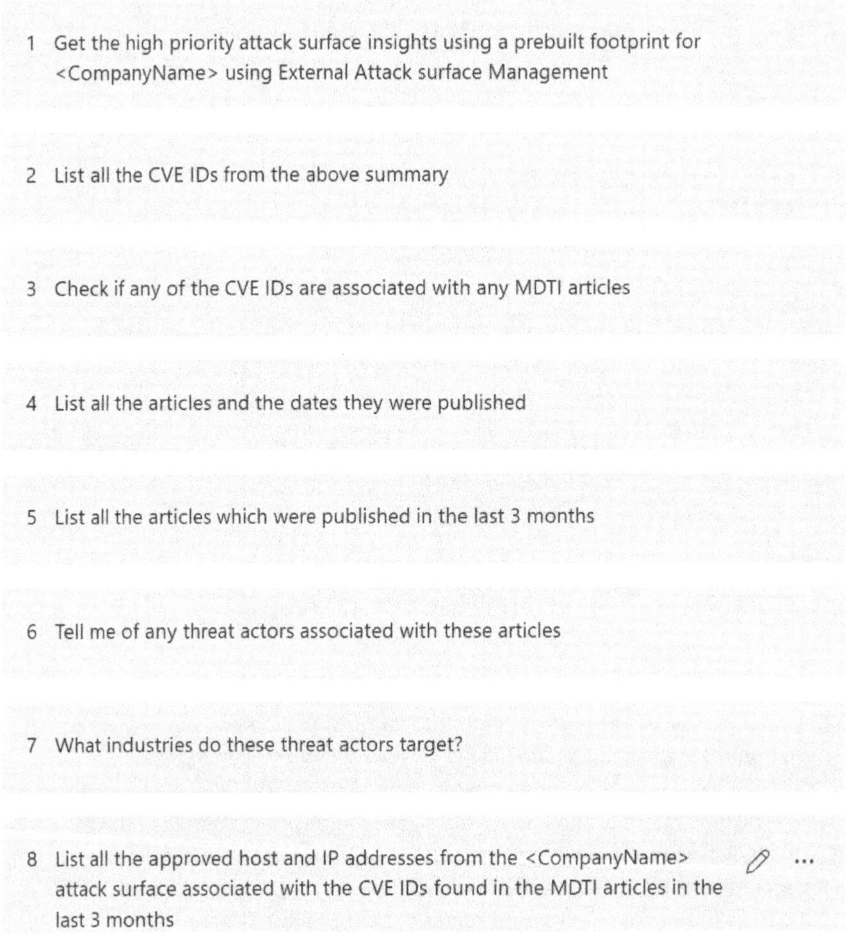

Figure 6.11 – The High Risk Assets from the External Attack Surface promptbook

Another noteworthy one is the **User Sign-In Analysis** promptbook available in the Microsoft GitHub repository. It utilizes the Microsoft Entra and Microsoft Intune plugins to analyze various user sign-in-related events and identify potential risky behaviors. The prompts in this promptbook are shown in the following screenshot:

1 What is <UPN> sign-in history?

2 Are there any failed sign-in attempts? If so, what are the details?

3 What applications has the user accessed during these sign-in events?

4 What device(s) has the user used for these sign-ins? Are these devices compliant and managed?

5 What is the sign-in location and IP address used for sign-in?

6 What is the risk level during sign-in? Are there any detected risk events?

7 What is the user's sign-in status? Are there any failures? If so, what are the reasons for these failures?

8 Does the user's sign-in satisfy the Multi-Factor Authentication (MFA) requirement?

9 What specific conditional access policies were applied during these sign-in events

10 When did the user last change their password?

11 Can you summarize the above investigation and provide a conclusion and recommendation

Figure 6.12 – The User Sign-In Analysis promptbook

Having reviewed many promptbook examples, you might be thinking that while these promptbooks are great, it would be nice to customize them for your own environment. And you can absolutely do that! The promptbook examples we've discussed so far are intended to provide you with ideas for modifying existing promptbooks or creating your own that suit your organization's needs. In the next section, let's look into how to create your own custom promptbooks.

Tailoring custom promptbooks for security needs

Security Copilot offers several options for developing a promptbook that fits your unique requirements. You can create a promptbook from scratch, use prompts from an existing session to assemble your own promptbook, or replicate another promptbook to adapt it to your needs. Let's jump in and discover how to use the different approaches to building promptbooks.

Designing and creating your own promptbook

As you grow more familiar and become skilled at using Security Copilot, you naturally have a list of your favorite prompts that you often rely on. You can turn these prompts into one or more promptbooks to streamline your workflow. The process of creating your own promptbook from scratch is simple and straightforward.

First, you need at least one prompt that has already run in a session to access the option for creating a promptbook. There isn't a direct menu path for creating a new promptbook.

When you go into a Security Copilot session and select one or more prompts, the **Create promptbook** icon at the top switches from being grayed out to active. This is illustrated in the next screen capture. For this example, let's select a single prompt, **Summarize incident 2807**:

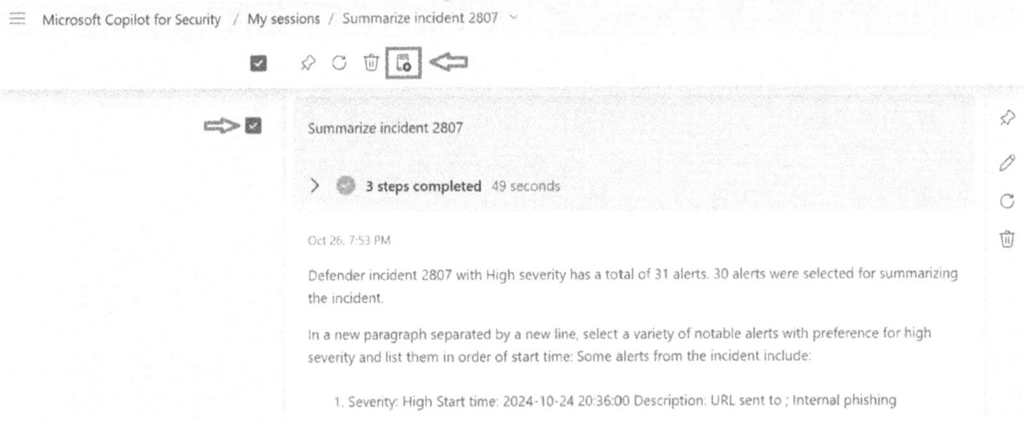

Figure 6.13 – The Create promptbook option

The **Create promptbook** icon looks like a notebook or a book symbol, accompanied by a plus sign (+), as shown next:

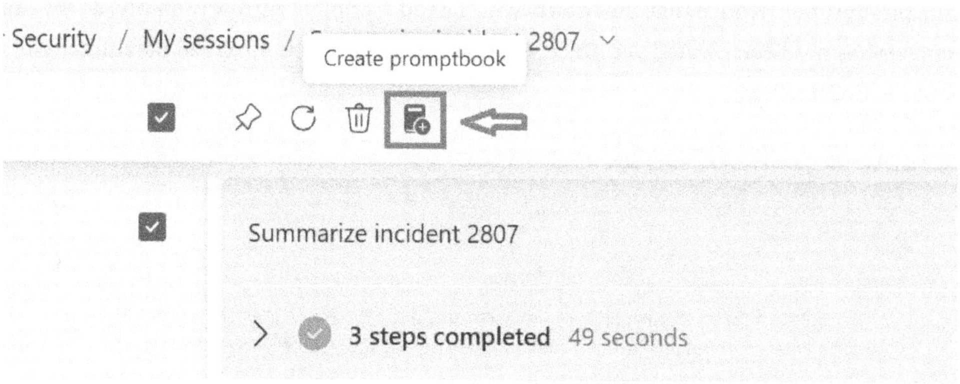

Figure 6.14 – The Create promptbook button

Clicking on this icon opens a new **Create a prompt book** dialog box. This is shown in the next screenshot:

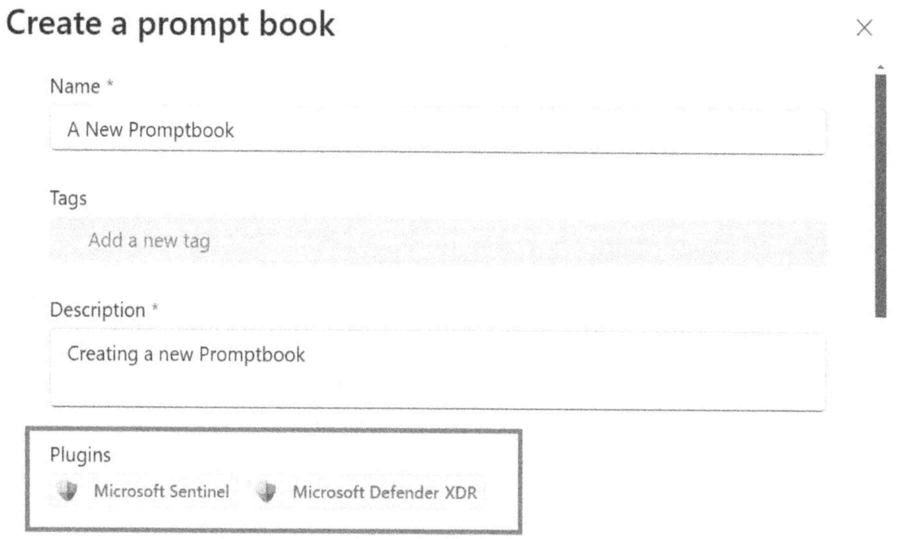

Figure 6.15 – The Create a prompt book dialog box

From the screenshot, you might have noticed that two plugins are prefilled for this new promptbook. This is because the **Summarize incident 2807** prompt is selected for this promptbook. Security Copilot automatically associates the prompt with the relevant plugins. Simply deleting the **Summarize incident 2807** prompt should remove the two plugins.

In the **Prompts** section of the promptbook creation window, shown in the next screen capture, you can modify, add, or delete the prompts. Within the prompt, you can also define the input for the promptbook. Notice that the **Inputs you'll need** section is currently empty, as the input parameter has not been created yet. Once you define the input, the specified parameter will appear in the **Input** section:

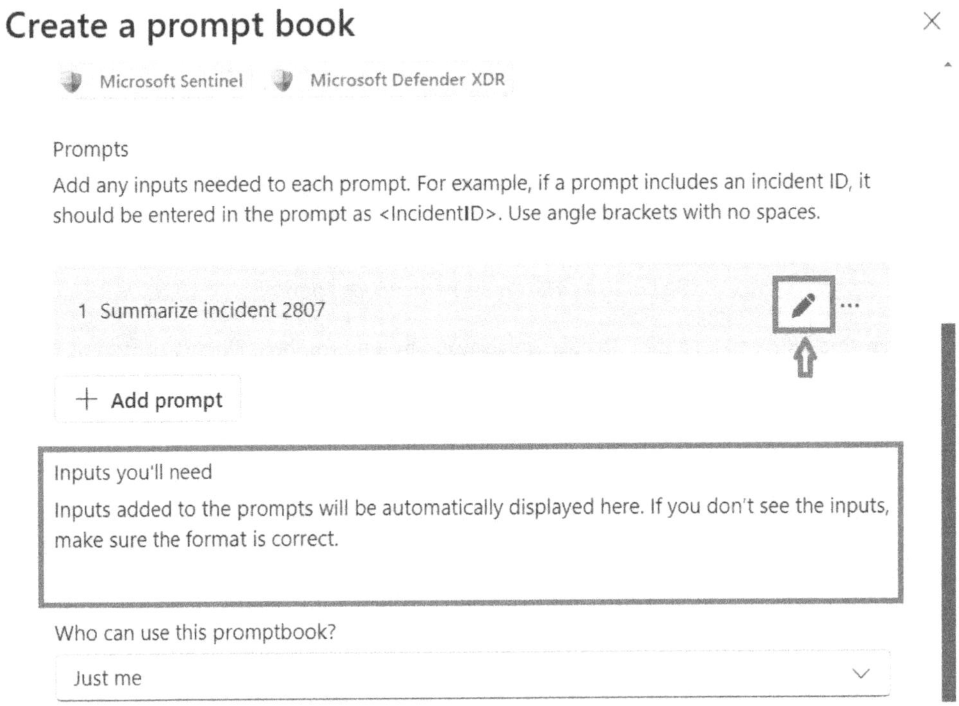

Figure 6.16 – Modifying the prompt and defining the promptbook input

For our example, the incident ID can be set as the input for the promptbook. To define this input parameter, you can edit the **Summarize incident 2807** prompt and replace **2807** with <Incident_ID>, as shown in the next screenshot:

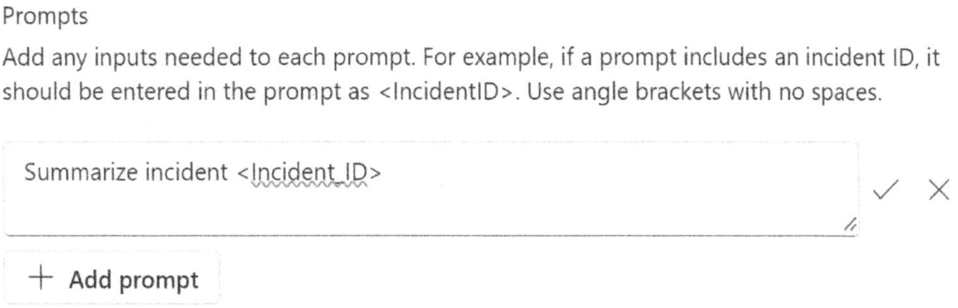

Figure 6.17 – Defining th input parameter

Once you save the updated prompt, the newly created input parameter will appear in the **Input** section of the promptbook creation window. The next screenshot displays the updated **Input** section:

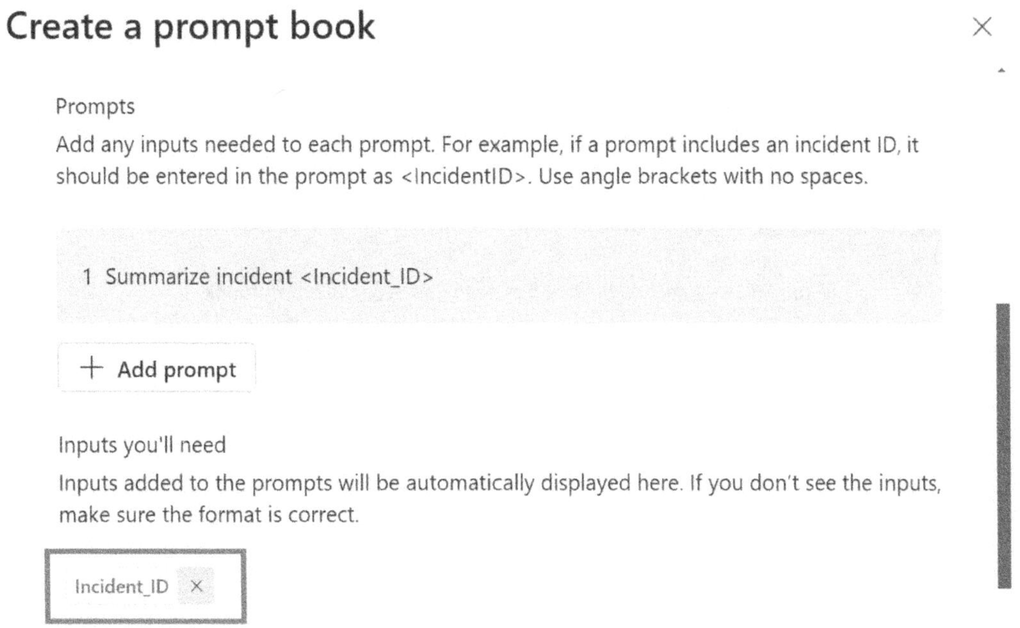

Figure 6.18 – The updated Input section

Important note

The **<Incident_ID>** parameter is used in this example. However, you can pick any parameter name as long as it doesn't contain spaces and is defined within angle brackets. You can also define multiple input parameters.

In the promptbook creation window, you can continue to add more prompts to complete your promptbook. In our example, a second prompt has been inserted, as shown next:

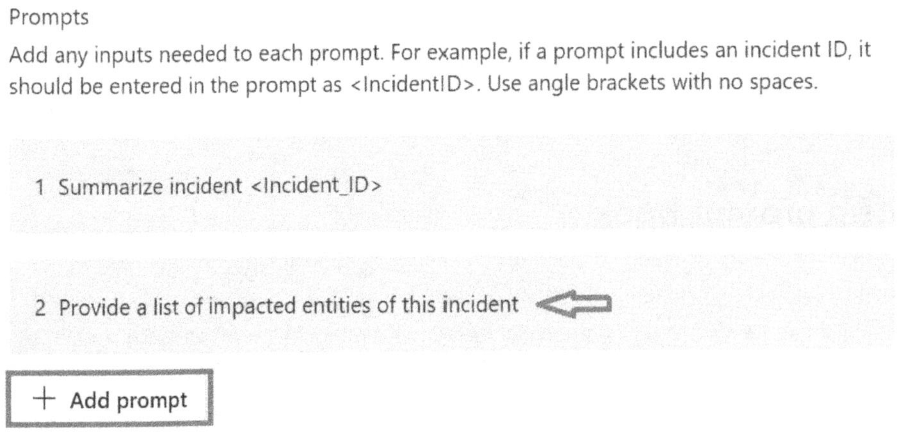

Figure 6.19 – A second prompt has been added to the promptbook

Lastly, in the promptbook creation window, you can choose who can view and use this new promptbook. It can be set to either just yourself or anyone in your organization, as displayed next:

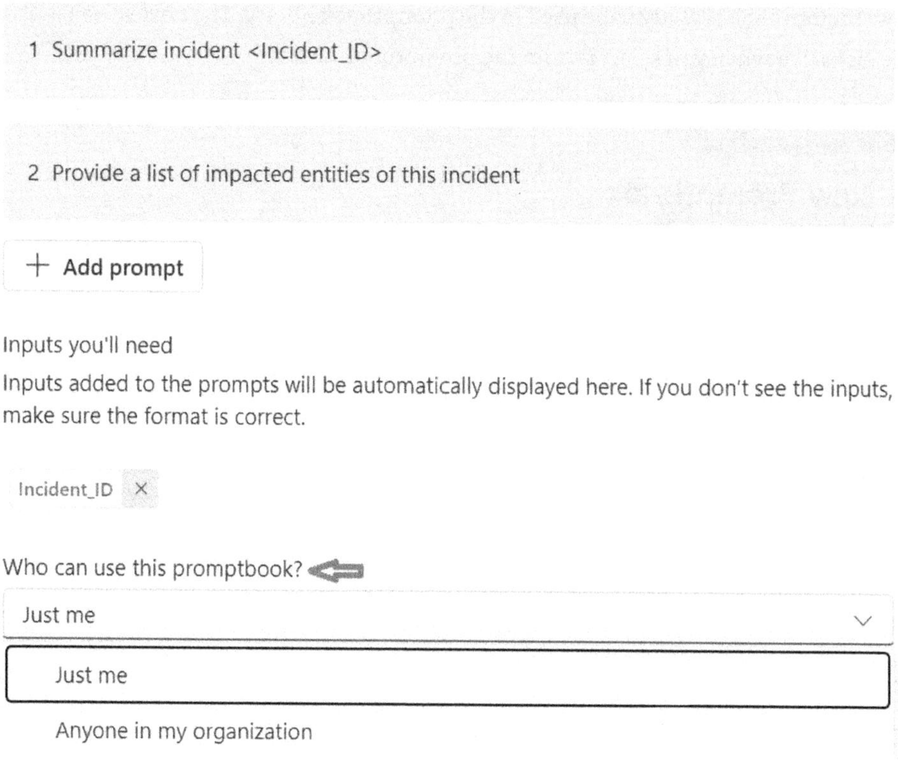

Figure 6.20 – Picking who can view and use this new promptbook

The final step is to save all your changes. And that's all there is to creating a new promptbook!

The new promptbook is ready to be used in the promptbook library. The next screenshot shows what it looks like when you select it from the promptbook library:

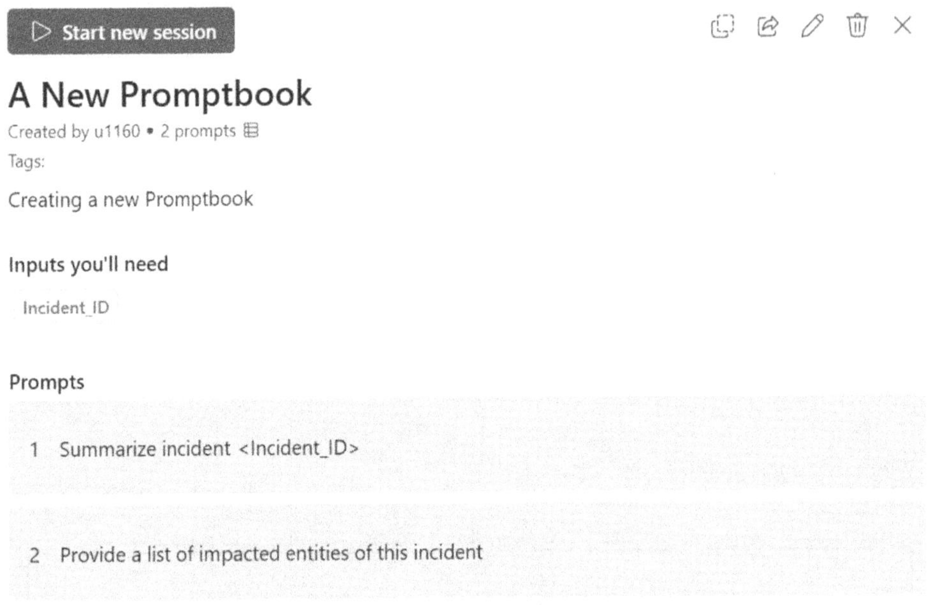

Figure 6.21 – The new promptbook

Upon clicking the **Start new session** button at the top, you are able to run the promptbook. As shown in the next screenshot, you can simply enter the **Incident_ID** number and then press **Submit** to execute this promptbook:

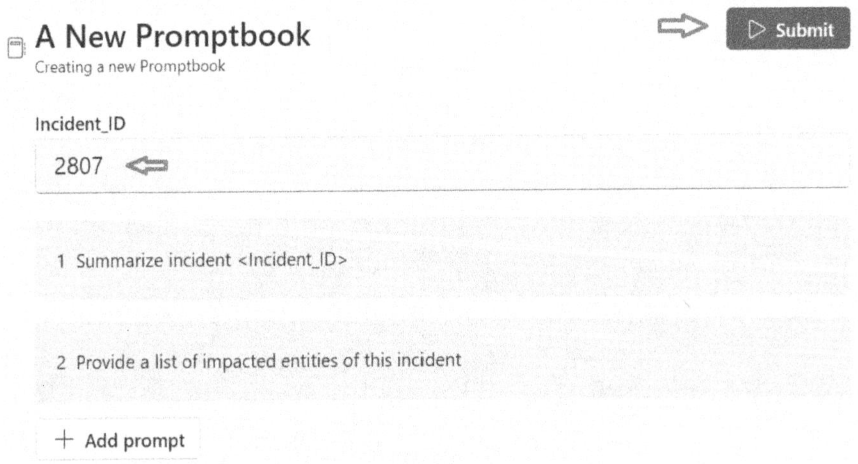

Figure 6.22 – Running the new promptbook

You can update this promptbook at any time by selecting the **Edit** option next to it in the promptbook library, as illustrated in the next screenshot:

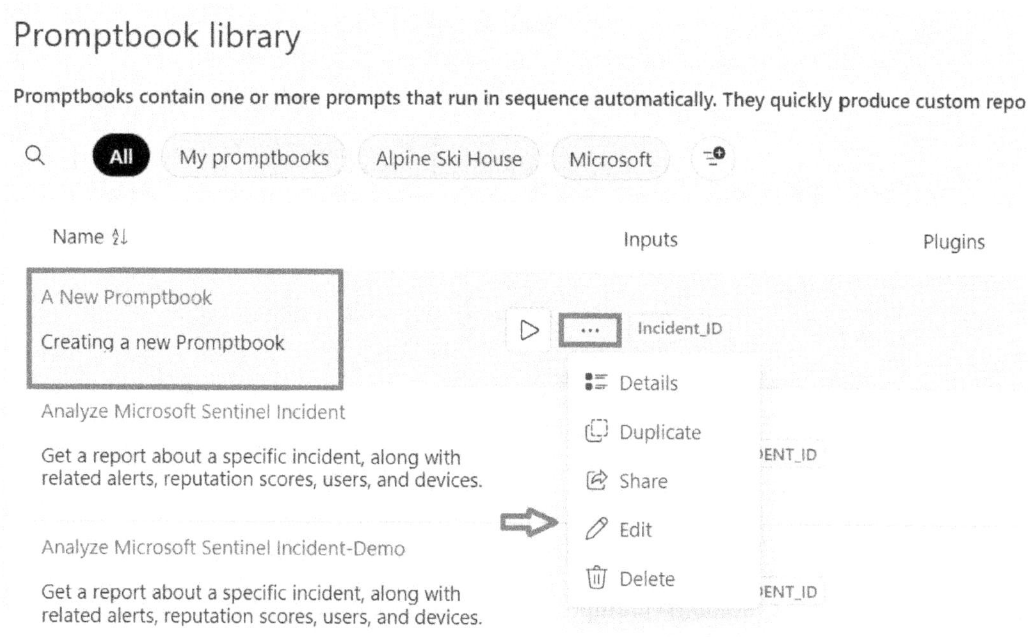

Figure 6.23 – Editing this promptbook

For instance, you can change the name of the promptbook, add a tag for easy filtering and identification, or update its description. In this case, the promptbook name has been changed to `Playbook - Incident Initial Review` and its description has been updated, as shown next:

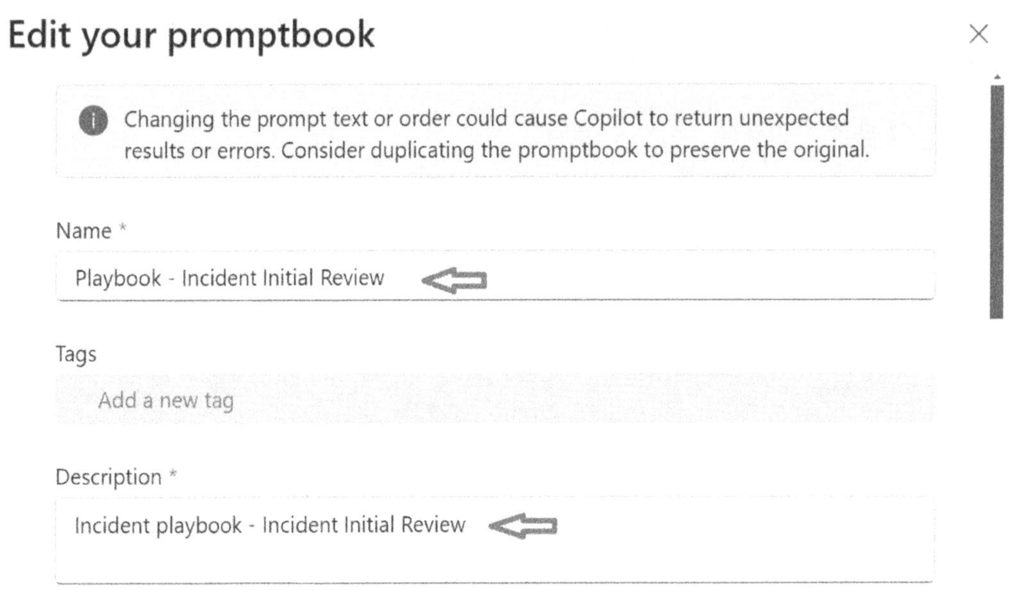

Figure 6.24 – Editing your promptbook

You can continue to add additional prompts, make changes to the existing prompts, and change the prompt order, as illustrated in the next screenshot:

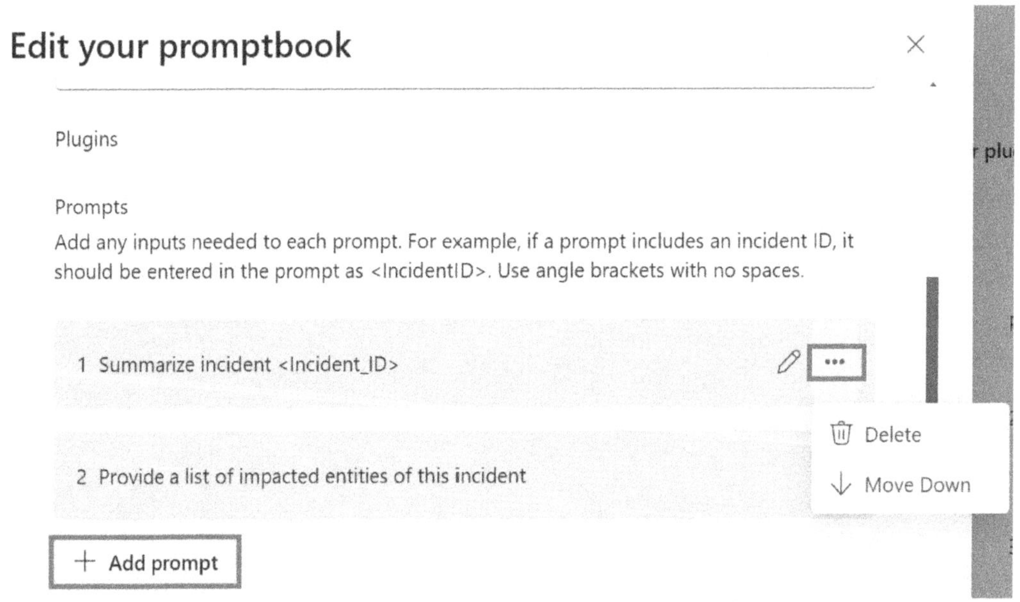

Figure 6.25 – Modifying existing prompts and adding additional prompts

Creating a promptbook from scratch lets you design and build a workflow tailored to your specific needs and interests. It allows you to organize and group your favorite prompts together to enhance investigation processes and automate repetitive tasks, thereby streamlining operations and boosting work efficiency.

Besides creating a new promptbook from the ground up, you also have the option to convert any of your existing Security Copilot session prompts into promptbooks. This allows you to preserve the successful workflows you've developed using specific sets of prompts that have worked well for you. Let's dive into it more in the next section.

Turning a session into a promptbook

In the standalone experience of Security Copilot, you typically start with a new session and execute various prompts to complete tasks. Some prompts may be created on the spot, while others are the ones you commonly use. Often, your tasks yield improved results thanks to these new prompts. You have the option to preserve this enhanced workflow by picking certain prompts from the session and converting them into a new promptbook. This allows you to formalize and retain the series of prompts that worked well for you.

In the previous section, we developed a new promptbook titled **Playbook - Incident Initial Review**, which offers a summary of the incident and the associated suspicious entities. When executing this promptbook for a specific incident, a few suspicious devices have been identified. At some point during the investigation, you need to gather more information about these devices, including details such as who logged on, the applications installed, known critical vulnerabilities, current and past IP addresses, and any alerts linked to the device.

This book includes a custom plugin designed to provide such device information. In a specific Security Copilot incident investigation session, prompts utilizing this custom plugin have retrieved relevant device data. We will use this session as an example to convert these prompts into a new promptbook focused on device information gathering.

The process for creating a promptbook from prompts in an existing Security Copilot session is quick and straightforward, and it follows similar steps of building a promptbook from scratch.

First, you need to identify the prompts in the session that you wish to convert into the new promptbook. For this example, let's pick the following prompts from this Copilot session:

- **Invoke "Device Users and Login Counts" skill in the "Custom Plugin Defender Device Info" plugin for device mb-winclient**

- **Invoke "Device Installed Applications" skill in the "Custom Plugin Defender Device Info" plugin for device mb-winclient**
- **Invoke "Device Critical Vulnerabilities" skill in the "Custom Plugin Defender Device Info" plugin for device mb-winclient**
- **Invoke "Device Alert Information" skill in the "Custom Plugin Defender Device Info" plugin for device mb-winclient**
- **Invoke "Device Current and Past IPs" skill in the "Custom Plugin Defender Device Info" plugin for device mb-winclient**
- **Invoke "Device OS Information" skill in the "Custom Plugin Defender Device Info" plugin for device mb-winclient**

Once you've selected the list of prompts from the Security Copilot session, click on the **Create promptbook** icon at the top, as shown next:

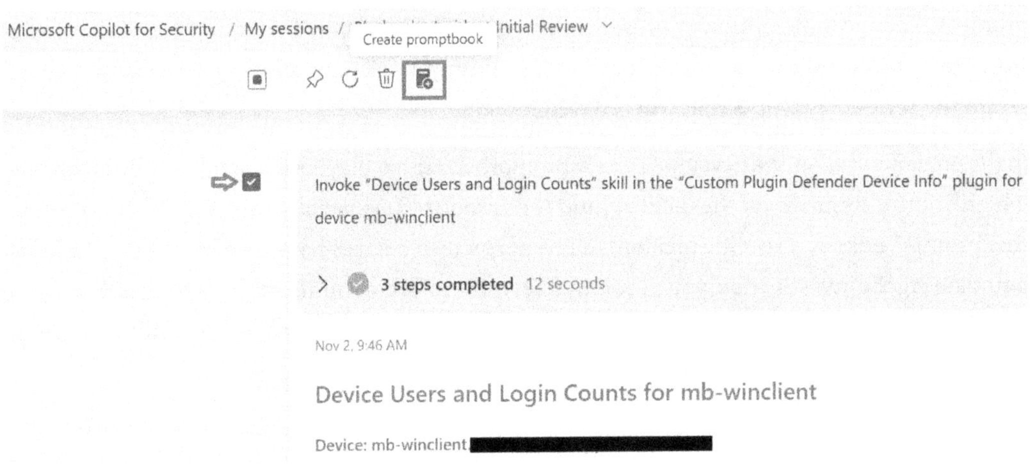

Figure 6.26 – Selecting prompts to create a new promptbook

The **Create a prompt book** dialog box then appears, as displayed in the next screen capture. You need to enter some basic information, such as the promptbook name and a description. Please note that the custom plugin for gathering device information is already prefilled in here:

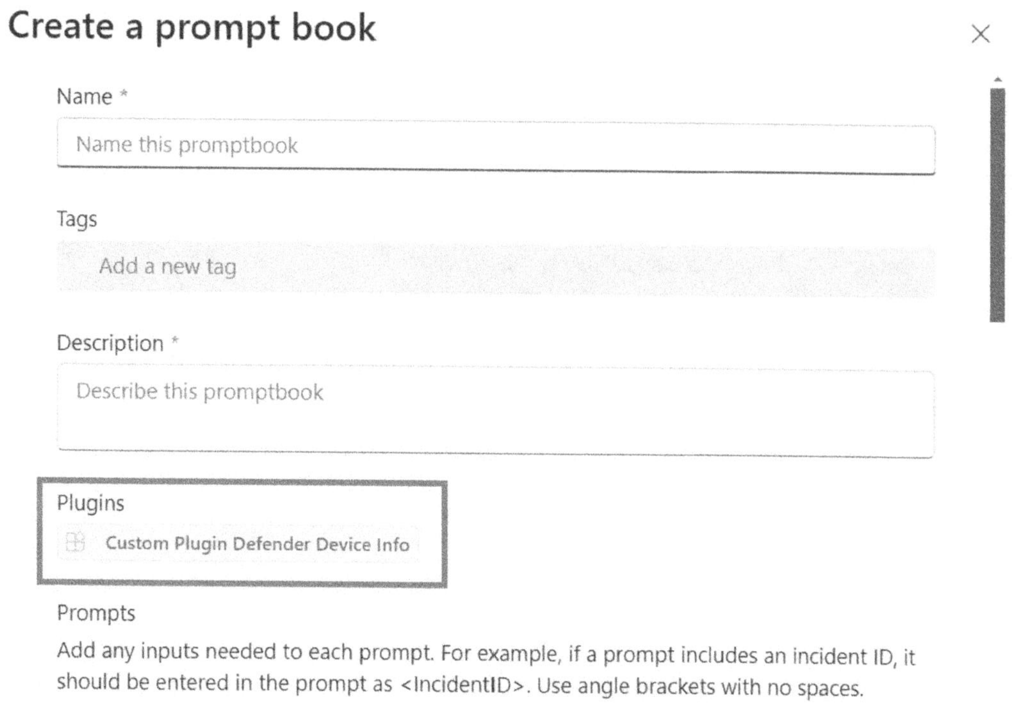

Figure 6.27 – The Create a prompt book dialog box

The prompts we selected earlier are already automatically filled in the **Prompts** section of the **Create a prompt book** dialog box, as illustrated in the next screenshot:

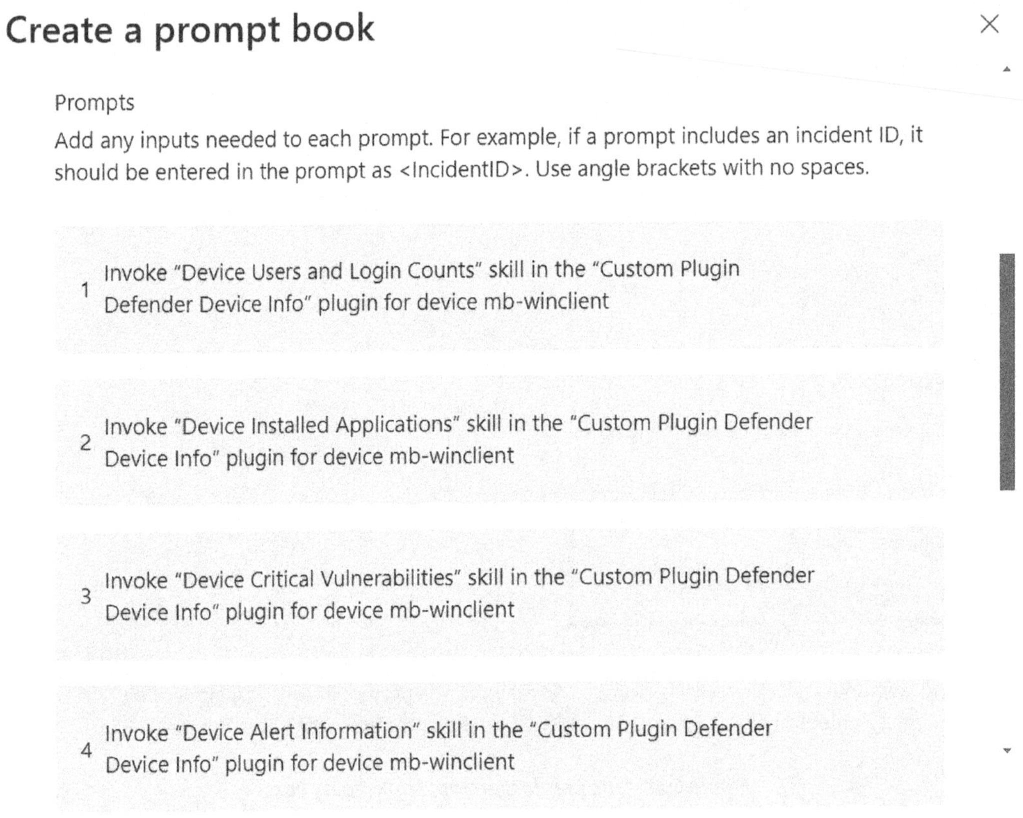

Figure 6.28 – The prepopulated prompts

Next, you need to define the input parameter. For this promptbook, let's use a new input parameter called `device_name`. This means that whenever this promptbook is invoked, the user will need to provide the device name in order for the promptbook to retrieve the corresponding device information.

To define this input, in the prompts, wherever the device name **mb-winclient** appears, you replace it with `<device_name>`. The next screenshot demonstrates that the first prompt is being edited, where the device name **mb-winclient** is about to be replaced:

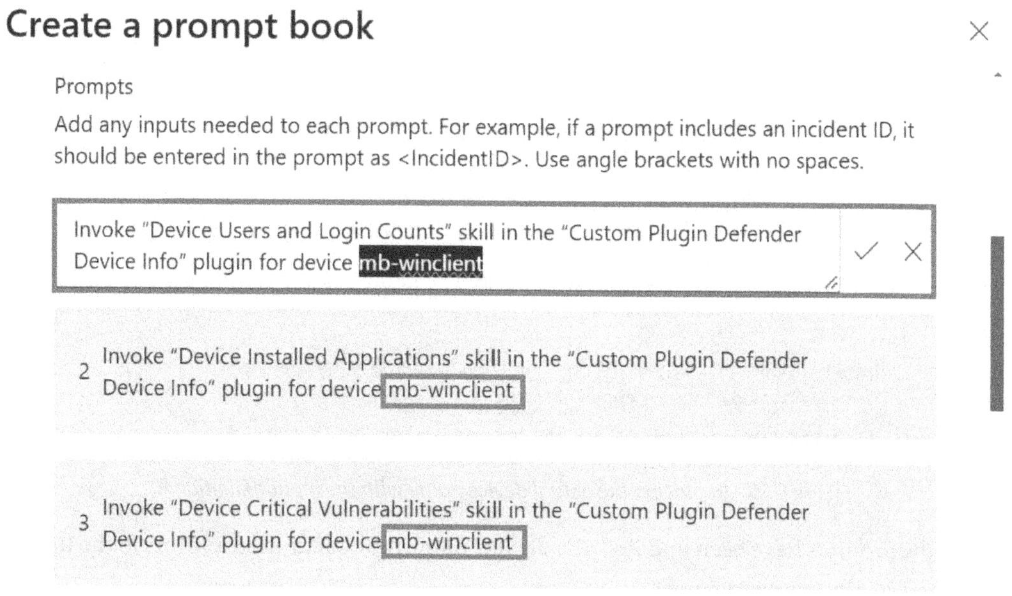

Figure 6.29 – Editing the prompt to define the input parameter

You need to edit each prompt that contains the actual device name and replace it with the input definition, `<device_name>`, as shown in the next screenshot. Note that the parameter name can be any word you choose, such as `device_name`, `DeviceName`, and so on, as long as there is no space and it is defined within angle brackets:

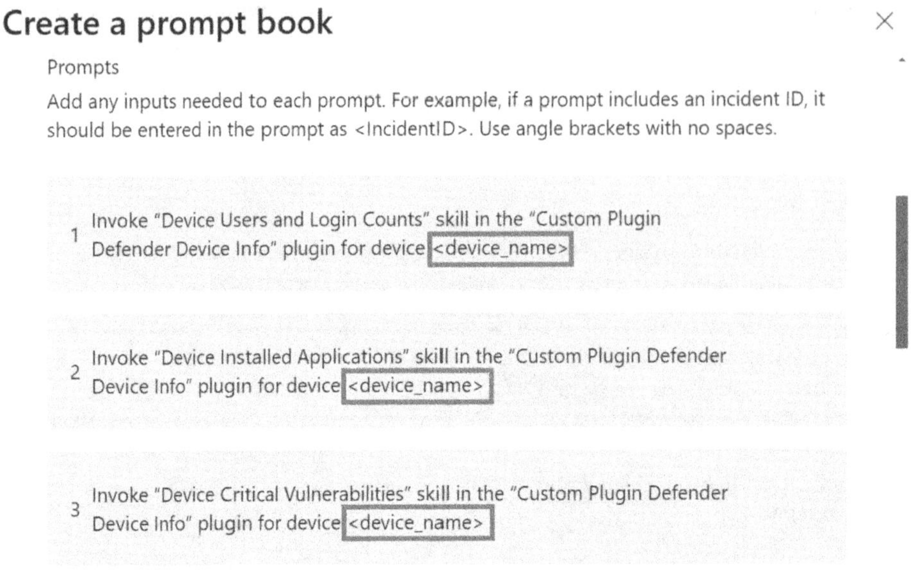

Figure 6.30 – Replacing the actual device name with the input definition

Once all the prompts have been updated, the **device_name** input definition appears in the **Inputs you'll need** section, as shown next:

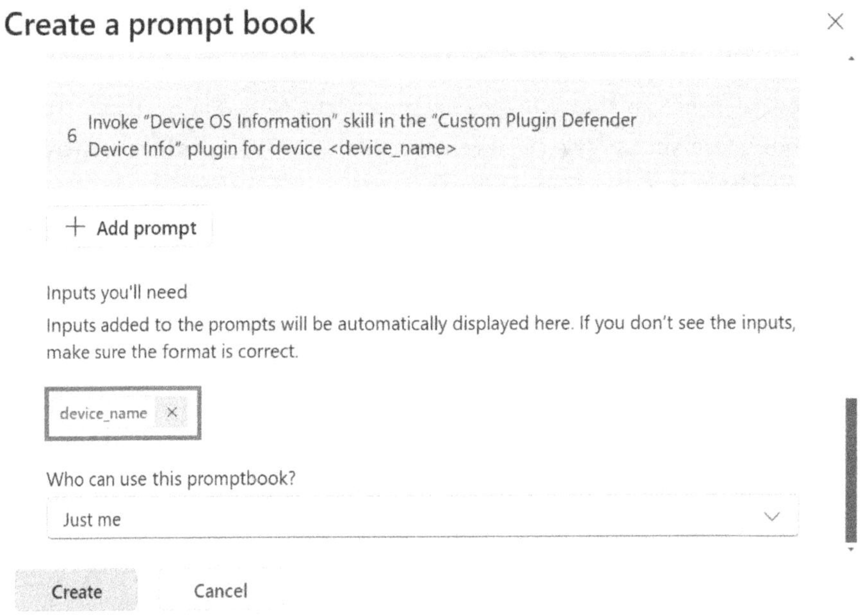

Figure 6.31 – The device_name input definition appears in the Input section

After specifying who can use this promptbook, just you or anyone in your organization, you can select **Create** to build this promptbook. The newly created promptbook is available in the promptbook library immediately, as shown in the next screenshot:

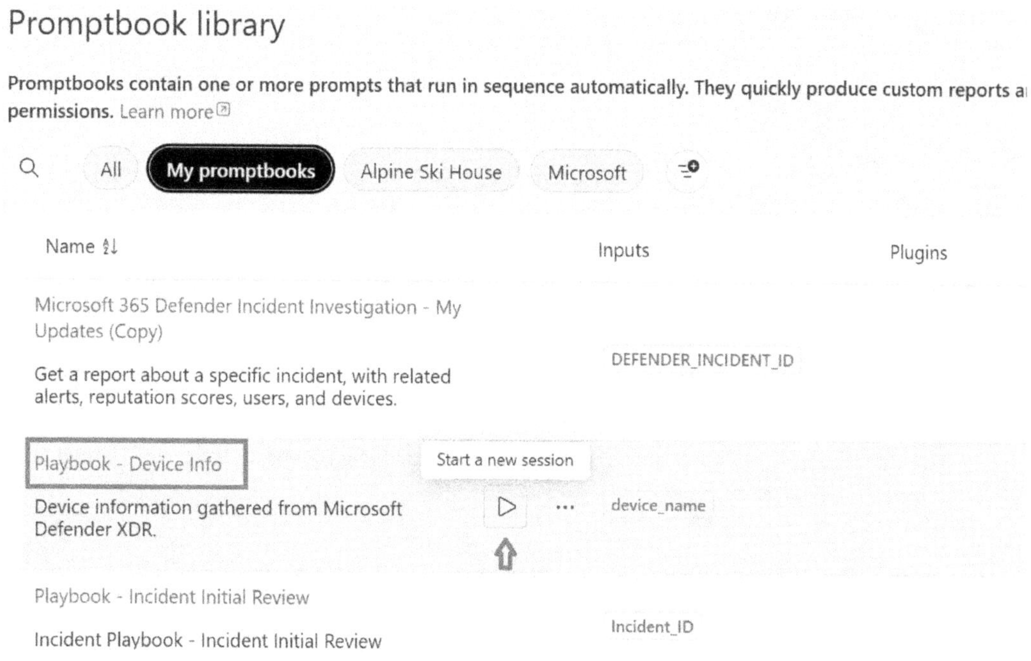

Figure 6.32 – Newly created promptbook seen in the promptbook library

You can run the promptbook in a new session or within an existing session. Additionally, you may edit, share, duplicate, or delete the promptbook as needed. For instance, you can add additional prompts to the promptbook if you see fit. For your reference, the next screenshot shows the complete promptbook that was just created:

Figure 6.33 – The newly created promptbook

In addition to creating a promptbook from prompts within an existing Security Copilot session, you also have the option to replicate and then modify an existing promptbook, allowing you to leverage the work of others.

There are already many promptbooks (`https://github.com/Azure/Copilot-For-Security/tree/main/Promptbook%20samples`) created for specific workflows and purposes. You can easily duplicate and customize them to fit your unique needs.

This way, you can build on existing ideas while adapting them to your workflow. In the next section, we'll explore how to duplicate and modify the promptbooks in detail.

Double the fun – duplicating a promptbook

Earlier in this chapter, you saw a list of promptbooks included in Security Copilot's promptbook library, developed by Microsoft and available for you to use. While these promptbooks serve as great resources, you can also modify and transform them into custom promptbooks. By using the **Duplicate** option in Security Copilot, you can make modifications in a copied Microsoft promptbook, allowing you to tailor it to your specific needs. The experience is simple and user-friendly. Let's take a look at how to do it.

In the promptbook library, when you navigate to the **Microsoft** tab, you'll find a list of promptbooks developed by Microsoft for your use. Clicking on the ellipses next to a specific promptbook expands the additional menu options. There, you'll see the **Duplicate** function, as illustrated next:

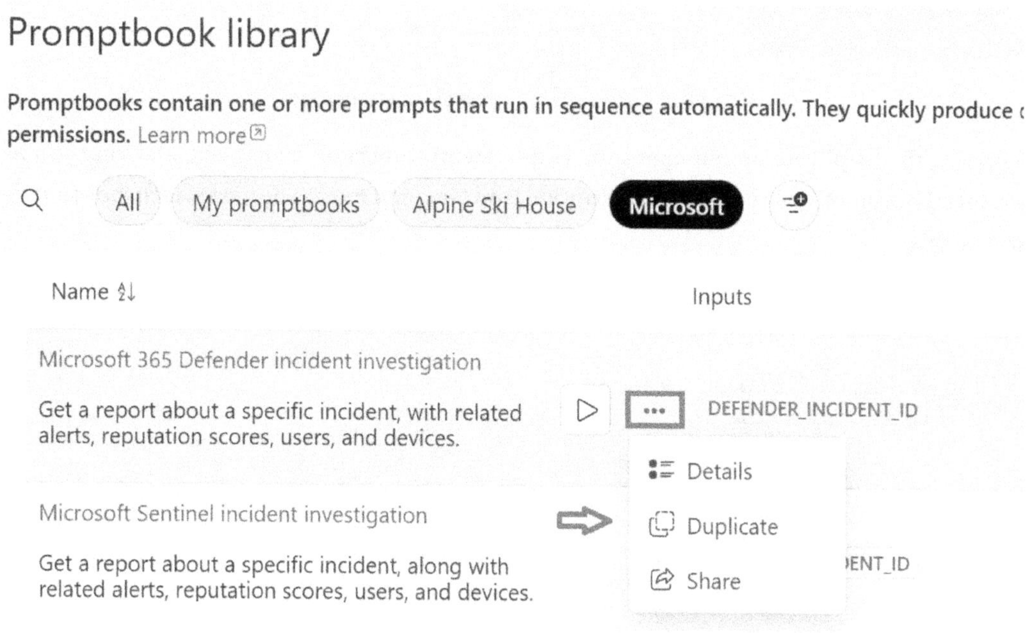

Figure 6.34 – The Duplicate option in the promptbook library

You can also find the same **Duplicate** option icon in the upper-right corner of the promptbook once you open it, as shown in the next screenshot:

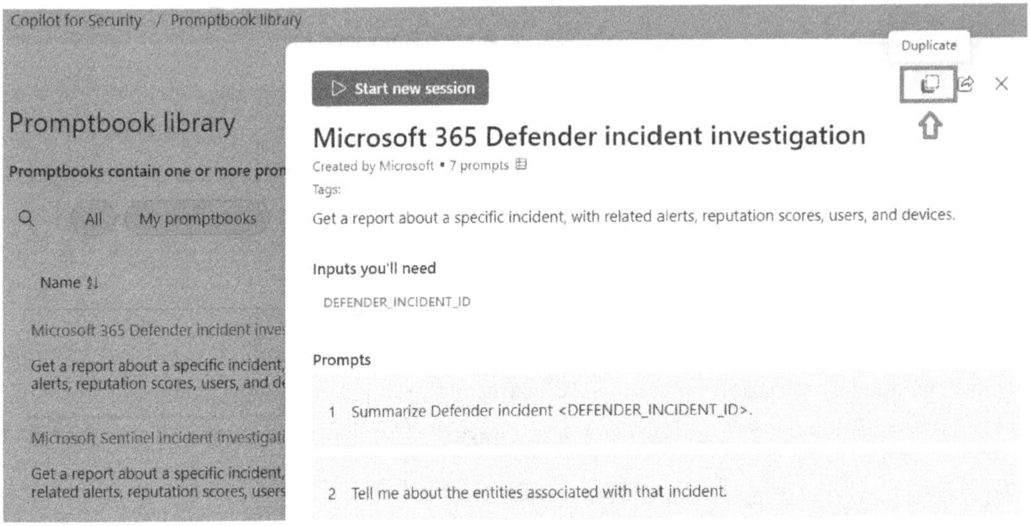

Figure 6.35 – The Duplicate icon in the promptbook

Selecting the **Duplicate** option opens the **Duplicate promptbook** dialog box, allowing you to rename the promptbook, update its description, add tags, and more. The next screenshot demonstrates this:

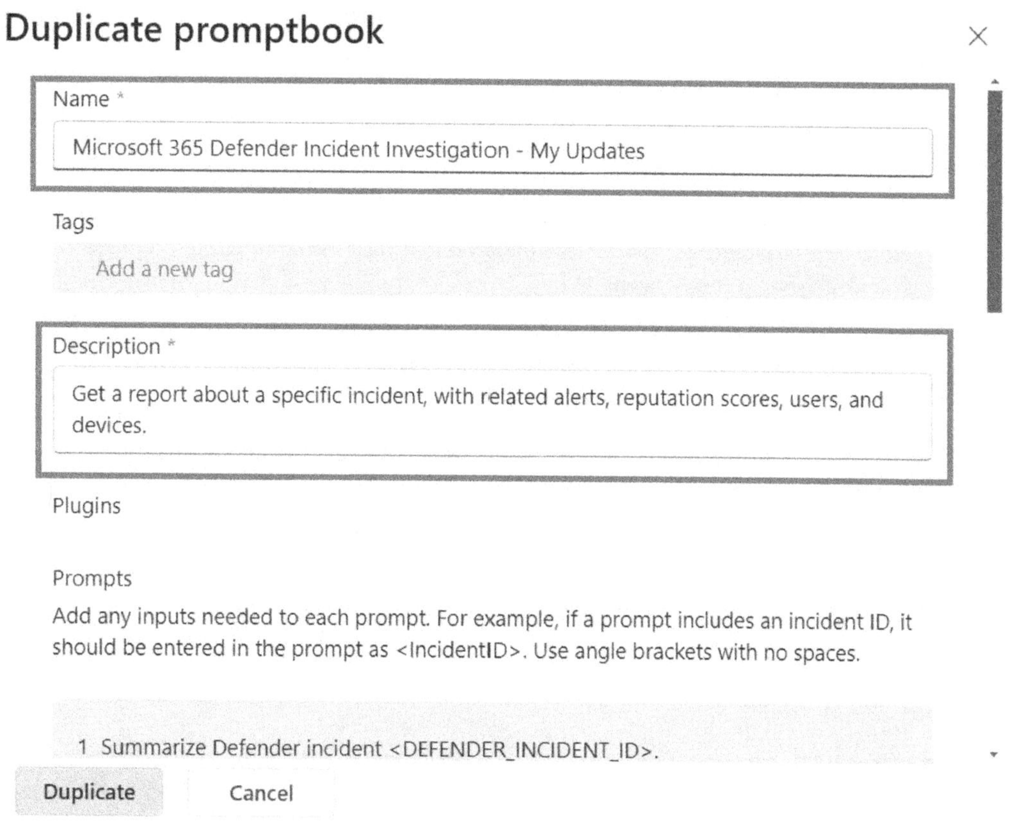

Figure 6.36 – Renaming the promptbook, updating its description, adding tags, and more

Most importantly, you can edit or delete the existing prompts in the copied promptbook, add new prompts, rearrange their order, or create additional input parameters, to fully customize the promptbook as shown next:

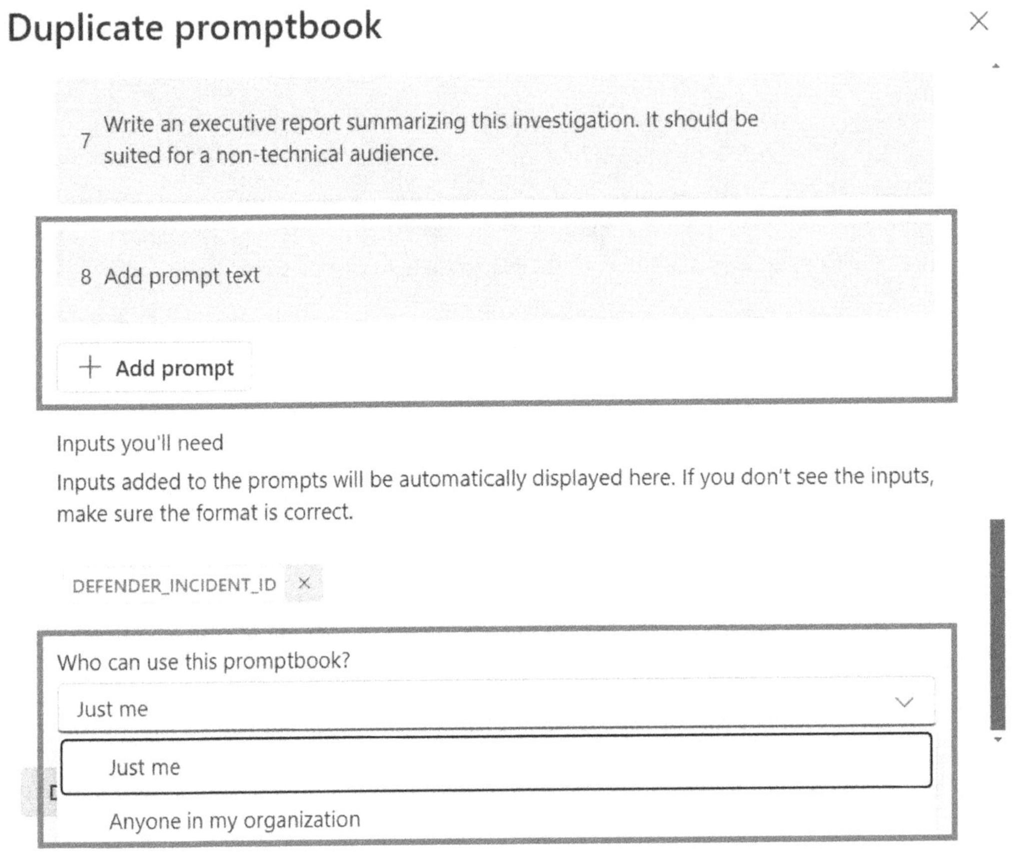

Figure 6.37 – Adding new prompts and other options

Once you've completed all your edits, click the **Duplicate** button to create the new promptbook. The duplicated promptbook then appears in the **My promptbooks** section of the promptbook library, with **(Copy)** added at the end of its name. This is displayed in the next screenshot:

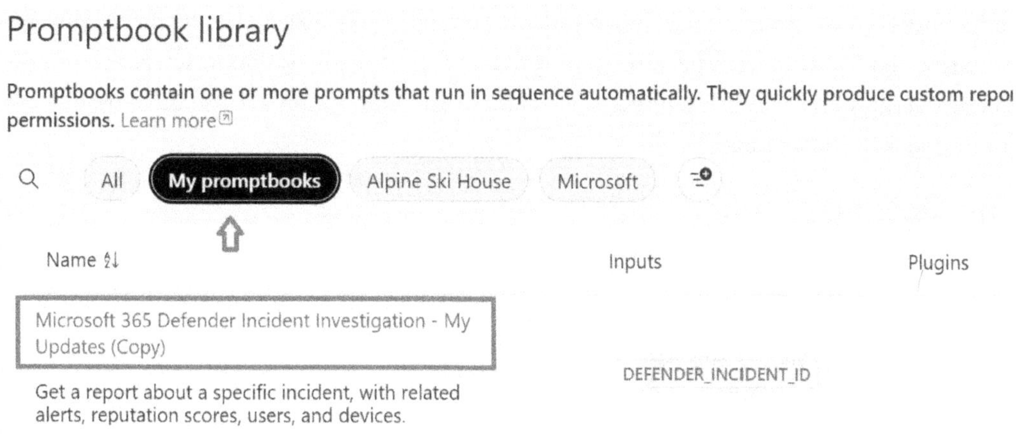

Figure 6.38 – Duplicated promptbook seen in the promptbook library

This new promptbook is now set up and ready for you to use. Note that you can again update the name of the promptbook to remove the word **(Copy)** that was added.

So far, we've discussed three different ways to develop your own promptbooks. For any promptbooks you've created, you have the option to modify them at any time. Let's take a closer look at this in the next section.

Polishing your promptbook

You can modify nearly every aspect of a promptbook that you've created. This includes changing the promptbook's name to enhance its clarity or to better reflect its purpose, updating tags for more effective categorization, and refining the description to provide clearer context for users. Additionally, you can adjust the prompts themselves and add or edit the input parameters. If you want a prompt to proceed to the next one if it fails, click the pencil icon next to the prompt. Then, turn on the **Continue on failure** option, which allows the promptbook to automatically move on to the next prompt if the current one fails. Furthermore, you can manage access permissions to determine who can use this promptbook.

However, for Microsoft promptbooks shared with you or those from your organization, you cannot modify them directly. Instead, you must first duplicate these promptbooks to create your own versions. Then, you can edit the copied promptbooks as needed.

In Security Copilot's promptbook library, your own promptbooks are listed under the **My promptbooks** section. Next to each personal promptbook, you have the option to select the ellipses to expand the additional menu options. From there, the **Edit** option allows you to modify the promptbook as shown next:

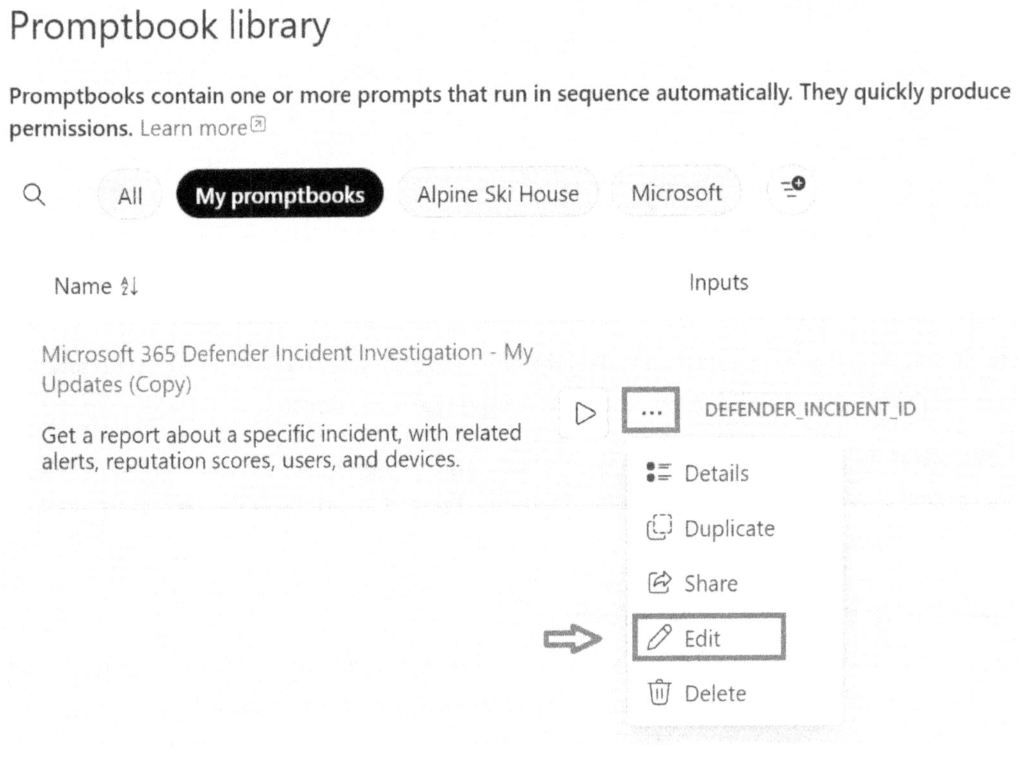

Figure 6.39 – The Edit feature for the promptbook

Note that when you make changes to a promptbook using this particular method, those changes are final. Once you save your changes, they cannot be undone. This underscores the importance of carefully considering your edits before finalizing them.

Security Copilot also offers another way for you to edit parts of the promptbook. *However, the changes made with this approach are not permanent.* When a promptbook is open in an active session, you can edit its prompts, delete existing ones, add new prompts, or rearrange their order, as shown in the next screenshot. Since the changes are not retained, they do not alter the original promptbook:

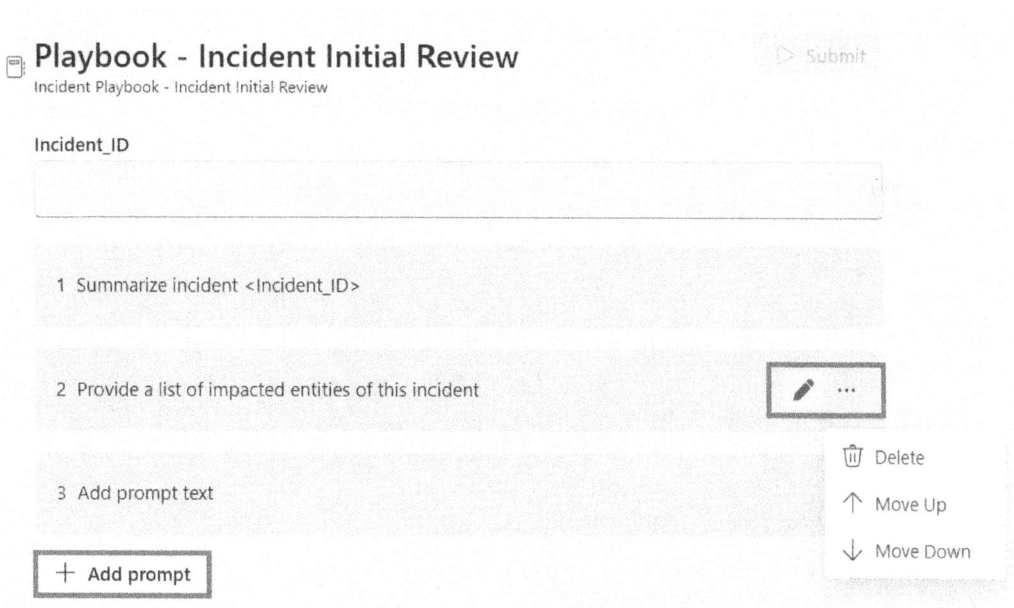

Figure 6.40 – Another way to edit the promptbook

This option is available for all promptbooks in the promptbook library, including those from Microsoft. It allows you to experiment with different prompt configurations in real time using an existing promptbook as its basis. If the outcome is satisfactory, you can then select both the modified and existing prompts in the session and convert them into a new promptbook.

For any promptbooks, especially your favorites, you are able to share them with others. Let's take a look at this next.

The joy of sharing

Sharing a promptbook with others is simple. In **Promptbook library**, clicking on the ellipses next to any promptbook lets you open the additional menu options, as seen in the next screenshot. From there, by selecting the **Share** option, the promptbook link is copied to your clipboard. You can then share this link with other analysts. When they open the shared link in their Security Copilot portal, they can save the promptbook. The shared promptbook will then appear in the **My Promptbooks** section of their Security Copilot console, with the other analyst designated as the promptbook owner:

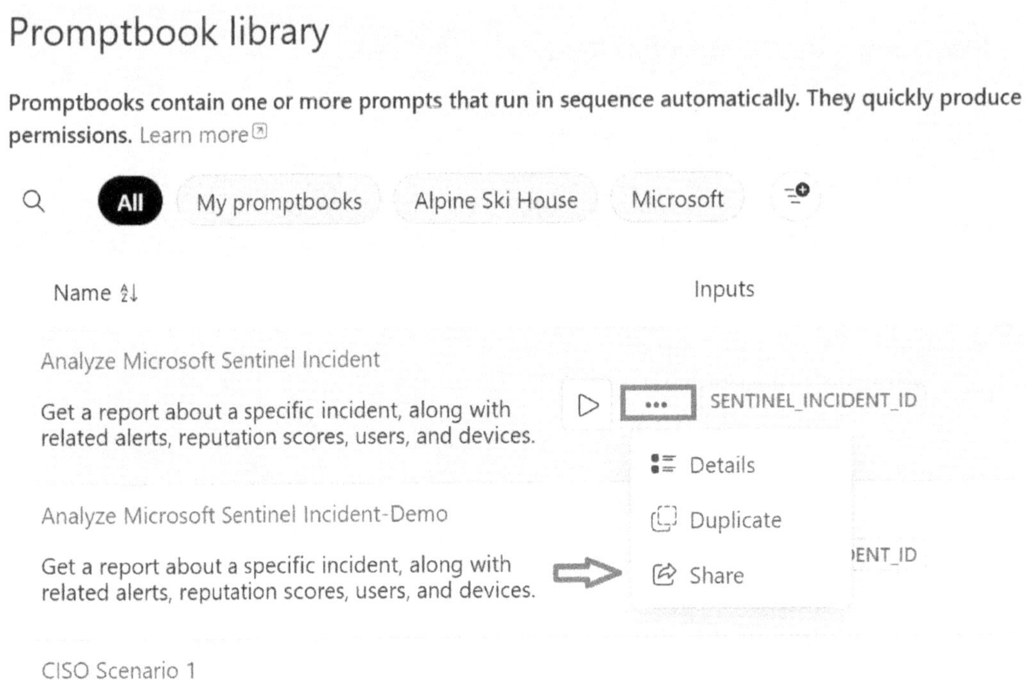

Figure 6.41 – The promptbook sharing option in Security Copilot

Please note that when you share a promptbook with a user who has different Security Copilot permissions or access, especially access to plugins, the user may receive a different response from Copilot when running the same promptbook. This is because the prompts in the promptbook are executed within the user's session, and Copilot processes data based on what is accessible to the user currently signed in.

Whether you're sharing a promptbook with others, using someone else's, or creating your own, promptbooks are valuable features within Security Copilot. They enhance productivity and efficiency across a range of security tasks, making them essential for supporting effective security workflows.

In the next section, we'll look into some additional promptbooks developed by the author, and discuss creative ways of building and utilizing promptbooks. We'll also share tips for using promptbooks effectively.

Promptbooks in action – sample promptbooks and tips

This book offers custom plugins available for you to download and set up in your own Security Copilot environment. *Chapter 4* details the steps for setting up the custom plugins, which can be completed in just a few clicks. *Chapter 5* further dives into some of these plugins. The custom plugins enable you to incorporate additional skills and capabilities into your prompts and promptbooks. Let's take a look at some of these plugins and the promptbooks that have been developed using them.

The promptbook playground

One of the custom plugins available in this book is **CUSTOM PLUGIN DEFENDER DEVICE INFO**. Some of its skills and capabilities are shown in the next screenshot:

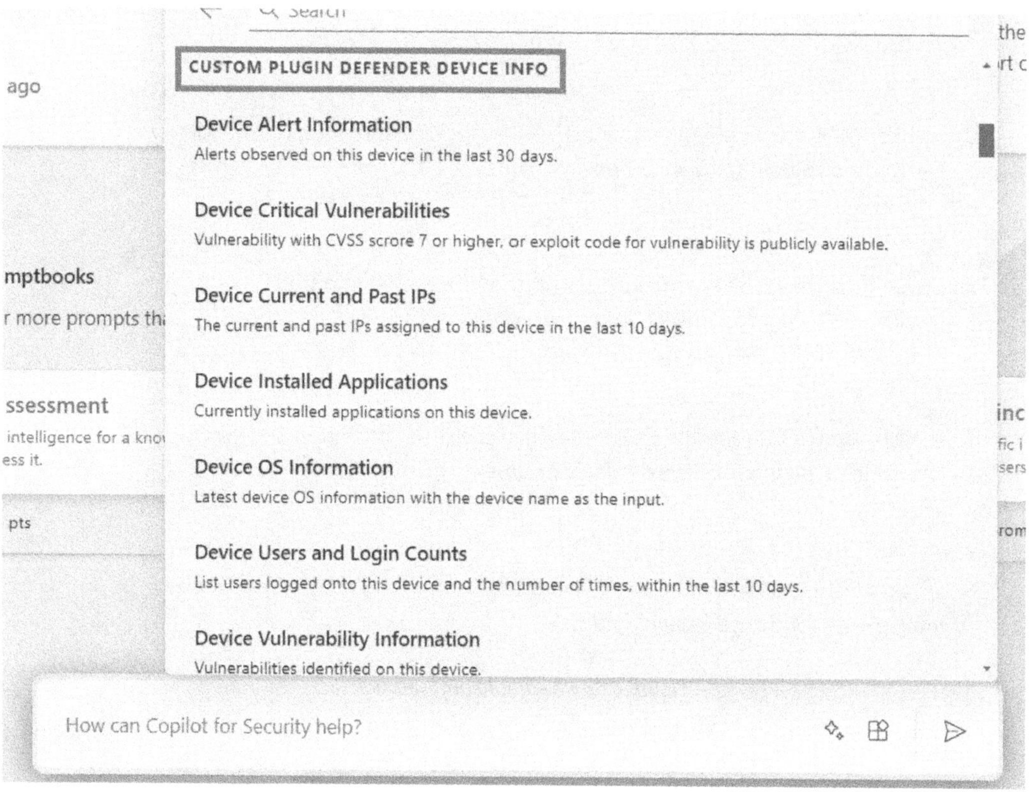

Figure 6.42 – The CUSTOM PLUGIN DEFENDER DEVICE INFO custom plugin

You can utilize the skills in this plugin to gather the device information that is often needed during an investigation. Even better, by transforming these skills into a promptbook, you are able to invoke these skills simultaneously in a session with just a single click.

The next screenshot displays a sample promptbook (also available at `https://github.com/PacktPublishing/Microsoft-Copilot-for-Security/blob/main/PromptBooks/Playbook%20-%20Device%20Info.md`) that you can replicate to take advantage of the skills offered in this custom plugin:

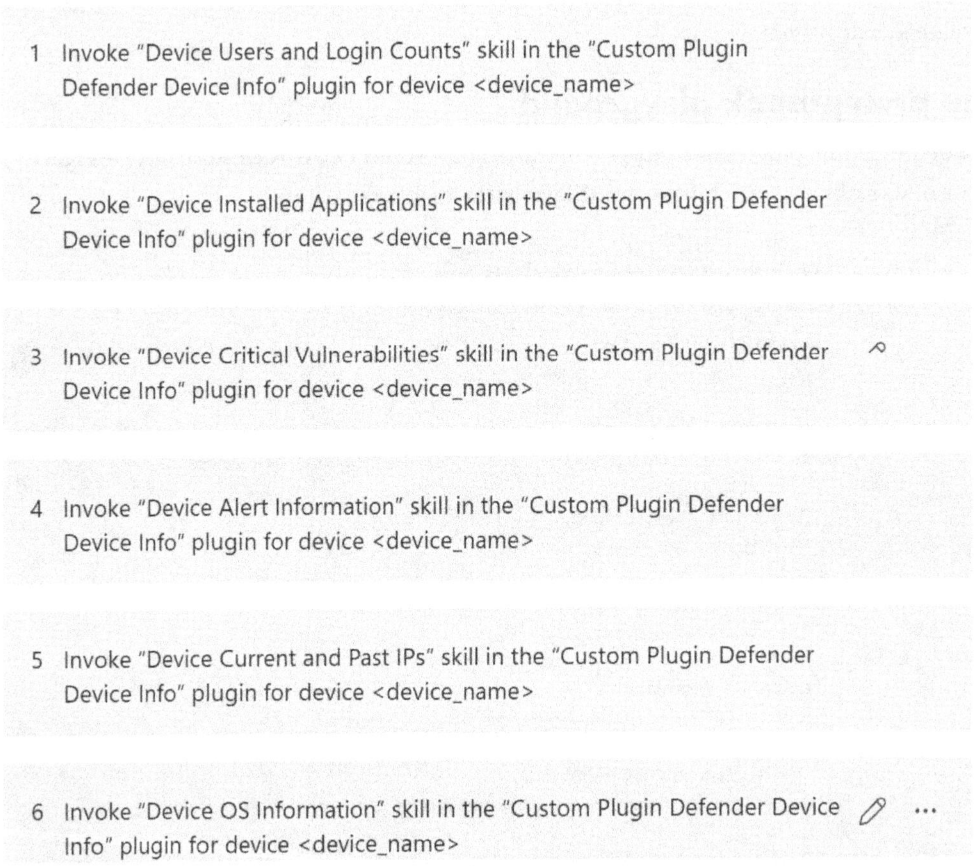

Figure 6.43 – A sample promptbook

This promptbook offers insights into who typically logs into the device, inferring the potential device owner. It also includes details about the device's installed applications, associated critical vulnerabilities, current and past IP addresses, relevant alerts, and basic operating system information.

Let's say you're using Security Copilot to help you to investigate an incident. During the session, Security Copilot generates a list of suspicious devices, as shown next:

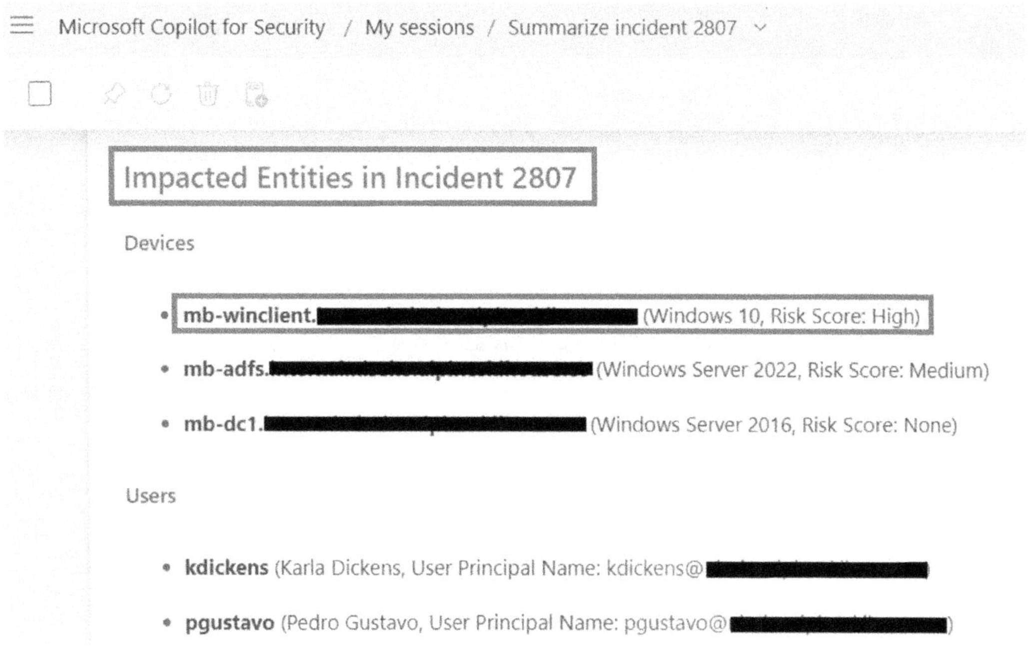

Figure 6.44 – A list of suspicious devices reported by Security Copilot

In this same Security Copilot session, through the prompt bar, you can invoke the promptbook just discussed to gather necessary device information for each suspicious device. The next screenshot illustrates this process of triggering the promptbook within the same session:

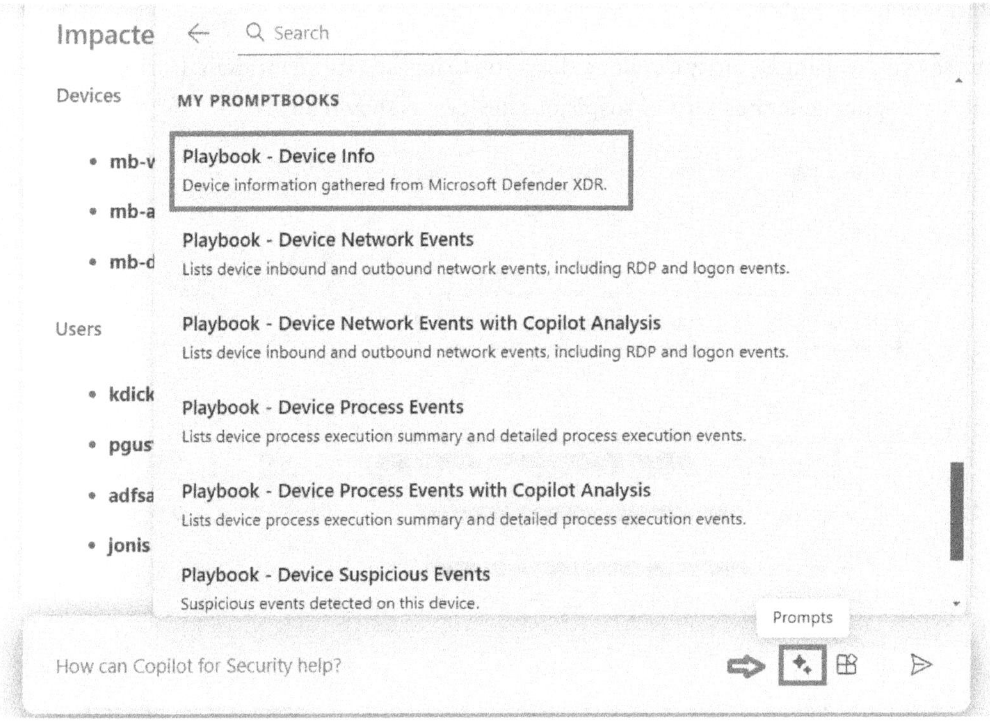

Figure 6.45 – Invoking the promptbook to gather necessary device information

Important note

Since Security Copilot is aware of the session content and retains context from previous interactions, the additional device data not only offers valuable insights for you but also allows Security Copilot to later build upon previous responses and tailor its responses accordingly, leading to better analysis and correlation.

To further illustrate the capabilities offered by this promptbook, here is some of the device information the promptbook provided for the first suspicious device, `mb-winclient`. The next screenshot shows that the user `kdickens`, typically logs into the device:

Device Users and Login Counts for mb-winclient

Device: mb-winclient[redacted]

Export to Excel

User Name	Domain	Login Count
kdickens	NISEKO	50

This table shows the user 'kdickens' logged onto the device 'mb-winclient' 50 times within the last 10 days.

Figure 6.46 – Device users and login counts

Following that, the next screenshot highlights the critical vulnerabilities associated with this device:

Critical Vulnerabilities on mb-winclient

Export to Excel

Software Name	Software Version	CVE ID
.net	6.0.0.0	CVE-2024-38095
.net	6.0.0.0	CVE-2024-38081
.net	7.0.5.0	CVE-2024-26190
.net	7.0.5.0	CVE-2024-21409

Figure 6.47 – Device critical vulnerabilities

Lastly, the alerts reported for this device are displayed next:

Figure 6.48 – Alerts reported for this device

Along with the plugin that gathers the device information, another custom plugin available in this book for your use is **CUSTOM PLUGIN DEFENDER DEVICE INVESTIGATION**, as shown next:

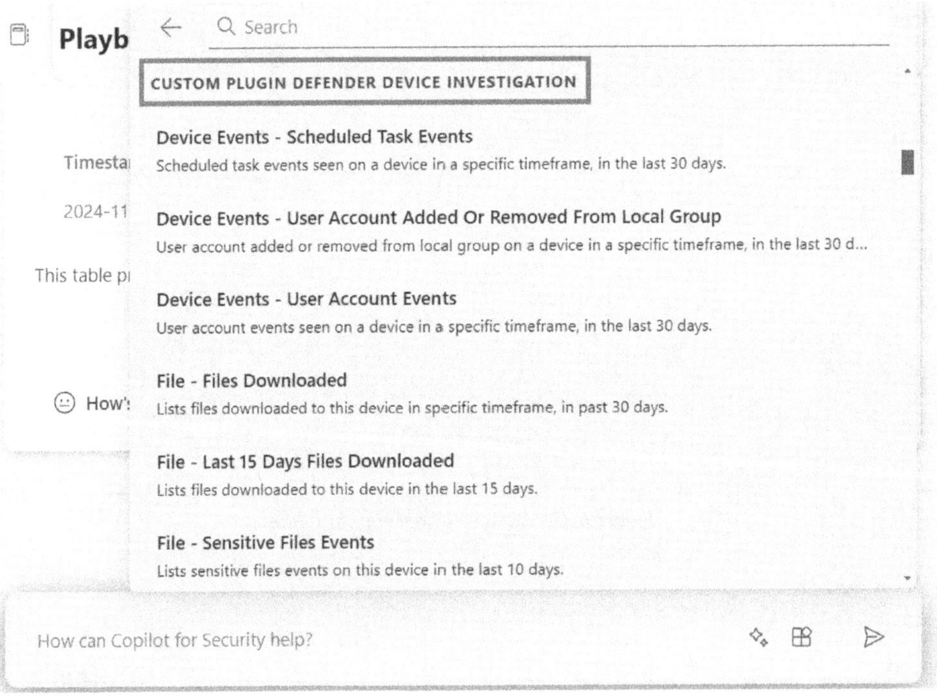

Figure 6.49 – Another custom plugin, CUSTOM PLUGIN DEFENDER DEVICE INVESTIGATION

This custom plugin (`https://github.com/PacktPublishing/Microsoft-Copilot-for-Security/blob/main/Plugins/Custom%20Plugin%20Defender%20Device%20Investigation.yml`) offers a range of skills and capabilities to assist you in investigating a suspicious device. The skills are as follows:

- **File - Files Downloaded**
- **File - Last 15 Days Files Downloaded**
- **File - Sensitive Files Events**
- **Process - Process Executions Summary**
- **Process - Detailed Process Executions**
- **Lateral Movement - RDP To Device**
- **Lateral Movement - Logon To Device**
- **Lateral Movement - Logons To Device In Last 10 Days**
- **Network - Outbound Network Events**
- **Network - Inbound Network Events**
- **Network - Device Listening Ports**
- **Device Events - Scheduled Task Events**
- **Device Events - User Account Events**
- **Device Events - User Account Added Or Removed From Local Group**
- **Suspicious Activities - ASR Rules Triggered**
- **Suspicious Activities - ASMSI Script Detection**
- **Suspicious Activities - Exploit Guard Events**
- **Suspicious Activities - Network Protection Events**
- **Suspicious Activities - Device Tampering Attempts**

By leveraging these skills, you should be able to create different promptbooks to enhance your investigation workflows. For example, the **Playbook - Device Suspicious Events** sample promptbook lets you examine some of the suspicious events reported on a device. This sample promptbook is available for you to copy and use through this book's GitHub repository at `https://github.com/PacktPublishing/Microsoft-Copilot-for-Security/blob/main/PromptBooks/Playbook%20-%20Device%20Suspicious%20Events.md`.

The prompts within this promptbook are displayed next:

1 Invoke "Suspicious Activities - ASR Rules Triggered" skill in the "Custom Plugin Defender Device Investigation" plugin for device <device_name>

2 Invoke "Suspicious Activities - ASMSI Script Detection" skill in the "Custom Plugin Defender Device Investigation" plugin for device <device_name>

3 Invoke "Suspicious Activities - Exploit Guard Events" skill in the "Custom Plugin Defender Device Investigation" plugin for device <device_name>

4 Invoke "Suspicious Activities - Network Protection Events" skill in the "Custom Plugin Defender Device Investigation" plugin for device <device_name>

5 Invoke "Suspicious Activities - Device Tampering Attempts" skill in the "Custom Plugin Defender Device Investigation" plugin for device <device_name>

Figure 6.50 – Promptbook titled Playbook - Device Suspicious Events

This promptbook is quite straightforward. Each prompt uses natural language to invoke a skill from the **CUSTOM PLUGIN DEFENDER DEVICE INVESTIGATION** custom plugin.

Since this custom plugin is a KQL-based plugin, the skills within it are developed using KQL queries. Therefore, instead of using natural language to invoke the skill for the promptbook, you also have the option to directly embed the associated KQL query in the prompt for the promptbook.

There are two key benefits to this approach. First, using natural language to invoke a specific skill within a plugin doesn't always guarantee that Security Copilot will select the desired plugin. Security Copilot analyzes the prompt content to determine which plugin it believes is the best match. But there are instances when a similar plugin is picked, preventing the promptbook from running as intended. By directly embedding the KQL query in the prompt for the promptbook, the likelihood of Security Copilot selecting the wrong plugin is greatly reduced.

Additionally, by directly embedding the KQL query in the prompt, you no longer rely on the custom plugin and its skills for your promptbooks. This may be preferred by some users for greater control and manageability.

As an example, here is a promptbook titled **Playbook - Device Process Events**, where the KQL query is defined within each prompt. This promptbook is available in the GitHub repository at `https://github.com/PacktPublishing/Microsoft-Copilot-for-Security/blob/main/PromptBooks/Playbook%20-%20Device%20Process%20Events.md` and is ready for you to use. The promptbook provides a summary of the processes executed on the device within a specific time period. It also includes any files downloaded to the device during that same time frame, allowing you to verify whether the downloaded file was executed. Additionally, this promptbook offers detailed process execution events for more thorough analysis.

There are three prompts in this promptbook, as shown next:

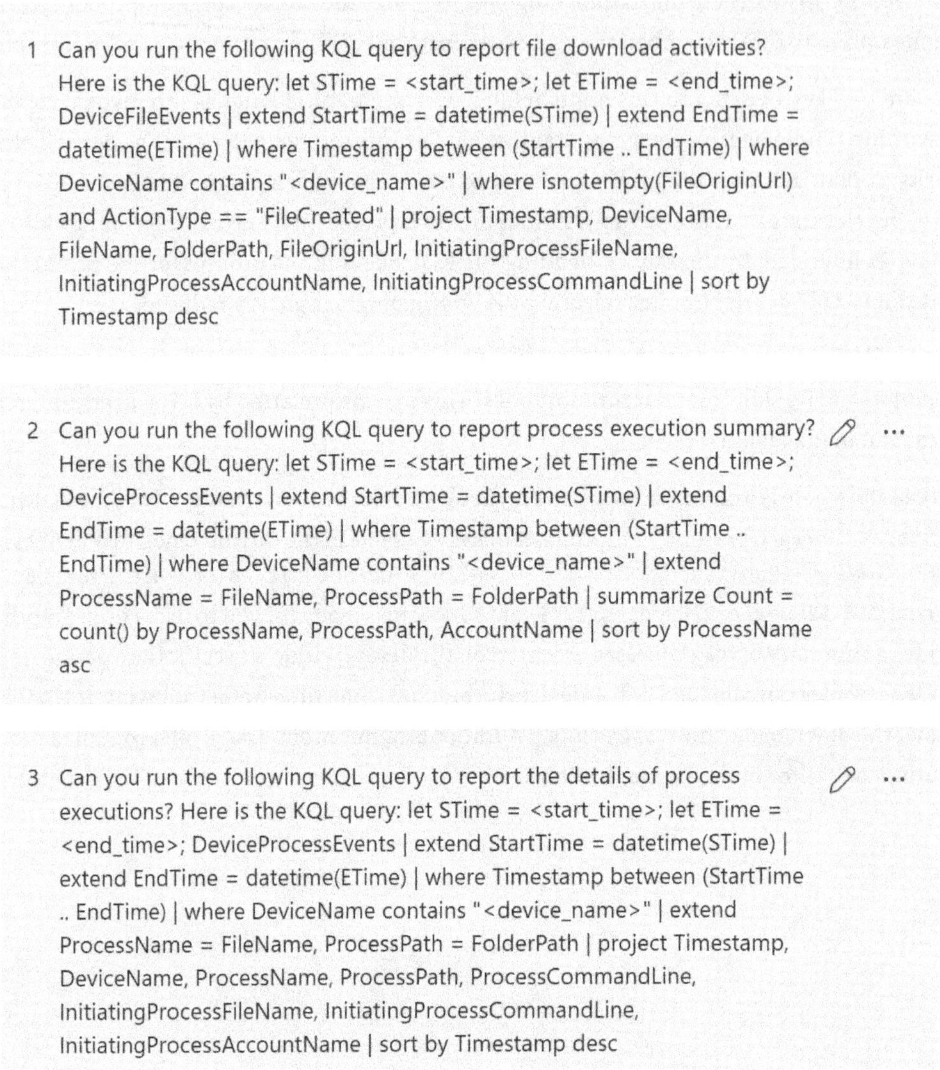

Figure 6.51 – Promptbook titled Playbook - Device Process Events

> Important note
>
> There are three input parameters defined for this promptbook: <start_time>, <end_time> and <device_name>. The KQL query in each prompt uses these parameters as input and executes them based on their values.

When you run this promptbook, you need to specify the start time, end time, and device name, as displayed in the next screenshot:

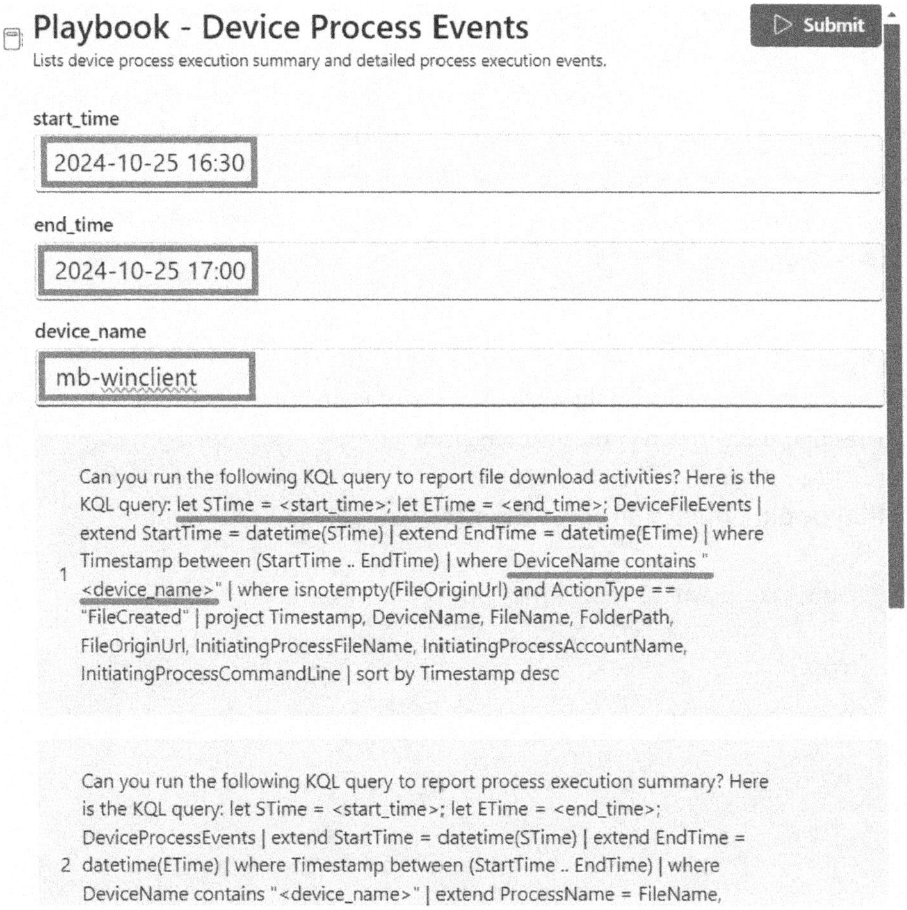

Figure 6.52 – Specifying inputs for the promptbook

Once the promptbook executes, Security Copilot automatically populates the input values into the corresponding fields in the KQL query in each prompt. The next screenshot demonstrates this, showing how the <start_time> field in the KQL query is replaced with the actual time value entered by the user:

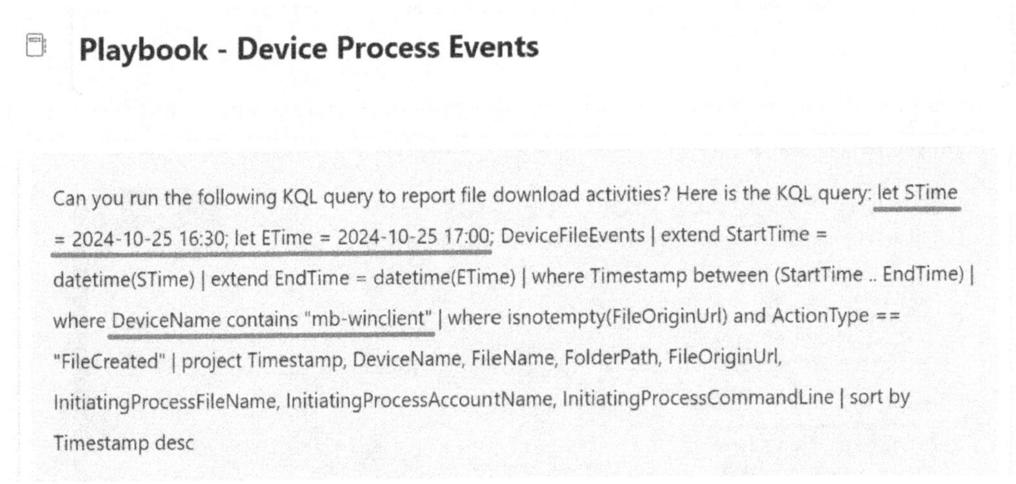

Figure 6.53 – Security Copilot automatically populates the input values

When the promptbook runs, it also shows the KQL query again in its response, prior to displaying the actual results, as illustrated in the next screenshot:

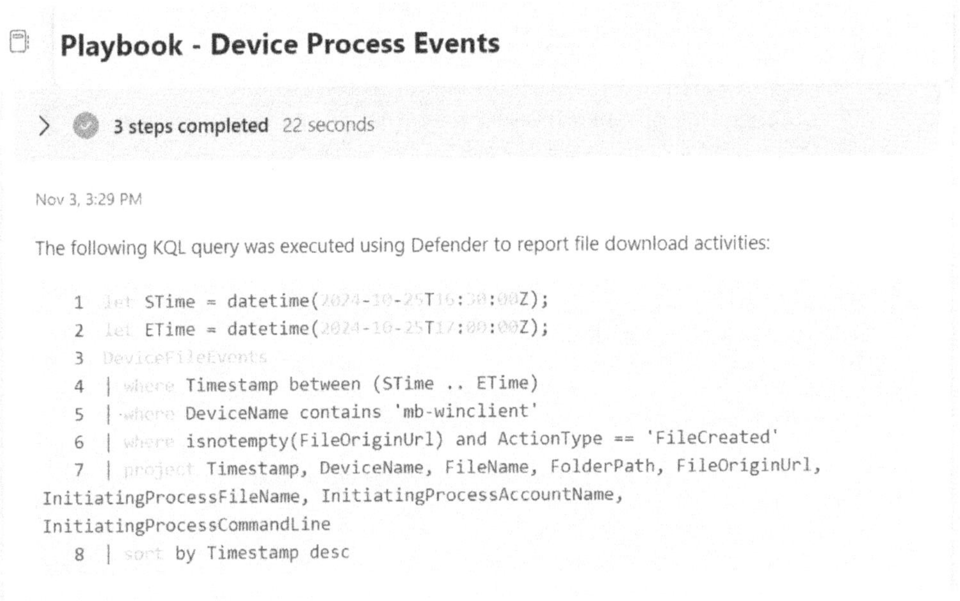

Figure 6.54 – The promptbook shows the KQL query again in its response

There are many promptbooks available online for reference and use. The GitHub repository for this book (`https://github.com/PacktPublishing/Microsoft-Copilot-for-Security/tree/main/PromptBooks`) offers additional promptbooks. Microsoft also adds new promptbooks to its Security Copilot GitHub at `https://github.com/Azure/Copilot-For-Security/tree/main/Promptbook%20samples`. Another good resource is Rod's GitHub at `https://github.com/rod-trent/Copilot-for-Security/tree/main/Prompts/Promptbooks`.

As you expand your collection of prompts and promptbooks, in the next section, let's dive into some useful tips and clever hacks that can enhance your promptbook experience.

Extra hacks and tips for your promptbooks

A promptbook is essentially a preconfigured workflow designed to automate tasks. Its ability to accept dynamic inputs, such as time ranges, device names, or other variables, makes a promptbook reusable in different scenarios, as it can be customized based on the specific needs of the investigation.

Promptbooks are particularly useful for automating repetitive tasks in a security investigation. *What's more, within a single Security Copilot session, you can invoke different promptbooks at various stages of your investigation. This modular approach allows you to use each promptbook for a specific task.* Whether it's gathering suspicious events on a compromised device or performing suspicious script analysis later on, the promptbooks make your overall investigation process more streamlined and efficient. In *Chapter 8*, we'll take a closer look at this modular approach and see its power in action.

As discussed earlier, using natural language to invoke a KQL-based plugin doesn't always guarantee Security Copilot will pick the right one, as it may choose a similar skill in another plugin instead. Embedding the KQL query directly in the prompt minimizes this risk, ensuring the promptbook runs as intended.

> Note
>
> To improve reliability, direct skill invocation from prompts and promptbooks is in development. This will guarantee Security Copilot invokes the specific skill within a plugin that you specify.

When creating promptbooks, it's important to ensure that they are built around the specific plugins you are using or have set up in your environment. If the promptbook is not aligned with or linked to the appropriate plugins, it won't be able to perform the intended tasks or provide relevant results, making it ineffective or useless.

As you are developing a new promptbook and changing the input parameter criteria, be sure to delete the existing input definitions in the **Inputs you'll need** section first. The next screenshot displays three input parameters that can all be deleted:

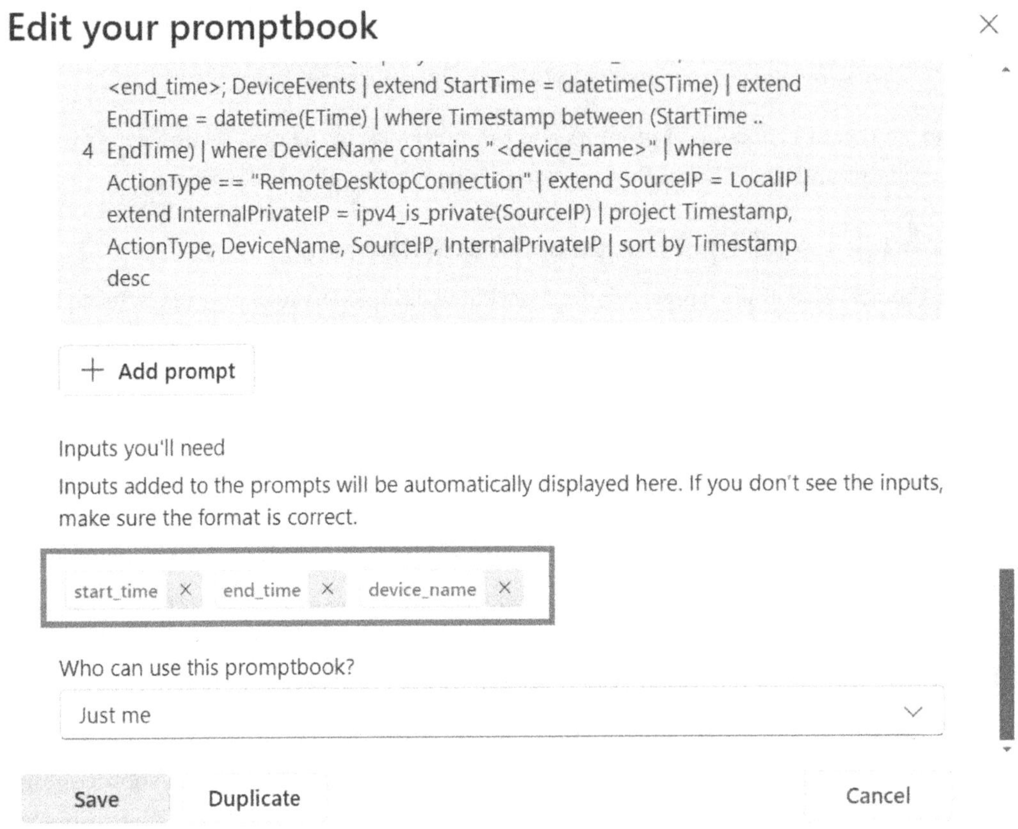

Figure 6.55 – Deleting the existing input definitions in the Inputs you'll need section

Once you save the updated prompt that contains the redefined input parameters, the new input definitions will again appear in the **Inputs you'll need** section. If you don't delete the previous input definitions, perhaps because you haven't changed the input parameter name, Security Copilot may retain the old settings. This could lead to issues, such as the promptbook not functioning as expected because it's not using the correct input parameter.

While modifying your promptbook, be sure to save it frequently, even if you're not finished with all the updates. Often, while editing the promptbook, you may accidentally click the scroll bar in the main Security Copilot window. This can cause the promptbook editing dialog box to disappear entirely, resulting in the loss of any unsaved changes.

There is no straightforward way to create a new promptbook from scratch. One option is to select at least one prompt within a Security Copilot session to get to the **Create promptbook** icon. Alternatively, you can navigate to an existing promptbook and use the **Duplicate** option to create a new one. To make this process more user-friendly and straightforward, you can prepare a template promptbook in advance. This template can then serve as a direct way for you to quickly start a new promptbook from scratch. It also acts as a foundation for starting a new promptbook with minimal modification from existing prompts or promptbooks.

For instance, as illustrated in the following screenshot, when you're ready to create a new promptbook, you can go directly to the pre-existing promptbook template named **New Promptbook Template** within the **My promptbooks** section. From there, simply select the **Duplicate** option to start developing a new promptbook from scratch:

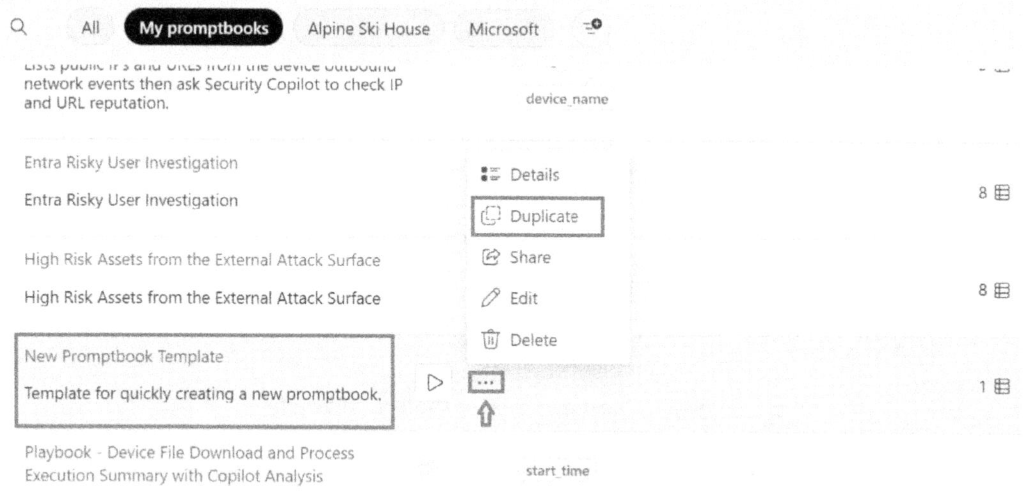

Figure 6.56 – New Promptbook Template within the My promptbooks section

The pre-existing promptbook template is a basic promptbook containing just one prompt, with no input parameters or predefined plugins. This allows you to quickly update the promptbook's name, description, and prompts, as well as add any necessary input parameters as needed for your new promptbook:

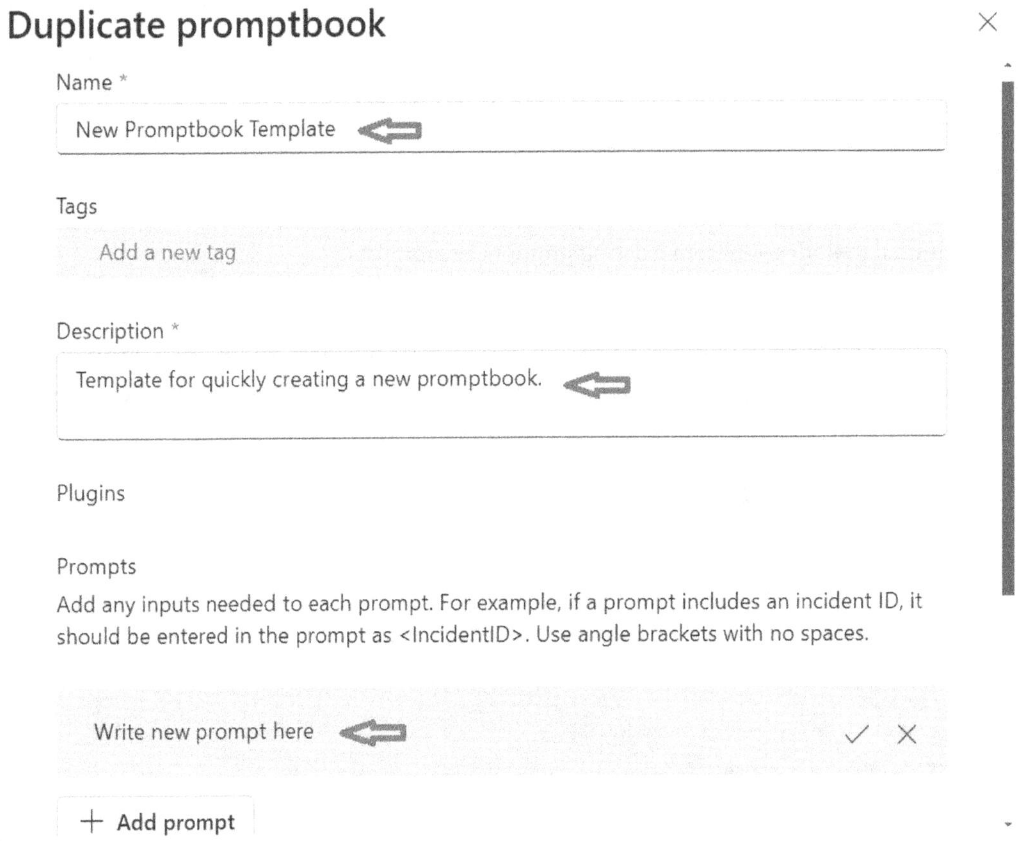

Figure 6.57 – The pre-existing promptbook template

Lastly, instead of clicking through multiple menu options to access the promptbook library each time, you can use `https://securitycopilot.microsoft.com/promptbooks` to get to the promptbook library faster. You can also easily access a specific promptbook by bookmarking the promptbook link you obtained through the promptbook sharing option.

Summary

This chapter unveiled the power of promptbooks and their role in Security Copilot. It showcased an array of prebuilt promptbooks, followed by detailed guidance on creating custom promptbooks. With this knowledge, you should now have a solid understanding of how promptbooks work. You should also be equipped to effectively use and create promptbooks. This will boost your efficiency and effectiveness in managing security operations while integrating promptbooks into your security workflows.

Looking ahead, in the next chapter, we will explore how Security Copilot integrates with **Logic Apps** to automate security workflows. We'll also discuss how to enhance Copilot with a custom knowledge base, including uploading files for Security Copilot to reference during responses.

7

Automation and Integration – The Next Frontier

The previous chapter focused on **promptbooks**, which are collections of pre-configured prompts chained together in a specific sequence to accomplish particular tasks. Essentially, the promptbook acts as a playbook, guiding Security Copilot through a series of actions to automate specific security workflows with minimal input. Since a promptbook can be reused repeatedly, it is particularly useful for automating routine security operations or responding to common incidents in a consistent and predefined manner.

While promptbooks are great, another powerful option for automation is to integrate Security Copilot directly into your **Azure Logic Apps** workflows. In this chapter, we'll introduce Azure Logic Apps and explore its capabilities. We'll take a closer look at the **Security Copilot Logic Apps Connector** and its functionalities. We'll also walk through examples to demonstrate how integrating Security Copilot into your Logic Apps workflows can offer a more flexible, scalable, and customizable approach to automation.

While Azure Logic Apps further helps to automate workflows and streamline security processes, Security Copilot's capabilities can be enhanced even more by integrating it with additional data sources, such as your enterprise knowledge base. This enables Security Copilot to leverage organization-specific insights for more tailored responses. Later in this chapter, we will take a look at how this can be achieved using Security Copilot's file upload option and the **Azure AI Search plugin**, which allows for powerful querying and analysis of large datasets.

In summary, this chapter will guide you through the following two key topics:

- Integrating Security Copilot with Logic Apps
- Empowering Security Copilot with custom knowledge base integration

> Want to try out the prompts, custom plugins, and promptbooks featured in this book? Take a look at the book's GitHub repository at `https://github.com/PacktPublishing/Microsoft-Copilot-for-Security`.

Integrating Security Copilot with Logic Apps

Promptbooks are typically ideal for automating simple and repetitive security tasks. However, integrating Security Copilot with Azure Logic Apps offers a more robust and scalable approach to automation. Azure Logic Apps allows for a high degree of customization, such as handling parallel tasks, applying conditional logic, and interacting with a wide range of services. With this, you can build end-to-end automation that combines Security Copilot with other applications, databases, and systems, automating security tasks while integrating them into broader business processes. For example, with Azure Logic Apps, you can send notifications through Microsoft Teams to ensure security teams are immediately informed about critical situations identified by Security Copilot. This integration allows organizations to create complex workflows that not only automate security actions but also integrate seamlessly with other business processes, providing greater customization, control, and scalability for complex automation needs.

To fully understand the power of this integration, let's begin by exploring what Azure Logic Apps is and how it works.

Azure Logic Apps – the brains behind automation

Azure Logic Apps (often referred to as Logic Apps) is a tool that helps to automate tasks, making it easier to streamline workflows without needing to write code. Imagine you have a repetitive task, such as moving files from one system to another, or getting notifications when certain events happen. Instead of doing these tasks manually, a logic app can handle them for you automatically.

Azure Logic Apps works by connecting to different applications and services and setting up workflows. These workflows are like a set of instructions that tell the system when to do something and what to do next. For example, if a new file is uploaded to an **SSH File Transfer Protocol server (SFTP server)**, a logic app can automatically move it to a secure storage location in the cloud.

Using Azure Logic Apps can save time by eliminating manual intervention and speeding up tasks. It also reduces errors since the processes are automated, meaning fewer mistakes. And the best part is, you don't need to be a programmer to use it. Anyone can create a workflow within a logic app using an easy, drag-and-drop visual designer.

To give you a clearer understanding of what a logic app looks like and how it works, let's take a look at a real-world example, which is displayed in the next screenshot:

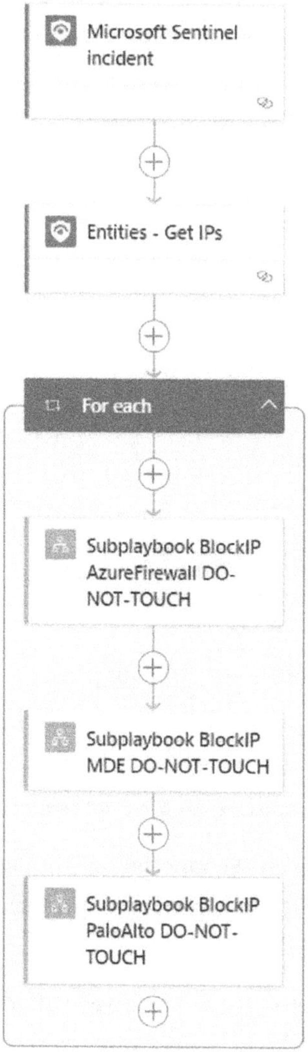

Figure 7.1 – An example of a logic app workflow

This is an example of a simple logic app workflow. First, IP address entities are extracted from a new security incident in Microsoft Sentinel, a **security information and event management (SIEM)** solution. Then each extracted IP is fed into three additional workflows: one is to block the extracted IP using **Azure Firewall**, the other is to block the IP with **Microsoft Defender for Endpoint** (**MDE**), and the third is to block the same IP in a **Palo Alto firewall.**

In this example, the logic app is connected with Microsoft Sentinel. When a new incident is created in Sentinel, the logic app workflow automatically receives **Microsoft Sentinel incident** as its input, including key information such as alerts and affected entities. This is shown in the next diagram:

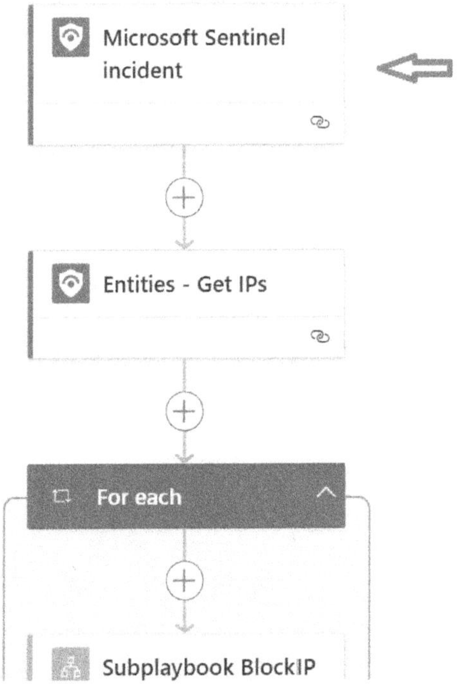

Figure 7.2 – The logic app receives Microsoft Sentinel incident as its input

The integration between Logic Apps and Sentinel is done through the **Sentinel connector** in Azure Logic Apps. This connector acts as the link that passes the incident data from Sentinel into Logic Apps, triggering a predefined workflow.

In addition to the Sentinel connector, Azure Logic Apps offers access to more than 1,000 other connectors. When creating a workflow in Logic Apps, you can use these connectors to interact with data, events, and resources across different applications, services, and systems, all without the need for coding. Each connector includes pre-configured actions that can be used within your workflow, streamlining the integration and automation process.

One of the connectors available in Azure Logic Apps is the **Microsoft Security Copilot connector**. In the next section, we'll take a closer look at how this connector lets you incorporate Security Copilot in your Azure Logic Apps workflows. You'll learn about the tasks the connector can perform, along with its available settings and options, to help you start using it in your security workflows.

The Security Copilot Logic Apps connector

As you create a workflow in Azure Logic Apps, you can use the Security Copilot connector to incorporate Security Copilot prompts and promptbooks into your security automation.

For example, you have the **Add an action** option when developing a new workflow in Azure Logic Apps, as shown in the next screen capture:

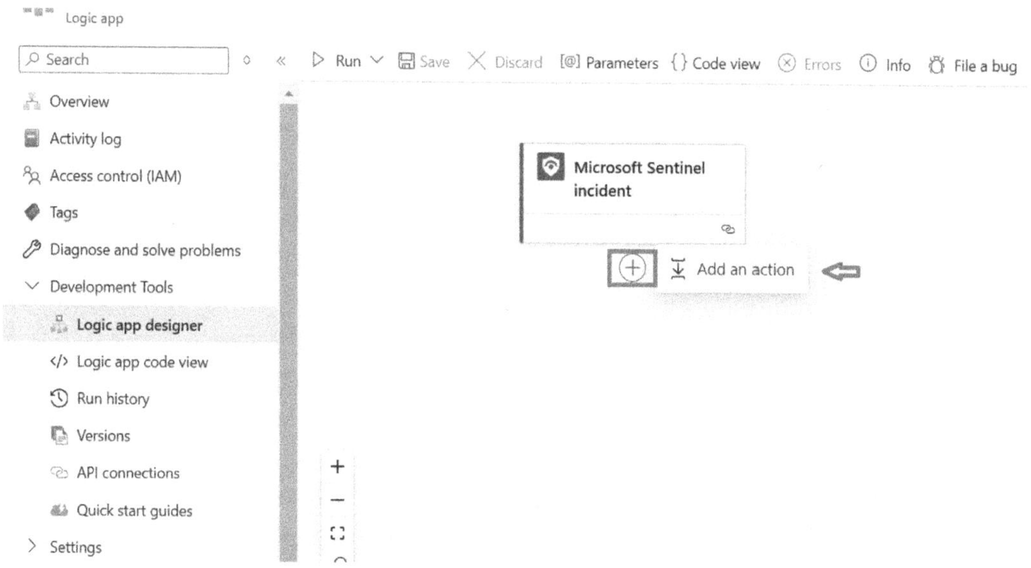

Figure 7.3 – The "Add an action" feature

After you click on the **Add an action** option, you can then search for different connectors to add. Let's enter the keyword `copilot` in the search bar. As shown in the next screenshot, two Security Copilot actions then appear: **Run a Copilot for Security promptbook** and **Submit a Copilot for Security prompt**.

Note

Microsoft changed the product name from **Copilot for Security** to **Security Copilot** in November 2024. While the updated name, Security Copilot, is used throughout the book, some screenshots may still show the earlier name, Copilot for Security. For example, by the time you begin working with Azure Logic Apps, the two Security Copilot actions should appear as **Run a Security Copilot promptbook** and **Submit a Security Copilot prompt.**

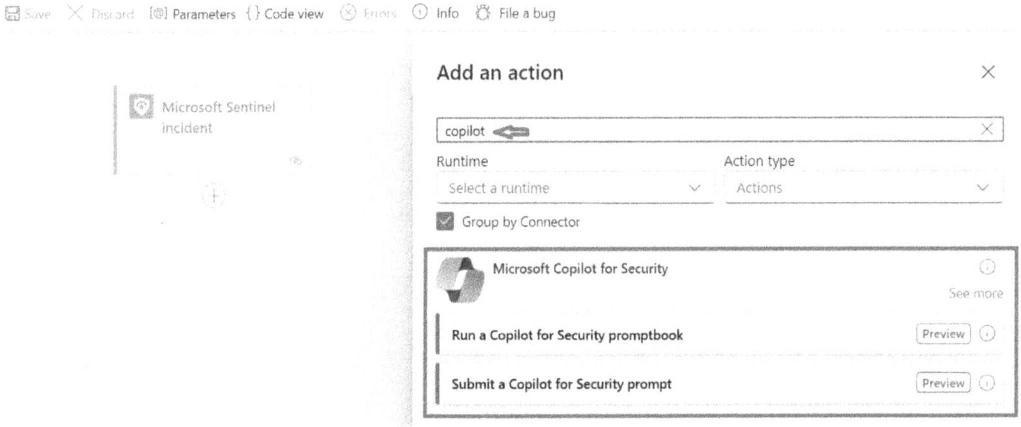

Figure 7.4 – Security Copilot actions

If you choose **Submit a Copilot for Security prompt**, this option is added to the existing workflow, and its side panel opens on the right, allowing you to enter the necessary parameters for the Security Copilot action. This is illustrated in the screenshot shown next:

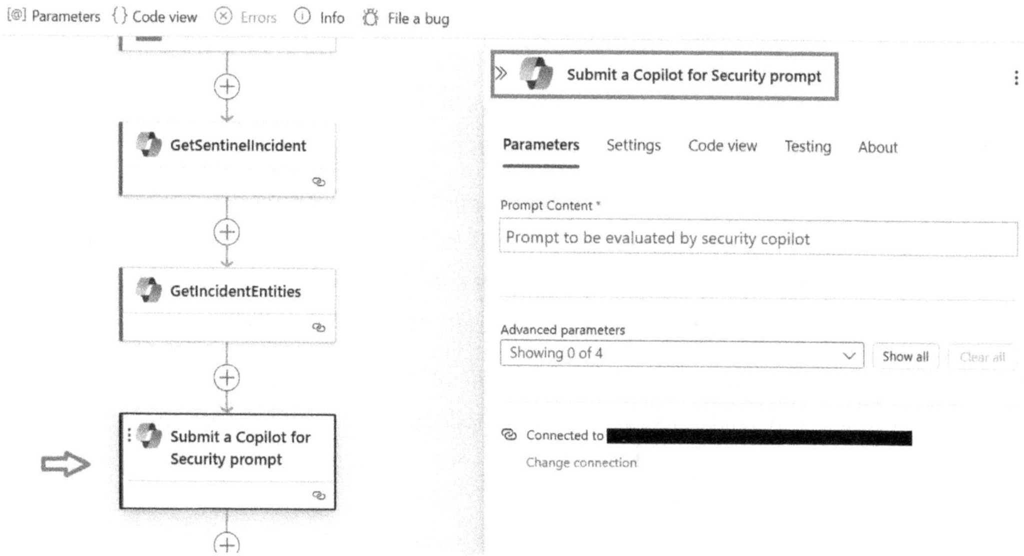

Figure 7.5 – The Submit a Copilot for Security prompt action

The key parameter to configure is the required **Prompt Content** input field, as shown in the next screen capture. This is where you enter the natural language prompt for Security Copilot to execute, as part of the automated workflow tasks:

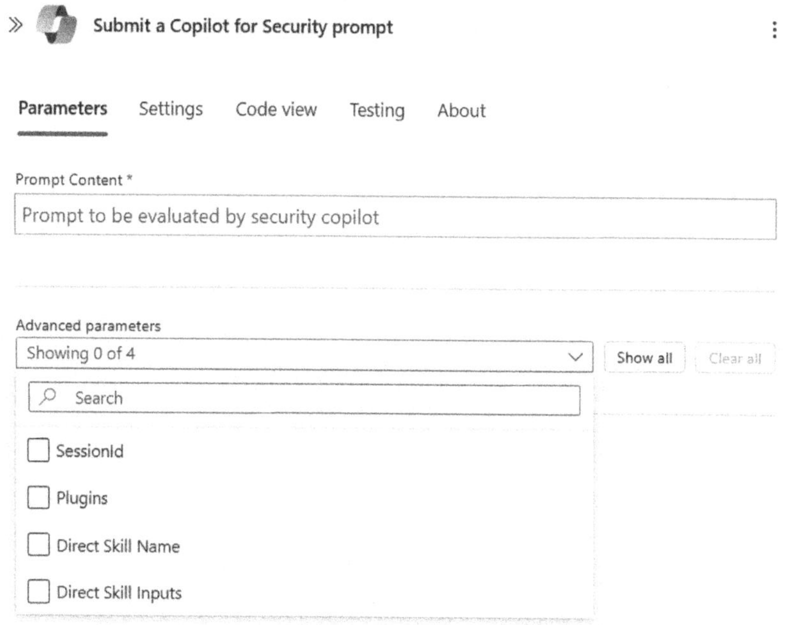

Figure 7.6 – The Submit a Copilot for Security prompt action UI

Also included in the side panel is the **Advanced parameters** option, illustrated in the previous screen capture. Expanding this section reveals four optional configuration settings: **SessionId**, **Plugins**, **Direct Skill Name**, and **Direct Skill Inputs**. These options are available for you to choose from, and you can select the ones that best suit your preferences for the setup.

SessionId is an optional field that lets you enter a Copilot session ID to maintain continuity across your tasks. By using the session ID, your prompts will be linked to the same session, allowing you to build on previous actions or queries. If you do not enter a session ID, Copilot will create a new investigation session, treating the task as in a separate and standalone session.

Plugins is another optional field. It gives you the flexibility to specify which plugin you'd like to use for the prompt, instead of letting Security Copilot automatically choose one for you. This gives you greater control, ensuring that the plugin you prefer is used for the specific task, and it also helps to prevent potential plugin collisions.

The third optional field, **Direct Skill Name**, allows you to refine your prompt even further by specifying the exact skill in a plugin that you'd like to use, rather than just specifying the plugin itself.

Finally, the **Direct Skill Inputs** field pairs with the third optional field, **Direct Skill Name**. A skill typically requires input parameters. This option allows you to define the input parameters for the specific skill you've selected.

You have the flexibility to choose which options you want to include. In this example, let's select all four, as shown next:

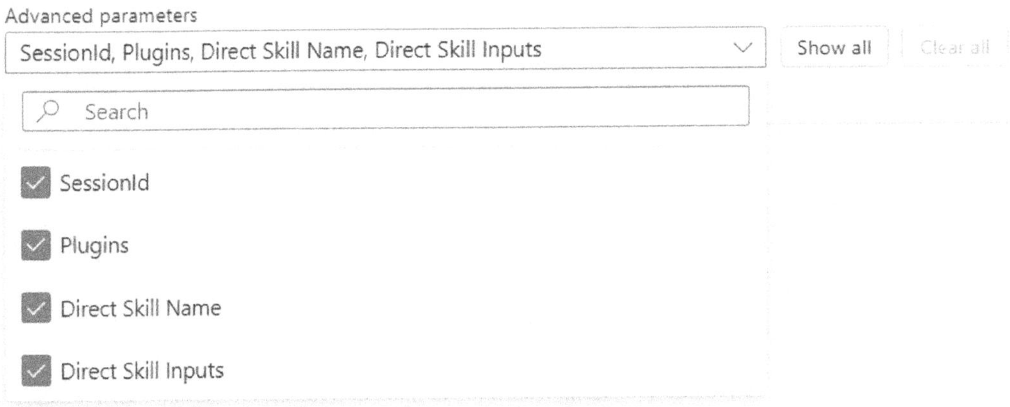

Figure 7.7 – The Advanced parameters options

The selected options are then populated in the side panel, as shown in the next screenshot:

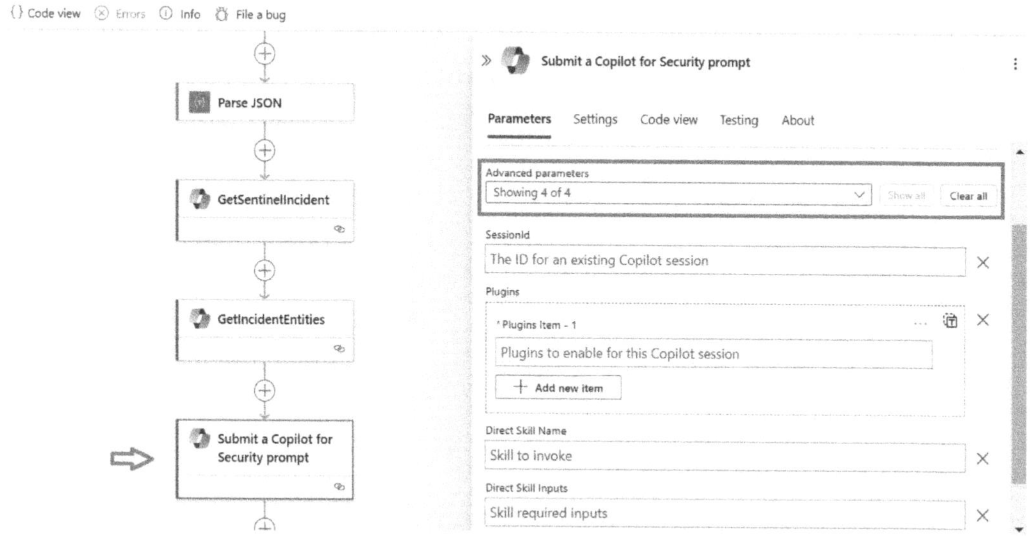

Figure 7.8 – The selected options populated in the side panel

Once you've filled in the different fields in the **Submit a Copilot for Security prompt** option, you can click the **Add an action** (the plus sign inside a circle) icon to add another option. In this example, let's choose **Run a Copilot for Security promptbook**. After selecting it, this option is added to the workflow and its side panel opens on the right. This is illustrated in the following screen capture:

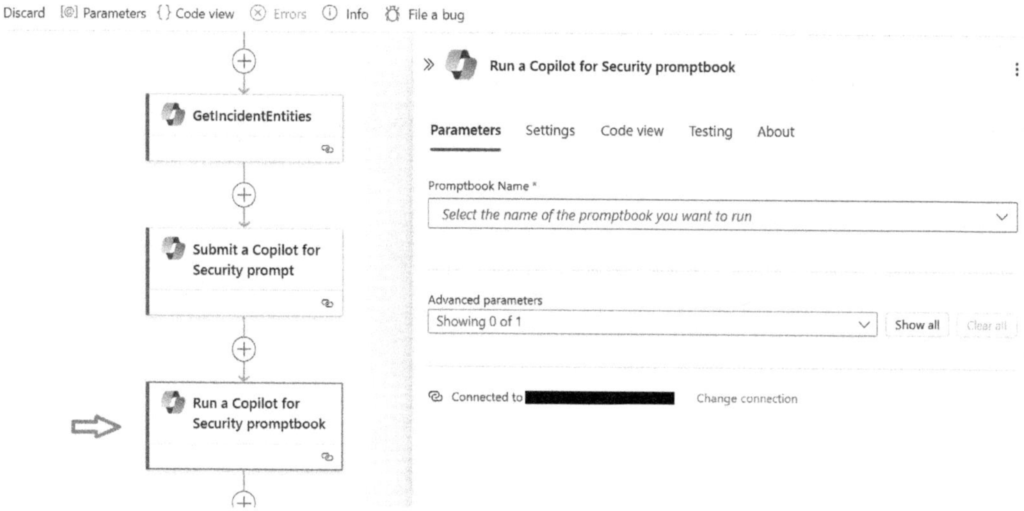

Figure 7.9 – The Run a Copilot for Security promptbook action

After specifying the name of a promptbook in the required **Promptbook Name** field, the **PromptbookInputs** field then appears, as shown in the next screenshot. Make sure the relevant promptbook inputs are entered, or the promptbook in the workflow will not run successfully. Additionally, you have the option to specify the Security Copilot session ID to maintain continuity across your tasks:

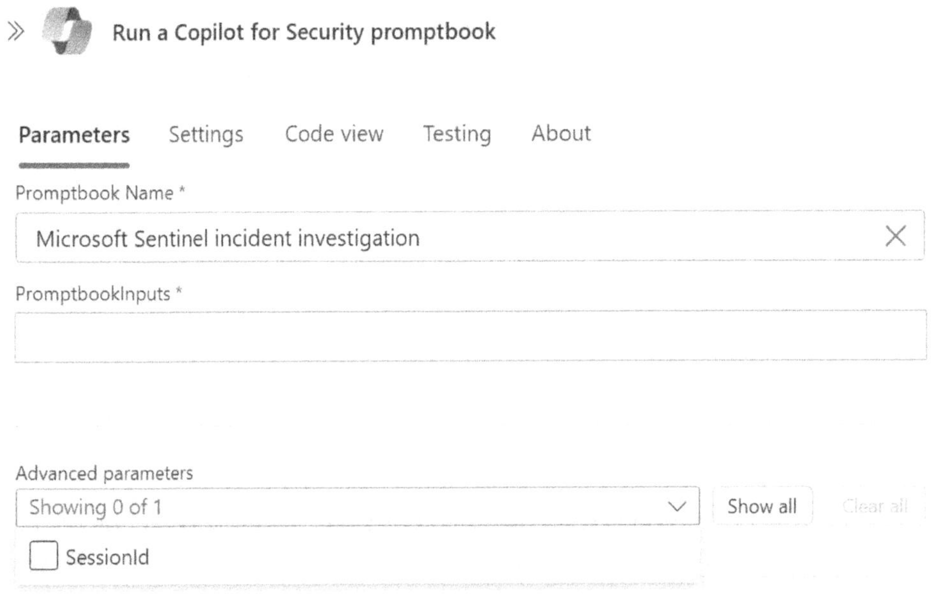

Figure 7.10 – Fields in the Run a Copilot for Security promptbook action

In short, within your Azure Logic Apps workflow, the Security Copilot connector lets you run prompts and promptbooks using the Security Copilot service. The responses you receive from Security Copilot can then trigger further actions in your workflow. This entire process is integrated seamlessly into Azure Logic Apps as part of the overall automation logic.

> Note
>
> Security Copilot is continuously improving with new features introduced regularly. By the time you're reading this, you may notice a third available action in the Security Copilot connector, **Fetch prompt status**, which is used to retrieve the evaluation status of a prompt.

Now that you have had a solid introduction to Azure Logic Apps and the Security Copilot connector, in the next section, let's take a look at a specific example of Azure Logic Apps using the Security Copilot connector to perform security-related automation.

Powering up automation with Logic Apps and Security Copilot

We will use an Azure Logic Apps workflow that hunts for suspicious PowerShell activity and automatically emails the findings as an example. It showcases how integrating Security Copilot with Logic Apps can enhance operational efficiency.

Let's first take a quick look at how the logic app works behind the scenes. Designed to run every hour, the first step in this logic app workflow prompts Security Copilot to identify detailed PowerShell execution events seen in the environment for the last hour. In the next step, Security Copilot analyzes these events and looks for anything suspicious. If no threats are found, the logic app workflow terminates itself. However, if any suspicious activity is detected, the workflow proceeds by instructing Security Copilot to draft an email to the security team. In its final step, the workflow calls Outlook to send out the email.

To better illustrate how these steps are connected in the workflow, the next screenshot provides a visual overview of the full logic app design:

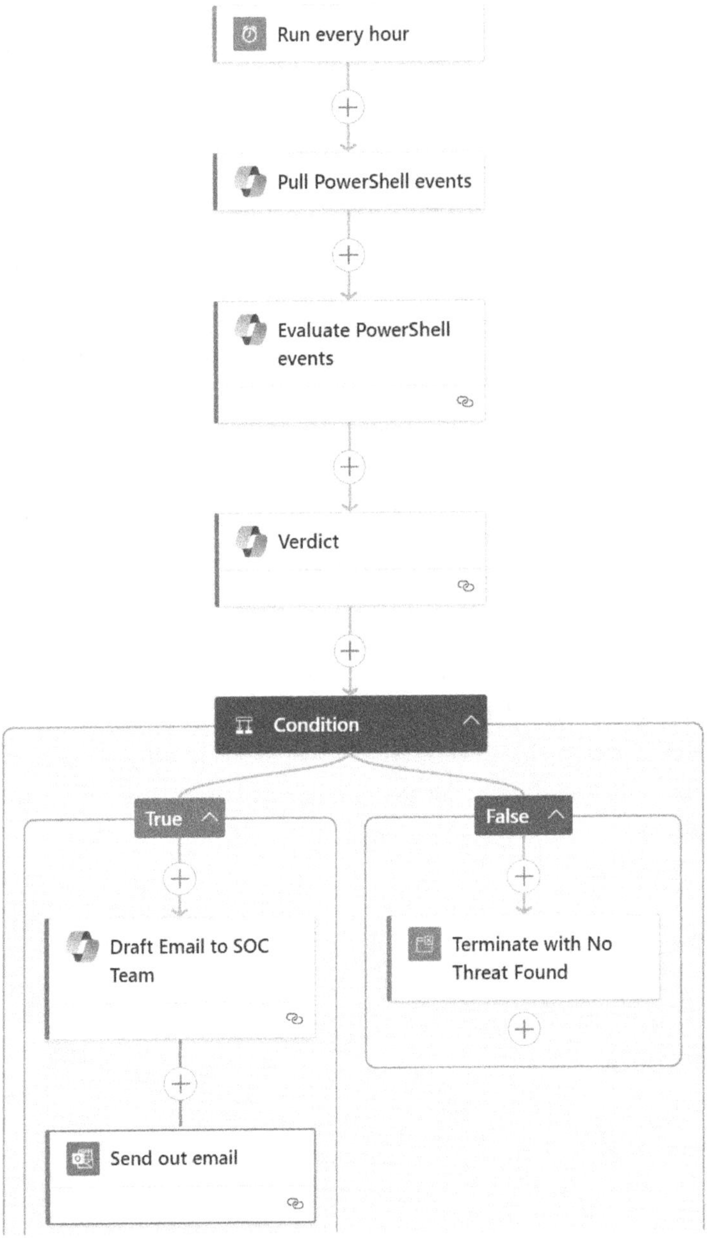

Figure 7.11 – The full logic app workflow

This logic app is relatively straightforward and easy to follow. Now let's take a closer look at it, especially the Security Copilot connector used in this workflow.

Every Logic Apps workflow starts with a trigger that defines when the logic app should run. For this workflow, the trigger is configured to activate every hour. As illustrated in the next screenshot, in the logic app designer pane, the workflow starts with a trigger named **Run every hour** and is displayed on the left side of the designer pane. When you select this trigger, its configuration pane appears on the right side. You can then review or configure the settings of this trigger:

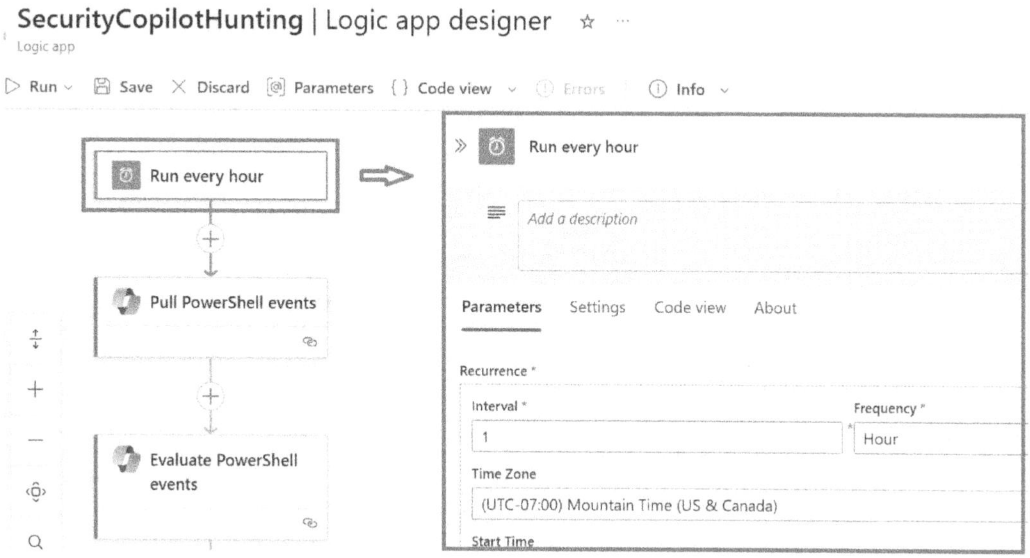

Figure 7.12 – Trigger in the Logic Apps workflow

Quick tip: Need to see a high-resolution version of this image? Open this book in the next-gen Packt Reader or view it in the PDF/ePub copy.

The next-gen Packt Reader and a **free PDF/ePub copy** of this book are included with your purchase. Scan the QR code OR visit `packtpub.com/unlock`, then use the search bar to find this book by name. Double-check the edition shown to make sure you get the right one.

Once the trigger is configured, the logic app workflow proceeds to its first action, instructing Security Copilot to retrieve detailed PowerShell execution events in the last hour. This action uses the Security Copilot connector to define and execute the prompt. As shown in the next screenshot, the action is labeled **Pull PowerShell events**. In its configuration pane, the Security Copilot prompt is set with an Advanced Hunting KQL query to collect the PowerShell event data:

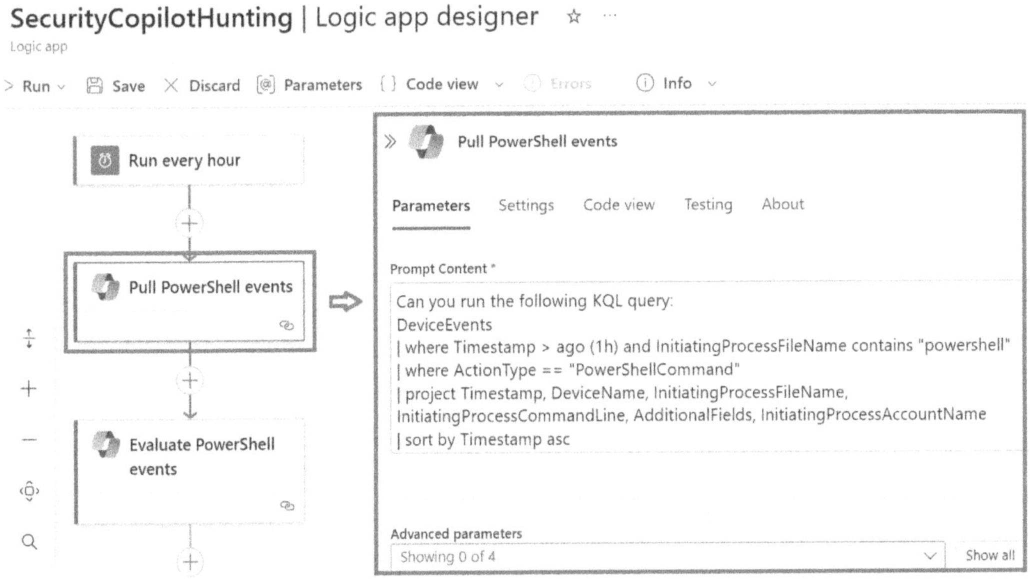

Figure 7.13 – The Pull PowerShell events action in the logic app workflow

The output of PowerShell events from this action is passed to the next step in the workflow – an action named **Evaluate PowerShell events**. This step also uses the Security Copilot connector. The prompt defined in this action is designed to analyze the retrieved PowerShell events and to identify any suspicious activity.

The next screenshot illustrates this action:

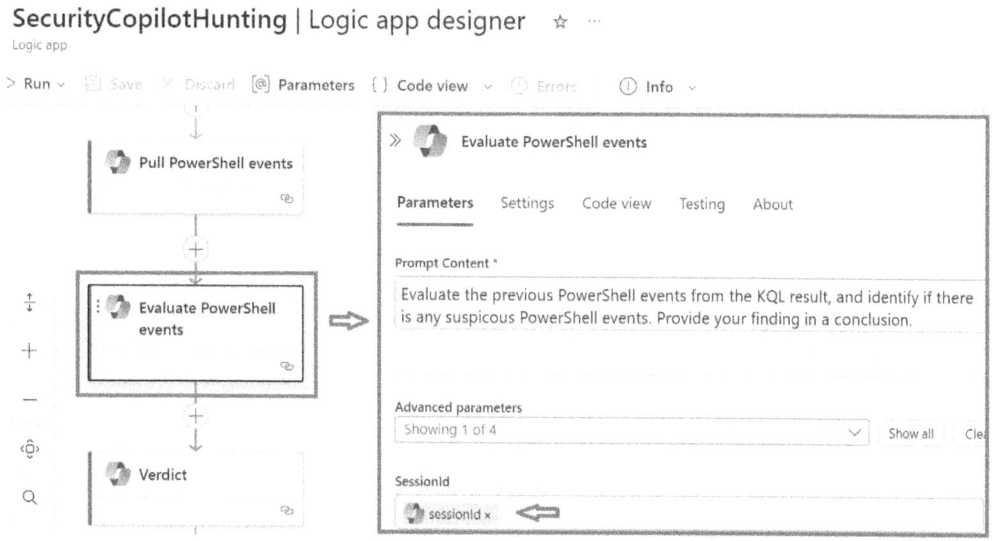

Figure 7.14 – The Evaluate PowerShell events action

Notice that from the previous screenshot, in addition to defining the Copilot prompt, **SessionId** is also selected. **SessionId** enables Security Copilot to maintain context and state across multiple steps within the same logic app workflow. This ensures continuity by allowing each action to build on the Security Copilot data in earlier steps.

Once the logic app completes the step of analyzing PowerShell events for suspicious activity, its next action calls the Security Copilot connector again. This time, it is to ask Security Copilot to summarize the analysis results with a simple verdict of either **threat found** or **no threat found.** This step prepares the workflow for the upcoming **Condition** action, which determines the appropriate follow-up actions based on the verdict. The action, named **Verdict**, along with its associated Security Copilot prompt, is illustrated next:

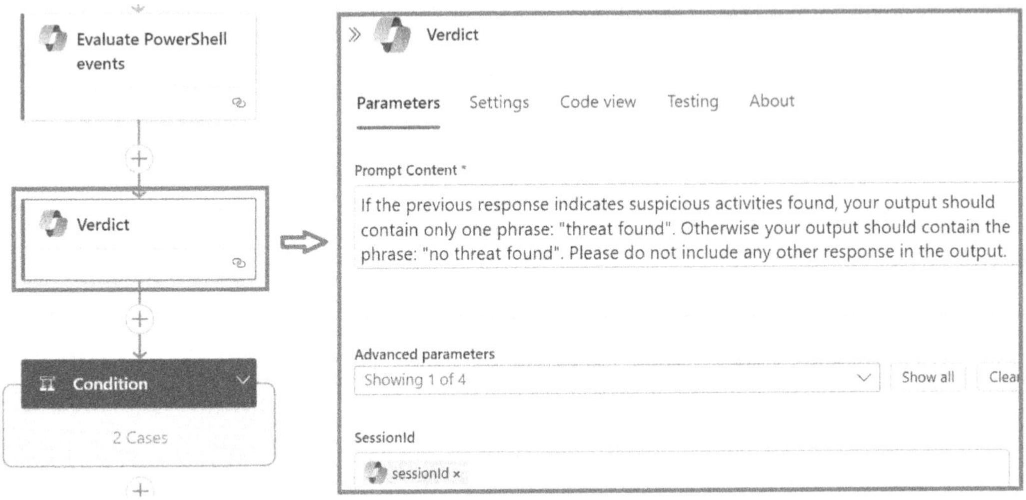

Figure 7.15 – The Verdict action in the logic app workflow

Every time the logic app workflow executes, you can review its run results. For reference, the next screenshot displays the results page from one such execution. As you can see, at the **Verdict** step of the execution, the result shown in the **EvaluationResultContent** field indicates a verdict of **threat found**:

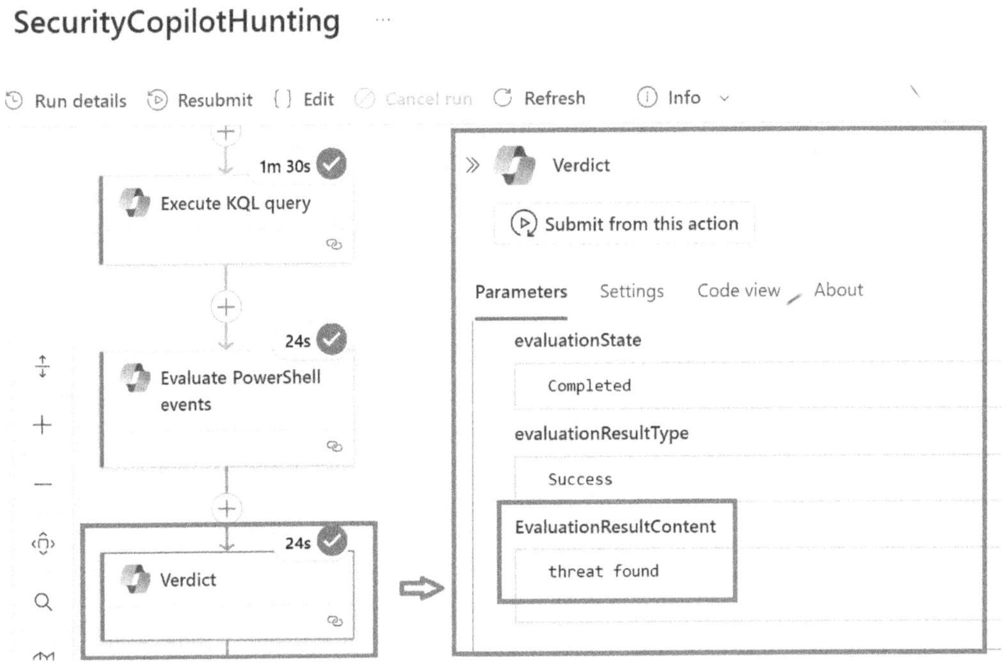

Figure 7.16 – The logic app workflow run result page

The value in the **EvaluationResultContent** field is passed to the next step in the workflow, a **Condition** action. The next screenshot shows the details of this action and the configuration pane of the subsequent action when the condition evaluates to **True**:

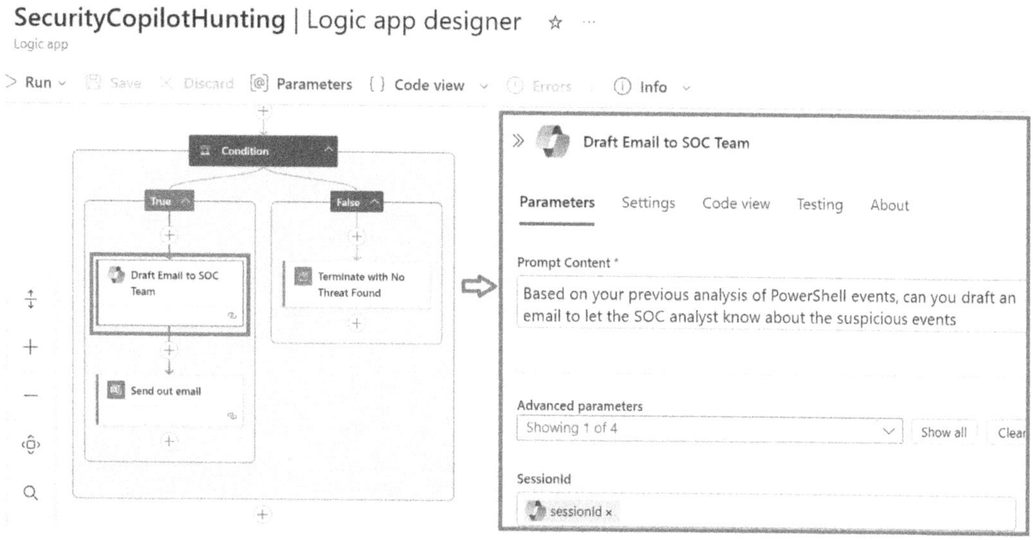

Figure 7.17 – The Condition action details

From the **Condition** action details, you can see that if the verdict is **threat found**, the logic app workflow calls Security Copilot to draft an email for the SOC team. Otherwise, it terminates the workflow.

The following screenshot displays a portion of the email generated by Security Copilot, as a result of the Security Copilot action named **Draft Email to SOC Team** being triggered during one of the workflow executions:

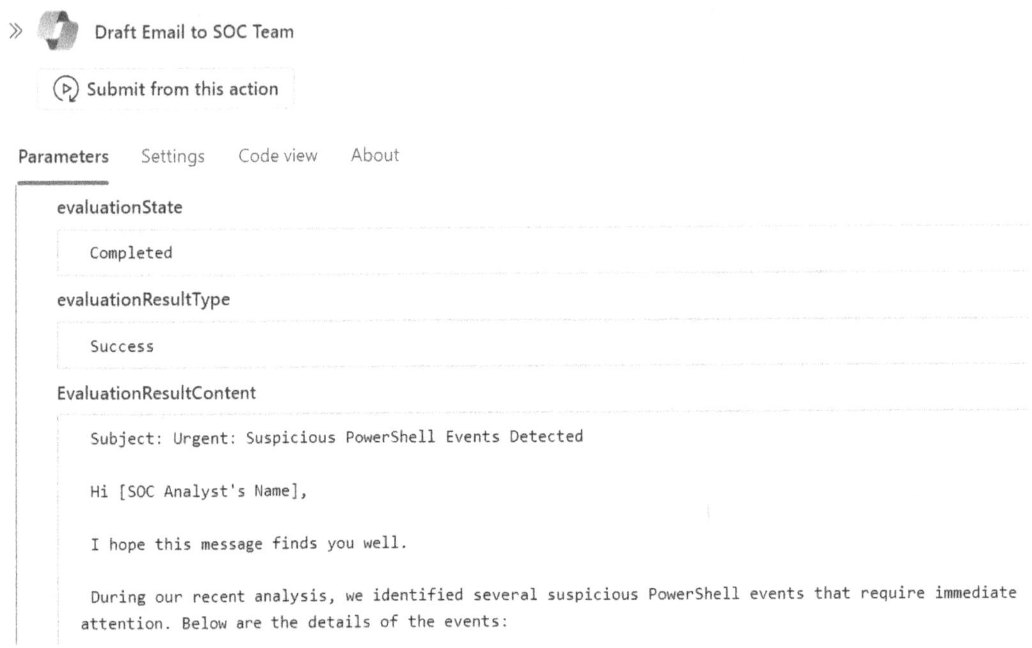

Figure 7.18 – A portion of the email generated by Security Copilot

The next and also the final step in the **Condition** action's **True** branch is to send out the drafted email using the Office 365 Outlook connector. This step also marks the end of the logic app workflow. This short and simple workflow is intended to demonstrate how integrating Security Copilot with Azure Logic Apps can unlock greater automation flexibility. As illustrated in this workflow, the **Condition** feature allows you to branch to different actions based on previous results, while connectors such as Outlook allow automated delivery of emails generated by Security Copilot. With Azure Logic Apps, you gain a broader range of automation capabilities beyond what Security Copilot provides on its own.

To further illustrate this, for instance, you can extend the workflow just discussed with additional automation. When sending the drafted email through the Outlook connector, you can include an adaptive card with **Approve** and **Reject** buttons in the email. This allows the security analyst to review the suspicious PowerShell activity and provide feedback. During this time, the logic app enters a waiting state until the analyst responds. Once a selection is made, the workflow resumes to trigger additional follow-up actions, such as automatically opening a ServiceNow ticket if the analyst clicks the **Approve** button.

There are already many logic app workflows created by the community, showcasing the automation potential unlocked by integrating Security Copilot with Azure Logic Apps. Reviewing these examples is a great way to explore how to leverage this integration to streamline your security operations.

One such community example that showcases more complex logic app operations using the Security Copilot connector is by Chaitanya Belwal, detailed in his blog post titled *Use LogicApps and Copilot for Security to Auto-Process ISAC Emails* on the Microsoft Tech Community site.

Chaitanya addresses a common challenge that security teams face: manually verifying CVEs listed in **Information Sharing and Analysis Center** (**ISAC**) threat bulletin emails. Typically, security analysts must manually verify whether each CVE listed in the email is present in their environment, then compile a list of affected CVEs for further action. Chaitanya demonstrates how Azure Logic Apps and the Security Copilot connector can automate this process.

The logic app begins by automatically retrieving the ISAC email from the analyst's inbox and extracting the CVEs mentioned. Using the Security Copilot connector, it determines which of those CVEs are present in the analyst's environment. It then enriches each identified CVE with additional threat data from **Microsoft Defender Threat Intelligence** (**MDTI**). Finally, the logic app instructs Security Copilot to generate a report summarizing the detected CVEs and their associated threat intelligence, and sends this report to one or more security analysts via email.

For a detailed, step-by-step explanation of how this logic app operates, be sure to read through its full write-up on the Microsoft Tech Community site at `https://techcommunity.microsoft.com/blog/securitycopilotblog/use-logicapps-and-copilot-for-security-to-auto-process-isac-emails/4243882`. If you'd like to deploy the logic app yourself, it's available on GitHub at `https://github.com/cbelwal/Copilot-For-Security/tree/main/Logic%20Apps/ISAC-Email-Processing`.

In addition to this community logic app example, there are many others featured in the Security Copilot blogs and GitHub repositories. These logic apps often include ready-to-use templates that you can download, install, and explore with minimal configuration. For example, many of the logic app templates that integrate with Security Copilot can be found in the GitHub repository at `https://github.com/Azure/Security-Copilot/tree/main/Logic%20Apps`.

By integrating Security Copilot into Azure Logic Apps, you can automate security tasks, streamline workflows, and enhance response times. This integration allows Security Copilot to trigger predefined actions based on insights, improving consistency and efficiency. Additionally, it offers customization to align with your organization's security protocols while fostering better collaboration across teams.

Building on this, you can further enhance Security Copilot's capabilities by incorporating additional data sources, which will enable Security Copilot to better understand and adapt to your organization's unique security needs. Let's explore this in the next section.

Empowering Security Copilot with custom knowledge base integration

Security Copilot is designed to leverage a vast amount of information, data, and insights to assist with cybersecurity tasks. Additionally, you can integrate extra data sources, such as your organization's internal policies, specific security playbooks, or other security-related documentation, to further enhance its capabilities. Incorporating your own knowledge base into Security Copilot allows Copilot to tailor its responses to provide contextually relevant insights that are specific to your unique security environment, improving the accuracy and usefulness of its recommendations and analysis.

There are two options to integrate additional data sources into Security Copilot:

- File upload
- Azure AI Search plugin

In the following sections, we'll explore each option in detail.

Using the file upload option to boost Security Copilot's knowledge base

You can upload various types of files containing different information and data to Security Copilot. Copilot can analyze and *reason over* these files, reference the associated information in order to respond to queries, and assist with tasks.

The files can be external reference materials, such as documentation on security investigations or threat hunting shared by others. An example is the *Hunt Evil* Poster from the *SANS Institute* (`https://www.sans.org/posters/hunt-evil/`), which outlines typical Windows behavior to help you identify anomalies. The files can also be the latest updates on emerging threats, vulnerabilities, and tactics used by threat actors. Or, they can be compliance and security standards detailing requirements relevant to risk management or incident handling.

Alternatively, the files can be your organization's internal knowledge base. They can be internal incident response plans, specific investigation processes, forensics guides, or detection playbooks. Other file examples include internal malware analysis reports, vulnerability assessment findings, and security tool documentation, or any other relevant knowledge specific to your organization.

Important note

Be sure to follow your organization's policies before uploading any file that may contain **Personally Identifiable Information** (**PII**) or other sensitive information. As a best practice, you should sanitize documents prior to uploading them to Security Copilot. Currently, **Data Loss Prevention** (**DLP**) protection is not integrated with this feature.

That said, the files uploaded to Security Copilot are private and can only be accessed by the specific user account that uploaded them. Other users, whether within the same organization (tenant) or outside of it, will not have access to these files. Security Copilot operates within Microsoft's controlled environment using OpenAI models, and Microsoft ensures that your prompts, responses, and uploaded data are not shared with other organizations or used to improve the underlying models.

The files uploaded to Security Copilot serve as additional sources of information that enhance Security Copilot's overall understanding and knowledge base. By incorporating such files, Security Copilot can tailor its responses to be more relevant, precise, and aligned with your organization's specific needs and operations. Essentially, these files help Security Copilot to be more effective at providing context and details that are unique to your environment, allowing Copilot to give more accurate and personalized assistance.

Lastly, a quick but important reminder: the file upload feature in Security Copilot is not intended for uploading or analyzing the malicious file itself. Support for malware analysis through sandboxing and detonation will be covered in the future.

Importing files into Security Copilot in a snap

Uploading a file to Security Copilot takes just a few clicks. For example, let's upload a file named `Cobalt Strike.docx`, which contains detailed information about **Cobalt Strike**, a penetration testing tool commonly used by cybercriminals, including ransomware attacks. Here are the steps to upload the file:

1. On the Security Copilot home page, in the prompt bar, select the **Sources** icon, as shown in the next screenshot:

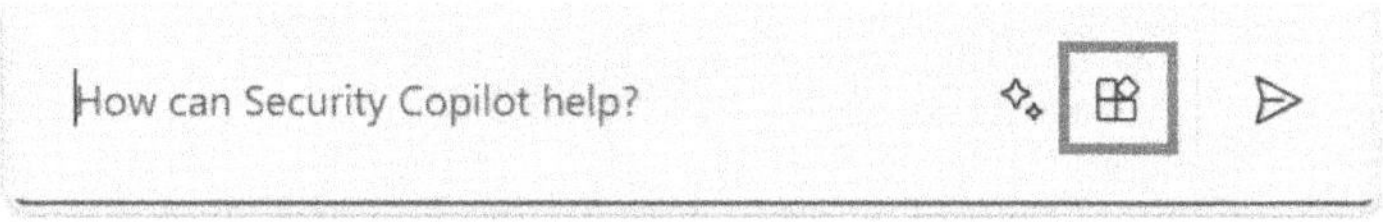

Figure 7.19 – The Sources icon

2. This takes you to the **Manage sources** page, as seen in the next screen capture:

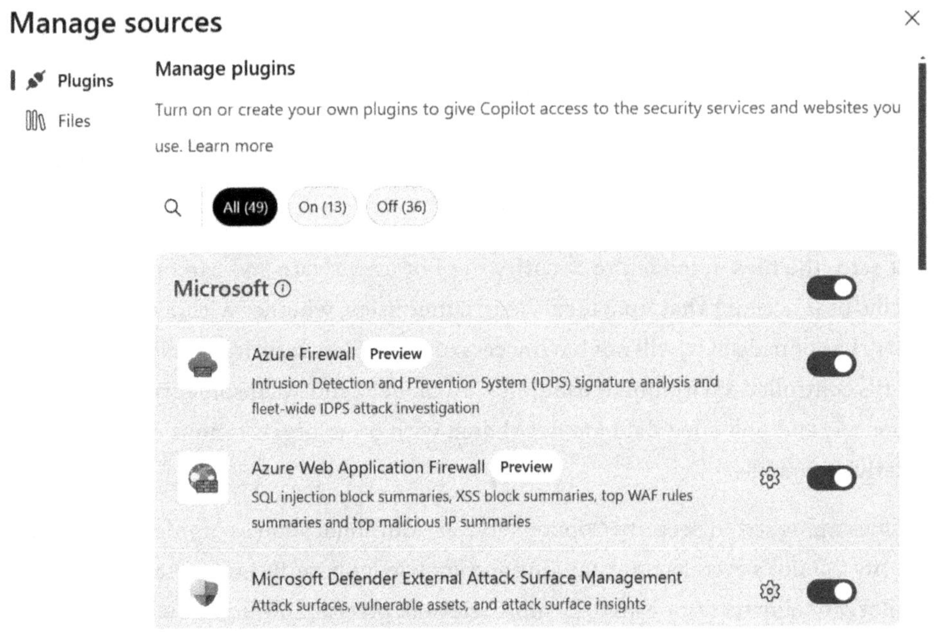

Figure 7.20 – The Manage sources page

3. Selecting the **Files** option on the left side takes you to the file upload section, as illustrated next:

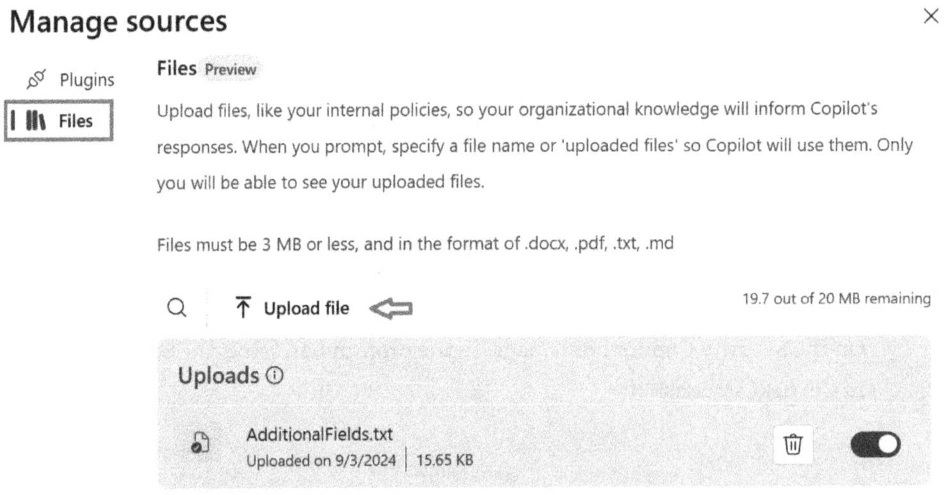

Figure 7.21 – The Files option and the file upload section

4. Click on the **Upload file** option to add a new file to Security Copilot. For this example, you can see the `Cobalt Strike.docx` file is being uploaded, as illustrated in the next screen capture:

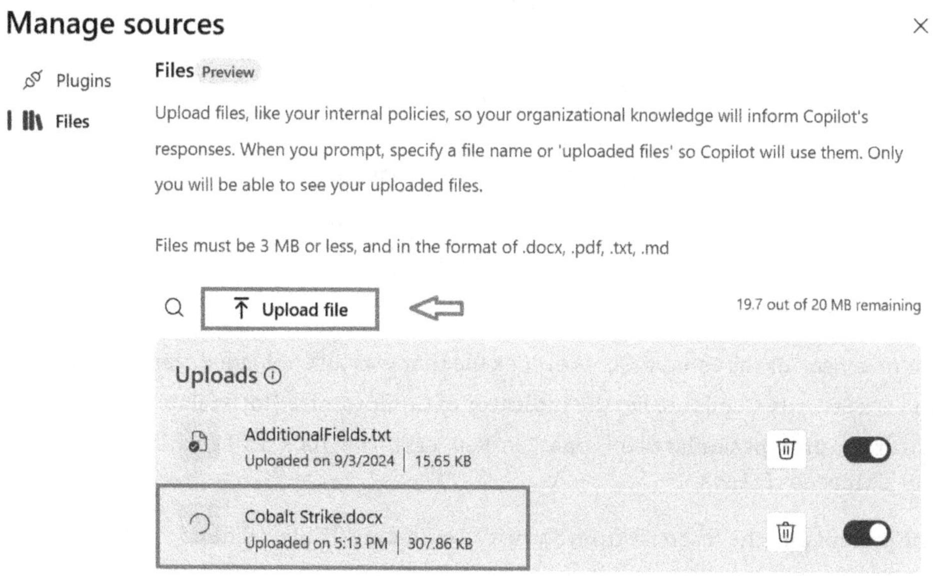

Figure 7.22 – Uploading the Cobalt Strike.docx file

5. The newly uploaded file then appears in the **Uploads** section, as displayed next:

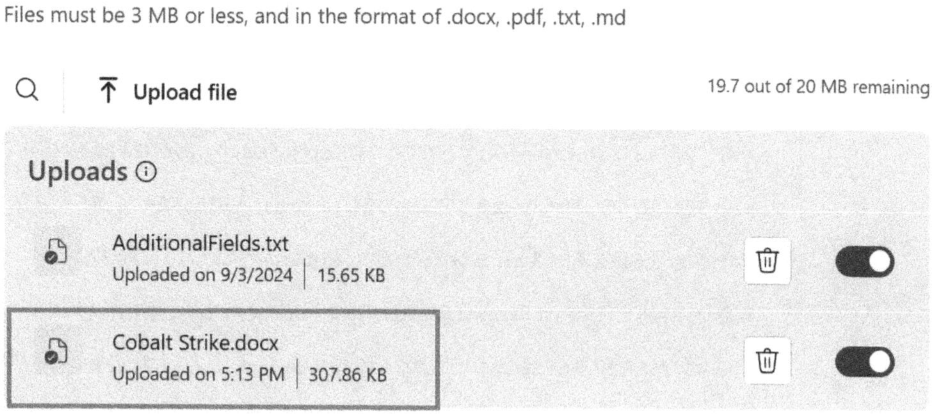

Figure 7.23 – The newly uploaded file seen in the Uploads section

Important note

When uploading files to Security Copilot, the files should be in standard text-based formats such as DOCX (Word documents), MD (Markdown files), PDF, or TXT. Additionally, each individual file must not be larger than 3 MB in size. You can upload multiple files as long as the total combined size does not exceed 20 MB.

Referencing the uploaded file in a prompt

For Security Copilot to use the contents of your uploaded files, you need to specifically mention the files in your prompt. It's best to include the file name in the prompt if you want Security Copilot to focus on a specific file.

For instance, for the `Cobalt Strike.docx` file that was just uploaded, you can reference the file and ask Security Copilot to list the **Indicator of Compromise** (**IoC**) related to Cobalt Strike. You can draft a prompt similar to this one: `Can you list the IOCs in "Cobalt Strike.docx" from the uploaded files?`

The prompt and the response from Security Copilot are displayed next:

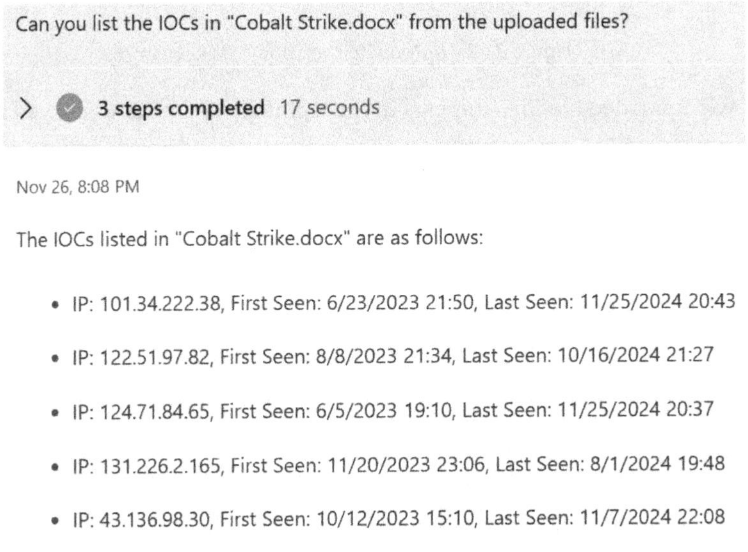

Figure 7.24 – The prompt and the response from Security Copilot

Using natural language, there are different options to refer to an uploaded file in your Security Copilot prompt. The next screenshot shows an alternative method for referencing the uploaded file named `Cobalt Strike.docx`:

In the uploaded files, referencing "Cobalt Strike.docx", can you list some of the common lateral movement techniques observed in Cobalt Strike activities?

> 3 steps completed 19 seconds

Nov 26, 2024

Common lateral movement techniques observed in Cobalt Strike activities include:

1. **Task Scheduler Activity**: Attackers use Task Scheduler to create tasks that execute malicious payloads.

   Examples include:

   - schtasks /create /tn ExampleTask /tr c:\users\W64.exe /sc once /st 00:00 /S ./RU System
   - schtasks /create /tn ExampleTask /tr <redacted>\users\W64.exe /sc once /st 00:00 /S ./RU System
   - schtasks /create /tn ExampleTask /tr <redacted>\C$\users\W64.exe /sc once /st 00:00 /S ./RU System
   - schtasks /create /tn ExampleTask /tr <redacted>\C$\users\W64.exe /sc once /st 00:00 /S ./RU <redacted> /RP Password$fun

2. **Suspicious File Creation and Transfer**: Attackers create and transfer suspicious files remotely, such as:

   - Tasked Beacon to copy <redacted>\C$\W64_Stageless_SMB.ps1 to <redacted>\C$\Users\W64.ps1
   - Suspicious file creation initiated remotely

Figure 7.25 – Another way of referencing the uploaded file in the Copilot prompt

Please note that Security Copilot uses the **File Uploads** plugin to reference the uploaded file and generate a response. This is illustrated in the next screen capture:

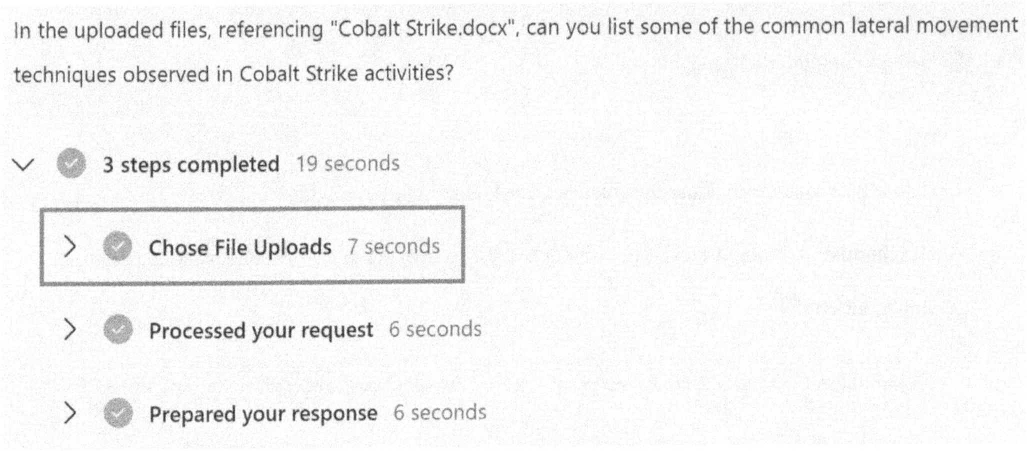

Figure 7.26 – The File Uploads plugin

The file upload option offers a fast and simple way to add extra data sources for Security Copilot to use. It enables you to integrate various data, especially from your organization's knowledge base, to improve Copilot's ability to deliver more customized and relevant responses.

It's important to note that the file upload option is limited to a total of 20 MB of data, which may not be sufficient for larger datasets. To address this limitation, Security Copilot also integrates with **Azure AI Search** to provide a more scalable solution for large volumes of data. By connecting to **Azure AI Search index**, Security Copilot can tap into your organization's vast data resources, offering more accurate and insightful responses tailored to your specific security needs. In the next section, we will take a closer look at Azure AI Search and its plugin offered by Security Copilot.

Supercharging Security Copilot with the Azure AI Search plugin

Azure AI Search is designed to help you search, retrieve information, and extract insights from large volumes of your enterprise data stored in diverse sources, such as databases, documents, or cloud storage.

Azure AI Search works by aggregating different types of data from various sources into a search index. This index acts as a structured catalog that organizes the data in a way that makes it easier and faster to search through. The index allows Azure AI Search to efficiently retrieve relevant information when you perform searches, providing quick and accurate results from large datasets.

Furthermore, with its built-in AI capabilities, Azure AI Search goes beyond simple keyword matching. It understands the context and meaning behind your queries. This enables it to deliver more accurate and relevant results, even when you're not sure of the exact terms you're searching for. For example, if you're looking for information on *summer vacation spots* within a collection of travel articles, a traditional search might only return results that exactly match the term *summer vacation*. Azure AI Search, however, can recognize related terms such as *beach resort* or *road trip*, ensuring you get a broader and more relevant set of results.

Azure AI Search also includes cognitive search capabilities that can analyze and extract information from unstructured data, which is often difficult to organize or categorize. For instance, if you have a bunch of photos of products and you want to find all the images with a particular item, such as a pen, cognitive search can help to recognize the pen in photos, even if they're not labeled or tagged. Similarly, if you have audio recordings, it can transcribe and extract key information from the content, making it searchable and easier to analyze.

The **Azure AI Search plugin** in Security Copilot allows you to seamlessly connect and interact with an Azure AI Search index directly within the Security Copilot interface. This integration combines Azure AI Search's capabilities with Security Copilot's advanced security features, enabling you to reference, analyze, and extract insights from large volumes of enterprise data stored in the Azure AI Search index. As a result, it enhances Security Copilot's ability to deliver tailored, relevant results, customized to meet your organization's needs.

Setup guide for the Azure AI Search plugin

In order to use the Azure AI Search plugin within Security Copilot, you must first configure it in your Security Copilot environment. Security Copilot can then query your organization's data stored in the Azure AI Search index, allowing it to retrieve information for tasks such as answering questions, analyzing content, and making decisions based on the knowledge in the index.

To start setting up the Azure AI Search plugin, you can follow the steps outlined next:

1. On the Security Copilot home page, in the prompt bar, select the **Sources** icon, as shown in the next screenshot:

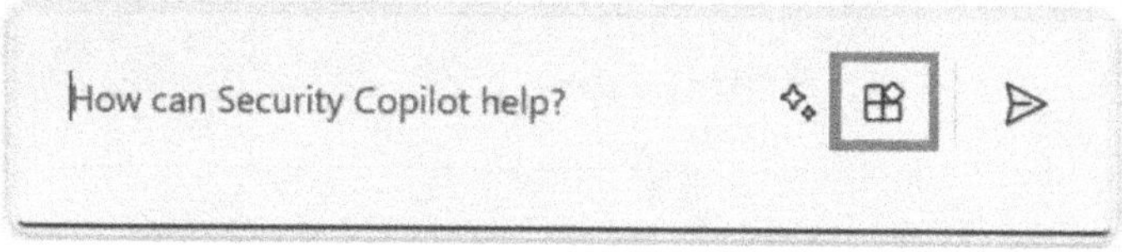

Figure 7.27 – The Sources icon in the prompt bar

2. This then takes you to the **Manage sources** page, where you can configure the Azure AI Search plugin, as displayed in the next screen capture:

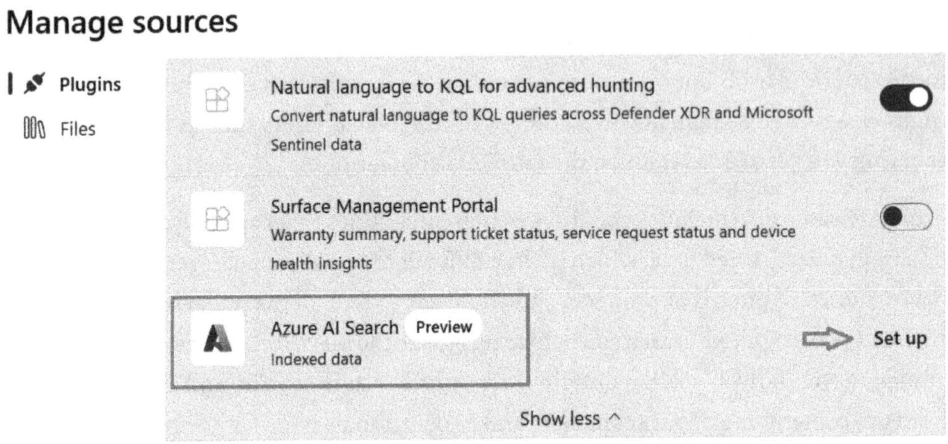

Figure 7.28 – The Azure AI Search plugin

3. The Azure AI Search setup page requires you to complete the mandatory fields to configure the Azure AI Search index. A screenshot of the setup page is displayed next:

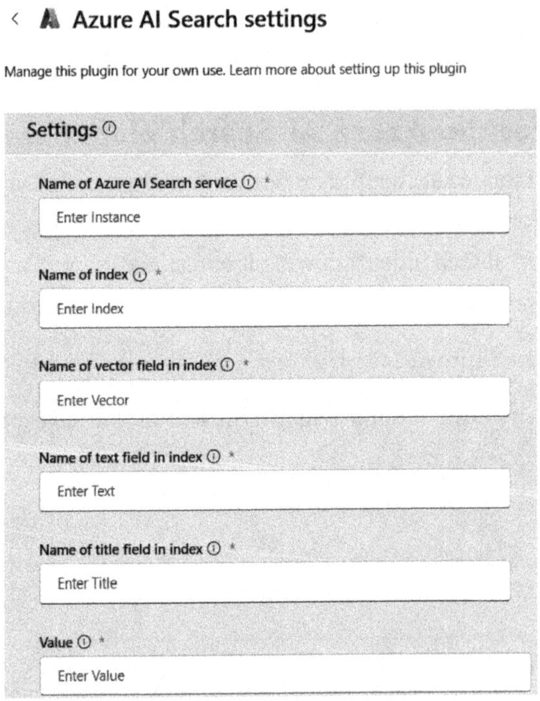

Figure 7.29 – The Azure AI Search settings

For your reference, the description of each field, provided by Microsoft at `https://learn.microsoft.com/en-us/copilot/security/plugin-azure-ai-search#connect-azure-ai-search-to-copilot`, is also listed here:

- **Azure AI Search instance**: The name of your search instance
- **Index**: The name of the index within your instance to search
- **Vector**: The name of the field label in the index containing the vector of embeddings
- **Text**: The name of the field label in the index containing the text to search
- **Title**: The title of each document to display as a source
- **Value**: The API key for authentication

> Important note
>
> The Azure AI Search plugin allows you to connect to only one Azure AI Search index. If you want to search or analyze data from a different index, you need to change the plugin's configuration settings to connect it to that new index.

Referencing Azure AI Search in a prompt

Once the Azure AI Search plugin is configured in Security Copilot, you can directly query and search the data stored in the Azure AI Search index. However, to let Security Copilot know that you want to use the Azure AI Search plugin, you must specifically include the phrase `Azure AI Search` in the prompt.

For instance, if a public-facing web server is compromised, you need to examine the web server logs to track the actions performed on the server, identify suspicious activities, and determine the time of the breach. You load the relevant web server logs into the Azure AI Search index. Then you can use a prompt similar to the one shown next to ask Security Copilot to analyze the logs for you:

```
Can you analyze the web server logs for server1 in Azure AI Search, to
identify any suspicious patterns or malicious activities such as unusual
HTTP request methods, or exploitation attempts, like SQL injections or
file inclusion attacks?
```

Let's look at another example. You have identified a commodity malware, not particularly harmful on its own, on a workstation. However, you've also discovered customer credit card information in one of the files on the system, which raises the incident's severity. To accurately assess the severity and criticality of the incident, you can leverage Security Copilot to cross-reference the findings with your organization's incident classification policy stored in the Azure AI Search index.

From there, you can ask Security Copilot to retrieve the relevant incident response procedures from the Azure AI Search index to guide you with the next steps. The sample prompt is shown next:

```
Considering the presence of the commodity malware and the results from
investigation steps completed so far, particularly the finding of the
credit card information, can you assess the criticality and severity of
this incident by referencing the organization's incident classification
policy in Azure AI Search? Then retrieve the corresponding IR procedures
in Azure AI Search to outline the next steps.
```

Integrating Azure AI Search with Security Copilot allows you to not only query and analyze large datasets but also enrich Security Copilot with your organization's unique knowledge base. This enables Security Copilot to deliver relevant insights tailored to your specific security context. The ability to cross-reference incident findings with your own incident classification policies and to retrieve precise incident response procedures empowers security teams to respond more effectively and efficiently to threats. Ultimately, this integration enhances the overall value of Security Copilot, improving its role in strengthening your organization's cybersecurity posture.

Summary

In this chapter, you learned how to integrate Security Copilot with Azure Logic Apps to automate security processes and streamline workflows. You saw a detailed example of an Azure Logic Apps workflow that leverages the Security Copilot connector to automatically hunt for suspicious PowerShell activity. You also learned how to use the upload files option to expand Copilot's knowledge base, enabling its responses to be more relevant to your specific environment. You then looked into the Azure AI Search plugin in Security Copilot, which allows you to tap into large datasets of your enterprise data, extract actionable insights, and obtain relevant responses tailored to your specific security context.

All these integrations serve to supercharge Security Copilot, empowering it to significantly enhance your overall security operations.

In the next chapter, we will explore real-world scenarios that demonstrate how Security Copilot excels in supporting cyber incident investigation and threat hunting. By leveraging the various Security Copilot features discussed so far, you will gain practical insights into how to effectively apply Security Copilot's capabilities to tackle specific security challenges.

8

Cyber Sleuthing with Security Copilot

The previous chapters have provided an in-depth look at key features and capabilities of Security Copilot, from its embedded experience to the standalone interface. You've explored how Security Copilot can be extended through plugins, looked into the nuances of prompt engineering, and seen firsthand how promptbooks can enhance security tasks. Additionally, you've discovered how Security Copilot integrates with Azure Logic Apps and is further strengthened by custom knowledge base integration. Now, let's tie it all together by exploring a series of real-world scenarios. For this chapter, we'll focus on **Microsoft Defender XDR** incident investigations, showcasing how various Security Copilot capabilities work together.

You will experience firsthand how Security Copilot can act as an intelligent assistant, supporting you throughout the investigation. Furthermore, this chapter will empower you with practical insights and strategies such as chaining promptbooks to effectively apply Security Copilot capabilities, including custom plugins, to tackle security challenges and improve overall security operations.

As we move through this chapter, we will focus on the following areas to enhance your expertise:

- Advancing XDR investigations with Security Copilot
- Streamlining incident response with promptbooks

> Want to try out the prompts, custom plugins, and promptbooks featured in this book? Take a look at the book's GitHub repository at `https://github.com/PacktPublishing/Microsoft-Copilot-for-Security`.

Advancing XDR investigations with Security Copilot

Let's explore a case study based on a real-world Microsoft Defender XDR incident, showcasing how Security Copilot can serve as an intelligent assistant in navigating complex security investigations. The incident involves privilege escalation across multiple endpoints, with 60 correlated alerts signaling suspicious activities. Its main incident page from the Microsoft Defender XDR console is displayed in the next screenshot:

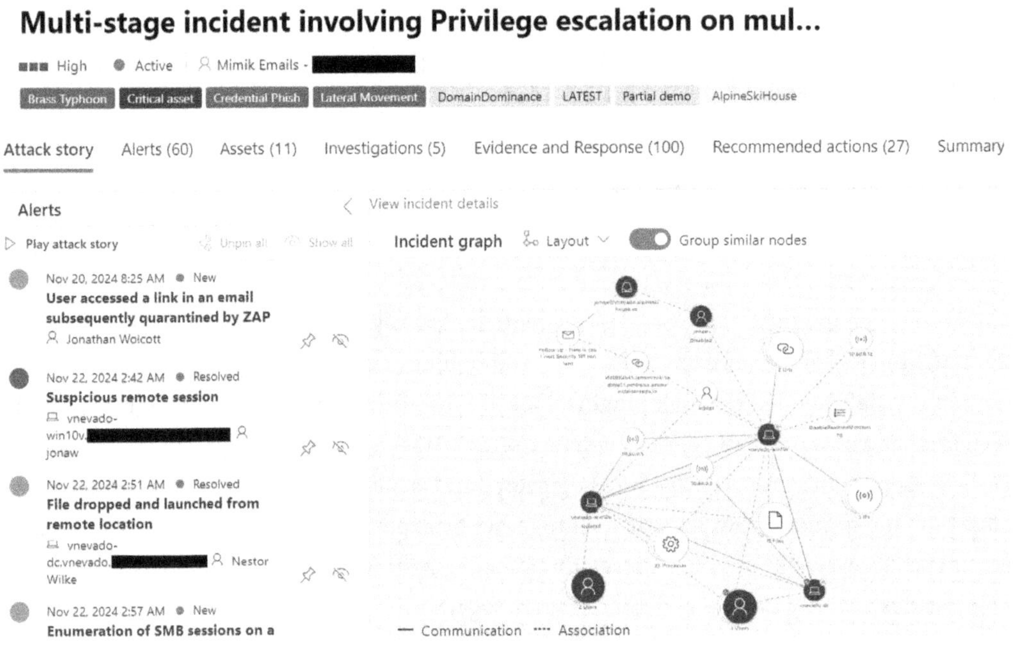

Figure 8.1 – The multi-stage incident in Microsoft Defender XDR

Over the next few sections, we'll take a detailed look at this incident and see how Security Copilot empowers analysts throughout each stage of the investigation. From uncovering suspicious remote sessions and identifying malicious processes to following the file trail and unmasking PowerShell activities, each step highlights how Security Copilot streamlines and strengthens the investigation process.

The Security Copilot incident summary

Security Copilot is seamlessly integrated with **Microsoft Defender** (commonly known as **Microsoft Defender XDR**) to enhance security operations. As soon as you start viewing the incident page in the Microsoft Defender portal, Security Copilot is set to automatically generate the incident summary, offering you a clear overview of the attack. The next screenshot shows this in action:

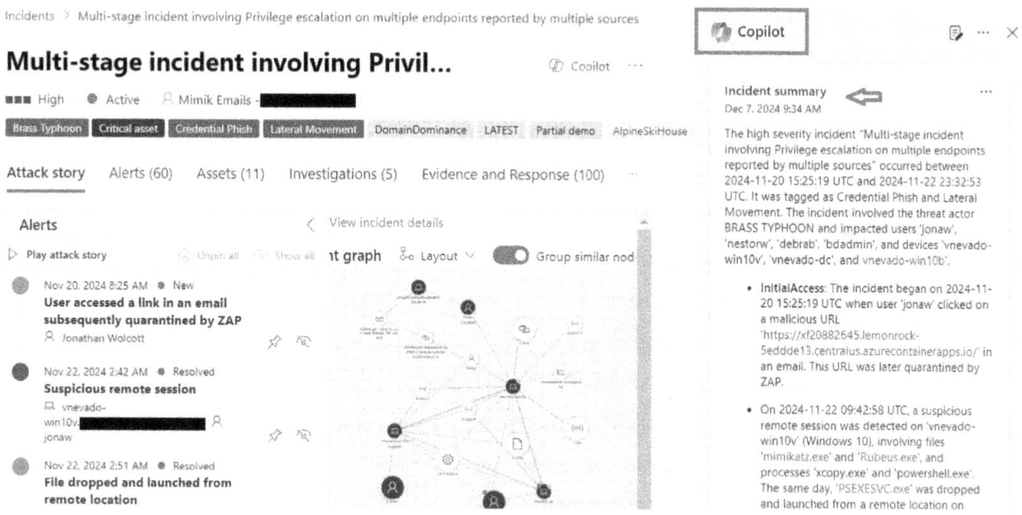

Figure 8.2 – The Security Copilot incident summary

This incident summary reveals that the threat actor, Brass Typhoon, used a credential phishing attack to gain initial access. Over the course of the attack, several instances of lateral movement, credential access, and privilege escalation were detected, impacting users and devices across the network. Key activities included the use of tools such as Mimikatz and Rubeus, suspicious remote sessions, and evidence of system manipulation.

The incident summary generated by Security Copilot helps security analysts quickly understand the scope of the attack, with key events highlighted and relevant details presented. To make it easier to review the incident summary, simply select the **Copy to clipboard** option in the Security Copilot side pane to copy the complete summary. In this case, the incident summary is provided next for your reference:

Incident summary

Dec 7, 2024 9:34 AM

The high severity incident "Multi-stage incident involving Privilege escalation on multiple endpoints reported by multiple sources" occurred between 2024-11-20 15:25:19 UTC and 2024-11-22 23:32:53 UTC. It was tagged as Credential Phish and Lateral Movement. The incident involved the threat actor BRASS TYPHOON and impacted users 'jonaw', 'nestorw', 'debrab', 'bdadmin', and devices 'vnevado-win10v', 'vnevado-dc', and vnevado-win10b'.

- **InitialAccess:** The incident began on 2024-11-20 15:25:19 UTC when user 'jonaw' clicked on a malicious URL 'https://xf20882645.lemonrock-5eddde13.centralus.azurecontainerapps.io/' in an email. This URL was later quarantined by ZAP.

- On 2024-11-22 09:42:58 UTC, a suspicious remote session was detected on 'vnevado-win10v' (Windows 10), involving files 'mimikatz.exe' and 'Rubeus.exe', and processes 'xcopy.exe' and 'powershell.exe'. The same day, 'PSEXESVC.exe' was dropped and launched from a remote location on 'vnevado-dc' (Windows Server 2019), involving IP 10.60.0.9 and processes 'ntoskrnl.exe' and 'PSEXESVC.exe' (running as SYSTEM).
- **Discovery:** At 2024-11-22 09:57:27 UTC, enumeration of SMB sessions on 'vnevado-dc' was detected from 'vnevado-win10v', involving processes 'powershell_ise.exe' and 'NetSess.exe'.
- **CredentialAccess:** On 2024-11-22 10:01:46 UTC, 'mimikatz.exe' was executed on 'vnevado-win10v', and Defender detected and prevented the execution of 'HackTool:PowerShell/Mimikatz!ams'. Multiple instances of 'mimikatz.exe' were detected throughout the incident.
- **LateralMovement:** On 2024-11-22 10:08:23 UTC, a suspected overpass-the-hash attack was detected involving user 'debrab' on 'vnevado-win10v' authenticating against 'vnevado-dc'. Multiple instances of lateral movement involving 'PSEXESVC.exe' and 'rubeus.exe' were detected.
- **DefenseEvasion:** On 2024-11-22 10:09:31 UTC, Microsoft Defender Antivirus tampering was detected on vnevado-win10b' involving 'powershell.exe'.
- **PrivilegeEscalation:** On 2024-11-22 10:19:28 UTC, SID history injection was detected on 'vnevado-win10v' involving 'powershell.exe'. Similar activity was detected on 'vnevado-dc' involving 'net1.exe' and 'ntds.dit'.
- **Persistence:** On 2024-11-22 10:19:06 UTC, suspicious account creation was detected on 'vnevado-win10v' involving 'net.exe' and 'powershell.exe'.

The incident summary is also available in Security Copilot's dedicated portal, known as the **standalone experience**. This allows you to easily switch between the Defender XDR console and Security Copilot's standalone interface while investigating the incident. Although Security Copilot is embedded within Microsoft Defender XDR, its standalone experience provides analysts with a unified interface to utilize additional Copilot features and is integrated with other security solutions, including third-party plugins.

To pivot from the Defender XDR portal to Security Copilot's standalone experience, you can either select the **Open in Security Copilot** option in Defender, as shown in the next screenshot, or log in directly at `https://securitycopilot.microsoft.com/`:

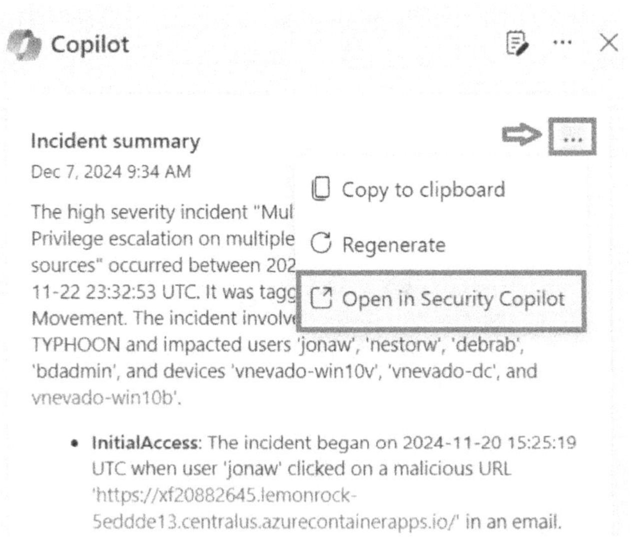

Figure 8.3 – Pivoting to Security Copilot's standalone experience

Once you have reviewed the incident summary and understand the key details, the next step is to start the investigation to determine what happened and identify additional indicators of compromise. In the following case study, we'll focus on using the standalone experience of Security Copilot to demonstrate how Copilot can quickly and efficiently support security analysts during the investigation. In the next few sections, let's dive into this incident and uncover the details step by step.

Cracking the case – uncovering suspicious remote sessions with Security Copilot

The Security Copilot incident summary reveals that the attack started when user `jonaw` clicked on a malicious URL in an email. Two days later, suspicious remote sessions were detected on the `vnevado-win10v` device, with the details shown in the next screenshot:

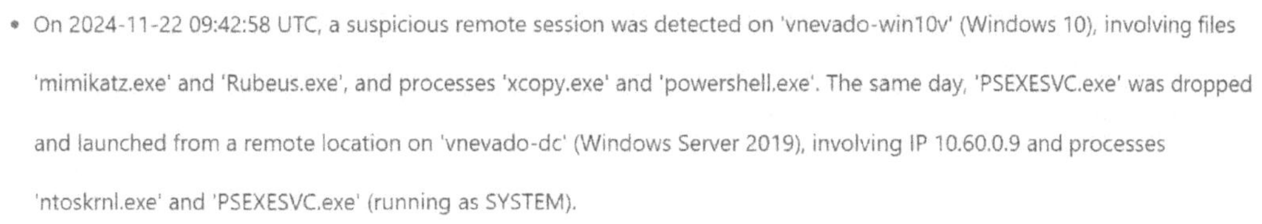

Figure 8.4 – Security Copilot incident summary snippet

The Microsoft Defender XDR incident page also presents the alerts related to remote sessions in its attack story, as shown in the next screenshot. Now, let's leverage Security Copilot to start the investigation:

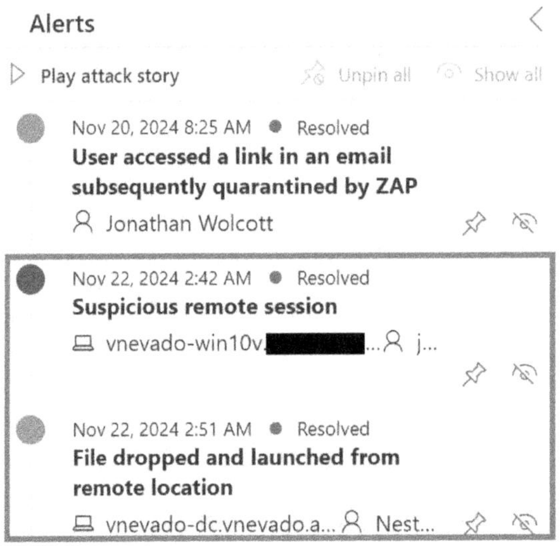

Figure 8.5 – The same alert seen from the Microsoft Defender XDR incident page

> Notice that the timestamp for the **Suspicious remote session** alert in the Defender XDR portal is Nov 22, 2024, at 2:42 a.m. Microsoft Defender XDR displays the time based on the analyst's local time. However, when using Security Copilot in its standalone mode, the timestamp is displayed in UTC instead, which, in this case, is Nov 22, 2024, at 9:42 UTC.

To investigate the suspicious remote session on a device, one way is to leverage the **Lateral Movement - Logon To Device** skill from the **CUSTOM PLUGIN DEFENDER DEVICE INVESTIGATION** plugin in Security Copilot's standalone mode. This skill presents a list of logon events that occurred on the device within a specified timeframe. The logon events include console logons, Remote Desktop logons, remote registry logons, scheduled task logons, and more. This custom plugin is available for download from the book's GitHub repository at `https://github.com/PacktPublishing/Microsoft-Copilot-for-Security/tree/main/Plugins`, ready for you to use. Detailed step-by-step guides on how to install and use the custom plugin can be found in *Chapters 4* and *5*.

You can invoke this skill by navigating to the **System Capabilities** menu option from the Security Copilot prompt bar. The skill is located under the plugin named **CUSTOM PLUGIN DEFENDER DEVICE INVESTIGATION**, as shown next:

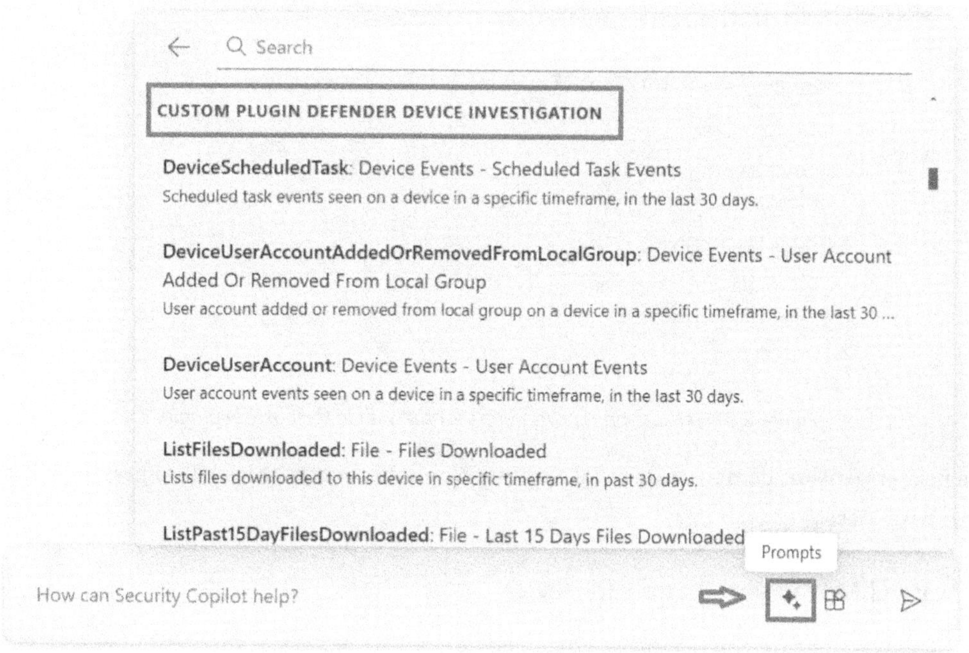

Figure 8.6 – Custom Plugin Defender Device Investigation

Once the skill is selected, you will need to fill in three input fields – the device name, start time, and end time – as shown in the next screenshot:

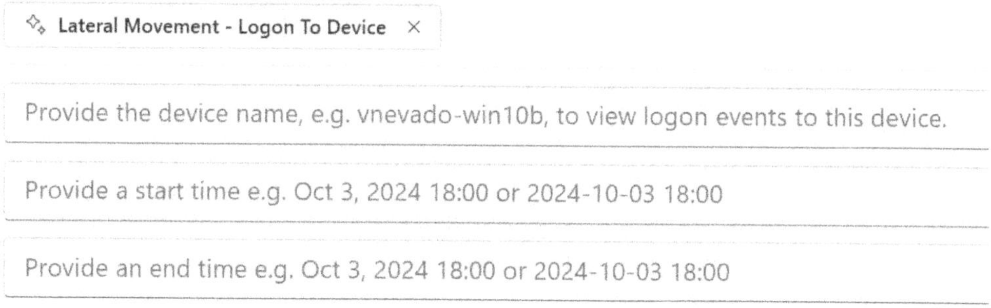

Figure 8.7 – Input fields for the skill within the custom plugin

For this case study, the alert for the suspicious remote session was triggered for the `vnevado-win10v` device occurring at approximately 9:42 UTC on November 22nd, 2024. For the investigation, let's set the start time to **2024-11-22 09:30** and the end time to **2024-11-22 09:50**, as shown in the next screenshot:

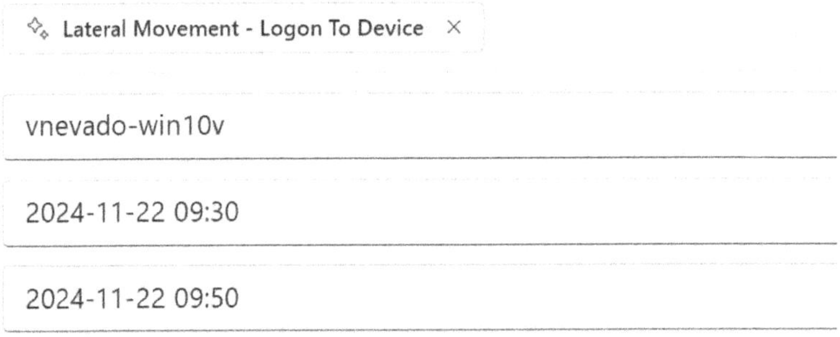

Figure 8.8 – Setting input parameters for the skill in the custom plugin

The next screenshot demonstrates that Security Copilot executes this skill to present a list of logon activities:

Figure 8.9 – Skill is executed by Security Copilot

In Security Copilot's response section, the **Export to Excel** option (see *Figure 8.9*) allows you to download the results generated by Copilot. In this case, you can use this feature to export a list of logon activities, and then manually review them. Upon inspection, it is discovered that for the `vnevado-win10v` device, there is a long list of logon events involving different user accounts within the 20-minute time frame. A screenshot showing a portion of the exported logon events is displayed next:

Timestamp	Source Device	Source IP	Destination Device	Action Type	Logon Type	Account Name
2024-11-22T09:45:12.237858Z			vnevado-win10v.[redacted]	LogonSuccess	Batch	debrab
2024-11-22T09:45:12.2378282Z		-	vnevado-win10v.[redacted]	LogonAttempted	Unknown	debrab
2024-11-22T09:45:12.2115336Z			vnevado-win10v.[redacted]	LogonSuccess	Batch	debrab
2024-11-22T09:42:58.0412787Z		10.0.0.132	vnevado-win10v.[redacted]	LogonSuccess	RemoteInteractive	jonaw
2024-11-22T09:42:58.0412586Z		10.0.0.132	vnevado-win10v.[redacted]	LogonSuccess	RemoteInteractive	jonaw
2024-11-22T09:42:58.041231Z		10.0.0.132	vnevado-win10v.[redacted]	LogonAttempted	Unknown	jonaw
2024-11-22T09:42:45.6343751Z			vnevado-win10v.[redacted]	LogonSuccess	Interactive	umfd-2
2024-11-22T09:42:45.6343437Z		-	vnevado-win10v.[redacted]	LogonAttempted	Unknown	umfd-2
2024-11-22T09:42:43.0673181Z	vm000000	10.0.0.132	vnevado-win10v.[redacted]	LogonSuccess	Network	jonaw
2024-11-22T09:42:33.1261191Z			vnevado-win10v.[redacted]	LogonSuccess	Batch	debrab
2024-11-22T09:42:33.1260934Z		-	vnevado-win10v.[redacted]	LogonAttempted	Unknown	debrab
2024-11-22T09:42:29.8658423Z		127.0.0.1	vnevado-win10v.[redacted]	LogonSuccess	Interactive	jonaw
2024-11-22T09:42:29.8658194Z		127.0.0.1	vnevado-win10v.[redacted]	LogonSuccess	Interactive	jonaw

Figure 8.10 – A portion of the logon events

You can then ask Security Copilot to summarize the logon events and highlight any suspicious activity for you. The next screenshot displays the Security Copilot prompt along with the beginning of its response:

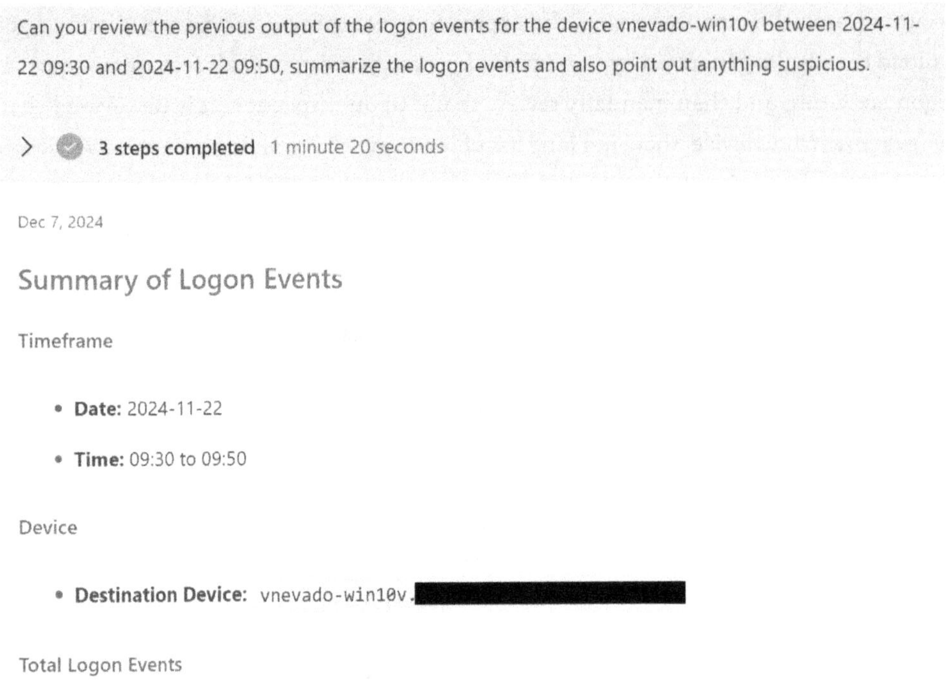

Figure 8.11 – Security Copilot compiles a summary of the logon events

The logon event summary provided by Security Copilot is thorough but a bit long. It also includes suspicious activities identified by Copilot. For your reference, the full Security Copilot response is shown next:

Summary of Logon Events

Timeframe

- **Date:** 2024-11-22
- **Time:** 09:30 to 09:50

Device

- **Destination Device:** vnevado-win10v.[redacted]

Total Logon Events

- **Total Events:** 31

Logon Types

- **Batch:** 4
- **Interactive:** 14

- **RemoteInteractive:** 2
- **Network:** 1
- **Unknown:** 10

Accounts Involved

- **debrab:** 4 logon events
- **dwm-3:** 3 logon events
- **umfd-3:** 2 logon events
- **jonaw:** 6 logon events
- **dwm-2:** 3 logon events
- **umfd-2:** 2 logon events
- **vnevado-win10v$:** 1 logon event
- **dwm-1:** 3 logon events
- **umfd-0:** 2 logon events
- **umfd-1:** 2 logon events

Protocols Used

- **Negotiate:** 26
- **NTLM:** 1
- **Unknown:** 4

Source IPs

- **10.0.0.132:** 5 logon events
- **127.0.0.1:** 3 logon events

Local Admin Status

- **Is Local Admin:** 1 (debrab)
- **Not Local Admin:** 30

Suspicious Activities

- **Multiple Logon Attempts:** There are several instances where logon attempts are followed by successful logons within milliseconds, which could indicate automated or scripted logon attempts.
- **Unknown Logon Types:** There are 10 logon events with an `Unknown` logon type, which is unusual and may warrant further investigation.
- **Local Admin Logon:** The account `debrab` has one logon event where it is marked as a local admin, which should be verified for legitimacy.

Note that Security Copilot's response suggests further investigation into the `debrab` user account, as she has one logon event marked as a local admin.

After reviewing the logon event summary for the `vnevado-win10v` device, let's find out who might be the owner of this device. The **Device Users and Login Counts** skill from the **Custom Plugin Defender Device Info** plugin provides a summary of how many times each user has logged in to the device over the past 30 days. Typically, the user with the most logins is likely the device owner.

As shown in the next screenshot, when this skill is invoked from the **System Capabilities** menu option, it requires the device name as input:

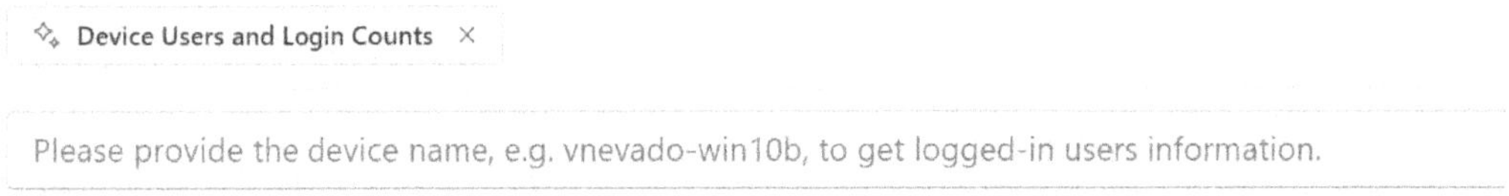

Figure 8.12 – The Device Users and Login Counts skill

Once the skill is executed for the `vnevado-win10v` device, Security Copilot reports that **The user jonaw has logged onto the device vnevado-win10v a total of 189 times in the last 30 days**, as shown in the next screenshot. This helps to identify user `jonaw` as the likely device owner, which, in turn, makes user `debrab` appear even more suspicious:

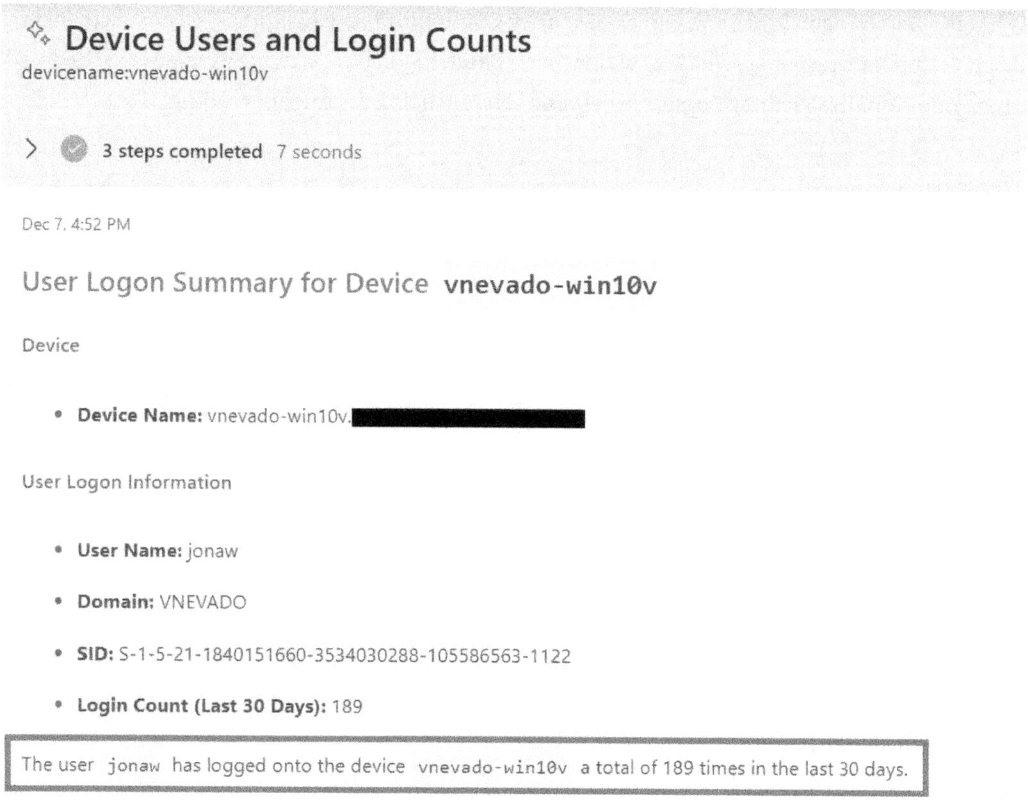

Figure 8.13 – Response from the Device Users and Login Counts skill

Let's go back to the detailed logon events provided by Security Copilot earlier and take another look at the `debrab` user account. The next screenshot shows the logon events for the `vnevado-win10v` device, filtered to display only those associated with the user `debrab`. One notable observation is that the logon type for user `debrab` is either **Batch** or **Unknown**, which appears suspicious as well, especially with one batch logon with local admin privilege:

Timestamp	Source Devi	Source IP	Destination Devic	Action Type	Logon Type	Account Nar	Is Local Admi
2024-11-22T09:45:12			vnevado-win10v	LogonSuccess	Batch	debrab	0
2024-11-22T09:45:12		-	vnevado-win10v	LogonAttempted	Unknown	debrab	0
2024-11-22T09:45:12			vnevado-win10v	LogonSuccess	Batch	debrab	1 ⇦
2024-11-22T09:42:33			vnevado-win10v	LogonSuccess	Batch	debrab	0
2024-11-22T09:42:33		-	vnevado-win10v	LogonAttempted	Unknown	debrab	0

Figure 8.14 – Logon events for user debrab

What is a **Batch** logon type? You can ask Security Copilot for more insights. The next screenshot displays Copilot's response, which explains that a **Batch** logon type is typically used for scheduled tasks. Additionally, Security Copilot provides a reference link for further reading:

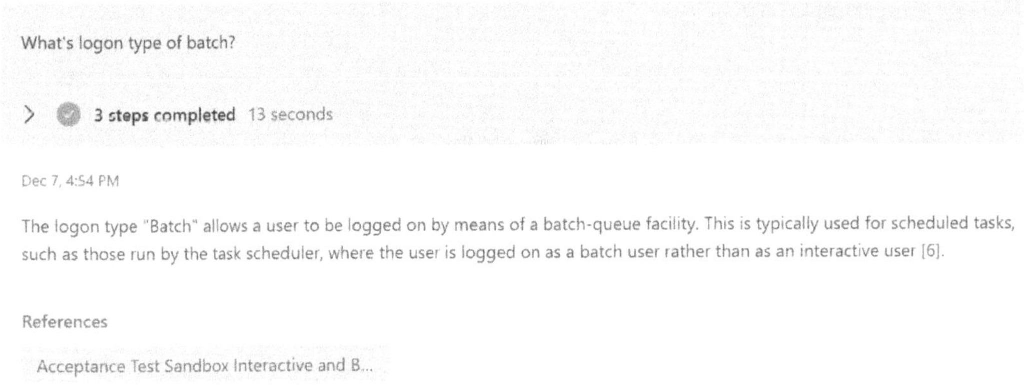

Figure 8.15 – The Batch logon type

The batch logon events for user `debrab` seem odd. Let's look at the logon events for user `jonaw`, who is likely the device owner, for comparison. As shown in the next screenshot, the filtered logon events reveal that user `jonaw` primarily logged onto the device through **Interactive** or **RemoteInteractive** logons:

Timestamp	Source Devic	Source IF	Destination Devic	Action Type	Logon Type	Account
2024-11-22T09:42:58		10.0.0.132	vnevado-win10v	LogonSuccess	RemoteInteractive	jonaw
2024-11-22T09:42:58		10.0.0.132	vnevado-win10v	LogonSuccess	RemoteInteractive	jonaw
2024-11-22T09:42:58		10.0.0.132	vnevado-win10v	LogonAttempted	Unknown	jonaw
2024-11-22T09:42:43	vm000000	10.0.0.132	vnevado-win10v	LogonSuccess	Network	jonaw
2024-11-22T09:42:29		127.0.0.1	vnevado-win10v	LogonSuccess	Interactive	jonaw
2024-11-22T09:42:29		127.0.0.1	vnevado-win10v	LogonSuccess	Interactive	jonaw
2024-11-22T09:42:29		127.0.0.1	vnevado-win10v	LogonAttempted	Unknown	jonaw

Figure 8.16 – Logon events for user jonaw

Let's again consult with Security Copilot to understand what kind of logons are defined as **Interactive** or **RemoteInteractive**. As seen in the Copilot response displayed in the next screenshot, an **Interactive** logon allows a user to log on to the device locally, which is typically used by users who are physically present at the computer. A **RemoteInteractive** logon lets a user log on to the device remotely over a network connection:

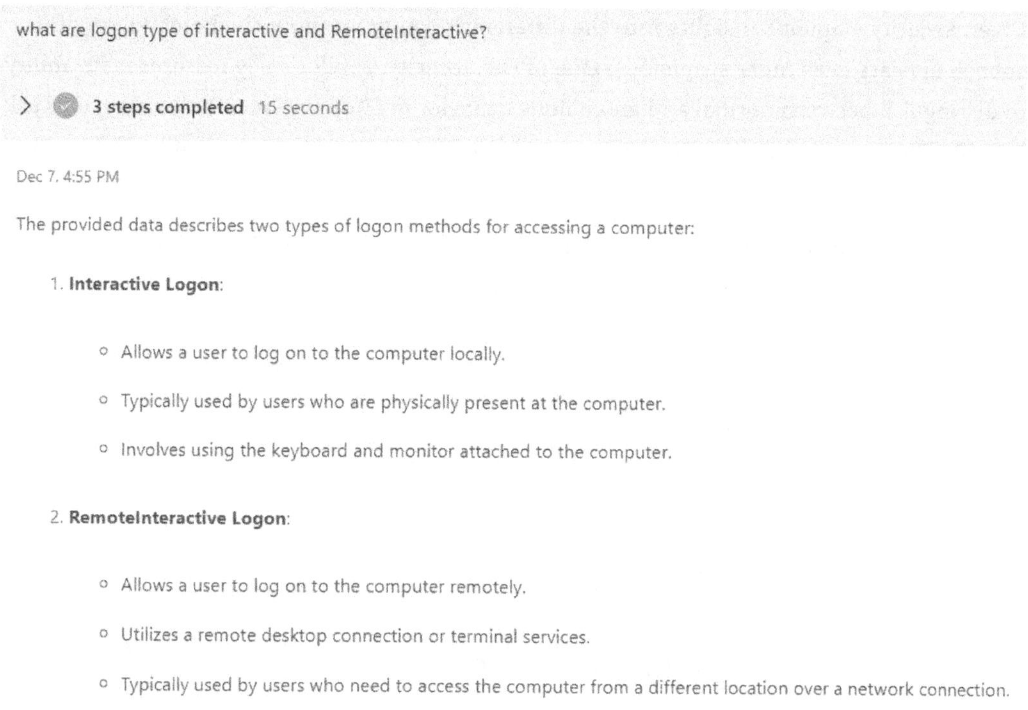

Figure 8.17 – Interactive and RemoteInteractive logon types

On a side note, Security Copilot also includes a section in its response mentioning the security relevance of the two logon types, as shown in the next screenshot:

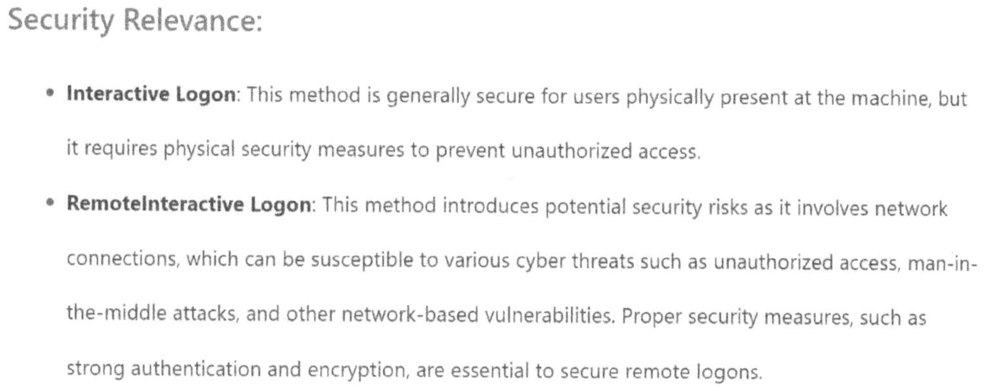

Figure 8.18 – Security relevance of the two logon types

Given Security Copilot's insights into the different logon types, now the batch logon of user `debrab` appears even more suspicious. One of the Security Copilot's key features is its ability to distinguish between normal and anomalous behavior in IT operations. In this case, let's ask Security Copilot whether it's common for someone with local admin privileges to log on to a device through a batch logon.

As seen in the next screenshot, Security Copilot points out that the batch logon is unusual, as it is typically not for interactive sessions by administrators:

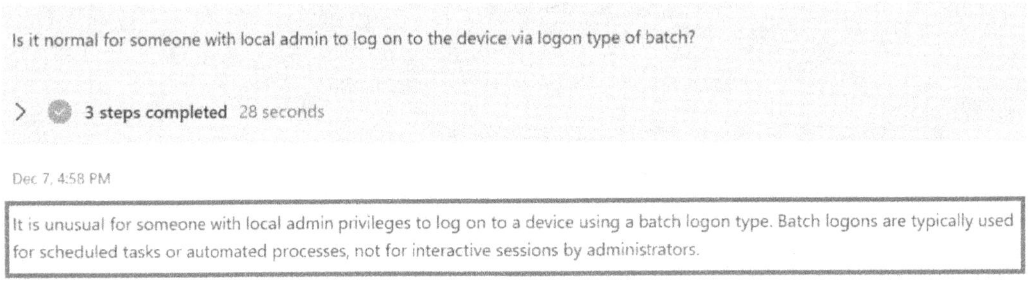

Figure 8.19 – Security Copilot's assessment of the batch logon events

Security Copilot's response further confirms that the batch logon events with user account `debrab` are suspicious and likely triggered the alert of suspicious remote sessions detected on the `vnevado-win10v` device.

Given the suspicious logon events with user `debrab`, the Security Copilot Entra plugin can be leveraged to gather additional information about this user account. The next screenshot displays the Security Copilot prompt that invokes the Microsoft Entra plugin:

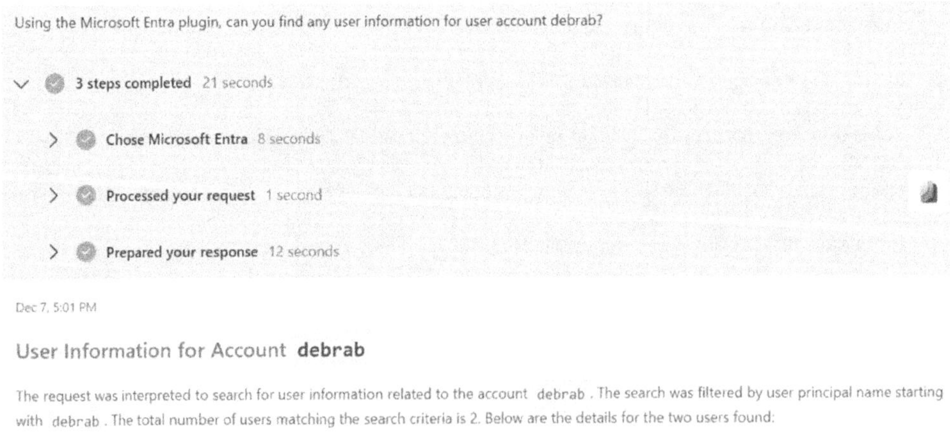

Figure 8.20 – Using the Microsoft Entra plugin to retrieve user information

Security Copilot's response reveals that this user account belongs to Debra Berger, a helpdesk administrator in the IT department, as shown next:

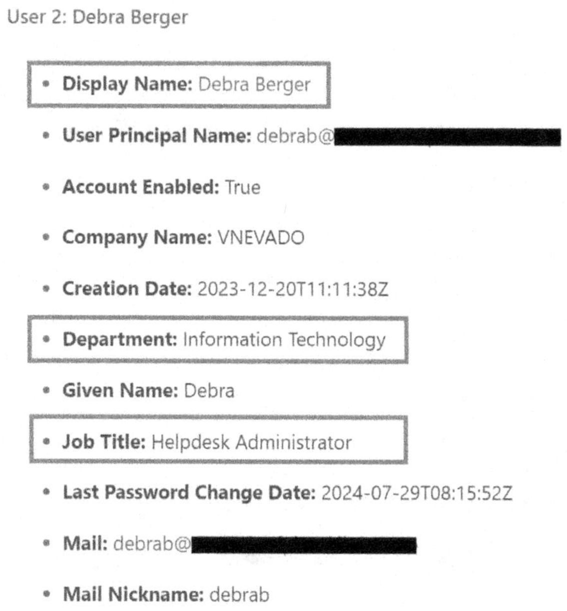

Figure 8.21 – Security Copilot's response

It would also be helpful to gather more information about user `jonaw`, who likely is the device owner. The next screenshot displays the Copilot prompt requesting to gather more information about user `jonaw`. The prompt is similar to the previous one, which triggers the Microsoft Entra plugin to present detailed user information:

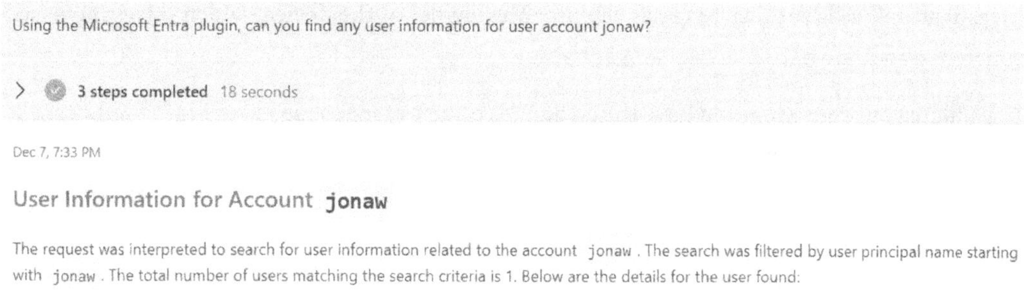

Figure 8.22 – Using the Entra plugin to retrieve user information

The information provided by Security Copilot, as seen in the next screenshot, reveals that the `jonaw` account belongs to Jonathan Wolcott, an account executive in the sales department:

User: Jonathan Wolcott

- **Display Name:** Jonathan Wolcott
- **User Principal Name:** jonaw@[redacted]
- **Account Enabled:** False
- **Company Name:** VNEVADO
- **Creation Date:** 2023-12-20T11:11:39Z
- **Department:** Sales
- **Given Name:** Jonathan
- **Job Title:** Account Executive
- **Last Password Change Date:** 2024-10-08T08:07:04Z
- **Mail:** jonaw@[redacted]
- **Mail Nickname:** jonaw

Figure 8.23 – Security Copilot's response

At this point, it has been determined that the user account `debrab`, a helpdesk administrator, initiated multiple logon attempts, including successful logons, to the `vnevado-win10v` device. Security Copilot's insights into logon types highlighted the unusual nature of the batch logon by this user, particularly one instance involving the local administrator privilege. Additional investigation has identified `jonaw` as the probable owner of the device, which raises increased concerns about the nature of `debrab`'s activities.

To validate your suspicion, you have the option to contact user `debrab` to confirm whether she is aware of the identified activities. You can also ask Security Copilot to draft the communication for you. The following screenshot shows the Security Copilot prompt and the plugin used:

Based on the suspicious activity associated with user "debrab," can you draft a message to reach out and confirm whether she is aware of these actions?

3 steps completed 13 seconds

Chose Generic 7 seconds

Figure 8.24 – The Security Copilot prompt

Using the investigation context within its session, Security Copilot drafts the following message for you to send to the user:

Subject: Urgent: Suspicious Logon Activities Detected on Your Account

Dear Debra,

I hope this message finds you well.

We have detected some suspicious logon activities associated with your account, including a batch logon type with local admin privileges on 2024-11-22. Could you please confirm if you are aware of these activities?

If you did not authorize these actions, please let us know immediately so we can take the necessary steps to secure your account.

Thank you for your prompt attention to this matter.

Best regards,

[Your Name]
[Your Position]
[Your Contact Information]

Figure 8.25 – The communication drafted by Security Copilot

While awaiting confirmation from user `debrab`, let's proceed with the investigation in the next section to see how Security Copilot can further assist in discovering relevant insights and conducting deeper analysis.

Uncovering malicious processes with Security Copilot promptbooks

The incident summary generated by Security Copilot not only mentions the detection of suspicious remote sessions on the `vnevado-win10v` device but also reports the presence of suspicious files, including `mimikatz.exe`, `rubeus.exe`, `xcopy.exe`, and `powershell.exe`, on the same device.

In the next few sections, we will investigate what occurred on the device involving these suspicious processes and see whether additional malicious entities can be uncovered. But before diving into that, in this section, let's first explore how Security Copilot can be leveraged to identify malicious processes.

Around the time of the incident, security analysts typically look for any files downloaded to the device and review the device's process execution events to identify downloaded malware and the execution of malicious files. Manually checking downloaded files and examining process execution events can be time-consuming and labor-intensive. However, with the help of Security Copilot, these tasks can be performed more quickly. Not only can you now execute the necessary steps with just a few prompts but, even better, these tasks can be automated with a promptbook that you can easily access during any investigation.

The next screenshot illustrates a promptbook where its first prompt is to identify downloaded files on a specific device within a given timeframe. Its second prompt then summarizes the device process executions during that period. Lastly, the third prompt instructs Security Copilot to analyze the processes to identify anything suspicious.

Figure 8.26 – A second Security Copilot promptbook

Notice that the first two prompts use embedded KQL queries to retrieve event data. These queries can be transformed into skills within a custom plugin. At the end of this section, you'll find an improved promptbook that serves the same purpose but leverages custom plugin skills for enhanced functionality.

Back to our incident investigation – let's use this promptbook to examine the same suspicious device, `vnevado-win10v`, within the same timeframe, to detect file downloads and analyze process executions. The next screenshot displays a portion of the promptbook with the required input parameters (device name, start time, and end time) filled in:

Figure 8.27 – Entering the required fields to run the promptbook

> Note that when the promptbook is executed, it automatically populates the KQL queries in the prompts with the inputs you provided, such as device name, start time, and end time. This enables all the prompts within the promptbook to run with the specific parameters you set, without the need for manual intervention.

Following the promptbook execution, Security Copilot reports that the `DomainDominance198.zip` file was downloaded to the `vnevado-win10v` device between 09:30 and 10:30 UTC on November 22, 2024, as shown next:

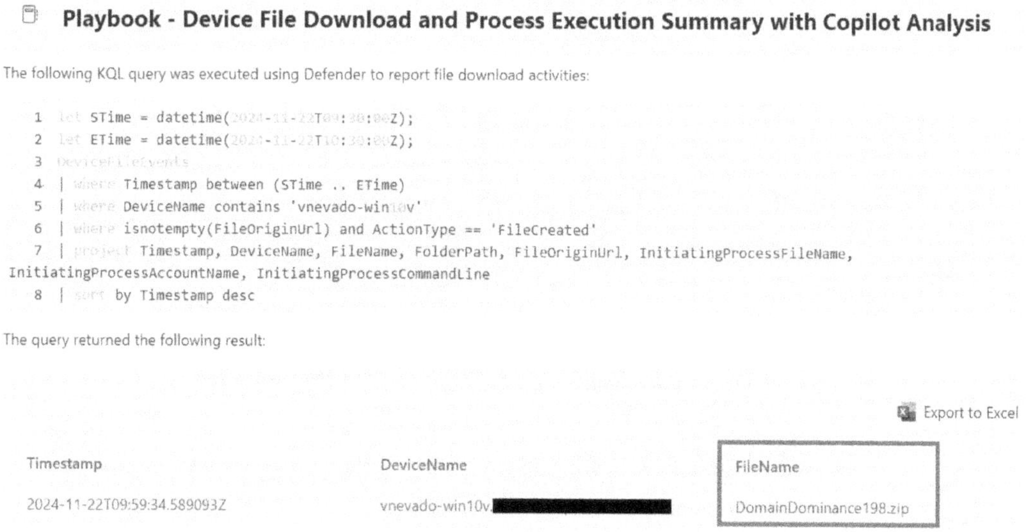

Figure 8.28 – A file named DomainDominance198.zip was downloaded

Keep in mind that not all details from Security Copilot's findings are visible in the console. To view the full result, you need to expand the output or export the data to Excel. Then, you can more thoroughly review the URL from which the file was downloaded, verify the file location through its folder path, and locate the user account associated with the download. The next screenshot displays some of these additional details seen in the Excel spreadsheet:

DeviceName	FileName	FolderPath	FileOriginUrl	Initiati
vnevado-win10v	DomainDominance198.zip	C:\Users\jonaw\Downloads\ DomainDominance198.zip	https://xf20882645.lemonrock-5eddde13.centralus.azurecontainerapps.io/	jonaw

Figure 8.29 – Additional details

From the same promptbook execution, the second prompt in this promptbook reports that 128 unique processes were executed on this device during the same time period. The corresponding file paths and user accounts are also displayed in the console, as displayed in the following screenshot:

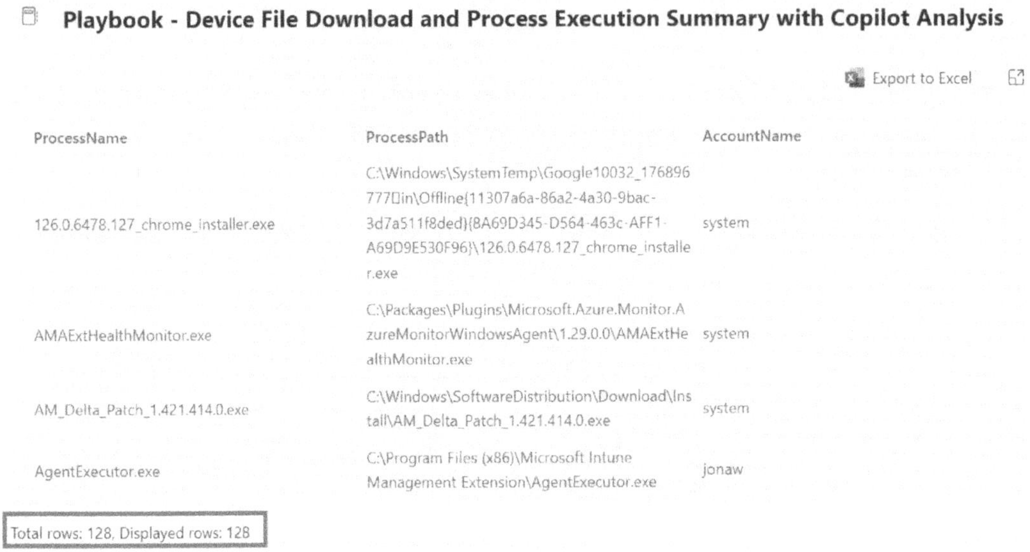

Playbook - Device File Download and Process Execution Summary with Copilot Analysis

Export to Excel

ProcessName	ProcessPath	AccountName
126.0.6478.127_chrome_installer.exe	C:\Windows\SystemTemp\Google10032_176896777□in\Offline{11307a6a-86a2-4a30-9bac-3d7a511f8ded}{8A69D345-D564-463c-AFF1-A69D9E530F96}\126.0.6478.127_chrome_installer.exe	system
AMAExtHealthMonitor.exe	C:\Packages\Plugins\Microsoft.Azure.Monitor.AzureMonitorWindowsAgent\1.29.0.0\AMAExtHealthMonitor.exe	system
AM_Delta_Patch_1.421.414.0.exe	C:\Windows\SoftwareDistribution\Download\Install\AM_Delta_Patch_1.421.414.0.exe	system
AgentExecutor.exe	C:\Program Files (x86)\Microsoft Intune Management Extension\AgentExecutor.exe	jonaw

Total rows: 128, Displayed rows: 128

Figure 8.30 – Security Copilot reports 128 unique processes executed

> Instead of manually reviewing all 128 processes, the third prompt in the promptbook directs Security Copilot to analyze the processes and flag any suspicious ones.

In this case, Security Copilot identifies three processes – `mimikatz.exe`, `PsExec.exe`, and `NetSess.exe` – that require further investigation. This is illustrated in the next screenshot:

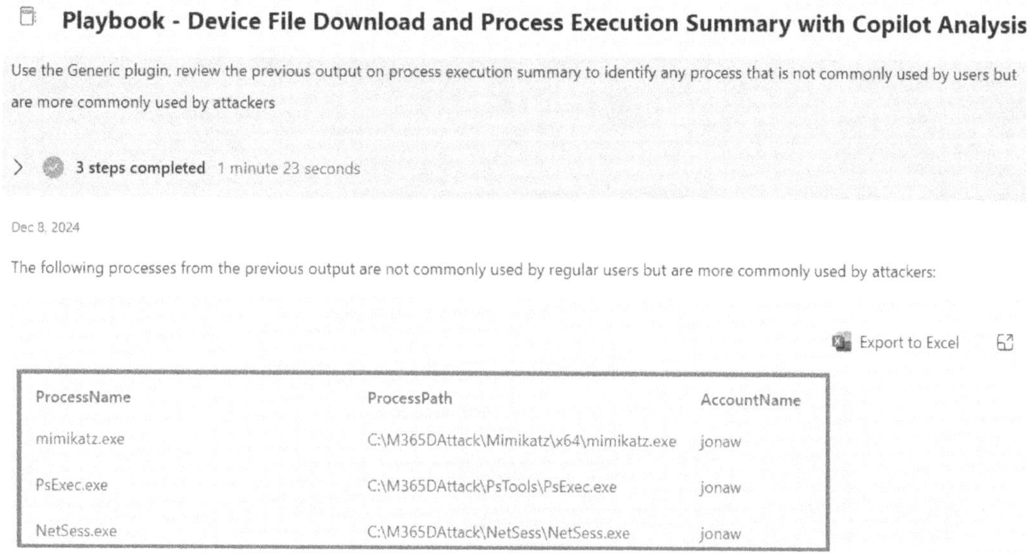

Figure 8.31 – The third prompt in the promptbook

After running the promptbook, you've identified one downloaded file that warrants further analysis and three suspicious processes that need to be examined more closely.

This promptbook executes a series of prompts commonly used in standard investigative workflows. However, you may follow up with additional prompts to perform further analysis. In this case, let's ask Security Copilot to list process executions to those associated with the `jonaw` user account. This way, we can further filter out the noisy processes such as the ones run by the operating system.

The Security Copilot prompt and its response are shown in the next screenshot:

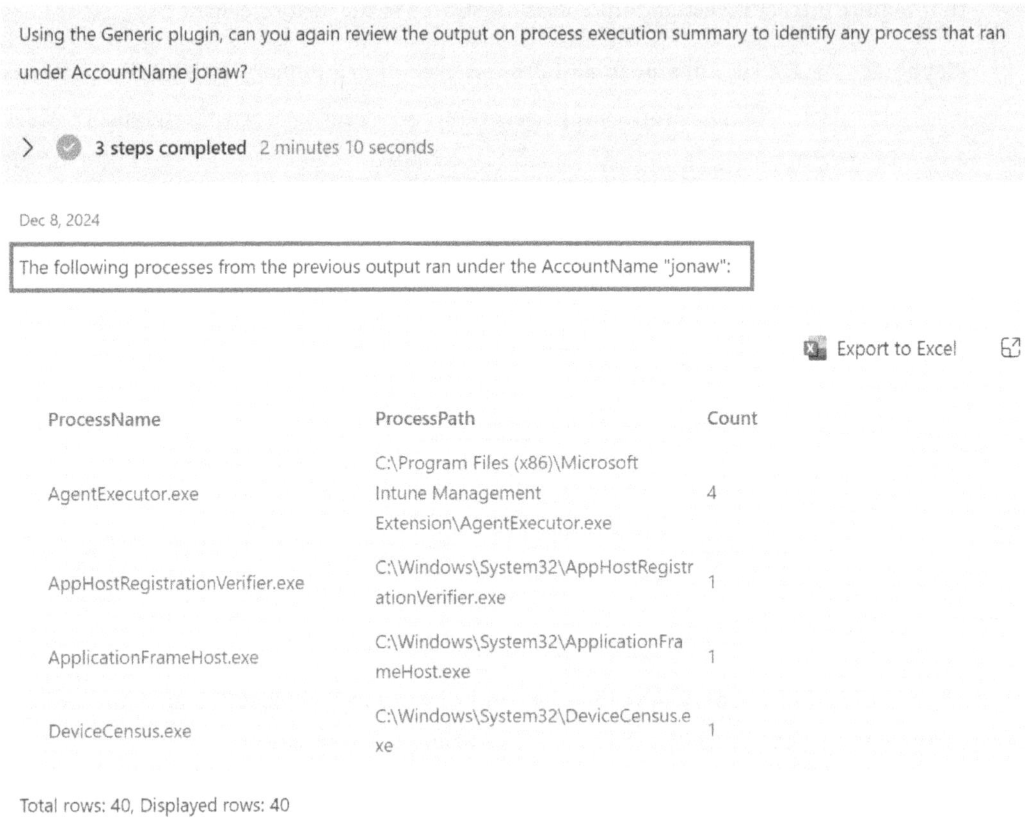

Figure 8.32 – Security Copilot to further filter the process execution events

As you can see from the screenshot, based on its previous output, Security Copilot identifies 40 processes running under the account name `jonaw`. Earlier in the investigation, leveraging the Microsoft Entra plugin, Security Copilot reported that the `jonaw` user account belongs to Jonathan Wolcott, an account executive in the sales department. With this information, let's ask Security Copilot to identify any process execution that typically should not be carried out by someone outside of the IT department.

Here's the Security Copilot prompt:

```
User jonaw is an account executive in the sales department, with this
information, can you identify any processes that typically should not be
carried out by someone outside of the IT department?
```

With this added context, Security Copilot then identifies several more suspicious processes and provides its reasoning along the way. The Copilot prompt and its response are seen in the next screenshot:

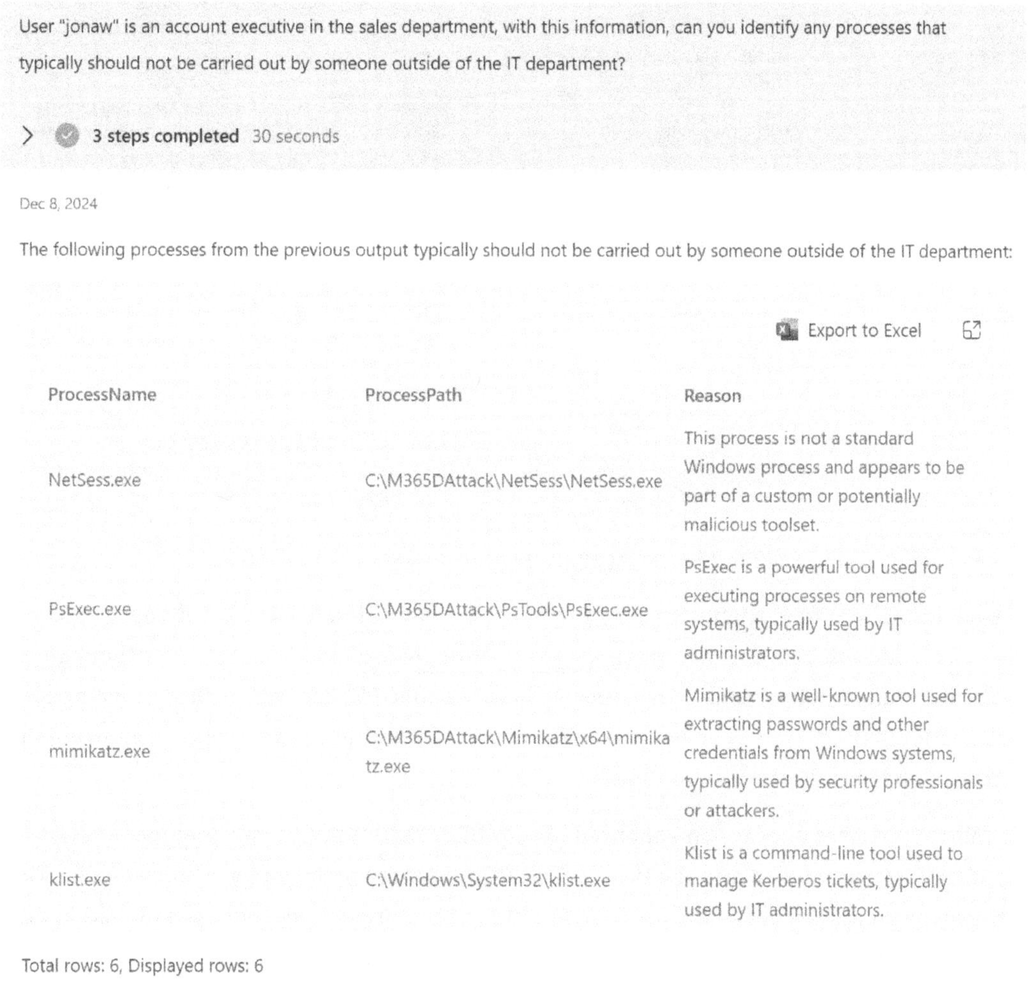

Figure 8.33 – Security Copilot identifies several more suspicious processes

Security analysts can manually identify these suspicious processes as well. However, by leveraging Security Copilot as an intelligent assistant, it can be faster and more efficient to detect such processes. It can also come in handy when the analyst needs to review a large number of processes in a short amount of time.

Once again, you can export the Security Copilot findings to Excel for a more thorough review. The next screenshot displays the results in Excel, showing all six suspicious processes:

ProcessName	ProcessPath	Reason
NetSess.exe	C:\M365DAttack\NetSess\NetSess.exe	This process is not a standard Windows process and appears to be part of a custom or potentially malicious toolset.
PsExec.exe	C:\M365DAttack\PsTools\PsExec.exe	PsExec is a powerful tool used for executing processes on remote systems, typically used by IT administrators.
mimikatz.exe	C:\M365DAttack\Mimikatz\x64\mimikatz.exe	Mimikatz is a well-known tool used for extracting passwords and other credentials from Windows systems, typically used by security professionals or attackers.
klist.exe	C:\Windows\System32\klist.exe	Klist is a command-line tool used to manage Kerberos tickets, typically used by IT administrators.
powershell.exe	C:\Windows\System32\WindowsPowerShell\v1.0\powershell.exe	PowerShell is a powerful scripting language and shell, often used by IT administrators for system management tasks.
powershell_ise.exe	C:\Windows\System32\WindowsPowerShell\v1.0\powershell_ise.exe	PowerShell ISE is an integrated scripting environment for PowerShell, typically used by IT administrators for scripting and automation tasks.

Figure 8.34 – The Security Copilot findings exported to Excel

The additional prompts enable Security Copilot to be more effective in identifying suspicious process executions. You can then integrate these prompts into the existing promptbook to enhance the promptbook's overall capabilities. To boost its effectiveness even further, the embedded KQL queries in the prompts can be transformed into skills within a custom plugin, allowing the promptbook to invoke these skills directly.

The next screenshot displays an enhanced promptbook, with the first two prompts leveraging the **ListFilesDownloaded** and the **ProcessExecutionSummary** skills in a custom plugin. The subsequent prompts identify the users behind the process executions and assess whether any process executions are unusual based on users' roles and departments:

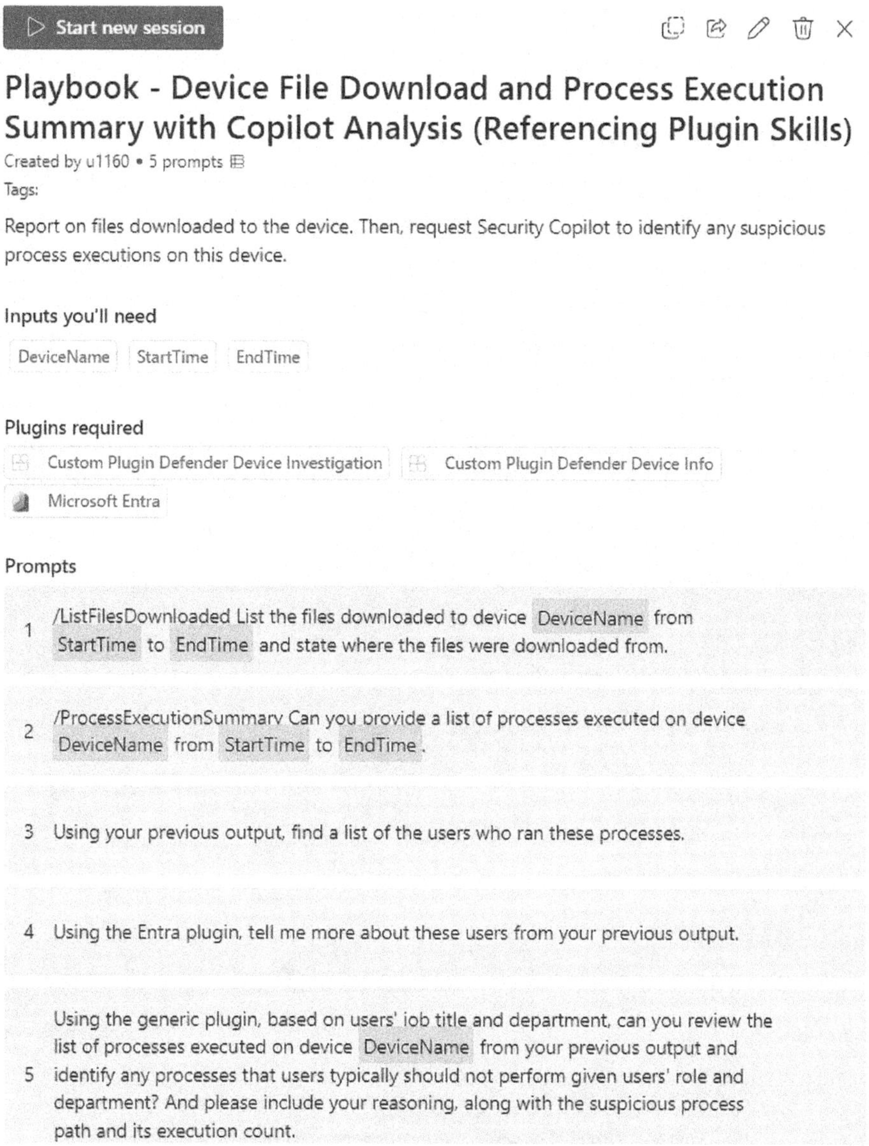

Figure 8.35 – The Security Copilot promptbook

Note that any custom plugins and promptbooks referenced in the book can be found in the GitHub repository of this book (`https://github.com/PacktPublishing/Microsoft-Copilot-for-Security`), available for you to install and use.

Now that a few more suspicious processes have been identified, let's revisit the downloaded file, `DomainDominance198.zip`, in the next section to see whether more details can be uncovered.

Following the file trail with Security Copilot

The **File - Any Device Events Related To This File** skill is part of the **Custom Plugin Defender XDR Hunting** plugin in Security Copilot. It is designed to report on any device events involving a specific file. It uses the filename as a keyword to filter and display only the device events containing this keyword within a defined time period. For the security incident we've been investigating in this chapter, let's use this skill to search for device events containing the name of the downloaded file, `DomainDominance198`.

The next screenshot shows this skill in action, returning a list of device events that include the keyword `DomainDominance198` during the same time period as the previous investigation:

Figure 8.36 – The skill executes and presents a list of device events

Upon reviewing the Security Copilot response exported to Excel, you can see that a new file, `DomainDominance198.ps1`, was created in the same directory as the downloaded file, `DomainDominance198.zip`:

Timestamp	ActionType	FileName	FolderPath	:ingProcessFile	ProcessAcco
2024-11-22T09:59:34.6319607Z	FileModified	DomainDominance198.zip	C:\Users\jonaw\Downloads\DomainDominance198.zip	msedge.exe	jonaw
2024-11-22T10:01:09.5377449Z	FileCreated	DomainDominance198.ps1	C:\Users\jonaw\Downloads\DomainDominance198\DomainDominance198.ps1	explorer.exe	jonaw
2024-11-22T10:03:33.4571438Z	FileCreated	DomainDominance198.ps1.lnk	C:\Users\jonaw\AppData\Roaming\Microsoft\Windows\Recent\DomainDominance198.ps1.lnk	explorer.exe	jonaw
2024-11-22T10:03:33.4719964Z	FileCreated	DomainDominance198.lnk	C:\Users\jonaw\AppData\Roaming\Microsoft\Windows\Recent\DomainDominance198.lnk	explorer.exe	jonaw

Figure 8.37 – A new file, DomainDominance198.ps1

Additionally, as seen in the next screenshot, there is a device event indicating that the Notepad process opened the `DomainDominance198.ps1` file, initiated by user `jonaw`:

Timestamp	ActionType	FileName	ProcessAcco	InitiatingProcessCommandLine
2024-11-22T10:03:33.1787891Z	ProcessCreated	notepad.exe	jonaw	"notepad.exe" "C:\Users\jonaw\Downloads\DomainDominance198\DomainDominance198.ps1"

Figure 8.38 – Device event related to DomainDominance198.ps1

Rather than manually reviewing all the device events, you can also ask Security Copilot to summarize them for you. The Security Copilot prompt is shown next:

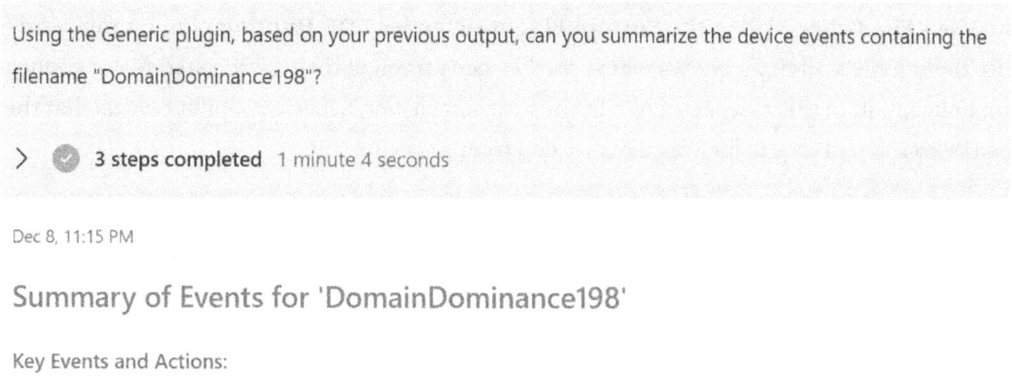

Figure 8.39 – Security Copilot summarizing the device events

Security Copilot offers a detailed summary of the device events, followed by its analysis of these events and a conclusion. The next screenshot displays a portion of the findings from Security Copilot:

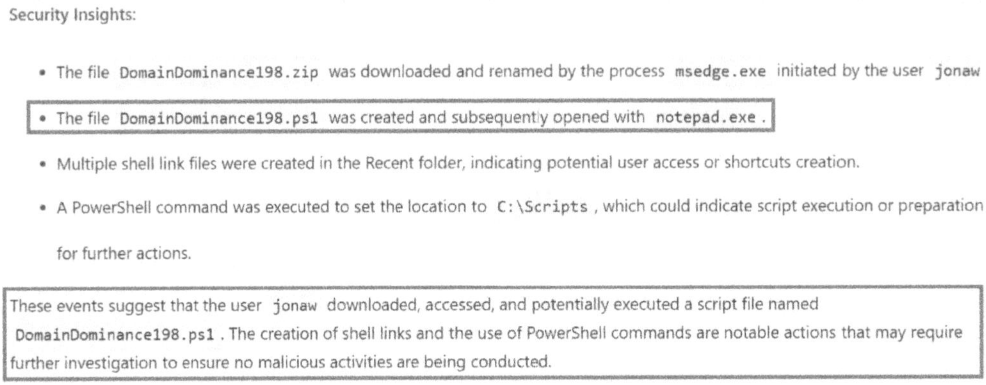

Figure 8.40 – Security Copilot's analysis of device events

Security Copilot's analysis points out the downloaded file and possible execution of `DomainDominance198.ps1`. It then mentions the implications of shell link creation and the use of PowerShell as notable actions that may require further investigation.

The **File - File Origin** skill in the **Custom Plugin Defender XDR Hunting** plugin provides details about a file's origin. It shows where the file came from, and any associated file or connection linked to it. In this case, as shown in the next screenshot, Security Copilot reveals that the `DomainDominance198.zip` file was downloaded from a specific URL:

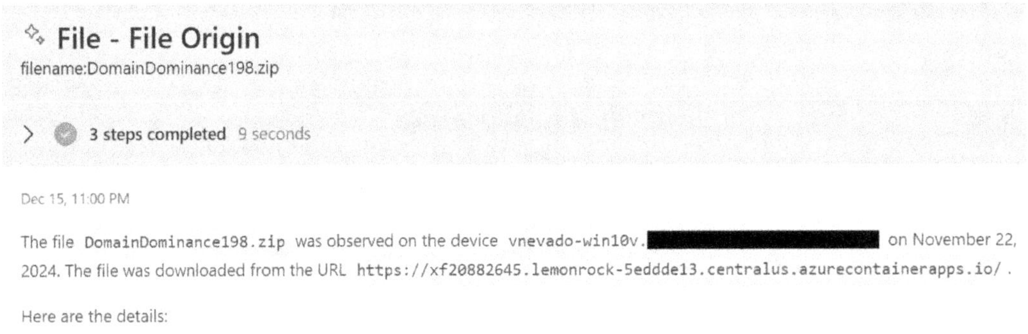

Figure 8.41 – The Security Copilot skill that shows file origin

It also shows that the `DomainDominance198.ps1` file is associated with the `DomainDominance198.zip` file, as shown next:

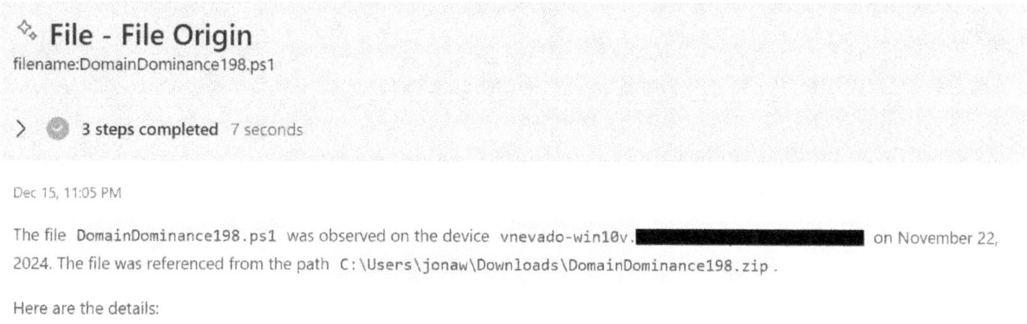

Figure 8.42 – The Security Copilot skill that shows file association

The additional details in Security Copilot's response highlight the direct association between `DomainDominance198.ps1` and `DomainDominance198.zip`, as shown in the next screenshot:

Figure 8.43 – File Origin Referrer URL

We started the investigation with the downloaded file, `DomainDominance198.zip`. With the help of Security Copilot, a newly created file, `DomainDominance198.ps1`, has been identified and it is linked back to the original download. Furthermore, Security Copilot flags potential threats related to this new file, especially its PowerShell execution. In the next section, let's continue to leverage Security Copilot to take a closer look at PowerShell activities for further analysis.

Unmasking PowerShell activities with Security Copilot

Based on Security Copilot's observation of PowerShell usage, let's use another Security Copilot skill to conduct a more in-depth examination of PowerShell execution events on the `vnevado-win10v` device. The **Process - Detailed Process Events** skill is also part of the **Custom Plugin Defender XDR Hunting** plugin. It retrieves detailed process execution events, including process command-line information and parent process execution details, for the specified process on a given device within a defined timeframe.

When this skill is invoked, it requires four mandatory fields to be filled, as shown next:

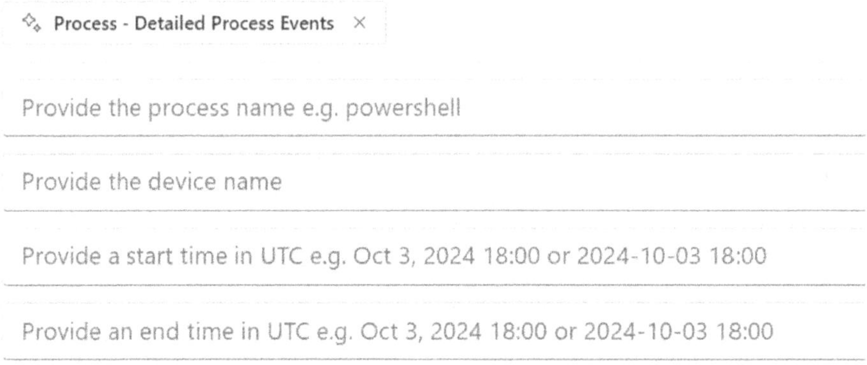

Figure 8.44 – The Process - Detailed Process Events skill

For this investigation, let's pull the detailed process execution events related to any PowerShell execution on the `vnevado-win10v` device. The required fields are filled in accordingly, as illustrated in the following screenshot:

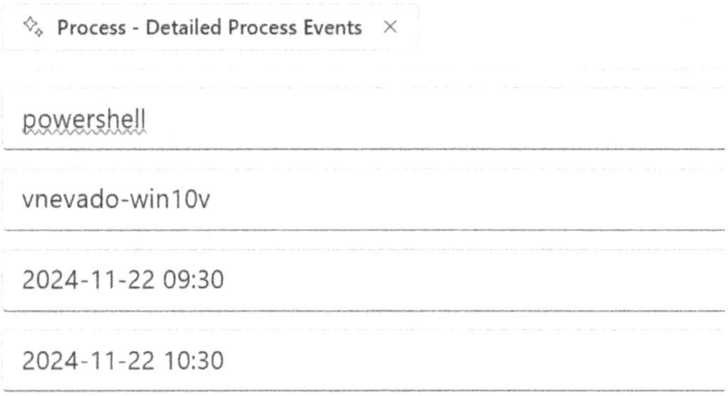

Figure 8.45 – Detailed process events related to PowerShell execution

Security Copilot then displays the PowerShell execution events identified on the `vnevado-win10v` device within the specified timeframe of 2024-11-22 between 09:30 and 10:30 UTC, as shown in the next screenshot. Note that in addition to the **Export to Excel** option, you can also select **Copy response** as an alternative way to export the output data from Security Copilot. This option, located in the lower-right corner of Security Copilot's response section, is also highlighted in the next screenshot:

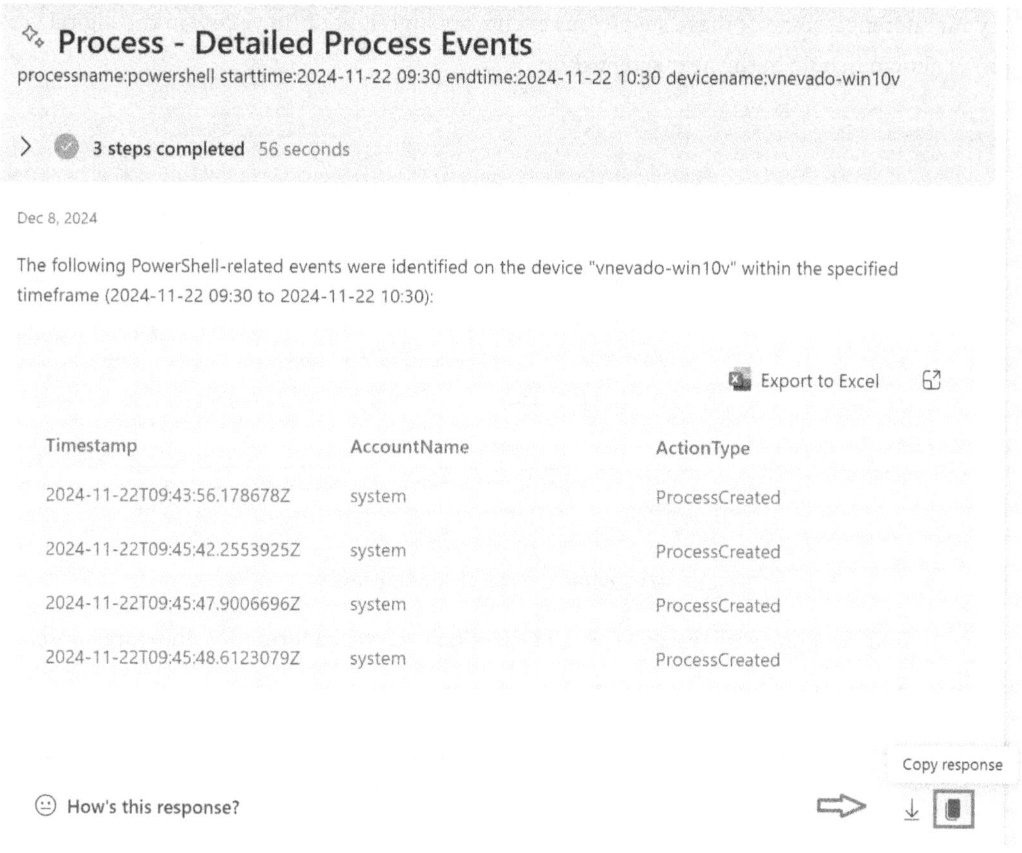

Figure 8.46 – PowerShell execution events on the vnevado-win10v device and the Copy response option

The **Copy response** option provides a more condensed text view of the response from Security Copilot, making it easier and faster to review the content. For this particular incident, a range of unusual or potentially harmful behaviors can be observed from Security Copilot's response, displayed in the condensed view format.

For your reference, some of these suspicious events are highlighted (in yellow in the digital version) or shown in bold in the next screenshot:

```
| 2024-11-22T09:57:27.1107941Z | jonaw | ProcessCreated | powershell.exe | "powershell.exe" -noexit -command Set-Location -literalPath 'C:\Scripts' | explorer.exe | E
| 2024-11-22T09:59:53.7104858Z | jonaw | ProcessCreated | powershell_ise.exe | "powershell_ise.exe" "C:\Scripts\Orchestrator.ps1" | explorer.exe | Explorer.EXE |
| 2024-11-22T10:02:18.3132755Z | jonaw | ProcessCreated | whoami.exe | "whoami.exe" | powershell.exe | "powershell.exe" -noexit -command Set-Location -literalPat
| 2024-11-22T10:02:18.5010146Z | jonaw | ProcessCreated | cmd.exe | "cmd.exe" /c "nslookup vnevado-dc.vnevado.alpineskihouse.co" | powershell.exe | "powershell.
| 2024-11-22T10:02:19.9104622Z | jonaw | ProcessCreated | net.exe | "net.exe" user /domain | powershell.exe | "powershell.exe" -noexit -command Set-Location -liter
| 2024-11-22T10:02:21.2379776Z | jonaw | ProcessCreated | net.exe | "net.exe" group /domain | powershell.exe | "powershell.exe" -noexit -command Set-Location -lit
| 2024-11-22T10:02:22.4289459Z | jonaw | ProcessCreated | net.exe | "net.exe" group "Domain Admins" /domain | powershell.exe | "powershell.exe" -noexit -commar
| 2024-11-22T10:02:23.7958601Z | jonaw | ProcessCreated | net.exe | "net.exe" group "Enterprise Admins" /domain | powershell.exe | "powershell.exe" -noexit -comn
| 2024-11-22T10:02:29.0566977Z | jonaw | ProcessCreated | NetSess.exe | "NetSess.exe" vnevado-dc | powershell.exe | "powershell.exe" -noexit -command Set-Locati
| 2024-11-22T10:02:34.6079262Z | jonaw | ProcessCreated | mimikatz.exe | "mimikatz.exe" privilege::debug sekurlsa::logonpasswords exit | powershell.exe | "powe
| 2024-11-22T10:02:34.9950496Z | jonaw | ProcessCreated | net.exe | "net.exe" user debrab /domain | powershell.exe | "powershell.exe" -noexit -command Set-Locati
| 2024-11-22T10:02:35.6219838Z | jonaw | ProcessCreated | mimikatz.exe | "mimikatz.exe" privilege::debug "sekurlsa::pth /user:debrab /ntlm:b75fb783d4b4eba91
| 2024-11-22T10:02:41.8364615Z | jonaw | ProcessCreated | mimikatz.exe | "mimikatz.exe" privilege::debug "sekurlsa::pth /user:debrab /ntlm:b75fb783d4b4eba9195b1
| 2024-11-22T10:08:18.5761879Z | jonaw | ProcessCreated | mimikatz.exe | "mimikatz.exe" privilege::debug "sekurlsa::pth /user:debrab /ntlm:b75fb783d4b4eba9195b1
| 2024-11-22T10:08:19.6905849Z | jonaw | ProcessCreated | powershell.exe | powershell.exe dir \\vnevado-win10b\C$ | mimikatz.exe | "mimikatz.exe" privilege::debug
| 2024-11-22T10:09:26.8416901Z | jonaw | ProcessCreated | mimikatz.exe | "mimikatz.exe" privilege::debug "sekurlsa::pth /user:debrab /ntlm:b75fb783d4b4eba9195b1
| 2024-11-22T10:09:26.9656562Z | jonaw | ProcessCreated | powershell.exe | powershell.exe C:\M365DAttack\Get-KRBTicket.ps1 | mimikatz.exe | "mimikatz.exe" privil
| 2024-11-22T10:09:29.8923388Z | jonaw | ProcessCreated | PsExec.exe | "PsExec.exe" \\vnevado-win10b -accepteula cmd /c "powershell -command Set-MpPreference
| 2024-11-22T10:09:35.0055142Z | jonaw | ProcessCreated | xcopy.exe | "xcopy.exe" C:\M365DAttack\Rubeus\Rubeus.exe \\vnevado-win10b\C$\Temp | powershell.ex
| 2024-11-22T10:09:35.1340313Z | jonaw | ProcessCreated | PsExec.exe | "PsExec.exe" \\vnevado-win10b -accepteula cmd /c "C:\Temp\Rubeus.exe dump /service:krbt
| 2024-11-22T10:09:35.6828423Z | jonaw | ProcessCreated | xcopy.exe | "xcopy.exe" \\vnevado-win10b\C$\Temp\AdminTicket.txt C:\M365DAttack\Admin-Tickets | pov
```

Figure 8.47 – Condensed text view of the response

The condensed view presents the PowerShell execution events in a format as illustrated here:

```
| Timestamp | AccountName | ActionType | ProcessName | ProcessCommandLine | InitiatingProcessFileName | InitiatingProcessCommandLine
```

Figure 8.48 – Format for the PowerShell execution events

For instance, *Figure 8.49* displays a portion of a PowerShell execution event that translates to the following:

- `ProcessName`: `xcopy.exe`
- `ProcessCommandLine`: `"xcopy.exe" C:\M365DAttack\Rubeus\Rubeus.exe \\vnevado-win10b\C$\Temp`
- `InitiatingProcessFileName`: `powershell.exe`
- `InitiatingProcessCommandLine`: `powershell.exe C:\M365DAttack\Get-KRBTicket.ps1`

```
| xcopy.exe | "xcopy.exe" C:\M365DAttack\Rubeus\Rubeus.exe \\vnevado-win10b\C$\Temp | powershell.exe | powershell.exe C:\M365DAttack\Get-KRBTicket.ps1
```

Figure 8.49 – Example of a portion of the PowerShell execution event

Essentially, it indicates that the initiating (parent) process, `powershell.exe`, executes a script called `Get-KRBTicket.ps1`. As a result, the `xcopy.exe` program is launched. The command line for `xcopy.exe` is `"xcopy.exe" C:\M365DAttack\Rubeus\Rubeus.exe \\vnevado-win10b\C$\Temp`.

One of the powerful features of Security Copilot is its ability to analyze scripts, command lines, registry keys, and more. In this case, you can ask it to explain the purpose of this command line for you. The Security Copilot prompt and its response are displayed in the next screenshot:

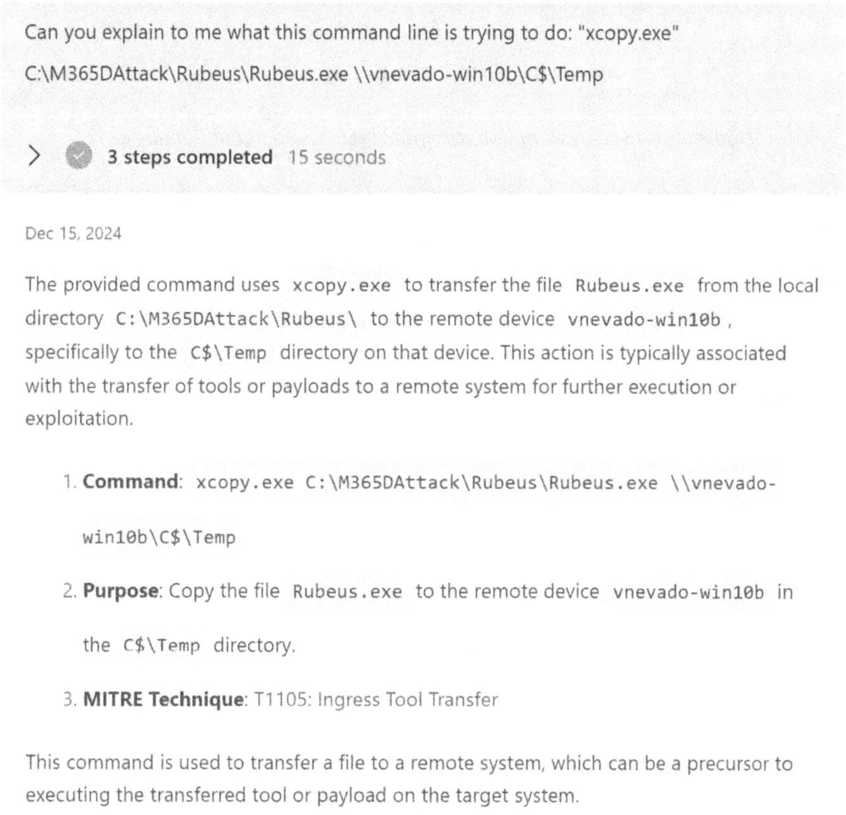

Figure 8.50 – Security Copilot analyzing a suspicious command line

With Security Copilot's explanation, it is clear that the user account, `jonaw`, belonging to an account executive in the sales department, is used to copy the `Rubeus.exe` file from the local directory, `C:\M365DAttack\Rubeus\`, to the `C$\Temp` directory on a remote device named **vnevado-win10b**.

You can then consult Security Copilot to learn more about the `Rubeus.exe` file that's being copied to the remote device. The Security Copilot prompt is shown in the next screenshot:

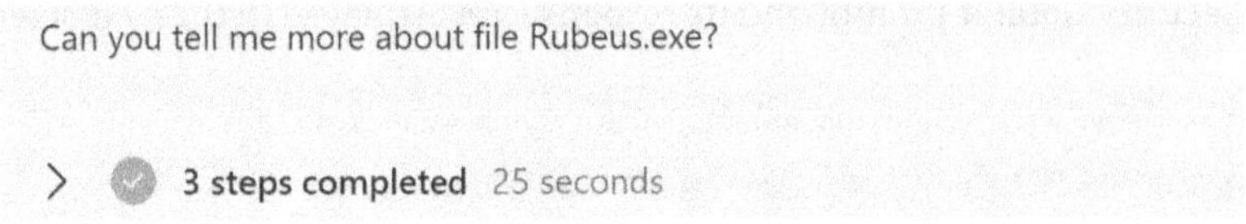

Figure 8.51 – Security Copilot prompt to learn more about Rubeus.exe

Security Copilot reveals that `Rubeus.exe` is a post-exploitation tool commonly used in Kerberos-related attacks. It outlines how this tool can be used in attacks such as extracting service account tickets for offline cracking or injecting Kerberos tickets into the current session. It also points out the associated security risks with this tool, including using stolen tickets to move laterally within a network or gaining higher privileges by exploiting Kerberos tickets. A portion of Security Copilot's response is displayed in the next screenshot:

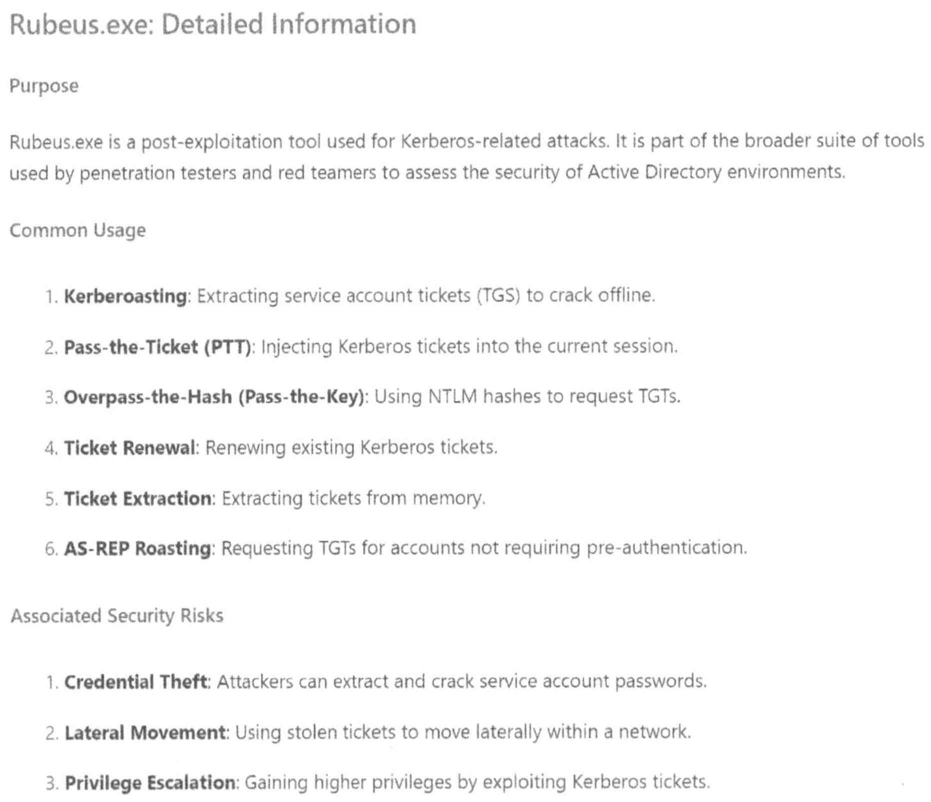

Figure 8.52 – Security Copilot reveals Rubeus.exe as an attacker tool

Immediately after the xcopy command was used to copy the `Rubeus.exe` file to the remote device, **vnevado-win10b**, a subsequent command involving `PsExec.exe` is observed in the detailed PowerShell execution events presented earlier by Security Copilot. A portion of the two command lines are shown in the next screenshot:

```
| xcopy.exe | "xcopy.exe" C:\M365DAttack\Rubeus\Rubeus.exe \\vnevado-win10b\C$\Temp | powershell.exe |
| PsExec.exe | "PsExec.exe" \\vnevado-win10b -accepteula cmd /c "C:\Temp\Rubeus.exe dump /service:krbtgt
```

Figure 8.53 – PowerShell events related to Rubeus.exe, PsExec.exe, and more

Consulting with Security Copilot reveals that `PsExec.exe` executed a command remotely on the **vnevado-win10b** device. This command launched `Rubeus.exe` to dump Kerberos tickets for user **nestorw** and saved the output to `C:\Temp\AdminTicket.txt`. Security Copilot notes that this action indicates credential dumping and potential lateral movement within the network. The next screenshot shows the prompt along with part of the response from Security Copilot:

Can you explain to me what this command line is trying to do: "PsExec.exe" \\vnevado-win10b -accepteula cmd /c "C:\Temp\Rubeus.exe dump /service:krbtgt /user:nestorw > C:\Temp\AdminTicket.txt"

> **3 steps completed** 19 seconds

Dec 15, 2024

The provided command uses `PsExec.exe` to remotely execute a command on the device `vnevado-win10b`. It runs `Rubeus.exe` from the `C:\Temp` directory to dump Kerberos tickets for the `krbtgt` service and the user `nestorw`. The output of this command is redirected to a file named `AdminTicket.txt` in the `C:\Temp` directory on the remote device. The command also automatically accepts the EULA for PsExec.

1. **Use PsExec to execute a command on a remote device**:

```
PsExec.exe \\vnevado-win10b -accepteula cmd /c "C:\Temp\Rubeus.exe dump /service:krbtgt /user:nestorw > C:\Temp\AdminTicket.txt"
```

   - *MITRE Technique*: T1021.002: SMB/Windows Admin Shares

2. **Accept the EULA for PsExec automatically**:

Figure 8.54 – Security Copilot analyzing suspicious command line

Many other potentially harmful behaviors are also observed in the detailed PowerShell execution events presented by Security Copilot earlier. You can submit each of these suspicious events to Security Copilot and ask for insights.

For instance, Security Copilot provides a straightforward explanation for the suspicious command involving the use of `mimikatz.exe` and with PowerShell as the parent process. While Mimikatz is well-known among security analysts as a powerful post-exploitation tool, understanding its actions on the device typically requires more research and familiarity with the tool. In this case, Security Copilot is able to assist by providing a clear explanation of the command's purpose, enabling the analysts to quickly grasp the intent and scope of the attack. The next screenshot displays the Security Copilot prompt requesting insights into the suspicious command line and part of the explanation provided by Security Copilot:

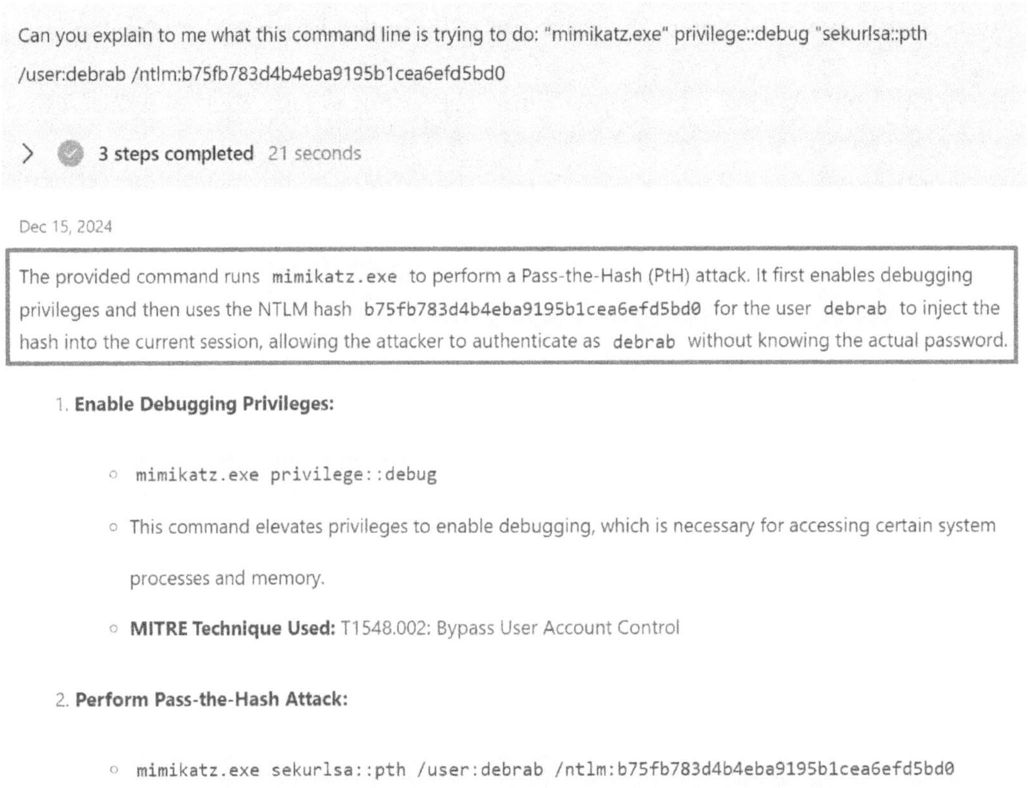

Figure 8.55 – Security Copilot analyzing a suspicious command line

After submitting the suspicious events for Security Copilot to provide insights, you can then request Security Copilot to summarize its findings, detailing the attacker's actions and potential impact. In this case, Security Copilot generates a long and detailed report. The next screenshot displays the prompt, along with the start of the report:

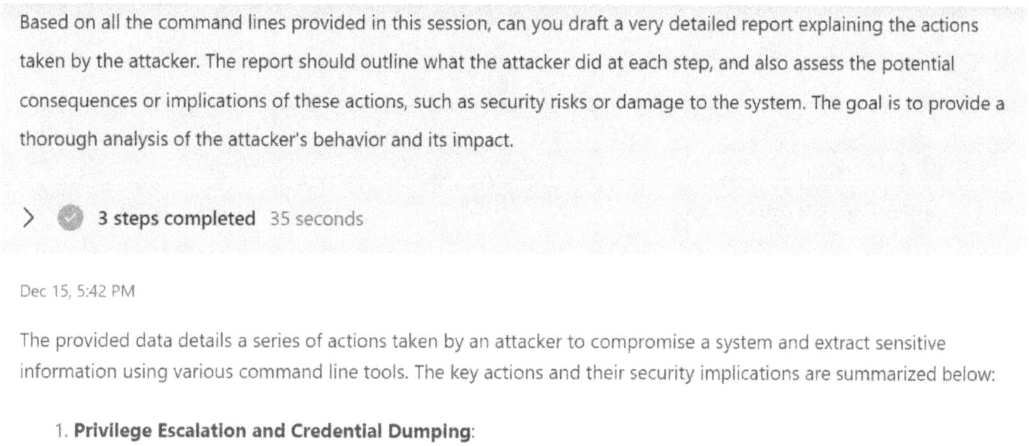

Figure 8.56 – Asking Security Copilot to generate a detailed report

Looking back at the Security Copilot incident summary and reviewing the investigation we've conducted so far, you can see just how effective Security Copilot is in acting as a smart assistant, guiding and supporting the analysts every step along the way.

For this incident, Security Copilot helps identify events related to remote sessions and provides insights into those events. Security Copilot also helps reveal detailed execution information about specific files and processes involved in the attack. It offers insights into `mimikatz.exe` and `Rubeus.exe`, which are commonly used by attackers for credential dumping and manipulating authentication tokens. Security Copilot not only identifies suspicious events but also provides crucial information that helps analysts quickly understand the attack and its potential impact.

Given the complexity of this security incident, we will not cover all the alerts. The purpose of examining part of the incident is to highlight Security Copilot's features and capabilities, demonstrating the different prompts and plugins that can be used and showcasing the value of promptbooks.

As you work on the incident, don't forget to leverage Security Copilot's **Guided Response** feature. This capability simplifies the response process by providing recommended incident classification, actions to contain the incident, steps to gather additional details, and recommended response actions.

Guided Response is available both as an embedded feature in Microsoft Defender XDR and in the Security Copilot standalone mode. The next screenshot presents the guided response for this incident seen from the Microsoft Defender XDR portal:

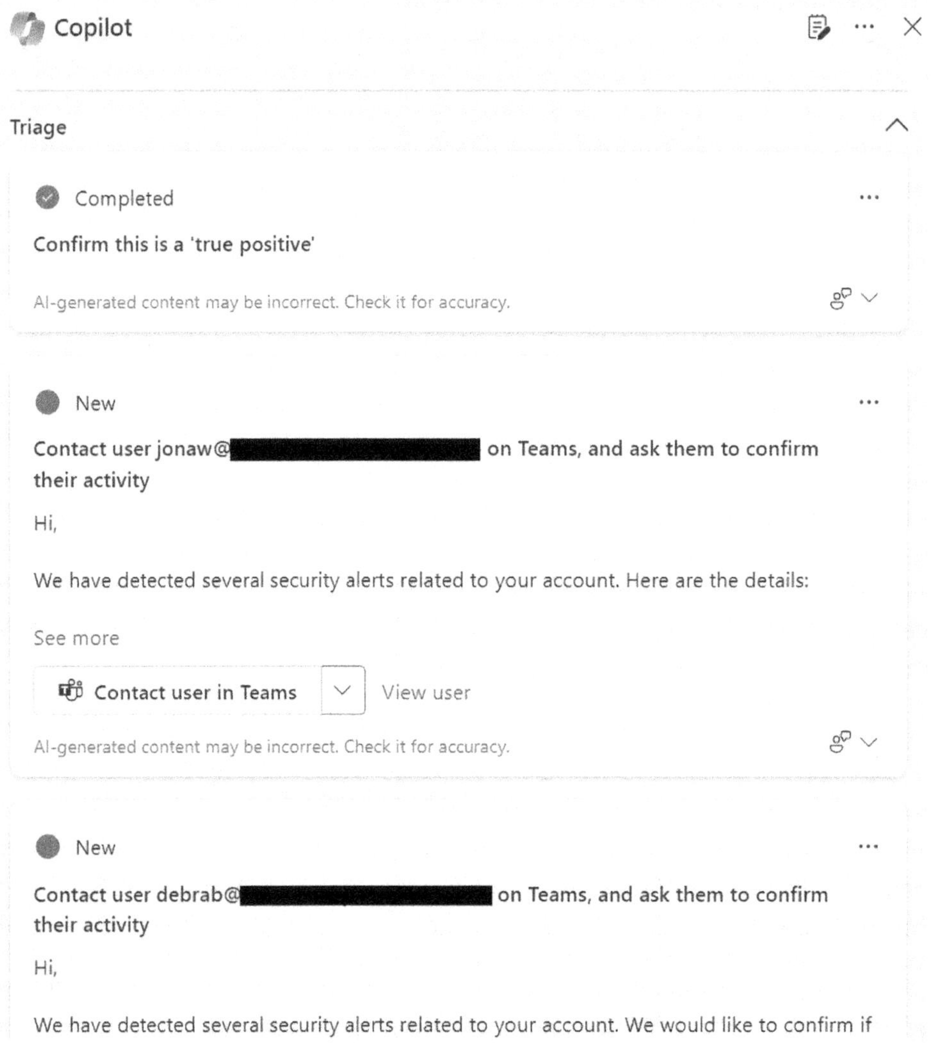

Figure 8.57 – Security Copilot's Guided Response feature

Last but not least, once the investigation is complete, you can request Security Copilot to generate an incident report. You have the option to either choose a generic report in the Microsoft Defender XDR portal or a more detailed and thorough report by providing specific requirements in a prompt within the standalone experience of Security Copilot.

The next screenshot displays a snippet of the generic incident report created by Security Copilot in the Microsoft Defender XDR portal:

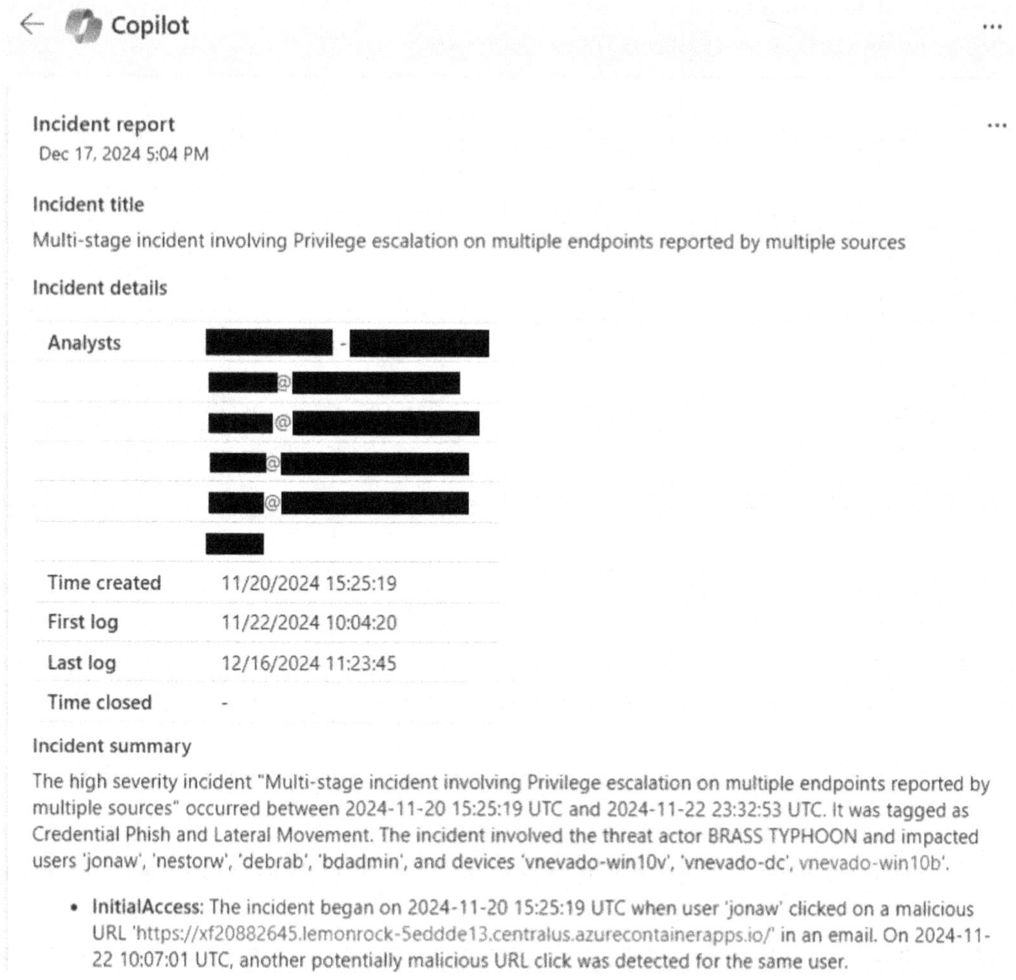

Figure 8.58 – The generic incident report

Within Security Copilot's embedded experience, you're limited to generating a standard report. However, when you switch to its standalone portal, you can tailor the report to your exact specifications using a simple prompt.

As a side note, all your Security Copilot investigation work is saved in sessions that you can access at any time from Security Copilot's standalone experience. These sessions are retained indefinitely unless you delete them. Additionally, you can share your sessions with others in your organization who have access to Security Copilot, as illustrated next:

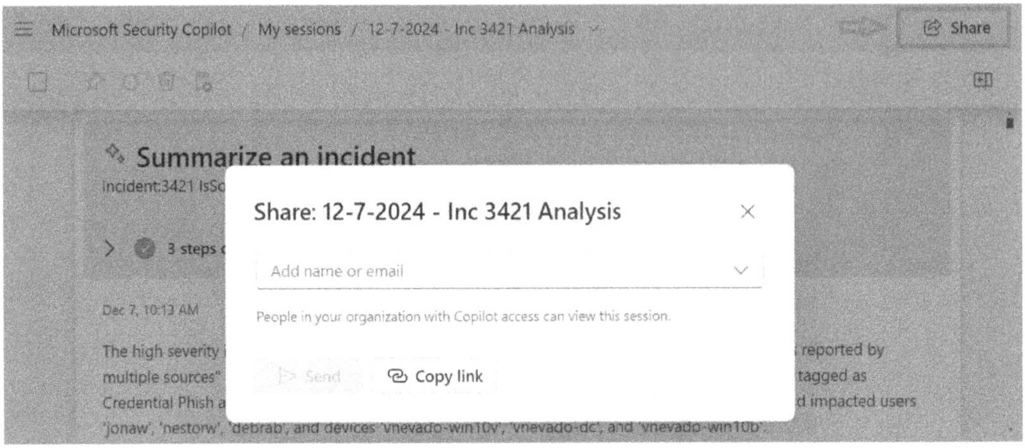

Figure 8.59 – Sharing a Security Copilot session

As we wrap up this case study, let's look ahead to how the investigative steps can be further optimized through the use of promptbooks. In the next section, we'll walk through a similar incident to demonstrate how a series of promptbooks can drive the investigation more efficiently.

Streamlining incident response with promptbooks

Earlier in this chapter, we touched on using promptbooks to streamline parts of the investigation process. However, there is more to promptbooks than just efficiency gains. For instance, many of the investigation techniques demonstrated in this chapter reflect common incident response practices that security teams can apply. As a result, these investigative prompts can be converted into reusable promptbooks. These promptbooks not only allow analysts to capture effective investigation methods tailored to their unique environments but also promote a more modular investigative approach. Within a Security Copilot session, an analyst can invoke different promptbooks, as pre-built workflows, to handle specific parts of an investigation. Rather than step-by-step manual investigation, the analyst can call on the appropriate promptbooks to automate different investigative tasks all within the same investigation session.

As an example, right before the start of an incident investigation, in Security Copilot's standalone portal, an analyst can launch a promptbook that automatically summarizes the incident and then provides a list of impacted entities of this incident for review. The next screenshot illustrates such a promptbook. It is configured with two prompts, one for summarizing the incident and another for retrieving the related entities:

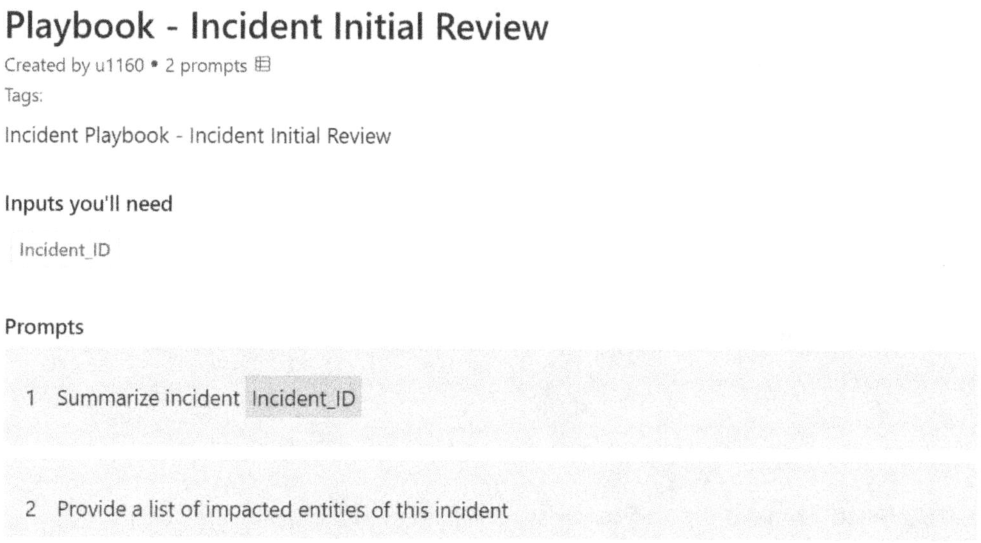

Figure 8.60 – The Incident Initial Review promptbook

The Security Copilot incident summary states that **the incident began at 2025-04-01 14:31:54 UTC when a malicious URL 'hxxps://xy015364077[.]victoriousdune-1cb66a73[.]westeurope[.]azurecontainerapps[.]io/' was clicked on 'mb-winclient'**. In response to any malicious URL click events, the analyst can launch a promptbook designed to detect malicious execution on the device, as the URL click action often leads to malware downloads and execution.

The promptbook, as shown next, checks for downloaded files and reviews process executions to identify suspicious ones:

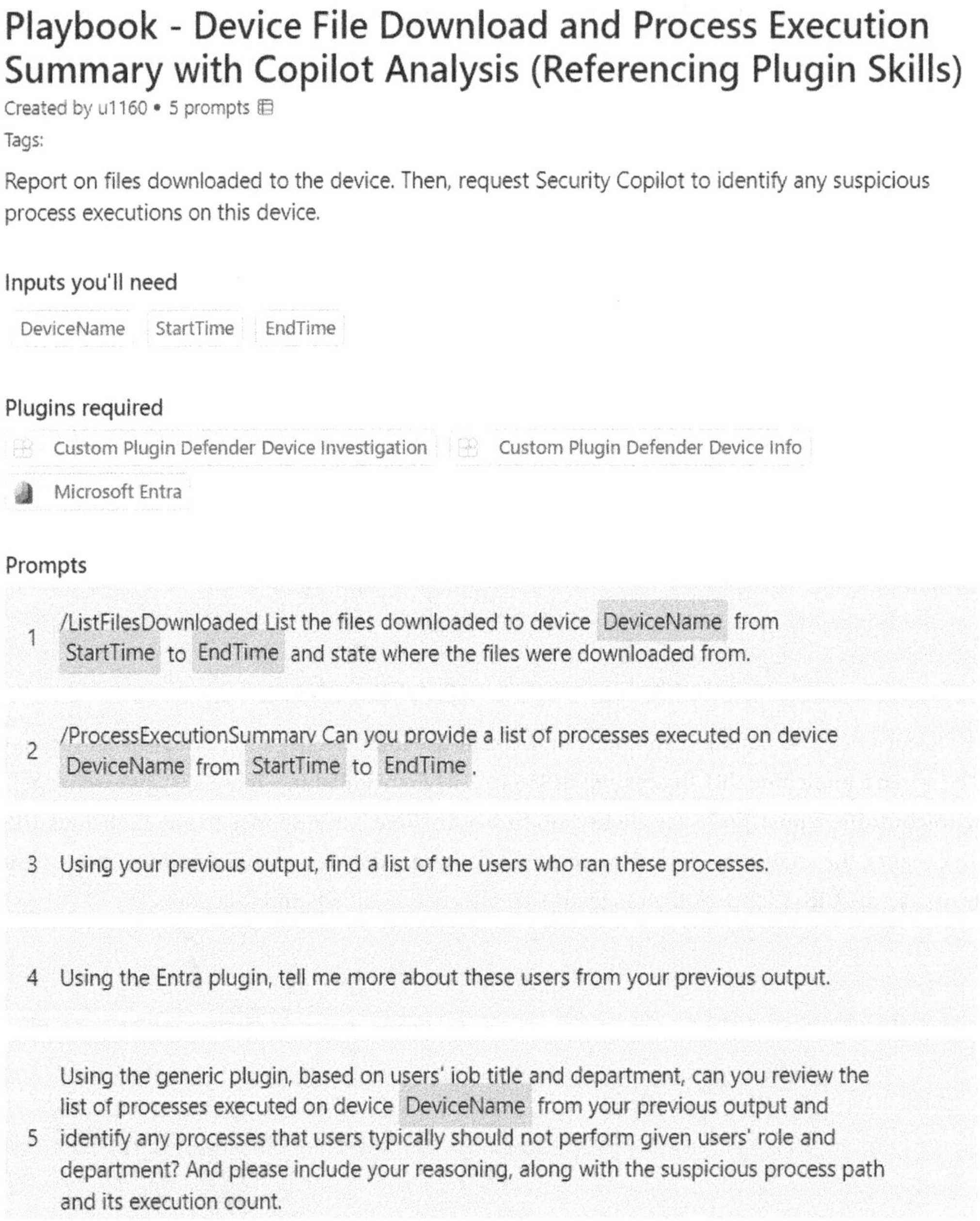

Figure 8.61 – The promptbook that checks for downloaded files and reviews process executions

Notice this promptbook not only captures user-initiated process executions but also leverages the Microsoft Entra plugin to retrieve these users' job titles and departments. It then instructs Security Copilot to analyze these processes to flag any that users typically do not initiate, given users' roles and departments.

For this incident, the promptbook reveals that a file named `Midnight56.zip` was downloaded. During the same time frame, user `kdickens` initiated multiple process executions on the device. Security Copilot points out that this user is an account manager in the sales department. It also flags three suspicious processes that are uncommon for someone in that role, suggesting potential unauthorized activities. The following screenshot displays a portion of the output from the Security Copilot promptbook:

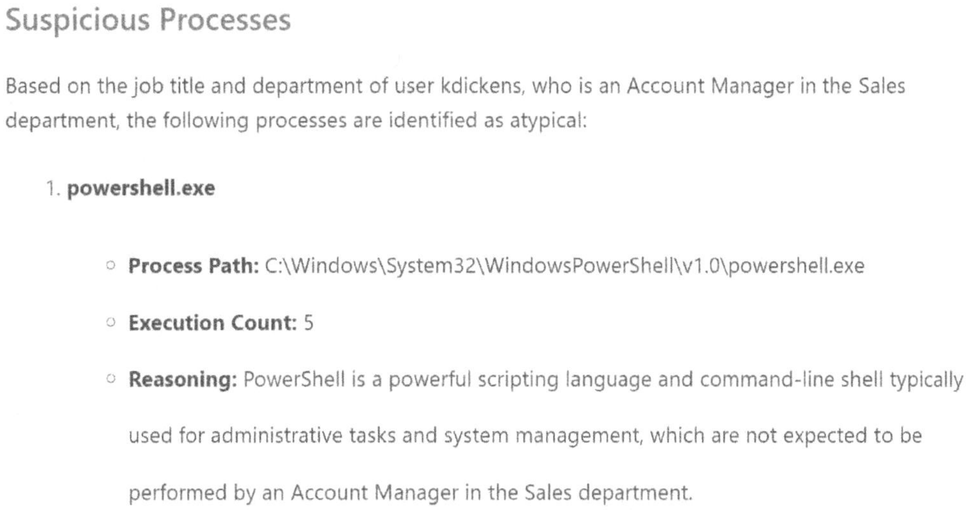

Figure 8.62 – A portion of the output from the promptbook

With PowerShell identified as one of the suspicious user-initiated processes, the analyst can then invoke an additional promptbook to analyze PowerShell executions, all within the same Security Copilot session. As shown in the following screenshot, this promptbook is designed to retrieve detailed PowerShell events from the device and then instruct Security Copilot to identify any suspicious activities.

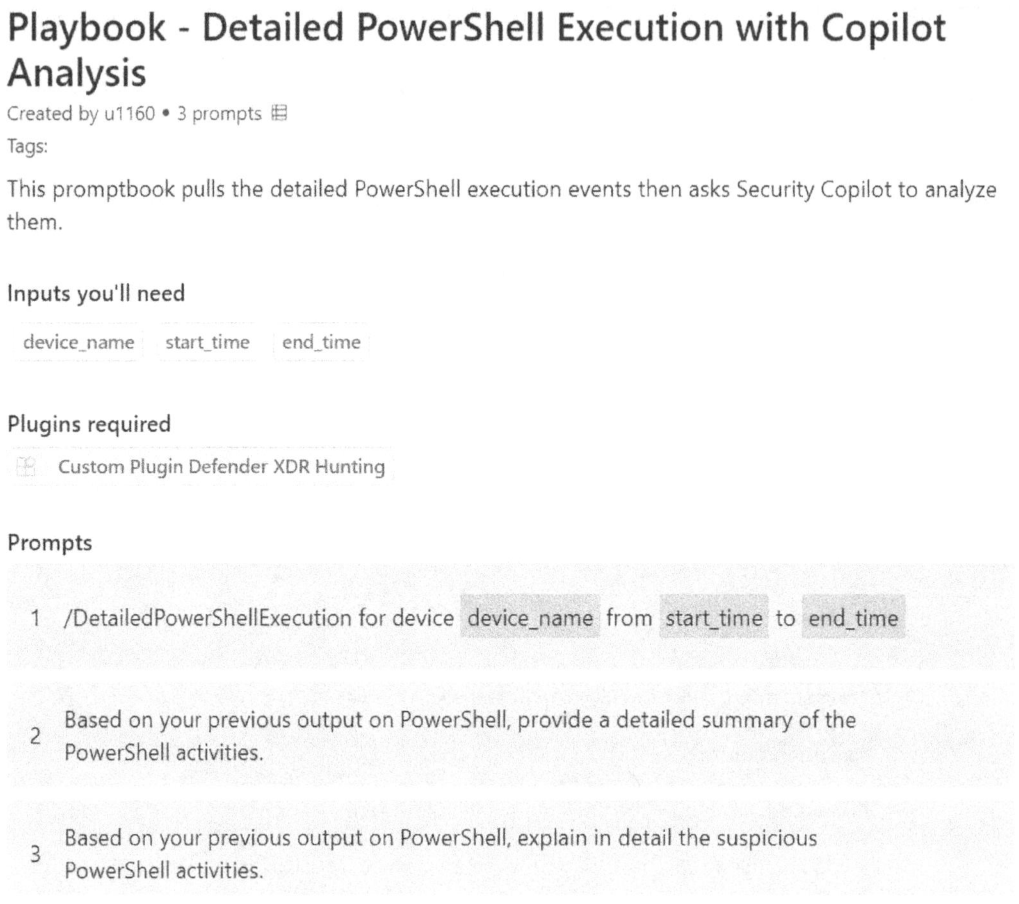

Figure 8.63 – Promptbook to identify suspicious PowerShell activities

The response from Security Copilot outlines the suspicious PowerShell activities. For each one, Security Copilot provides the specific PowerShell command deemed as suspicious, the associated known malicious technique, and an explanation of why the command is considered suspicious.

The next screenshot displays the first three suspicious PowerShell actions identified by Security Copilot. This example highlights Security Copilot's ability to cut through noisy data to pinpoint suspicious activities, which reduces the time analysts need to spend on manual review. Additionally, it demonstrates Security Copilot's strength in analyzing scripts, command lines, and more, allowing analysts to quickly gain deeper insights into potentially harmful activities. Keep in mind that it's always a good idea to double-check Security Copilot's responses, as AI-generated insights may miss context or produce inaccuracies:

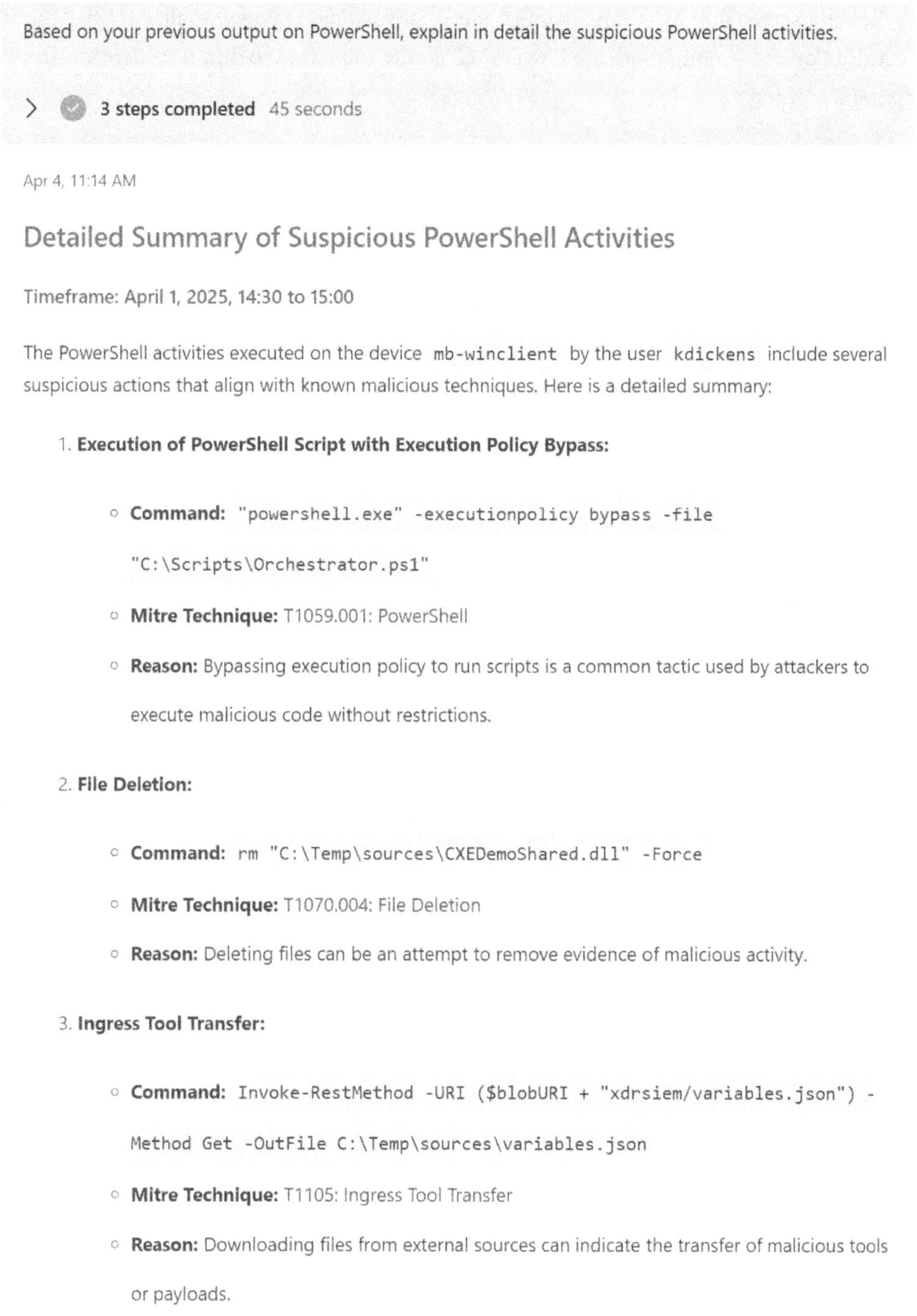

Figure 8.64 – The first part of Security Copilot's response

The following screenshot highlights some additional suspicious PowerShell activities reported by Security Copilot. Among them are PowerShell commands used to dump credentials from the computer's memory:

4. **Execution of Malicious Script:**
   - **Command:** `"powershell.exe" -ExecutionPolicy bypass -File C:\Users\kdickens\Downloads\Midnight56\Midnight56.ps1`
   - **Mitre Technique:** T1059.001: PowerShell
   - **Reason:** Running a script from the Downloads folder with execution policy bypass is highly suspicious and indicative of malicious intent.

5. **Credential Dumping:**
   - **Command:** `Invoke-Expression $module` (part of the Invoke-Mimikatz script)
   - **Mitre Technique:** T1003.001: LSASS Memory
   - **Reason:** Using Mimikatz to dump credentials from memory is a known technique for stealing user credentials.

6. **Use of Windows API for Memory Manipulation:**
   - **Commands:**
     - `$VirtualAllocAddr = Get-ProcAddress kernel32.dll VirtualAlloc`
     - `$memcpyAddr = Get-ProcAddress msvcrt.dll memcpy`
   - **Mitre Technique:** T1106: Native API
   - **Reason:** Using native Windows API functions for memory allocation and manipulation is often associated with advanced malware techniques.

Figure 8.65 – Additional suspicious PowerShell activities

Based on the malicious PowerShell execution observed, the device is likely compromised or under the attacker's control. The analyst can then invoke an additional promptbook to gather more information about the device, such as the owner and IP address, while preparing to isolate it. The following screenshot displays the promptbook, which features six prompts that are designed to retrieve various pieces of information about the device:

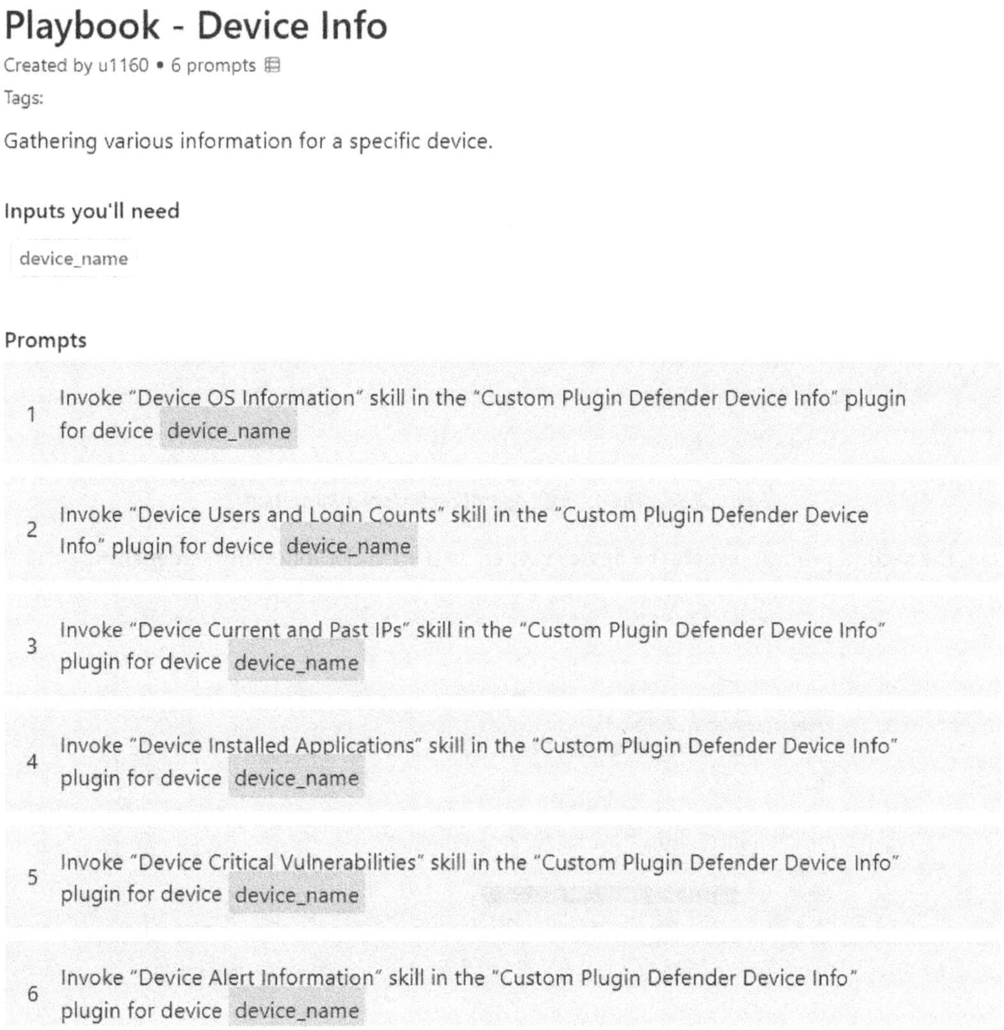

Figure 8.66 – The promptbook that gathers device information

Once the promptbook executes its first prompt, shown in the next screenshot, Security Copilot displays the device's operating system information:

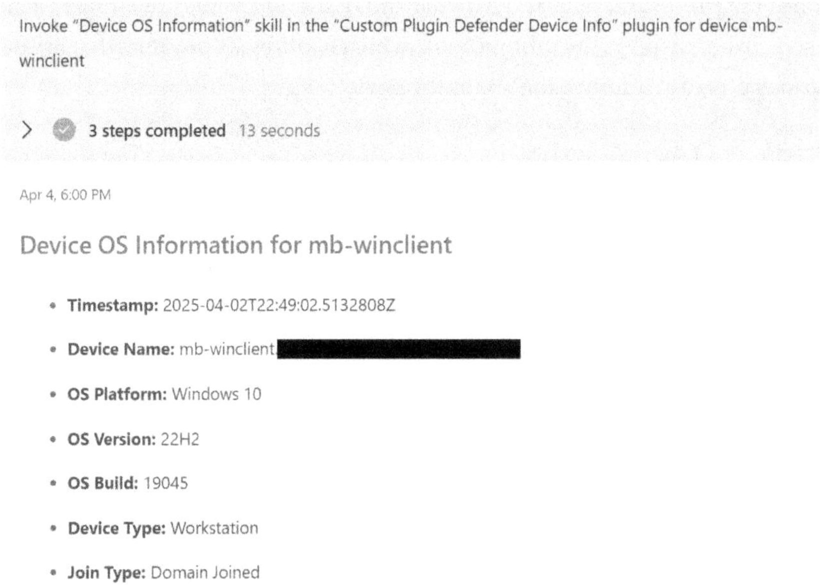

Figure 8.67 – The device's operating system information

Next, the second prompt reveals the device owner, as seen in the following screenshot:

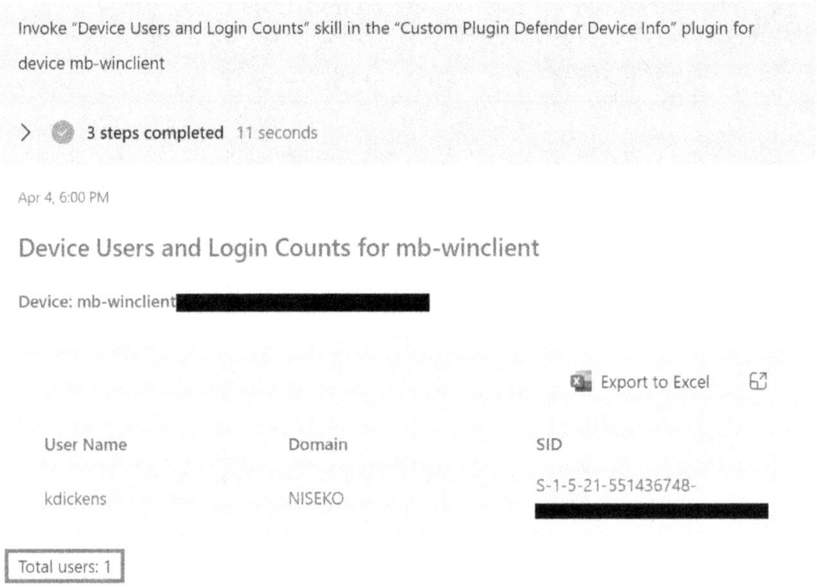

Figure 8.68 – The device owner's information

The third prompt in the promptbook reveals the device's current and past IP addresses. For this incident, only one IP address has been assigned to the device over the past 10 days. This is illustrated in the following screenshot:

Figure 8.69 – The device's current and past IPs

As the investigation moves forward, the analyst can continue to invoke additional promptbooks as needed. In essence, promptbooks enhance incident response efficiency by enabling the analyst to launch multiple targeted investigative workflows, each tailored to a specific investigative task, all within the same Security Copilot session. This modular approach reduces manual effort, accelerates response times, and promotes more consistent, thorough investigations.

Up to this point, we've highlighted how Security Copilot can support you throughout incident investigations in Microsoft Defender. As we conclude the case studies and reflect on the investigation journey, it's also important to emphasize that Security Copilot is highly customizable. Although the examples shared here focus on specific scenarios and may differ from your workflows, you can leverage the same underlying approach and core principles to customize your prompts, promptbooks, or plugins accordingly to meet your operational needs.

Summary

In this chapter, we explored real-world Microsoft Defender XDR incident investigations, showcasing how Security Copilot enhances and streamlines the cyber incident investigation process. Through this exploration, this chapter also equipped you with the knowledge and practical insights to effectively leverage Security Copilot's capabilities to address security challenges.

Looking ahead, the next chapter will delve into additional real-world scenarios, demonstrating how the integration of Microsoft Threat Intelligence, Entra, and Intune with Security Copilot can further strengthen your security operations.

9

Harnessing Security Copilot within the Microsoft Ecosystem

Over the course of this book, you have been introduced to key features and capabilities of **Security Copilot**. The previous chapter used a **Microsoft Defender XDR** incident scenario to showcase how various Security Copilot capabilities work together.

In this chapter, we will continue with additional case studies to illustrate the practical application of Security Copilot, particularly its integration with **Microsoft Entra** and **Intune** within the broader Microsoft ecosystem. We will explore how Security Copilot, leveraging its Entra plugin, assists user account investigations. In particular, we'll look at how it supports analysts in analyzing user behaviors, tracking suspicious activities, and identifying signs of account compromise. Additionally, we'll examine how Intune, when enhanced by Security Copilot, can provide valuable support to IT administrators and security teams. This includes using Security Copilot for device comparisons, as well as identifying policy conflicts, to ensure more efficient and secure device management.

This chapter is divided into two main sections, each focusing on the practical application of Security Copilot in different contexts:

- Identifying and investigating user threats with Entra and Security Copilot
- Showcasing Intune capabilities enhanced by Security Copilot for IT admins and SOC analysts

Want to try out the prompts, custom plugins, and promptbooks featured in this book? Take a look at the book's GitHub repository at `https://github.com/PacktPublishing/Microsoft-Copilot-for-Security`.

Identifying and investigating user threats with Entra and Security Copilot

Investigating risky or suspicious users with Microsoft Entra has become easier with the help of Security Copilot, which enables faster and more streamlined detection and analysis. Embedded directly in Microsoft Entra, Security Copilot provides actionable insights and recommendations in real time. Through its standalone experience, Security Copilot enables access to critical Entra data points such as users, groups, sign-in logs, audit logs, and more, all within a unified interface. This integration allows security teams to quickly gain a deeper understanding of user behaviors and correlate events across various datasets, including those from other security solutions.

In the next few sections, let's take a closer look at an identity-based case study to highlight how Security Copilot can empower security teams.

Harnessing Security Copilot for user account investigations

We will start by exploring how Security Copilot provides user context, offering insights into user activities and behaviors to assist with investigations. To illustrate this in action, let's walk through a case study. It starts with Security Copilot, leveraging the Microsoft Entra plugin, to identify high-risk users. Through a series of investigative steps, including analysis of user sign-in activities and additional threat intelligence, suspicious logins from an IP address in Luxembourg are uncovered.

Now let's take a closer look at how this unfolds step by step. In the standalone experience of Security Copilot, using the Entra plugin, you can request Security Copilot to automatically identify recent high-risk users in the organization, as shown in the following screenshot:

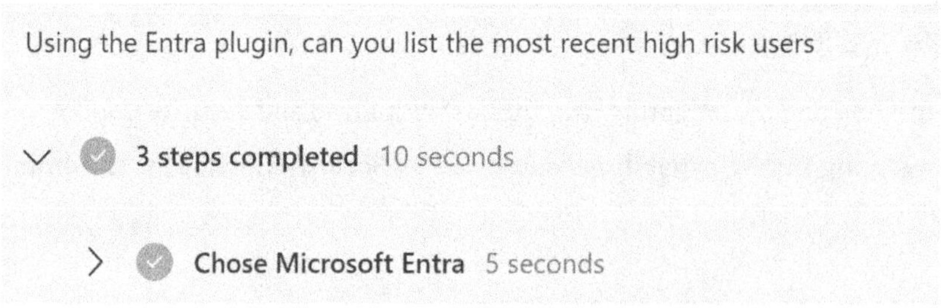

Figure 9.1 – Identify recent high-risk users

The response from Security Copilot provides a list of at-risk users, displaying key details such as the users' display names, principal names, risk states, risk details, and more. Part of the response is shown in the next screenshot:

Most Recent High Risk Users

Here are the most recent high-risk users identified in Microsoft Entra:

Export to Excel

Display Name	User Principal Name	Risk State
[redacted]	[redacted]@[redacted]	atRisk
[redacted]	[redacted]@[redacted]	atRisk
Lynne Robbins	[redacted]@[redacted]	atRisk

Figure 9.2 – Key details about high-risk users

The at-risk users identified are categorized into different risk states. For this case study, for demonstration purposes, let's focus on a user with a **'confirmed compromised** 'risk state and investigate this account to understand the reasons behind the compromise.

> **Note**
>
> Security Copilot prompts used in this case study can also be applied to examine other types of risky users.
>
> In cases where there are no **high-risk** users present in the organization, the Copilot response may look something like **I have retrieved the most recent high-risk users, but it appears there are no current entries in the system.**

Back to the case study, within the same Copilot session, you can issue a follow-up prompt, asking Security Copilot to identify **'confirmed compromised'** users in the organization. The prompt is displayed next:

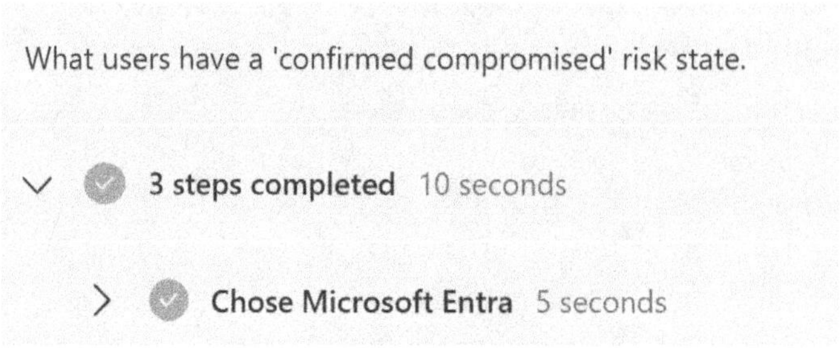

Figure 9.3 – The Security Copilot prompt

In this case, Security Copilot returns a few users with a **Confirmed Compromised** risk state, as illustrated in the following screen capture. Let's take a closer look at the first user, Lee Gu, from the list in Copilot's response:

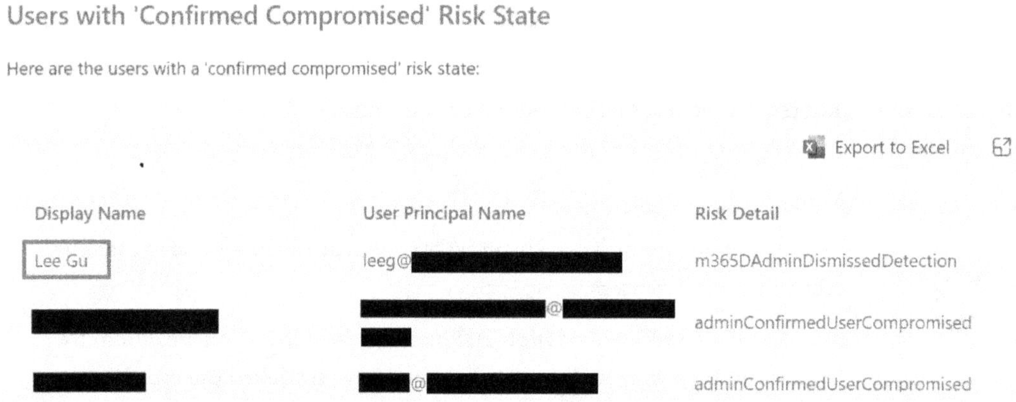

Figure 9.4 – Users with a 'Confirmed Compromised' risk state

Leveraging the Microsoft Entra plugin, you ask Security Copilot to explain what could trigger Lee Gu's account to be flagged as **'confirmed compromised'**. As shown in the following screenshot, Security Copilot responds with an explanation: **the account has been confirmed as compromised by an administrator or through automated detection mechanisms**. Also, from the additional user details provided by Security Copilot in its response, shown next, you find out that Lee Gu is a finance analyst:

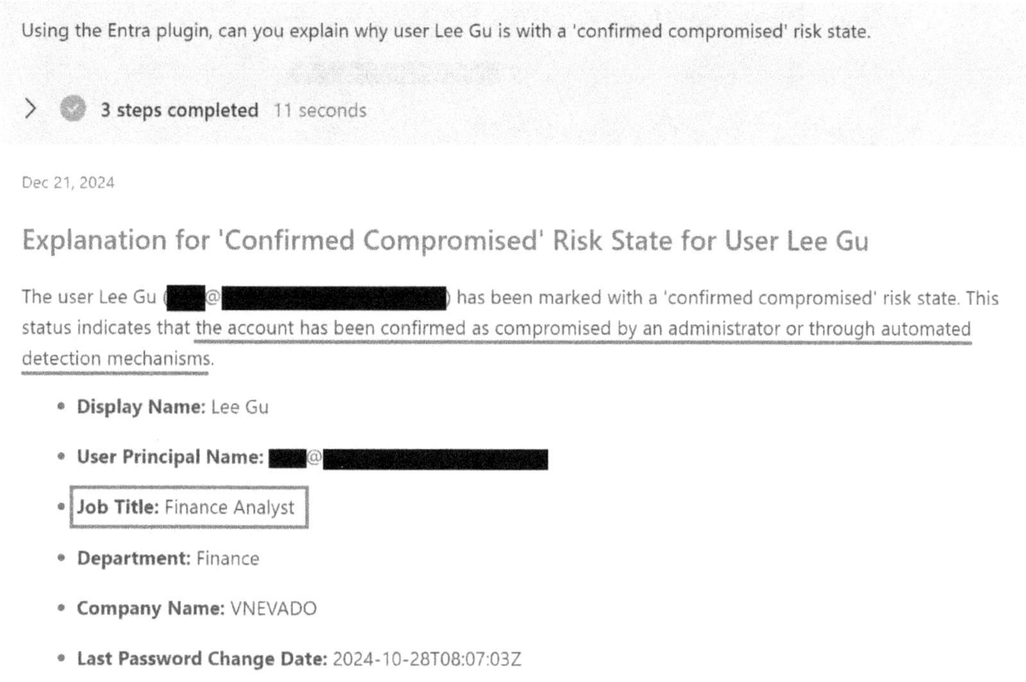

Figure 9.5 – The Security Copilot prompt and response

To investigate a user account, you can start by reviewing the user's sign-in events to look for any unusual behaviors or patterns. For quick access to the sign-in logs, you simply ask Security Copilot to gather Lee Gu's sign-in activities for you. Please note that, as of December 2024, Security Copilot can only retrieve the last 30 days of user sign-in logs from Microsoft Entra.

The Security Copilot prompt and the first part of its response are displayed in the next screenshot:

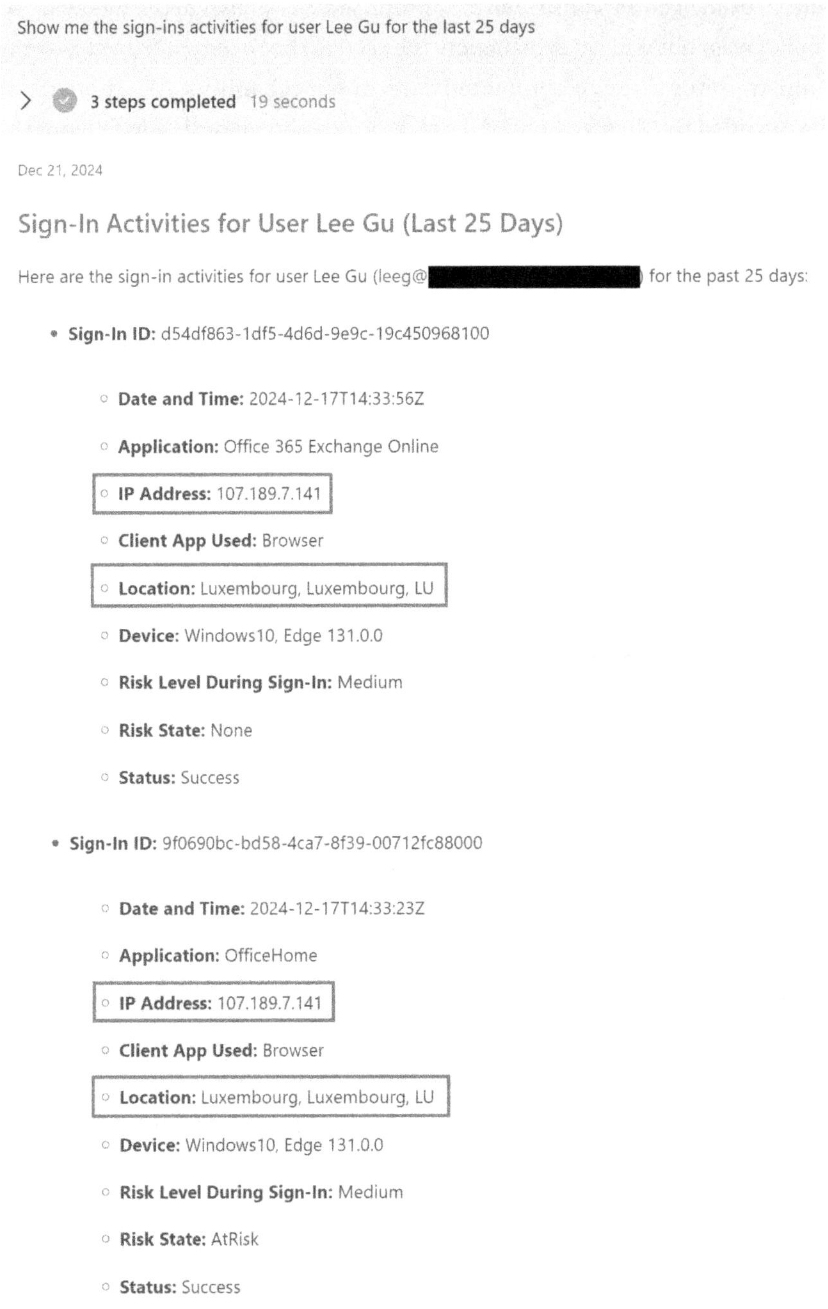

Figure 9.6 – Sign-in activities for user Lee Gu

After quickly reviewing the sign-in events, you notice that Lee Gu's recent sign-ins are from IP 107.189.7.141, an address located in Luxembourg, LU.

Are there any failed sign-in attempts? You can request Security Copilot to retrieve those logs for you. In this case, Security Copilot reports that there have been no recent failed sign-ins for user Lee Gu:

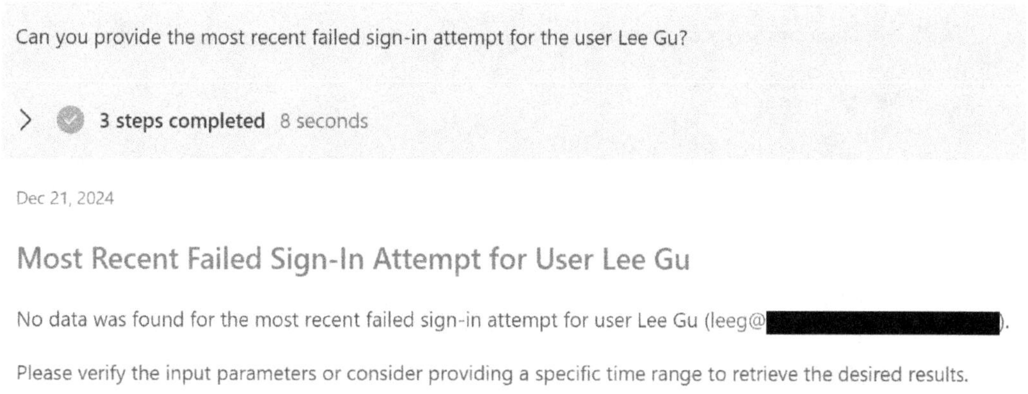

Figure 9.7 – Most recent failed sign-in attempts

With this information, let's focus on the IP address 107.189.7.141, as it's strange for Lee Gu to sign in from Luxembourg, Europe. Using the **Microsoft Defender Threat Intelligence** (**MDTI**) plugin in Security Copilot, you request Security Copilot to gather threat intelligence related to this IP address.

As shown in the following screenshot, Security Copilot presents the MDTI data, indicating that this IP is classified as neutral and belongs to **ASN AS53667**. An **Autonomous System Number** (**ASN**) is a unique identifier for a network on the internet. ASNs facilitate routing and communication between different networks. It's worth noting that through the MDTI plugin, Security Copilot also reports that **Infrastructure hosted by this ASN frequently exhibits suspicious behavior**. This could be the first indication that the IP address **107.189.7.141** might be suspicious.

From the same Security Copilot response, also shown in the next screenshot, you notice that the DNS records for this IP address indicate **107.189.7.141** would resolve to different, uncommon domains over time, which is also unusual and concerning:

Figure 9.8 – Information on IP Address 107.189.7.141

To further validate your suspicion, you request that Security Copilot gathers more information about these domains. In response to your prompt, Copilot invokes the MDTI plugin, as shown in the next screenshot:

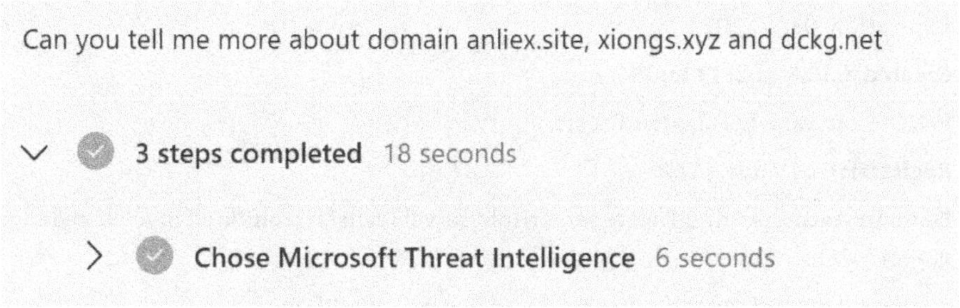

Figure 9.9 – The Security Copilot prompt

Security Copilot returns detailed information for each domain queried in the prompt. The full response from Security Copilot is provided next for your reference:

Information on Domains

Domain: anliex.site

- **Record updated:** 05/18/2022 20:21:37
- **Last scanned:** 05/26/2022 19:53:18
- **Expiration:** 03/19/2022 23:59:59
- **Created:** 03/19/2021 10:00:58
- **WHOIS server:** whois.dnspod.com
- **Registrar:** DNSPod, Inc.
- **Domain status:** serverTransferProhibited
- **Email:** abuse@dnspod.com - (abuse)
- **Name:** Abuse Contact - (abuse), DNSPod, Inc. - (registrar)
- **Organization:** wangzheng - (tech, admin, registrant, billing), DNSPod, Inc. - (abuse)
- **State:** bei jing shi - (tech, admin, registrant, billing)
- **Country:** China - (tech, admin, registrant, billing)
- **Phone:** +86.4009100100 - (abuse)
- **Nameservers:** wall.dnspod.net, thera.dnspod.net

Domain: xiongs.xyz

- **Record updated:** 05/07/2023 08:14:37
- **Last scanned:** 06/27/2023 19:13:55
- **Expiration:** 03/26/2023 23:59:59
- **Created:** 03/26/2021 19:13:08
- **WHOIS server:** whois.godaddy.com
- **Registrar:** Go Daddy, LLC
- **Domain status:** pendingDelete serverHold serverTransferProhibited inactive redemptionPeriod
- **Country:** UNITED STATES - (tech, admin, registrant, billing)
- **State:** Arizona - (registrant)

Domain: dckg.net

- **Record updated:** 09/17/2024 04:16:49
- **Last scanned:** 12/23/2024 21:30:33
- **Expiration:** 09/18/2025 12:26:57
- **Created:** 09/18/2023 12:26:57
- **WHOIS server:** whois.ename.com
- **Registrar:** eName Technology Co., Ltd.
- **Domain status:** clientDeleteProhibited clientTransferProhibited
- **Email:** 1252577398@QQ.com - (tech, admin, registrant)
- **Name:** ZhangJian - (tech, admin, registrant)
- **Organization:** Zhang Jian - (tech, admin, registrant)
- **Street:** JiangSuSheng ChangZhouShi WuJinQu Niu Tang Zhen - (tech, admin, registrant)
- **City:** ChangZhouShi - (tech, admin, registrant)
- **State:** JiangSu - (tech, admin, registrant)
- **Postal code:** 213000 - (tech, admin, registrant)
- **Country:** CHINA - (tech, admin, registrant)
- **Phone:** 18915883666 - (tech, admin, registrant)
- **Nameservers:** jm1.dns.com, jm2.dns.com

Upon reviewing the Copilot response, you notice that the domains associated with IP 107.189.7.141 are registered by different organizations, in various locations, and with differing contact details. This inconsistency could be another red flag. Typically, end users connect to the internet through their **Internet Service Providers (ISPs)**, which usually results in a consistent IP address range and domain usage. However, the domains linked to 107.189.7.141 are uncommon and have been registered with different registrars, locations, and so on, which may suggest potentially fraudulent activity, especially since this behavior deviates from typical ISP patterns.

At this point, you suspect that the IP address 107.189.7.141 is likely used by malicious actors and user Lee Gu did not log in from this IP address.

Let's check with Security Copilot to see whether there are any sign-in events from other IPs. The Copilot prompt is shown in the next screenshot:

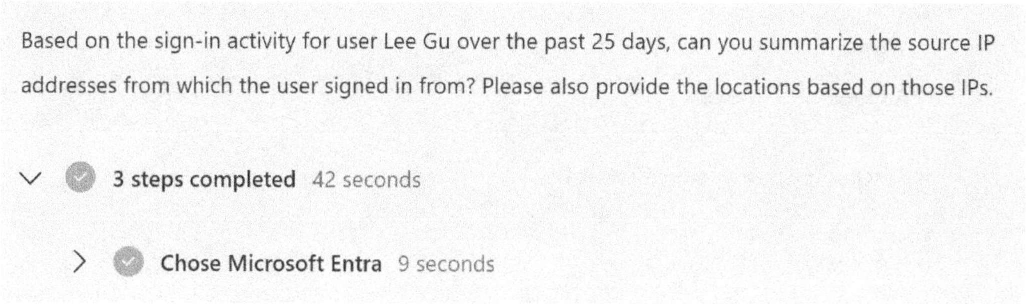

Figure 9.10 – The Security Copilot prompt

Security Copilot identifies two additional IP addresses, **137.117.84.85** and **20.185.147.193**, from which Lee Gu signed in. Both IPs are located in the US. The Copilot response is displayed in the following screen capture:

Source IP Addresses and Locations for User Lee Gu's Sign-In Activities (Last 25 Days)

Here are the source IP addresses and their corresponding locations from which user Lee Gu (leeg@[redacted]) signed in over the past 25 days:

- **IP Address:** 107.189.7.141
    - **Location:** Luxembourg, Luxembourg, LU
    - **Sign-In Count:** 10
- **IP Address:** 137.117.84.85
    - **Location:** Washington, Virginia, US
    - **Sign-In Count:** 1
- **IP Address:** 20.185.147.193
    - **Location:** Washington, Virginia, US
    - **Sign-In Count:** 1

Figure 9.11 – Two additional IP addresses identified

You then ask Security Copilot to find the exact date and time when Lee Gu signed in from IP **137.117.84.85**. This is done through the following prompt:

```
For the past 25 days, based on the sign-in activity for user Lee Gu,
can you provide the date and time when user Lee Gu signed in from IP
137.117.84.85?
```

As shown in the next screenshot, Lee Gu signed in from IP **137.117.84.85**, located in the US, on the same day and within the same hour as his sign-in from IP **107.189.7.141**, which is based in Luxembourg, Europe:

Sign-In Activity for User Lee Gu from IP 137.117.84.85

Here is the sign-in activity for user Lee Gu (leeg@[redacted]) from IP address 137.117.84.85 over the past 25 days:

- **Sign-In ID:** 84c475d8-dc37-42ee-82c9-48ef01fb6e00
    - **Date and Time:** 2024-12-17T14:12:40Z
    - **Application:** Office 365 Exchange Online
    - **IP Address:** 137.117.84.85
    - **Client App Used:** Browser
    - **Location:** Washington, Virginia, US
    - **Device:** Windows10, Edge 131.0.0
    - **Risk Level During Sign-In:** None
    - **Risk State:** None
    - **Status:** Success

Total items shown: 1.

Figure 9.12 – Sign-In activity for user Lee Gu from IP 137.117.84.85

In theory, it's impossible for Lee Gu to sign in from two different locations across the Atlantic Ocean within the same hour. This raises further suspicion, especially considering your earlier investigation of IP address 107.189.7.141, which appears to be associated with a malicious actor.

What about the other IP, 20.185.147.193? Using a similar prompt, you ask Security Copilot for the exact date and time of Lee Gu's sign-in from it. Security Copilot reveals that Lee Gu signed in from 20.185.147.193 within the same hour on the same day as the other two IPs. However, both this IP address and IP 137.117.84.85 are located in Washington, Virginia, US.

As of now, you know Lee Gu signed on from three different IPs within the same hour on December 17, 2024. Two of the IPs are located in Washington, Virginia, US, while the third IP is based in Luxembourg, Europe. Your previous investigation indicates that the third IP is likely used by malicious actors. All these factors lead you to suspect that Lee Gu did not sign in from the third IP address.

A quick way to confirm your suspicion is to contact the end user directly. You ask Security Copilot to draft an email for you to send to the user for confirmation. The following screenshot displays the Security Copilot prompt along with the plugin that is selected for the query:

Can you draft an email to follow up with user Lee Gu, asking him to share his usual working location for the month of December 2024? This will help to verify whether he was the one who logged in from Luxembourg, Europe around December 17th, 2024.

3 steps completed 10 seconds

Chose Generic 6 seconds

Figure 9.13 – Asking Security Copilot to draft an email

The email generated by Security Copilot is displayed in the next screenshot:

Subject: Verification of Login Activity

Dear Lee Gu,

I hope this email finds you well.

We are conducting a routine security check and noticed a login attempt from Luxembourg, Europe around December 17th, 2024. To ensure the security of your account, could you please confirm your usual working location for the month of December 2024?

Your prompt response will help us verify the legitimacy of this login attempt and take necessary actions if required.

Thank you for your cooperation.

Best regards,

[Your Name]
[Your Position]
[Your Contact Information]
[Your Company]

Figure 9.14 – The email generated by Security Copilot

While waiting for user Lee Gu to confirm his location, let's continue the investigation. In the next section, we will explore what additional insights can be uncovered with the help of Security Copilot.

Uncovering authentication and account changes with Security Copilot

Security Copilot can quickly access the authentication methods assigned to the user and track changes made to the user's account. For instance, you can ask Security Copilot to provide the authentication methods configured for user Lee Gu. In this case, as shown in the next screenshot, Security Copilot reveals that only password authentication is set up for Lee Gu:

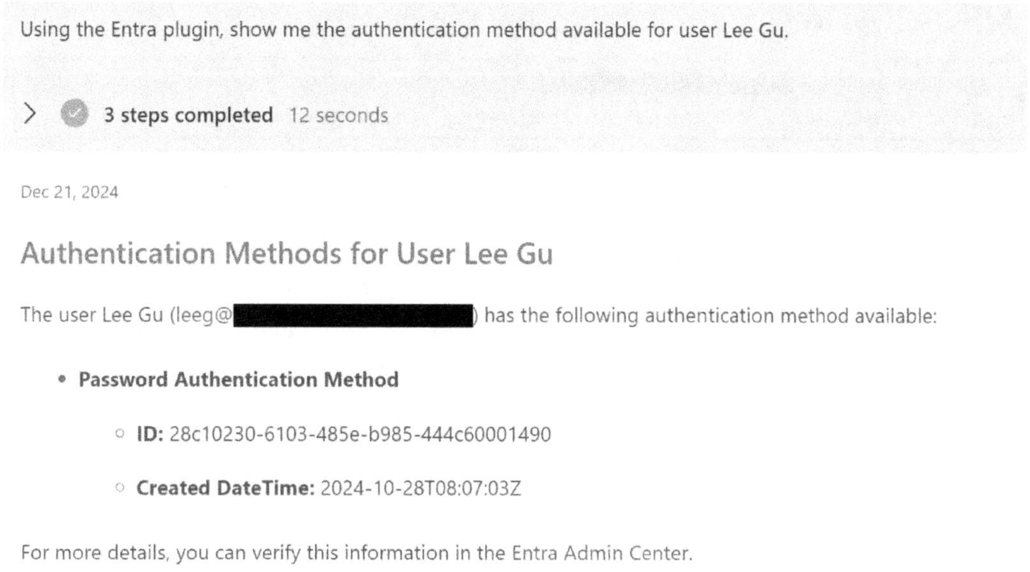

Figure 9.15 – Authentication method for user Lee Gu

Password authentication allows users to log in using only their username and password. If a malicious actor obtains the compromised password, possibly by purchasing it from the dark web, the intruder can use this information to sign in as a legitimate user.

Given the potential security risk, you request that Security Copilot confirms whether any **Multi-Factor Authentication** (**MFA**) policies are assigned to user Lee Gu. As shown next, Security Copilot confirms that the only available authentication method for this user is password authentication, as no MFA method has been assigned to Lee Gu:

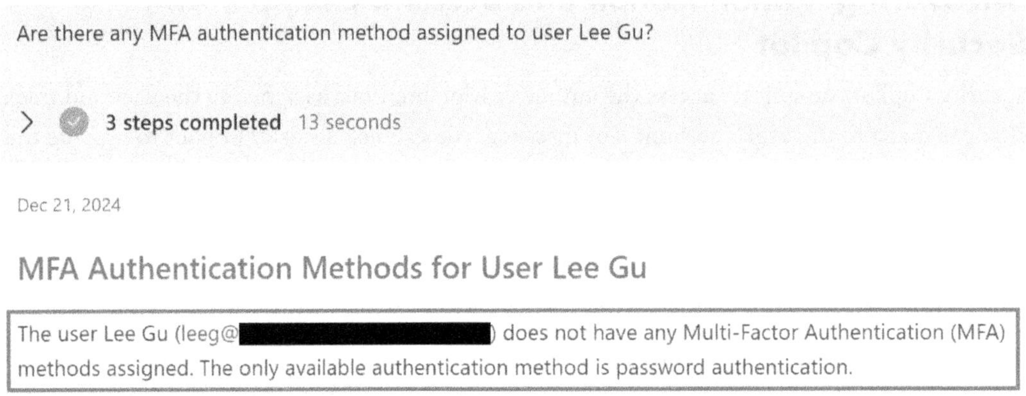

Figure 9.16 – Verifying MFA for user Lee Gu

The investigation findings so far are concerning. It appears a malicious actor may have signed in as Lee Gu to access his corporate resources. Additionally, Lee Gu's account is secured only with password authentication, which significantly increases the risk of unauthorized access. Without MFA in place, a compromised password becomes a simple entry point for malicious actors.

Let's continue with the investigation. The Entra plugin within Security Copilot can access and retrieve information from account audit logs to track changes made to a user's account. In this case, you ask Security Copilot to list changes or updates made to Lee Gu's account. The Security Copilot prompt is displayed next:

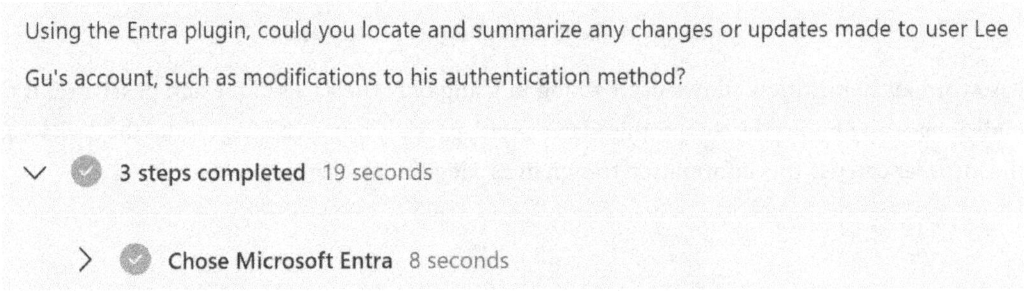

Figure 9.17 – The Security Copilot prompt

Security Copilot reveals a number of changes made to Lee Gu's account, as shown in the following screen capture. Notably, Lee Gu's account was added to the **MFA_Demo_Exclusion** group and then removed from this group. Also, notice these account changes occurred on December 17, 2024 – the same day Lee Gu's account signed in from IP 107.189.7.141, which is located in Luxembourg, Europe:

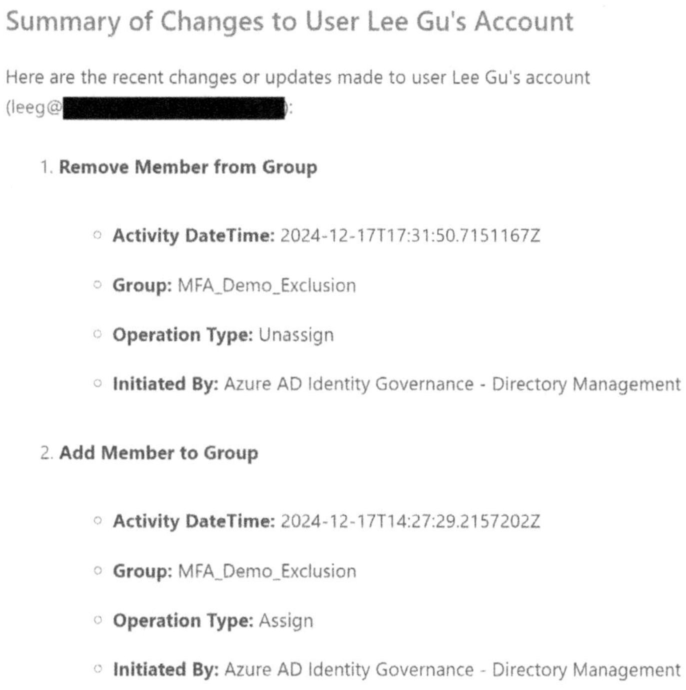

Figure 9.18 – Changes to Lee Gu's account

Given that there are a number of account changes, instead of examining each one in detail by yourself, you can have Security Copilot explain the security implications of these changes for you first. This allows you to quickly review the changes and then focus on the ones that are most relevant. The next screenshot displays the Security Copilot prompt along with the plugin invoked:

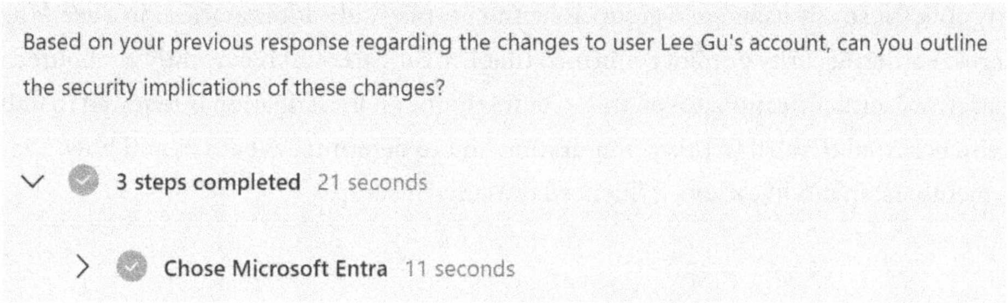

Figure 9.19 – The Security Copilot prompt

Then, as shown next, Security Copilot presents the security impacts for each one:

Security Implications of Recent Changes to User Lee Gu's Account

Here are the security implications of the recent changes or updates made to user Lee Gu's account (leeg@[redacted]):

1. **Remove Member from Group (MFA_Demo_Exclusion)**
   - **Activity DateTime:** 2024-12-17T17:31:50.7151167Z
   - **Implication:** Removing Lee Gu from the MFA_Demo_Exclusion group means that he is no longer excluded from Multi-Factor Authentication (MFA) policies. This enhances the security of his account by ensuring that MFA is enforced.
2. **Add Member to Group (MFA_Demo_Exclusion)**
   - **Activity DateTime:** 2024-12-17T14:27:29.2157202Z
   - **Implication:** Adding Lee Gu to the MFA_Demo_Exclusion group temporarily excluded him from MFA policies. This could have reduced the security of his account by bypassing MFA requirements during this period.

Figure 9.20 – The security implications of recent changes

Security Copilot's analysis shows that on 2024-12-17 at 14:27, the action **Add Member to Group (MFA_Demo_Exclusion)** added Lee Gu to the **MFA_Demo_Exclusion** group. As the group name implies, this action possibly excluded Lee Gu from MFA policies. Then, on the same day, at 17:31, the action **Remove Member from Group** removed Lee Gu from the **MFA_Demo_Exclusion** group, presumably re-enabling MFA policies for him.

While group membership doesn't always directly correspond to the configuration applied to the end user, the changes made to a user account often provide valuable context that can aid the investigation. Group membership is commonly used to control access to certain resources or security policies, so any changes in group assignments may indicate alterations in a user's access privileges. Earlier, Security Copilot confirmed that Lee Gu's account is currently configured with only password authentication. Given this, a more thorough investigation is required to uncover what else occurred that led to this configuration and to determine whether, and how, Lee Gu's group membership modifications influenced the current setup.

For this case study, we will not delve into further investigation details as this scenario could represent a complex incident requiring substantial additional analysis. However, keep in mind that you can always rely on Security Copilot to support your investigation. As an example, you can prompt Security Copilot with the following:

```
Using the Entra plugin, can you list the groups currently assigned to user
Lee Gu?
```

The Security Copilot response is displayed next:

Here are the groups currently assigned to user Lee Gu (leeg@[redacted]):

- **Group Name:** Vallee Nevado
- **Group Name:** DemoUsers
- **Group Name:** MFA exclusion eligibility
- **Group Name:** All Users - No Guest
- **Group Name:** Conference Planning

Figure 9.21 – Groups assigned to user Lee Gu

You can then follow up to learn more about a specific group by using a prompt such as this:

```
What is the group description and group type for group MFA exclusion
eligibility?
```

Or, you can simply ask Security Copilot:

```
Fetch details of the group Vallee Nevado.
```

Alternatively, in addition to using Security Copilot to assist with your investigation, you may also ask Copilot to provide you with additional reference materials. In the next section, let's look at some of these scenarios, using the existing case study.

Turning investigation insights into action with Security Copilot

Security Copilot can also provide guidelines, including process outlines, procedures, and more. For instance, you can consult Security Copilot on how to enable MFA authentication for a user.

Leveraging the Microsoft Document plugin, Security Copilot provides detailed steps and multiple approaches for enabling MFA for user Lee Gu. Part of the Security Copilot response is shown next:

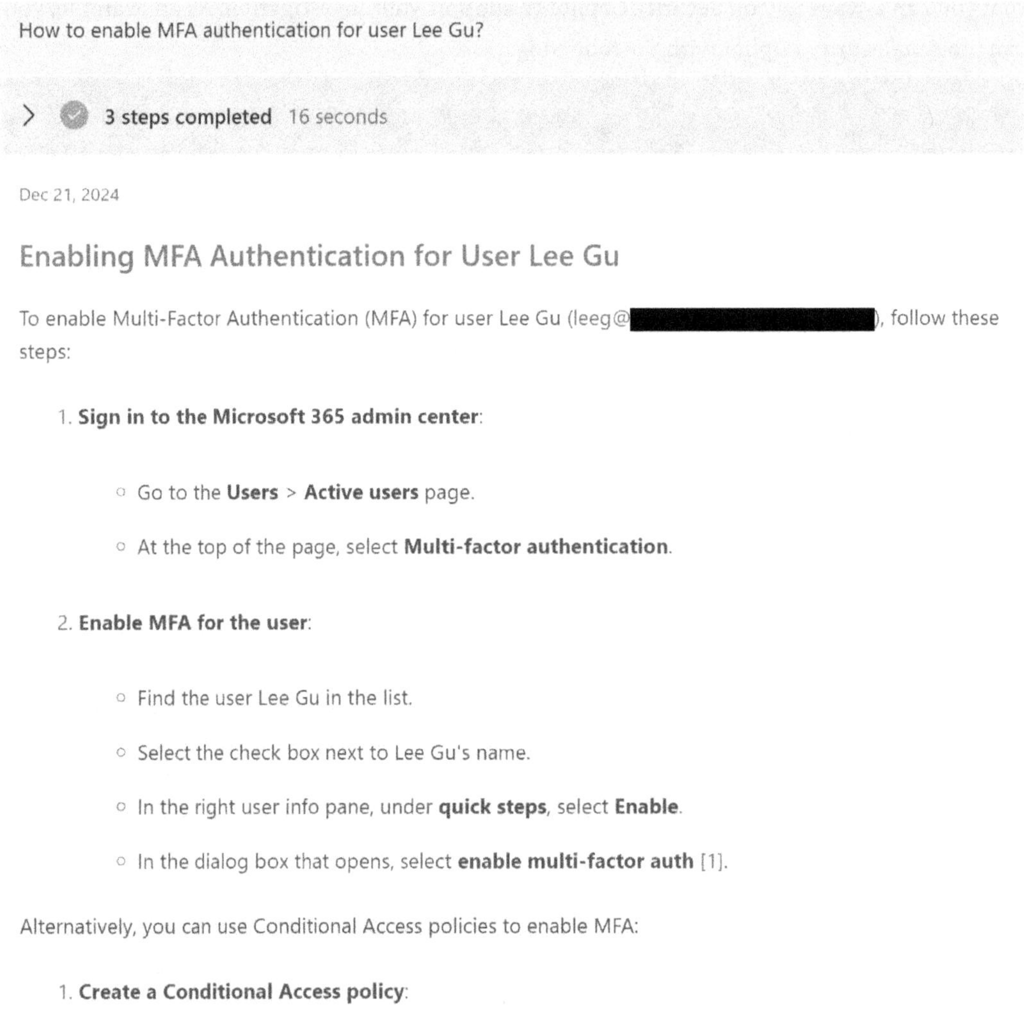

Figure 9.22 – How to enable MFA for user Lee Gu

For your reference, the rest of the Security Copilot response, particularly regarding the use of Conditional Access policies to enable MFA, is provided next:

Alternatively, you can use Conditional Access policies to enable MFA:

1. **Create a Conditional Access policy:**

- Sign in to the Microsoft Entra admin center as at least a Conditional Access Administrator.
- Browse to **Protection > Conditional Access**, select **+ New policy**, and then select **Create new policy**.

2. **Configure the policy:**

- Enter a name for the policy, such as *MFA Pilot.*
- Under **Assignments**, select **Users or workload identities.**
- Choose **Select users and groups**, and then select **Users and groups.**
- Browse for and select the group or user, such as Lee Gu.

3. **Set conditions and access controls:**

- Under **Cloud apps or actions**, select **Select resources.**
- Choose the apps or actions that require MFA.
- Under **Access controls**, select **Grant access** and **Require multifactor authentication.**

4. **Activate the policy:**

- Under **Enable policy**, select **On.**
- Select **Create** to apply the policy [2].

These instructions not only offer reference guidance for analysts, but they may also come in handy during investigation. Using this same example, understanding the different ways for applying MFA may assist analysts in identifying different areas where an attacker could have altered configuration settings.

Optionally, after the investigation, you may also consult Security Copilot for recommendations, such as how to protect the compromised user account and prevent unauthorized access. A sample prompt and part of Security Copilot's response are shown in the following screen capture:

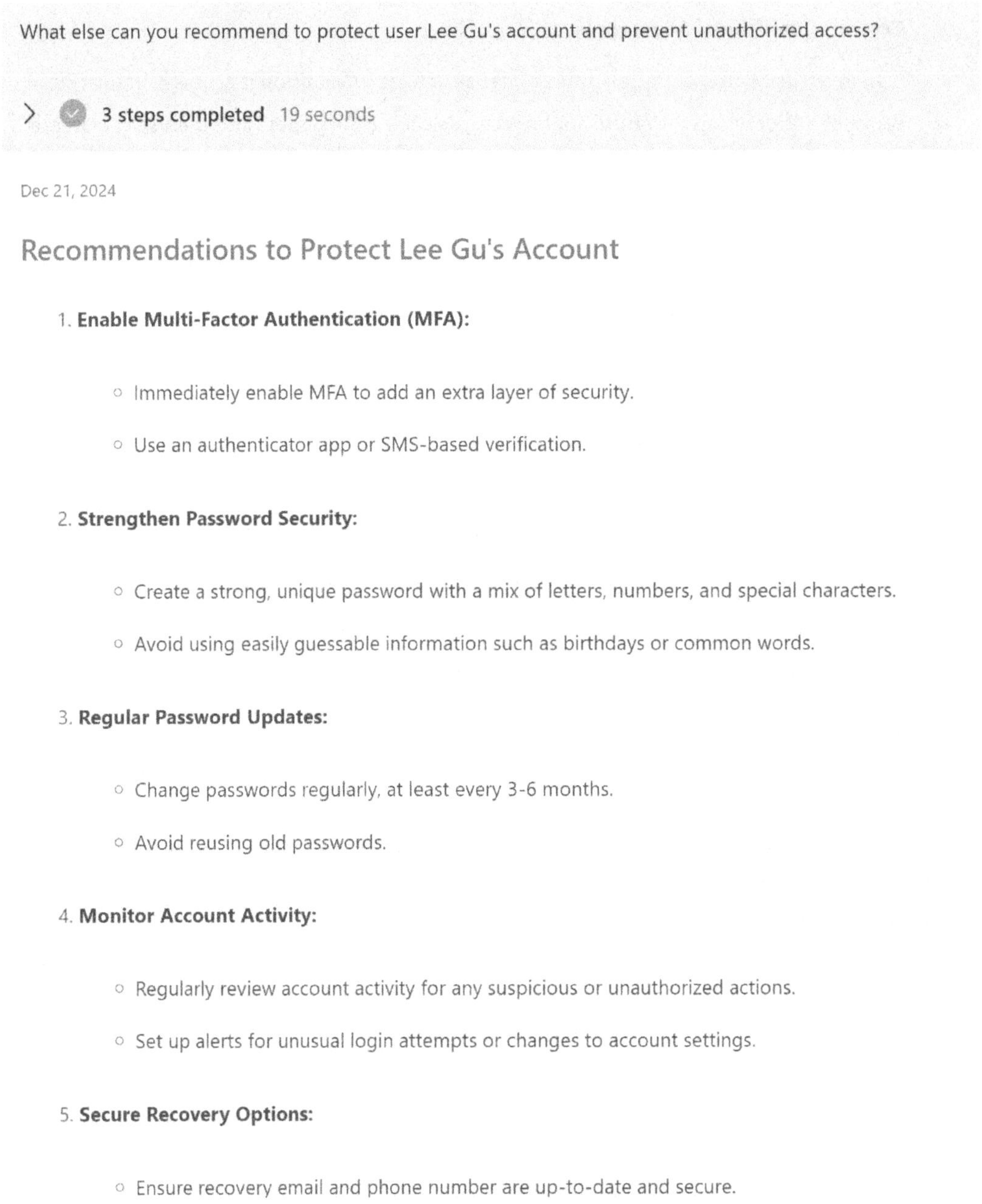

Figure 9.23 – Recommendations for protecting Lee Gu's account

You may also consult Security Copilot for other security-related recommendations. As an example, you can ask Copilot for suggestions on monitoring suspicious activities and configuring alerting, as illustrated next:

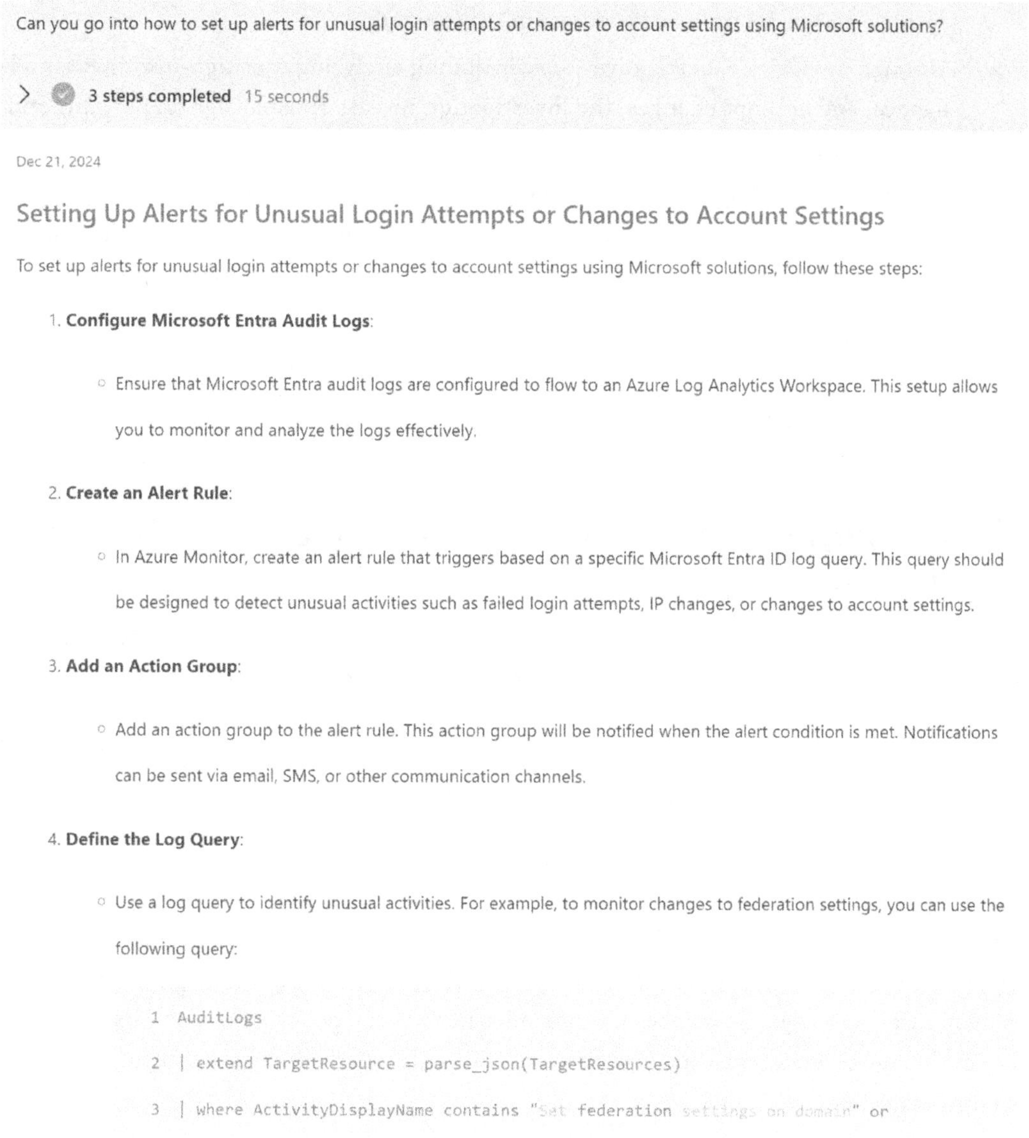

Figure 9.24 – Monitoring suspicious activities and configuring alerting

With these recommendations in mind, let's now recap the key insights explored so far in this case study:

- The case study starts with Security Copilot identifying high-risk users and uncovering suspicious sign-ins from an IP address in Luxembourg.
- Through a series of investigative steps, including analyzing user sign-ins, threat intelligence, and account changes, the investigation reveals unusual sign-in patterns and potential account compromise.
- The case study highlights how Security Copilot assists in investigating compromised user accounts, reviewing authentication methods, and tracking account changes. Additionally, it offers actionable recommendations, such as enabling MFA to mitigate risks.
- This case study concludes with insights on turning investigation findings into proactive actions, such as securing compromised accounts and monitoring suspicious activities.

As we move into the next section, we'll dive into how Intune capabilities, enhanced by Security Copilot, can further support IT admins and security teams.

Showcasing Intune capabilities enhanced by Security Copilot for IT admins and SOC analysts

Microsoft Intune provides businesses with robust device and application management. It enables organizations to secure and manage a wide range of devices, while also overseeing the applications used by employees. Security Copilot further enhances Intune's efficiency by providing AI-powered insights and assisting with real-time visibility into device compliance and security posture, offering greater control over Intune-managed environments.

For instance, Security Copilot allows security analysts and IT administrators to easily and quickly access data on Intune-managed devices, helping to improve decision-making and response times. The Intune plugin in Security Copilot also simplifies the tracking of configuration policies and applications by allowing administrators to query policy assignments and deployment status using natural language. This makes it more efficient to check policy states, understand how they are being assigned across the organization, and verify whether they are applying correctly to targeted devices.

Another key feature of the Security Copilot's Intune plugin is its ability to compare two devices, such as a working and a non-working (status) device. This feature is particularly useful for troubleshooting or investigating devices' status, as it helps to identify discrepancies between devices that are functioning as expected and those that may have issues related to policy enforcement, configuration, or app deployment.

In the next few sections, we'll illustrate the Security Copilot Intune features through a case study. This will offer practical examples of how Security Copilot can be used to streamline device management and strengthen security operations.

Unlock device insights with Security Copilot

The case study starts with a multi-stage incident detected on an endpoint, ash-irvins, as shown next:

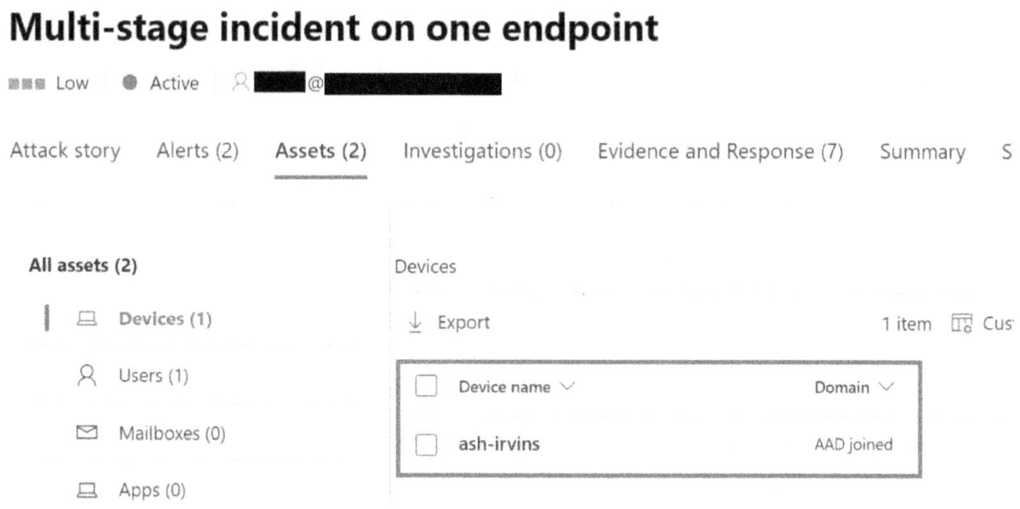

Figure 9.25 – A multi-stage incident on one endpoint

Using the Intune plugin, a single Security Copilot prompt lets you quickly gather detailed information about the device. As illustrated in the next screen capture, Security Copilot provides a range of information for `device ash-irvins`.

This includes the device name, type, model, manufacturer, serial number, operating system, storage details, compliance state, and more:

Using the Intune plugin, can you tell me more about device ash-irvins?

> **3 steps completed** 12 seconds

Jan 7, 10:36 PM

Device Information for ASH-IrvinS

- **Intune Device ID**: f907637e-fe24-4b9d-87fb-74df8b8a0abb
- **Device Name**: ASH-IrvinS
- **Azure AD Device ID**: 39443e72-6c8b-46f0-9f6c-92f2db82f587
- **Operating System**: Windows 10.0.26100.2605
- **Compliance State**: Compliant
- **Management State**: Managed
- **Owner Type**: Company
- **Device Type**: WindowsRT
- **Manufacturer**: Microsoft Corporation
- **Model**: Virtual Machine
- **Serial Number**: 7273-7359-8146-2595-9192-0810-06
- **Total Storage Space**: 135,565,148,160 bytes
- **Free Storage Space**: 102,285,443,072 bytes
- **Last Sync Date**: 2025-01-07T22:59:27.9357651Z
- **Enrolled Date**: 2024-12-27T20:23:30.0838971Z

Figure 9.26 – Device Information for ash-irvins

In the same response, Security Copilot also includes details about the device owner and the device's last logon time. In this case, the device is linked to user Irvin Sayers, as shown next:

- **Enrolled Date**: 2024-12-27T20:23:30.0838971Z
- **User Principal Name**: [redacted]@[redacted]
- **User Display Name**: Irvin Sayers
- **User ID**: [redacted]
- **Last Logon Time**: 2025-01-07T22:41:28.3878679+00:00

Figure 9.27 – Device owner and device's last logon time

After gathering the basic device information, you can issue a follow-up prompt to quickly identify and assess the different policies assigned to the device. In the case of device ash-irvins, Security Copilot reveals that it is managed by 30 device configuration policies and 2 compliance policies. The prompt and part of the policy assignment details can be viewed in the following screen capture:

Using the Intune plugin, can you provide all the policies assigned to this device?

> **3 steps completed** 13 seconds

Jan 7, 10:38 PM

Policies Assigned to Device ASH-IrvinS

The device ASH-IrvinS with id 39443e72-6c8b-46f0-9f6c-92f2db82f587 has a total of 30 device **configuration** policies and 2 **compliance** policies.

Device Configuration Policies

Export to Excel

Policy Name	Status
RealPolicy_Chrome extensions	Succeeded
RealPolicy_Chrome extensions	Succeeded
RealPolicy_Cloud PKI Root CA	Succeeded
RealPolicy_Cloud PKI Root CA	Succeeded

Figure 9.28 – Policies assigned to the device

While the Security Copilot Intune plugin provides details about the device's information and policies, the Defender XDR plugin offers insights into the device's security state, including its security posture and vulnerabilities. These two sets of information, device policies and security state, often complement each other, providing a more complete picture of the device's overall status.

For device ash-irvins, the Security Copilot prompt used to fetch the device's security state, along with the initial part of the response, are shown next:

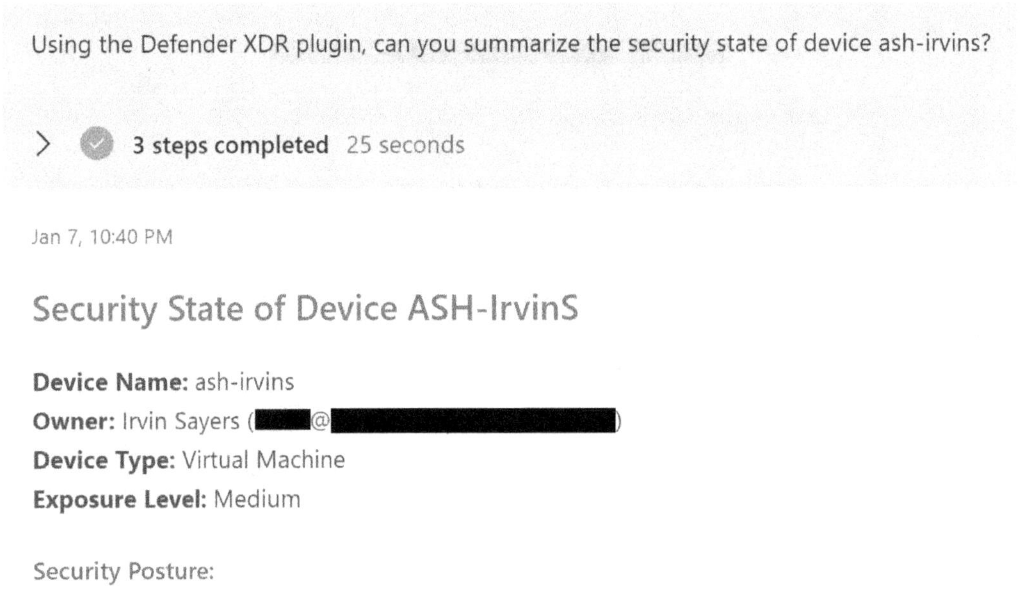

Figure 9.29 – Security state of device ash-irvins

The remaining portion of the Security Copilot response is displayed in the next screen capture for your reference. As you can see, Security Copilot identifies that the **PUA Protection** setting (**PUA** being short for **Potentially Unwanted Applications**) in the device's antivirus configuration is set to non-blocking and comments: **Not having PUA in Block mode enabled leaves the machine vulnerable to unwanted applications with potentially malicious behavior**. Security Copilot also flags several firewall configuration settings for review, indicating that these settings are not securely configured. Furthermore, it points out that the **Microsoft Defender Attack Surface Reduction** (**ASR**) setting is also turned off and explains why it's concerning:

Security Posture:

- **Antivirus:**
  - **PUA Protection:** Non-blocking. Not having PUA in Block mode enabled leaves the machine vulnerable to unwanted applications with potentially malicious behavior.
- **Firewall:**
  - **Disable Microsoft Defender Firewall notifications when programs are blocked for Domain profile:** Off. An attacker may be more easily able to remotely exploit a weakness in a network service.
  - **Disable merging of local Microsoft Defender Firewall connection rules with group policy firewall rules for the Public profile:** Off.
  - **Disable Microsoft Defender Firewall notifications when programs are blocked for Public profile:** Off.
  - **Disable Microsoft Defender Firewall notifications when programs are blocked for Private profile:** Off.
- **Attack Surface Reduction:** Off. ASR rules are the most effective method for blocking the most common attack techniques being used in cyber attacks and malicious software.

Vulnerabilities:

- **firefox 127.0.2.0:** Critical
- **chrome 131.0.6778.205:** High
- **openssl 3.0.13.0:** High
- **python 3.13.1.0:** High

This summary includes the security posture and vulnerabilities for the device ASH-IrvinS.

Figure 9.30 – Security posture and vulnerabilities information

With Security Copilot highlighting the antivirus, firewall, and ASR configuration settings for device ash-irvins, you can take a moment to further review the associated policies assigned to the device. Rather than manually retrieving each configuration policy from Intune, you simply prompt Security Copilot to fetch the policy settings for you.

As an example, you ask Security Copilot to identify the antivirus policy assigned to device ash-irvins and retrieve the corresponding policy settings. The Security Copilot prompt and part of the response are displayed in the next screenshot. In its response, Security Copilot provides the name of the antivirus policy along with the policy settings. A short description of each policy setting is included as well:

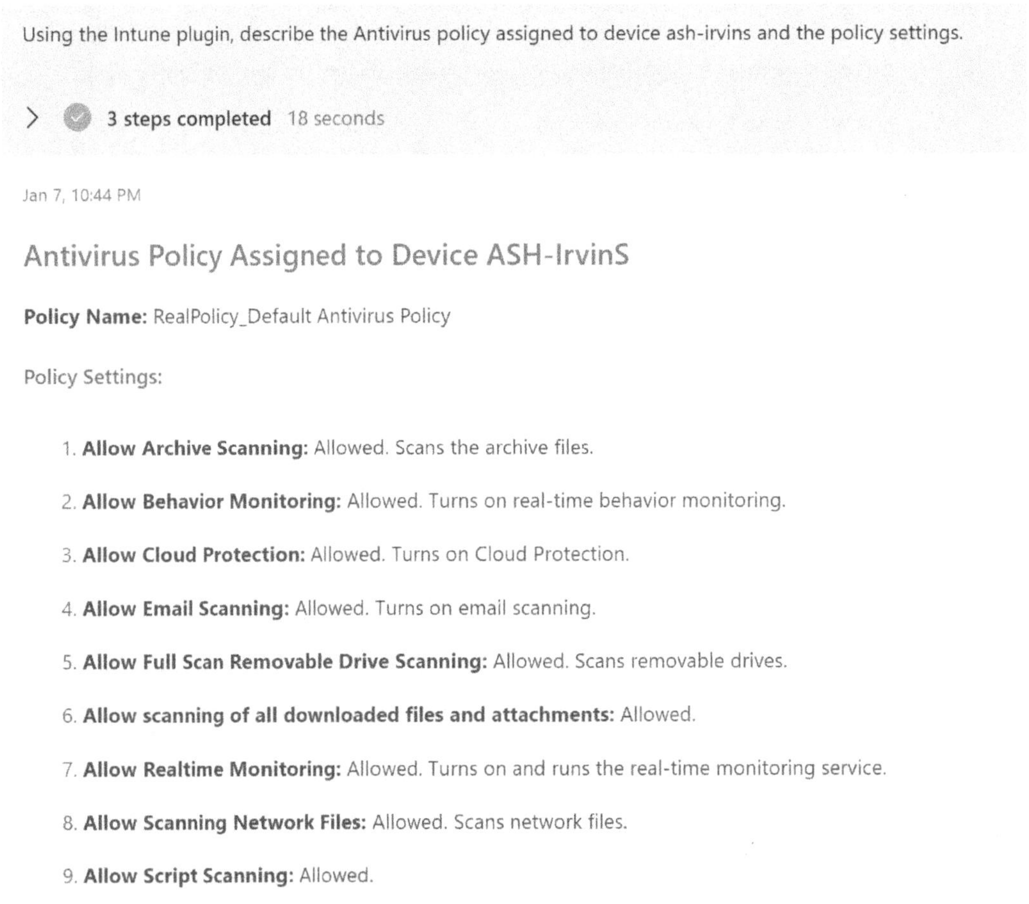

Figure 9.31 – AV policy and its settings

In the same response, Security Copilot also lists the assignment scope of this antivirus policy, as shown next:

Assignment Scope:

- **Included Groups:**
  - **All Devices:** All devices are included in this policy.
- **Excluded Groups:**
  - **MDE disabled:** 4 devices.
  - **MDE notconfigured:** 1 device.
  - **MDE harden:** 2 devices.

This summary includes the policy settings and assignment scope for the Antivirus policy assigned to the device ASH-IrvinS.

Figure 9.32 – Assignment scope of the AV policy

Next, using a similar prompt, you ask Security Copilot to retrieve the policy name and settings for the firewall policy assigned to device ash-irvins. Both the prompt and part of the response from Security Copilot are displayed in the next screen capture. Again, Security Copilot provides the name of the firewall policy, the individual policy settings, and a brief description of each setting.

The policy assignment is also included in the response, though it is not shown in the screen capture:

Using the Intune plugin, describe the firewall policy assigned to device ash-irvins and the policy settings.

> 3 steps completed 15 seconds

Jan 7, 10:45 PM

Firewall Policy Assigned to Device ASH-IrvinS

Policy Name: RealPolicy_Default Firewall Policy

Policy Settings:

1. **Object Access Audit Filtering Platform Connection:** Success+ Failure. This setting allows you to audit connections that are allowed or blocked by the Windows Filtering Platform (WFP). It generates audit events for various connection activities, enhancing security visibility.
2. **Object Access Audit Filtering Platform Packet Drop:** Success+ Failure. This setting allows auditing of packets dropped by the WFP, which can help identify potential threats or issues.
3. **Enable Domain Network Firewall:** True. This setting enables the firewall for domain networks, enhancing security by blocking unauthorized access.
4. **Enable Domain Network Firewall - Default Inbound Action for Domain Profile:** Block. This setting specifies that the default action for inbound connections on domain networks is to block them.
5. **Enable Domain Network Firewall - Log File Path:** %systemroot%\system32\LogFiles\Firewall\pfirewall.log. This setting specifies the file path for the firewall log.

Figure 9.33 – Firewall policy and policy settings

Some of the firewall policy settings may require more effort to review than the antivirus configuration settings. Therefore, you ask Security Copilot to first analyze the firewall settings from its previous response and to identify any that could potentially be exploited by an attacker. As illustrated in the next screenshot, Security Copilot lists several configuration settings that could be vulnerable to exploitation if not properly monitored or configured:

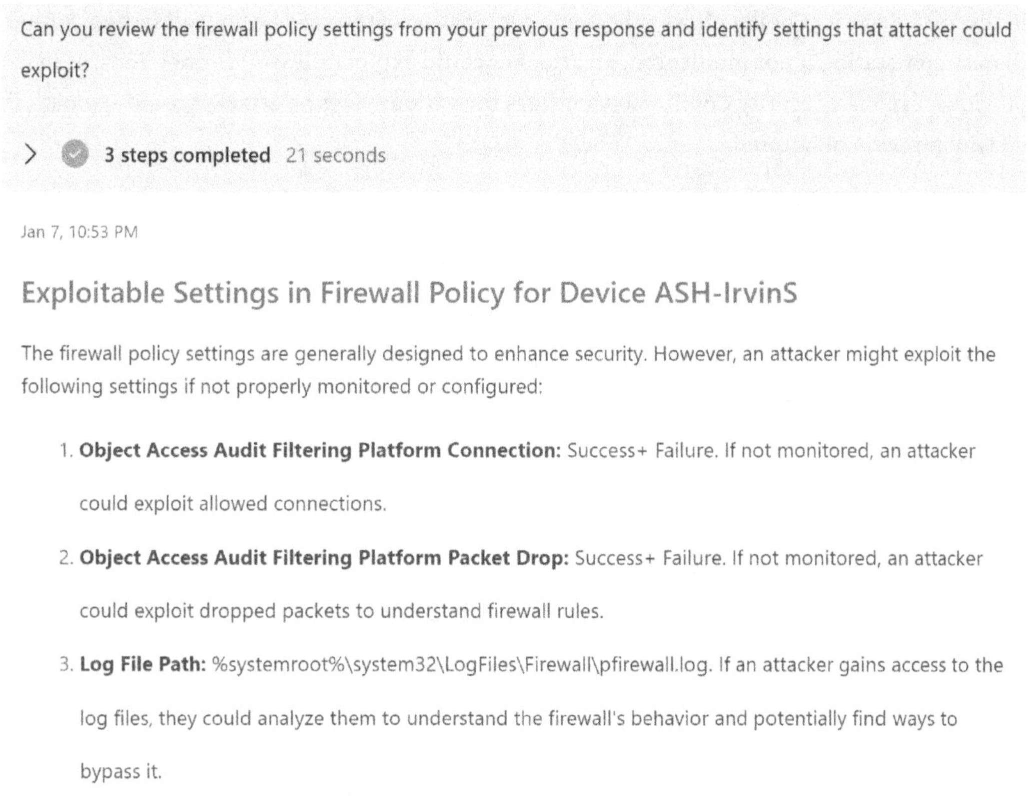

Figure 9.34 – Exploitable settings in firewall policy

You can also ask Security Copilot for a detailed explanation of a specific firewall setting and request further clarification on why an attacker could exploit it. This is shown next:

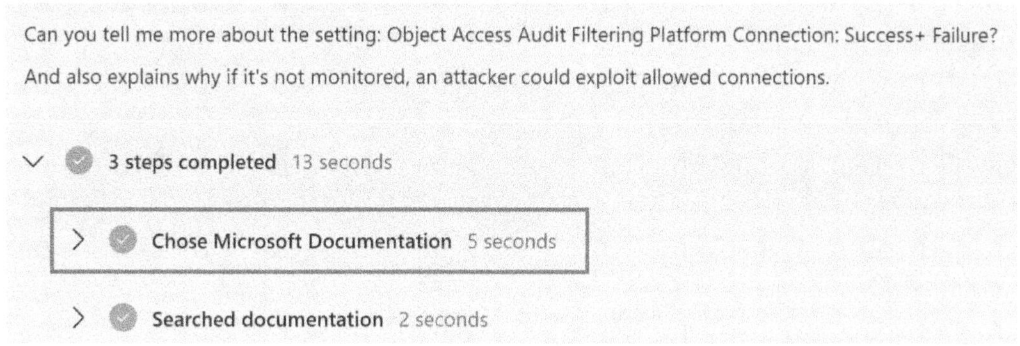

Figure 9.35 – The Security Copilot prompt and the plugin invoked

In this case, Security Copilot offers a thorough explanation of the specific firewall setting. Rather than simply stating **If not monitored, an attacker could exploit allowed connections**, as in its previous response, Security Copilot now outlines the various ways an attacker could exploit it if it is not properly monitored.

For your reference, the full response from Security Copilot is provided next:

Object Access Audit Filtering Platform Connection: Success+ Failure

This policy setting allows you to audit connections that are allowed or blocked by the Windows Filtering Platform (WFP). The following events are included:

- The Windows Firewall service blocks an application from accepting incoming connections on the network.
- The WFP allows a connection.
- The WFP blocks a connection.
- The WFP permits a bind to a local port.
- The WFP blocks a bind to a local port.
- The WFP allows a connection.
- The WFP blocks a connection.
- The WFP permits an application or service to listen on a port for incoming connections.
- The WFP blocks an application or service to listen on a port for incoming connections.

If you configure this policy setting, an audit event is generated when connections are allowed or blocked by the WFP. Success audits record events generated when connections are allowed, and Failure audits record events generated when connections are blocked. If you don't configure this policy setting, no audit event is generated when connections are allowed or blocked by the WFP [1].

Potential Exploitation by Attackers

If this setting is not monitored, an attacker could exploit allowed connections in the following ways:

- **Undetected Malicious Connections:** Without monitoring, malicious connections allowed by the WFP might go unnoticed, providing an attacker with a persistent foothold in the network.
- **Reconnaissance:** An attacker could analyze allowed connections to understand the network's structure and identify potential targets for further exploitation.
- **Lateral Movement:** By exploiting allowed connections, an attacker could move laterally within the network, accessing sensitive resources and data.

Regular monitoring and analysis of audit logs are essential to detect and respond to suspicious activities promptly.

Earlier, when Security Copilot presents the security state for device `ash-irvins`, it also includes the vulnerabilities detected on the device, such as the following:

- firefox `127.0.2.0`: Critical
- chrome `131.0.6778.205`: High
- openssl `3.0.13.0`: High
- python `3.13.1.0`: High

You can ask Security Copilot to quickly list the applications installed on the device, allowing you to assess both the applications and their associated vulnerabilities. For instance, if the application with a critical vulnerability is managed by Intune, you can take immediate action to implement proper security measures, such as applying updates, enforcing policies, or removing the application if necessary.

By using the Intune plugin, Security Copilot displays the managed applications installed on the device. As seen in the next screen capture, Security Copilot shows that the device ash-irvins has 11 managed applications assigned to the primary user, Irvin Sayers:

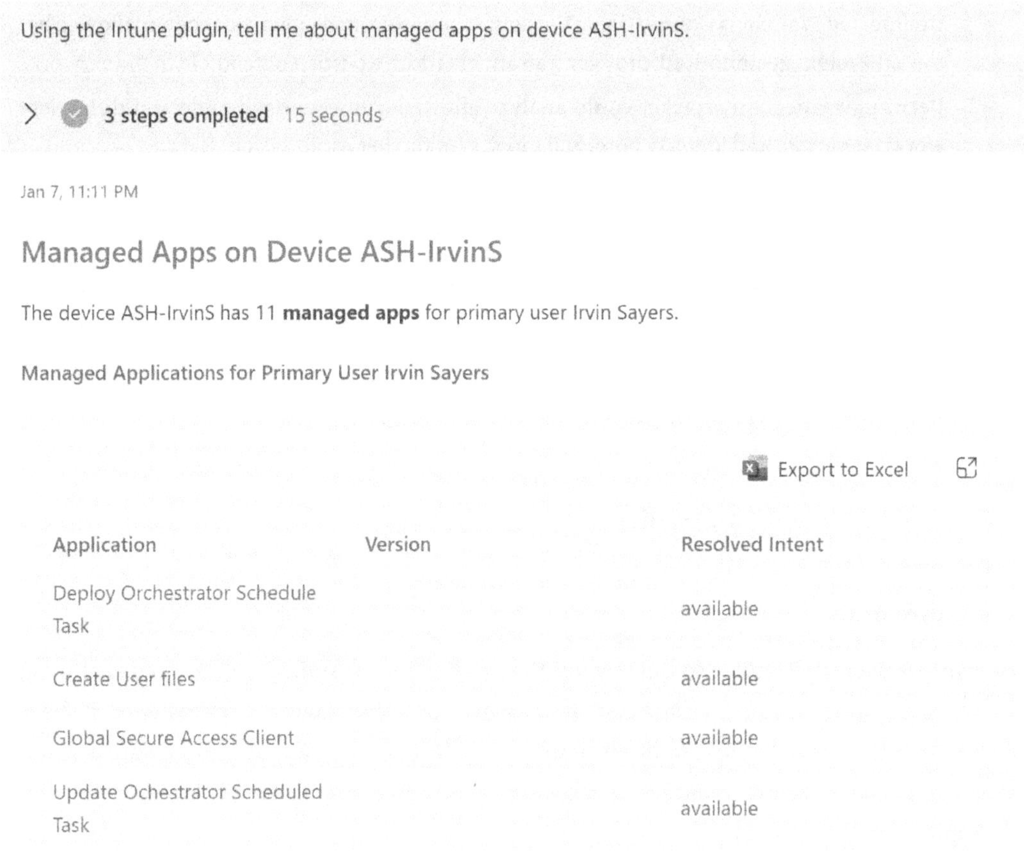

Figure 9.36 – Managed apps on device ash-irvins

Using a similar prompt, you then ask Security Copilot to display the discovered applications on device ash-irvins to gain an overview of both the corporate and third-party applications installed. As shown from the following screen capture, Security Copilot identifies 75 discovered applications on device ash-irvins:

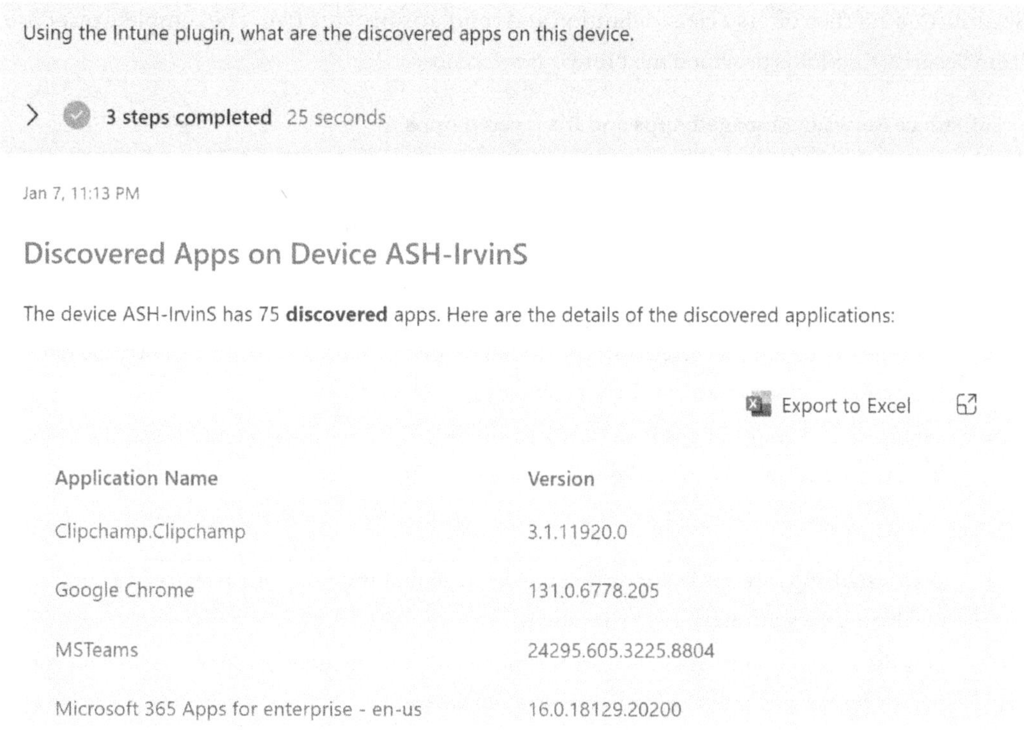

Figure 9.37 – Discovered apps on device ash-irvins

If you need clarification on the difference between discovered apps and managed apps, there's no need to research it yourself. Security Copilot, utilizing the Microsoft Documentation plugin, can present the relevant information for you. The sample prompt and the plugin invoked are displayed in the next screen capture:

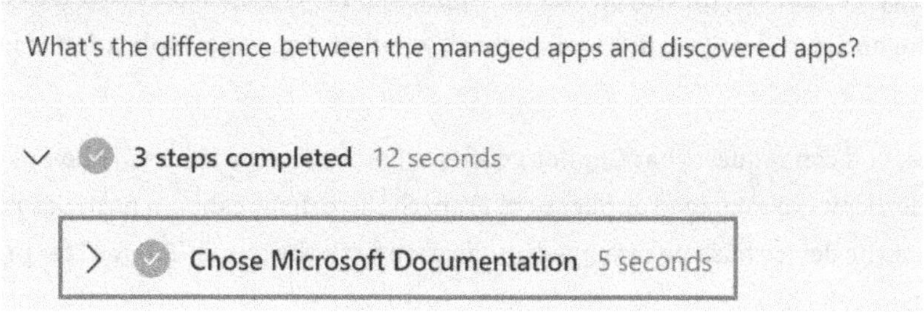

Figure 9.38 – The Security Copilot prompt and the plugin invoked

Security Copilot then offers a clear definition and comparison of the two. The complete response from Security Copilot is provided next for your reference:

Difference Between Managed Apps and Discovered Apps

Managed Apps:

- Managed apps are applications that are specifically deployed, configured, and managed by Intune.
- These apps can be store apps, web apps, or line-of-business (LOB) apps.
- Managed apps are protected and controlled by Intune policies, which can include data protection, access control, and app configuration settings.
- Examples of managed apps include Microsoft 365 apps, custom in-house apps, and apps from the Microsoft Store that are assigned to users or devices through Intune [2].

Discovered Apps:

- Discovered apps are applications that are detected on Intune-enrolled devices, regardless of whether they are managed by Intune.
- This list acts as a software inventory for the tenant and includes all apps installed on corporate devices and managed apps on personal devices.
- The discovered apps report is refreshed every seven days from the time of enrollment, except for Win32 apps collected through the Intune Management Extension, which are updated every 24 hours [1].

In summary, managed apps are those that are actively managed and protected by Intune policies, while discovered apps are simply detected on devices and listed for inventory purposes.

While Security Copilot can quickly list all the applications on the device for you to review, you also have the option to let Security Copilot check whether a specific application is installed on the device.

For instance, you can request that Copilot verifies whether Firefox is installed on device ash-irvins and whether it is a managed application. From the screenshot shown next, Security Copilot confirms that the device has one managed application with the name "Firefox" for primary user Irvin Sayers:

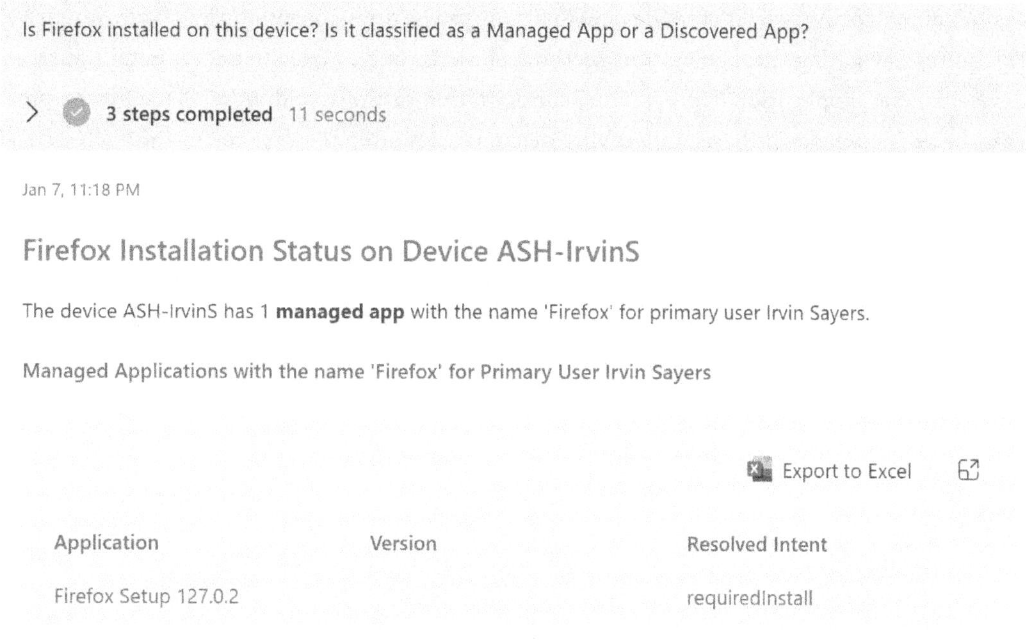

Figure 9.39 – Verifying Firefox installation status

To summarize what's been discussed so far, you start with an unknown device, ash-irvins, that is flagged in a security incident. Security Copilot lets you quickly gather detailed information about the device, including its policies, security state, vulnerabilities, and more. Security Copilot also helps you assess the device's configuration settings and applications, enabling you to efficiently evaluate and address potential risks.

In addition to these features, the Intune plugin within Security Copilot offers even more capabilities that boost efficiency. In the next section, let's dive into its device comparison feature, which reduces manual effort and enhances your overall efficiency.

Accelerating device comparisons with Security Copilot

This case study starts when device ASH-IrvinS is identified in a multi-stage incident. Security Copilot is able to provide detailed information about this device. To further identify anomalies or discrepancies on this device, a quick and easy approach is to compare this device's settings and applications with another known and trusted device.

Manually comparing two different devices in Intune can be time-consuming and labor-intensive. It requires navigating through various sections of the Intune console to gather details such as device policies, application deployments, configuration settings, and more. Since Intune presents data on a per-device basis, identifying discrepancies often requires reviewing each device individually across various settings.

The Intune plugin within Security Copilot includes a feature that identifies the similarities and differences in the configurations of two managed devices, which greatly speeds up the comparison process. This skill is listed in the **System Capabilities** function under **Microsoft Intune**, as shown next (note, the **System Capabilities** function can be accessed through the prompt icon as indicated by the arrow):

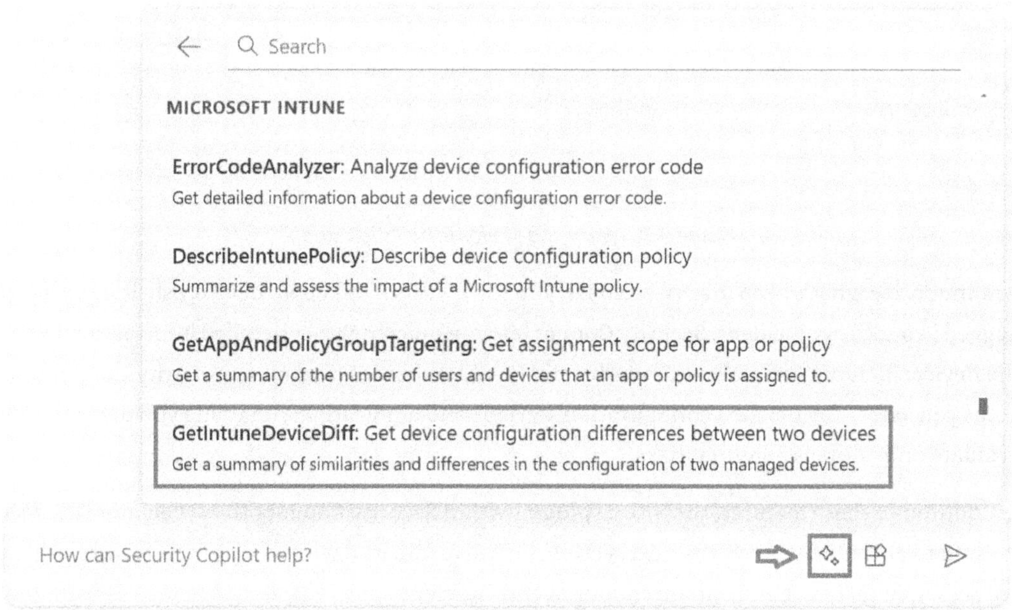

Figure 9.40 – The GetIntuneDeviceDiff skill

Let's now again take a look at device ASH-IrvinS, which has been flagged in the incident described in this case study. You will compare it with a known good device named ASH. You can start by comparing the managed applications installed on both devices. The Security Copilot prompt is displayed in the following screenshot. Notice that when the Intune plugin is triggered, it uses its **Summarized differences between devices** skill to gather the necessary information:

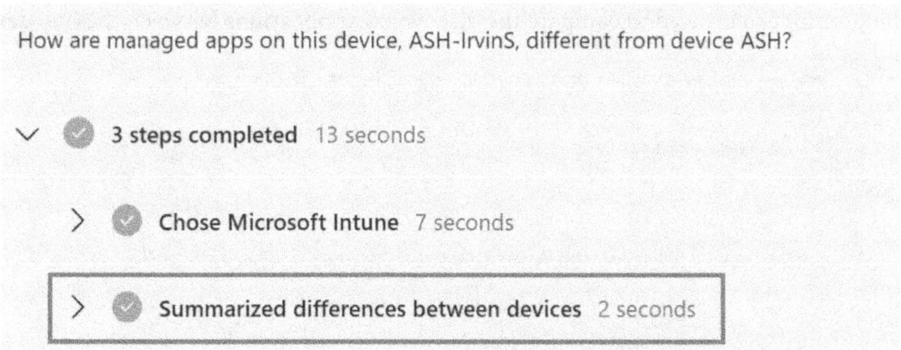

Figure 9.41 – The Summarized differences between devices feature

Security Copilot then reports the differences in managed applications, as shown next:

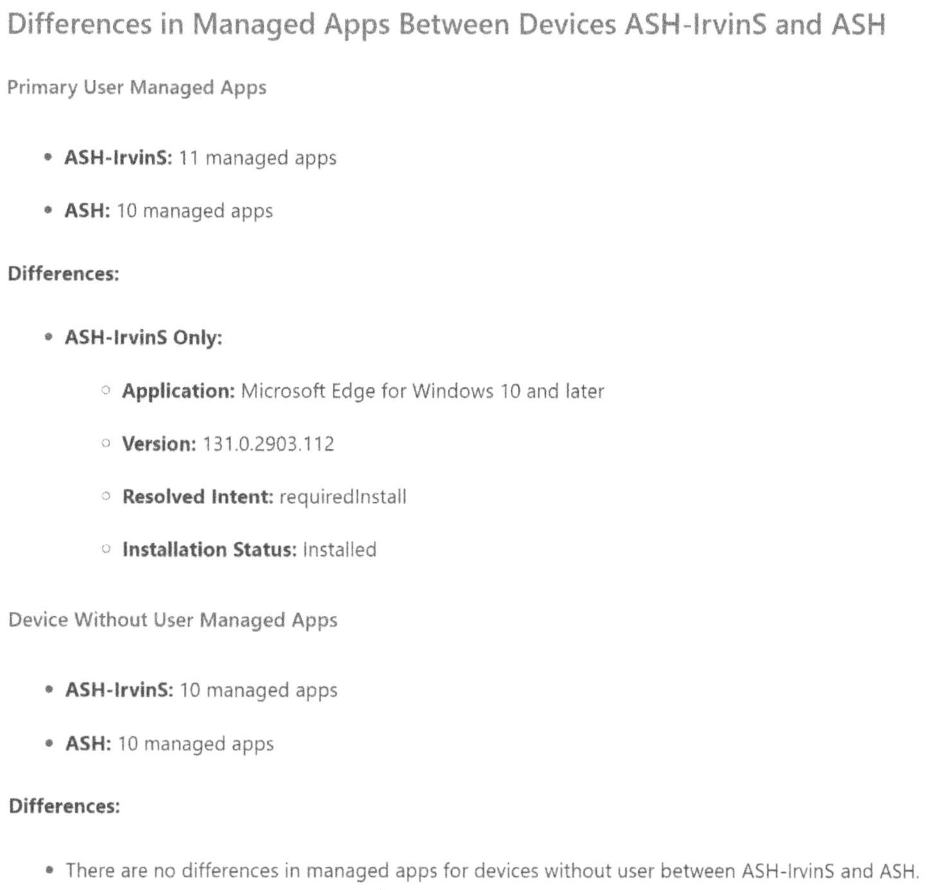

Figure 9.42 – Differences in managed applications

A similar prompt can be used to compare the discovered applications between the two devices:

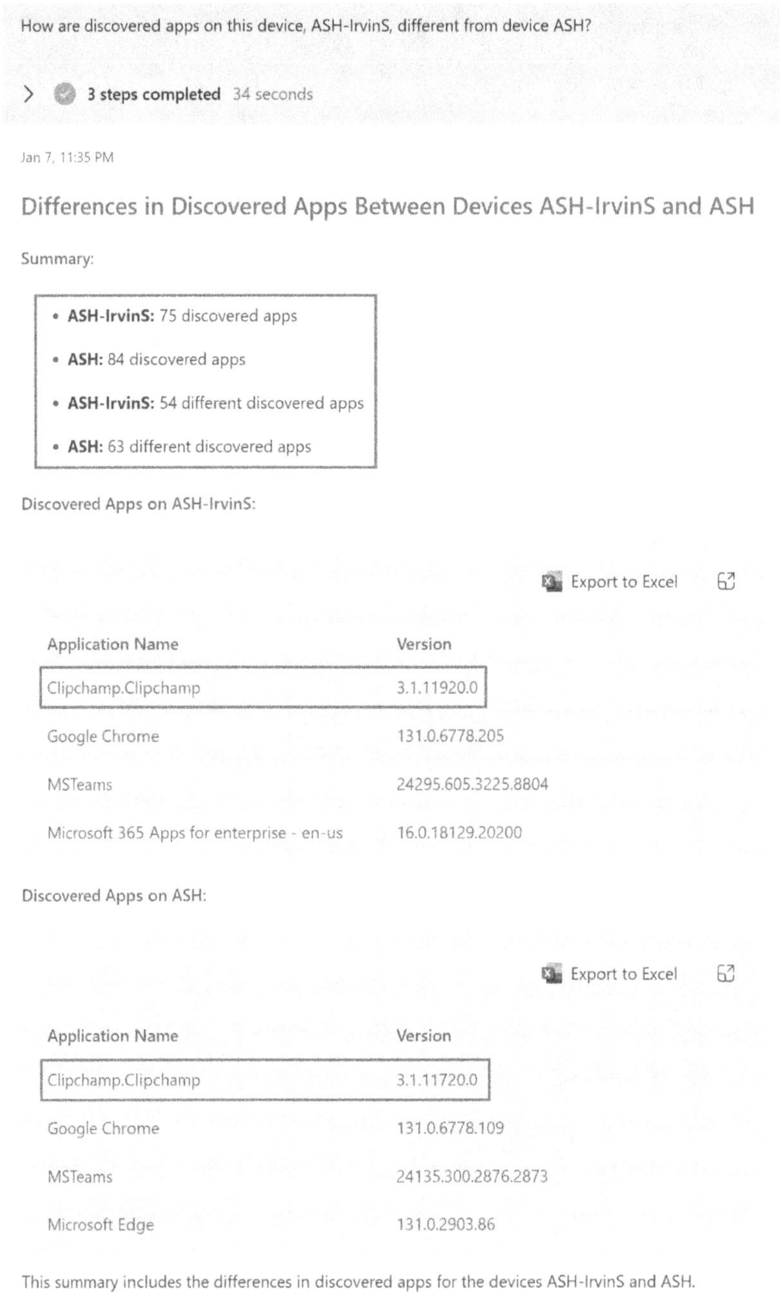

Figure 9.43 – Differences in discovered applications

You also have the option to compare policies assigned to the devices, as shown next:

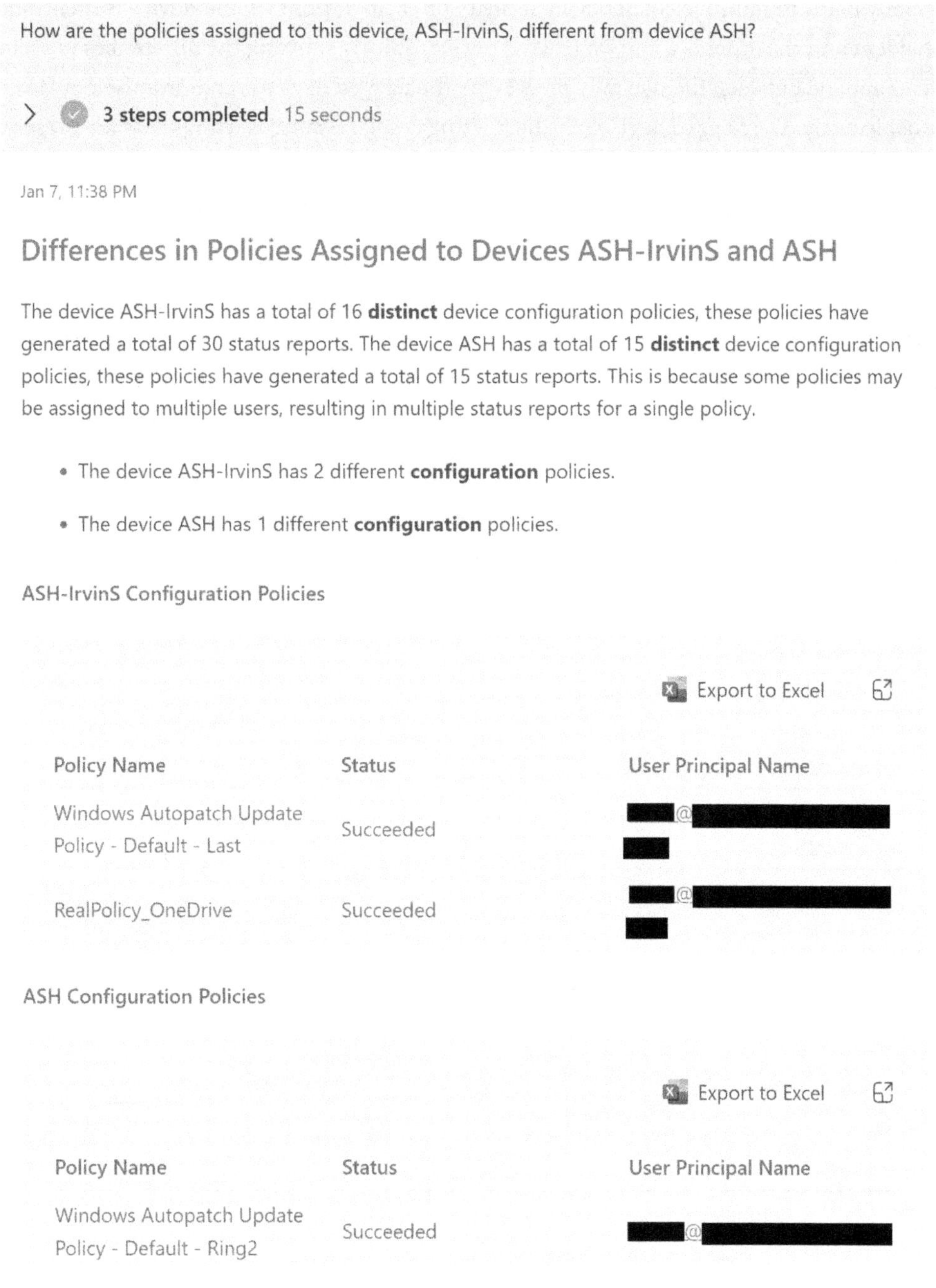

Figure 9.44 – Compare policies assigned to devices

Using Security Copilot to compare the policies allows you to quickly find discrepancies. This especially helps to improve efficiency in security or IT operations. If one device is identified in an incident and the other is a known trusted device, quickly spotting the differences in security policies applied between the two may reveal why the flagged device is compromised or is behaving suspiciously. The flagged device may be missing crucial security settings that are present on the trusted device, allowing you to address those gaps and reduce the risk of further incidents. Alternatively, if the flagged device has outdated policies, aligning its settings with the trusted device ensures both are secured to the same standard.

Similarly, using Security Copilot to compare the applications installed on both devices helps you quickly identify any unauthorized or suspicious applications on the flagged device that could be linked to the incident. You may also discover outdated applications or applications missing critical updates on the flagged device, allowing you to take necessary actions to ensure it is protected from potential threats.

Optionally, if needed, you can request Security Copilot to also compare the hardware for devices ASH-IrvinS and ASH, as illustrated in the next screen capture:

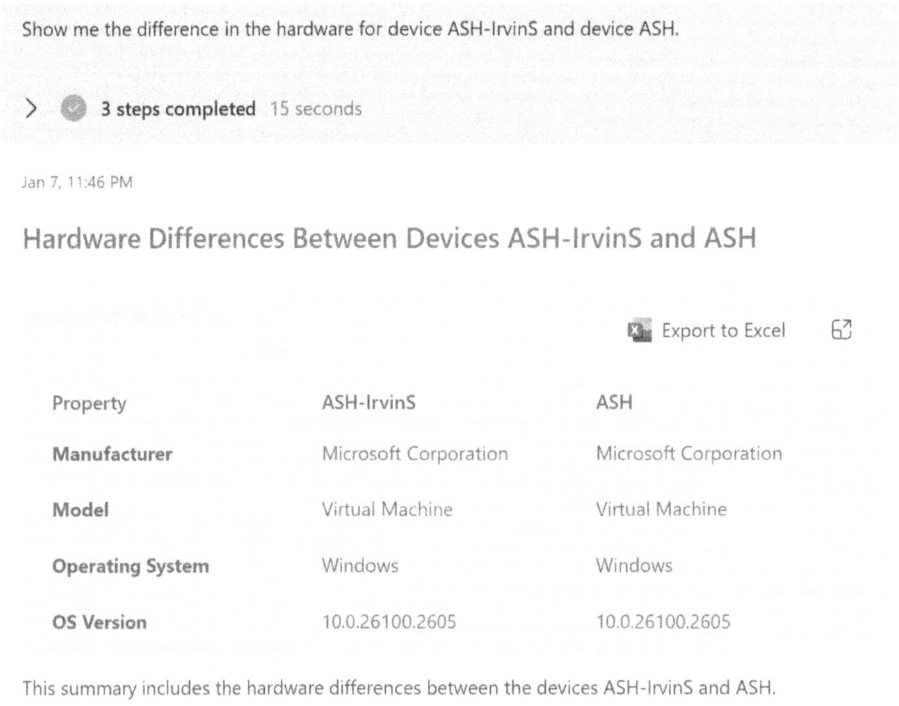

Figure 9.45 – Hardware differences between two devices

The next screenshot displays some additional details from the Copilot response that appear when you expand the initial reply from Security Copilot:

Management Agent	Mdm	Mdm
Device Category		
Physical Memory	10,485,760,000 bytes (10 GB)	8,388,608,000 bytes (8 GB)
Total Storage Space	135,565,148,160 bytes (126.2 GB)	135,380,598,784 bytes (126.1 GB)
Free Storage Space	102,285,443,072 bytes (95.2 GB)	84,851,818,496 bytes (79 GB)
Is Encrypted	False	False
Compliance State	Compliant	Compliant
Device Enrollment Type	WindowsAzureADJoin	WindowsAzureADJoin

Figure 9.46 – Additional details from Copilot response

Often, the ability to quickly identify how the device in question differs from other functioning devices can help both security and IT teams find discrepancies and uncover potential vulnerabilities or misconfigurations. As demonstrated in this section, Security Copilot greatly simplifies the device comparison process. Another challenge IT and security admins face is when the same device setting is defined in multiple Intune policies, potentially leading to policy conflicts. In the next section, we'll explore how Security Copilot can quickly identify duplicate settings in Intune.

Say goodbye to Intune policy conflicts with Security Copilot

In Intune, a single device setting can often be configured in different policies, leading to policy conflicts. This has been a known issue and a pain point for both IT and security teams. Policy conflicts can result in inconsistent device configurations, causing devices to behave unpredictably or leaving them with weaker protection. For instance, endpoint security policies, device configuration policies, and security baselines in Intune can all be the source of device configuration settings, and conflicts among these policies must be resolved manually.

Identifying these duplicate settings across policies can be difficult, time-consuming, and frustrating. Analysts need to carefully review each policy to pinpoint where the conflicts are occurring, often requiring manual cross-referencing of settings and navigating through various sections within the Intune console.

The complexity of these conflicts increases when different teams manage different policies, creating additional coordination challenges and a lack of consistency across the organization's device management. This can lead to delays in addressing issues and, in some cases, cause the underlying conflicts to go unnoticed, further escalating security risks or compliance gaps.

Security Copilot can assist in identifying Intune policies that include specific settings, helping you to pinpoint the conflicts. It's a proactive way to detect duplicate or potentially conflicting settings in your environment before they lead to bigger issues.

For example, the Microsoft Defender Network Protection setting can be configured across multiple Intune policies. Instead of manually searching through each policy to find where this setting is applied, you can simply ask Security Copilot with a natural language prompt such as **Where have I set the enable network protection setting in Intune?** As illustrated in the following screenshot, the Intune plugin in Security Copilot then uses its **Got policies containing this setting** skill to quickly locate the policies that include this setting:

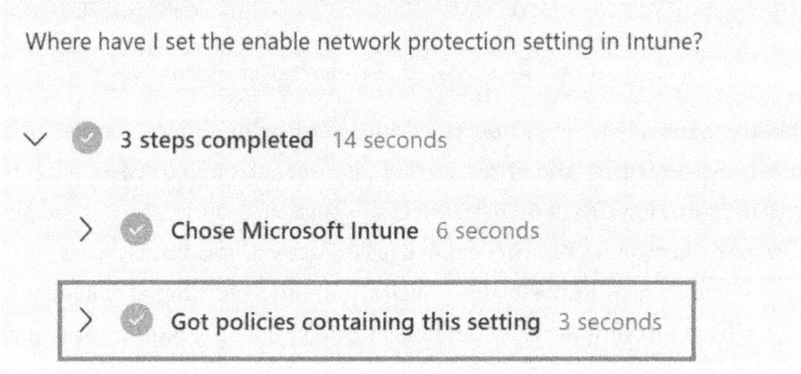

Figure 9.47 – The Got policies containing this setting feature

As seen from Security Copilot's response shown in the next screen capture, Copilot successfully identifies the **Enable Network Protection** setting in two Intune policies, **RealPolicy_Default Antivirus Policy** and **RealPolicy_MDE Harden.** Additionally, Security Copilot adds in a comment: **the "Enable Network Protection" setting is enabled in block mode in both policies."**

The "Enable Network Protection" setting is configured in two policies in your Intune account:

1. **Policy Name:** RealPolicy_Default Antivirus Policy
   - **Platform:** Windows 10 and later
   - **Policy Type:** Settings Catalog
   - **Last Modified:** 2024-12-17T09:58:51.130503Z
   - **Is Assigned:** True
   - **Policy Link:** Policy Link
   - **Setting Value:** Enabled (block mode)
2. **Policy Name:** RealPolicy_MDE Harden
   - **Platform:** Windows 10 and later
   - **Policy Type:** Settings Catalog
   - **Last Modified:** 2024-12-17T10:05:16.1536872Z
   - **Is Assigned:** True
   - **Policy Link:** Policy Link
   - **Setting Value:** Enabled (block mode)

In summary, the "Enable Network Protection" setting is enabled in block mode in both policies.

Figure 9.48 – The same setting in two different policies

Once you have located the policies containing this specific setting, you can then ask Security Copilot to find which device groups these policies are assigned to. Understanding the assignments for the policies allows you to compare which devices are affected by these configurations and verify policy conflicts.

The prompt for gathering assignments for **RealPolicy_Default Antivirus Policy**, along with the Security Copilot's response, are displayed in the following screen capture. Notice Security Copilot provides both the included and excluded device groups in its response:

What are the assignments for RealPolicy_Default Antivirus Policy?

> 3 steps completed 10 seconds

Jan 11, 8:25 PM

The assignments for the "RealPolicy_Default Antivirus Policy" are as follows:

Included Groups

Export to Excel

Display Name	Group ID	User Count
All Devices	adadadad-808e-44e2-905a-0b7873a8a531	N/A

Excluded Groups

Export to Excel

Display Name	Group ID	User Count
MDE disabled	0e58cf65-41cd-4dce-ac20-3d64dc429436	0
MDE notconfigured	0e7a39cf-704c-450e-b3b7-30e077716475	0
MDE harden	78a296c8-8a0d-4225-8577-55aadb4d5eca	0

A group can have users, organizational contacts, devices, service principals, and other groups as members, but only the breakdown of Users and Devices are shown.

References

Figure 9.49 – Assignments for RealPolicy_Default Antivirus Policy

You can then ask Security Copilot for assignments related to the other policy, **RealPolicy_MDE Harden**, which also has the **Enable Network Protection** setting configured. This is shown in the next screen capture:

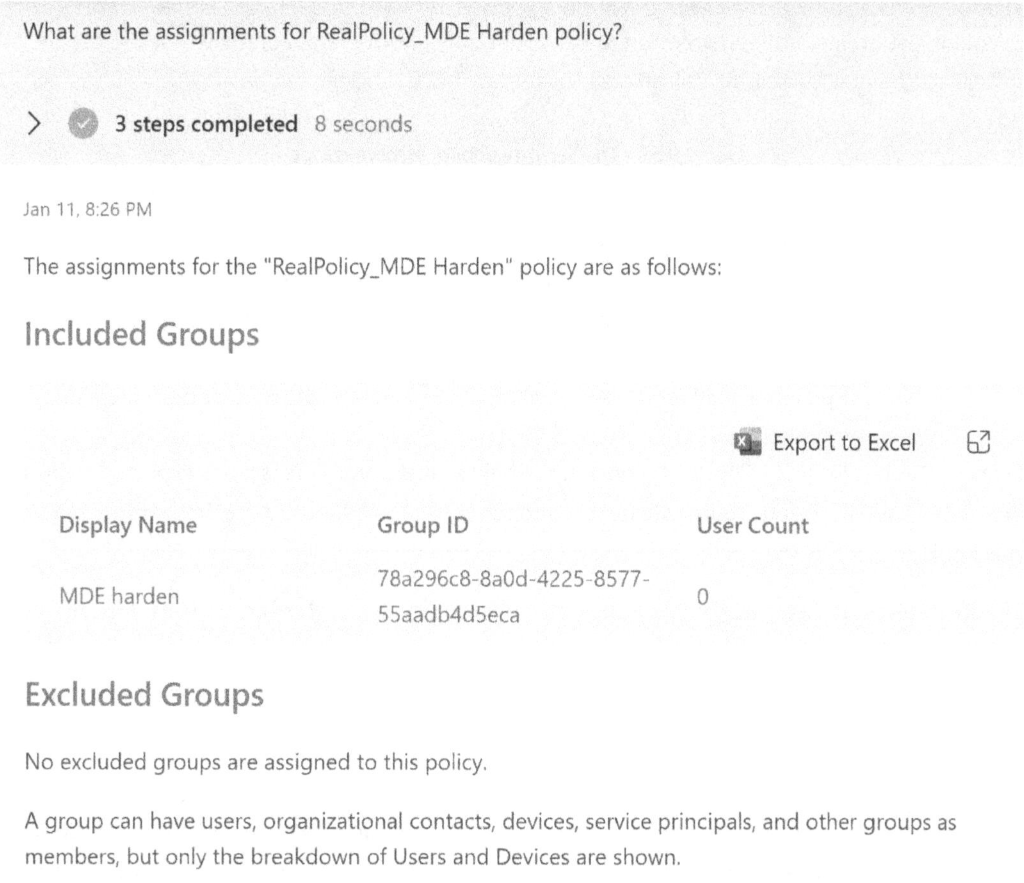

Figure 9.50 – Assignments for RealPolicy_MDE Harden policy

Based on Security Copilot's responses, you learn that the **RealPolicy_MDE Harden** policy is only assigned to the **MDE harden** device group, and this device group is excluded from **RealPolicy_Default Antivirus Policy**. Although the **Enable Network Protection** setting is configured in both policies, there is no inherent policy conflict since each policy targets different device groups.

You may be wondering why policy assignments need to be requested individually. In this case, Security Copilot is not able to pull assignments for both policies simultaneously. Its error message is shown in the following screenshot:

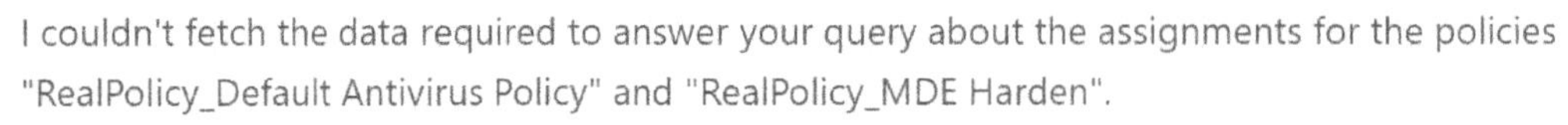

Figure 9.51 – The Security Copilot error message

> Tip: If you encounter an issue with Security Copilot not providing the expected response, you can always try to break your request into smaller, individual queries. Security Copilot sometimes may have difficulty processing multiple requests at once. By asking for data on just one item at a time, such as requesting assignments for one policy instead of two, Security Copilot can more easily retrieve the information.

Please note that Security Copilot is continually being enhanced. This issue is expected to be addressed by the Multi-Step Planner feature, which should be available by the time you are reading this book.

The **RealPolicy_Default Antivirus Policy** and **RealPolicy_MDE Harden** policies appear to be similar and share many of the same configuration settings. To quickly learn more about them, you can ask Security Copilot to compare the two policies and highlight the similarities and differences between the two.

For example, you can start by requesting that Security Copilot identifies common settings that are configured in both policies. As illustrated in the following screen capture, Security Copilot presents a list of settings in both policies, along with a note stating **there are 17 common settings between the two policies, with some differences in their values.**

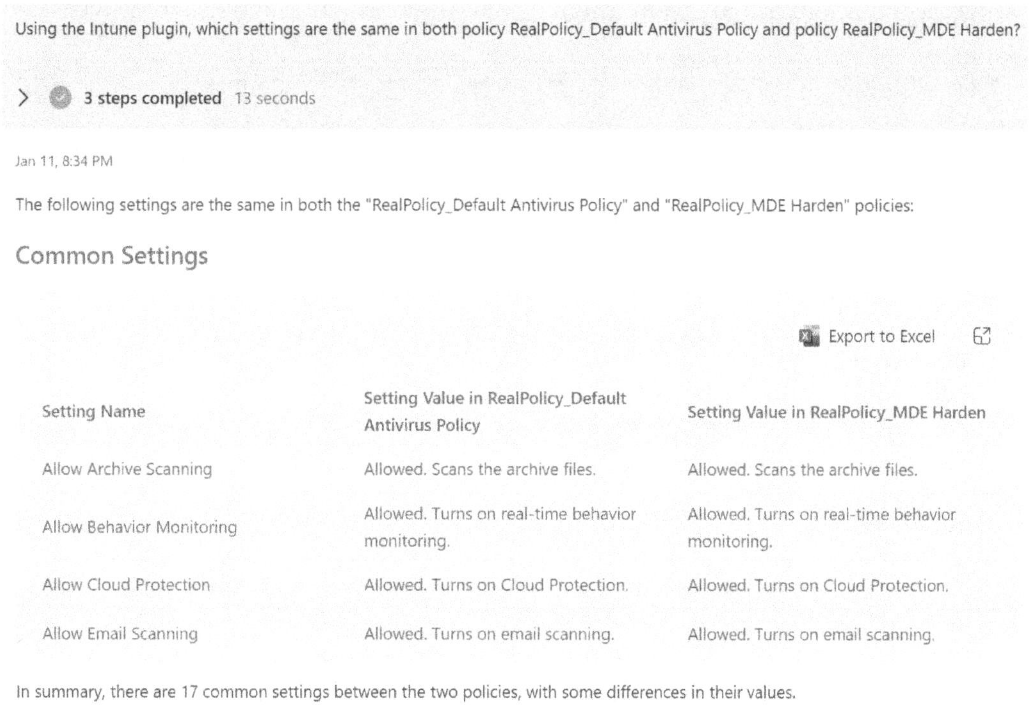

Figure 9.52 – Security Copilot presents a list of common settings in both policies

Next, you ask Security Copilot to compare these two policies and identify any settings that are configured differently between them. As seen from the next screenshot, Security Copilot provides a list of five settings that vary between the policies.

It also includes the details of the differences.

Using the Intune plugin, which settings are different in both policy RealPolicy_Default Antivirus Policy and policy RealPolicy_MDE Harden?

> 3 steps completed 15 seconds

Jan 11, 8:35 PM

The following settings are different between the "RealPolicy_Default Antivirus Policy" and "RealPolicy_MDE Harden" policies:

Different Settings

1. **Cloud Block Level**
   - **RealPolicy_Default Antivirus Policy:** High
   - **RealPolicy_MDE Harden:** Zero Tolerance
2. **PUA Protection**
   - **RealPolicy_Default Antivirus Policy:** Audit mode. Windows Defender will detect potentially unwanted applications, but take no action.
   - **RealPolicy_MDE Harden:** PUA Protection on. Detected items are blocked. They will show in history along with other threats.
3. **Signature Update Interval**
   - **RealPolicy_Default Antivirus Policy:** 3
   - **RealPolicy_MDE Harden:** 2
4. **Submit Samples Consent**
   - **RealPolicy_Default Antivirus Policy:** Send safe samples automatically.
   - **RealPolicy_MDE Harden:** Send all samples automatically.
5. **Disable Catchup Full Scan**
   - **RealPolicy_Default Antivirus Policy:** Enabled
   - **RealPolicy_MDE Harden:** Disabled

In summary, there are 5 settings that differ between the two policies.

Figure 9.53 – Different settings

While reviewing both policies, you can see that they each include settings for **Microsoft Defender Antivirus (Defender AV)**. If you prefer, you can consult Security Copilot for the recommended Defender AV settings.

Security Copilot invokes the Microsoft Documentation plugin to fetch this information for you. The Security Copilot prompt you can use is shown next:

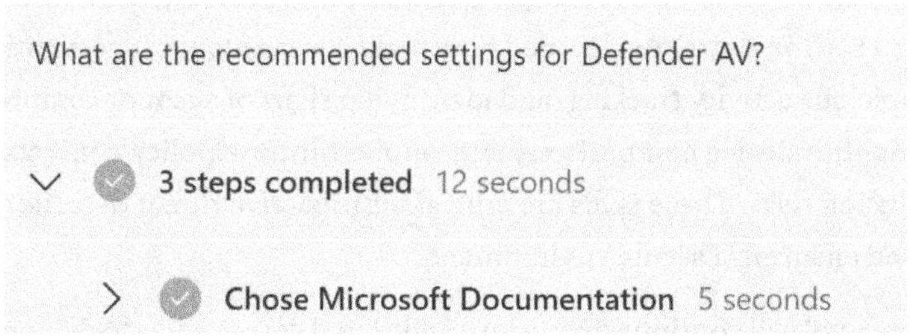

Figure 9.54 – The Security Copilot prompt and the plugin invoked

In its response, Security Copilot outlines the recommended settings for Microsoft Defender Antivirus in Intune. A portion of Copilot's response is shown in the following screen capture:

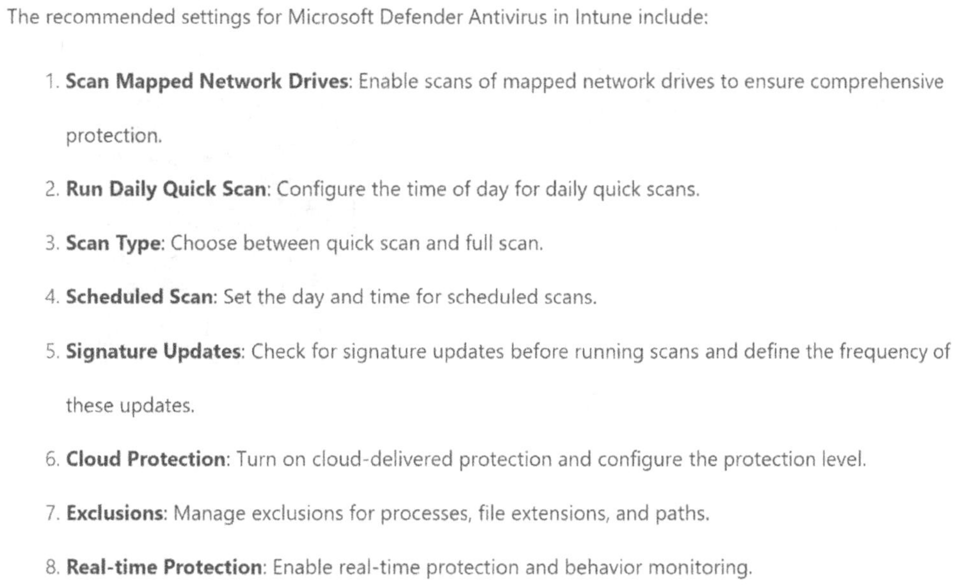
The recommended settings for Microsoft Defender Antivirus in Intune include:

1. **Scan Mapped Network Drives**: Enable scans of mapped network drives to ensure comprehensive protection.
2. **Run Daily Quick Scan**: Configure the time of day for daily quick scans.
3. **Scan Type**: Choose between quick scan and full scan.
4. **Scheduled Scan**: Set the day and time for scheduled scans.
5. **Signature Updates**: Check for signature updates before running scans and define the frequency of these updates.
6. **Cloud Protection**: Turn on cloud-delivered protection and configure the protection level.
7. **Exclusions**: Manage exclusions for processes, file extensions, and paths.
8. **Real-time Protection**: Enable real-time protection and behavior monitoring.

Figure 9.55 – The recommended settings for Defender Antivirus in Intune

In summary, managing Intune policy conflicts can be challenging and time-consuming. However, with the help of Security Copilot, you can now quickly and easily identify duplicate or conflicting settings across multiple Intune policies. This feature is especially valuable for IT and security teams. It simplifies Intune policy management and ultimately enhances both security and operational efficiency.

Summary

To recap, this chapter covered how Security Copilot enhances security and device management for IT admins and SOC analysts. You learned how it aids user account investigation, user behavior analysis, suspicious activity tracking, and identifying signs of account compromise. Security Copilot also simplifies device comparisons and resolves Intune policy conflicts, improving efficiency and reducing risks. These skills are crucial for proactive threat detection, better device management, and ensuring a secure environment.

In the next chapter, we will continue diving into additional case studies to demonstrate how the Microsoft Threat Intelligence plugin within Security Copilot strengthens security operations. You'll learn how it tracks threats, identifies attacker infrastructures, uncovers hidden connections, and transforms intelligence into actionable insights. Additionally, you will see how Security Copilot supports CISOs by providing strategic insights for proactive defense and informed decision-making.

10

Frontline Tales with Security Copilot

In this chapter, let's continue exploring additional case studies. We will first focus on **Microsoft Defender Threat Intelligence** (**MDTI**) within Security Copilot, exploring how it enhances an organization's security operations and offers a deeper understanding of complex threats. Through practical examples, you'll gain insight into tracking malicious infrastructures, uncovering hidden connections, and turning threat intelligence into actionable insights. We'll also look at how MDTI can help streamline security operations, improving overall efficiency. These case studies will provide you with a clearer picture of how the MDTI plugin within Security Copilot can support and strengthen your organization's security efforts.

Security Copilot not only supports security analysts but also delivers strategic insights to help **Chief Information Security Officers** (**CISOs**) stay ahead of emerging threats. You will explore how Security Copilot offers actionable intelligence, enabling CISOs to develop proactive defense strategies and respond quickly to evolving risks. Additionally, you will observe how detailed incident insights provide CISOs with the data needed for informed decision-making.

As we proceed through this chapter, we will cover different case studies focusing on the following two key areas:

- Enhancing security incident investigations with MDTI and Security Copilot
- Empowering CISOs with proactive defense and actionable insights

Want to try out the prompts, custom plugins, and promptbooks featured in this book? Take a look at the book's GitHub repository at `https://github.com/PacktPublishing/Microsoft-Copilot-for-Security`.

Enhancing security incident investigations with MDTI and Security Copilot

The Microsoft Threat Intelligence plugin was featured in *Chapter 4*, highlighting its integration with Security Copilot. MDTI goes beyond traditional detection methods by gathering and analyzing threat intelligence from various sources to identify threats, particularly emerging **tactics, techniques, and procedures** (**TTPs**) used by cybercriminals. It tracks attackers' behavior, tactics, **indicators of compromise** (**IOCs**), malicious infrastructure, and more. By continuously updating its threat intelligence data, MDTI provides proactive insights that help organizations to stay ahead of evolving cyber threats.

The MDTI plugin in Security Copilot lets you harness the power of AI to more efficiently tap into the vast threat intelligence data available in MDTI. In this section, we will look into different case studies that showcase some of the key features of the MDTI plugin, demonstrating how it can enhance threat detection, improve incident response, and strengthen overall cybersecurity posture.

Harnessing Security Copilot to uncover cyber risks and drive proactive defense

Let's first look at a use case to illustrate a common application of the MDTI plugin. In this particular case, the plugin is used to identify the latest threats specific to an organization. It then extracts the IOCs and TTPs from the threat. Following that, Security Copilot further breaks down the detection rule written in KQL for proactive defense.

The use case starts with a prompt asking Security Copilot to identify the top three threats relevant to your organization. Security Copilot responds with the most pertinent threats: **Golden SAML**, **OAuth apps used in BEC and phishing**, and **on-premises credential theft**. Each threat is supported with insights and references for further reading. The next screenshot displays the Security Copilot prompt and part of its response:

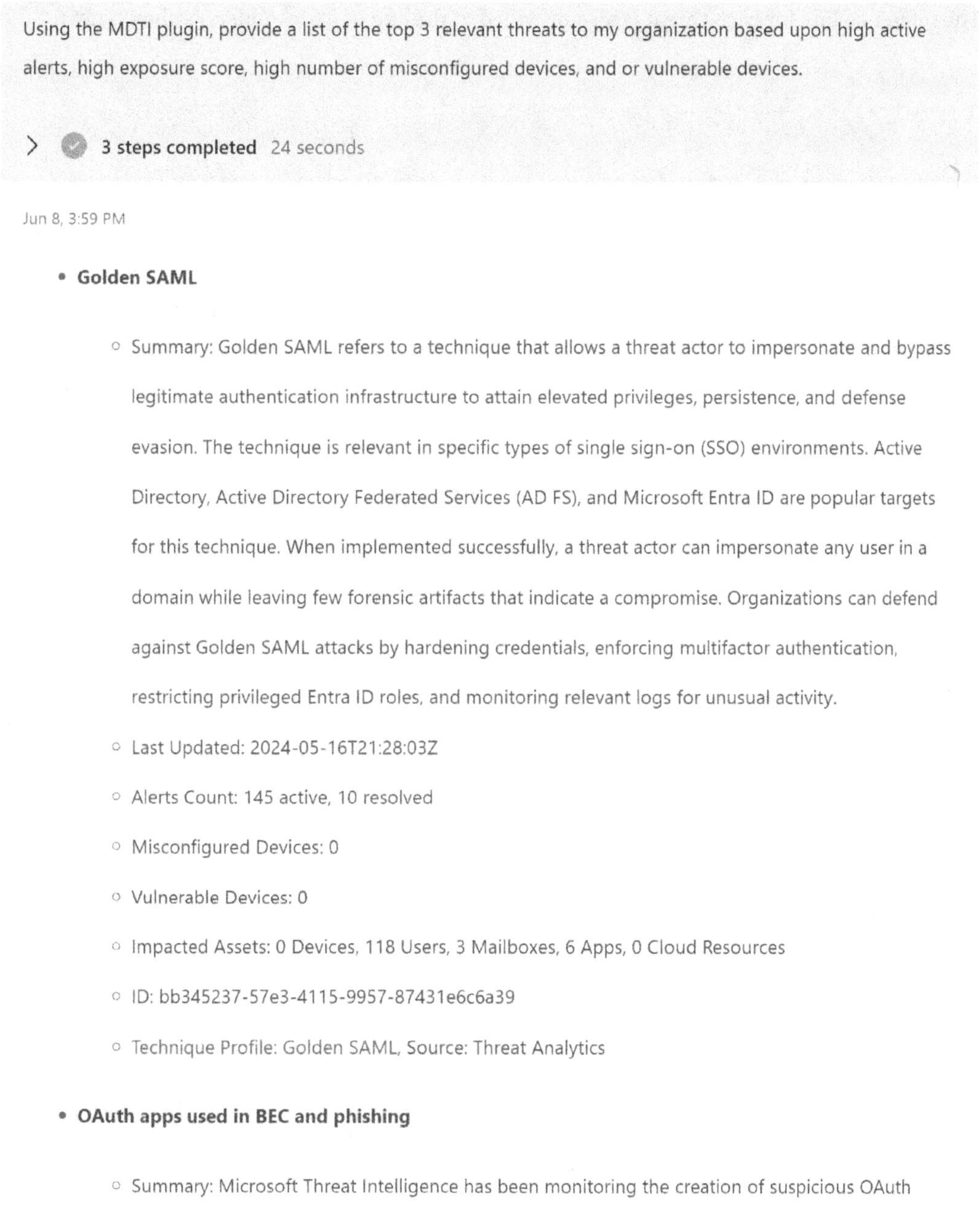

Figure 10.1 – Top three threats specific to the organization

The reference link for each threat is also provided at the end of its response, as shown next:

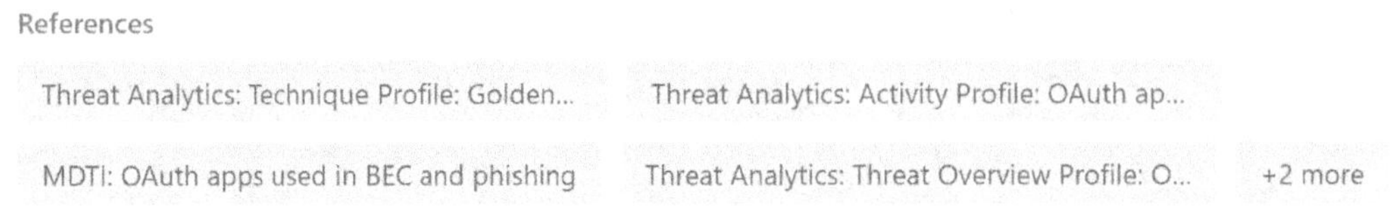

Figure 10.2 – References for each threat

You can always request that Security Copilot gathers more detailed information about a specific threat from its previous response. For instance, the following screenshot illustrates the prompt used to learn more about the **OAuth apps used in BEC and phishing** threats, along with the start of the Security Copilot response:

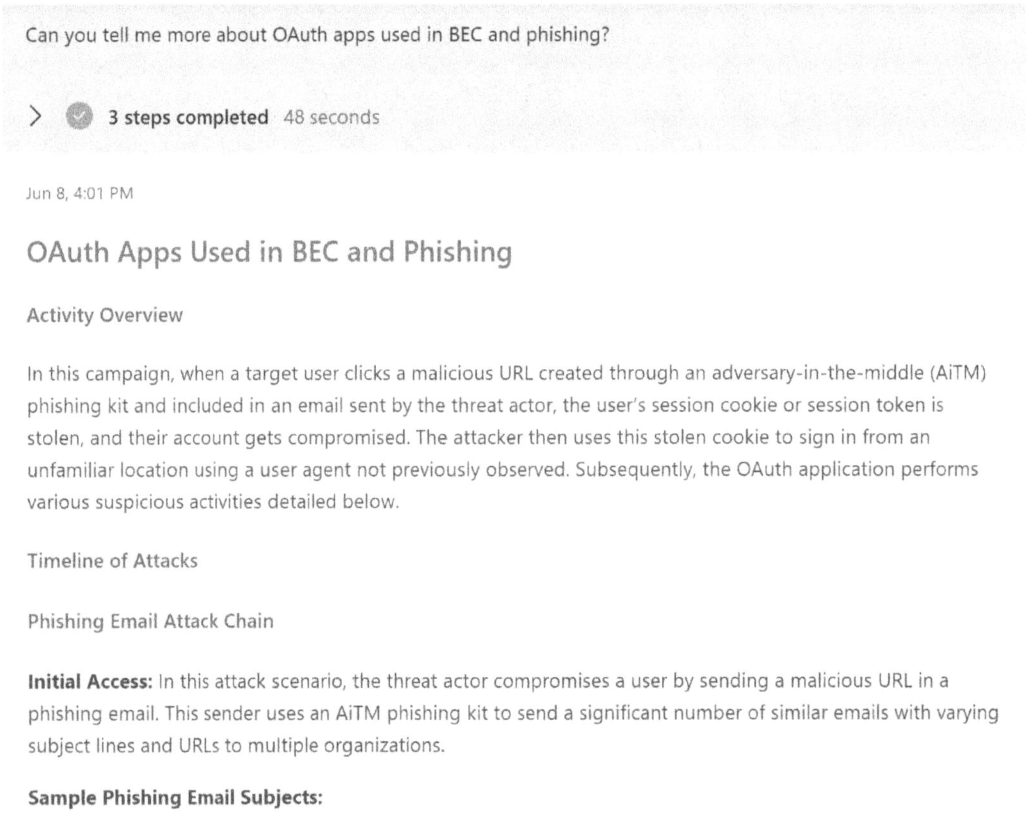

Figure 10.3 – The OAuth apps used in BEC and phishing threat

Security Copilot delivers detailed insights into the OAuth apps used in BEC and phishing threats, including the email attack chain, relevant MITRE ATT&CK techniques, recommended actions, and as well as detection and hunting queries. The full response is too long to include here; instead, you can read the complete output at `https://github.com/PacktPublishing/Microsoft-Copilot-for-Security/blob/main/Other/OAuth%20apps%20used%20in%20BEC%20and%20phishing%20-%20Chapter%2010.png`.

Additionally, you can specifically request that Security Copilot provides the IOCs and TTPs associated with the threat. The next screenshot displays the prompt and a portion of the response:

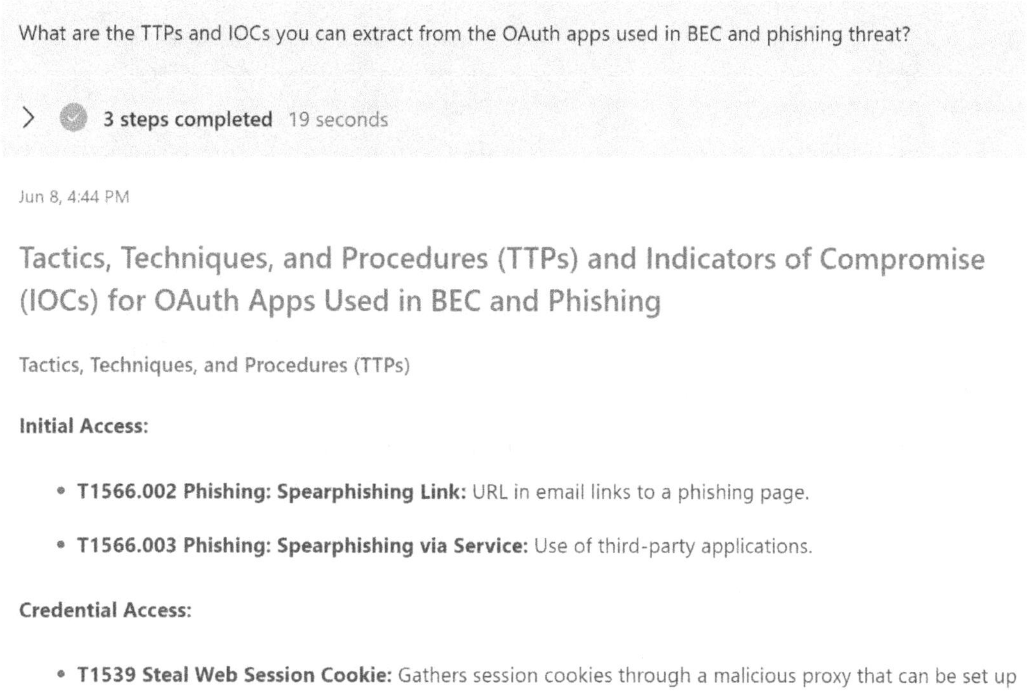

Figure 10.4 – TTPs for the threat

The IOCs included in the same Security Copilot response are shown next:

Indicators of Compromise (IOCs)

Export to Excel

IoC Type	IoC Value
User Agent	Mozilla/5.0 (Windows NT 10.0; Win64; x64; rv:109.0) Gecko/20100101 Firefox/114.0
User Agent	Mozilla/5.0 (Windows NT 10.0; Win64; x64) AppleWebKit/537.36 (KHTML, like Gecko) Chrome/114.0.0.0 Safari/537.36
User Agent	python/3.10.10 (Windows-10-10.0.20348-SP0) AZURECLI/2.50.0 (MSI)

Figure 10.5 – IOCs for the threat

The full response from Copilot is also available for viewing in the GitHub repository at `https://github.com/PacktPublishing/Microsoft-Copilot-for-Security/blob/main/Other/IOCs%20and%20TTPs%20for%20the%20threat%20-%20Chapter%2010.png`.

In its earlier response, Security Copilot also includes several detection queries written in KQL, targeting OAuth apps involved in BEC and phishing activities. One of these queries is shown next:

OAuth Application Creation or Modification by a User with Suspicious Sign-in Activities: Look for OAuth applications created or modified by a user with suspicious sign-in activities. Run query

```
AADSignInEventsBeta
| where Timestamp >ago (7d)
| where ErrorCode == 0
| where RiskLevelDuringSignIn >= 50
| project SignInTime=AccountUpn, AccountObjectId, SessionId, RiskLevelDuringSignIn, ApplicationId, Application
| join kind=leftouter (CloudAppEvents | where Timestamp > ago(7d)
| where ActionType in ("Add application.", "Update application.", "Update application - Certificates and secrets management ")
| extend appId = tostring(parse_json(RawEventData.Target[4].ID))
| project
    Timestamp,
    ActionType,
    Application,
    ApplicationId,
    UserAgent,
    ISP,
    AccountObjectId,
    AppName=ObjectName,
    OauthApplicationId=appId,
    RawEventData ) on AccountObjectId
| where isnotempty(ActionType)
```

Figure 10.6 – A detection query written in KQL

As this is a rather complex KQL query, you can ask Security Copilot to break it down for you. This can help you to quickly understand the query and allow you to customize it for your environment later on.

The corresponding Security Copilot prompt is shown in the next screen capture:

Can you break down the following KQL query? AADSignInEventsBeta | where Timestamp >ago (7d) | where ErrorCode == 0 | where RiskLevelDuringSignIn >= 50 | project SignInTime=AccountUpn, AccountObjectId, SessionId, RiskLevelDuringSignIn, ApplicationId, Application | join kind=leftouter (CloudAppEvents | where Timestamp > ago(7d) | where ActionType in ("Add application.", "Update application.", "Update application – Certificates and secrets management ") | extend appId = tostring(parse_json(RawEventData.Target[4].ID)) | project Timestamp, ActionType, Application, ApplicationId, UserAgent, ISP, AccountObjectId, AppName=ObjectName, OauthApplicationId=appId, RawEventData) on AccountObjectId | where isnotempty(ActionType)

Figure 10.7 – The prompt to break down a KQL query

The following screenshot illustrates how Security Copilot first provides a summary of the KQL query before explaining it line by line:

Explanation of the Kusto query

The Kusto query is designed to analyze sign-in events and related cloud application events over the past 7 days. It filters for successful sign-ins with a high risk level and joins this data with specific cloud application events to provide a comprehensive view of potentially risky activities.

Breakdown of the Kusto query

- `AADSignInEventsBeta` : Specifies the primary data source, which contains Azure Active Directory sign-in events.
- `| where Timestamp > ago(7d)` : Filters the sign-in events to include only those that occurred in the last 7 days.
- `| where ErrorCode == 0` : Filters the sign-in events to include only those that were successful (no error).
- `| where RiskLevelDuringSignIn >= 50` : Filters the sign-in events to include only those with a high risk level during sign-in.
- `| project SignInTime=AccountUpn, AccountObjectId, SessionId, RiskLevelDuringSignIn, ApplicationId, Application` : Selects specific columns to include in the output for the sign-in events, renaming `AccountUpn` to `SignInTime` .
- `| join kind=leftouter (` : Initiates a left outer join with another data source, `CloudAppEvents` .
- `CloudAppEvents` : Specifies the secondary data source, which contains cloud application events.

Figure 10.8 – Explanation of the KQL query

This use case highlights Security Copilot's ability to identify the latest threats to an organization. It showcases how Copilot can provide deep insights into specific risks and break down complex detection queries for you. Building on this, in the next section, let's look at how Security Copilot can leverage its Public Web plugin to gather intelligence from publicly available online resources.

Extracting IOCs from the open web

Besides requesting Security Copilot to extract threat information from MDTI, you can also ask it to gather data from external web pages. For example, there is an external threat article that offers detailed insights into a malware named Gootloader. Let's ask Security Copilot to analyze the article and extract the relevant IOCs associated with this malware. By leveraging Security Copilot's capabilities to read both internal and external sources, you can streamline the process of gathering threat intelligence data from a broader range of resources.

Security Copilot utilizes the **Public web** plugin to analyze and collect information from publicly available sources online (More information about this plugin is covered in *Chapter 4*). Here, you can ask Security Copilot to analyze the external web page about the Gootloader malware, located at `https://darktrace.com/blog/gootloader-malware-detecting-and-containing-multi-functional-threats-with-darktrace`, then extract the IOCs from it. The Security Copilot prompt and the plugin used are displayed in the next screen capture:

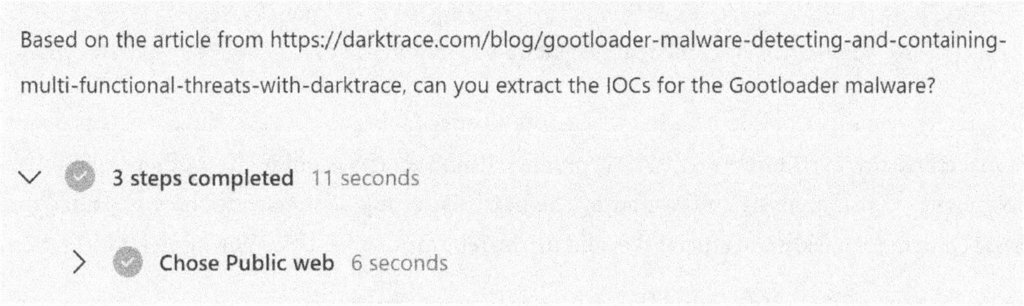

Figure 10.9 – Analyzing external web page using the public web plugin

Security Copilot extracts a long list of IOCs from the web page and displays a selection of them on its main results page, as seen next:

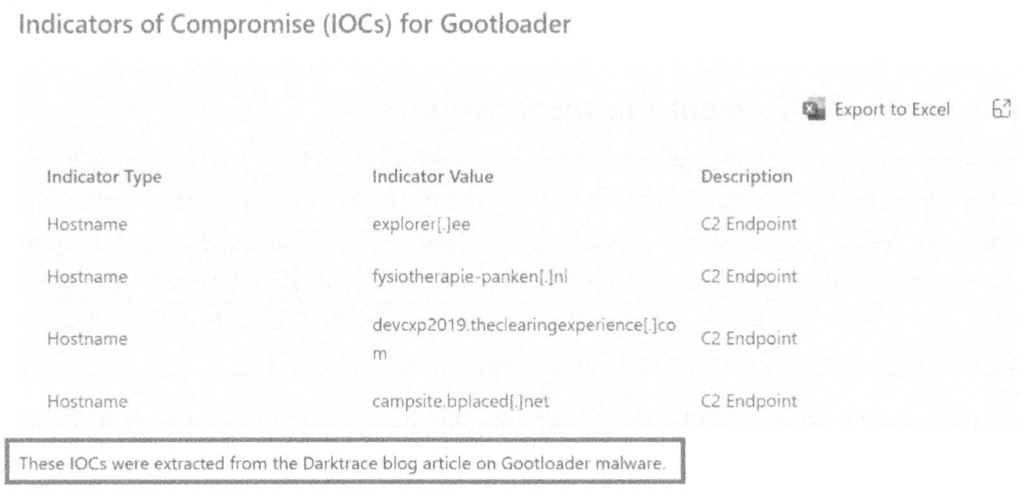

Figure 10.10 – IOCs extracted from external web page

> Tip: You can request that Security Copilot collects different information from the public web page; it's not limited to extracting IOCs. Additionally, Security Copilot can summarize the content of the public web resource or even generate a report for you.

Leveraging Security Copilot to gather threat intelligence for organizational threats boosts operational efficiency. Furthermore, the MDTI plugin within Security Copilot offers other capabilities to enhance threat analysis and response. The next case study demonstrates how to utilize the MDTI plugin to quickly and efficiently validate the reputation of entities during an investigation.

Optimizing and streamlining threat validation

While investigating an incident and sifting through large volumes of logs, such as device events, web logs, network traffic, and more, you can leverage the MDTI plugin to validate the reputation of processes, files, IP addresses, or domains, helping you to quickly identify suspicious entities. Even better, the step of calling the MDTI plugin can be integrated into promptbooks for added efficiency (Promptbooks are covered thoroughly in *Chapter 6*, including how to create and use promptbooks).

For instance, the promptbook shown in the next screenshot retrieves a device's outbound network events within a specific timeframe. It then instructs Security Copilot to invoke the MDTI plugin to check the reputation of the IPs and URLs listed in the network events:

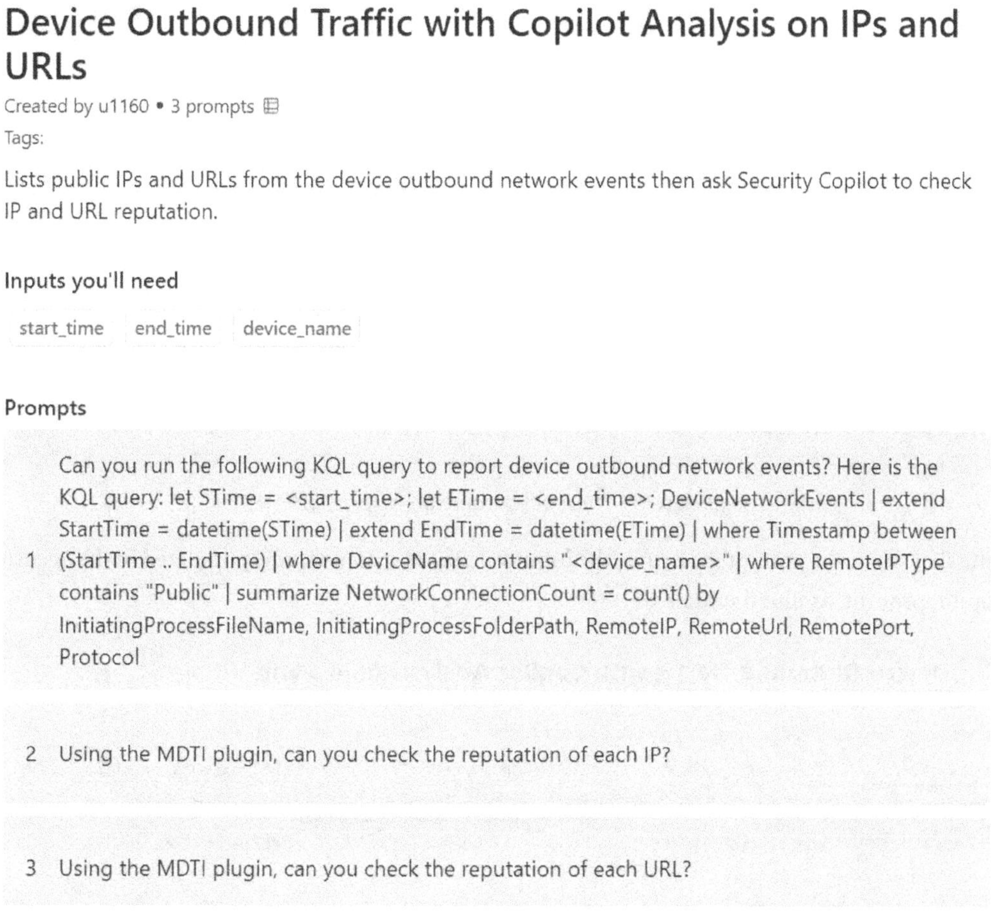

Figure 10.11 – The promptbook that uses MDTI to check reputation of IPs and URLs

This promptbook comes in handy during investigations. Let's say a malicious executable is found on a device. The malware, or related processes, may initiate outbound traffic to its **Command and Control (C2)** server for further instructions. To verify whether any C2 traffic occurred, one way is to examine the device's network activities, specifically the outbound IPs and URLs around the time of the incident. In the past, analysts often had to manually extract and review these outbound IPs and URLs. Now, the promptbook in Security Copilot can automate this process, greatly enhancing the speed and efficiency.

As an example, let's run this promptbook for device `vnevado-win10v`, with the timeframe set to all day of December 9th, 2024. The input parameters for this promptbook are shown in the next screen capture:

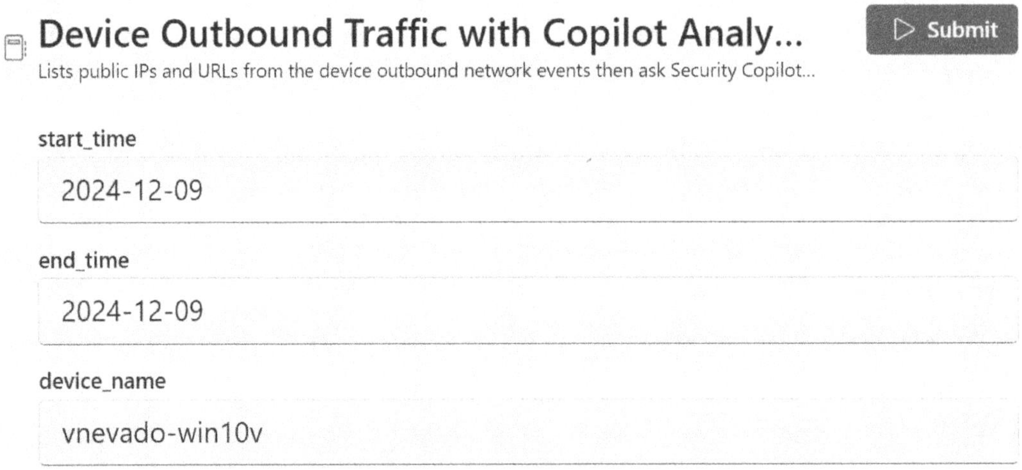

Figure 10.12 – The input parameters for promptbook

Note that when the promptbook runs, the input values are automatically populated in the Security Copilot prompt, as illustrated next:

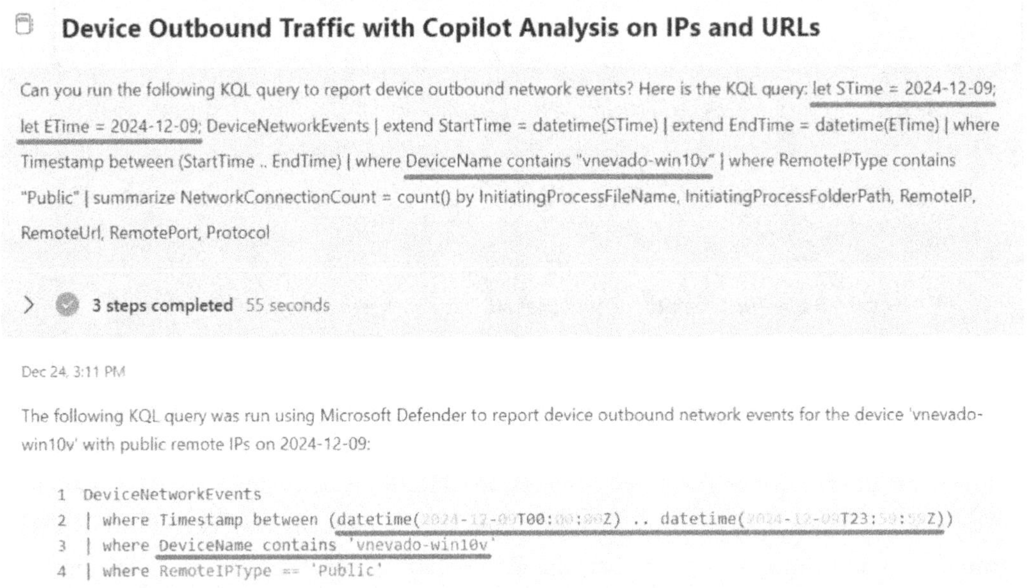

Figure 10.13 – Input values automatically populated in prompt

The first prompt in this promptbook returns a list of outbound connections, including external IPs and URLs. The main result page, as shown in the next screenshot, displays the processes that initiated the outbound connections and the corresponding external IPs:

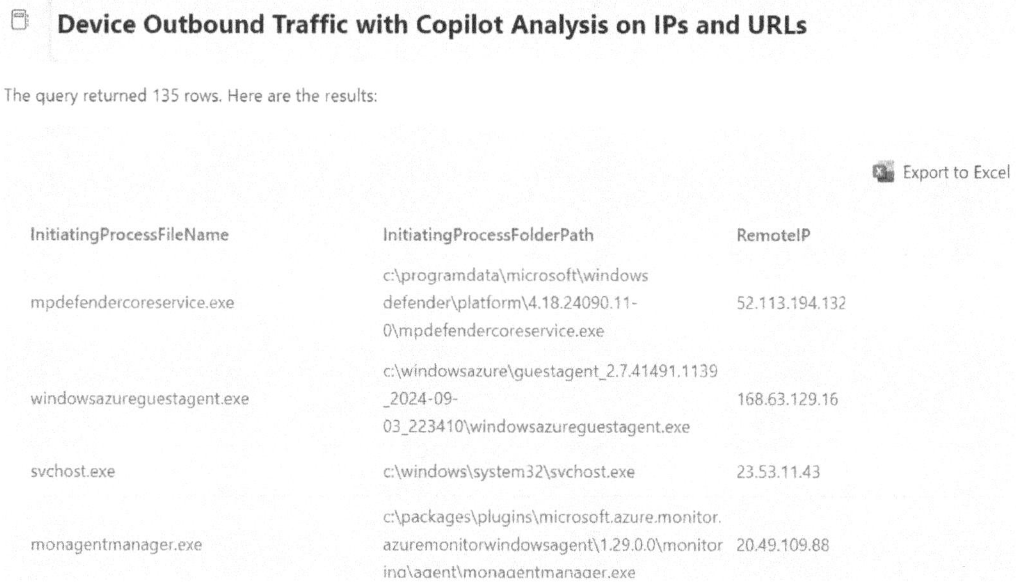

Device Outbound Traffic with Copilot Analysis on IPs and URLs

The query returned 135 rows. Here are the results:

Export to Excel

InitiatingProcessFileName	InitiatingProcessFolderPath	RemoteIP
mpdefendercoreservice.exe	c:\programdata\microsoft\windows defender\platform\4.18.24090.11-0\mpdefendercoreservice.exe	52.113.194.132
windowsazureguestagent.exe	c:\windowsazure\guestagent_2.7.41491.1139_2024-09-03_223410\windowsazureguestagent.exe	168.63.129.16
svchost.exe	c:\windows\system32\svchost.exe	23.53.11.43
monagentmanager.exe	c:\packages\plugins\microsoft.azure.monitor.azuremonitorwindowsagent\1.29.0.0\monitoring\agent\monagentmanager.exe	20.49.109.88

Figure 10.14 – Outbound connections with external IPs listed

The next prompt in the promptbook invokes the MDTI plugin to assess the reputation of each IP in the outbound connections from the first prompt. For this example, as shown in the next screen capture, Security Copilot identifies one IP address with a slightly suspicious reputation:

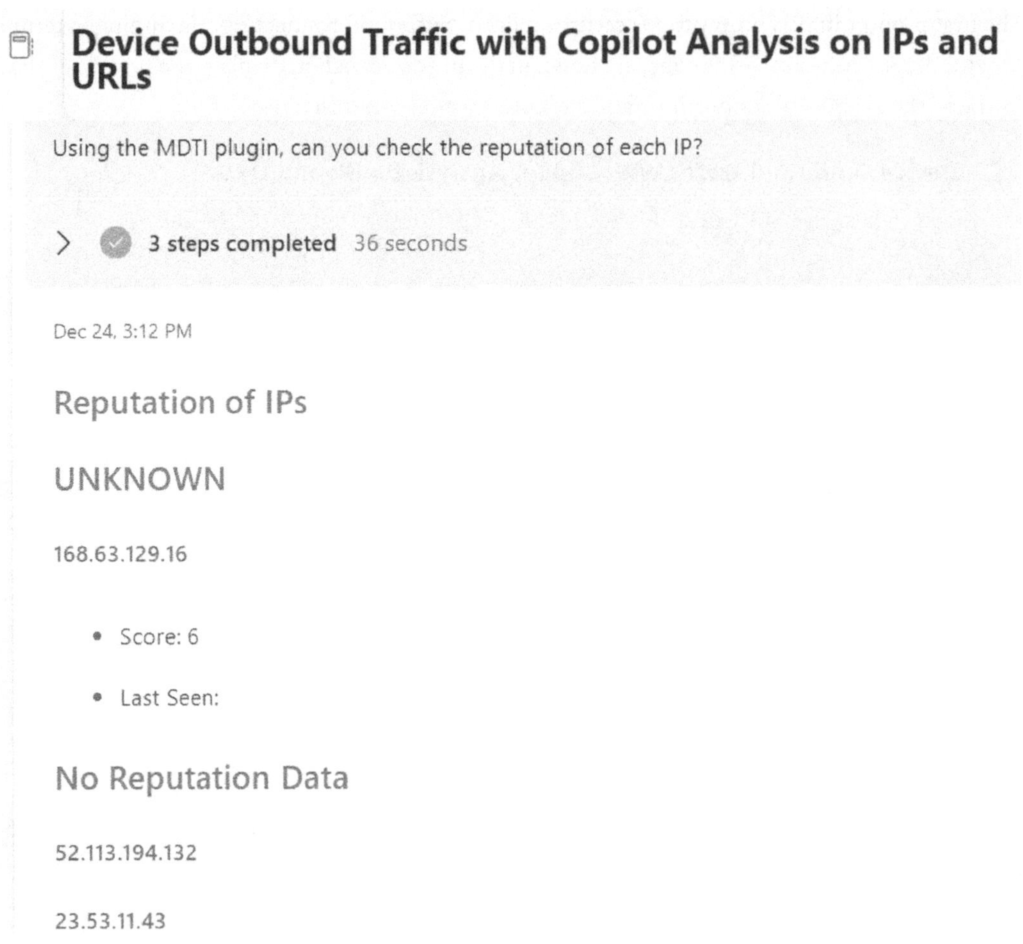

Figure 10.15 – Reputation of the IPs

The third prompt uses the MDTI plugin to check the reputation of each URL identified in the outbound connections, with results shown in the next screen capture:

Reputation of URLs

UNKNOWN

v10.events.data.microsoft.com

- Score: 1
- Last Seen:
- Rule:
  - Name: Resolving IP Address
  - Description: 20.189.173.9

No Reputation Data

ctldl.windowsupdate.com

global.handler.control.monitor.azure.com

manage.microsoft.com

settings-win.data.microsoft.com

go.microsoft.com

agents.amsub0502.manage.microsoft.com

e34d562e-ef12-4c4e-9bc0-7c6ae357c015.ods.opinsights.azure.com

2ae55c3e-0750-47b1-8ec1-e6c0fe2c89cb.ods.opinsights.azure.com

Figure 10.16 – Reputation of the URLs

The workflow in this promptbook serves as one example of how the MDTI plugin can be utilized in promptbooks for enhanced efficiency. Another similar promptbook involves gathering a list of processes executed on the device around the time of the incident, then using the MDTI plugin to check the reputation of each process based on its file hash value. Alternatively, a different promptbook can identify all files created on the device during the incident timeframe and leverage MDTI to check the reputation of those files through their hash values.

Note

These promptbooks are provided in the GitHub repository of this book.

Now, let's move on to the next case study showcasing some powerful yet lesser-known features offered by the MDTI plugin in Security Copilot.

Tracking and uncovering threat actor infrastructures

MDTI is a powerful tool that provides a wide range of capabilities. One of its key features is the ability to track attackers' infrastructures as they move or change. Attackers frequently shift their infrastructure to avoid detection, such as by changing their IP addresses, domains, or even cloud environments. MDTI not only tracks changes in threat actors' infrastructures but also provides a wealth of associated historical data points and indicators. This information helps analysts to uncover hidden connections and relationships, allowing them to link threat actors and infrastructures across multiple attacks or campaigns.

For instance, a common method for tracking malicious infrastructure is through WHOIS records, which contain information about the ownership and registration details of domain names and IP addresses. The MDTI plugin in Security Copilot enables users to extract and analyze these WHOIS records for insights. By leveraging this data, as an example, analysts can trace connections and possibly identify new C2 domains related to the same threat actor by correlating the shared email address across different domains found in the WHOIS records.

Another common way to track attacker infrastructure is to leverage the passive DNS data, also available through the MDTI plugin. Passive DNS works by providing historical DNS query data, which can help track and analyze domain activities, IP addresses, and their associations over time. For instance, if a threat actor frequently registers domains with similar naming conventions or consistently resolves to the same set of IP addresses, these recurring behaviors can form a pattern. By analyzing this historical DNS data, analysts can correlate these domains and IPs with known threat actor TTPs.

While both WHOIS records and passive DNS are commonly used by analysts, some of the less familiar but equally effective methods for infrastructure analysis involve the examination of SSL/TLS certificates, web components, host-pair relationships, subdomains, trackers, and cookies. These datasets can often provide deeper insights into attacker infrastructures. The Security Copilot MDTI plugin offers a set of skills for retrieving and analyzing these datasets to support different security use cases, as shown next:

- **Get SSL certificates by indicators:** Get the SSL certificates of a list of IP addresses and hostnames
- **Get host pairs by indicators:** Get the host pairs of a list of IP addresses and hostnames
- **Get trackers by indicators:** Get the trackers of a list of IP addresses and hostnames
- **Get web components by indicators:** Get the web components of a list of IP addresses and hostnames
- **Get Subdomains for indicators:** Get the subdomains for a list of hostnames
- **Get cookies by indicators:** Get the cookies of a list of IP addresses and hostnames
- **Get indicators by indicators:** Get the indicators of compromise (IOCs) related to another indicator of compromise (IOCs).

Important note

SSL/TLS certificates are used to secure data exchanged between user devices and websites. These certificates can reveal relationships between network infrastructures that passive DNS or WHOIS data may miss. They're another effective way to correlate and identify malicious infrastructures, helping analysts to uncover hidden connections.

MDTI can link an SSL/TLS certificate to the IP address hosting it, providing visibility into where the certificate is located. Through large-scale internet scans, MDTI gathers certificates from all IP addresses, building a historical database for the certificate data. With this repository of IP addresses to TLS certificate mappings, analysts can identify overlaps in infrastructures. For instance, if an attacker's infrastructure is detected and flagged as malicious, they can quickly set up a new one. Instead of developing everything from scratch, the attacker may replicate the contents of the old infrastructure to the new server, using the same TLS certificate for the new IP address. At this point, through visibility of the IP address to TLS certificate mapping, the security analyst can recognize the connection between the old, known malicious web server and the new one, revealing a potential link in the attacker's evolving infrastructure.

By utilizing the MDTI plugin, Security Copilot helps to facilitate the discovery process, enabling analysts to trace connections between malicious IPs by examining the shared certificate. This allows one malicious IP to serve as a starting point for uncovering other related suspicious IP addresses.

For instance, during a ransomware investigation, you identified the malicious IP address 91.109.176.4. Now, let's see how its certificate data can assist in correlating this IP to other malicious IP addresses and uncovering connections to other attackers' infrastructure.

You start by reviewing the threat intelligence data that Security Copilot has gathered about this IP address. The prompt and the MDTI plugin used by Security Copilot are shown in the next screen capture:

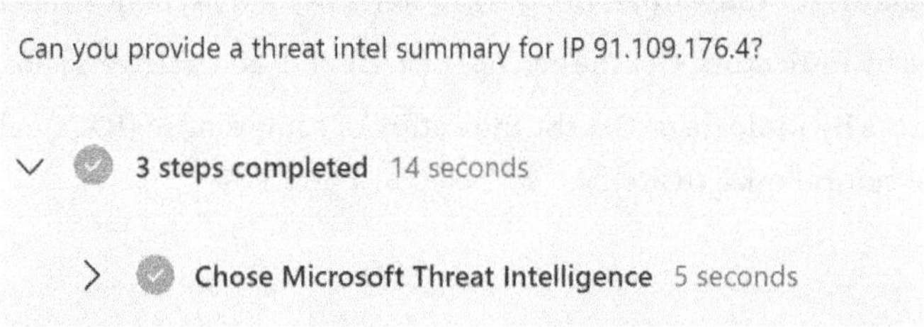

Figure 10.17 – Prompt to gather information for IP 91.109.176.4

> Important note
>
> Since the MDTI plugin isn't explicitly referenced in this prompt, it is possible for Security Copilot to pick other available threat intelligence plugins if they are enabled. As a result, the response could differ from one generated specifically using the MDTI plugin. This applies to any threat intelligence prompt when multiple TI plugins are enabled.

In its response, as illustrated next, Security Copilot indicates that the reputation of this IP is unknown but adds a note stating, **Infrastructure hosted by this ASN exhibits suspicious behavior**:

Threat Intel Summary for IP: 91.109.176.4

Reputation and Meta Data

- **Score**: 7
- **Classification**: UNKNOWN
- **First Seen**: 07-27-2013
- **Last Seen**: 05-07-2024
- **Netblock**: 91.109.176.0/20
- **Organization**: IELO-LIAZO SERVICES SAS
- **ASN**: AS29075 - IELO
- **Country**: FR
- **Description**: Infrastructure hosted by this ASN frequently exhibits suspicious behavior

Figure 10.18 – Threat intel summary for IP 91.109.176.4

Security Copilot also provides past DNS resolutions for this IP address in its response. Notice the domain `duckdns.org` appears a couple of times, as shown next:

Intelligence Profiles

No intelligence profiles available.

Articles

No articles available.

DNS Resolutions

Export to Excel

Indicator	Resolve	Last seen
91.109.176.4	dwumdwww.xxxvt.duckdns.org	05-07-2024
91.109.176.4	xxxvt.duckdns.org	04-23-2024
91.109.176.4	mantruck95.ddns.net	02-14-2024
91.109.176.4	milla.publicvm.com	01-28-2024

Figure 10.19 – DNS resolutions for IP 91.109.176.4

Now let's invoke the **Get SSL certificates by indicators** skill from Security Copilot's System Capability function to identify the certificates associated with IP 91.109.176.4. The following screenshot illustrates that this IP address is provided as input for the skill. Note that you can also use natural language in your prompt to activate the same skill:

Figure 10.20 – The Get SSL certificates by indicators skill

As seen in the next screen capture, Security Copilot has identified a long list of certificates linked to this IP address. Additionally, each certificate has a number of other IP addresses associated with it:

Export to Excel

Indicator	SHA1	Last seen	First seen	Infrastructure
91.109.176.4	2140c33a7a24ca83deb99bc6b7d8da3b5f06f32c	12-14-2023	12-14-2023	4 IP addresses
91.109.176.4	85f1958540cbe005a06523ec3f12a5d8be45a8e1	11-28-2023	11-05-2023	28 IP addresses
91.109.176.4	e0dde06914c9eb79c3ccc4f2f806b7c7a4090eab	10-17-2023	10-17-2023	8 IP addresses
91.109.176.4	092ad7bfdd4ba88eda3468ea46ec0e10268f7815	10-01-2023	10-01-2023	10 IP addresses
91.109.176.4	b0238c547a905bfa119c4e8baccaeacf36491ff6	09-04-2023	05-06-2020	3,457,588 IP addresses
91.109.176.4	b20f72559fb30748324e1f9845b86dc70c0611a2	07-26-2023	01-06-2023	14,581 IP addresses
91.109.176.4	489783390ab3fa7c3a979d87baa1ddd652c09b31	07-16-2023	07-16-2023	28 IP addresses

Figure 10.21 – List of certificates linked to this IP

Based on the list of certificates provided in a previous response, let's ask Security Copilot to find the certificate with the most IP addresses linked to it. As shown in the following screenshot, an SSL certificate with its SHA1 hash value ending in 91ff6 is identified by Security Copilot as the one with the most associated IP addresses:

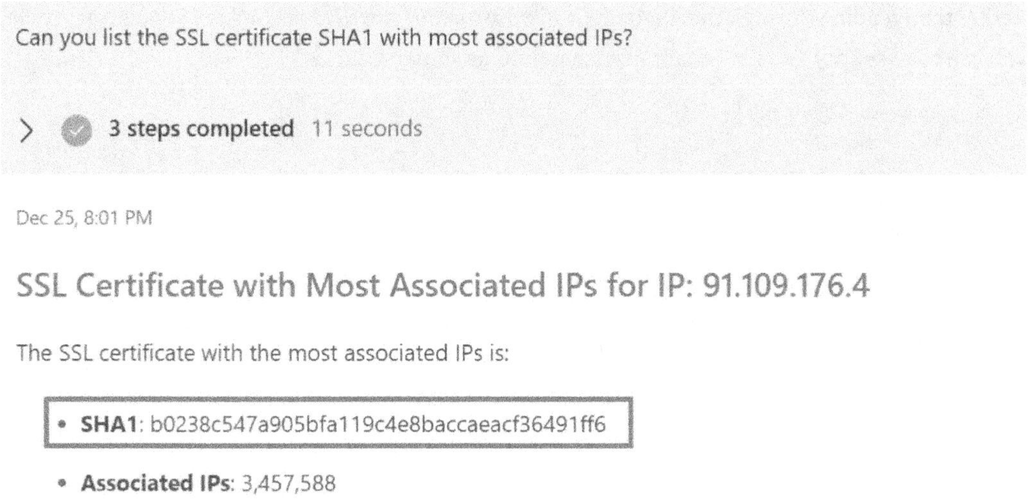

Figure 10.22 – Certificate with the most IP addresses linked to it

This certificate appears unusual due to the large number of IP addresses linked to it. When checking with Copilot to see what it knows about this certificate, Security Copilot provides a threat article tied to it. This is illustrated in the following screen capture:

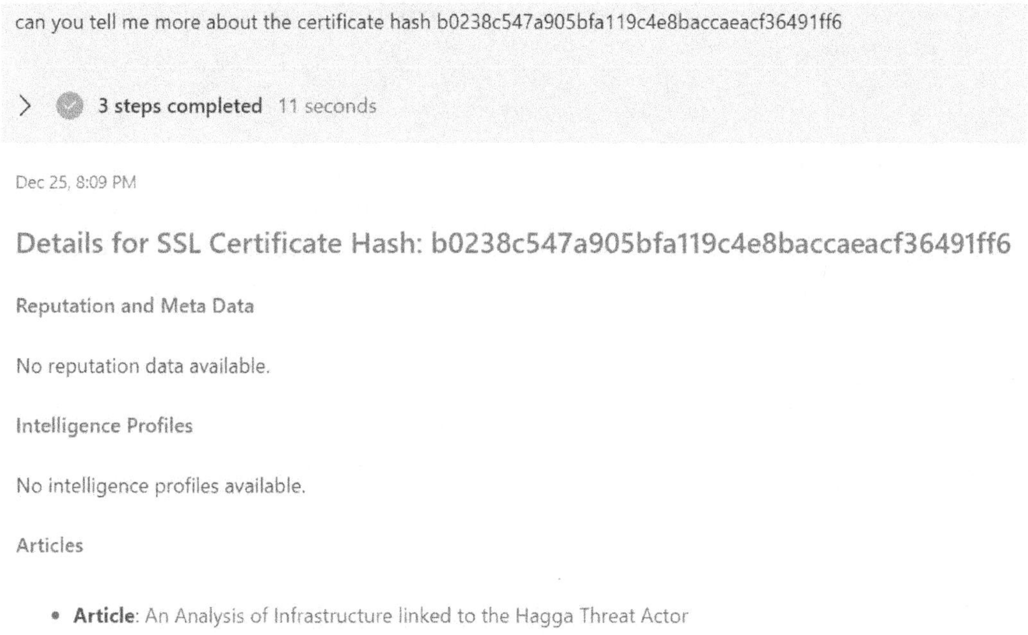

Figure 10.23 – Threat article tied to this certificate

Rather than reading through the *An Analysis of Infrastructure linked to the Hagga Threat Actor* article, you can ask Security Copilot to summarize it first, as shown next:

Can you provide a summary for the threat article from your previous response?

> **3 steps completed** 17 seconds

Dec 25, 2024

This is what we found for the search query `An Analysis of Infrastructure linked to the Hagga Threat Actor`

Summary of the Article

Description

Team Cymru researchers describe how they were able to pivot in threat telemetry, using IOCs from Yoroi Security's blog as seeds, to identify several other C2s. From the starting point of an IP address (69.174.99.181) associated with an Agent Tesla command and control server, it was possible to pivot and identify a backend server hosting a MySQL database operated by the threat actor Hagga. From this point, a further pivot led Team Cymru researchers to the identification of additional C2s hosting the Mana Tools C2 panel along with a common certificate that can be used to increase confidence in attributing future infrastructure to this threat actor.

Figure 10.24 – Summary of the threat article

In the same summary overview, Security Copilot also provides a list of indicators extracted from the threat article. These indicators include the exact same certificate you've reviewed, with its hash ending in 91ff6, as well as multiple domains associated with `duckdns.org`. These specific indicators are marked with a red outline and shown in the following screenshot:

Community Indicators

- **Certificate SHA1**: b0238c547a905bfa119c4e8baccaeacf36491ff6
- **URL**: http://69.174.99.181/webpanel-reza/login.php
- **Domains**: abotherrdpajq.duckdns.org, bakuzamokala.duckdns.org, bot.statusupdate.one, cdec22.duckdns.org, heavy-dutyindustry.shop, microsoftiswear.duckdns.org, mobibagugu.duckdns.org, mobibanewdan.duckdns.org, mobinomomuam.duckdns.org, mohbeebnew.duckdns.org, mubbibun.duckdns.org, newbotv4.monster, statusupdate.one, update.newbotv2.monster, update.newbotv4.monster, vncgoga.duckdns.org, warnonmobina.duckdns.org, workflowstatus.live
- **IPs**: 103.133.105.61, 103.151.122.110, 103.153.77.98, 155.94.209.50, 161.129.64.49, 192.154.226.47, 194.31.98.108, 207.32.217.137, 42.201.155.21, 42.201.155.40, 64.188.20.198, 64.188.21.227, 64.188.27.104, 69.174.99.181, 72.11.143.125, 72.11.143.47, 72.11.157.208, 78.138.105.142

Figure 10.25 – Indicators from the threat article

🔍 **Quick tip**: Need to see a high-resolution version of this image? Open this book in the next-gen Packt Reader or view it in the PDF/ePub copy.

🔒 **The next-gen Packt Reader** and a **free PDF/ePub copy** of this book are included with your purchase. Scan the QR code OR visit `packtpub.com/unlock`, then use the search bar to find this book by name. Double-check the edition shown to make sure you get the right one.

At the start of the Security Copilot session, remember that the DNS resolutions for the malicious IP address 91.109.176.4 also include `duckdns.org`. Now, things are starting to come together. The various URLs containing `duckdns.org`, both in the DNS resolution earlier and now as indicators in the threat summary, suggest a potential connection between the two.

Also shown in the previous screenshot is a list of IP indicators provided by Security Copilot in the same summary writeup. Let's request that Security Copilot retrieves the certificates linked to the first IP from the indicator list, 103.133.105.61. The Security Copilot skill and its response are displayed in the following screen capture:

Figure 10.26 – Certificates for IP 103.133.105.61

From Security Copilot's response, you quickly notice that the first certificate linked to this IP address is the same TLS certificate you've been examining, with its SHA1 hash ending in 91ff6. This indicates that the two IP addresses, 91.109.176.4 and 103.133.105.61, are both tied to the same certificate, suggesting that this TLS certificate was hosted in both infrastructures at one point.

As shown in the next screenshot, the DNS resolutions for IP address 103.133.105.61 are primarily linked to `duckdns.org`. Remember that some of the DNS resolutions for the IP address 91.109.176.4 are also associated with `duckdns.org`? This establishes another connection between the two IP addresses, as they are not only tied to the same certificate but are also associated with the same `duckdns.org` domain name:

DNS Resolutions

Export to Excel

Indicator	Resolve	Last seen
103.133.105.61	abotherrdpajq.duckdns.org	06-02-2022
103.133.105.61	mubbibun.duckdns.org	06-01-2022
103.133.105.61	mobibagugu.duckdns.org	06-01-2022
103.133.105.61	vncgoga.duckdns.org	05-31-2022

Figure 10.27 – DNS resolutions for IP 103.133.105.61

The IP address 103.133.105.61 originates from Vietnam, with an ASN number of AS135905, as shown next:

Threat Intel Summary for IP: 103.133.105.61

Reputation and Meta Data

- **Reputation**: No reputation data
- **First Seen**: 05-07-2022
- **Last Seen**: 06-02-2022
- **Netblock**: 103.133.104.0/22
- **Organization**: VIETNAM POSTS AND TELECOMMUNICATIONS GROUP
- **ASN**: AS135905 - VNPT-AS-VN
- **Countrv**: VN

Figure 10.28 – IP address 103.133.105.61

In contrast, IP address 91.109.176.4 is registered in France and has a different ASN number, as illustrated in the following screen capture:

Threat Intel Summary for IP: 91.109.176.4

Reputation and Meta Data

- **Score**: 7
- **Classification**: UNKNOWN
- **First Seen**: 07-27-2013
- **Last Seen**: 05-07-2024
- **Netblock**: 91.109.176.0/20
- **Organization**: IELO-LIAZO SERVICES SAS
- **ASN**: AS29075 - IELO
- **Country**: FR

Figure 10.29 – IP address 91.109.176.4

At first glance, the two IP addresses may appear unrelated. However, leveraging the MDTI plugin in Security Copilot, you can now confirm that they were both likely being used by the same threat actors at some point.

Now let's summarize what's been covered in this case study so far. It began with the identification of the malicious IP address 91.109.176.4. Using the MDTI plugin in Security Copilot, you retrieved a list of certificates associated with this IP. Upon examining one of these certificates, Security Copilot linked it to a relevant threat intelligence article, which contained a list of indicators. When Security Copilot provided certificates for one of the IP indicators, you discovered that the certificate associated with this IP was the same one for IP 91.109.176.4. Additionally, both IP addresses had resolved to various `duckdns.org` domains at some point, further linking them together.

The Security Copilot MDTI plugin enables analysts to quickly connect the dots among various data points, such as certificates, IP addresses, and domains. However, this is just one of the key features that highlight the MDTI plugin's ability to uncover less obvious relationships and connections.

In the next section, let's use another case study to introduce one more key feature, the host-pair relationship, to further illustrate how these data points can enhance the investigation process and support more informed decision-making during cybersecurity investigations.

Uncovering hidden connections with host pair relationships

The term host pairs refers to two pieces of online infrastructure that are linked together in some way. One of the pieces is called the *parent* and the other is the *child*. Think of the parent as the main website that a user first connects to. The child is a secondary site or service that the parent interacts with. The child host could be another page on the same website or an external third-party service that is being called by the parent host.

For example, imagine you're browsing an online shopping site (the parent). You click a link that takes you to a page to enter your payment information (the child). This payment page could be part of a third-party service integrated into the website. The connection between the parent and child sites is referred to as a host pair. It's a way of identifying how different pieces of online infrastructure are connected and how data or functionality flows between them.

In a phishing attack, a cybercriminal can send a fake login request or password reset email that appears to be from a legitimate source, such as a bank or online retailer. The email contains a link to the malicious website (the parent) designed to mimic the legitimate site, but is actually set up to steal sensitive information. This phishing website (the parent) can pull content from the legitimate site (the child) to make the scam more convincing. The MDTI plugin in Security Copilot identifies such host pair relationships, offering further support for analysts in their investigations and threat-hunting efforts.

Let's consider a scenario in which you're investigating a suspicious domain, apple.id-19.top, identified from a phishing email. You start by requesting that Security Copilot provides a threat intelligence summary for this domain.

As shown in the following screenshot, in addition to basic details such as the WHOIS registrar and DNS resolution, Security Copilot also provides host pair records for this domain.

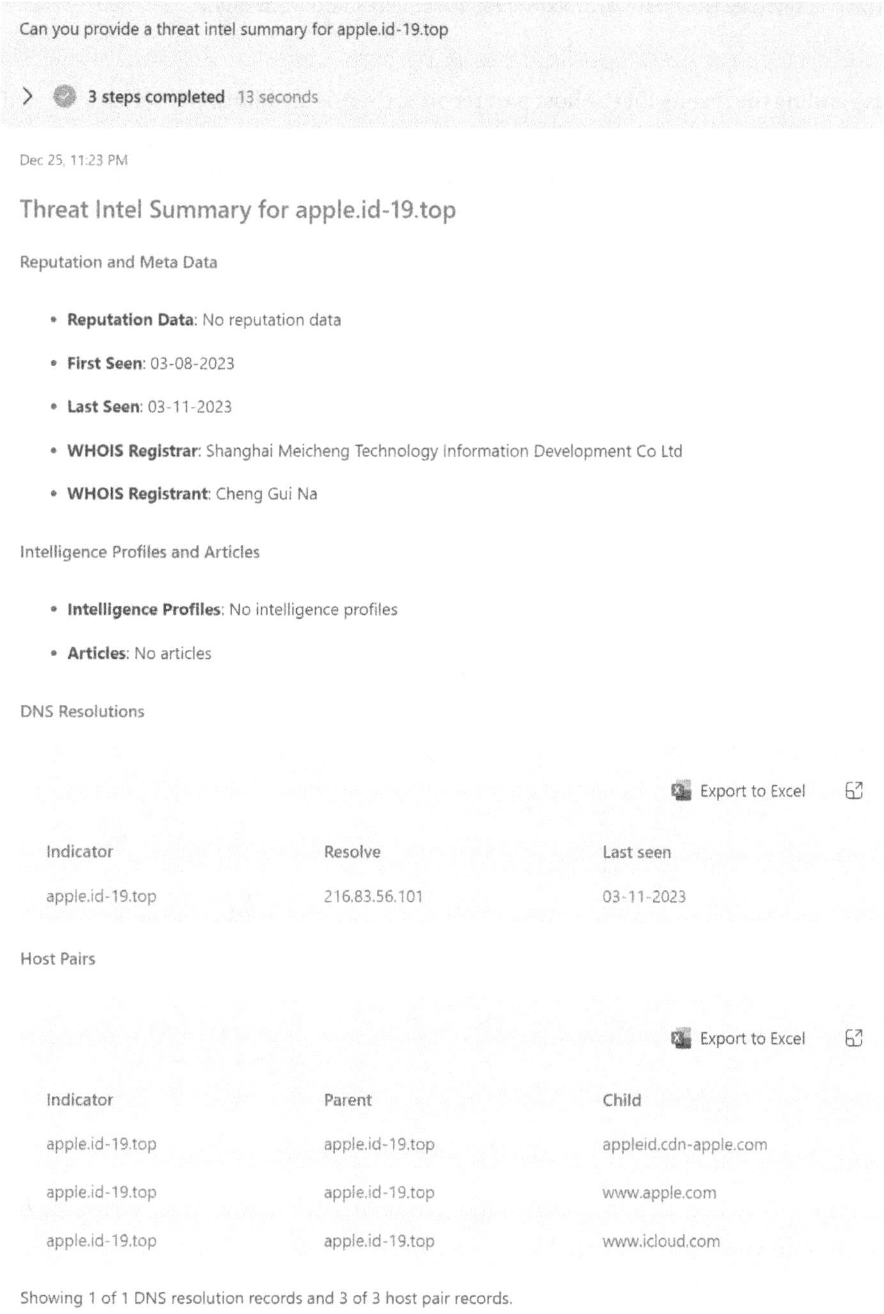

Figure 10.30 – Threat intel summary for apple.id-19.top

> Tip: You can also invoke the **Get host pairs by indicators** skill in Security Copilot to retrieve the host pair records for specific IPs and domains.

When expanding the results for the host pair records, there is an additional column labeled **Cause**. This column indicates the type of connection between the parent and child hosts. As shown in the next screen capture, for this particular domain, there are three different causes: img.src, css.import, and script.src:

Export to Excel

Indicator	Parent	Child	Last seen	First seen	Cause
apple.id-19.top	apple.id-19.top	appleid.cdn-apple.com	03-11-2023	03-11-2023	img.src
apple.id-19.top	apple.id-19.top	www.apple.com	03-11-2023	03-11-2023	css.import
apple.id-19.top	apple.id-19.top	www.icloud.com	03-11-2023	03-11-2023	script.src

Figure 10.31 – The Cause column specifying the connection type

What does each cause mean exactly? As shown in the next screenshot, Security Copilot provides a clear and easy-to-understand explanation for the script.src cause:

Can you explain what it means from your first response where the parent is apple.id-19.top, the child is www.icloud.com and the cause is script.src

2 steps completed 13 seconds

Dec 25, 11:24 PM

The entry where the parent is `apple.id-19.top`, the child is `www.icloud.com`, and the cause is `script.src` indicates that the domain `apple.id-19.top` included a script from `www.icloud.com` in its web content. This means that when a user visited `apple.id-19.top`, a script hosted on `www.icloud.com` was loaded and executed in the user's browser. This type of relationship can be used to track how different domains interact with each other, which can be important for understanding potential security risks or the spread of malicious content.

Figure 10.32 – The script.src cause

Reading through Security Copilot's explanation, particularly the statement **script.src indicates that the domain apple.id-19.top included a script from www.icloud.com in its web content. This means that when a user visited apple.id-19.top, a script hosted on www.icloud.com was loaded and executed in the user's browser**, makes it easier to understand how the `script.src` function operates between the parent and child hosts.

To further understand the security implications of the behavior when a user visits a suspicious site such as apple.id-19.top, and a script hosted on www.icloud.com executes alongside other content on apple.id-19.top, let's consult with Security Copilot again.

The next screenshot shows that Security Copilot outlines several potential ways this behavior could be connected to a threat actor's exploit. The first scenario involves phishing, where Security Copilot explains **The attacker can create a convincing phishing page that appears to be part of the legitimate www.icloud.com site. Users might be tricked into entering their credentials, thinking they are on a legitimate Apple site.**

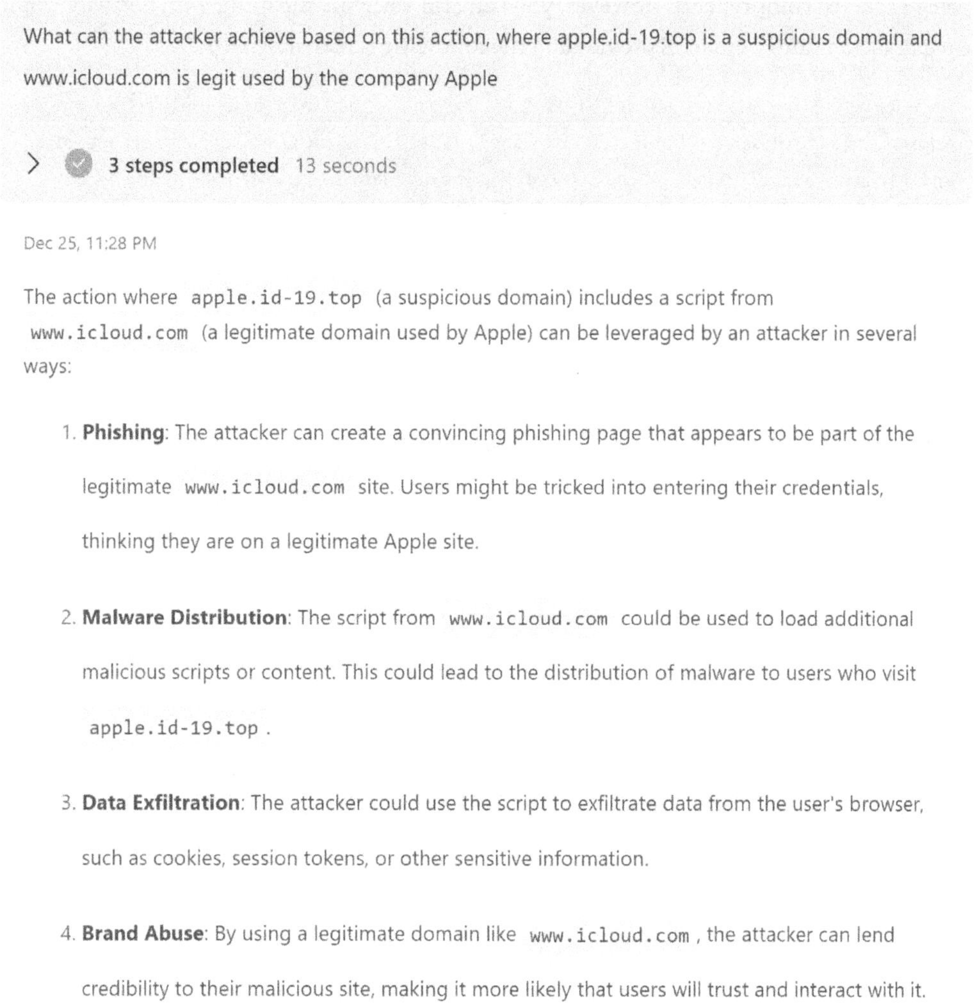

Figure 10.33 – Security risks associated with the script.src cause

Also outlined in Security Copilot's response are two other scenarios, **Malware Distribution** and **Data Exfiltration**, as shown in the previous screenshot. These scenarios provide additional useful insights and help to reveal other malicious behaviors. For instance, in a different scenario not related to this case study, it is possible for a compromised child host to serve malicious content or scripts that distribute malware to users visiting the parent host. This technique is commonly used in drive-by downloads, where users unknowingly download malicious software while visiting a seemingly legitimate website.

After reviewing the script.src cause with Security Copilot, the reasoning behind the img.src cause appears easier to comprehend. However, you can still verify its meaning with Security Copilot. The explanation from Copilot is provided in the following screenshot:

> The entry where the parent is `apple.id-19.top`, the child is `appleid.cdn-apple.com`, and the cause is `img.src` indicates that the domain `apple.id-19.top` included an image source from `appleid.cdn-apple.com` in its web content. This means that when a user visited `apple.id-19.top`, an image hosted on `appleid.cdn-apple.com` was loaded and displayed in the user's browser. This type of relationship can be used to track how different domains interact with each other, which can be important for understanding potential security risks or the spread of malicious content.

Figure 10.34 – The img.src cause

When the domain apple.id-19.top is analyzed by Security Copilot, three host pair records are identified, each representing a different type of connection. You've already looked into the script.src and img.src causes. Now, let's turn to Security Copilot to learn more about the third cause, css.import.

When you prompt Security Copilot to gather more information about css.import, Copilot reveals that **when a user visited apple.id-19.top, a CSS file hosted on www.apple.com was loaded and applied to the user's browser**, as shown in the following screen capture:

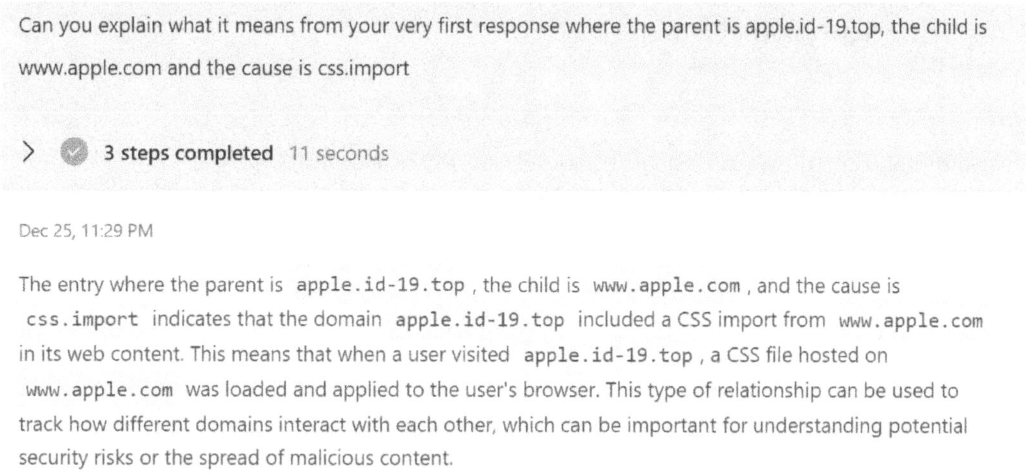

Figure 10.35 – The css.import cause

Next, you can ask Security Copilot to explain the security implications of this observed behavior. Security Copilot again highlights a phishing scenario in its response, stating that **the attacker can create a visually convincing phishing page that mimics the appearance of a legitimate Apple site, increasing the likelihood that users will enter sensitive information.**

The prompt and response from Security Copilot are shown in the following screenshot:

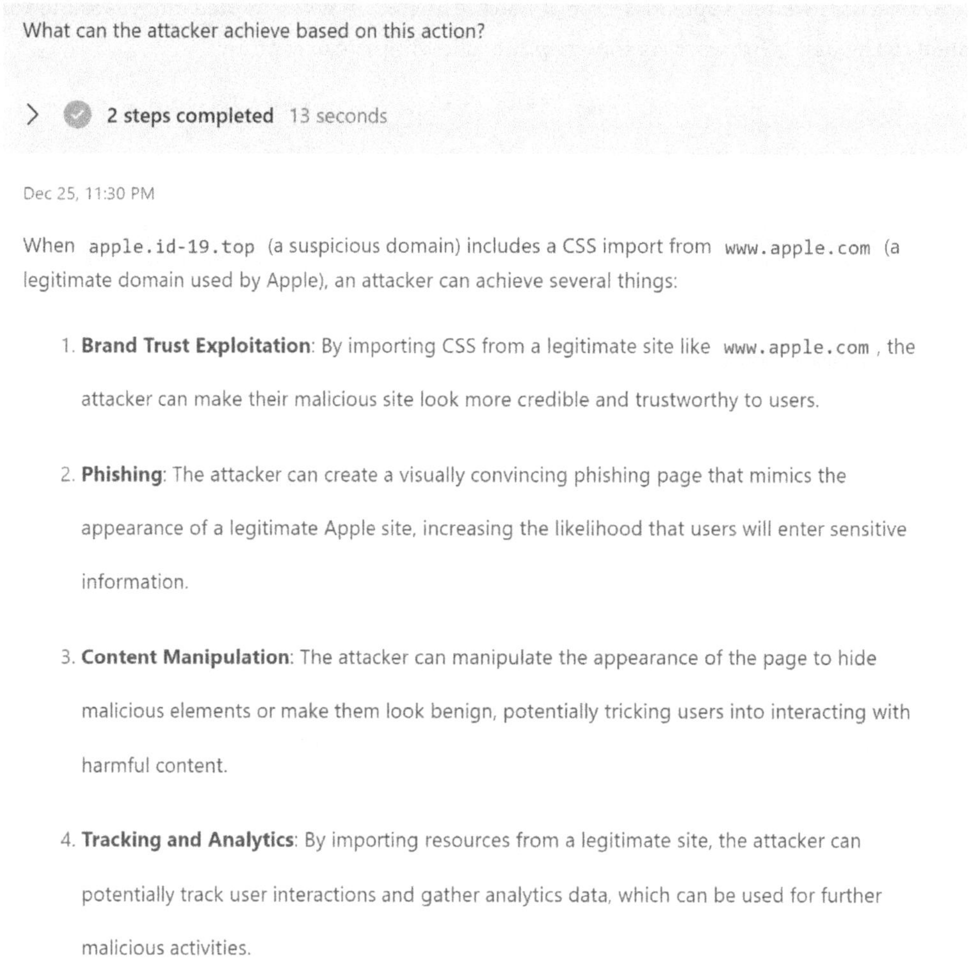

Figure 10.36 – Security implications of the css.import cause

To verify and further understand the role CSS import played in the phishing scenario, you can request that Security Copilot gathers more information about it. As shown in the next screenshot, Security Copilot, using the Microsoft Documentation plugin, explains that **the @import rule in CSS is used to import one stylesheet into another.** Given that CSS is a styling language used in web development to control the presentation and layout of HTML elements, Security Copilot's explanation supports the details in the phishing scenario. The CSS import function enables the attacker to **create a visually convincing phishing page that mimics the appearance of a legitimate Apple site.**

In web development, what function does CSS Import serve?

3 steps completed 9 seconds

Chose Microsoft Documentation 4 seconds

Searched documentation 2 seconds

Prepared your response 3 seconds

Dec 29, 9:21 AM

In web development, the `@import` rule in CSS is used to import one stylesheet into another. This allows developers to modularize their CSS by splitting it into multiple files and then combining them as needed. The `@import` rule must be placed at the top of the CSS file, before any other rules.

For example:

```
@import url("styles2.css");
@import url("styles3.css");

body {
  font-family: Arial, sans-serif;
}
```

In this example, the styles from `styles2.css` and `styles3.css` are imported into the main stylesheet. This can help in organizing and maintaining CSS code, especially in larger projects [1].

Figure 10.37 – Additional details on CSS import

At this stage, the host pair relationship identified by Security Copilot, along with its explanation of different types of connections and their implications, helps to uncover and confirm additional tactics attackers may use in phishing attacks. Each host pair relationship acts as a valuable artifact during the investigation and can be crucial evidence to gather. These artifacts can also be used in future threat-hunting efforts. They can help to identify similar attack patterns and strengthen proactive security measures.

What's great about the MDTI plugin in Security Copilot is that it not only identifies host pair relationships but also provides explanations and their implications. Information about these host pair connections is not always readily available online, but you can always turn to Security Copilot for answers. Think of Copilot as your smart assistant that is equipped with a wealth of cybersecurity knowledge, including insights from MDTI.

You may be wondering if an MDTI license is required to access the threat intelligence resources in Security Copilot. As of January 2025, purchasing a single **Security Compute Unit** (**SCU**) for Security Copilot provides full access to MDTI's threat intelligence features, excluding API access, at no additional cost.

With this in mind, next, let's explore how Security Copilot can benefit the security leadership team. The case studies reviewed so far have been designed for security analysts, illustrating how Security Copilot can assist and support them in their daily tasks. In the next section, we will shift our focus to explore how Security Copilot can deliver value to **Chief Information Security Officers** (**CISOs**).

Empowering CISOs with proactive defense and actionable insights

As cyber threats continue to evolve at an unprecedented pace, CISOs are facing mounting pressure to strengthen their organization's security posture and stay ahead of emerging risks. In the next few sections, let's explore three different case studies, highlighting how Security Copilot can support CISOs in navigating this complex landscape. From offering insights into emerging threats to recommending effective defense strategies and providing visibility into critical incident metrics, Security Copilot empowers CISOs to take proactive steps toward protecting their organization.

Empowering CISOs to tackle emerging threats with proactive defense strategies

New threats are constantly emerging, and staying ahead of them is crucial. Security Copilot helps CISOs do just that by continuously informing them of the most relevant threats to their industry. Furthermore, Security Copilot can provide additional insights into these emerging threats, followed by detailed steps to implement defense measures for them. Additionally, Security Copilot offers a clear, step-by-step plan that serves as a reference for CISOs to effectively execute these defense strategies and protect their organization.

In this case study, as the CISO for an **Independent Software Vendor** (**ISV**) company, you ask Security Copilot to inform you about the latest emerging threats. The following screenshot displays the Security Copilot prompt and illustrates how Copilot responds to your request by providing a list of emerging threats impacting ISVs, including Golden **SAML** (**Security Assertion Markup Language**), Cloud Identity Abuse, and others:

I am a CISO for an ISV company, can you provide a summary of new emerging threats I should be aware of?

> **3 steps completed** 29 seconds

Dec 31, 2024

Emerging Threats Summary

Golden SAML

Golden SAML refers to a technique that allows a threat actor to impersonate and bypass legitimate authentication infrastructure to attain elevated privileges, persistence, and defense evasion. The technique is relevant in specific types of single sign-on (SSO) environments. Active Directory, Active Directory Federated Services (AD FS), and Microsoft Entra ID are popular targets for this technique. When implemented successfully, a threat actor can impersonate any user in a domain while leaving few forensic artifacts that indicate a compromise. Organizations can defend against Golden SAML attacks by hardening credentials, enforcing multifactor authentication, restricting privileged Entra ID roles, and monitoring relevant logs for unusual activity.

- **Exposure Score:** 0
- **Last Updated:** 2024-05-16
- **Alerts Count:** 88 active, 33 resolved
- **Misconfigured Devices:** 0
- **Vulnerable Devices:** 0
- **Impacted Assets:** 0 Devices, 80 Users, 1 Mailbox, 6 Apps, 1 Cloud Resource
- **ID:** bb345237-57e3-4115-9957-87431e6c6a39

Cloud Identity Abuse

With more organizations moving to hybrid or cloud-only models, it is becoming increasingly important to secure both cloud resources as well as cloud identities. Cloud identity compromise was initially thought to be a technique reserved for only a handful of advanced actors in the past such as Midnight Blizzard with the Solar Winds supply chain compromise. However, other tracked actors including Peach Sandstorm, Storm-0219, and Octo Tempest have recently shown sophisticated competency in the cloud across a large variety of industry verticals. By implementing the best practices commonly seen on-premises such as multifactor authentication, disabling legacy authentication, following the principles of least privilege and zero trust, and continuous monitoring for suspicious or malicious usage of an identity, an organization can drastically decrease their attack surface for cloud identity abuse.

Figure 10.38 – Emerging threats impacting ISVs

Note

Due to the evolving threat landscape and different challenges across industries, the results you receive from this prompt are likely to differ.

Next, you ask Security Copilot to summarize the top three new attack techniques from the threats. As shown next, Copilot highlights Golden SAML as the first technique to tackle. Additionally, Security Copilot outlines the defense measures for Golden SAML, which include hardening credentials, enforcing multifactor authentication, restricting privileged Entra ID roles, and monitoring logs for unusual activity:

Can you summarize the top three new attack techniques that I need to focus on?

> 3 steps completed 34 seconds

Dec 31, 2024

Top Three New Attack Techniques to Focus On

1. Golden SAML

- **Description**: Golden SAML is a technique that allows threat actors to impersonate and bypass legitimate authentication infrastructure to gain elevated privileges, persistence, and defense evasion. It targets specific single sign-on (SSO) environments, including Active Directory, AD FS, and Microsoft Entra ID.
- **Impact**: Can impersonate any user in a domain with minimal forensic artifacts.
- **Defense Measures**: Harden credentials, enforce multifactor authentication, restrict privileged Entra ID roles, and monitor logs for unusual activity.
- **Current Status**:
  - **Exposure Score**: 0
  - **Alerts**: 88 active, 33 resolved
  - **Impacted Assets**: 80 Users, 1 Mailbox, 6 Apps, 1 Cloud Resource

Figure 10.39 – Top three new attack techniques

After reviewing Security Copilot's response, you request a breakdown of the steps to implement each defense measure. The following screenshot illustrates the actionable implementation guidelines recommended by Security Copilot for each one:

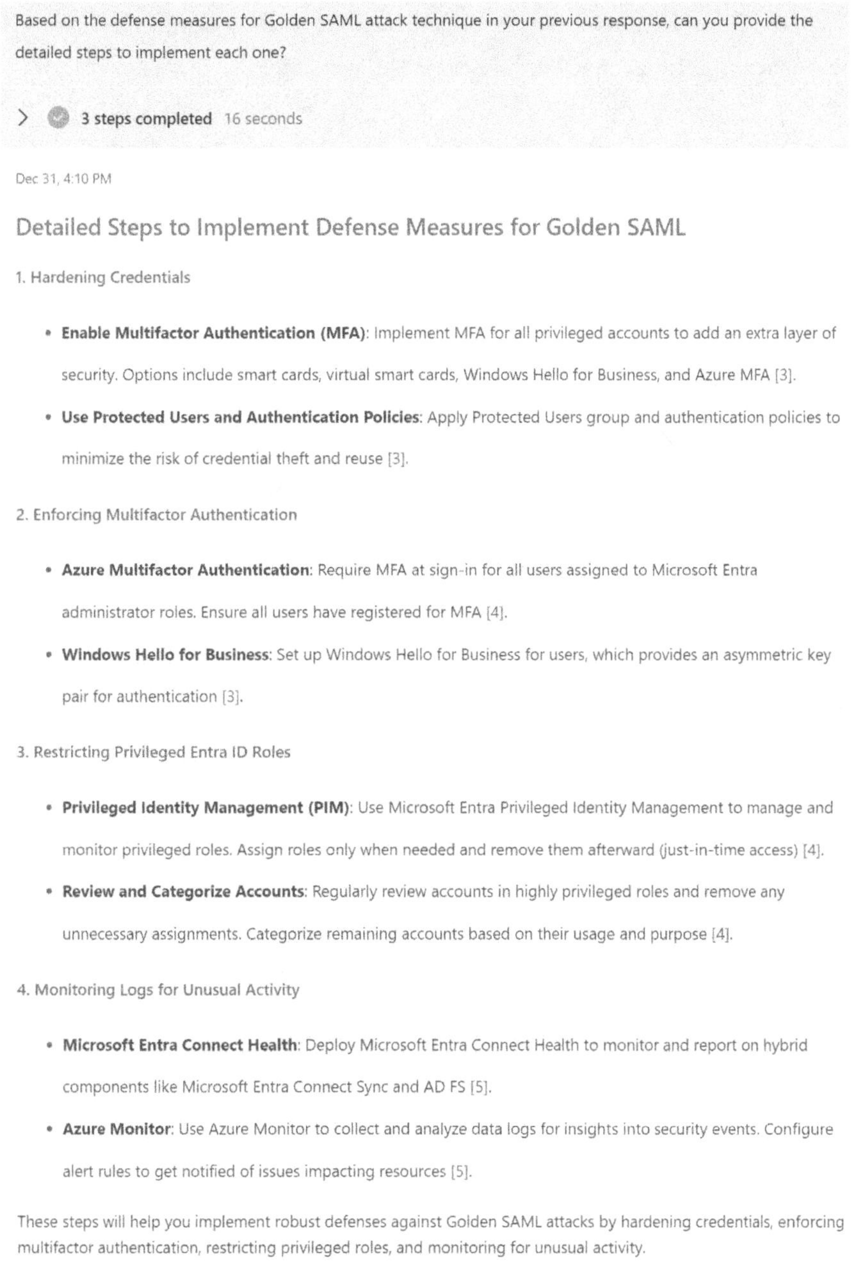

Figure 10.40 – Implementation guidelines recommended by Security Copilot

Optionally, you can ask Security Copilot to suggest additional best practices for implementing security measures. Copilot provides an extensive list of recommendations, with the first few highlighted in the next screenshot:

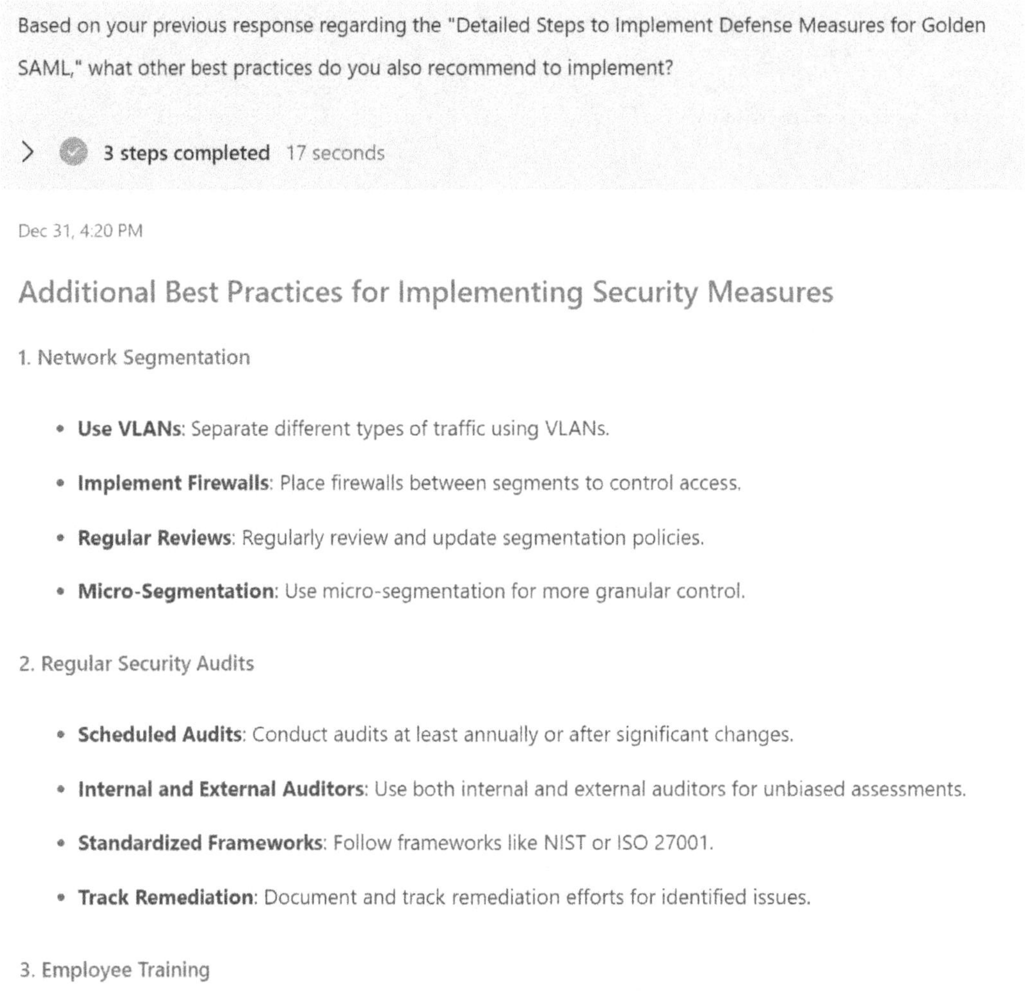

Figure 10.41 – Additional best practices

For your reference, here is the complete list of the additional best practices suggested by Security Copilot:

Additional Best Practices for Implementing Security Measures

1. Network Segmentation

- **Use VLANs:** Separate different types of traffic using VLANs.
- **Implement Firewalls:** Place firewalls between segments to control access.
- **Regular Reviews:** Regularly review and update segmentation policies.
- **Micro-Segmentation:** Use micro-segmentation for more granular control.

2. Regular Security Audits

- **Scheduled Audits:** Conduct audits at least annually or after significant changes.
- **Internal and External Auditors:** Use both internal and external auditors for unbiased assessments.
- **Standardized Frameworks:** Follow frameworks like NIST or ISO 27001.
- **Track Remediation:** Document and track remediation efforts for identified issues.

3. Employee Training

- **Security Awareness Sessions:** Conduct regular security awareness training.
- **Phishing Simulations:** Include phishing simulations to test and educate employees.
- **Role-Specific Training:** Provide training for high-risk positions.
- **Updated Materials:** Keep training materials updated with the latest threat information.

4. Multi-Factor Authentication (MFA)

- **Implement MFA:** Use MFA for all critical systems and applications.
- **Combination of Factors:** Use something you know (password), something you have (token), and something you are (biometrics).
- **Policy Reviews:** Regularly review and update MFA policies.
- **User Education:** Educate users on the importance and use of MFA.

5. Zero Trust Architecture

- **Verify Users and Devices:** Verify all users and devices before granting access.
- **Least Privilege Access:** Implement least privilege access controls.
- **Continuous Monitoring:** Continuously monitor and log all network traffic.
- **Strong Authentication:** Use strong authentication and authorization mechanisms.

6. Cloud Security Posture Management (CSPM)

- **Continuous Monitoring:** Continuously monitor cloud environments for misconfigurations.
- **Automated Tools:** Use automated tools to enforce security policies.
- **Policy Reviews:** Regularly review and update cloud security policies.
- **Compliance:** Ensure compliance with relevant regulations and standards.

7. Endpoint Detection and Response (EDR)

- **Deploy EDR Solutions:** Deploy EDR solutions on all endpoints.
- **Regular Updates:** Regularly update EDR software to protect against new threats.
- **Monitor Alerts:** Monitor EDR alerts and respond promptly to incidents.
- **Threat Hunting:** Conduct regular threat hunting exercises.

8. Identity and Access Management (IAM)

- **Role-Based Access Control (RBAC):** Implement RBAC.
- **Access Reviews:** Regularly review and update user access rights.
- **Single Sign-On (SSO):** Use SSO to simplify access management.
- **Access Logging:** Monitor and log all access activities for auditing purposes.

The list of additional best practices can offer useful information with further insights for you to reference, but it may be a bit long and overwhelming to go through. Instead, you can ask Security Copilot to create a prioritized implementation plan, combining the recommended defense measures and additional best practices. The plan would start with quick wins and progress to more complex tasks, making it easier for you to reference. The Security Copilot prompt and the start of its response are shown next:

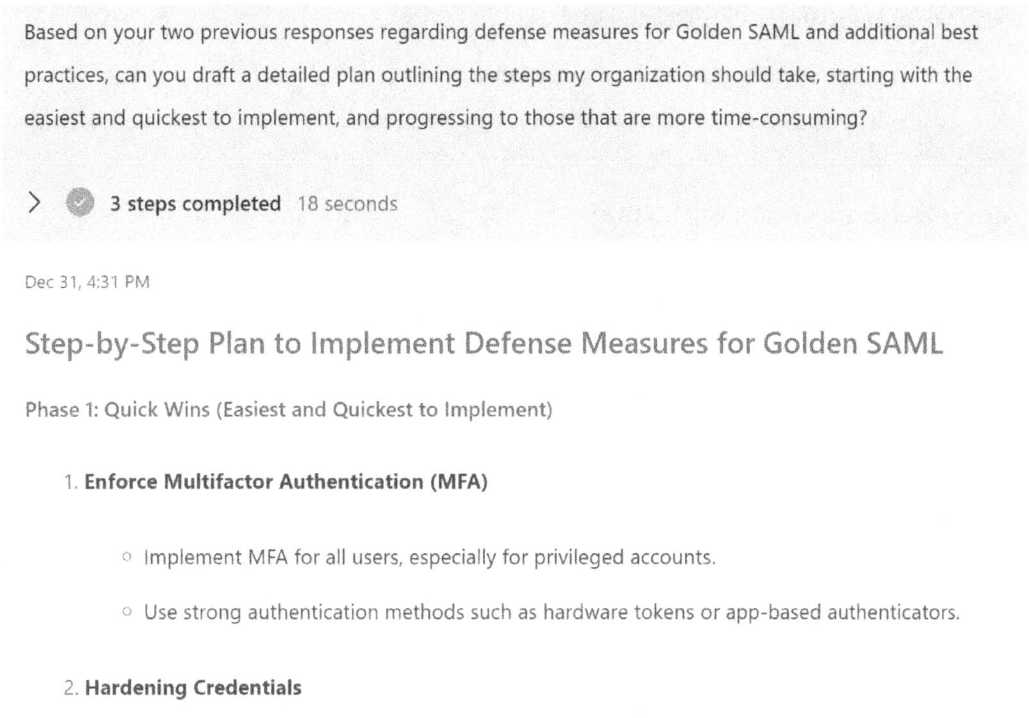

Figure 10.42 – A prioritized implementation plan

The complete prioritized implementation plan generated by Security Copilot is outlined here. The recommendations are divided into three phases, starting with the quick win of enforcing MFA for all users, particularly for privileged accounts:

Step-by-Step Plan to Implement Defense Measures for Golden SAML

Phase 1: Quick Wins (Easiest and Quickest to Implement)

1. **Enforce Multifactor Authentication (MFA)**

- Implement MFA for all users, especially for privileged accounts.
- Use strong authentication methods such as hardware tokens or app-based authenticators.

2. **Hardening Credentials**

- Ensure all passwords meet complexity requirements.
- Implement password expiration policies.
- Disable unused accounts and remove unnecessary privileges.

3. **Restrict Privileged Entra ID Roles**

- Limit the number of users with administrative privileges.
- Use **role-based access control** (**RBAC**) to assign permissions based on the principle of least privilege.

4. **Monitor Logs for Unusual Activity**

- Enable logging for all authentication and authorization events.
- Set up alerts for suspicious activities such as multiple failed login attempts or logins from unusual locations.

Phase 2: Intermediate Measures

5. **Employee Training**

- Conduct regular security awareness training sessions.
- Educate employees on recognizing phishing attempts and other social engineering attacks.

6. **Network Segmentation**

- Segment the network to isolate critical systems and sensitive data.
- Implement firewalls and access controls between segments.

7. **Regular Security Audits**

- Schedule regular security audits and vulnerability assessments.
- Address any identified vulnerabilities promptly.

8. **Identity and Access Management (IAM)**

- Implement a robust IAM solution to manage user identities and access rights.
- Regularly review and update access permissions.

Phase 3: Advanced Measures (More Time-Consuming)

9. **Endpoint Detection and Response (EDR)**

- Deploy EDR solutions to monitor and respond to threats on endpoints.
- Ensure continuous monitoring and incident response capabilities.

10. **Cloud Security Posture Management (CSPM)**

- Implement CSPM tools to continuously monitor and manage cloud security configurations.
- Ensure compliance with security best practices and regulatory requirements.

11. **Zero Trust Architecture**

- Adopt a Zero Trust security model where no entity is trusted by default.
- Implement continuous verification of user and device identities.

12. **Multi-Factor Authentication (MFA) for All Services**

- Extend MFA to all services and applications, not just Entra ID.
- Ensure MFA is enforced for both on-premises and cloud-based services.

Lastly, you can ask Security Copilot to summarize the session and generate a report that reviews all the key points discussed so far. The next screenshot shows the Copilot prompt and part of its response.

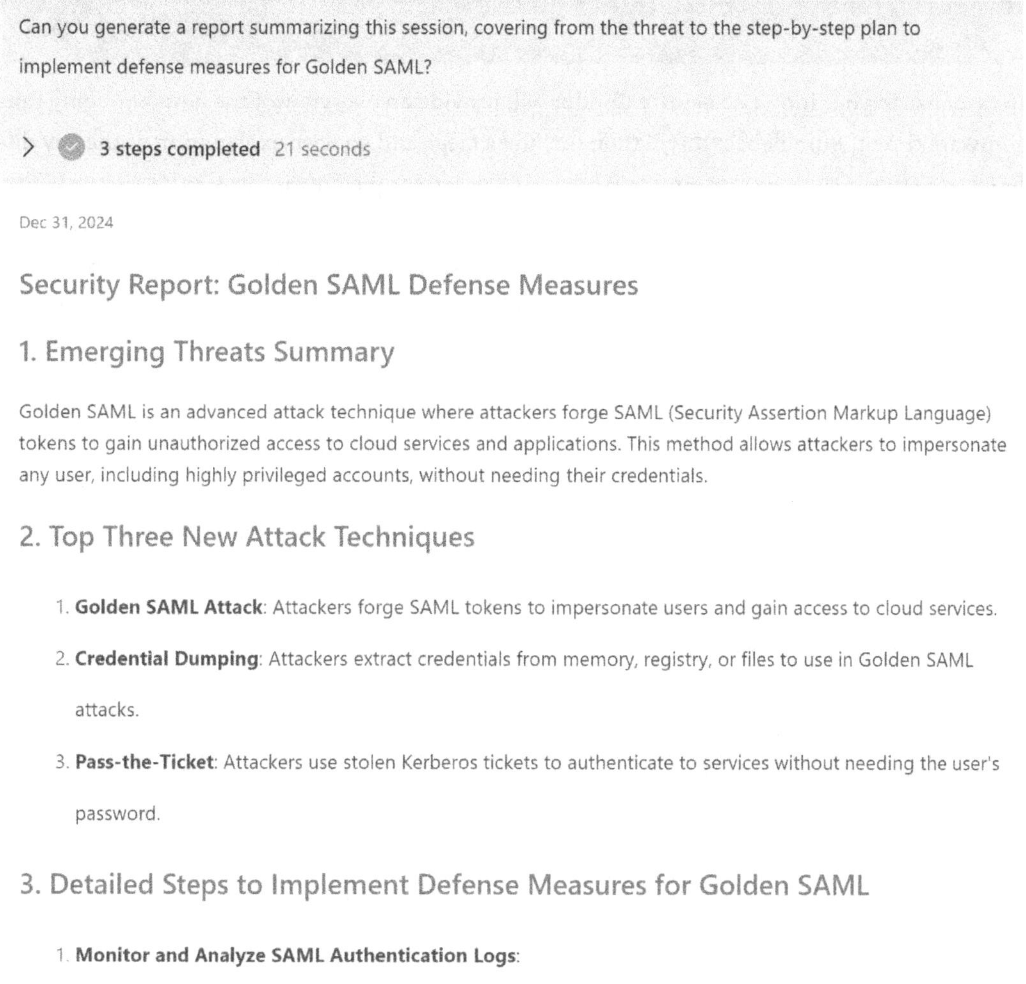

Figure 10.43 – A report to summarize the session

This case study starts with the CISO seeking insights from Security Copilot on emerging threats. However, it's not limited to just emerging threats; you can also inquire about other risks, such as threat actors, vulnerabilities, ransomware, and more. Let's take a quick look at such a use case next.

Insights into emerging ransomware threats

Ransomware continues to be a growing concern for organizations across industries. As cybercriminals become increasingly sophisticated, ransomware attacks remain a top security priority. As a CISO, you can turn to Security Copilot for insights into new and emerging ransomware threats, helping you to stay informed and prepared. For example, you can ask Security Copilot:

```
As a CISO, can you provide a summary of new, emerging ransomware threats
and explain how they differ from previous attacks that I should be aware
of?
```

In response to your inquiry, Security Copilot will provide an overview of the new, emerging ransomware threat, Bumblebee. It will then include a clear and concise explanation of the key differences between the new ransomware threat and previous ransomware attacks. As shown in the next screen capture, Security Copilot highlights that Bumblebee uses **disc images, VHD files, and legitimate file-sharing services like OneDrive and Google APIs to host malicious files** while previous ransomware attacks often **relied on direct email attachments or links to malicious websites** for delivery mechanisms:

Emerging Ransomware Threats: Bumblebee

Overview

The Bumblebee malware, distributed by threat actors such as Storm-0455 and Storm-0249, represents a significant evolution in ransomware tactics. This malware is delivered through spear-phishing emails that trick users into mounting a disc image (.img or .iso) containing a malicious Windows shortcut (.lnk) that launches a DLL. The delivery techniques include HTML smuggling, CVE-2021-40444 exploitation, and URL links in emails.

Key Differences from Previous Ransomware Attacks

1. **Delivery Mechanisms**:
   - **Bumblebee**: Uses disc images, VHD files, and legitimate file-sharing services like OneDrive and Google APIs to host malicious files, evading traditional email security measures.
   - **Previous Ransomware**: Often relied on direct email attachments or links to malicious websites.
2. **Execution Techniques**:
   - **Bumblebee**: Employs living-off-the-land binaries (LOLBin) like ODBCCONF.exe and PowerShell scripts to load the malware DLL, making detection more challenging.
   - **Previous Ransomware**: Typically used more straightforward executable files or scripts.
3. **Persistence and Evasion**:
   - **Bumblebee**: Copies the malware DLL to the ProgramData folder, creates a VBS script for persistence, and uses WMI scripts for system reconnaissance.
   - **Previous Ransomware**: Often relied on registry modifications or scheduled tasks for persistence.

Figure 10.44 – New, emerging ransomware threats

In the same response, but not shown in the previous screenshot, Security Copilot also includes a section on observed MITRE ATT&CK techniques, along with recommendations, detection and hunting queries, and a long list of references.

Optionally, you can ask Security Copilot to provide an action plan for addressing the techniques used in emerging ransomware threats such as Bumblebee. For instance, consider using a prompt such as:

```
Based on your previous response about new delivery mechanisms, execution
techniques, persistence and evasion, etc., what steps can my organization
take to strengthen its defenses and minimize the risk?
```

For your reference, the complete action plan generated by Security Copilot in response to the prompt is included here:

Detailed Steps and Best Practices for Strengthening Defenses Against Ransomware Attacks

Regular Backups

1. **Frequency:** Perform daily incremental backups and weekly full backups.
2. **Storage:** Store backups in multiple locations, including offsite and cloud storage.
3. **Testing:** Regularly test backup restoration processes to ensure data integrity.
4. **Automation:** Use automated backup solutions to reduce human error.
5. **Encryption:** Encrypt backups to protect data from unauthorized access.

Patch Management

1. **Inventory:** Maintain an up-to-date inventory of all software and hardware.
2. **Assessment:** Regularly assess and prioritize patches based on criticality.
3. **Automation:** Use automated patch management tools to deploy updates.
4. **Testing:** Test patches in a controlled environment before deployment.
5. **Schedule:** Establish a regular patching schedule and adhere to it.

Endpoint Protection

1. **Antivirus:** Install and regularly update antivirus software on all endpoints.
2. **EDR:** Implement Endpoint Detection and Response (EDR) solutions.
3. **Configuration:** Configure endpoint protection settings to block suspicious activities.
4. **Updates:** Ensure all endpoint protection tools are regularly updated.
5. **Monitoring:** Continuously monitor endpoints for signs of compromise.

Network Segmentation

1. **Design:** Design the network with separate segments for different functions.
2. **Access** Control: Implement strict access controls between network segments.
3. **Firewalls:** Use firewalls to enforce segmentation policies.
4. **Monitoring:** Monitor traffic between segments for unusual activity.
5. **Review:** Regularly review and update segmentation policies.

Email Security

1. **Filtering:** Implement email filtering solutions to block malicious emails.
2. **Authentication:** Use email authentication protocols like SPF, DKIM, and DMARC.
3. **Awareness:** Train users to recognize phishing and suspicious emails.
4. **Attachments:** Scan email attachments for malware.
5. **Links:** Disable automatic link previews and scan URLs for threats.

User Training and Awareness

1. **Programs:** Develop and implement a comprehensive security awareness program.
2. **Phishing Simulations:** Conduct regular phishing simulations to test user awareness.
3. **Updates:** Provide regular updates on new threats and security practices.
4. **Policies:** Educate users on company security policies and procedures.
5. **Feedback:** Encourage users to report suspicious activities and provide feedback.

Multi-Factor Authentication (MFA)

1. **Implementation:** Implement MFA for all critical systems and applications.
2. **Methods:** Use a combination of authentication methods (e.g., SMS, app-based, hardware tokens).
3. **User Education:** Educate users on the importance and use of MFA.
4. **Enforcement:** Enforce MFA policies across the organization.
5. **Review:** Regularly review and update MFA configurations.

Incident Response Plan

1. **Development:** Develop a detailed incident response plan.
2. **Team:** Establish an incident response team with defined roles and responsibilities.
3. **Training:** Regularly train the incident response team on the plan.
4. **Testing:** Conduct regular incident response drills and simulations.
5. **Review:** Continuously review and update the incident response plan.

Network Monitoring and Logging

1. **Tools:** Implement network monitoring and logging tools.
2. **Logs:** Collect and store logs from all critical systems and devices.
3. **Analysis:** Regularly analyze logs for signs of suspicious activity.
4. **Alerts:** Set up alerts for unusual or unauthorized activities.
5. **Retention:** Maintain log retention policies in compliance with regulations.

Access Controls

1. **Principle of Least Privilege:** Grant users the minimum access necessary for their roles.
2. **Role-Based Access Control (RBAC):** Implement RBAC to manage permissions.
3. **Review:** Regularly review and update access controls.
4. **Authentication:** Use strong authentication methods for access control.
5. **Monitoring:** Monitor access logs for unauthorized access attempts.

Application Whitelisting

1. **Policy:** Develop an application whitelisting policy.
2. **Tools:** Use application whitelisting tools to enforce the policy.
3. **Inventory:** Maintain an inventory of approved applications.
4. **Updates:** Regularly update the whitelist to include new approved applications.
5. **Monitoring:** Monitor for attempts to run unapproved applications.

Threat Intelligence

1. **Sources:** Subscribe to reputable threat intelligence sources.
2. **Integration:** Integrate threat intelligence into security tools and processes.
3. **Analysis:** Regularly analyze threat intelligence data for relevant threats.
4. **Sharing:** Share threat intelligence with relevant stakeholders.
5. **Response:** Use threat intelligence to inform incident response and mitigation efforts.

Vulnerability Management

1. **Scanning:** Regularly scan systems and applications for vulnerabilities.
2. **Assessment:** Prioritize vulnerabilities based on risk and impact.
3. **Remediation:** Develop and implement a remediation plan for identified vulnerabilities.
4. **Verification:** Verify that vulnerabilities have been successfully remediated.
5. **Reporting:** Maintain detailed records of vulnerability management activities.

Secure Configuration

1. **Baseline:** Establish secure configuration baselines for all systems and devices.
2. **Guidelines:** Follow industry best practices and guidelines for secure configuration.
3. **Automation:** Use automated tools to enforce secure configurations.
4. **Review:** Regularly review and update configuration settings.
5. **Monitoring:** Monitor configurations for unauthorized changes.

Data Encryption

1. **Encryption:** Encrypt sensitive data at rest and in transit.
2. **Keys:** Use strong encryption keys and manage them securely.
3. **Protocols:** Use secure encryption protocols (e.g., TLS, AES).
4. **Compliance:** Ensure encryption practices comply with relevant regulations.
5. **Review:** Regularly review and update encryption practices and policies.

Reading through the action plan, it's impressive to see the wealth of information Security Copilot can provide based on the scenario. Furthermore, as a CISO, you can always follow up with additional prompts to dive deeper into specific topics mentioned in the response. For now, let's shift gears and explore one more case study in the next section to uncover other ways Security Copilot can support CISOs.

Enabling CISOs with actionable incident insights

In today's rapidly evolving threat landscape, managing incidents effectively helps to maintain a strong security posture. Security Copilot provides CISOs with visibility into incidents detected over a specific period, covering key metrics such as the total number of incidents, the number of active and resolved incidents, incident severity levels, resolution statuses, and response times. These insights ensure efficient resource allocation and provide a clear picture of the overall performance of security operations. They also help CISOs to fine-tune incident response strategies and enhance overall security workflows.

There are various Security Copilot prompts that retrieve different incident metrics. For instance, the prompt shown in the following screenshot reports the total number of Defender incidents from the past 7 days, with the results organized by severity, incident name, status, and creation date in descending order:

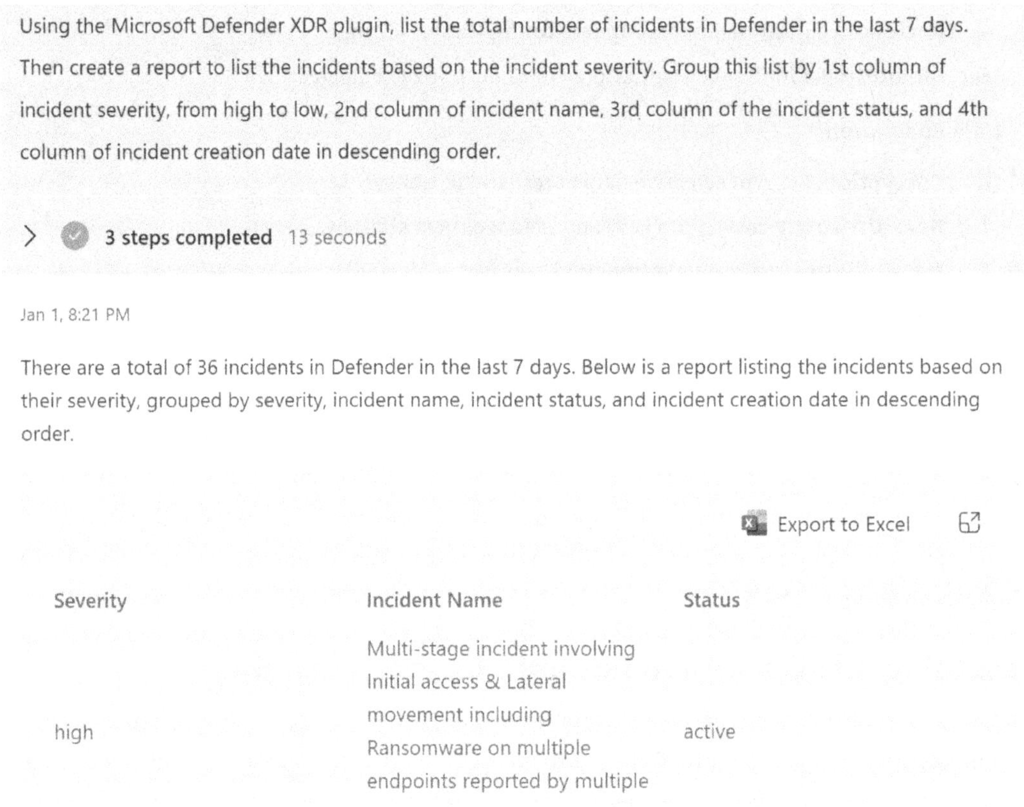

Figure 10.45 – Defender incidents from the past 7 days

Selecting the icon next to **Export to Excel** opens the full, detailed Security Copilot response. A portion of this output is displayed next:

Severity	Incident Name	Status	Creation Date
high	Multi-stage incident involving Initial access & Lateral movement including Ransomware on multiple endpoints reported by multiple sources	active	2024-12-06T12:30:08.633:
high	A potentially malicious URL click was detected	active	2025-01-01T17:28:27.81Z
high	DLP policy (U.S. Financial Data) matched for email with subject (Document) involving one user	active	2025-01-01T17:03:47.83Z
high	A potentially malicious URL click was detected	active	2025-01-01T10:37:27.736€
medium	Multi-stage incident involving Defense evasion & Discovery on one endpoint	active	2024-12-17T13:58:16.843:

Figure 10.46 – The detailed, expanded Security Copilot response

> Note
>
> With ongoing updates to Security Copilot, by the time you test this or a similar prompt, it may return only the top 10 incidents due to potential volume constraints. For example, you might see a message such as **There are a total of 300 incidents available. The table above shows the top 10 incidents based on severity from high to low.**

The next prompt lists the number of active Defender incidents in the last 7 days, as shown in the following screen capture:

Using the Microsoft Defender XDR plugin, list number of Defender incidents with active status in the last 7 days.

> **3 steps completed** 12 seconds

There are a total of 27 active incidents in Defender in the last 7 days. Below is a report listing some of these incidents based on their severity, grouped by severity, incident name, incident status, and incident creation date in descending order.

Severity	Incident Name	Status
high	Multi-stage incident involving Initial access & Lateral movement including Ransomware on multiple endpoints reported by multiple	active

Figure 10.47 – Number of active Defender incidents in the last 7 days

Other similar prompts could be as follows:

```
Using the Microsoft Defender XDR plugin, list number of Defender incidents
with resolved status in the last 7 days
```

This could also be a prompt:

```
Using the Microsoft Defender XDR plugin, list number of Defender incidents
with inProgress status in the last 7 days
```

Security Copilot can analyze time-based data, such as timestamps, and perform calculations. In this case, you can request that Copilot determines how long each incident has been active using the prompt shown in the next screen capture:

Using the Microsoft Defender XDR plugin, can you provide a list of active Defender incidents from the last 7 days and indicate how long each has been active? Please sort the results by duration, from longest to shortest.

Figure 10.48 – The Security Copilot prompt

Security Copilot calculates the duration of each active incident by comparing the incident's start time to the current time, then reports this information in the **Duration** column. This is illustrated next:

Incident Name	Status	Creation Date	Duration (days)
Multi-stage incident involving Initial access & Lateral movement including Ransomware on multiple endpoints reported by multiple sources	active	2024-12-06T12:30:08.6333333Z	26
Multi-stage incident involving Defense evasion & Discovery on one endpoint	active	2024-12-17T13:58:16.8433333Z	15
Multi-stage incident involving Execution & Discovery on one endpoint	active	2024-12-16T14:41:55.79Z	16
DLP policy (Audit emailing sensitive information externally) matched for email with subject (Lee do you still would like to work with us?)	active	2025-01-01T21:30:44.79Z	1
A potentially malicious URL click was detected	active	2025-01-01T17:28:27.81Z	1
DLP policy (U.S. Financial Data) matched for email with subject (Document) involving one user	active	2025-01-01T17:03:47.83Z	1

Figure 10.49 – Duration of each active incident

Similarly, Security Copilot can report the time it takes to resolve each incident. The prompt is displayed next:

> Using the Microsoft Defender XDR plugin, can you provide a list of resolved Defender incidents from the last 7 days and indicate the average time to resolve each one? Please sort the results by resolution duration, from longest to shortest.

Figure 10.50 – The Security Copilot prompt

The following screenshot shows the Security Copilot response, which includes a **Resolution Duration (days)** column:

Incident Name	Status	Creation Date	Resolution Duratic
Hands-on keyboard attack was launched from a compromised account (attack disruption)	resolved	2024-10-25T17:11:20.9133333Z	67
Unfamiliar sign-in properties involving one user	resolved	2024-12-31T08:33:52.4366667Z	0.3
Unfamiliar sign-in properties involving one user	resolved	2024-12-31T08:34:51.14Z	0.1
Unfamiliar sign-in properties involving one user	resolved	2024-12-31T08:32:41.8233333Z	0.1
Automated investigation started manually on one endpoint	resolved	2024-12-30T16:15:04.37Z	0.1

Figure 10.51 – Defender incident resolution duration (days)

Rather than running these prompts one by one each time, you can group them into a promptbook, allowing you to gather incident metrics with just a few clicks. The following screenshot demonstrates a promptbook that includes the previously discussed prompts.

Plus, there is one additional prompt at the end of this promptbook, asking Security Copilot to consolidate all the incident statistics into a concise report:

Plugins required

Microsoft Defender XDR

Prompts

1	Using the Microsoft Defender XDR plugin, list the total number of incidents in Defender in the last <NumberOfDay> days. Then create a report to list the incidents based on the incident severity. Group this list by 1st column of incident severity, from high to low, 2nd column of incident name, 3rd column of the incident status, and 4th column of incident creation date in descending order.
2	Using the Microsoft Defender XDR plugin, list number of Defender incidents with active status in the last <NumberOfDay> days.
3	Using the Microsoft Defender XDR plugin, list number of Defender incidents with resolved status in the last <NumberOfDay> days.
4	Using the Microsoft Defender XDR plugin, list number of Defender incidents with inProgress status in the last <NumberOfDay> days.
5	Using the Microsoft Defender XDR plugin, can you provide a list of active Defender incidents from the last <NumberOfDay> days and indicate how long each has been active? Please sort the results by duration, from longest to shortest.
6	Using the Microsoft Defender XDR plugin, can you provide a list of resolved Defender incidents from the last <NumberOfDay> days and indicate the average time to resolve each one? Please sort the results by resolution duration, from longest to shortest.
7	Based on all your previous response about various incident stats, can you summarize them into a concise report?

Figure 10.52 – The Security Copilot promptbook

Another benefit of converting prompts into a promptbook is the ability to easily adjust the time period for gathering various incident metrics. As demonstrated in the next screen capture, you first start the promptbook by clicking the **Run** button next to it in the promptbook library:

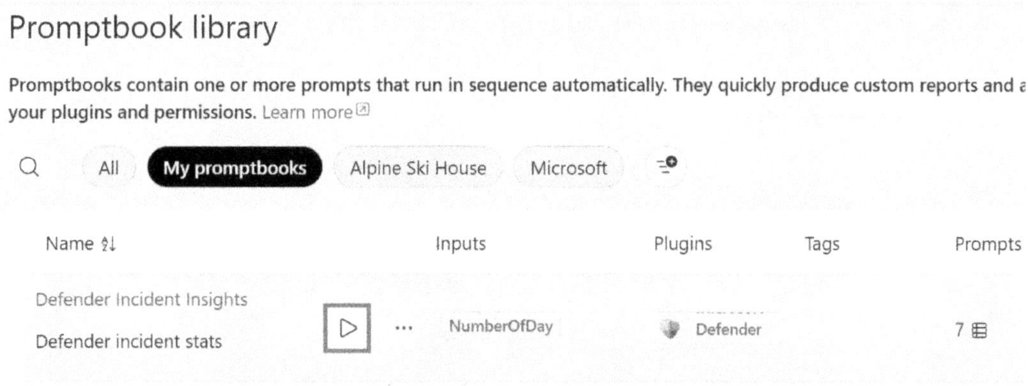

Figure 10.53 – Click the Run button to start a promptbook

This opens the promptbook in a new Copilot session, where you can enter the number of days for which you want to pull incident data. In this example, 7 is entered to gather incident data from the past 7 days:

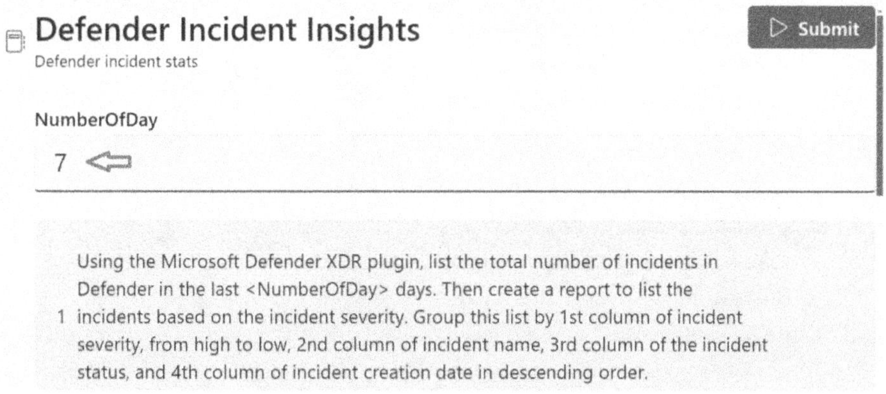

Figure 10.54 – The promptbook input

Once this promptbook executes, you can review the incident metric data, especially the report generated by the final prompt. A screenshot of the summary report for this promptbook is provided next for reference:

Summary Report of Defender Incidents in the Last 7 Days

Total Incidents

- **Total number of incidents:** 36

Active Incidents

- **Total number of active incidents:** 27
- **Duration of active incidents:** Sorted from longest to shortest
    - Multi-stage incident involving Initial access & Lateral movement including Ransomware on multiple endpoints reported by multiple sources (26 days)
    - Multi-stage incident involving Defense evasion & Discovery on one endpoint (15 days)
    - Multi-stage incident involving Execution & Discovery on one endpoint (16 days)
    - DLP policy (Audit emailing sensitive information externally) matched for email with subject (Lee do you still would like to work with us?) (1 day)
    - A potentially malicious URL click was detected (1 day)
    - DLP policy (U.S. Financial Data) matched for email with subject (Document) involving one user (1 day)
    - DLP policy (Audit emailing sensitive information externally) matched for email with subject (New design spec Process | SpecDis-625) (1 day)
    - Email messages containing malicious URL removed after delivery involving one user (1 day)
    - A potentially malicious URL click was detected (1 day)
    - User accessed a link in an email subsequently quarantined by ZAP involving one user (1 day)

Resolved Incidents

- **Total number of resolved incidents:** 8
- **Average time to resolve incidents:** Sorted from longest to shortest
    - Hands-on keyboard attack was launched from a compromised account (attack disruption) (67 days)
    - Unfamiliar sign-in properties involving one user (0.3 days)
    - Unfamiliar sign-in properties involving one user (0.1 days)
    - Unfamiliar sign-in properties involving one user (0.1 days)
    - Automated investigation started manually on one endpoint (0.1 days)
    - Automated investigation started manually on one endpoint (0.1 days)
    - Automated investigation started manually on one endpoint (0.1 days)
    - Administrative action submitted by an Administrator (0.1 days)

InProgress Incidents

- **Total number of inProgress incidents:** 1
    - An active 'Malgent' malware in a PowerShell script was prevented from executing via AMSI on one endpoint (duration not specified)

Figure 10.55 – Summary report for Defender incidents

This promptbook enables seamless gathering of incident insights and metrics with just a few clicks. It is not only fast but also minimizes manual effort. For a CISO, this means quicker access to actionable insights, allowing for more informed decision-making and a more efficient approach to security management.

Summary

This chapter covered strategies for strengthening security operations through the MDTI plugin in Security Copilot. It dived into case studies such as transforming threat intelligence into proactive detection, optimizing threat validation, tracking threat actor infrastructures, and uncovering hidden connections. The chapter showcased how Security Copilot provides enhanced visibility and strategic insights. Furthermore, Security Copilot was introduced as a tool that empowers CISOs in tackling emerging threats with proactive defense strategies. It demonstrated how CISOs can utilize Security Copilot to gather actionable incident insights that support informed decision-making to strengthen security posture.

The case studies presented in this and earlier chapters provide a strong foundation for understanding how to leverage Security Copilot across diverse scenarios. Naturally, the next question arises: "*This all sounds great, but how much does it cost to run Security Copilot?*" The next chapter answers this by exploring the Security Copilot pricing model in depth. It introduces the pivotal role of **Security Compute Units (SCUs)** within the ecosystem and breaks down the SCU pricing structure. The chapter also addresses the challenges of forecasting costs amid unpredictable workloads and offers practical strategies for optimizing SCU usage—covering forecasting, cost control, and scalable deployment.

11

The Pricing Model in Security Copilot

Over the past three chapters, we went through practical case studies that offered a deeper understanding of Security Copilot's real-world applications. Now, let's shift focus to another key aspect of Security Copilot: its pricing model. At the heart of Security Copilot's cost structure lies the **security compute unit (SCU)**. The SCU represents the computational resources needed to carry out tasks within Security Copilot, and understanding how it functions is essential for both cost efficiency and optimal performance.

In this chapter, we will explore the integral role of SCUs within the Security Copilot ecosystem. We will break down the pricing structure associated with SCUs and offer a detailed look at its consumption-based cost model. Since the unpredictability of workloads can introduce uncertainty into Security Copilot's cost planning and budgeting, we'll share practical strategies to address these challenges and optimize costs, including improving forecasting, leveraging overage options, and scaling SCUs efficiently.

To guide you through these topics, this chapter is structured into four key sections:

- The role of the SCU
- Understanding the Security Copilot pricing model
- A guide for practitioners in monitoring and managing SCUs
- Maximizing value and efficiency in SCU usage

The role of the SCU

Security Copilot relies on computing power to execute tasks, and the SCU is the unit used to measure and allocate this power. You can think of SCUs like tokens at an arcade. You purchase a bundle in advance. Just like how each game you play costs a certain number of tokens, each Security Copilot prompt you run consumes a certain number of SCUs. In essence, SCUs offer a trackable and scalable way to manage the computing capacity that powers Security Copilot's operations.

The number of SCUs consumed for each Security Copilot task varies based on the complexity of the operation. More complex tasks, such as script analysis, tend to use more SCUs compared to simpler actions such as incident summarization. You can track the overall SCU usage, as well as how many SCUs are used for specific prompts, promptbooks, and more, through the SCU **Usage monitoring** dashboard within Security Copilot. For reference, a portion of this dashboard is shown next, where the **Units used** column reflects the number of SCUs used for each prompt, promptbook, and other activities:

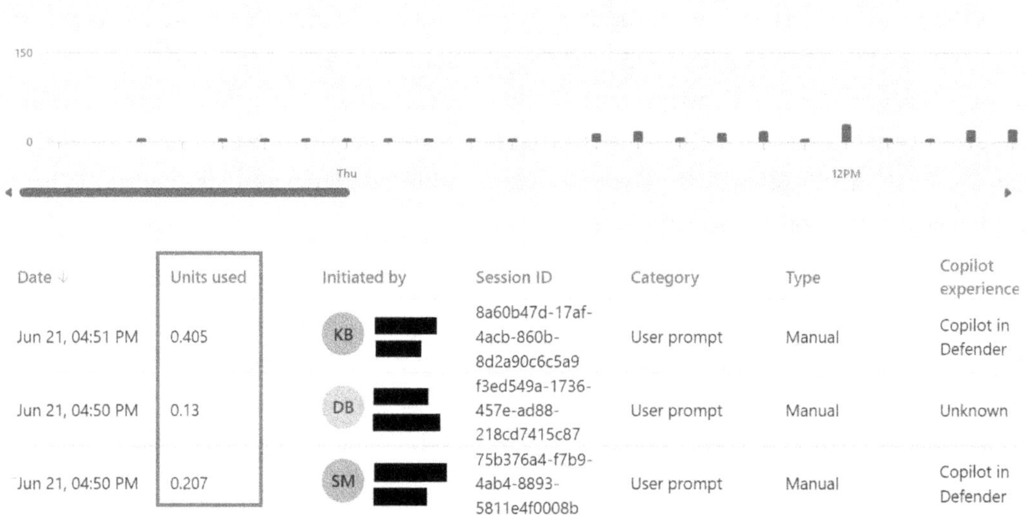

Figure 11.1 – A section of the SCU Usage monitoring dashboard

The Security Copilot pricing model is also based on SCUs. Unlike other Microsoft licenses, which are priced per user or per device, Security Copilot is offered as a provisioned service where you purchase the necessary SCUs based on your expected usage. The provisioning process starts with you estimating the number of SCUs you need to perform tasks in Security Copilot. After you purchase the necessary SCUs, they are allocated, and the Security Copilot service is then ready for you to use.

Those allocated SCUs will power the security tasks you carry out. At the same time, your billing is tied to the number of SCUs you've provisioned each hour, regardless of the number of SCUs you actually consume. Let's say you've provisioned 5 SCUs for a given hour. You run a prompt that consumes 1.5 SCUs, then later in that same hour, you run a second prompt that uses 1 SCU. Although your total usage is 2.5 SCUs, you're still billed for the full 5 SCUs you've allocated for that hour. For your reference, the following table offers a visual breakdown of the scenario:

Task performed	SCUs consumed
1st prompt	1.5 SCUs
2nd prompt	1 SCU
Total SCU consumption	2.5 SCUs
Total billing	5 SCUs

As SCUs are provisioned and billed on a per-hour basis, the number of SCUs allocated can vary from hour to hour. This enables you to adjust SCU provisioning to match workload demands. You can scale up to accommodate periods of high demand or scale down the number of SCUs during times of low usage. By doing so, you avoid overprovisioning during low-usage periods while ensuring enough capacity is available when demand is high. As a result, SCU provisioning also plays a key role in managing costs effectively. More details on this cost-optimization approach will be covered in the next section, *Understanding the Security Copilot pricing model.*

Furthermore, insights into past SCU consumption can help you uncover trends in how your organization has utilized Security Copilot over time. This data often offers valuable context when you are planning for future SCU provisioning. Additionally, by providing visibility into the SCUs consumed for each task, Security Copilot enables you to pinpoint inefficiencies and identify opportunities to optimize your Security Copilot tasks. We will discuss this in detail in the upcoming section, *A guide for practitioners in monitoring and managing SCUs.*

Ultimately, SCUs are designed to offer transparency into how Security Copilot is billed and scaled. Security Copilot is powered by advanced AI models and cloud-scale infrastructure. By tying usage to SCUs rather than users or seats, the Security Copilot costs are based on the estimated workload. You're not paying for access to the tool itself, but rather the estimated compute power it consumes, measured in SCUs. This model allows you to tailor your provisioning to meet your security needs while Microsoft manages the compute-intensive workloads in the background. However, this model can also introduce confusion and uncertainty. Estimating workload in advance can be challenging, especially when the volume of incoming security incidents is unpredictable.

Throughout this chapter, we will discuss strategies to address this uncertainty, such as improving workload predictions, using overage as a safety net for unexpected spikes, and scaling SCUs effectively to meet changing demands.

> Note
>
> SCUs can be provisioned through either the Security Copilot standalone portal or the Azure portal. Currently, SCUs are available for purchase in four regions (US East, UK South, West Europe, and Australia East), with additional regions to be added in the future.

In essence, SCUs play a key role in improving planning, budgeting, and optimizing Security Copilot resource management. Understanding how SCUs work is crucial because they directly impact the performance, cost, and scalability of your Security Copilot usage. In the following sections, let's explore these topics in greater detail.

Understanding the Security Copilot pricing model

Previously, we discussed how Security Copilot is offered as a provisioned service. Its cost is determined by the number of SCUs you allocate, which is charged at a fixed rate of **$4 per SCU per hour**. You're billed based on the number of SCUs you commit to, regardless of how many SCUs you actually consume.

During periods of increased demand, such as a major cyberattack or an unexpected surge in activity, your team might require more SCUs than initially reserved. To accommodate these scenarios, you have the option to configure a specific number of overage SCUs to cover the unexpected usage spike and to ensure Security Copilot continues to run without interruption. Overage SCUs are priced at a higher rate of **$6 per SCU per hour**, but you're only charged based on the actual usage, down to one decimal place (e.g., 0.5 SCUs). This pay-as-you-go approach helps to guarantee service availability when it's needed.

Therefore, Security Copilot's overall pricing model consists of a base cost tied to the provisioned capacity and an overage charge for extra usage exceeding the reserved capacity. Since security teams typically work within a defined budget, it's important for many to understand and plan for the costs associated with Security Copilot upfront. To support that planning, let's walk through how to estimate Security Copilot usage and costs, starting with the base cost, followed by how overage charges are applied when usage exceeds the provisioned capacity.

Understanding base cost

Under Security Copilot's provisioned capacity model, you're billed at a fixed rate of $4 per SCU per hour based on the number of SCUs you purchase in advance. This pricing applies to both the standalone and the embedded experiences across all geographies. In order to utilize Security Copilot, you must provision a minimum of 1 SCU per hour, and you have the option to scale up to 100 SCUs per hour to meet changing business needs.

To calculate the Security Copilot cost each month based on the number of SCUs provisioned, you can refer to the following Security Copilot cost estimation formula:

# SCUs/hour	x	$4 SCU hourly price	x	730 hours/month

With each SCU priced at $4 per hour, and an average of 730 hours per month, Security Copilot's monthly cost based on 1 SCU is calculated as shown next:

1 x 4 x 730 = $2,920

Note that this monthly bill estimate is for 1 SCU provisioned for 24 hours daily for the entire month.

Based on the same pricing formula, the minimum annual cost for Security Copilot with 1 SCU provisioned year-round would be approximately $35,040.

Microsoft recommends starting with 3 SCUs per hour for an introductory exploration of Security Copilot. With 3 SCUs provisioned per hour for 24 hours a day, 365 days a year, the estimated cost is $8,760 per month, or $105,120 annually.

SCUs are provisioned on a per-hour basis. This allows for hourly adjustments to SCUs at any time. Let's say in the Security Copilot portal, you set your allocation to 10 SCUs. From that moment on, you're charged for 10 SCUs each hour until you update the allocation again, say down to 3 SCUs. At that point, billing adjusts to 3 SCUs per hour. This flexibility allows you to scale SCUs up during periods of high demand and scale down when usage is lower, helping you manage costs more effectively based on actual needs. For instance, you might start with 1 SCU, increase to 5 SCUs for a 5-hour high-demand period, then scale back to 1 SCU afterward. Keep in mind that billing is based on the allocated amount, not actual usage. So, even if you only use 1 SCU in an hour with 3 allocated, you'll still be billed for all 3.

As an example, assume your security teams work from 8 a.m. to 5 p.m., Monday to Friday. During these hours, you allocate 3 SCUs per hour for analysts to run Security Copilot tasks. Outside of regular working hours, from 5 p.m. to 8 a.m. on weekdays, as well as all day on Saturdays and Sundays, you reduce the allocation to just 1 SCU.

As mentioned earlier, with 3 SCUs per hour for 24 hours a day, your monthly bill is $8,760. However, with 3 SCUs per hour from 8 a.m. to 5 p.m., Monday to Friday, and 1 SCU for the off-hours, including weekends, your monthly Security Copilot bill is reduced to $4,464, almost half of the cost compared to before. The calculation for the reduced bill is shown next:

- **Weekday peak hours**:

  3 SCUs/hour x $4 SCU hourly price x 9 hours a day x 22 weekdays = $2,376

- **Weekday off-hours**:

  1 SCU/hour x $4 SCU hourly price x 15 hours a day x 22 weekdays = $1,320

- **Weekend hours**:

  1 SCU/hour x $4 SCU hourly price x 24 hours a day x 8 weekend days = $768

- **Total monthly bill**:

  $2,376 + $1,320 + $768 = $4,464

Note

By taking advantage of the fact that SCUs are provisioned on an hourly basis and by setting the number of SCUs to the minimum of 1 during periods of low Security Copilot usage, you can significantly lower your Security Copilot cost.

This approach may not be practical for all SOC operating models, particularly those with 24/7 operations, which may have limited flexibility to scale SCUs down during off-hours. This also means that having visibility into when your security teams are actively using Security Copilot, understanding the typical SCU consumption at different times of day, and identifying periods of inactivity are essential. It enables you to more accurately adjust SCU provisioning to reduce cost.

At the same time, tracking SCU consumption can be challenging. It is not straightforward to map SCU consumption directly to the number of tasks performed in Security Copilot. The prompts you submit vary in complexity, scripts to be analyzed differ in length, and promptbooks come in various sizes. Each of these factors influences how many SCUs are consumed, making it difficult to draw a one-to-one correlation between SCU usage and the number of tasks executed. Also, keep in mind that the total SCUs consumed each hour depend on the overall number of prompts submitted by various members of the security teams, regardless of whether those prompts use Microsoft or third-party plugins.

The good news is that Security Copilot provides several options for monitoring SCU usage and tracking consumption. You can leverage these solutions to understand your Security Copilot usage patterns. Over time, this can help you establish the SCU consumption baseline. As an example, an organization new to Security Copilot can try it out in a pilot program over a period of time. This allows the organization to assess its typical usage scenarios and to better understand its SCU demands. This, in turn, helps them develop a more accurate forecast for SCU provisioning. We will dive into these solutions in greater detail in the next section.

In the meantime, if you're just getting started with Security Copilot, it's recommended to begin with 3 to 5 SCUs, depending on your requirements and the number of analysts using Security Copilot. In general, you would want to provision around 1 SCU per hour for the embedded experience and approximately 3 SCUs per hour for the standalone experience. If you have promptbooks and logic apps in place, plan for an additional 3 to 5 SCUs.

Understanding overage charges

Rather than overprovisioning SCUs from the start as a precaution, consider starting with a modest SCU number. You can then monitor the SCU consumption patterns closely and scale up as necessary. In the meantime, overage SCUs can provide flexibility to handle unexpected workload spikes, giving you the opportunity to adjust your SCU allocation later on. For teams that are new to Security Copilot or still learning their usage patterns, this approach offers a safe buffer that allows you to start small and scale based on real needs.

Here is an example illustrating how overage can help to prevent overprovisioning of SCUs, keeping costs down while still meeting operational needs. Assume you have provisioned 3 SCUs per hour for a 5-hour period. During that time, your SCU consumption spikes to 5.1 SCUs after running a promptbook. This results in an additional 2.1 SCUs consumed through overage in that specific hour. The total Security Copilot cost for the 5 hours increases from $60 (*3 provisioned SCUs × $4 × 5 hours*) to $72.60, after factoring in the overage charge (*2.1 overage SCUs × $6*).

In comparison, if you had provisioned 6 SCUs for each hour within the same 5-hour period, without any overage to cover the same promptbook execution, the cost would have been $120 (*6 SCUs × $4 × 5 hours*). In this case, using overage while keeping your baseline at 3 SCUs reduces the total cost from $120 to $72.60. This example illustrates how overage SCUs can offer a more cost-effective alternative to overprovisioning.

However, since overage charges are based on actual consumption, its cost advantage decreases as the frequency of SCU usage spikes. If the same promptbook that consumes 5.1 SCUs runs every hour over the 5-hour period and you've only provisioned 3 SCUs, your total cost would increase to $123 (*3 provisioned SCUs × $4 × 5 hours + 2.1 overage SCUs × $6 × 5*). In this case, using overage ends up being more expensive than simply provisioning 6 SCUs upfront for the same duration, which would cost $120. Therefore, while overage SCUs offer flexibility and cost savings in scenarios with occasional usage spikes, they may become more expensive than baseline provisioning if high-consumption workloads occur consistently. This is where you would again fine-tune your baseline SCUs and overage limits to align with observed usage patterns.

When configuring overage for Security Copilot, it's recommended to start with a conservative limit, typically around 50% to 100% of your provisioned SCUs. Regularly monitoring usage, ideally on a weekly basis, can help you to identify peak patterns. As your team's workload stabilizes or grows, you can adjust the overage cap to better align with your operational needs. Furthermore, during your pilot or learning phase, you might consider setting overage to unlimited to get a sense of your maximum usage and determine what overage limits you may need. However, keep in mind that this setting can lead to unexpectedly high costs during periods of sustained high usage.

As shown in the next screen capture, you can activate overage SCU by toggling the **Use overage units when needed** option to *on* in the same area where you provision SCUs in the Security Copilot standalone experience. From there, you can adjust your overage limit as needed.

Note

Since overage charges are based on actual usage, you will not be billed for any overage SCUs that are allocated but remain unused. Another point to keep in mind is that if you do not enable overage, throttling will occur once you exceed your provisioned limit.

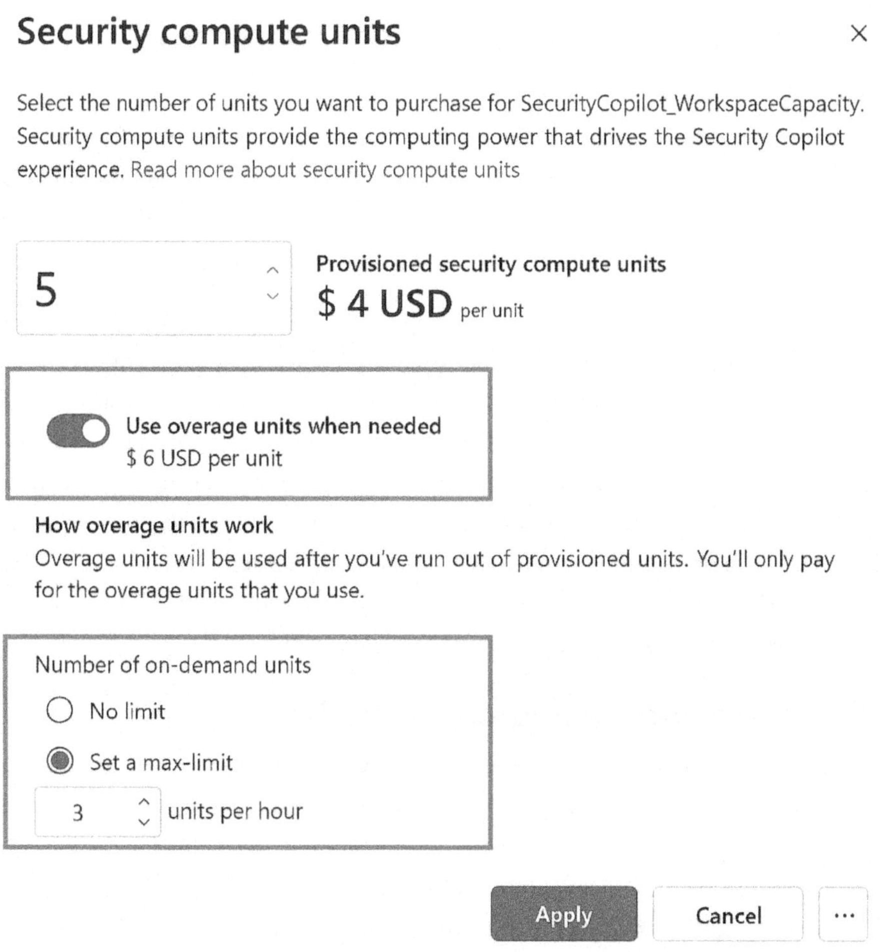

Figure 11.2 – Configuring Security Copilot overage units

Now that we've covered the Security Copilot pricing model in detail and shared more information about SCU cost estimation, in the next section, we will focus on how to monitor SCU usage and discuss different ways for tracking user activities within Security Copilot.

A guide for practitioners in monitoring and managing SCUs

As previously mentioned, you can optimize the Security Copilot cost by adjusting the number of provisioned SCUs to align with the actual usage. For instance, you could reduce the number of active SCUs to one when Security Copilot usage is minimal. However, to apply this strategy effectively, it's important to have a good understanding of your SCU consumption and user activity patterns to more accurately estimate the number of SCUs needed.

Security Copilot includes an in-product SCU usage dashboard that provides visibility into SCU consumption over time, allowing you to identify periods of high demand and low usage. The Security Copilot audit log tracks user and administrator activities, further assisting you in understanding Security Copilot consumption and usage patterns. Additionally, you can leverage the **Advanced Hunting** feature in Microsoft Defender XDR to quickly analyze user events presented in the Security Copilot audit log by running various KQL queries. These queries can also be transformed into custom Security Copilot plugins or Sentinel dashboards for greater flexibility and efficiency. In the next few sections, let's dive into each of these features in more detail.

The SCU Usage monitoring dashboard

Available in Security Copilot's standalone portal, the SCU **Usage monitoring** dashboard offers various SCU consumption insights to assist you in tracking and managing SCUs. The dashboard displays SCU consumption over time, with the exact usage data provided for every hour of the day. It also shows the exact SCU consumption for each individual prompt or promptbook. Additionally, the dashboard highlights the SCU usage associated with various plugins. It lets you filter SCU consumption by different embedded experiences or the standalone experience. It also provides visibility into SCU usage by individual users. Up to 90 days of Security Copilot data are accessible through this dashboard.

Before we dive into the dashboard features, it's important to quickly go over who can access this dashboard. In Security Copilot, there are two primary role types: owner and contributor. Only users assigned the owner role have permission to access the Security Copilot SCU **Usage monitoring** dashboard.

When the user with the *owner* role signs into Security Copilot's standalone portal and navigates to the **Home** menu, a dedicated menu section specifically for Security Copilot owners is displayed. This is illustrated in the following screenshot. The **Usage monitoring** option in the **Owner** menu takes you to the Security Copilot SCU **Usage monitoring** dashboard:

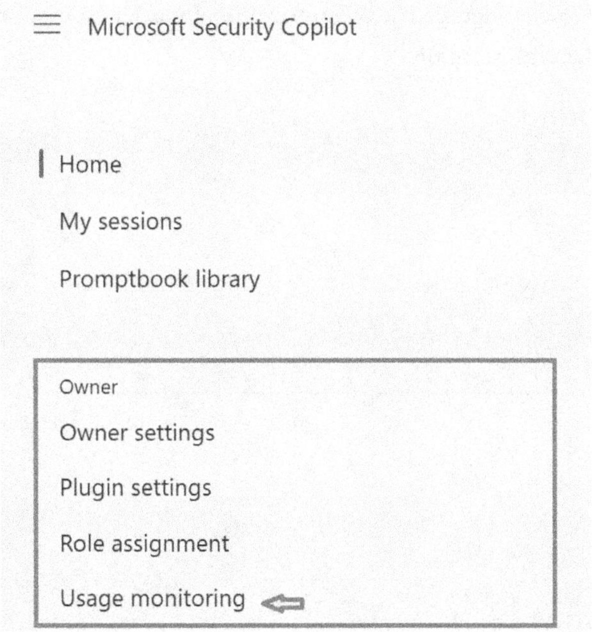

Figure 11.3 – The Usage monitoring option in the Owner menu section

Important note

As shown in the previous screenshot, the **Owner** menu section includes options such as **Owner settings**, **Plugin settings**, **Role assignment**, and **Usage monitoring**. These features are only accessible and manageable by users with the *owner* role. Users assigned the *contributor* role do not have access to this section of the menu. This means they are not able to view the SCU usage dashboard or provision SCUs through the **Owner settings** option. However, outside of these owner-specific settings, users with the *contributor* role can access and use the core operational features of Security Copilot. This includes executing prompts, creating and running promptbooks, or managing personal custom plugins.

The SCU **Usage monitoring** dashboard, shown in the next screenshot, is divided into two main sections. The top section features a bar chart, displaying the number of SCUs consumed over a specific time period, broken down by the hour.

The bottom section provides detailed SCU consumption for each prompt or promptbook, along with additional relevant information:

Figure 11.4 – The SCU Usage monitoring dashboard

In the top section of the dashboard, hovering your mouse over a specific SCU usage bar reveals the exact number of SCUs consumed during that hour. The corresponding time period during which SCUs were consumed is also displayed, as illustrated in the next screenshot. This enables you to view not only the total SCU usage but also the specific hours of consumption. These consumption details can reveal trends such as peak usage times, sustained activity periods, or low usage windows that may indicate underutilization. These insights can uncover patterns in how your organization has leveraged Security Copilot over time and offer a meaningful perspective when planning for future SCU provisioning:

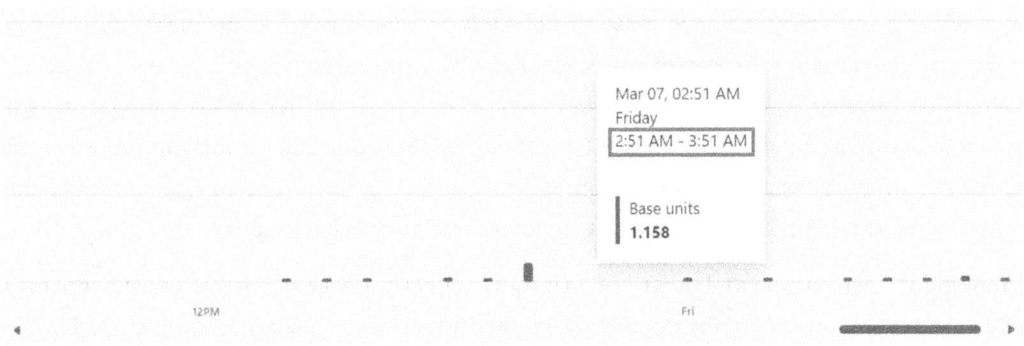

Figure 11.5 – Exact number of SCUs consumed during the hour

The bottom section of the usage dashboard, displayed in the following screen capture, offers more detailed and specific SCU consumption insights:

Date ↓	Units used	Initiated by	Session ID	Category	Type	Copilot experience	Plugins used
Mar 07, 09:22 AM	1.535	AB [redacted] (SECCOPILOT)	e38d0544-59d9-4ab6-9c46-ff7a8f759032	User prompt	Manual	Security Copilot portal	Microsoft Defender XDR
Mar 07, 09:17 AM	0.932	AM [redacted]	a1e268ef-fcf9-4e2f-ac15-2fa7987bbdb1	User prompt	Manual	Security Copilot portal	Microsoft Purview
Mar 07, 09:17 AM	0.015	AM [redacted]	a1e268ef-fcf9-4e2f-ac15-2fa7987bbdb1	User prompt	Manual	Security Copilot portal	
Mar 07, 09:16 AM	0.014	AM [redacted]	a1e268ef-fcf9-4e2f-ac15-2fa7987bbdb1	User prompt	Manual	Security Copilot portal	
Mar 07, 09:16 AM	0.086	AM [redacted]	e20e2ae3-6150-479e-ac7f-699d5eb34e6e	User prompt	Manual	Copilot in Microsoft Purview	Microsoft Purview

Figure 11.6 – The bottom section of the usage dashboard

The **Units used** column indicates the number of SCUs consumed by a specific user prompt or a promptbook execution. Since prompts vary in complexity, more complex operations consume more SCUs. As illustrated in the previous screenshot, the user prompt SCU usage varies from as low as 0.014 to as high as 1.535.

Also shown in the previous screenshot, in addition to displaying the number of SCUs used for each prompt or promptbook, the **Usage monitoring** dashboard provides other detailed information about the prompt or promptbook. It includes the date and time the prompt or promptbook was executed, along with its **Session ID** value. Furthermore, it identifies the user who initiated the operation, the Copilot experience from which the session was started, whether in an embedded experience, the standalone portal, or logic apps, and the corresponding plugin used.

By analyzing how many SCUs are consumed by individual prompts or entire promptbooks, you can identify which tasks are resource-intensive and which are more efficient. This level of visibility helps you to evaluate whether certain workflows or prompt structures are delivering sufficient value relative to their compute cost. Over time, these insights can guide optimization efforts, such as refining prompt wording, consolidating steps, or adjusting usage patterns, to maximize the impact of Security Copilot while minimizing unnecessary SCU consumption.

In addition to per-prompt and promptbook insights, the SCU **Usage monitoring** dashboard also allows you to focus on SCU consumption over a specific period of time, which is illustrated in the next screen capture. You can view up to 90 days of metrics data:

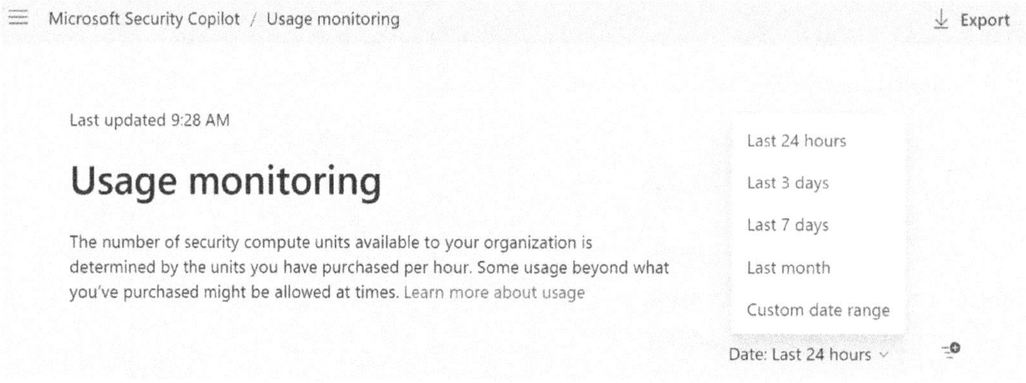

Figure 11.7 – View SCU usage within a specific timeframe

Furthermore, the SCU **Usage monitoring** dashboard offers additional filtering for you to narrow down the Security Copilot data. The filtering icon can be found near the upper-right corner of the main dashboard interface, as illustrated next:

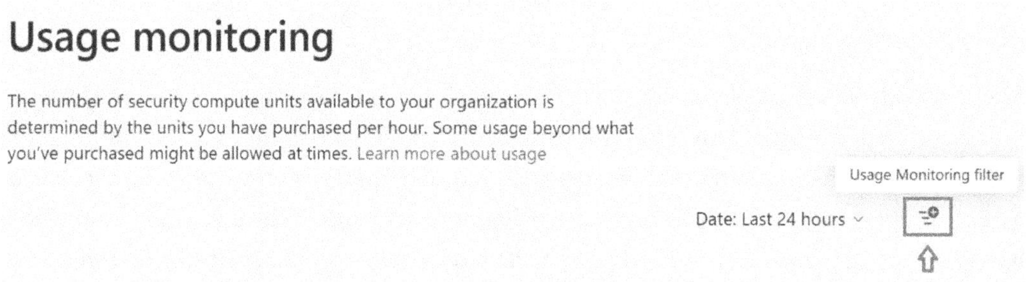

Figure 11.8 – The filtering icon

There are five filtering options available in the SCU **Usage monitoring** dashboard:

- **Copilot experience**: This option filters SCU usage based on the specific Security Copilot environment, whether it's the standalone portal or any of the embedded experiences, such as Defender XDR, Purview, Entra, Intune, and others. It helps distinguish how SCUs are consumed across different Security Copilot experiences.
- **Users**: This allows you to filter SCU usage by specific users. It is useful for tracking individual usage patterns, identifying users with high SCU consumption, and further investigating their actions.
- **Plugins used**: This one filters SCU usage based on specific Security Copilot plugins. It includes Microsoft, custom, third-party plugins, and agents. It is helpful for assessing plugin efficiency and identifying underutilized or high-consumption plugins.
- **Type**: This filter offers two options, **Manual** or **Automated**. It lets you identify SCU usage triggered by either direct user actions or automated processes and workflows. This helps you understand how much SCU consumption comes from hands-on analyst activity versus system-driven automation.
- **Category**: This option distinguishes SCU usage based on the category of **User prompt** or **Promptbook**. It helps differentiate between one-time user interactions from structured, multi-step workflows executed through promptbooks. This distinction allows you to further analyze SCU consumption patterns.

Overall, the filtering options in the SCU **Usage monitoring** dashboard enable you to gain further insights into how SCUs are being consumed across your organization. As an example, the next screenshot illustrates some of the **Copilot experience** filtering options available, such as the specific embedded experience, the standalone portal, or logic apps:

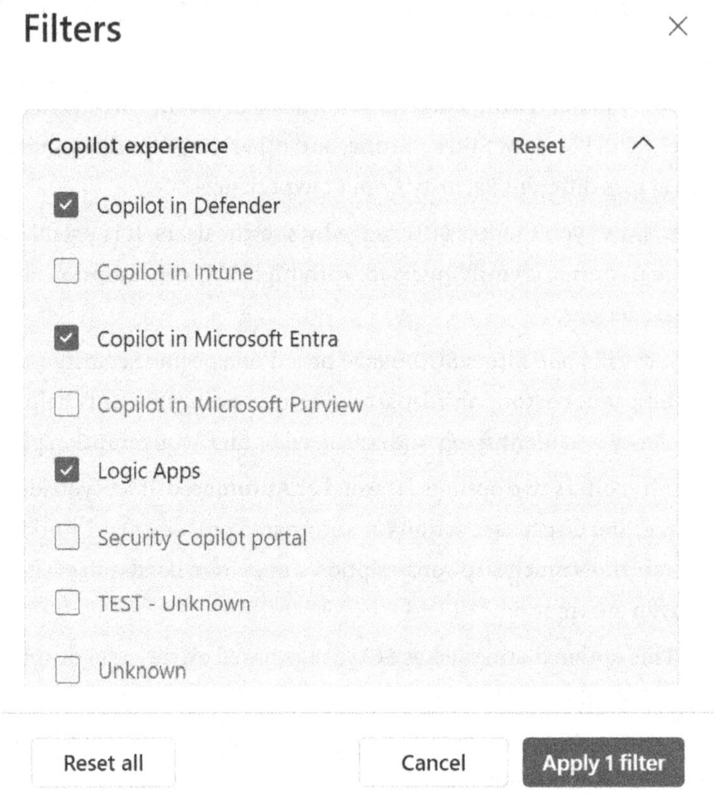

Figure 11.9 – The Copilot experience filtering option

Notice that, as seen from the previous screenshot, you can select multiple **Copilot experience** options. This allows you to view the SCU consumption data from a set of Copilot experiences at once.

Furthermore, you can apply multiple filters simultaneously. The next screenshot demonstrates how you can narrow down the SCU consumption data to focus only on the promptbook executed by a specific user:

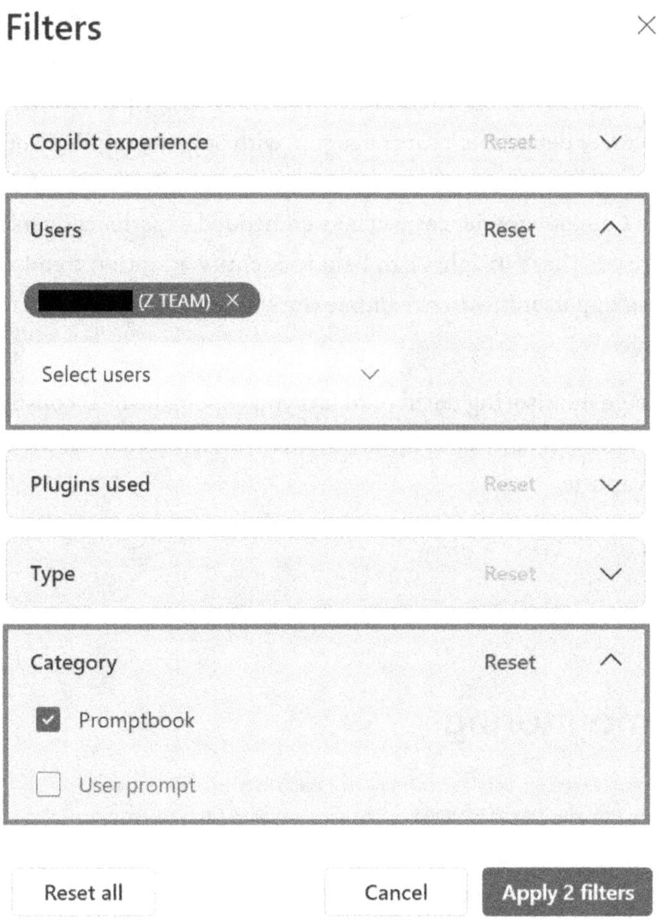

Figure 11.10 – Applying multiple filters simultaneously

The following screenshot captures the outcome after applying these two filters. It displays the SCU usage data specifically for the promptbook that this user has just run:

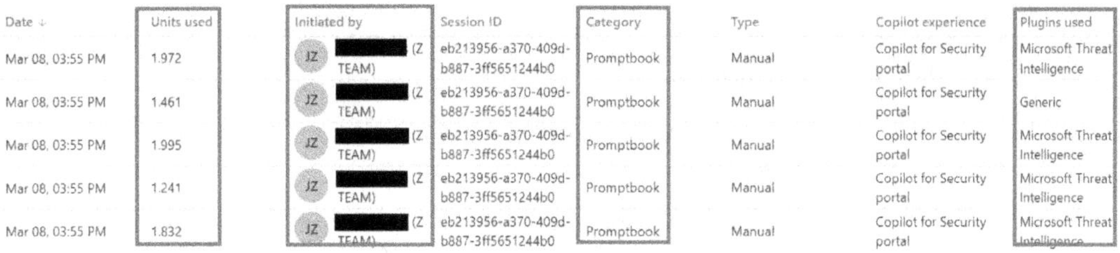

Date ↓	Units used	Initiated by	Session ID	Category	Type	Copilot experience	Plugins used
Mar 08, 03:55 PM	1.972	JZ [redacted] (Z TEAM)	eb213956-a370-409d-b887-3ff5651244b0	Promptbook	Manual	Copilot for Security portal	Microsoft Threat Intelligence
Mar 08, 03:55 PM	1.461	JZ [redacted] (Z TEAM)	eb213956-a370-409d-b887-3ff5651244b0	Promptbook	Manual	Copilot for Security portal	Generic
Mar 08, 03:55 PM	1.995	JZ [redacted] (Z TEAM)	eb213956-a370-409d-b887-3ff5651244b0	Promptbook	Manual	Copilot for Security portal	Microsoft Threat Intelligence
Mar 08, 03:55 PM	1.241	JZ [redacted] (Z TEAM)	eb213956-a370-409d-b887-3ff5651244b0	Promptbook	Manual	Copilot for Security portal	Microsoft Threat Intelligence
Mar 08, 03:55 PM	1.832	JZ [redacted] (Z TEAM)	eb213956-a370-409d-b887-3ff5651244b0	Promptbook	Manual	Copilot for Security portal	Microsoft Threat Intelligence

Figure 11.11 – Results after filters are applied

In general, the filtering options enable you to analyze SCU consumption by individual users, across different Copilot experiences, and by workload or activity type, providing a holistic view of user behavior and tool adoption. You can drill down into usage patterns and understand how different teams, roles, or departments are engaging with Security Copilot. For example, you can compare how usage differs between security analysts and incident responders, or evaluate how frequently specific Copilot experiences, such as embedded experiences versus the standalone portal, are being used. These insights can help to identify adoption trends, uncover training needs, and highlight opportunities to streamline workflows or reallocate SCU resources for better operational efficiency.

Lastly, the SCU **Usage monitoring** dashboard lets you export the SCU consumption data in an Excel file format. The **Export** button is located in the top-right corner of the dashboard, shown in the next screen capture:

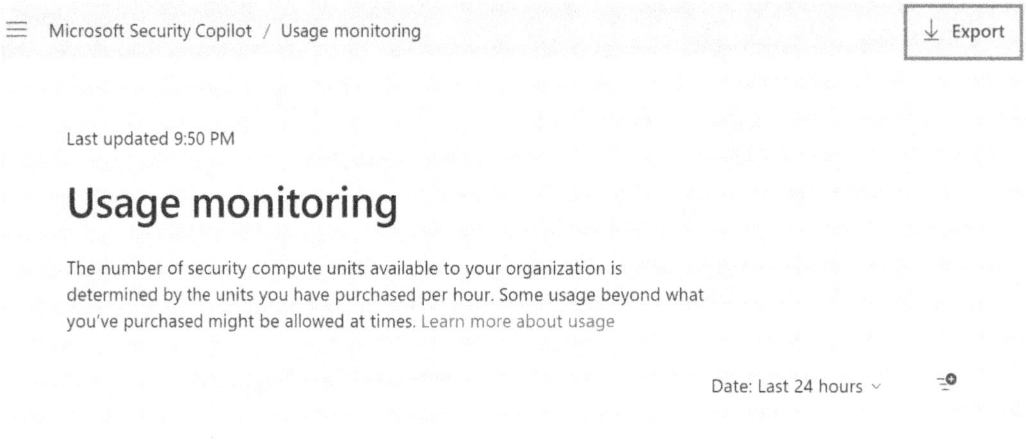

Figure 11.12 – The Usage monitoring dashboard's Export feature

Overall, the SCU **Usage monitoring** dashboard within Security Copilot offers insights to help you effectively track SCU consumption.

Key points to remember

- Access to the **Usage monitoring** dashboard is limited to users with the owner role.
- This access level allows you to see detailed information on SCU usage over time, including consumption for specific prompts and promptbooks.
- You can leverage the advanced filtering options to identify additional usage patterns and extract more insights.

Alongside the SCU usage dashboard, Security Copilot also allows you to review both user and administrator activities through its auditing feature. Its audit log lets you track and assess user interactions and administrative actions for improved visibility and security management. Let's dive into this feature next.

The Security Copilot audit log

Microsoft provides a variety of audit logs that allow you to track and analyze user interactions with Microsoft security products. These logs document user and administrator operations across services and solutions, including Security Copilot. The logs are stored in the unified audit log, accessible through the Purview portal.

The audit log offers visibility into the following activities carried out in Security Copilot:

- Common interactions with Copilot, such as users executing prompts, promptbooks, or logic apps
- Captures events when users enable or disable built-in plugins
- Tracks actions such as creating, modifying, or deleting custom plugins or promptbooks
- Logs administrative actions, such as tenant-level configuration changes
- Offers visibility into activities and events related to third-party partner integrations

> Note
>
> Auditing of Security Copilot prompts and responses is available through **Data Security Posture Management for AI**, a premium Microsoft Purview capability with additional costs associated.

By tracking these user events through the audit log, you can more quickly and efficiently identify user usage patterns and establish different usage baselines based on various criteria. This helps optimize resource allocation and detect anomalies. Additionally, it aids in compliance reporting and ensures that administrative actions are transparent and accountable.

In Security Copilot, users with the owner role have the ability to enable or disable the audit logging feature. To do so, you simply navigate to the **Owner settings** menu section from the **Home** menu. In there, the **Logging audit data in Microsoft Purview** option allows you to turn on or off the ability for Security Copilot to process and store user activity data in Microsoft Purview.

This is illustrated in the following screen capture:

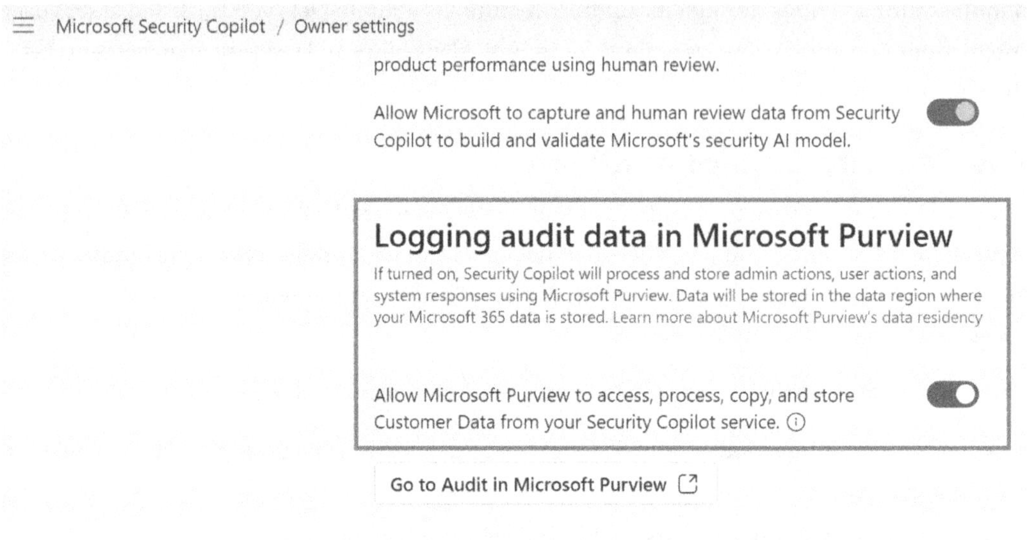

Figure 11.13 – The Logging audit data in Microsoft Purview option

Typically, the audit log becomes accessible in Microsoft Purview within 24 hours of being enabled in Security Copilot. However, having owner permissions in Security Copilot doesn't automatically grant you access to search those logs in Purview. Purview uses a separate **role-based access control** (**RBAC**) system, so you must be assigned the appropriate permissions within Purview to view or query audit log entries.

Once you have the necessary access to view and search the audit log, navigate to the Microsoft Purview portal at `https://purview.microsoft.com/`. Next, select the **Audit** menu option from the left-hand navigation bar. This then expands to reveal additional options. Click **Search** to proceed with searching through the audit log. The following screenshot illustrates this process:

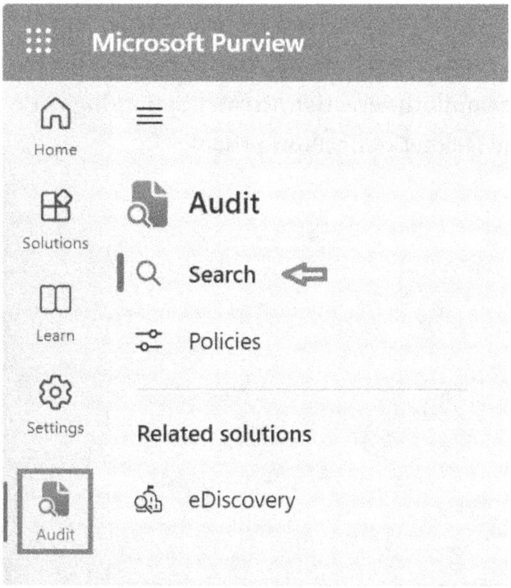

Figure 11.14 – The audit log search feature in Microsoft Purview

The **Search** page for the audit log offers a variety of search criteria for you to choose from. Let's start with the **Record Types** search option, as shown next:

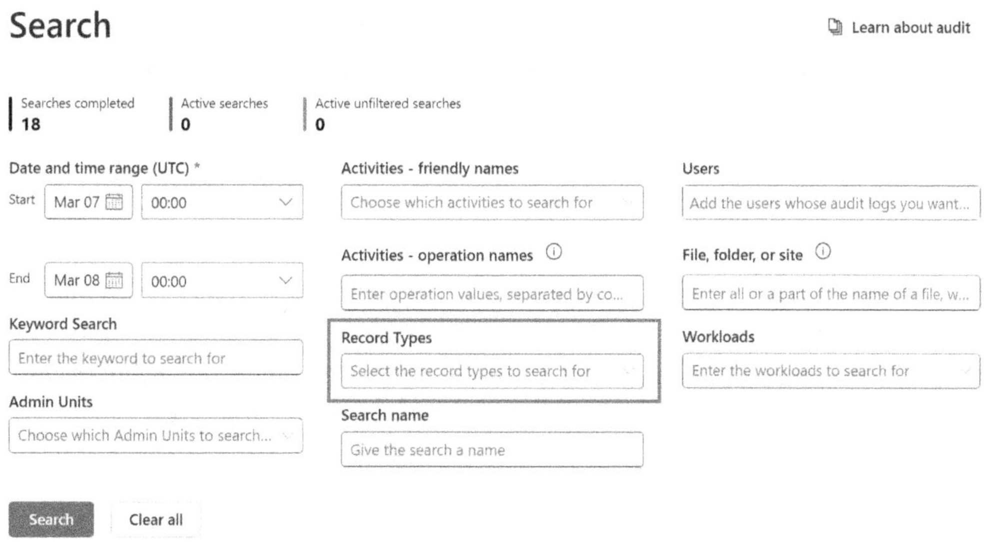

Figure 11.15 – The audit log search page

Within the **Record Types** search option, look for record type names that contain the keyword `copilot`. As shown in the following screenshot, the drop-down list displays several Security Copilot record types, such as **CopilotInteraction**, **CreateCopilotPlugin**, **CreateCopilotPromptBook**, **DeleteCopilotPlugin**, and **DeleteCopilotPromptBook**:

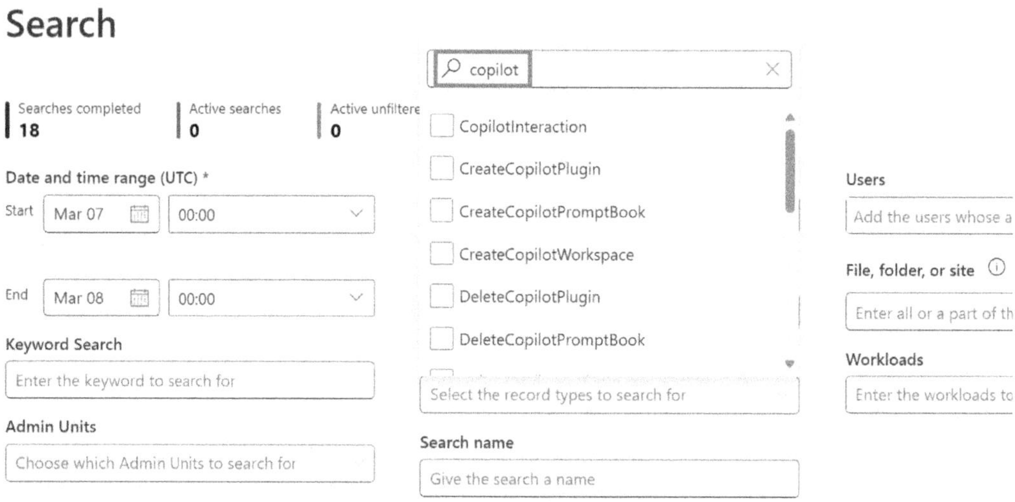

Figure 11.16 – Some Security Copilot record types available for search in the audit log

By scrolling further down the drop-down list, you can view additional Security Copilot record types, including **EnableCopilotPlugin**, **UpdateCopilotPlugin**, **EnableCopilotPromptBook**, and more. This is shown in the next screen capture:

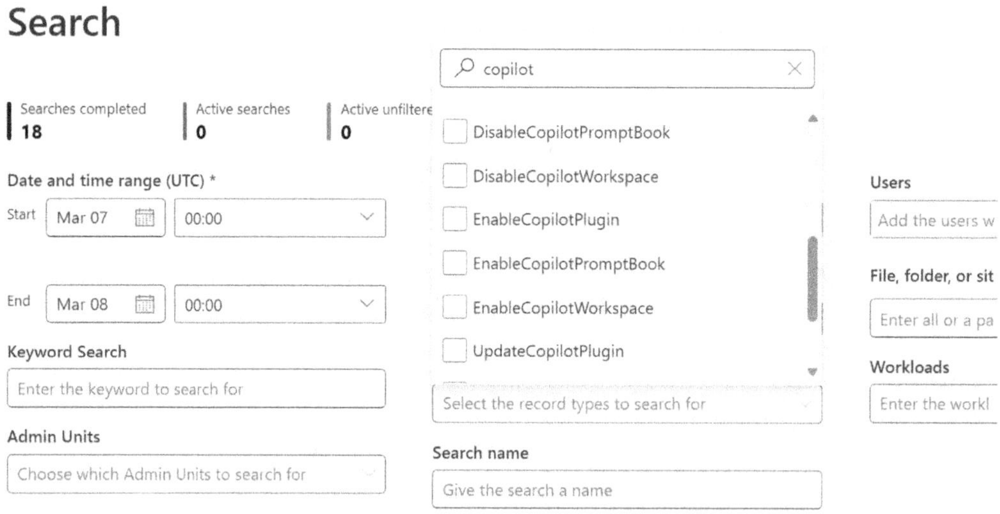

Figure 11.17 – Additional record types available for search in the audit log

You are able to select one or more record types as part of your search criteria to find the corresponding user events. In this example, let's search events with the record type of **CopilotInteraction** performed by a specific user, as illustrated in the next screen capture:

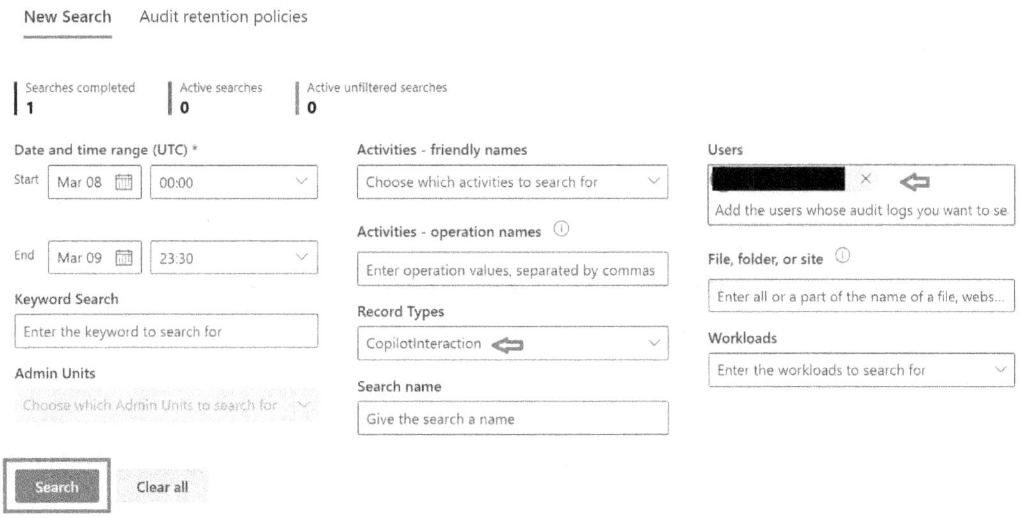

Figure 11.18 – Searching for CopilotInteraction events performed by a specific user

The **CopilotInteraction** record type tracks events related to user interactions with Security Copilot, such as when a user executes a prompt or a promptbook. In this example, once the search criteria are entered and the search is initiated, the status of the search job is then displayed, as shown in the following screen capture:

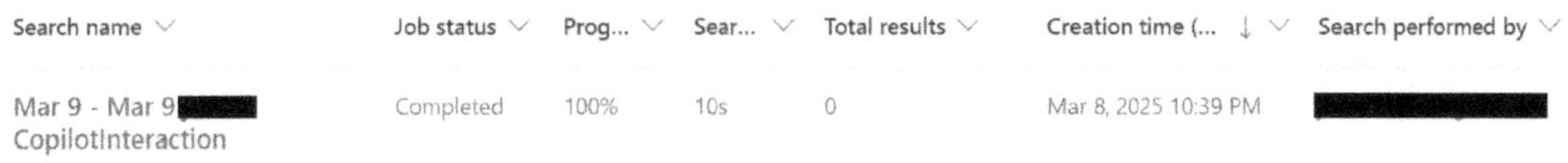

Figure 11.19 – Status of the search job

When the search status shows as **Completed**, clicking anywhere on the search status page takes you to the detailed search results page, as shown next:

Figure 11.20 – The detailed search results page

This search returns two Security Copilot user interaction events, with each event containing details such as the date and time, user name, specific activity, operation names, details, and more. Typically, the user's IP address is also displayed. Although there are exceptions, such as when a user executes a promptbook.

From the previous screen capture, you may have noticed a **Filter** option in the upper-right corner. If your search returns too many events, the **Filter** option enables you to narrow down the results or to focus on a specific set of search results. The available filtering criteria include the following:

- **Date range**
- **IP address**
- **User**
- **Activity**
- **Activities – operation names**
- **Details**
- **Admin units**

Most of the filtering criteria are self-explanatory. However, the **Activities – operation names** filtering option may require more clarification. The Microsoft audit log offers both a user-friendly name and the official operation name for the same activity. You can search specific activities using either option. The screenshot shown next highlights the difference between the two for a few activities.

A list of Security Copilot's operation names can be found at `https://learn.microsoft.com/en-us/purview/audit-log-activities?view=o365-worldwide#copilot-activities`:

Friendly Name	Operation	Description
Created a new Copilot plugin	CreateCopilotPlugin	A user (or admin or system on behalf of a user) created a new Copilot plugin.
Created a new Copilot promptbook	CreateCopilotPromptBook	A user (or admin or system on behalf of a user) created a new promptbook in Copilot.
Deleted a Copilot plugin	DeleteCopilotPlugin	A user (or admin or system on behalf of a user) deleted a Copilot plugin.

Figure 11.21 – Difference between the user-friendly name and the official operation name

Back to the search results page, clicking on any event allows you to view more event details in the **Details** side pane:

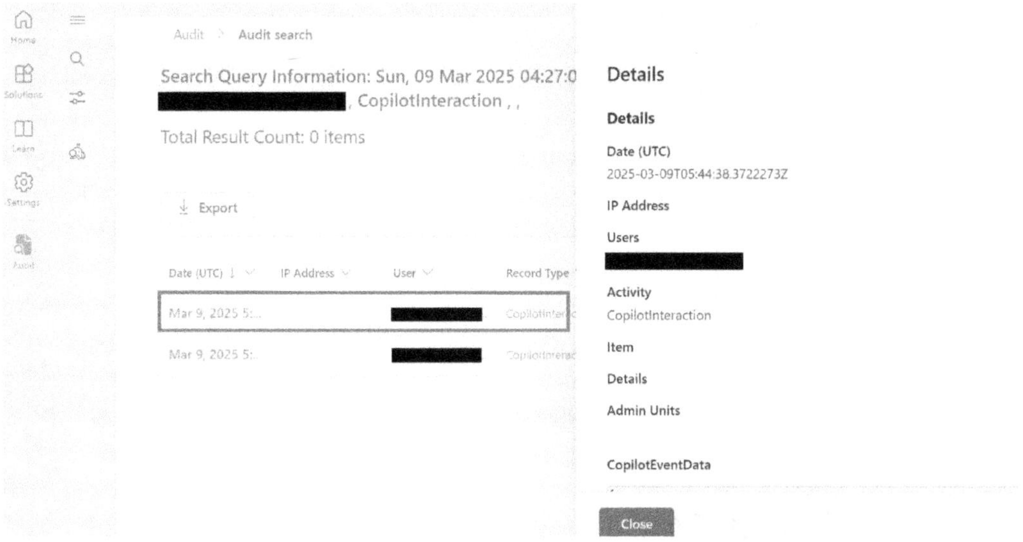

Figure 11.22 – More event details in the side pane

The **Details** side pane can display information such as the **CopilotEventData** information, prompt ID, correlation ID, user ID, and more. A portion of the side pane is shown next:

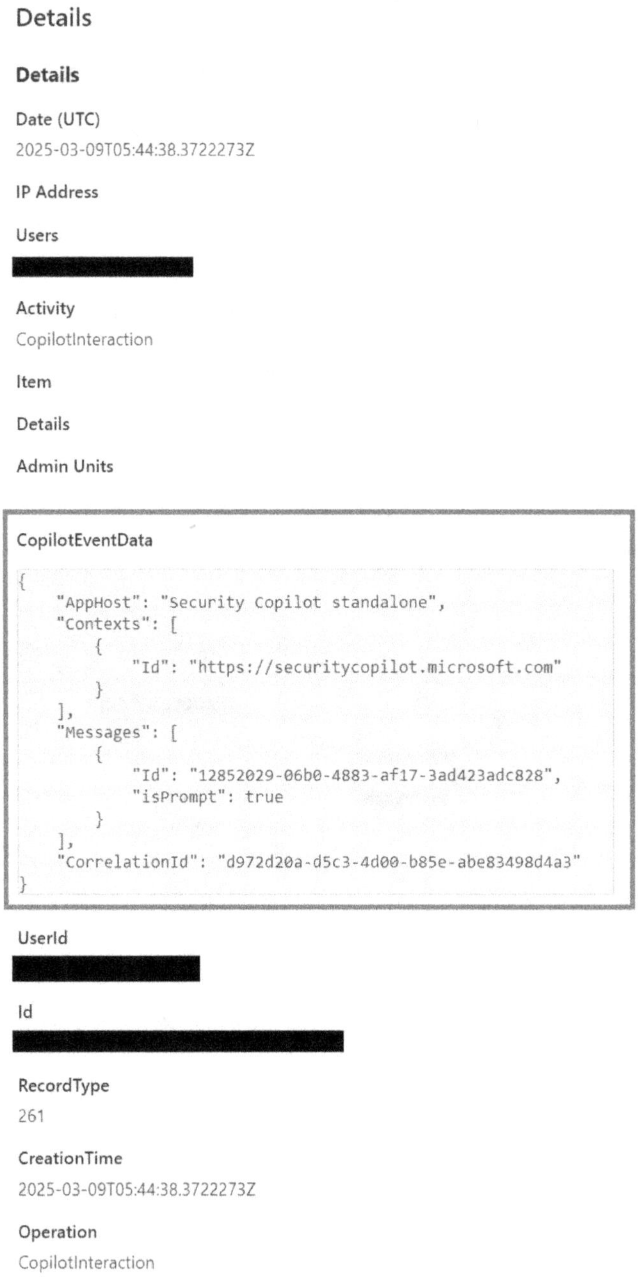

Figure 11.23 – A portion of the Details side pane

The audit log provides detailed visibility into user activities within Security Copilot. By tracking these user events, you can analyze how different teams or roles interact with Security Copilot. For instance, you can compare how frequently security analysts run promptbooks versus how often IT administrators trigger logic apps. You may also observe whether certain users consistently initiate high-SCU-consuming operations. This can help to identify opportunities to optimize prompts or workflows.

Additionally, audit log entries for actions such as creating, enabling, or disabling Copilot plugins or promptbooks can provide valuable context when assessing changes in SCU usage. As an example, if a newly created or enabled plugin results in a spike in SCU consumption, you can trace that back to the user or team that deployed it. Similarly, disabling an underused or inefficient plugin may correspond with a noticeable drop in SCU usage. Monitoring these types of events helps you evaluate the operational impact of new tools or configurations, identify resource-heavy custom components, and ensure that deployments align with performance and cost-efficiency goals.

The audit log search capability is also available in the Microsoft Defender XDR portal, with the same user interface as in Purview. Furthermore, the same underlying audit log data for Security Copilot can also be accessed through the `Search-UnifiedAuditLog` cmdlet in PowerShell or by using the **Advanced Hunting** feature in Microsoft Defender XDR. Both advanced query options offer more flexibility and greater control for extracting targeted insights from the audit log, but require familiarity with PowerShell or **Kusto Query Language** (**KQL**). In the next section, let's take a look at how different KQL queries in Advanced Hunting can quickly retrieve and analyze the Security Copilot audit log data.

Advanced Hunting in Microsoft Defender XDR

The Advanced Hunting feature in Microsoft Defender XDR provides powerful querying and analytics capabilities across a wide range of data sources, including the Security Copilot audit log. It leverages KQL queries to perform fast, precise, and customizable searches across large volumes of data.

For the same underlying audit logs seen in Microsoft Purview, Advanced Hunting allows you to quickly identify patterns, correlations, and outliers. Rather than manually reviewing rows of events or running repetitive searches, KQL queries in Advanced Hunting help to surface insights in seconds. These insights enable you to quickly and accurately pinpoint where SCUs are being heavily consumed and whether that consumption aligns with business value. With this information, you can refine workflows, adjust prompt structures, or establish usage policies that reduce unnecessary SCU spending. As a result, this makes Advanced Hunting a powerful tool for driving more efficient and strategic use of SCUs.

For instance, with KQL queries, you can filter audit logs based on specific criteria such as user actions, time ranges, plugin activity, or promptbook execution, thereby making it easier to isolate the exact events you're looking for. You may run a query to identify all promptbook executions by a specific user within a defined timeframe, allowing you to identify usage trends, particularly if certain users are consistently initiating high-SCU operations. Or you can track how frequently custom plugins are created or modified across the tenant, helping to detect configuration changes that may affect usage or security posture. Additionally, KQL queries can highlight trends in how different Copilot experiences, such as embedded experience, the standalone portal, or logic apps, are being used across your organization, which helps you understand SCUs consumption across various workflows and interfaces.

As an example, the previous section showcased how to search events such as **CopilotInteraction** in the audit log from the Microsoft Purview portal. Now, let's look at searching for the same events in Advanced Hunting using KQL queries. The following screenshot displays a KQL query in action, along with its results in **Advanced hunting**:

Figure 11.24 – The Advanced hunting feature in Microsoft Defender XDR

The KQL query, shown next in a more readable format, retrieves Security Copilot audit log events from an event table called **CloudAppEvents**. It then filters these events to show only the `CopilotInteraction` logs. Next, the query presents the results in a spreadsheet-like format, with columns showing key event details. These include the event timestamp, the user account, and the specific Copilot environment (e.g., standalone experience, the different embedded experiences, or logic app). It also includes the user's IP address, the user's location based on the IP, and the user's **internet service provider** (**ISP**) name:

```
// User Security Copilot Interaction
CloudAppEvents
| extend AppId = parse_json(RawEventData)["AppIdentity"]
| where AppId == "Copilot.Security.SecurityCopilot"
| extend EventType = parse_json(RawEventData)["Operation"]
| where EventType == "CopilotInteraction"
| extend UserIP = parse_json(RawEventData)["ClientIP"]
| extend Time= tostring(parse_json(RawEventData)["CreationTime"])
| extend User = parse_json(RawEventData)["UserId"]
| extend Events = parse_json(RawEventData)["CopilotEventData"]
| extend CopilotExperience = parse_json(Events)["AppHost"]
| project Time, User, EventType, CopilotExperience, UserIP, City, CountryCode, ISP
| sort by Time desc
```

Figure 11.25 – The KQL query in Advanced Hunting

The results from the KQL query are displayed in the following screen capture:

Time	User	EventType	CopilotExperience	UserIP	City	CountryCode	ISP
> 2025-03-09T	[redacted]	CopilotInteraction	Copilot in Intune	96.237.171.24	natick	US	verizon
> 2025-03-09T	[redacted]	CopilotInteraction	Security Copilot standalone	96.237.171.24	natick	US	verizon
> 2025-03-09T	[redacted]	CopilotInteraction	Security Copilot standalone	96.237.171.24	natick	US	verizon
> 2025-03-09T	[redacted]	CopilotInteraction	Security Copilot standalone	96.237.171.24	natick	US	verizon
> 2025-03-09T	[redacted]	CopilotInteraction	Security Copilot standalone	96.237.171.24	natick	US	verizon
> 2025-03-09T	[redacted]	CopilotInteraction	Copilot in Microsoft Purview	2600:1700:d87a:5eb0:b1...	plano	US	at&t enterpri
> 2025-03-09T	[redacted]	CopilotInteraction	Copilot in Microsoft Purview	2600:1700:d87a:5eb0:b1...	plano	US	at&t enterpri
> 2025-03-09T	[redacted]	CopilotInteraction	Security Copilot standalone	96.237.171.24	natick	US	verizon
> 2025-03-09T	[redacted]	CopilotInteraction	Security Copilot standalone	96.237.171.24	natick	US	verizon
> 2025-03-09T	[redacted]	CopilotInteraction	Logic App	102.132.161.66	randburg	ZA	ftth gauteng

Figure 11.26 – The results from the KQL query

By adding just one extra line of code to this KQL query, as shown next, you can further filter the results to only display events associated with a specific user:

```
// User Security Copilot Interaction
CloudAppEvents
| extend AppId = parse_json(RawEventData)["AppIdentity"]
| where AppId == "Copilot.Security.SecurityCopilot"
| extend EventType = parse_json(RawEventData)["Operation"]
| where EventType == "CopilotInteraction"
| extend UserIP = parse_json(RawEventData)["ClientIP"]
| extend Time= tostring(parse_json(RawEventData)["CreationTime"])
| extend User = parse_json(RawEventData)["UserId"]
| where User == [redacted]
| extend Events = parse_json(RawEventData)["CopilotEventData"]
| extend CopilotExperience = parse_json(Events)["AppHost"]
| project Time, User, EventType, CopilotExperience, UserIP, City, CountryCode, ISP
| sort by Time desc
```

Figure 11.27 – Additional filtering by specific user

Or, based on the first KQL query discussed, simply modifying the last two lines of its code allows you to categorize and quantify user `CopilotInteraction` events according to the specific Security Copilot environments in which they occurred. The updated KQL query is displayed in the following screen capture:

```
// Summarize Security Copilot User Interaction
CloudAppEvents
| extend AppId = parse_json(RawEventData)["AppIdentity"]
| where AppId == "Copilot.Security.SecurityCopilot"
| extend EventType = tostring(parse_json(RawEventData)["Operation"])
| where EventType == "CopilotInteraction"
| extend UserIP = tostring(parse_json(RawEventData)["ClientIP"])
| extend Time= tostring(parse_json(RawEventData)["CreationTime"])
| extend User = tostring(parse_json(RawEventData)["UserId"])
| extend Events = parse_json(RawEventData)["CopilotEventData"]
| extend CopilotExperience = tostring(parse_json(Events)["AppHost"])
| summarize UserInteractionCount = count() by User, EventType, CopilotExperience
| sort by User asc, CopilotExperience asc
```

Figure 11.28 – Updated KQL query to categorize and quantify user CopilotInteraction events

A portion of the results is displayed in the next screenshot, highlighting event summaries for two users. For the first user with a username starting with e384, Security Copilot in its Microsoft Defender XDR sessions was triggered 16 times, either automatically or manually, over the last 30 days. During the same period, Security Copilot was invoked twice in its Microsoft Entra sessions and 36 times in Microsoft Purview.

Additionally, this user interacted with Security Copilot through its standalone experience eight times:

User	EventType	CopilotExperience	UserInteractionCount
> e384[redacted]	CopilotInteraction	Copilot in Defender	16
> e384[redacted]	CopilotInteraction	Copilot in Microsoft Entra	2
> e384[redacted]	CopilotInteraction	Copilot in Microsoft Purview	36
> e384[redacted]	CopilotInteraction	Security Copilot standalone	8
> e385[redacted]	CopilotInteraction	Copilot in Defender	170
> e385[redacted]	CopilotInteraction	Copilot in Microsoft Entra	6
> e385[redacted]	CopilotInteraction	Copilot in Microsoft Purview	6
> e385[redacted]	CopilotInteraction	Security Copilot standalone	1212

Figure 11.29 – KQL query results highlighting event summaries for two users

Based on the user's activity summary from the past 30 days, it is clear that this user frequently interacts with Microsoft Purview and Defender XDR, both of which have triggered Security Copilot either automatically or manually. The moderate user interaction with Security Copilot's standalone experience suggests that this user likely prefers the convenience and integrated support offered by Security Copilot's embedded experiences.

On the contrary, the second user, whose username starts with e385, interacted with Security Copilot in the standalone environment 1,212 times during the same period. This suggests that this user prefers using Security Copilot features in the standalone portal, rather than within the embedded environments.

> Note
>
> This KQL query, along with others covered in this book, is available for download from the book's GitHub repository at `https://github.com/PacktPublishing/Microsoft-Copilot-for-Security/tree/main/KQL`.

Additionally, based on the first KQL query, you can change from == to != in the code to filter for user events other than the `CopilotInteraction` event. This is illustrated in the next screen capture:

```
//Other Security Copilot Events Excluding User Interaction
CloudAppEvents
| extend AppId = parse_json(RawEventData)["AppIdentity"]
| where AppId == "Copilot.Security.SecurityCopilot"
| extend EventType = tostring(parse_json(RawEventData)["Operation"])
| where EventType != "CopilotInteraction"
| extend User = tostring(parse_json(RawEventData)["UserId"])
| extend EventDetail = tostring(parse_json(RawEventData)["CopilotSettingsEventData"])
| project Timestamp, ActionType, User, EventDetail, IPAddress, City, CountryCode, ISP
| sort by Timestamp desc
```

Figure 11.30 – Filter user events excluding the CopilotInteraction event

The following screenshot displays the results generated by the updated KQL query. It highlights various user actions, such as `EnablePlugin`, `DisablePlugin`, and `CreatePlugin`, that are linked to different users. The query also provides details of each user action, for example, the name of the plugin that was enabled or disabled:

Timestamp	ActionType	User	EventDetail
Mar 9, 2025 6:47:4...	EnablePlugin	u1[redacted]...	{"Resource":[{"NewValue":"Enabled","OriginalValue":"Disabled","Property":"FileUploads"}],"Workspace":{"Name":"Secu
Mar 9, 2025 6:47:4...	DisablePlugin	u1[redacted]...	{"Resource":[{"NewValue":"Disabled","OriginalValue":"Enabled","Property":"EASM"},{"NewValue":"Disabled","OriginalV
Mar 9, 2025 6:47:4...	EnablePlugin	u1[redacted]...	{"Resource":[{"NewValue":"Enabled","OriginalValue":"Disabled","Property":"FileUploads"}],"Workspace":{"Name":"Secu
Mar 9, 2025 6:47:3...	DisablePlugin	u1[redacted]...	{"Resource":[{"NewValue":"Disabled","OriginalValue":"Enabled","Property":"AzureFirewall"},{"NewValue":"Disabled","O
Mar 9, 2025 6:47:3...	EnablePlugin	u1[redacted]...	{"Resource":[{"NewValue":"Enabled","OriginalValue":"Disabled","Property":"FileUploads"}],"Workspace":{"Name":"Secu
Mar 9, 2025 6:47:3...	DisablePlugin	u1[redacted]...	{"Resource":[{"NewValue":"Disabled","OriginalValue":"Enabled","Property":"WAF"},{"NewValue":"Disabled","OriginalVa
Mar 9, 2025 6:47:3...	EnablePlugin	u1[redacted]...	{"Resource":[{"NewValue":"Enabled","OriginalValue":"Disabled","Property":"FileUploads"}],"Workspace":{"Name":"Secu
Mar 9, 2025 6:47:3...	EnablePlugin	u1[redacted]...	{"Resource":[{"NewValue":"Enabled","OriginalValue":"Disabled","Property":"FileUploads"}],"Workspace":{"Name":"Secu
Mar 9, 2025 4:49:0...	CreatePlugin	e6[redacted]...	{"Resource":[{"Property":"Skillsets.Summarize Sentinel Cost details for a specified time and date range."}],"Workspace
Mar 9, 2025 8:08:1...	EnablePlugin	u6[redacted].	{"Resource":[{"NewValue":"Enabled","OriginalValue":"Disabled","Property":"Purview"},{"NewValue":"Enabled","Original
Mar 9, 2025 4:18:3...	EnablePlugin	49[redacted].	{"Resource":[{"NewValue":"Enabled","OriginalValue":"Disabled","Property":"Purview"},{"NewValue":"Enabled","Original

Figure 11.31 – Output from the updated KQL query

There are also KQL queries available online that are tailored for monitoring and managing Security Copilot usage. As an example, the Microsoft Security Copilot GitHub repository provides a query to report on who enabled Security Copilot, as shown next:

```
AzureActivity
| where TimeGenerated >= ago(30d)
| where ResourceProviderValue == "MICROSOFT.SECURITYCOPILOT"
| extend resourceName = tostring(parse_json(Properties).resource)
| extend resourceGroupName = tostring(parse_json(Properties).resourceGroup)
| extend resourceActivity = tostring(parse_json(Properties).message)
| where resourceActivity == "Microsoft.SecurityCopilot/capacities/write"
| project Caller, resourceName, resourceGroupName, resourceActivity, TimeGenerated
```

Figure 11.32 – KQL query to report on who enabled Security Copilot

> Note
>
> This KQL query is intended to run in Azure. Currently, it is not supported within the Microsoft Defender XDR portal.

More information about this KQL query can be found at `https://github.com/Azure/Security-Copilot/tree/main/Monitoring/KQL%20query%20to%20see%20who%20enabled%20CFS`.

From the same GitHub repository, another KQL query that reports on who deleted the Security Copilot instance is available at `https://github.com/Azure/Security-Copilot/blob/main/Monitoring/KQL%20to%20see%20who%20deleted%20CFS/WhoDeletedCFS.kql`.

As demonstrated in *Chapter 4*, you can easily convert a KQL query into a Security Copilot custom plugin. More information on custom plugins powered by KQL can also be found in *Chapters 5* and *8*. Besides leveraging KQL queries to monitor and track SCU usage, you also have the option to transform them into specific custom plugins for enhanced flexibility and efficiency. In the next section, let's dive into this option and explore other similar offerings.

Leveraging custom plugins and Sentinel workbooks

The Microsoft Security Copilot GitHub repository offers a KQL-based custom plugin that enables you to track changes to the number of SCUs provisioned in your Security Copilot environment. With this plugin, you can directly prompt Security Copilot for SCU capacity changes over the past three days right within the Security Copilot standalone experience.

The KQL query that is used to power this custom plugin is displayed in the following screen capture:

```
AzureActivity
| where TimeGenerated >= ago(3d)
| where ResourceProviderValue == "MICROSOFT.SECURITYCOPILOT"
| extend resourceName = tostring(parse_json(Properties).resource)
| extend resourceGroupName = tostring(parse_json(Properties).resourceGroup)
| extend resourceActivity = tostring(parse_json(Properties).message)
| where resourceActivity == "Microsoft.SecurityCopilot/capacities/write"
| distinct Caller, CallerIpAddress, resourceName, resourceGroupName, resourceActivity
```

Figure 11.33 – KQL query used to power the custom plugin

The custom plugin's YAML file, which references this KQL query, along with the prerequisites and setup instructions, can be found at `https://github.com/Azure/Security-Copilot/tree/main/Plugins/Community%20Based%20Plugins/SCU%20Changes`.

After installing the custom plugin, in Security Copilot, you can use a prompt such as `Have there been any SCU changes recently?` to quickly track SCU provisioning changes. For more detailed information about this plugin and sample prompt outputs, you can also read through the *Copilot for Security Custom Plugin to Track SCU Changes* blog at `https://rodtrent.substack.com/p/copilot-for-security-custom-plugin`.

KQL queries serve as the foundation for developing KQL-based custom plugins in Security Copilot. They also play a key role in building interactive dashboards within Sentinel, a Microsoft **security information and event management (SIEM)** solution. As noted in the previous section, in the Defender XDR portal, you can run various KQL queries, each helping you analyze and interpret audit logs in different ways. Microsoft Sentinel takes this a step further by executing multiple KQL queries in the background and presenting all the results on a single interactive and visually appealing dashboard using the Sentinel workbook feature.

A Sentinel workbook enables you to easily view and analyze data from various sources, including those related to Security Copilot. The Microsoft Security Copilot GitHub repository offers a pre-built Sentinel workbook that provides various insights and information on how Security Copilot has been utilized.

Displayed in a single dashboard, this workbook offers visibility into key metrics such as the total number of Security Copilot users in your organization, the total number of prompts, the number of disabled Security Copilot plugins, and more.

It also features different visualizations that track prompt execution over time, the number of prompts across different Security Copilot experiences, and user activities (such as enabling or disabling plugins, creating, updating, or deleting promptbooks, and changes at both the user and tenant levels).

Additionally, the workbook includes a visual representation of successful and failed sign-ins by location, along with a diagram illustrating the different reasons for unsuccessful sign-ins. Furthermore, the workbook also highlights changes in the provisioned SCU count.

This workbook, much like other approaches covered earlier, supports identifying usage patterns and providing insights into how users are interacting with Security Copilot. For instance, by displaying the total number of users, prompt activity over time, and usage across different Copilot experiences, it highlights trends in how frequently and in what contexts Security Copilot is being used. The visualizations of user actions, such as plugin enablement, promptbook modifications, and sign-in attempts, offer a detailed view into engagement levels and operational behavior.

The configuration files for this workbook, along with its prerequisites and other relevant information, can be found in the Microsoft Security Copilot GitHub repository at `https://github.com/Azure/Security-Copilot/tree/main/Monitoring/IngestSecurityCopilotAuditlogs`. In there, the **Deploy to Azure** button allows you to directly deploy this workbook to your Microsoft Sentinel environment.

There is also a Microsoft technical community blog (`https://techcommunity.microsoft.com/blog/securitycopilotblog/monitor-user-activities-and-system-events-with-security-copilot-and-microsoft-se/4303368`) that thoroughly describes this Sentinel workbook, including relevant screenshots for added clarity.

Please note that since the visual summaries or charts in the workbook are generated by KQL queries, you can create similar visual representations in Advanced Hunting within the Defender XDR portal. However, the benefit of using the Sentinel workbook is that it consolidates all these visuals into one central dashboard.

With a variety of log data and analysis methods available to understand SCU usage patterns, it's equally important to apply these insights through actionable strategies. In the next section, we'll explore practical ways to optimize SCU consumption and improve overall efficiency.

Maximizing value and efficiency in SCU usage

As organizations scale their use of Security Copilot, optimizing SCU consumption becomes increasingly important. SCUs directly affect both the performance and cost of Security Copilot, and thoughtful management can lead to meaningful operational and financial gains.

There are practical strategies you can employ to maximize the value and efficiency of SCU usage. These approaches include prompt optimization, workflow refinement, automation, and adapting to ongoing platform changes. Each is designed to reduce unnecessary compute usage while maintaining or even improving security operation outcomes. Let's go through each one in detail next.

Direct skill invocation is more efficient in SCU consumption

After a prompt is submitted, Security Copilot interprets it and selects the appropriate plugin and skill to generate a response. However, letting Security Copilot decide which skill to use adds extra processing, which can lead to more SCU consumption. A more efficient way is to directly specify the desired skill in your prompt. This bypasses the additional processing and helps to reduce SCU usage.

For example, let's say an analyst wants to get a summary of a specific incident. A general prompt, such as `Can you provide a summary for incident #12345?`, requires Security Copilot to process the request and then select the **Incident Summarization** skill to generate a response. A more efficient approach is to directly invoke the skill within the prompt, for instance, by using a prompt such as `GetIncident 12345`, where `GetIncident` is the skill name. This tells Security Copilot exactly which skill to use and skips the decision-making process.

Direct skill invocation can reduce SCU consumption by varying degrees, depending on the complexity of the prompt. This is particularly effective in high-volume environments where analysts frequently use specific skills.

Furthermore, Security Copilot supports a growing library of plugins from both Microsoft and third-party providers. The skills within these plugins are purpose-built to handle specific security tasks and are optimized for particular data sources. Think of them as intelligent shortcuts. They know exactly what data to access, where to find it, and how to return results, all without requiring the AI model to perform unnecessary processing. Therefore, whenever possible, leverage specific plugins in your prompts, as they are designed for both performance and efficiency. This further helps to reduce SCU usage while maintaining speed and accuracy.

Not all prompts need to be handled by Security Copilot

Security Copilot consumes SCUs and is more computationally expensive than simpler automation tools. For repetitive or straightforward tasks, alternatives such as Azure Logic Apps, Azure Functions, or predefined workflows can handle the job more efficiently and at a fraction of the cost.

Here's a scenario to consider: a security analyst needs to convert Unix timestamps in a log file into human-readable dates and times for a daily audit report. The analyst could use Security Copilot's `ConvertUnixTimestamp` skill by entering a timestamp (e.g., `1733356800`) and receiving a readable output (e.g., `2025-07-05 07:00:00 UTC`). However, for a large log file containing many Unix timestamps, repeatedly using this skill can quickly lead to increased SCU consumption.

A more efficient alternative is to set up an Azure Logic Apps app with a connector to parse the log file, extract Unix timestamps, and convert them to a human-readable format using a basic function. The logic app can then call the Security Copilot connector only when needed, such as for further analysis to support the final report.

Security Copilot's `ConvertUnixTimestamp` skill is powerful for dynamic, complex workflows where analysts need to combine timestamp conversion with other AI-driven tasks, for example, correlating timestamps with threat patterns. However, for the repetitive, straightforward task of converting Unix timestamps to human-readable dates, Azure Logic Apps or similar tools such as Azure Functions are more cost-effective.

Logic apps to streamline prompts and responses

Furthermore, you can leverage Azure Logic Apps to clean and organize data before it's sent to Security Copilot, or use them to handle simple follow-up actions after Copilot responds. This helps reduce SCU consumption by offloading preprocessing and post-processing tasks to logic apps.

For instance, when analyzing incoming emails from the **Information Sharing and Analysis Center (ISAC)**, a logic app can be used to extract CVE numbers from the email and remove duplicates. Then, this short and clean list of CVEs is sent to Security Copilot to determine which of the CVEs are present in the analyst's environment.

By using a logic app to prepare the data in advance, you simplify the input data sent to Security Copilot for processing. This cuts down on prompt complexity and, in turn, lowers SCU consumption. It's a smart approach to ensure you're leveraging Security Copilot where it really adds value, not on tasks that can be easily automated.

Well-tuned promptbooks use fewer SCUs and deliver better results

Promptbooks are reusable workflows designed to perform tasks within Security Copilot. An inefficient promptbook may contain redundant logic, verbose prompts, or unnecessarily broad requests, all of which can lead to increased SCU consumption. By refining promptbooks iteratively, organizations can make prompts more precise, reducing SCU consumption and improving response accuracy.

As an example, consider a promptbook that starts with a vague prompt such as `Provide details on recent phishing campaigns`. Its lack of specificity can lead to broad processing and higher SCU consumption. An improved prompt in the promptbook would be `Summarize phishing campaigns from the last 7 days and focus on email-based attacks`. This refined prompt reduces ambiguity, allowing Security Copilot to execute a targeted query, lowering SCU usage while delivering clearer, more actionable insights.

Regularly reviewing SCU usage per prompt within promptbooks, combined with iterative testing and feedback from analysts, can help fine-tune promptbook performance over time. Analyzing which prompts consume the most SCUs can highlight areas of inefficiency. Meanwhile, feedback from frontline analysts adds important context by identifying which outputs are genuinely useful. Together, this data-driven and human-centered approach helps organizations continuously refine promptbooks to be more precise, cost-efficient, and aligned with real-world operational needs.

Scheduling non-urgent tasks during off-peak hours

During peak operational hours, multiple users or systems may access Security Copilot around the same time. This can lead to increased SCU contention, which impacts performance and drives up costs. One effective strategy with Security Copilot is to schedule non-urgent or routine tasks, such as report generation or data summarization, during off-peak hours. Running these lower-priority workflows during quieter periods avoids competition with high-priority or time-sensitive tasks during peak usage times. This not only improves overall system responsiveness but can also help to flatten resource usage patterns and avoid unexpected SCU spikes.

In practice, this might mean configuring logic apps or automation scripts to run such low-priority Security Copilot tasks overnight or on weekends when analyst activity is minimal. By shifting non-urgent workloads to off-peak windows, organizations can reduce performance bottlenecks, optimize their SCU usage, and better control their Security Copilot operating costs, all without compromising security operations.

Streamlining SCU allocation through scheduled automation

As mentioned in the earlier section, SCUs are provisioned on an hourly basis, giving you the flexibility to adjust SCU allocation based on Security Copilot usage patterns. You can then take this a step further by implementing automation strategies to dynamically adjust SCU provisioning. This provides a more streamlined way to manage resources to match demand while freeing up teams from routine administrative overhead.

For example, you start by defining the desired number of SCUs and overage SCUs to be allocated for designated peak and off-peak periods. Then, you run a logic app to automatically adjust SCU provisioning based on these criteria. For this example, the logic app sets the SCU allocation to 7 SCUs each hour on weekdays from 5 a.m. to 10 p.m., with an additional 5 overage SCUs. During off-peak hours (weekdays from 10 p.m. to 5 a.m. and throughout the weekend), the logic app reduces the allocation to 1 SCU, while still allowing up to 5 SCUs for overage.

This ensures SCU allocation scales effectively with demand. You avoid overprovisioning during low-usage periods, which helps control costs while ensuring enough compute power is available during critical times to maintain performance. This approach not only optimizes SCU efficiency but also supports a more predictable and cost-effective operational model.

Adjusting workflows and promptbooks as AI models change

Security Copilot continues to evolve through ongoing updates and feature enhancements. As the underlying AI models and capabilities advance, these changes may require adjustments to existing prompts, promptbooks, or logic apps to maintain optimal performance.

For instance, as of this writing, direct skill invocation for prompts and promptbooks has just been introduced and is in private preview. This feature allows you to explicitly invoke specific Security Copilot skills within prompts, offering greater precision, control, and more efficient SCU consumption. While it opens up new opportunities for building more targeted and efficient prompt workflows, it also requires refactoring existing prompts or promptbooks to ensure compatibility and to take full advantage of the enhanced capability. The prompts and promptbooks presented in this book do not yet utilize this feature. To optimize SCU consumption, you will need to update them to incorporate direct skill invocation.

In summary, applying strategies to optimize SCU utilization in Security Copilot allows you to reduce unnecessary compute overhead while improving the cost-efficiency of your security operations. As Security Copilot continues to evolve, taking a proactive approach to managing SCU consumption will ensure your environment remains both agile and sustainable.

Summary

This chapter began by introducing the concept of SCUs and their role in powering Microsoft Security Copilot. You learned how the Security Copilot pricing model works, including how SCUs are provisioned, consumed, and monitored. Practical guidance was provided for managing SCUs effectively, with a focus on using the SCU **Usage monitoring** dashboard and audit logs to gain insight into consumption patterns and user activity.

This chapter also covered tools such as Advanced Hunting in Microsoft Defender XDR and demonstrated how KQL queries, custom plugins, and Microsoft Sentinel workbooks can be leveraged to enhance visibility, analytics, and operational decision-making.

Lastly, strategies for maximizing SCU value and efficiency were discussed, including automation, workload scheduling, and prompt optimization. Together, these approaches help ensure that Security Copilot runs at peak performance while supporting cost control and long-term operational sustainability.

And with that, we've reached the end of the final chapter of this book. However, your journey with Security Copilot doesn't stop here. As AI continues to advance at an unprecedented pace, Security Copilot is evolving right alongside it. Leveraging AI to protect, detect, and respond to threats is poised to become a core component of resilient security operations. You can expect to see more powerful AI models integrated into Security Copilot, new capabilities rolled out in the platform, broader integrations with other solutions, and much more.

To continue to adapt to this fast-changing landscape, it's essential to stay informed about emerging developments and continually sharpen your skills. Therefore, before we close this book, a selection of resources has been included in the following add-on section to support your ongoing learning journey.

Stay connected and keep learning

Connecting with a community of like-minded professionals is a great way to stay current, exchange ideas, and grow your expertise in Security Copilot. From forums and discussion groups to online channels, you'll find plenty of opportunities to learn, collaborate, and stay inspired. To get started, you can take a look at the following list of community resources and learning platforms:

- The LinkedIn Security Copilot Community at `https://www.linkedin.com/groups/14345161/` is a public group with over 5,000 members.

- There is also a Security Copilot newsletter you can sign up for at `https://aka.ms/TheCfSPrompt`.
- The Microsoft Security Copilot **Customer Connection Program** (**CCP**) offers free technical training webinars and an early preview of the Security Copilot product roadmap. You also have opportunities to contribute insights through surveys and focus groups, and direct collaboration with Microsoft engineering teams. You can join this program at `https://aka.ms/JoinCommunity`.
- Microsoft collaborates with partners to enhance and customize Security Copilot's features. The **Microsoft Security Partners** program at `https://securitypartners.transform.microsoft.com/security-copilot` offers a range of Security Copilot resources to facilitate better collaboration.
- The Microsoft Security YouTube channel has a dedicated playlist specifically on Security Copilot available at `https://www.youtube.com/watch?v=11bBgGU5Nc0&list=PL3ZTgFEc7LyuQRLD61q9YqPKEDlZj4j5u`.
- You can stay informed on Security Copilot's latest developments and best practices by following its blog posts on Microsoft Tech Community at `https://techcommunity.microsoft.com/category/security-copilot/blog/securitycopilotblog`.
- The Microsoft Security Copilot GitHub repository (`https://github.com/Azure/Security-Copilot`) offers a variety of resources designed to help you make the most of Security Copilot. These resources include sample prompts, promptbooks, plugins, logic apps, customer guides, and even technical workshops.

In addition to community resources, you also have the option to access hands-on training through live Security Copilot sessions in a simulated lab environment. This interactive experience, available at `https://learn.microsoft.com/en-us/training/modules/security-copilot-exercises/`, allows you to engage directly with Security Copilot and gain practical hands-on experience. You can either navigate freely to get a feel for how Security Copilot works or follow the detailed, step-by-step guides included in the training modules.

Furthermore, attending conferences that feature Security Copilot and AI also offer opportunities for you to gain practical insights and network with experts in the field. Microsoft hosts several key events throughout the year that showcase the latest advancements in security, AI, and cloud technologies.

Notable among these are Microsoft Ignite, Microsoft Secure, and Microsoft Build conferences:

- The **Microsoft Ignite** conference is an annual event that unveils the latest tools, technologies, and innovations from Microsoft, including new Security Copilot features and updates:
    - Conference official home page: `https://ignite.microsoft.com/en-US/home`
    - Conference blog link: `https://ignite.microsoft.com/en-US/blog`
    - Conference session archives: `https://ignite.microsoft.com/en-US/archives`
    - 2025 Ignite conference link: `https://moscone.com/events/microsoft-ignite-2025`
    - 2024 Ignite conference link: `https://news.microsoft.com/ignite-2024/`
- The **Microsoft Secure** conference focuses on cybersecurity, where discussions on the latest trends, technologies, and best practices in the field of security are conducted:
    - Conference official home page: `https://register.secure.microsoft.com/`
- **Microsoft Build** is an annual developer conference where Microsoft showcases the latest tools, technologies, and innovations for building applications across the Microsoft ecosystem, including Azure, AI, Windows, and Microsoft 365:
    - Conference official home page: `https://build.microsoft.com/en-US/home`
    - Conference blog link: `https://build.microsoft.com/en-US/blog`
    - Conference session archives: `https://build.microsoft.com/en-US/archives`

As we wrap up the list of resources to support your continued growth, remember that whether you're learning independently or collaborating with peers, there are always tools and community offerings available to support you. They'll help you to stay connected, current, and confident as you continue your journey with Security Copilot in an ever-evolving cybersecurity landscape.

Looking ahead

This book covered the Security Copilot features and capabilities available at the time of writing. However, by the time the book reaches your hands, Microsoft will have already rolled out additional updates and enhancements. One of the most notable developments is the introduction of **Security Copilot agents**. These agents represent a significant addition to the many ways Security Copilot supports security teams. Designed as intelligent and task-oriented assistants, agents bring even greater automation, precision, and scalability to core security operations such as threat detection, investigation, and risk assessment.

These agents are likely to become an increasingly central part of the Security Copilot experience, empowering security professionals to do more, with greater speed and confidence.

With AI advancing at an alarming speed, it's natural that some see it as a threat. However, to succeed in a world increasingly shaped by AI, it's essential to understand it, work alongside it, and learn how to use it to your advantage. Do not let AI be here to replace you, but rather learn to leverage it as a powerful ally that can complement your strengths, minimize your weaknesses, and help you reach the next level by amplifying your potential. Embrace it as a tool that can empower you to take on bigger challenges and unlock new opportunities.

As we conclude this book, one thing is clear: the way we approach cybersecurity is fundamentally changing. With AI entering the scene, you are now equipped with a force multiplier, one that augments decision-making, strengthens security operations, and empowers defenders to act with speed and precision. Security Copilot brings advanced AI-driven capabilities to the forefront and leads the way into the next generation of cyber defense.

But this is just the beginning. With the evolution of AI, Security Copilot will keep advancing, becoming smarter, more capable, and better prepared to tackle the ever-changing landscape of tomorrow's cyber threats.

So stay curious. Keep experimenting. Continue learning.

12

Unlock Your Book's Exclusive Benefits

Your copy of this book comes with the following exclusive benefits:

Next-gen Packt Reader

AI assistant (beta)

DRM-free PDF/ePub downloads

Use the following guide to unlock them if you haven't already. The process takes just a few minutes and needs to be done only once.

How to unlock these benefits in three easy steps

Step 1

Have your purchase invoice for this book ready, as you'll need it in *Step 3*. If you received a physical invoice, scan it on your phone and have it ready as either a PDF, JPG, or PNG.

For more help on finding your invoice, visit https://www.packtpub.com/unlock-benefits/help.

Note: Did you buy this book directly from Packt? You don't need an invoice. After completing Step 2, you can jump straight to your exclusive content.

Step 2

Scan this QR code or go to packtpub.com/unlock.

On the page that opens (which will look similar to Figure 12.1 if you're on desktop), search for this book by name. Make sure you select the correct edition.

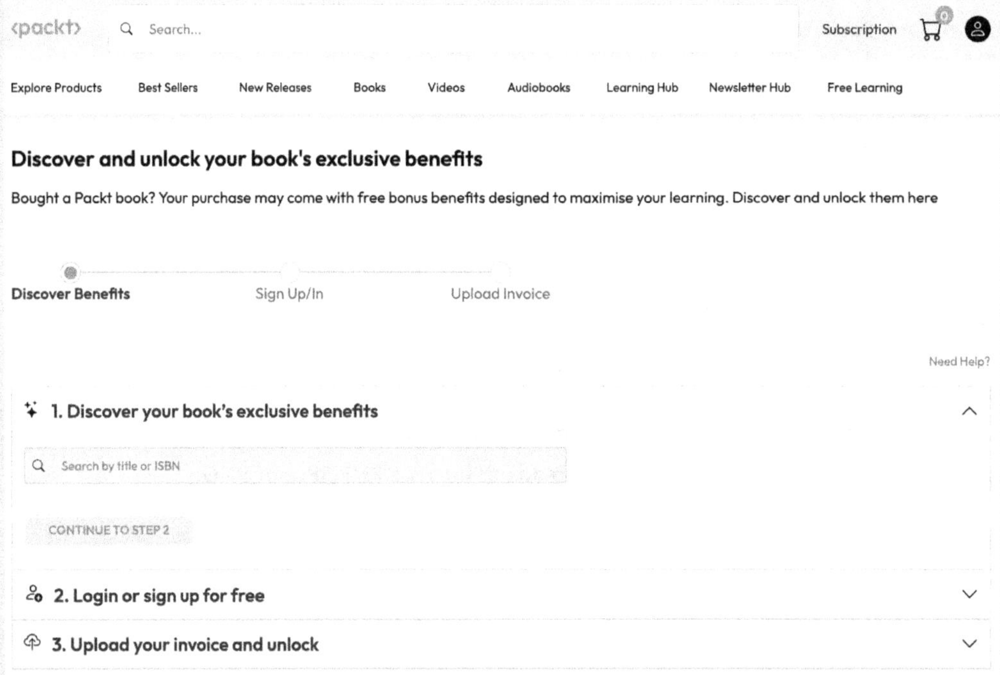

Figure 12.1: Packt unlock landing page on desktop

Step 3

Once you've selected your book, sign in to your Packt account or create a new one for free. Once you're logged in, upload your invoice. It can be in PDF, PNG, or JPG format and must be no larger than 10 MB. Follow the rest of the instructions on the screen to complete the process.

Need help?

If you get stuck and need help, visit `https://www.packtpub.com/unlock-benefits/help` for a detailed FAQ on how to find your invoices and more. The following QR code will take you to the help page directly:

Note: If you are still facing issues, reach out to `customercare@packt.com`.

Appendix A – Security Copilot Agents

An **Artificial Intelligence** (**AI**) agent is a system designed to act on its own with minimal supervision to complete tasks. It's called an "agent" because it acts on behalf of a person or system. An agent is typically designed to perceive its environment, gather dynamic, real-time data, and apply AI techniques for reasoning and decision-making. Based on this, it executes actions to achieve defined goals.

Security Copilot agents are specialized applications of AI agents designed for the cybersecurity domain. Like other AI agents, they operate with minimal supervision and act on behalf of human users to carry out security-focused tasks. For example, the Security Copilot Threat Intelligence Briefing Agent generates threat intelligence reports based on an organization's unique context. It filters through an extensive array of threat data, highlights the most pertinent trends, explains their potential impact, and delivers an actionable briefing to the security team. This allows teams to stay informed and make proactive decisions, without spending hours manually sifting through threat data.

In essence, Security Copilot agents extend the core concept of AI agents by applying it to real-world cybersecurity challenges. They consist of predefined workflows and capabilities tailored to address particular security challenges. As of the time of writing, the Security Copilot portfolio includes six Microsoft-developed agents and five partner agents. Let's take a closer look at each of them in the next section.

Microsoft-developed agents

Currently, Security Copilot offers six Microsoft-developed agents, with additional ones expected to be introduced over time. These agents take on high-volume, time-consuming tasks, such as threat intelligence briefings or **Conditional Access** (**CA**) optimization. They integrate seamlessly with Microsoft Security solutions to automate various routine tasks on your behalf with minimal human intervention.

The following list presents the six agents, outlining how each is designed to address a distinct cybersecurity need:

- Threat Intelligence Briefing Agent
- Phishing Triage Agent in Microsoft Defender
- Microsoft Entra CA optimization agent
- Vulnerability Remediation Agent in Microsoft Intune
- Data loss prevention triage agent
- Insider Risk Management triage agent

Threat Intelligence Briefing Agent

As mentioned earlier, the Threat Intelligence Briefing Agent helps organizations by providing relevant threat intelligence briefings tailored to their specific context. Rather than overwhelming security teams, the agent analyzes large volumes of threat information to surface the latest threats and vulnerability information.

This agent leverages the Microsoft Threat Intelligence plugin to access relevant threat information. Optionally, other plugins, such as Defender External Attack Surface Management and Defender Vulnerability Management, add more context to further enrich the agent with additional insights. Drawing on the extensive threat intelligence knowledge base and applying advanced AI techniques, the agent develops each threat intelligence briefing by evaluating the information analyzed at each step and, based on that outcome, dynamically determines what information to gather next. This real-time, adaptive approach allows the agent to decide what threat information is most relevant and important to include and prioritize in each unique briefing.

You can execute the agent manually at any time or configure it to run on a scheduled basis. Be aware that the agent requires a dedicated identity, such as a user account, to be connected to operate within the Microsoft Security Copilot environment. This account connection ensures the agent operates with appropriate permissions and can access organization-specific data.

After the agent is executed, it creates a threat intelligence briefing that includes an executive summary of the identified threats, along with a detailed technical analysis and their potential impact on your organization.

Phishing Triage Agent in Microsoft Defender

Similarly, Phishing Triage Agent in Microsoft Defender XDR leverages advanced AI models to apply dynamic reasoning when analyzing the content of user-reported phishing emails. It uses both the Microsoft Defender XDR plugin and the Microsoft Threat Intelligence plugin to understand and learn from the organization's environment. Based on the knowledge it gathers, the context of the organization, and its training, the agent autonomously identifies phishing attempts and classifies emails as either phishing or legitimate.

After identifying a phishing email, the triage agent explains why it made that decision using easy-to-understand natural language. It outlines the reasoning behind its verdict and highlights the specific evidence it referenced. In addition, it provides a visual representation of its decision-making process, helping you to follow its logic and better understand how the conclusion was reached.

As you and other analysts review its decisions and provide feedback, the agent learns from that input to enhance its future accuracy. This continuous learning process gradually fine-tunes the agent, making it increasingly precise over time.

Microsoft Entra CA optimization agent

The CA optimization agent is a Security Copilot agent built into Microsoft Entra. The primary function of this agent is to monitor for new users and applications within your Microsoft Entra tenant that are not covered by existing CA policies. It identifies security gaps, such as users or apps missing **multifactor authentication** (**MFA**) or device compliance controls, and recommends policy updates or new CA policies to secure them.

The agent runs automatically every 24 hours, though you can also run it manually at any time. You can review the agent's recommendations, understand how the agent reached its conclusions, and examine the details of the proposed policies. The agent only proceeds with changes once you've approved its suggestions.

Vulnerability Remediation Agent in Microsoft Intune

The Vulnerability Remediation Agent, integrated into Microsoft Intune as part of Microsoft Security Copilot, leverages data from **Microsoft Defender Vulnerability Management** (**MDVM**) to detect both CVEs and Windows-specific vulnerabilities on managed devices.

The agent runs on demand and then generates a prioritized list of remediation suggestions based on MDVM data, factoring in risk severity, exploitability, and organizational exposure (e.g., the number of affected devices and potential impact). Each suggestion includes detailed instructions to guide IT administrators through remediation using Intune. The Intune admin center displays these suggestions along with CVSS scores, affected devices, actionable links to create or deploy policies, and more.

The Vulnerability Remediation Agent reduces the time required for threat investigation and remediation.

By streamlining vulnerability management and prioritizing threats based on real-world risk, the agent helps organizations to reduce their attack surface, minimize the time to remediation, and improve overall security posture, while also decreasing the operational burden on IT teams.

Data loss prevention triage agent

The **Data Loss Prevention** (**DLP**) agent in Microsoft Security Copilot is designed to help security teams to streamline their alert review process by intelligently evaluating and prioritizing data loss prevention alerts. Using signals such as sensitivity risk, exfiltration risk, and policy risk, the agent automatically triages alerts and organizes them into categories to support faster, more informed decision-making. These categories, **All**, **Needs attention**, **Less urgent**, and **Not triaged**, are presented directly on the DLP solution's **Alerts** page. Note that the **All** category includes every alert the agent is either actively analyzing or has already reviewed. The **Needs attention** category surfaces alerts that the agent has flagged as high priority for your review. This categorization makes it easier for teams to focus on what matters most without getting overwhelmed by alert volume. Additionally, you have the option to either schedule the agent to run at a specific time or trigger it manually whenever needed.

By reducing the time and effort required to sort through large volumes of alerts, the DLP agent enables security teams to respond more quickly to high-risk incidents and proactively reduce the risk of data loss across the organization.

Insider Risk Management triage agent

The Insider Risk Management agent is designed to help security teams stay ahead of potential internal threats by intelligently evaluating and prioritizing insider risk alerts seen in Microsoft Purview. By analyzing signals such as user risk, file risk, and activity risk, the agent triages alerts and sorts them into clearly defined categories to support more efficient and focused investigations.

These categories, **All**, **Needs attention**, **Less urgent**, and **Not triaged**, mirror the same categorization used by the DLP agent but are displayed in the Insider Risk Management solution under the **Alerts** tab. This agent also supports scheduled or manual execution, providing a structured and intuitive way to assess potential insider threats. This approach not only streamlines the alert review process but also empowers security teams to respond more effectively to high-risk behaviors while minimizing time spent on low-priority activity.

Partner agents

Microsoft Security Copilot also integrates with a growing ecosystem of partner agents, designed to help security teams automate and accelerate specialized workflows across privacy, operations, and threat response. Whether it's identifying the regulatory obligations of a data breach, diagnosing network issues, or reducing alert fatigue through intelligent prioritization, these partner agents extend the capabilities of Security Copilot and enable teams to act faster and more confidently in high-pressure environments. The following list presents an overview of each partner-developed agent:

- **Privacy Breach Response Agent by OneTrust**

  This agent helps privacy teams navigate the complex regulatory landscape following a data breach. By analyzing the type of compromised data, the jurisdictions involved, and applicable privacy laws, it generates tailored guidance to ensure organizations meet relevant compliance obligations. This automation enables privacy teams to respond more quickly and consistently, reducing both legal risk and response time.

- **Network Supervisor Agent by Aviatrix**

  Focused on network reliability, this agent investigates failures related to VPNs, gateways, and Site2Cloud connections. It identifies the root cause of connectivity issues and provides clear, actionable insights to network administrators, helping them resolve incidents faster and with greater confidence.

- **SecOps Tooling Agent by BlueVoyant**

  This agent evaluates the current state of an organization's Security Operations Center (SOC) and its controls. Based on its assessment, it offers practical recommendations to improve operational efficiency, strengthen controls, and enhance overall compliance. It's particularly useful for teams looking to optimize SOC performance and align with industry best practices.

- **Alert Triage Agent by Tanium**

  Designed to reduce the burden on analysts, this agent adds valuable context to security alerts. It enables faster, more confident decision-making by providing detailed background, associated risks, and recommended actions for each alert—helping analysts prioritize their efforts and respond more effectively.

- **Task Optimizer Agent by Fletch**

  This agent uses intelligent forecasting to identify and prioritize the most critical threat alerts. By filtering out low-risk noise and surfacing high-impact risks, it helps security teams reduce alert fatigue and focus their efforts where they matter most. The result is improved incident response and better resource allocation.

Understanding agent pricing and SCU consumption

Security Copilot agents are powered by SCUs. Each time an agent is initiated, it consumes SCUs based on the complexity, duration, and type of task it performs. The number of SCUs required may vary across agents. For instance, agents handling alert triage or vulnerability remediation may consume fewer SCUs compared to those performing deeper analytics or assessments across larger datasets. You can again leverage the **SCU Usage Monitoring** dashboard to track the number of SCUs consumed for resource planning and cost management. Understanding how agents consume SCUs not only helps optimize your organization's usage but also enables security teams to balance automation with budget considerations. It's also important to note that agents typically consume more SCUs than prompts or promptbooks, due to the scale and depth of their automated workflows.

Summary

Security Copilot agents, both Microsoft-developed and partner-provided, are transforming security operations by automating complex workflows, improving threat detection, and streamlining response efforts across diverse areas. These agents help security teams to work more efficiently and confidently, reducing the manual workload and accelerating incident resolution. As the ecosystem of agents continues to expand, you can expect even greater coverage, deeper specialization, and more seamless integration.

One example of this evolving ecosystem is the Copilot Studio Connector for Security Copilot, which is available today. This connector enables seamless integration between Security Copilot and Copilot Studio, allowing you to extend and automate workflows by connecting Security Copilot insights with other tools and data sources.

Looking ahead, additional integrations and capabilities are planned. Notably, you will soon be able to develop your own custom agents within Security Copilot, allowing for tailored solutions that meet your unique needs and use cases. This growth will further empower security teams to scale their operations, adapt to evolving threats, and optimize resource use.

Appendix B – Additional Resources

In the fast-paced world of cybersecurity, staying ahead of new threats and technologies is essential for professionals looking to succeed. The right training resources are key in helping you to sharpen your skills and advance your career. This appendix highlights a selection of them to support your learning journey. They are organized into the following key areas to help you find the relevant resources more easily:

- Power up your skills with training resources
- Explore and collaborate through GitHub repositories
- Bootcamps and technical training skill building
- The path to expertise: The certification journey

Power up your skills with training resources

There is a wealth of Security Copilot training resources tailored to different skill levels. The following list highlights some of them to get you started:

A comprehensive Security Copilot learning path is available at `https://learn.microsoft.com/en-us/training/paths/security-copilot-and-ai/`.

Another helpful Security Copilot training resource can be found at `https://learn.microsoft.com/en-us/training/modules/unlock-insights-microsoft-copilot-security/`.

Additionally, Microsoft Security Copilot Flight School offers an in-depth look at Security Copilot through a series of advanced training videos at `https://learn.microsoft.com/en-us/shows/microsoft-security-copilot-flight-school/`.

You can also refer to the Microsoft Security Copilot video hub at `https://adoption.microsoft.com/en-us/security-copilot/video-hub/` as another dynamic way to explore Security Copilot in action.

For a complete level 400 training on Security Copilot and to become a Microsoft Security Copilot ninja, you can dive into the expert-level tutorials at `https://techcommunity.microsoft.com/blog/securitycopilotblog/how-to-become-a-microsoft-security-copilot-ninja-the-complete-level-400-training/4106928`.

Another great resource for Security Copilot is the official Microsoft learning portal available at `https://learn.microsoft.com/en-us/copilot/security/`.

The Microsoft Security YouTube channel has a dedicated playlist on Security Copilot at `https://www.youtube.com/watch?v=11bBgGU5Nc0&list=PL3ZTgFEc7LyuQRLD61q9YqPKEDlZj4j5u`.

Additionally, the Microsoft Security Partners program provides many Security Copilot training resources at `https://securitypartners.transform.microsoft.com/security-copilot`. Note that within the same portal, there is also a collection of recorded demos available for viewing.

Furthermore, the Microsoft Adoption program offers enablement resources, which includes a wide range of Security Copilot content, at `https://adoption.microsoft.com/en-us/security-copilot/`.

Lastly, you can stay up to date on the latest developments and best practices for Security Copilot by following the blog posts published by the Microsoft Tech Community at `https://techcommunity.microsoft.com/category/security-copilot/blog/securitycopilotblog`.

Explore and collaborate through GitHub repositories

The official public GitHub repository for Microsoft Security Copilot is available at `https://github.com/Azure/Security-Copilot`.

For your reference, here is a list of direct links to some of the resources within the repository:

- **Prompting tips with Microsoft Security Copilot**: `https://github.com/Azure/Security-Copilot/tree/main/Customer%20Guides/Prompting%20Tips%20for%20Copilot%20For%20Security`
- **Sample prompts**: `https://github.com/Azure/Security-Copilot/tree/main/Sample%20Prompts`
- **Sample promptbooks**: `https://github.com/Azure/Security-Copilot/tree/main/Promptbook%20samples`
- MSFT plugin samples: `https://github.com/Azure/Security-Copilot/tree/main/Plugins/MSFT_Plugin_Samples`
- Community-based plugins: `https://github.com/Azure/Security-Copilot/tree/main/Plugins/Community%20Based%20Plugins`

- Published plugins: https://github.com/Azure/Security-Copilot/tree/main/Plugins/Published%20Plugins
- Logic Apps: https://github.com/Azure/Security-Copilot/tree/main/Logic%20Apps
- Monitoring Security Copilot: https://github.com/Azure/Security-Copilot/tree/main/Monitoring
- Technical Workshops: https://github.com/Azure/Security-Copilot/tree/main/Technical%20Workshops
- Customer Guide: https://github.com/Azure/Security-Copilot/tree/main/Customer%20Guides

Additionally, there are other GitHub repositories created by individual contributors. They also offer useful content, tools, and information related to Security Copilot. One such example is Rod Trent's repository, available at https://github.com/rod-trent/Copilot-for-Security.

Bootcamps and technical training skill building

Bootcamps and technical sessions typically offer a structured way for you to develop practical skills with Security Copilot.

The Microsoft Security Bootcamp is a free digital event offering Microsoft Virtual Training Days. These sessions are designed to help you to hone your security skills and protect your organization in the age of AI. They're led by Microsoft experts and feature live Q&As. More detailed information on the Microsoft Security Bootcamp can be found at https://www.microsoft.com/en-in/indiasecuritybootcamp/.

Furthermore, there is also the Microsoft Security Copilot Partner Bootcamp. It offers insights into Security Copilot's capabilities and more. You can read about its 2024 bootcamp at https://techcommunity.microsoft.com/discussions/modernworksecurityswitzerland/microsoft-copilot-for-security-partner-bootcamp--february-21-22/4056724. Its on-demand training materials are available at https://gateway.on24.com/wcc/eh/4557503/category/138224/on-demand?filters=40404.

The path to expertise – The certification journey

As you continue to develop your Security Copilot skills, besides bootcamps and technical sessions, pursuing certifications can further solidify and showcase your knowledge. Microsoft offers certification programs designed to prepare you for the certification exams through training and practice tests.

However, currently, there isn't a specific certification solely for Microsoft Security Copilot. The closest option is the Security Operations Analyst Associate certification, also referred to as SC-200. It includes in-depth coverage of Security Copilot.

If you're looking to demonstrate your expertise with Security Copilot, pursuing the SC-200 certification would be a good option. Its module titled *Mitigate threats using Microsoft Security Copilot* specifically dives into Security Copilot.

You can find more information and explore the SC-200 learning path at `https://learn.microsoft.com/en-us/training/paths/sc-200-mitigate-threats-using-microsoft-copilot-for-security/`.

In addition, the Microsoft Certified: Azure AI Fundamentals certification, also known as AI-900, is designed for individuals who want to demonstrate their knowledge of machine learning and AI concepts, as well as related Microsoft Azure services. More information on AI-900 can be found at `https://learn.microsoft.com/en-us/credentials/certifications/azure-ai-fundamentals/`.

Lastly, if you want to further enhance and showcase your AI skills, the Microsoft Certified: Azure AI Engineer Associate certification, or AI-102, is intended for professionals who want to demonstrate their expertise in designing, developing, and implementing AI solutions using Azure AI services, Azure AI Search, and Azure OpenAI. To gather more details of this certification, you can visit its learning path at `https://learn.microsoft.com/en-us/credentials/certifications/azure-ai-engineer/?practice-assessment-type=certification`.

Index

A

B

C

I

K

L

M

R

S

T

U

V

W

X

Y

Other Books You May Enjoy

If you enjoyed this book, you may be interested in these other books by Packt:

Microsoft Security, Compliance, and Identity Fundamentals Exam Ref SC-900

Dwayne Natwick

ISBN: 978-1-80181-599-4

- Become well-versed with security, compliance, and identity principles
- Explore the authentication, access control, and identity management capabilities of Azure Active Directory
- Understand the identity protection and governance aspects of Azure and Microsoft 365
- Get to grips with the basic security capabilities for networks, VMs, and data
- Discover security management through Microsoft Defender for Cloud
- Work with Microsoft Sentinel and Microsoft 365 Defender
- Deal with compliance, governance, and risk in Microsoft 365 and Azure

Microsoft Identity and Access Administrator SC-300 Exam Guide

Aaron Guilmette, James Hardiman, Doug Haven, Dwayne Natwick

ISBN: 978-1-83620-039-0

- Implement an identity management solution using Microsoft Entra ID
- Manage identity with MFA, conditional access and identity protection
- Design, implement, and monitor the integration single sign-on (SSO)
- Deploy the new Global Secure Access features
- Add apps to your identity and access solution with app registration
- Design and implement identity governance for your identity solution

Looking for more on cybersecurity? Browse our full collection at `https://www.packtpub.com/en-us/security`.

Packt is searching for authors like you

If you're interested in becoming an author for Packt, please visit authors.packtpub.com and apply today. We have worked with thousands of developers and tech professionals, just like you, to help them share their insight with the global tech community. You can make a general application, apply for a specific hot topic that we are recruiting an author for, or submit your own idea.

Share your thoughts

Now you've finished *Microsoft Security Copilot*, we'd love to hear your thoughts! Scan the QR code below to go straight to the Amazon review page for this book and share your feedback or leave a review on the site that you purchased it from.

https://packt.link/r/1835884539

Your review is important to us and the tech community and will help us make sure we're delivering excellent quality content.

www.ingramcontent.com/pod-product-compliance
Lightning Source LLC
LaVergne TN
LVHW081736071126
851857LV00042B/1860